GLOBAL RESOURCES

This book, part of a radio/audio college course series in international studies, is a cooperative venture of National Public Radio, the Foreign Policy Association and the University of Texas at Austin. Funds for the preparation of print and audio material were provided by the Corporation for Public Broadcasting, the Exxon Education Foundation and the Fund for the Improvement of Post-Secondary Education (U.S. Department of Education).

GLOBAL RESOURCES

Challenges of Interdependence

Edited by
Martin I. Glassner

Supervising Editor
Nancy L. Hoepli

Published for the
Foreign Policy Association

PRAEGER SPECIAL STUDIES • PRAEGER SCIENTIFIC

Library of Congress Cataloging in Publication Data

Main entry under title:

Global resources.

Includes bibliographical references and index.
1. Natural resources—Addresses, essays, lectures.
I. Glassner, Martin Ira, 1932–
HC59.G576 1983 333.7 83-12169
ISBN 0-03-068782-9
ISBN 0-03-068783-7 (pbk.)

Published in 1983 by Praeger Publishers
CBS Educational and Professional Publishing
a Division of CBS Inc.
521 Fifth Avenue, New York, NY 10175, U.S.A.

456789 052 98765432

Printed in the United States of America.

For one brief, shining moment, four men
gave us a vision of a better world.
To their memories and their vision
this book is dedicated.

Dag Hammarskjold *29 July 1905–18 September 1961*
Pope John XXIII *25 November 1881–3 June 1963*
John Fitzgerald Kennedy *29 May 1917–22 November 1963*
Martin Luther King, Jr. *15 January 1929–4 April 1968*

Preface

In the closing years of the twentieth century our thinking about resources must be based not on fantasy or panic or blind optimism or ideology or simplistic slogans, but on a clear understanding of the subject. It is the purpose of this book to contribute to that understanding. The three main themes that emerge from the readings are, briefly:

1. There are many points of view about resources, and, although none of them may be "true" in any meaningful way, all have some validity and are therefore worthy of consideration.
2. Resources, however defined, and taken together, still constitute only one element in an intricately complex and interrelated web of environmental, political, economic, and cultural elements, none of which may safely be ignored.
3. All of mankind is by now quite interdependent; not even the largest or richest political or cultural entity can survive at an acceptable level in isolation from other communities, and this elementary fact of modern life is nowhere clearer than in the realm of resources.

The ramifications of this relatively new interdependence are already bewildering and are likely to become even more so in the unpredictable future.

I have made no effort to include in this book all points of view on all resources. Indeed, my most difficult task was deciding what had to be left out because of space limitations. What remains is a sampling of a wide range of opinions on resources in general and on some of our most critical individual resources. Not singled out for detailed treatment but mentioned in various places in the book are such vital resources of modern life and the human spirit as good soil, clean air, variety and abundance of plant and animal species, natural beauty, open space, and solitude. None of these is free any longer, or even cheap. Are we willing to pay the price for them?

While preparing this book I had the good fortune to work with some very fine people. Nancy L. Hoepli, editor of the Foreign Policy Association, asked me to do the book originally and has been a stalwart support even through the difficult periods. Frankie Westbrook of the University of Texas at Austin, head of the development team for the global resources project, was a warm, talented, and dedicated collaborator. While working on the study guide and instructor's manual, she helped me in many ways. Brian Brightly, director of education services for National Public Radio, was the creative spirit and business manager of the whole project. Allen Hundley, who produced the accompanying audiocassettes under contract to NPR, was perceptive and good-humored as we worked to make our respective contributions complementary. Special thanks go to Professors Ian Manners and Tom Januzzi of the University of Texas at Austin for their most helpful criticisms and suggestions in their roles as consultants to the project. And Professors Kempton E. Webb, chairman of the department of geography of Columbia University, and Geoffrey J. Martin, my colleague in the department of geography of Southern Connecticut State University, were most patient and professional as they produced fine essays-to-order within rather rigorous constraints. I also wish to thank the Corporation for Public Broadcasting, the Exxon Education Foundation and the Fund for the Improvement of Post-Secondary Education (U.S. Department of Education) for their recognition of the importance of international studies and for their generous funding of this project.

Martin Ira Glassner
New Haven, Connecticut

Contents

IV

TERRESTRIAL RESOURCES

Food

TERRESTRIAL RESOURCES

Energy

V
MARINE RESOURCES

VI
CONCLUSION

APPENDIX

Prologue

This excerpt from the prologue to Swedish economist and Nobel Laureate Gunnar Myrdal's splendid book Asian Drama *refers specifically to Westerners' attitudes toward economic development in South Asia, but its message is universal. We all have biases that emerge from our backgrounds and frames of reference. Even when we cannot overcome our biases, we can at least recognize them, understand them, and try to prevent them from distorting too badly the world we see. Our notions of time, space, wealth, happiness, scarcity, progress—indeed, resources—may not always be applicable in other cultures and other circumstances. It would be well to keep Myrdal's cautionary note in mind as we journey through this book.*

The Beam in Our Eyes

Gunnar Myrdal

Our main interest in this prologue is in the sociology of knowledge, which is concerned with causation. The point is that we could better avoid biases, and could therefore expect more rapid progress in the social sciences, if we were a little less naive about ourselves and our motivations. A minimal desideratum is that we be always aware of the problem and attain some degree of sophistication about the operation of the personal and social conditioning of our research activity.[1] From this should rationally follow systematic inquiry into this important part of social reality. That would require the firmer establishment of a hitherto much neglected discipline: the sociology of knowledge.

These forces working on our minds, which cause irrationality if not recognized and controlled, are exceptionally strong and insidious in our approach to the problems of underdevelopment, development, and planning for development in the underdeveloped countries of South Asia. On this fact rests the defense for beginning our book with the general observations just made. [. . .]

A major source of bias in much economic research on poor countries is thus the endeavor to treat their internal problems from the point of view of the Western political and military interest in saving them from communism. Sometimes this intention is stated, though not in the form of a reasoned presentation of specific value premises logically related to the definition of the concepts used. More often it remains implicit in the approach, though the study is interspersed with suggestive formulations. This type of reasoning must often make the public and scholars in the underdeveloped countries suspicious and irritated, as they naturally want their problems analyzed from the point of view of their own inter-

---

Gunnar Myrdal, *Asian Drama: An Inquiry into the Poverty of Nations.*

ests and valuations. The taking of an outside view does not in itself constitute a fault in the methodology of scientists, whose criterion of validity cannot be the acceptability of approaches and conclusions to the people concerned. What is important is that the practice usually goes hand in hand with a retreat from scientific standards, which permits the entrance of uncontrolled biases—and this, of course, gives substance to the suspicion and irritation in underdeveloped countries.

Consideration of Western political and military interests in saving the underdeveloped countries from communism invites inhibitions, for instance, about observing and analyzing the shortcomings of political regimes in those countries—provided, let it be noted, that they are not friendly with the enemy in the cold war. An indication of such tortuous reasoning, which lends itself to opportunistic arrangement of the facts, is the use even in scholarly writings of labels like "the free world" or "the free Asian countries" to denote, not that people are free in the ordinary sense of the word, but the purely negative fact that a country's foreign policy is not aligned to that of the communist bloc or blocs. This is not an innocent terminological matter; such practice hides shifts in the meaning of concepts. And, as the literature abundantly proves, this kind of reasoning tends to give strength by association to an assortment of loosely argued and inexplicitly stated value preferences even in matters of internal policy—economic policy in regard to foreign trade and exchange, public versus private enterprise, and so on.

This opportunistic approach to a research task is not necessarily, or even ordinarily, egoistic and hard-hearted in its conclusions. A study may have as its purpose to discover better based and politically appealing reasons for giving more generous aid to the underdeveloped countries. The political influences on Western social research do not usually encourage unkind treatment of underdeveloped countries—as long as they are not hopelessly lost to the enemy bloc. On the contrary, what national communities more or less overtly demand from their social scientists are essays in practical diplomacy pleading certain directions of external and internal policy and giving a more solid and scholarly foundation to such pleas. When, as often happens, social scientists resist having their work turned into diplomacy, the pressures on them may nevertheless force them to engage in research on particularly innocuous problems in an underdeveloped country that have less immediate connection with political issues. They become accustomed to bypass facts that raise awkward problems, to conceal them in technical terminology, or to treat them in an "understanding" and forgiving manner. These are also biases in research. Conditioning that results in omissions rather than commissions nonetheless erodes the basis for objective research. The scholar should not be made to speak with tongue in cheek.

These remarks are not intended to isolate the economic problems of underdeveloped countries from the ideological and power constellations of world politics. The cold war has, of course, considerable bearing on events in the underdeveloped countries of South Asia; and their political allegiance to a power bloc, or their neutrality, is worth studying. Most certainly, the drift of its economy and the social and economic policies it pursues can affect such a country's alignment in the cold war, though this problem is often oversimplified. An underdeveloped country that, for whatever reason, comes under communist rule will apply Soviet methods of planning for economic development, and this will bring about a major change in the situation under study. In the same way a country's dependence on credits and gifts from the Western bloc may influence its internal policies and thereby affect the social reality we are studying. But to recognize these causal relations is not to say that the Western interest in winning the underdeveloped countries as allies or at least keeping them neutral is an appropriate value premise for the study of their development problems. If it *is* chosen as a value premise, it should be chosen openly and operate in a logical way that does not detract from scientific objectivity. Diplomacy is essential to national policy, but it is disastrous when it dominates the work of social scientists.

The tendency to think and act in a diplomatic manner when dealing with the problems of the underdeveloped countries of South Asia has, in the new era of independence, become a counterpart to the "white man's burden" in colonial times. No one with any critical sense can be unaware of this trend. I can myself testify that British and American and other Western scholars confess and defend as a principle—when speaking "among ourselves," that is, among us who are from the rich and progressive countries—the necessity to "bend over backwards." Not only politicians but also scholars, in public appearances, will apologize for making even slightly derogatory remarks and suggest that as foreigners they should not venture to express a view on the matter. In the literature such discretion leads to the avoidance of certain problems and the deliberate understatement of negative findings. I have often heard writers explain that they did this in order not to hurt feelings. A Russian scholar addressing a South Asian audience is equally tactful now that the policy of the Soviet Union has become friendly to the "bourgeois-nationalist" regimes in the region. [. . .]

Another primary source of bias of special importance to the study of the underdeveloped countries of South Asia may appear to be more mechanical, a function merely of the rapidity with which we have undertaken massive research in a previously almost uncultivated field. As research must of necessity start from a theory, a set of analytical preconceptions, it was tempting to use the tools that were forged in the West and that in the main, served a useful purpose there,[2] without careful consideration of their suitability for South Asia. Thus a Western approach became incorporated into the mainstream of the discussion of development problems in South Asia, both within the region and outside it. Indeed, Western theoretical approaches have assumed the role of master models. For reasons we shall go into at considerable length in the body of the book, a

Western approach must be regarded as a biased approach. Let us attempt to understand how the transfer came to pass.

Economic theorists, more than other social scientists, have long been disposed to arrive at general propositions and then postulate them as valid for every time, place, and culture. There is a tendency in contemporary economic theory to follow this path to the extreme. For such confidence in the constructs of economic reasoning, there is no empirical justification. But even apart from this recent tendency, we have inherited from classical economics a treasury of theories that are regularly posited with more general claims than they warrant. The very concepts used in their construction aspire to a universal applicability that they do not in fact possess. As long as their use is restricted to our part of the world this pretense of generality may do little harm. But when theories and concepts designed to fit the special conditions of the Western world—and thus containing the implicit assumptions about social reality by which this fitting was accomplished—are used in the study of underdeveloped countries in South Asia, where they do *not* fit, the consequences are serious.

There is a conservatism of methodology in the social sciences, especially in economics, that undoubtedly has contributed to the adherence to familiar Western theories in the intensive study of underdeveloped countries. Economists operate to a great extent within a framework that developed early in close relationship with the Western philosophies of natural law and utilitarianism and the rationalistic psychology of hedonism. Only with time has this tradition been adapted to changing conditions, and then without much feeling of need for radical modifications. That economists work within a methodologically conservative tradition is usually not so apparent to the economists themselves, especially as the tradition affords them opportunity to display acumen and learning and, within limits, to be inventive, original, and controversial. Even the heretics remain bound by traditional thought in formulating their heresies. As circumstances, particularly political ones, changed, there was room for a shifting of emphasis and approach. When theoretical innovations lagged far behind events, such adjustments sometimes took on the appearance of definite breaks, as in the so-called Keynesian "revolution." The new thoughts were soon integrated into the traditional mold, slightly modified to better suit the environment, the changes in which were themselves largely responsible for inspiring fresh thinking.

Occasionally a breakthrough established new lines of thought that contrasted more sharply with tradition. The most important challenge came, of course, from Marx and his followers. But Marx, at the base of his constructs, retained much of classical economic theory. And gradually economists remaining within the fold incorporated large parts of what was or seemed novel in Marx's approach, not least in regard to the problems of development, as we shall see. For both these reasons we should not be surprised to find that the biases operating on Western economists often tend to converge with those conditioning economists in the communist countries. These assertions will be exemplified in various contexts in this book.

When we economists, working within this tenacious but variegated and flexible tradition of preconceptions that admittedly are not too badly fitted to our own conditions, suddenly turn our attention to countries with radically different conditions, the risk of fundamental error is exceedingly great.[3] This risk is heightened by the dearth of empirical data on social realities in the underdeveloped countries of South Asia, which enables many biases to be perpetuated that might be questioned and corrected if concepts and theories could be exposed to the challenge of concrete facts. The problem is compounded by another consequence of the Western-biased approach. When new data are assembled, the conceptual categories used are inappropriate to the conditions existing, as, for example, when the underutilization of the labor force in the South Asian countries is analyzed according to Western concepts of unemployment, disguised unemployment, and underemployment. The resulting mountains of figures have either no meaning or a meaning other than that imputed to them. Empirical research then becomes faulty and shallow, and, more important in the present context, less valuable for testing the premises latent in the Western concepts that have guided the production of new statistics. The very fact that the researcher gets figures to play with tends to confirm his original, biased approach. Although it is the confrontation with the facts that ultimately will rectify our conceptual apparatus, initially the paucity and flimsiness of data in underdeveloped countries leave ample opportunity for biases, and the continuing collection of data under biased notions only postpones the day when reality can effectively challenge inherited preconceptions.

The danger of bias does not necessarily arise from the fact that students from the rich countries in the West inevitably face the problems of underdeveloped countries in South Asia as strangers. If anything, the outsider's view has advantages in social research. There are two ways of knowing a toothache: as a patient or as a dentist, and the latter is usually not the less objective. The white southerner's conviction that he, and he alone, "knows" the American Negroes because of his close association with them has been proved erroneous. The stranger's view may be superficial, it is true, but superficiality is not the monopoly of strangers; it is a matter of the intensity and effectiveness of research. There is thus no necessary connection between superficiality and the extent of bias. Indeed, biases in research have no relation to superficiality per se. They emanate from the influences exerted by society, from our personal involvement in what we are studying, and from our tendency to apply approaches with which we are familiar to environments that are radically different. Biases can be present or absent as much when we are strangers to the country we are studying as when we are its nationals and as much when the research undertaken stretches over long periods and is conducted with a huge apparatus as when it is simply a journalist's attempt to put his impressions and reflections in order.

Nor are Western economists uniquely subject to the specific biases emanating from our methodological conservatism. Our confreres in the South Asian countries are afflicted as much, if not more, with them. Many have been trained at Western centers of learning or by teachers who acquired their training in the West. All have been thoroughly exposed to the great economic literature in the Western tradition. Familiarity with, and ability to work in accordance with, that tradition is apt to give them status at home. Their motivations for sharing in this bias are fairly independent of their political attitudes. Part of the explanation, as will be shown in the next section, is that application of the Western approach serves both conservative and radical needs for rationalization in the South Asian countries. [. . .]

The two main sources of bias in the Western countries thus strengthen each other in that their influences tend to converge. As we saw, the international power conflict and the tensions and emotions associated with it have influenced the study of the problems of the underdeveloped countries in South Asia in the general direction of diplomatic kindness and tolerance—again, provided that these countries are not on the wrong side in that conflict. Many of the conditions peculiar to these countries are highly undesirable; indeed, this is what is meant by their being underdeveloped. Therefore, the other source of bias with which we dealt in the last section—the tendency to use the familiar theories and concepts that have been used successfully in the analysis of Western countries—exerts influences in the same direction. For when using the Western approach one can more easily soften the bite of these peculiar and undesirable conditions.

We have wanted to stress the political urges behind these tendencies that affect research on underdeveloped countries in the region. But these tendencies have at their core a compassion that makes them almost irresistible. Quite aside from the cold war and the opportunistic tendencies to bias emerging from it, we of the West are by tradition disposed to be friendly to peoples in distress, once we begin to take an interest in their condition. And it is our earnest hope, apart from all selfish interests, that they will succeed in their development efforts. That we wish them to develop into national communities as similar to our own as possible is a natural ethnocentric impulse that would make itself felt in the calmest world situation. Perhaps it should be stressed again that the concern of the West about the possibility of communist expansion in underdeveloped countries is also understandable, and from the viewpoint of our own interests valid. And these interests justify using our influence to stop it. Still less can one criticize the human sympathy that characterizes the Western attidude toward these countries.

Nevertheless, we must not let these understandable and genuine feelings influence our perception of the facts. It is the ethos of scientific inquiry that truth and blunt truth-speaking are wholesome and that illusions, including those inspired by charity and good will, are always damaging. Illusions handicap the pursuit of knowledge and they must obstruct efforts to make planning for development fully effective and successful. For this reason, the present book is intended to be undiplomatic. In our study we want to step outside the drama while we are working. We recognize no legitimate demand on the student to spare anybody's feelings. Facts should be stated coldly: understatements, as well as overstatements, represent biases.[4]

One more point should be mentioned before we leave this attempt to characterize briefly the forces tending to create biases in research on development problems in South Asia. As these biases engender an overoptimistic view of development prospects, they sometimes provide encouragement; but mainly they are apt to create undue complacency. In any case, a more realistic view makes it clear that *development requires increased efforts: speedier and more effective reforms in South Asia and greater concern in the West.* [. . .]

NOTES

1. The American novelist Richard Wright, who in his book *White Man Listen!* tried to deal with a problem in general terms, was conscious of the need to watch the way he was conditioned in his views: "I state that emotion here precedes the idea, that attitudes select the kind of ideas in question. . . . We are human; we are the slaves of our assumptions, of time and circumstances, we are the victims of our passions and illusions, and . . . our critics can ask of us . . : Have you taken your passions, your illusions, your time, and your circumstances into account? This is what I am attempting to do." (Richard Wright, *White Man Listen!*, Doubleday and Company, New York, 1957, p 64.)

A social scientist should not be less humble and assume that he is purely "factual and objective." He cannot, in any case, escape valuations, as he needs explicit, or implicit, value premises even to ascertain the facts.

2. Throughout this book I am making the generous assumption that the Western approach is fairly adequate to Western conditions. This might be an overstatement. In any case, this is a book on South Asia, and I have not felt it to be my task to go into a critical analysis of the use of Western concepts and theories outside the region I am studying.

3. "One ever-present problem is the possibility that a conceptual scheme will imprison the observer, allowing him to see only what the scheme directs him to see and ruling out other interpretations of data. It is readily admitted that this danger is implicit in all a priori thinking." (Richard C. Snyder and Glenn D. Paige, "The United States Decision to Resist Aggression in Korea: The Application of an Analytic Scheme," in *Administrative Science Quarterly*, Vol. 3, No. 3, December, 1958, p. 358.)

4. In regard to issues that have been felt to be awkward and threatening—for instance, the Negro problem in America—biases toward forbearance and optimism have been quite general in the social sciences. A "balanced view" on such

issues tends to be a view that soft-pedals difficulties and causes for worry. Understatements, though in principle just as damaging to the establishment of truth as overstatements, are considered more "objective" and certainly give more respectability. When working without explicit value premises, "the optimistic bias becomes strengthened, paradoxically enough, by the scientist's own critical sense and his demand for foolproof evidence. The burden of proof is upon those who assert that things are bad in our society; it is not the other way around. Unfortunate facts are usually more difficult to observe and ascertain, as so many of the persons in control have strong interests in hiding them. The scientist in his struggle to detect truth will be on his guard against making statements which are unwarranted. His very urge to objectivity will thus induce him to picture reality as more pleasant than it is." (Gunnar Myrdal, *An American Dilemma, The Negro Problem and Modern Democracy*, Harper, New York, 1944, p. 1039.)

"I have often observed that social scientists who are responsible for the publication of other authors' works or who utilize them in their own writings, when they apprehend biases, believe that these can be 'edited away,' by modifying certain expressions used or cutting out or revising certain practical conclusions drawn. Similarly, a general tendency toward understatement is observable in most social science literature. When an author has set down something which he feels to be unfavorable about a social class or a region, he looks for something favorable to say in order to 'balance the picture.' A 'balanced view,' a colorless drawing, is considered to be more 'scientific.' Particularly in governmental investigations great care is usually taken to spare the readers. The deliberate attempt that is made in such reports not to offend anyone will often make them difficult to use for scientific purposes. This tendency is, of course, not only ineffective in mitigating biases, but, even worse, it is itself one of the main types of bias in research." (*Ibid*., p. 1043.)

GLOBAL RESOURCES

I
Introduction

This section introduces two fundamental ideas that must underlie any discussion of natural resources: what they are and their place in the ecosystem of our planet. Geographers Robert P. Larkin, Gary L. Peters and Christopher H. Exline graphically elaborate the basic truth that resources, like beauty, are in the eye of the beholder, an example of the point made by Myrdal in the prologue. Perceptions of resources vary not only in different cultures but in different physical environments and at different periods in history. In any physical environment all elements exist naturally in complete harmony. Only human interference disrupts this natural harmony as the resources in the environment are exploited. The inevitable effects of this exploitation conform to what ecologist Barry Commoner calls the four laws of ecology. This is not to say that people should not exploit resources. People are part of the natural world, as are all other animals, and need not apologize for existing or for utilizing the environment for survival. They must do so wisely, however, keeping in mind Commoner's laws.

1

Natural Resources: The Basis for Economic Development

Robert P. Larkin, Gary L. Peters and Christopher H. Exline

RECOGNIZING NATURAL RESOURCES

Resources are the foundation of wealth and power because people are material-using animals. Everything we use, from the food we eat to keep us alive to the objects we manufacture, comes from substances found on this planet. Our concern over resources, however, is nothing new. Throughout history people have wondered where tomorrow's bread would come from. The hunger for land, water, and mineral supplies is as old as the ages.

No consensus exists, however, on the exact meaning of the term ***resource***; many popular misconceptions do exist. One common misconception identifies resources as only tangible things or substances. Of course, substances can function as resources and play an important role as such, but there are many less tangible resources, like knowledge, wise policies, or social harmony. This preoccupation with resources as tangible phenomena in nature creates the false impression that resources are fixed or static. In his classic study Erich W. Zimmermann defined resources as

> living phenomena, expanding and contracting in response to human effort and behavior. . . . To a large extent, they are man's own creation. Man's own wisdom is his premier resource—the key resource that unlocks the universe. . . . The word "re-

Reprint of "Natural Resources: The Basis for Economic Development," Chapter 9 in *People, Environment, and Place: An Introduction to Human Geography* by Robert P. Larkin, Gary L. Peters and Christopher H. Exline. Copyright 1981 by the Charles E. Merrill Publishing Company, Columbus, Ohio. Reprinted by permission of the publisher. Pp. 170–93.

source" does not refer to a thing or a substance but to a function which a thing or a substance may perform. (1951, p.7)

Resources are an expression or reflection of human appraisal, and without people, there would be no resources. Resources are not static, but expand and contract in response to human needs and human actions.

Resource Creation and Destruction

Resources are the result of human culture; the materials of the physical environment become resources only when they fulfill a human want or need. "Natural" resources, therefore, exist only in conjunction with human culture. According to Zimmermann, human culture forges further into the realm of nature converting more and more ***neutral stuff*** into resources.

Because resources are a creation of human culture, they can be destroyed by human culture. A good example of ***resource creation and destruction*** is the development of rubber in the Amazon Basin of Brazil. For many centuries rubber had been familiar to the people of the western hemisphere, but little could be done with it until Charles Goodyear developed vulcanization in 1839. As a result, rubber could be used to satisfy human needs, and many manufactured articles made of vulcanized rubber began to appear on world markets. The worldwide demand for rubber products determined the process by which neutral stuff in the Amazon Basin could be converted into a rubber resource. According to Zimmermann, this complex resource-creating setup was composed of many parts, including "invention and technology, business enterprise, market demand, labor, capital equipment, the social and political institutions governing international trade and regulating human relationships both intranationally and internationally" (1951, p. 14).

The case of rubber in Brazil is not an isolated incident; the same story could be told over and over again in different parts of the world with different resources. Resource creation, therefore, stems from the interaction of natural and cultural processes.

The process can also be reversed. Modern science and technology not only can create the needs and wants that make neutral stuff into resources but can also destroy these resources, turning them back into neutral stuff. The case of Brazilian rubber is once again a good example. As the internal combustion engine and the automobile became an important part of world technology, a tremendous demand for cheap rubber tires developed. Geneticists developed new strains of rubber trees, which were much more productive than the indigenous varieties of the Brazilian jungle. These new varieties of rubber trees were cultivated in plantations primarily in Ceylon (Sri Lanka), Indonesia, and the Malay Peninsula. Rubber plantations could produce more rubber at cheaper prices than the wild trees in the Amazon Basin. Eventually Brazilian rubber was squeezed out of the world market and the rubber resources of the Amazon Basin were little more than a memory. Ironically, even the rubber plantations eventually were hurt by the development of synthetic rubber.

Types of Natural Resources

As we have mentioned, defining a natural resource can be a very complex matter. On the broadest scale we have defined a natural resource as something available from the physical environment that meets human needs. This definition may seem simple, but consider the question, What are human needs? We know that cultural systems and environmental perception have much to do with the definition of a resource. The level of technology of a given people is the primary factor in the determination of importance of various resources.

The pre-Columbian Indians of the American Southwest had no real use or means of recovering the fossil fuels that lay beneath their land. Does this mean that the fossil fuels were not a resource? There are vast oil shale formations in Colorado, Utah, and Wyoming. Many predict that one day we will mine and process most of the oil shale, but there is currently only marginal use. Does this mean that oil shale is not yet a resource? We see once again the importance of the cultural perspective in both space and time. The same consideration is important when we discuss the types of resources, resource availability, and the present distribution of resources.

The two basic types of resources are ***renewable*** and ***nonrenewable*** resources. The nature of resource renewability is simply a question of whether or not the resource in question can be readily renewed or reproduced. A forest is a renewable resource because most varieties of trees grow rapidly (relative to the replacement time of other resources). Fossil fuels and minerals, such as gold, silver, or copper, obviously do not renew themselves; thus once extracted from the earth and consumed, they are not replaced. Many minerals can be recycled, of course, as evidenced by the collection of aluminum cans.

We can add another term to our discussion of renewable and nonrenewable resources, the concept of ***recoverability***. Recoverability is similar to the notion of renewability in that it refers to the length of time involved in the replenishment and viability of the resource. Fossil fuels and minerals have essentially no recoverability; that is, once used the resource will not recover to its original condition (Luten, 1972). Forests are variable in recoverability. A forest of pine trees, especially Monterey pine, will recover rapidly after the original forest has been cut. Forests of trees important for commerical lumbering operations, such as the ponderosa pine, recover relatively rapidly. Human influence, such as replanting a forest after trees have been removed and reforesting in such a way that the young trees receive optimum growing conditions, hastens recoverability. The redwood forests of coastal California and Oregon recover extremely slowly regardless of human influence.

Water as a resource may recover very quickly. A rapidly flowing river will recover once pollution sources are eliminated; but a large lake with little inflow and outflow may take thousands of years to recover. Animals also demonstrate a variable nature in recoverability. The California condor, or any one of a number of the great whales, replenish their population very slowly. If the population of one of these types of animals decreases, the species may not survive because their recoverability is a slow process. If the population of many microscopic organisms was reduced to just a handful of individuals, in a matter of hours, the populations would climb rapidly. The questions we must deal with are whether or not a resource is renewable and, if it is, what is the recoverability rate.

There are other concepts to consider within the major categories of land, water, mineral, and energy resources: *stretchability, flexibility,* and *vulnerability* (Luten 1972).

Stretchability is a term given to the ability of the resource to produce greater yields as the result of more efficient methods of resource manipulation. For example, we may increase the production from farmlands through the use of chemical fertilizers. The question and attendant problems of resource definition appear again at this point. There is a certain amount of land on the earth, and of this surface, only a portion is suitable for agriculture. If we increase the amount of land in agricultural use, is this not an example of resource stretchability? The answer is yes, and we will view any exploitation of a natural resource that produces greater yield as stretching the resource.

Greater returns of products from fossil fuels can be accomplished in many ways. At the most basic level, fluids are pumped into some oil fields in an attempt to force all possible crude oil out of the ground. In the processing stage, research is currently focused on substances that might be mixed with gasoline to stretch the amount of fuel produced from each barrel of crude oil. Attempts by automobile manufacturers to produce vehicles with better fuel mileage are another example of the stretchability of fossil fuels.

Perhaps one of the most discussed potential sources of fossil fuels is oil shale. This particular type of rock material can be processed mainly through the use of extreme heat to precipitate the oil material from this unique sedimentary rock. The stretchability of this source of fossil fuel is great. The present level of technology produces only about 25 gallons of crude oil per ton of quality grade shale. Researchers believe that significantly more crude will be produced per ton of shale as technology in this area progresses. The search for methods of yielding greater returns from fossil fuels results from increases in demand for this resource.

Demand is generally referred to as the need or desire for a resource. We will add to that definition the concept of ***flexibility*** as being a measure of the ability to find adequate substitutions for a resource to satisfy demand. Basically, we are asking how flexible a resource is, given a particular cultural system. The flexibility of farmland illustrates this principle. In the United States we have a great flexibility in demand for farmland. Large tracts of this part of the American resource base are removed from production every year as a result of urban sprawl. Agriculturalists continue to produce greater amounts of food, however, because they are able to stretch the returns from the remaining land. In Southeast Asia the demand for agricultural land is very inflexible. If significant amounts of agricultural lands were changed from that particular land use, the overall production of food would likely decline.

Fossil fuels are very inflexible. We have no widely used substitute for this resource. Forests, on the other hand, are highly flexible, since many substitutes for wood can be found. It should be noted that the concept of flexibility is used in reference to the current level of technology and style of life found in world societies. Many argue that great economic investment in energy resources could produce many substitutes for fossil fuels, but no major technological breakthroughs are on the horizon. However, petroleum shortages and high prices are stimulating increased research efforts. In order to maintain current societal status, great quantities of fossil fuels must be consumed, and without realistic substitutes available, we maintain that the fossil fuel resource is very inflexible.

Vulnerability is a measure of how susceptible the resource is to destruction. Land is a highly vulnerable resource. Agricultural land converted to urban or suburban uses is removed from the food producing resource base. Wilderness as a resource of both ecological and aesthetic importance is highly vulnerable. The impact of human activity on wilderness areas changes the character and basic value of the resource. The problems of perception of resources and resource utilization are culminated in the issues of wilderness land use and conservation. Anyone who has recently visited Yosemite Valley knows something of the human impact on the visual and aesthetic qualities of natural environments.

Resource vulnerability

Hawkes has summarized the basic elements in the conflict of how to use the land through his discussion of Gifford Pinchot, a famous forester, and John Muir, the mountaineer (1960). Pinchot is characterized as representative of those having a utilitarian perception of the wilderness and resources in general. The ***utilitarian viewpoint*** is fundamentally that resources are to be used and should serve the general economy.

Muir is perhaps most famous for his writings about the Sierra Nevada of California and Nevada. Near the turn of the twentieth century Muir inspired the founding of the Sierra Club, an organization originally devoted to resource preservation in California, and which continues to be a powerful voice for the environment. Muir represented the ***preservationist movement*** in Hawkes's dichotomy.

Eighty years ago the main confrontation between preservationists and utilitarians was over the use of forest lands (Hawkes 1960). There followed a series of conflicts over petroleum, soil erosion following the dust bowl years, and water and wildlife management. There seem to have been shifts in public attitudes toward resources, with utilitarian concerns dominating prior to the Second World War. In the years following World War II, the preservationists seem to have been the strongest group. In the last years of the decade of the 1970s, utilitarian arguments seemed to be gaining in popularity. The battle over the Alaskan Pipeline was fought along utilitarian and conservationist lines. Those favoring resource utilization finally were able to dominate this issue.

Questions of the best use of lands where strip mining and agriculture compete, and the future of wilderness areas, will be discussed later in this chapter. Resource vulnerability, stretchability, and renewability must all be considered when we estimate resource availability.

Measuring and Estimating Resource Availability

You have undoubtedly heard or read that the world will deplete its supply of coal or oil within a given number of years. These estimates are made for nearly every individual country and obviously for the earth as a whole. One fact that will not escape the attentive reader is that the amount of time remaining before resource depletion takes place varies remarkably. Why the difficulty in estimating ***resource availability***?

Consider for a moment the complexities involved in every aspect of cultural systems. The economic, political, historical, social, and psychological factors that make so many issues difficult to deal with are also involved in estimating resources. Combine these factors with some of the difficulty inherent in defining resources, assessing the perception of resources, and the continuous reappraisal of existing resources, and it is not difficult to imagine why there is such a wide range of estimates of future resources. [. . .] We should consider the factors originally used to make these estimates and discuss events that have acted to influence actual consumption and availability.

In making projections for future resource needs, Landsberg considered the following factors: populations; gross national product; individual, government, and business investment; and advances in technology (1964). Estimating population, as we have seen, is a difficult proposition; the baby boom following World War II produced a sharp upward deviation in actual population as compared with population estimates. Likewise, the present decline in population growth rates in Anglo-America and Western Europe was not foreseen in long-range estimates. Planning based on the extrapolation of short-term trends is a hazardous business.

Population is the essential element in the estimation of resource consumption and subsequent needs. Obviously a population exhibiting a growth pattern will demand more natural resources. The habits of cultural groups are equally as important as pure numbers of people; a person born and raised in India, for example, will generally consume far less than the average citizen of the United States. Population and cultural systems, as well as the economic subsystem and modernization, must all be considered in estimating for the future.

The principal measure of the economic activity of a nation is the total range of goods and services produced in the nation. In the United States we use a measure referred to as the gross national product (GNP). In many nations, however, an accurate reflection of all production is impossible to calculate. The trend toward modernization can be used as an estimator in these countries.

A high gross economic output reflects a need for the consumption of resources. This is a generalization, of course, but it is difficult to argue that more goods and services can be produced without some increased input of raw materials. The resources that drive the economic output of our world society come from the land, water, and minerals of the earth and are processed by the use of energy. Future estimates of need are based upon the rate of growth in the use of basic natural resources. In the United States, for example, the consumption of electrical energy was growing by 8 percent per year during the 1970s. This means that as a nation the United States will nearly double its consumption of electrical energy every eight and one-half years.

Based upon exponential growth rates in the consumption of fossil fuels, Hubbard estimated that a child born in 1935 would live to see 80 percent of the petroleum in the United States consumed (1969). He further predicted that, within the life span of a child born in 1973, 80 percent of the world's petroleum reserve would be consumed. Nothing takes into account possible new discoveries of petroleum, innovative technology that may stretch the resource, or a change in lifestyle in favor of conservation; this is not a severe criticism, because estimates of future resource availability are perhaps more accurately made excluding these three factors. It is more responsible to be conservative in future estimates than to promise a cornucopia of long-term resources that may or may not exist. Two other aspects of prediction of resource availability that must be considered are the issues of quality versus quantity and the costs of providing resources.

Landsberg cites individual spending, governmental spending, and business investment as major factors in future resource availability. If the costs of urban sprawl become so high that consumer demand diminishes, perhaps sprawl would be reduced and agriculturally productive land preserved. If U.S. gasoline prices rise to two or three dollars per gallon, it is possible that consumption of petroleum would be reduced.

In virtually all studies dealing with the availability of resources, the cost input is a major factor. As the price of energy increases, more money is expended for obtaining resources. If the nations of the world are willing and able to divert much of their economic output into resources, especially energy, then resources will continue to be available for some time. However, there may be limits. Gas prices have risen phenomenally in some parts of Europe. The days when the economic cost of obtaining and processing resources was very small are a part of history. The term *economic cost* may be used to describe one aspect of meeting future resource needs. However, there are other costs—social costs—that must be considered as well.

The quality of the environment and the quantity of resources produced often are in conflict. For example, the production of oil shale, as well as coal, often requires extensive strip mining. Increasing the world's food supply through sea-harvesting poses the potential for the loss of some species of sea animals. These are only a few examples of the dichotomy between environment and economy. When estimates of future resources are given, regardless of the source, we should question the economic and environmental costs of resource production. It could be claimed that, with enough money and monumental environmental sacrifice, the world production of coal would be virtually infinite, but this is an unrealistic estimate. In the assessment of resource availability we must consider the anticipated needs for the future, the environmental and economic costs of production, and population factors. The interrelations between these components of the question offer the opportunity for a systems approach to problem analysis.

Estimates of the need for, and cost of, fossil fuels made during the early 1960s by Landsberg and others have proven generally inaccurate, mainly because of unforeseen events that are impossible to work into an equation. The systems dynamics of economics, politics, new developments in technology, and the discovery of new resources make long-range predicting difficult. For example, who could have forecast in 1960 that, by the mid-1970s, those Middle Eastern nations that control so much of the world's oil reserves would, through economic and cultural solidarity, be able to dictate a policy of great impact on virtually every nation? The rise of OPEC (Organization of Petroleum Exporting Countries) has literally altered the distribution of wealth in a short time as "petro dollars" have accumulated at unprecedented rates since 1973. In 1979 a change in the political leadership in one nation, Iran, led, through interaction of cultural systems, to a number of economic consequences, especially in the United States. In 1979 the new government restricted the export of oil, and gas prices rose rapidly in the United States. These are representative of the types of events that influence resource availability and of costs that often go unrecognized when estimating future availability. We can, however, examine a few broad generalizations of existing world resources that influence the analysis of the resource base.

THE MATERIAL BASIS OF DEVELOPMENT

No simple relationship exists between economic growth and natural resources. Many areas of the world are endowed with a variety of natural resources, yet they are relatively poor (India, China, parts of Africa). On the other hand, nations like Japan or Switzerland have a paucity of natural resources yet a high level of development. According to geographer Norton Ginsburg, the important questions to ask are, "How important are natural resources in the course of economic development, and what relationships do they bear to other factors which enter into the developmental complex?" (1957, p. 197). In its broadest sense, the resource base would include all the material phenomena of nature, including land, air, sea, and the nonmaterial quality of location or situation.

If all things were equal (*ceteris paribus*), the larger and more varied the resource base of a particular state, the greater the likelihood that it would modernize or develop. Ginsburg offered several preliminary ideas concerning the relationship between natural resources and economic growth (1957, p. 212):

1. An ample supply and diversity of natural resources is a major advantage to a country attempting to modernize.
2. Although it is not necessarily critical to have natural resources within the political boundaries of a country, those resources must be accessible. This means facilities must be available to transport those resources.
3. An easily exportable natural resource can be the source of wealth for capital accumulation. Large quantities of a natural resource such as oil can provide enormous amounts of development capital.
4. Even if abundant natural resources are available, they cannot determine the kinds of uses, if any, to which they will be put.
5. The particular stage of development of a country will be an important factor in resource use. Natural resources play an especially important role in the early stages of the development process because they can supply capital necessary for the acceleration of economic growth.
6. Natural resources, although important, do not play as crucial a role in the developed nations because these wealthier nations have larger

supplies of skilled labor, capital, technology, and development experience.

7. Any economic development program of a comprehensive nature must begin with a sophisticated inventory of the resource base.

Though Ginsburg's ideas may seem appropriate, we might argue that they represent neither necessary nor sufficient conditions for economic development and modernization in the 1980s. Abundant resources in poor countries have often been controlled by rich countries, thus hindering development. On the other hand, Japan has modernized with a minimum of natural resources. Services are increasingly important and require less than manufacturing in terms of natural resources. Look, for example, at the importance of banking in the Swiss economy. Furthermore, the relationship today between rich and poor countries restrains development, as does rapid population growth.

Natural Resources and Economic Development: The Case of Japan

Perhaps more than any other modern nation, Japan's rise to international prominence illustrates the interrelationship between resource availability and economic development. The beginning of modern Japanese development can be traced back to the fall of the shogunate and the restoration of the emperor in 1867. Prior to this time Japan was a nation virtually isolated from the rest of the world.

By most objective standards of resource endowment, Japan would be classified as a nation with a paucity of resources. Less than 20 percent of its total land area is arable; soil fertility is high in some areas but overall it is not exceptional; and, though it contains a variety of mineral resources, most are in small quantities and have little commercial value. At the fall of the shogunate, Japan had a population of approximately 35 million, which had remained unchanged for a number of years. Also, at the time of the Meiji Restoration, Japan was using its resource base at a level appropriate for its technological development. How, then, was Japan able to increase dramatically its economic base and become a world power in a relatively short period of time?

Most analysts agree that the initial source of capital came from within the country. Foreign investments, although important in some areas, were very small. The internal resource base was the source of capital, which was used to fuel productivity increases. Small investments in sericulture enabled Japan to displace China as the world's principal supplier of silk. Also, investments in agriculture increased productivity in that sector, and the government, through forced savings techniques of taxation, transferred capital from agriculture to other productive sectors of the economy.

It was primarily the textile industry, initially silk and later cotton, that permitted rapid economic growth. The textile industry was developed through the application of already available technology to the production process. The resultant increase in production helped supply the capital to initiate the Japanese program of heavy-industry expansion. The development of heavy industry was initially financed internally but later was aided by foreign investment. Japan is thus a successful example of a nation using its limited resource endowment, in conjunction with improved technology, to supply the capital to finance further development.

RESOURCES: A GEOGRAPHIC SURVEY OF MAJOR CATEGORIES

Land

Land as a resource may be assessed in many ways. The basic determinants of what makes land a resource are found in the composition of soil and in environmental conditions. Soils provide the home for bacteria, fungi, and a variety of other organisms; they are composed of organic materials and inorganic components, such as weathered rock particles, along with water and gases, mainly oxygen and nitrogen. The organic and inorganic elements are acted upon by sunlight, water, plant and animal communities, and human activities, with the product of this process being a particular type of soil.

The surface of the earth is roughly 30 percent land area, only some of which is suitable for agriculture; the rest is too wet, too dry, too warm, or too cold, or too acidic or alkaline, too rocky or sandy, or covered with urban settlements. Further, of the soils in production, only a small percentage is in intensive use. Areas of great agricultural productivity are generally limited to certain physical locations—river valleys, areas of volcanic soil, intensively irrigated rice lands, or in the prairie (chernozemic) soil regions, where extensive cultivation is common.

Forests are another land-based natural resource, providing such things as fuel, lumber, paper, wildlife habitats, and recreation. We have discussed forests as a renewable resource. Anyone who has traveled in regions noted for forest industries has probably seen reforestation. In most industrialized nations, even with reforestation, large expanses of forests have already disappeared. Deforestation is also occurring rapidly in developing countries. In Brazil, for example, a program is underway to clear tropical forests in order to provide new agricultural lands. The cutting of tropical forests, a frequently proposed source of new farmlands, presents several environmental problems. First, once trees are removed, the ground is directly exposed to water from the constant tropical rain, leading to accelerated erosion and leaching. Leaching is the process by which the minerals and nutrients in the soil are washed out of the top layers of soil by the action of moving water. In the natural tropical ecosystem, the leached minerals and nutrients are constantly being replaced, but if forests are removed, massive amounts of chemical fertilizers must be added, increasing the cost of farming.

A second problem with this type of forest removal is that a very complex ecosystem is replaced by a simple one. A tropical ecosystem may have hundreds of types of plants and animals in a small area, whereas an agricultural ecosystem would have only a small variety of plants and animals in a given area. If a pest or plant disease moves through an area in which the ecosystem has been simplified to this extent, widespread damage results. By sheer strength of numbers, a complex ecosystem will absorb this damage, whereas a simple ecosystem may be destroyed. The potato blight of the mid-1800s in Ireland is an example of the devastation that can occur when a simple ecosystem is overcome by disease; it resulted in the death by starvation of thousands and the migration of thousands more to North America.

Water

Water is a renewable resource in both an absolute sense, as in the hydrologic cycle, and in a relative sense, as in a polluted stream being cleaned of pollutants. The stretchable nature of the resource is evident by the vast number of water quality standards that exist. Water is principally used by people for industrial activity (46 percent in the United States), irrigation (46 percent), and municipal uses (8 percent) (Luten 1972). Water as a renewable resource is not consumed but can be polluted until it is virtually useless. Pollution has been a factor of human use of the earth for nearly as long as there have been settlements. Accounts of almost every water-based city in history describe waste materials being dumped into water systems. The problem became especially acute during the Industrial Revolution, as suggested in the following comment:

> And sprinklings of water a little cooled the main streets and the shops but the mills, and the courts and alley, baked at a fierce heat. *Down by the river that was black and thick with dye*, some Coke town boys who were large—a rare sight there—rowed a crazy boat, *which made a spumous tract upon the water as it jogged along, every drop of the oar stirred up vile smells.* (Dickens, 1854; as quoted in Salter, 1971, pp. 217–18. Emphasis added.)

In the modern era pollution continues to be a problem. A myriad of federal, state, and local laws to curb water pollution have been passed in recent years, both in the United States and elsewhere.

Development of energy resources often acts to pollute water systems. The chemical residue from strip mining adds a pollutant to the water of surrounding streams. Water discharge from nuclear power plants creates thermal, or heat, pollution.

In the contemporary urban world, a frequent problem is the lack of water resources at specific urban sites. Los Angeles is a prime example, where water to serve the needs of the metropolitan area must be imported from great distances. The lesson to be learned from Los Angeles might be that resource availability should govern the growth and ultimately the size of urban areas, but growth patterns do not follow such a rational plan. One of the fastest growing areas in the United States is the urban corridor along the Front Range of the Colorado Rockies from Fort Collins in the north to Colorado Springs in the south, where vast quantities of water must be imported.

Water policy in much of the world seems to equate progress with growth and growth with the provision of water, almost regardless of economic or environmental cost. Water is so inexpensive and has traditionally been in such great supply that conservation has never seemed like a real necessity. However, this may not be the case in the future; conservation may become a more attractive alternative to continual expansion of the resource base.

CASE STUDY: THE CALIFORNIA DROUGHT OF 1976–77

Severe drought conditions existed in the western United States during 1976 and 1977. California in general and Marin County in particular were especially adversely affected by the lack of precipitation.

Marin County receives most of its water from reservoir systems located in the foothills along the Pacific Ocean. During the drought period the normal pattern of Pacific storms was disrupted for two consecutive winters. Marin County has a Mediterranean type of climate, which typically features a summer drought. The lack of rainfall in the winters meant that this particular area, with a population of over 200,000, had no new water added to its reservoirs for several years. The only immediate answer was water conservation.

The local water district began an immediate campaign to inform residents of the magnitude of the problem. A great many attempts were made to conserve water on a voluntary basis, which were somewhat successful; however, the water shortage became so acute that rationing was needed. An allocation of water for each resident in the house was assigned. The rationing system was designed to cut water use to approximately 40 percent of the consumption levels of the previous years. Each household was given a specific number of gallons per day; this amount was translated into cubic feet for a two-month period (Table 1). People in Marin County learned to read the water meters at their homes and could easily calculate the rate of their consumption.

There were no exceptions to the rationing plan. This, coupled with the nature of the resource shortage—the residents obviously knew these were drought conditions—prompted community action on a broad scale. Special newspaper issues were devoted to water-saving tips. Bumper stickers appeared urging conservation. All conceivable manner of water-saving devices were sold in stores. The main topic of conservation became how to cope with the drought. A number of lists comparing normal water use and conservative use were widely distributed (Table 2).

An esprit de corps developed in Marin County, because the nature of the problem was quite clear and everyone was involved equally. Marin County residents actually brought consumption below the ration level. At one point residents were averaging a use of only 23.3 gallons per person per day for *all* purposes; Table 2 shows that, through normal household activities, 23 gallons of water could be consumed very quickly. The extent to which Marin County residents conserved can be brought into sharper focus if you calculate the water usage of your household for a period of time and compare that with an allotment of 23.3 gallons per person per day.

The only immediate detrimental impact of the water conservation effort was that some ornamental vegetation (lawns, some shrubs, and so on) did badly without constant watering. A lawn brown from lack of water became something of a status symbol. This example illustrates that conservation of some resources is possible with minimal change in lifestyle. One resource, which people in most parts of the world are being urged to conserve, is energy, though so far results have been rather poor.

Energy

Energy is perhaps the most complex of all resources. It may be defined simply as the ability to do work; although we speak of energy in a wide range of contexts, we are essentially describing the ability to perform some task. It may be said that one has little energy on a particular day, or that energy is obtained from the burning of coal, or that energy is potential, kinetic, or latent in nature. All of these concepts involve generating force to do work. Our concern with energy is in the realm of the broad overview of major energy sources in the world. Energy as a resource is nonrenewable, with the exception of solar, wind, and tidal energy (Luten 1972). There are seven basic steps in utilizing energy: discovery, harvest, transport, storage, conversion, use, and waste disposal (Luten 1971, p. 109).

Discovery and *harvest* have become increasingly more efficient through technological innovation. It is possible to estimate where energy

TABLE 1. Water Allotments for Single-Family and Duplex Homes During the California Drought

No. of Permanent Residents in Household	Gallons per Day for Each Resident	Gallons per Day for Household	Cubic Feet for Two-Month Period per Household
1	49	49	400
2	43	86	700
3	41	123	1,000
4	37	148	1,200
5	34	170	1,400
7	32	224	1,800

TABLE 2. "How to Save Water": An Example of Guidelines Issued During the California Drought

Activity	Normal Use	Conservation Use
Shower	Water running 25 gallons	Wet down, soap up, rinse off 4 gallons
Brushing teeth	Tap running 10 gallons	Wet brush, rinse briefly 0.5 gallon
Tub bath	Full 36 gallons	Minimal water level 10 to 12 gallons
Shaving	Tap running 20 gallons	Fill basin 1 gallon
Dishwashing	Tap running 30 gallons	Wash and rinse in dishpans or sink 5 gallons
Automatic dishwasher	Full cycle 16 gallons	Short cycle 7 gallons
Washing hands	Tap running 2 gallons	Fill basin 1 gallon
Toilet flushing	Depending on tank size 5 to 7 gallons	Using tank displacement bottles 4 to 6 gallons
Washing machine	Full cycle, top water level 60 gallons	Short cycle, minimal water level 27 gallons
Outdoor watering	Average hose 10 gallons per minute	Lowest priority Eliminate

might be obtained from the earth through satellite imagery, a vast improvement over previous forms of analysis. Oil can now be pumped from wells over 10,000 feet deep. The techniques becoming common now are far more expensive than those of the past.

How much energy resource remains to be discovered? We have detailed the problems inherent in attempting to estimate such things earlier in this chapter. Suffice it to say that there are undoubtedly large quantities of energy resources that are yet to be harvested.

Transport is the process that follows discovery and harvest. Large electrical wires transport electrical energy from a point of generation to places a great distance away. Oil is moved by pipeline, ship, rail, truck, and most recently, supertanker. Natural gas may move through pipelines, and coal may be transported through slurry pipelines (coal through a pipeline propelled by moving water) or by truck, train, or sometimes ship.

Storage of most major resources from which we obtain energy is often not difficult, but once a material has been converted to energy, storage becomes a more challenging problem.

Conversion is the term given to the use of a material to generate energy. Coal or fuel oil is burned to generate electrical energy. The problems in storing electrical energy come from the "free" nature of this source of energy. Electrical energy cannot be placed in piles or storage tanks, so it must be essentially used as generated. Demand for electrical energy is greatest in the early evening, declines at night, then begins a gradual climb in the early morning to its evening peak. If large-scale storage of electricity were possible, peak usage could be more efficiently handled.

When a resource is converted to form an energy source, a question of efficiency is involved. If coal or oil is burned to generate other types of energy, much of the potential energy held in oil or coal is lost as waste heat. One way in which energy resources may be stretched in the future is in minimizing this loss.

The final stage in our process of energy utilization is the *disposal of waste material*. In most cases waste material is heat. Energy generated by nuclear power produces heat, which is either released into the environment through cooling (evaporation) towers or discharged into water systems. The by-product of using uranium for fuel is a radioactive waste that can be harmful for many thousands of years. Until adequate methods of nuclear waste disposal are found, this potential source of energy may not be fully utilized.

Disposal of waste products from energy production illustrates one of the basic conflicts produced by modernization. It is essential to generate more energy, but as this occurs, so does environmental deterioration.

RESOURCE CONFLICTS

Because natural resource policy decisions are made in conjunction with economic, social, and political factors, it is inevitable that conflicts will arise (Leonardo Scholars 1975, p. 71). For example, a decision to exploit one resource at the expense of another could lead to conflicts at the local, national, or international level.

The increased demand for both food and energy contains the seeds of several conflicts: (1) more ocean fisheries are threatened by the potential for massive spills that accompanies oil companies' reliance on oceanic transport; (2) strip-mining high-sulfur coal in Illinois, Indiana, and Iowa will disrupt farmlands that supply much of the nation's and, for that matter, the world's supply of corn, wheat, and soybeans; and (3) strip-mining in the western United States will destroy land valuable for wheat production and grazing. The use of one resource that is desperately needed by one group of people can therefore preempt the use of another resource needed equally badly by another group.

Oceanic transport and marine fisheries

The impact of oil pollution on marine fisheries is already widespread, and the increased demand for crude oil will most certainly add to the problem. People in the oil industry argue that increased reliance on supertankers will decrease the probability of an oil spill because there will be fewer tankers. However, supertankers contain much more oil—on the average, five times as much as a traditional tanker—and present the possibility of much larger oil spills. At any rate, increased reliance on supertankers will certainly increase the total volume of oil shipped via oceanic transport.

The exact impact of oil spills on marine life varies according to the type of organism and its habitat. Oil spills are more detrimental to marine life in inshore areas, such as estuaries, than in the open ocean, because they are important for spawning, shelter, and juvenile rearing for more than two-thirds of the food fish (Longwood 1972, p. 40).

The coal–wheat conflict

An increasing demand for energy resources in the United States, brought about by a growing and more affluent population, will lead to a concomitant increase in mining activities in the final quarter of the twentieth century. The United States has abundant supplies of coal, which is likely to be of major importance in America's future energy policy (Tregarthen et al. 1978, p. 351). Of concern to many planners are the land-use implications and conflicts associated with increased production of coal, especially the increasing percentage and the changing spatial pattern of production from strip mines. Every state in the United States has at one time experienced some form of surface mining, although the largest reserves of strippable coal are found in the Appalachian region, the Midwest, and just east of the Rocky Mountains in Montana, Wyoming, Colorado, and North Dakota.

Current estimates are that, of all the land that has been disturbed by strip mining, more than half has not been reclaimed. Fortunately, most of the land affected in recent years has been reclaimed, but the definition of reclamation is simply that local, state, or federal laws were complied with in whatever effort was undertaken. Although small experimental plots can be made to grow almost anything, there is little evidence to show that agricultural lands in the United States can be restored to their former productivity. Even if they could, the cost involved would most likely be prohibitive.

Much of the land where strippable coal is found is presently used for cropland. Large areas of primary wheat land—where wheat is at least 30 percent of planted crop acreage, and in most cases is at least 45 percent—overlie strippable beds of bituminous, subbituminous, and lignite coal in eastern Montana; secondary wheat lands—with wheat at less than 30 percent of planted crop acreage—overlie strippable coal in south-central Illinois (U.S.D.A. 1971, pp. 3–6). These two states are already encountering difficulty because of the land-use conflicts associated with wheat and coal development.

Estimates are that, by the time the lignite and low-sulfur coal reserves are depleted in Montana, about 800,000 acres will have been strip mined. The coal in Montana is primarily found in the eastern part of the state, and approximately 85 percent of that land is pasture, cropland, or range. According to the United States Geological Survey, part of the coal lies under a piece of the Northern Plains spring wheat region, one of the nation's prime wheat-producing areas.

Like Montana, Illinois has a similar land-use conflict. Illinois is one of the oldest and largest coal-producing states in the nation. The principal crops grown in Illinois are corn and soybeans, although it also ranks high in wheat production. Some of the better wheat lands found in the state, as well as areas that are large producers of soybeans and corn, lie over strippable coal reserves.

It is difficult to assess the exact parameters of this land-use conflict. According to a study by the Leonardo Scholars:

> With the increasingly delicate balance of world food supplies and the rising significance of food-stuffs as export commodities for the United States, a number of unpredictable variables could affect the picture immensely. One could be a greater reliance upon coal than foreseen. . . .
>
> Another variable is the relative productivity of land lying over coal fields. Some of the world's most productive land and most favorable climatic conditions occur in the Midwest. (1975, p. 80)

A Faustian Bargain

An unexpected shortage in an important natural resource or energy supply can lead to shortsighted resource policy decisions with possibly long-lasting, regrettable effects. Perhaps this type of decision making is excusable under conditions of stress; however, it is inexcusable when there is sufficient lead time for more thoughtful policies.

The use of any resource involves a trade-off or payment, even at the most basic level. For example, a boy who wants to get an apple from the upper branches of a tree must "pay" for that apple in several ways:

> First, he will make a very real payment on the spot in the form of energy he expends in climbing the tree. Second, he will take risks. One might be that of falling out of the tree. Another might be that from his vantage point on the ground he cannot be sure that the apple does not contain a worm. If the boy actually acquired the apple and ate it with satisfaction, we can assume that the expenditure of energy and risk-taking were worth it. (Leonardo Scholars, 1975, p. 60)

We could not know if the energy and risk involved were worth it until after the boy had climbed the tree and eaten the apple. Therefore, only through hindsight can we determine if the boy profited from his efforts.

Unfortunately, not all the risks and trade-offs associated with resource exploitation and use are so clear-cut. In the totality of resource use, the boy becomes our global society, and the apple, losing its exact definition, becomes a nebulous concept such as a "high living standard" or a "pristine environment." The price or payment made for the use of the resource is also obscured. Part of the payment, a polluted environment, may be delayed until later generations. Detrimental side effects may be an accepted consequence of resource exploitation or may have been unforeseen at the time of resource development.

The development of nuclear power highlights several important resource development issues. Most of the environmental costs associated with the development of nuclear power are natural science problems dealing with potential cost of a tangible nature. There are, however, intangible costs; these were outlined by Alvin Weinberg, director of the Oak Ridge National Laboratory, in his article "Social Institutions and Nuclear Energy" (1972).

According to Weinberg, the development of nuclear power had far-reaching social implications and was a direct threat to a cherished western value, individual freedom. He called it a ***Faustian bargain*** in which future societies would pay dearly for an inexhaustible source of energy, much like the bargain in the familiar German legend in which Faust sold his soul to the devil in exchange for temporal influence and power.

> We nuclear people have made a Faustian bargain with society. On the other hand we offer—in the catalytic nuclear burner [the breeder reactor]—an inexhaustible source of energy. . . . But the

> price that we demand of society for this magical energy source is both a vigilance and a longevity of our social institutions that we are quite unaccustomed to. . . .
>
> We make two demands. The first . . . is that we exercise in nuclear technology the very best techniques and that we use people of high expertise and purpose. . . . The second demand is less clear, and I hope it may prove to be unnecessary. This is the demand for longevity in human institutions. We have relatively little problem dealing with [nuclear] wastes if we can assume always that there will be intelligent people around to cope with eventualities we have not thought of.

Finally, Weinberg asked:

> Is mankind prepared to exert the eternal vigilance needed to ensure proper and safe operation of its nuclear energy situation? This admittedly is a significant commitment that we ask of society. (pp. 33–34)

Social institutions must therefore watch over the dangerous lifespan of radioactive wastes which could be around for over 200,000 years, yet human institutions have endured for only a few thousand years. The nuclear power issue is a dramatic example of the Faustian bargain because the magnitude of time associated with the disposal of nuclear wastes is clear. There are, however, many other "bargains" where the true nature of the future payment is questionable.

REFERENCES

Ginsburg, N. (1957), "Natural Resources and Economic Development," *Annals of the Association of American Geographers* 47, No. 3, 197–212.

Hawkes, H. (1960), "The Paradoxes of the Conservation Movement," *Bulletin of the University of Utah* 51.

Hubbard, M. (1969), "Energy Resources," in *Resources and Man: National Academy of Sciences—National Research Council, Report of Committee on Resources and Man*. San Francisco: W. H. Freeman & Co., 157–242.

Landsberg, H. (1964), *Natural Resources for U.S. Growth*. Baltimore, MD: Johns Hopkins University Press.

The Leonardo Scholars (1975), *Resources and Decisions*. North Scituate, MA: Duxbury Press/Wadsworth Publishing Co., Inc.

Longwood, W. (1972), *The Darkening Land*. New York: Simon & Schuster, Inc.

Luten, D. B. (1971), "The Economic Geography of Energy," in *Energy and Power*. San Francisco: W. H. Freeman & Co., 109–120.

Luten, D. B. (1972), Based on a series of lectures given in Berkeley, California, and San Diego, California, in 1972 and 1973.

Tregarthen, T. D., Larkin, R. P., and Peters, G. L. (1978), "Mining, Markets, and Land Use," *The Geographical Review* 68, No. 3, 351–358.

U.S. Dept. of Agriculture (1971), *Commercial Wheat Production*. Economic Research Service Bulletin ERS 480, September.

Weinberg, A. W. (1972), "Social Institutions and Nuclear Energy," *Science* 177, 27–34.

Zimmermann, E. W. (1951), *World Resources and Industries*, rev. ed. New York: Harper & Bros., Publishers.

2

The Ecosphere

Barry Commoner

THE FIRST LAW OF ECOLOGY: EVERYTHING IS CONNECTED TO EVERYTHING ELSE

This generalization [. . .] reflects the existence of the elaborate network of interconnections in the ecosphere: among different living organisms and between populations, species, and individual organisms and their physicochemical surroundings.

The single fact that an ecosystem consists of multiple interconnected parts, which act on one another, has some surprising consequences. Our ability to picture the behavior of such systems has been helped considerably by the development, even more recent than ecology, of the science of cybernetics. We owe the basic concept, and the word itself, to the inventive mind of the late Norbert Wiener.

The word "cybernetics" derives from the Greek word for helmsman; it is concerned with cycles of events that steer, or govern, the behavior of a system. The helmsman is part of a system that also includes the compass, the rudder, and the ship. If the ship veers off the chosen compass course, the change shows up in the movement of the compass needle. Observed and interpreted by the helmsman this event determines a subsequent one: The helmsman turns the rudder, which swings the ship back to its original course. When this happens, the compass needle returns to its original, on-course position and the cycle is complete. If the helmsman turns the rudder too far in response to a small deflection of the

---

compass needle, the excess swing of the ship shows up in the compass—which signals the helmsman to correct his overreaction by an opposite movement. Thus the operation of this cycle stabilizes the course of the ship.

In quite a similar way, stabilizing cybernetic relations are built into an ecological cycle. Consider, for example, the freshwater ecological cycle: fish–organic waste–bacteria of decay–inorganic products–algae–fish. Suppose that due to unusually warm summer weather there is a rapid growth of algae. This depletes the supply of inorganic nutrients so that two sectors of the cycle, algae and nutrients, are out of balance, but in opposite directions. The operation of the ecological cycle, like that of the ship, soon brings the situation back into balance. For the excess in algae increases the ease with which fish can feed on them; this reduces the algal population, increases fish waste production, and eventually leads to an increased level of nutrients when the waste decays. Thus, the levels of algae and nutrients tend to return to their original balanced position.

In such cybernetic systems the course is not maintained by rigid control, but flexibly. Thus the ship does not move unwaveringly on its path, but actually follows it in a wavelike motion that swings equally to both sides of the true course. The frequency of these swings depends on the relative speeds of the various steps in the cycle, such as the rate at which the ship responds to the rudder.

Ecological systems exhibit similar cycles, although these are often obscured by the effects of daily or seasonal variations in weather and environmental agents. The most famous examples of such ecological oscillations are the periodic fluctuations of the size of fur-bearing animal populations. For example, from trapping records in Canada it is known that the populations of rabbits and lynx follow ten-year fluctuations. When there are many rabbits the lynx prosper; the rising population of lynx increasingly ravages the rabbit population, reducing it; as the latter become scarce, there is insufficient food to support the now numerous lynx; as the lynx begin to die off, the rabbits are less fiercely hunted and increase in number. And so on. These oscillations are built into the operation of the simple cycle, in which the lynx population is positively related to the number of rabbits and the rabbit population is negatively related to the number of lynx.

In such an oscillating system there is always the danger that the whole system will collapse when an oscillation swings so wide of the balance point that the system can no longer compensate for it. Suppose, for example, in one particular swing of the rabbit–lynx cycle, the lynx manage to eat *all* the rabbits (or, for that matter, all but one). Now the rabbit population can no longer reproduce. As usual, the lynx begin to starve as the rabbits are consumed; but this time the drop in the lynx population is not followed by an increase in rabbits. The lynx then die off. The entire rabbit–lynx system collapses.

This is similar to the ecological collapse which accompanies what is called "eutrophication." If the nutrient level of the water becomes so high as to stimulate the rapid growth of algae, the dense algal population cannot be long sustained because of the intrinsic limitations of photosynthetic efficiency. As the thickness of the algal layer in the water increases, the light required for photosynthesis that can reach the lower parts of the algal layer becomes sharply diminished so that any stong overgrowth of algae very quickly dies back, releasing organic debris. The organic matter level may then become so great that its decay totally depletes the oxygen content of the water. The bacteria of decay then die off, for they must have oxygen to survive. The entire aquatic cycle collapses.

The dynamic behavior of a cybernetic system–for example, the frequency of its natural oscillations, the speed with which it responds to external changes, and its overall rate of operation—depends on the relative rates of its constituent steps. In the ship system, the compass needle swings in fractions of a second; the helmsman's reaction takes some seconds; the ship responds over a time of minutes. These different reaction times interact to produce, for example, the ship's characteristic oscillation frequency around its true course.

In the aquatic ecosystem, each biological step also has a characteristic reaction time, which depends on the metabolic and reproductive rates of the organisms involved. The time to produce a new generation of fish may be some months; of algae, a matter of days; decay bacteria can reproduce in a few hours. The metabolic rates of these organisms—that is, the rates at which they use nutrients, consume oxygen, or produce waste—is inversely related to their size. If the metabolic rate of a fish is 1, the algal rate is about 100, and the bacterial rate about 10,000.

If the entire cyclical system is to remain in balance, the overall rate of turnover must be governed by the slowest step—in this case, the growth and metabolism of the fish. Any external effect that forces part of the cycle to operate faster than the overall rate leads to trouble. So, for example, the rate of waste production by fish determines the rate of bacterial decay and the rate of oxygen consumption due to that decay. In a balanced situation, enough oxygen is produced by the algae and enters from the air to support the decay bacteria. Suppose that the rate at which organic waste enters the cycle is increased artificially, for example, by dumping sewage into the water. Now the decay bacteria are supplied with organic waste at a much higher level than usual; because of their rapid metabolism they are able to act quickly on the increased organic load. As a result, the rate of oxygen consumption by the decay bacteria can easily exceed the rate of oxygen production by the algae (and its rate of entry from the air) so that the oxygen level goes to zero and the system collapses. Thus, the rates of the separate processes in the cycle are in a natural state of balance which is maintained only so long as there are no external intrusions on the system. When such an effect originates outside the cycle, it is not controlled by the self-governing cyclical relations and is a threat to the stability of the whole system.

Ecosystems differ considerably in their rate characteristics and therefore vary a great deal in the speed with which they react to changed situations or approach the point of collapse. For example, aquatic ecosystems turn over much faster than soil ecosystems. Thus, an acre of richly populated marine shoreline or an acre of fish pond produces about seven times as much organic material as an acre of alfalfa annually. The slow turnover of the soil cycle is due to the rather low rate of one of its many steps—the release of nutrient from the soil's organic store, which is very much slower than the comparable step in aquatic systems.

The amount of stress an ecosystem can absorb before it is driven to collapse is also a result of its various interconnections and their relative speeds of response. The more complex the ecosystem, the more successfully it can resist a stress. For example, in the rabbit–lynx system, if the lynx had an alternative source of food they might survive the sudden depletion of rabbits. In this way, branching—which establishes alternative pathways—increases the resistance of an ecosystem to stress. Most ecosystems are so complex that the cycles are not simple circular paths, but are crisscrossed with branches to form a network or a fabric of interconnections. Like a net, in which each knot is connected to others by several strands, such a fabric can resist collapse better than a simple, unbranched circle of threads—which if cut anywhere breaks down as a whole. Environmental pollution is often a sign that ecological links have been cut and that the ecosystem has been artificially simplified and made more vulnerable to stress and to final collapse.

The feedback characteristics of ecosystems result in amplification and intensification processes of considerable magnitude. For example, the fact that in food chains small organisms are eaten by bigger ones and the latter by still bigger ones inevitably results in the concentration of certain environmental constituents in the bodies of the largest organisms at the top of the food chain. Smaller organisms always exhibit much higher metabolic rates than larger ones, so that the amount of their food that is oxidized relative to the amount incorporated into the body of the organism is thereby greater. Consequently, an animal at the top of the food chain depends on the consumption of an enormously greater mass of the bodies of organisms lower down in the food chain. Therefore, any *non*metabolized material present in the lower organisms of this chain will become concentrated in the body of the top one. Thus, if the concentration of DDT (which is not readily metabolized) in the soil is 1 unit, earthworms living in the soil will achieve a concentration of from 10 to 40 units, and in woodcocks feeding on the earthworms the DDT level will rise to about 200 units.

All this results from a simple fact about ecosystems—everything is connected to everything else: the system is stabilized by its dynamic self-compensating properties; these same properties, if overstressed, can lead to a dramatic collapse; the complexity of the ecological network and its intrinsic rate of turnover determine how much it can be stressed, and for how long, without collapsing; the ecological network is an amplifier, so that a small perturbation in one place may have large, distant, long-delayed effects.

THE SECOND LAW OF ECOLOGY: EVERYTHING MUST GO SOMEWHERE

This is, of course, simply a somewhat informal restatement of a basic law of physics—that matter is indestructible. Applied to ecology, the law emphasizes that in nature there is no such thing as "waste." In every natural system, what is excreted by one organism as waste is taken up by another as food. Animals release carbon dioxide as a respiratory waste; this is an essential nutrient for green plants. Plants excrete oxygen, which is used by animals. Animal organic wastes nourish the bacteria of decay. Their wastes, inorganic materials such as nitrate, phosphate, and carbon dioxide, become algal nutrients.

A persistent effort to answer the question "Where does it go?" can yield a surprising amount of valuable information about an ecosystem. Consider, for example, the fate of a household item which contains mercury—a substance with serious environmental effects that have just recently surfaced. A dry-cell battery containing mercury is purchased, used to the point of exhaustion, and then "thrown out." But where does it really go? First it is placed in a container of rubbish; this is collected and taken to an incinerator. Here the mercury is heated; this produces mercury vapor which is emitted by the incinerator stack, and mercury *vapor* is toxic. Mercury vapor is carried by the wind, eventually brought to earth in rain or snow. Entering a mountain lake, let us say, the mercury condenses and sinks to the bottom. Here it is acted on by bacteria which convert it to methyl mercury. This is soluble and taken up by fish; since it is not metabolized, the mercury accumulates in the organs and flesh of the fish. The fish is caught and eaten by a man and the mercury becomes deposited in his organs, where it might be harmful. And so on.

This is an effective way to trace out an ecological path. It is also an excellent way to counteract the prevalent notion that something which is regarded as useless simply "goes away" when it is discarded. Nothing "goes away"; it is simply transferred from place to place, converted from one molecular form to another, acting on the life processes of any organism in which it becomes, for a time, lodged. One of the chief reasons for the present environmental crisis is that great amounts of materials have been extracted from the earth, converted into new forms, and discharged into the environment without taking into account that "everything has to go somewhere." The result, too often, is the accumulation of harmful amounts of material in places where, in nature, they do not belong.

THE THIRD LAW OF ECOLOGY: NATURE KNOWS BEST

In my experience this principle is likely to encounter considerable resistance, for it appears to contradict a deeply held idea about the unique competence of human beings. One of the most pervasive features of modern technology is the notion that it is intended to "improve on nature"—to provide food, clothing, shelter, and means of communication and expression which are superior to those available to man in nature. Stated baldly, the third law of ecology holds that any major man-made change in a natural system is likely to be *detrimental* to that system. This is a rather extreme claim; nevertheless I believe it has a good deal of merit if understood in a properly defined context.

I have found it useful to explain this principle by means of an analogy. Suppose you were to open the back of your watch, close your eyes, and poke a pencil into the exposed works. The almost certain result would be damage to the watch. Nevertheless, this result is not *absolutely* certain. There is some finite possibility that the watch was out of adjustment and that the random thrust of the pencil happened to make the precise change needed to improve it. However, this outcome is exceedingly improbable. The question at issue is: why? The answer is self-evident: there is a very considerable amount of what technologists now call "research and development" (or, more familiarly, "R & D") behind the watch. This means that over the years numerous watchmakers, each taught by a predecessor, have tried out a huge variety of detailed arrangements of watch works, have discarded those that are not compatible with the overall operation of the system and retained the better features. In effect, the watch mechanism, as it now exists, represents a very restricted selection, from among an enormous variety of possible arrangements of component parts, of a singular organization of the watch works. Any random change made in the watch is likely to fall into the very large class of inconsistent, or harmful, arrangements which have been tried out in past watch-making experience and discarded. One might say, as a law of watches, that "the watchmaker knows best."

There is a close, and very meaningful, analogy in biological systems. It is possible to induce a certain range of random, inherited changes in a living thing by treating it with an agent, such as x-irradiation, that increases the frequency of mutations. Generally, exposure to x-rays increases the frequency of all mutations which have been observed, albeit very infrequently, in nature and can therefore be regarded as *possible* changes. What is significant, for our purpose, is the universal observation that when mutation frequency is enhanced by x-rays or other means, nearly all the mutations are harmful to the organisms and the great majority so damaging as to kill the organism before it is fully formed.

In other words, like the watch, a living organism that is forced to sustain a random change in its organization is almost certain to be damaged rather than improved. And in both cases, the explanation is the same—a great deal of "R & D." In effect there are some two to three billion years of "R & D" behind every living thing. In that time, a staggering number of new individual living things have been produced, affording in each case the opportunity to try out the suitability of some random genetic change. If the change damages the viability of the organism, it is likely to kill it before the change can be passed on to future generations. In this way, living things accumulate a complex organization of compatible parts; those possible arrangements that are not compatible with the whole are screened out over the long course of evolution. Thus, the structure of a present living thing or the organization of a current natural ecosystem is likely to be "best" in the sense that it has been so heavily screened for disadvantageous components that any new one is very likely to be worse than the present ones.

This principle is particularly relevant to the field of organic chemistry. Living things are composed of many thousands of different organic compounds, and it is sometimes imagined that at least some of these might be improved upon if they were replaced by some man-made variant of the natural substance. The third law of ecology suggests that the artificial introduction of an organic compound that does not occur in nature, but is man-made and is nevertheless active in a living system, is very likely to be harmful.

This is due to the fact that the varieties of chemical substances actually found in living things are vastly more restricted than the *possible* varieties. A striking illustration is that if one molecule each of all the possible types of proteins were made, they would together weigh more than the observable universe. Obviously there are a fantastically large number of protein types that are *not* made by living cells. And on the basis of the foregoing, one would reason that many of these possible protein types were once formed in some particular living things, found to be harmful, and rejected through the death of the experiment. In the same way, living cells synthesize fatty acids (a type of organic molecule that contains carbon chains of various lengths) with even-numbered carbon chain lengths (i.e., 4, 6, 8, etc., carbons), but no fatty acids with odd-numbered carbon chain lengths. This suggests that the latter have once been tried out and found wanting. Similarly, organic compounds that contain attached nitrogen and oxygen atoms are singularly rare in living things. This should warn us that the artificial introduction of substances of this type would be dangerous. This is indeed the case, for such substances are usually toxic and frequently carcinogenic. And, I would suppose from the fact that DDT is nowhere found in nature, that somewhere, at some time in the past, some unfortunate cell synthesized this molecule—and died.

One of the striking facts about the chemistry of living systems is that for every organic substance produced by a living organism, there exists, somewhere in nature, an enzyme capable of breaking that substance down. In effect, no organic substance is synthesized unless there is provision for its degradation; recycling is thus enforced. Thus, when a new man-made organic substance is synthesized with a molecular structure that departs significantly from the types which occur in nature, it is probable that no degradative enzyme exists, and the material tends to accumulate.

Given these considerations, it would be prudent, I believe, to regard every man-made organic chemical *not* found in nature which has a strong action on any one organism as potentially dangerous to other forms of life. Operationally, this view means that all man-made organic compounds that are at all active biologically ought to be treated as we do drugs, or rather as we *should* treat them—prudently, cautiously. Such caution or prudence is, of course, impossible when billions of pounds of the substance are produced and broadly disseminated into the ecosystem where it can reach and affect numerous organisms not under our observation. Yet this is precisely what we have done with detergents, insecticides, and herbicides. The often catastrophic results lend considerable force to the view that "Nature knows best."

THE FOURTH LAW OF ECOLOGY: THERE IS NO SUCH THING AS A FREE LUNCH

In my experience, this idea has proven so illuminating for environmental problems that I have borrowed it from its original source, economics. The "law" derives from a story that economists like to tell about an oil-rich potentate who decided that his new wealth needed the guidance of economic science. Accordingly he ordered his advisers, on pain of death, to produce a set of volumes containing all the wisdom of economics. When the tomes arrived, the potentate was impatient and again issued an order—to reduce all the knowledge of economics to a single volume. The story goes on in this vein, as such stories will, until the advisers are required, if they are to survive, to reduce the totality of economic science to a single sentence. This is the origin of the "free lunch" law.

In ecology, as in economics, the law is intended to warn that every gain is won at some cost. In a way, this ecological law embodies the previous three laws. Because the global ecosystem is a connected whole, in which nothing can be gained or lost and which is not subject to over-all improvement, anything extracted from it by human effort must be replaced. Payment of this price cannot be avoided; it can only be delayed. The present environmental crisis is a warning that we have delayed nearly too long.

The preceding pages provide a view of the web of life on the earth. An effort has been made to develop this view from available facts, through logical relations, into a set of comprehensive generalizations. In other words, the effort has been scientific.

Nevertheless, it is difficult to ignore the embarrassing fact that the final generalizations which emerge from all this—the four laws of ecology—are ideas that have been widely held by many people without any scientific analysis or professional authorization. The complex web in which all life is enmeshed, and man's place in it, are clearly—and beautifully—described in the poems of Walt Whitman. A great deal about the interplay of the physical features of the environment and the creatures that inhabit it can be learned from *Moby Dick*. Mark Twain is not only a marvelous source of wisdom about the nature of the environment of the United States from the Mississippi westward, but also a rather incisive critic of the irrelevance of science which loses connection to the realities of life. As the critic Leo Marx reminds us, "Anyone familiar with the work of the classic American writers (I am thinking of men like Cooper, Emerson, Thoreau, Melville, Whitman, and Mark Twain) is likely to have developed an interest in what we recently have learned to call ecology."

Unfortunately, this literary heritage has not been enough to save us from ecological disaster. After all, every American technician, industrialist, agriculturalist, or public official who has condoned or participated in the assault on the environment has read at least some of Cooper, Emerson, Thoreau, Melville, Whitman, and Mark Twain. Many of them are campers, bird-watchers, or avid fishermen, and therefore to some degree personally aware of the natural processes that the science of ecology hopes to elucidate. Nevertheless, most of them were taken unawares by the environmental crisis, failing to understand, apparently, that Thoreau's woods, Mark Twain's rivers, and Melville's oceans are *today* under attack.

The rising miasma of pollution has helped us to achieve this understanding. For, in Leo Marx's words, "The current environmental crisis has in a sense put a literal, factual, often quantifiable base under this poetic idea [i.e., the need for human harmony with nature]." This is perhaps the major value of the effort to show that the simple generalizations which have already emerged from perceptive human contact with the natural world have a valid base in the facts and principles of a science, ecology. Thus linked to science, these ideas become tools for restoring the damage inflicted on nature by the environmental crisis.

In the woods around Walden Pond or on the reaches of the Mississippi, most of the information needed to understand the natural world can be gained by personal experience. In the world of nuclear bombs, smog, and foul water, environmental understanding needs help from the scientist.

II
Historical Overview

Perceptions of resources vary not only among cultures and physical environments but also through time. Geographer Geoffrey J. Martin illustrates this idea in the following essay, and he summarizes some of the changing perceptions of resources that have arisen out of changing circumstances. Yet if change is one theme of this essay, constancy is another. Concern about food scarcity is thousands of years old, and we still use some of our original techniques to ensure adequate supplies. President Harry S. Truman tried to make the United States independent of foreign oil supplies a generation before President Jimmy Carter did. The environmental movement began not on Earth Day in 1970, nor in the days of naturalist John Muir, nor even a century earlier with Henry David Thoreau. It began many millennia ago in ancient Sumer, where water was husbanded, and in China, where soil was carefully nurtured.

What is new is the rapidity of change and the resultant instability in the world despite the fundamental constancy of basic human needs and responses to the environment. The rapidity of population growth, technological development, decolonization, the rise and fall of great powers, armaments production and distribution, growth of the gap between rich and poor—all have placed far greater stress than ever before on our store of resources of all kinds. Is it now possible to avoid investigating the possible utility of any portion of the earth's surface or any element of our environment? Can we any longer simply leave something or some place alone, as it was before we discovered it?

3

Global Resources in Historical Perspective

Geoffrey J. Martin

For all but a tiny fraction of human history, the earth's population has grown at a very slow pace. After two to four million years on earth, the human population probably did not exceed five million. Throughout those millennia people lived as hunters and gatherers. Speech, tools, and fire were not discovered until Paleolithic time (approximately the last two million years). Only in the last 100,000 years (the Upper Paleolithic) were bone and ivory implements developed, and then the spear and the bow and arrow, which enabled people to become successful hunters.

In the Neolithic period (approximately the last 10,000 years) people learned to make more sophisticated tools as well as pottery, and, most importantly, in several areas of the tropical world they domesticated plants and animals. Gradually, human manipulation of, and domination over, the biotic world became more thorough. A producing economy replaced a collecting economy. Ingenuity led to invention. The plow was developed about 5000 B.C., the wheel about 3500 B.C., and bronze implements and weapons very soon thereafter. The camel was domesticated about 5000 B.C. and the horse in 3000 B.C. Some 1500 years later the introduction of the alphabet, and in 1000 B.C. iron working, contributed to human advance.

Coincident with cultural progress came the advance of agriculture. By the Neolithic era hunters and gatherers had proliferated throughout the world, and increasing population pressure demanded a system that provided a larger caloric return per unit of earth space. It was one of mankind's great decisions to choose agriculture over hunting and gathering, and it did so universally in a brief span of time. By the beginning of the Christian era, the population had increased to some 250 million, concentrated in three great centers: Greco-Roman (the Mediterranean region), the Chin and Han dynasties (China, but extending into Southeast Asia), and the successors of the Mauryan Empire (northern India).

Between the first and mid-seventeenth centuries A.D., the world population doubled to half a billion, though net growth was erratic owing to the devastation of pandemic diseases. This first sustained and substantial advance of world population coincided with the diversification of agriculture. Most notable among the new forms of agricultural practice that emerged were shifting cultivation, livestock domestication, intensive subsistence agriculture, and plantation agriculture. Each developed in its own environmental niche, and there were numerous variations in practice among different cultures. Critical to the development of agriculture were the plant seeds that were carried from one area to another and, by a process of trial and error, were established and then perpetuated themselves in suitable physical environments. Basic technology helped transform planters into farmers, and superior tools enabled them to work the soil in a manner not previously possible. The more successful this agriculture, the more sedentary became the population. Having learned that the physical environment was a critical resource, people settled in warm areas and shunned cold, preferred river valleys to bleak uplands, sought climates with long growing seasons, and learned that soils had different properties.

Preindustrial society was largely rural, although there were the beginnings of urban settlements. The latter were few in number and small in population. In times of drought, when pasture was poor and livestock did not flourish, wandering nomads would attack the settled areas. They recognized them as centers of resource surplus.

Preindustrial society predated the rule of law and was racked by conflict—Greeks versus Persians, Romans versus Carthaginians, Christians versus Muslims. The quest for greater material wealth inspired expansion by military conquest. A warring group was usually well endowed with able-bodied men, possessed appropriate equipment and weaponry, and was usually experienced in some form of military strategy. Those were the attributes of the Roman Empire at the height of its power. Military success was rewarded by new territory, new subjects, new weaponry, and new agricultural environments. Governmental apparatus evolved for the exercise of political control and the maintenance of stability. Trade expanded within the empire and beyond with other peoples. More trade usually meant more wealth as the comparative cost advantages worked to the benefit of each trader. The wealth of empires grew as their comprehension of environments slowly developed.

TERRITORIAL AND ECONOMIC EXPANSION

The quest for trade and exploratory discoveries stimulated the agricultural and scientific innovation that ushered in the industrial age. Modern European expansion may be said to have begun with the Portuguese conquest of Ceuta, Morocco, in 1415. It was the search for a route to the East that brought Columbus to the Americas. Conquistadores, missionaries, settlers, and craftsmen from Europe followed in search of gold and silver, religious freedom, free land, bases near excellent fishing grounds, and an escape from political oppression. By 1650, Spain, Portugal, France, England, and the Netherlands had colonies in the Americas. Portugal, followed by France, England, and the Netherlands, also acquired coastal bases from which to ply profitable trade.

A second cycle of colonial empire building began in the 1760s. Within 60 years, the European colonies in the New World had dwindled to holdings of little significance. Much of British North America had achieved independence by revolution in 1783. France lost Haiti in 1804, and Spain had lost all its continental possessions by 1825, the same year that Portugal recognized the independence of Brazil.

In the late 1800s there was a new burst of enthusiasm to secure "places in the sun." Nationalism was on the rise. Its moral counterpart was Rudyard Kipling's notion that Europe should assume the "white man's burden." Expansion was thought to be appropriate, attainable, and beneficial. The tropics offered a variety of products, among them tea and coffee, which were already established as favored beverages. These lands also represented markets for certain products now emerging from European factories. Some of the colonial powers were especially anxious to secure territories with potential strategic significance. Between 1880 and 1910 the pace of annexation quickened, and by 1914 Europe dominated all the continents with the exception of the Americas.

THE MECHANICAL REVOLUTION

The principal stimulus for European colonialism was doubtless industrialization. There was an attendant felt need to expand and acquire economies of scale at a time when a rapidly growing population had reached substantial density. Britain was in the forefront of the Industrial Revolution. With the end of the Thirty Years' War in 1648 and the return of peace and order, Britain experienced a period of unprecedented economic growth. Its population and trade increased rapidly. Sugar, tobacco, and cotton from colonial America were unloaded at docks in Liverpool and Bristol, and textiles from British factories were shipped overseas. British advances in technology and industrial production were diffused throughout Western Europe and North America, then to southern and Eastern Europe, and to much of the remainder of the world through colonialism.

The Industrial Revolution that began in Britain was fundamentally social. It brought people from the countryside into the factory and urban environment—eloquently portrayed in Oliver Goldsmith's "The Deserted Village." The factories themselves were the result of the division of labor, so well written about in Adam Smith's *The Wealth of Nations*. The concurrent mechanical revolution, on the other hand, was the product of a new technology that made possible the substitution of machine power for human muscle and animal power.

The year 1769, when James Watt announced his steam engine, is frequently cited as the beginning of the Industrial Revolution, but the real revolution did not begin until the development of metallurgical processes, more particularly the process for making sheet iron. Sheet iron had been developed in the early eighteenth century, but decades would pass before the introduction of rods and bars. To produce sheet iron, factories were built near coalfields. The coal was needed to feed the steam engine, which then helped fashion machinery, which helped miners take yet more coal from the ground.

Discovery of the practical application of coal to the smelting and manufacture of iron had been made in the early eighteenth century, when the depletion of the British woodland was becoming apparent. Coal had a number of advantages over lumber: It was easier to transport, it burned more slowly than wood, and provided more heat. With the exploitation of coal, industrial production increased enormously. The mining, transport, storage, and utilization of coal became an industry in itself. The locomotive was a product of the revolution, as was the network of railroads, bridges, canal works, and steamboats. The transportation system expanded vastly, and hitherto remote parts of the globe became accessible.

Coal was responsible for all this and much more. Long before the mechanical revolution entered its second phase, scientists, including Alessandro Volta, Luigi Galvani, and Michael Faraday, were investigating the properties of electricity. The electric telegraph was developed about 1835 and the first undersea cable in 1851. By the 1880s, electric light, electric traction, and transmission of electric power were secrets no longer.

The third phase of the mechanical revolution came in the 1880s with a new type of engine in which the expansive force of an explosive mixture replaced the expansive force of steam. This led, of course, to the automobile, the airplane, and the oil industry. To maintain these industries required a continuous movement of labor from farm to factory in the urban area and a new arrangement for the use of land. Mechanization of agriculture had left a poorly paid surplus of laborers in the rural area, who migrated to coal mine or textile mill. Towns grew, and some became cities. Both suffered from overcrowding as people needed to live near their places of work. With the coming of the streetcar, poor housing followed the tracks radiating outward from the city center. In these conditions of overcrowding, long hours of work, and inadequate diet, diseases spread rapidly; improvements came slowly. Railroads and the settlements and factories that flanked them spread across the industrializing nations. The "civilizing rails" they were called. Formerly inaccessible areas were opened up. Agriculture was stimulated, and such resources as coal and timber could now be brought from afar to the city. Agricultural products could be transported to the urban community swiftly to meet demand. A symbiotic relationship had been achieved.

The population of the industrializing countries—and, indeed, the world—increased almost five times during the last two centuries. The consumption of water power, coal, electricity, oil, solar energy, nuclear power, and other forms of energy grew enormously. Raw material consumption escalated to such a startling degree that modern blast furnaces produce in less than one day the world's total output of iron in 1750.

Labor, inventive capacity, raw material, plus energy together produced a number of mass consumption societies. The economist W. W. Rostow calculates that economic "maturity" was achieved by Great Britain by 1850, the United States by 1900, Germany and France by 1910, Sweden by 1930, Japan by 1940, and the USSR and Canada by 1950.

A mark of maturity was the cities. Whereas early cities were strictly places of consumption, since the beginning of the Industrial Revolution they have also been centers of production. They include both the apparatus of production and the living quarters for vast numbers of people. This has brought about a revision of social structure, occupational structure, transportation, and housing. Whether production is attempted in a small town or large city, circulation is vital. Hence, the success of the transportation industry has become essential to the well-being of economically developed society. In the case of Los Angeles, approximately 50 percent of the area is given to the automobile—expressways, roadways, parking lots, garages, and the like (and this does not include the vast areas required by airports, railway lines, gas and oil pipelines, vehicle testing grounds, etc.).

Throughout the developed world we are covering over several thousand square miles of earth surface each year. In the urban context this brings air, water, earth, and noise pollution—a pattern that cannot continue indefinitely. The notion that expansion means growth and that all growth is good is no longer accepted wisdom.

THE POSTWAR ECONOMIC ORDER

At the end of World War II the United States and the Soviet Union emerged as the new military-industrial giants. The once splendidly developed economies of Western Europe were ruined. Clearing the rubble of war and rebuilding factories, houses, schools, churches, railroads, highways, and bridges were the order of the day.

The hitherto unprecedented consumption of resources of all kinds during the war led to many postwar policy changes that resulted in stockpiling, preemptive buying, and intensive exploration for new ore bodies. One of the most far-reaching of the new policies was expressed in the Truman Proclamation of September 28, 1945, in which the U.S. government laid claim to all of the resources on and under the continental shelf adjacent to its coasts. This initiated a still-continuing extension of coastal-state jurisdiction far out to sea.

By the late 1950s, Western Europe, with the help of the U.S. Marshall Plan and subsequent aid programs, was well on the road to recovery. In 1961, the Organization for European Economic Cooperation, founded in 1948, changed its name and function to become the Organization for Economic Cooperation and Development (OECD). A new emphasis was placed on the development of global trade. The relationships among the European states, the United States, Canada, Japan, Australia and New Zealand and the developing countries were given special emphasis. Six of these countries—Belgium, the Netherlands, Luxembourg, France, Italy, and West Germany—had already begun to work closely together. They had established the European Coal and Steel Community in 1952 to reduce the cost of steel making, and in 1957 they formed the European Economic Community, or Common Market. Seven countries—Austria, Denmark, Norway, Portugal, Sweden, Switzerland, and the United Kingdom—formed the European Free Trade Association in 1959. The principles of the free enterprise system were encouraged, and economic growth was the result. The military counterpart of these economic associations was the North Atlantic Treaty Organization (NATO).

In Eastern Europe there was a similar grouping of countries. The USSR, in 1949, organized the Council of Mutual Economic Assistance (CMEA) consisting of itself and the other Communist East European countries, with the exception of Yugoslavia. The same countries later formed the Warsaw Pact military alliance, the Eastern counterpart to NATO.

A few similar economic units were organized elsewhere. In Latin America, the Latin American Free Trade Association and the Central American Common Market were formed, and in Africa, the East African Community.

Each of these regional groupings represented a desire on the part of its members for security and protection, initially economic in nature. Peace and social and economic progress were also the objectives of the United Nations organization, founded in San Francisco in 1945. The preamble to the UN Charter is worthy of recollection: "We the peoples of the United Nations determined . . . to promote social progress and better standards of life in larger freedom, and for these ends . . . to employ international machinery for the promotion of the economic and social advancement of all peoples. . . ." Since 1945, the UN has developed a variety of committees, councils, offices, organizations, and commissions. Among the best known are the Food and Agriculture Organization (FAO), the UN Educational, Scientific and Cultural Organization (UNESCO), and the World Health Organization (WHO). Two key multilateral financial institutions are the International Bank for Reconstruction and Development (IBRD or World Bank) and the International Monetary Fund (IMF).

One of the areas in which UN efforts have been unsuccessful is in breaking down trade barriers. Although efforts to establish an International Trade Organization to deal with world trade problems failed, 23 major trading countries signed the General Agreement on Tariffs and Trade (GATT) in 1947. GATT's current membership is 88 countries. In order to enable the developing countries to increase their share of the benefits of trade, the first UN Conference on Trade and Development (UNCTAD) was held in Geneva in 1964. UNCTAD is now a permanent UN agency.

The U.S. and Soviet competition for allies and partners that began after World War II has not abated. In the 1950s and 1960s, both the United States and the USSR adopted foreign aid policies designed to win influence and allies. They spent vast sums of money, some wisely, some foolishly. Veiled competition in the form of cultural activities also took place—theater, opera, chess, sports events. The ever-escalating competition—political, economic, and cultural—led to still greater distrust and suspicion. And this was accompanied by an arms race that absorbed vast resources.

Post–World War II Decolonization and Effects

A principal source of the industrialized world's resources was the former European colonies. World War II had intensified nationalism throughout the world, and after the war colonial empires began to shrink. There were numerous reasons for decolonization in the postwar period. First, there was the new alignment of world power, with the United States and the Soviet Union dominating the world scene and both claiming to support independence for colonies. Second, the colonial powers, seriously weakened by the war years, no longer had the ability to retain authority and control overseas. Third, in many of the dependent countries, there were strong independence and resistance movements that the colonial authorities found difficult to combat. By 1981, some 100 colonies had become independent.

Some of the former colonial powers attempted to maintain indirect domination by retaining a division of labor between themselves, the manufacturing powers, and those supplying food, fuels, and raw materials, their former colonies. This indirect foreign domination, which ex-colonies sometimes refer to as neocolonialism, may assume many forms:

retention of former currency, language, economic ties, administrative systems, marketing arrangements, and even place-names and military assistance. Indeed this type of activity may be beneficial to the former colonials, and may be a necessary transitional stage of growth prior to the assumption of full economic independence.

CHANGING VIEWPOINTS AND ACTIVITIES OF DEVELOPING COUNTRIES DURING THE 1960s AND 1970s

The distinguishing characteristic of the new countries was their poverty, and a vast gap existed in the material standard of living between the "haves" and the "have-nots." Different terms have been used to describe the have-nots, each term euphemistically catering to sensitivities—hence, undeveloped, underdeveloped, developing, and less developed. This division between rich and poor is one of the most fundamental schisms of the twentieth century, and one that holds great portent for humanity, for two-thirds of humanity "have not."

An analysis of the differences in the two groups' accomplishments is a study in the history of resource exploitation. Those countries clustered around the North Sea were the first to benefit from the fruits of industrialization. They were followed in the nineteenth century by other temperate-latitude countries. People in those countries found it hard to penetrate the tropics because of the very real climatic barrier. As the years passed, temperate-latitude countries accumulated vast stores of capital, experience, and trained people to work with new technologies. They multiplied their advantages with advantages already won. But people living in many of the undeveloped countries continued life patterns that had not changed for centuries. A system of international exchange and capital flow developed that favored the developed world through the system of colonialism. Even after independence, much of the old pattern remains.

All too frequently underdeveloped countries have no industry, inefficient agricultural systems, low per capita incomes, high illiteracy rates, and high rates of population growth. Hunger and malnutrition are the rule, not the exception, and life expectancy is low. In many of these countries nearly half the population is under 15 years of age and is largely unemployed. These young people, because they are consumers and not producers, are a cost to society. They, too, will probably have large families, starting at an early age. Weaknesses in the economic order are revealed in the occupational structure of the labor force. Per capita consumption of energy and use of metal are very low, and transportation facilities are poor. The list is coextensive with the indices of societal growth.

Gunnar Myrdal has applied the principle of circular and cumulative causation to the plight of these countries. Malnourished people are not healthy people and are subject to disease, which means they will not be as economically productive as would otherwise be the case. This, in turn, makes their escape from poverty and hunger all the more unlikely. Outside capital is brought in only at higher interest rates because of perceived risks, and this slows investment in capital projects. Slowed capital projects mean reduced employment opportunities. This in turn reduces incomes and savings. In despair, the better educated, who may also be the more intelligent, may choose to migrate to the developed world. This further worsens the plight of the less developed economy, which cannot afford to lose educated people. But is the situation all gloom and doom? Or are there grounds for optimism?

Developing Countries' Prospects

There are three circumstances that, although not irrevocable, are at least somewhat determinative. The first of these is size. Some countries are so small that they are not able to achieve the economies of scale and simply find it very difficult to shoulder the costs of government, at least in a form comparable to that which they enjoyed under British rule, for example. It is not by chance that the Falklands, Gibraltar, and Pitcairn have remained with the British Empire. It is difficult for small states to acquire more territory. Expansion by conquest is most unlikely. However, expansion via a form of federation is practical and has been successfully accomplished in the past, for example, by Malaysia and the United Arab Emirates.

The second circumstance that is difficult to change is the physical environment. Some physical environments are hostile. Desert states, such as Mali, Mauretania, and Chad, can do little to compensate for regoliths or a climate characterized by a great diurnal range of temperature. Other states, such as Zaire and Brazil (in large part), which are located in the tropical rain forest, can do as little to overcome heavy rainfalls and leached soils.

The third circumstance somewhat determinative of growth is the way in which a country secured its independence and the resulting political climate, that is, its stability, or instability. Some states secured independence via negotiation, and some secured it only after violence. Some had experience with self-government, others had none. The transition from colony to independent state was frequently complicated by local parochialism, tribalism, and regionalism. If fragmentation occurred (Balkanization), the state almost certainly emerged weakened and this could lead to civil war (as in the case of Nigeria). The success of a new nation depends upon the adequacy of its leadership, but in the longer run it depends on sustained economic development.

The countries of the developing world can be grouped into three categories. In the first group are the oil producers, which have formed the

Organization of Petroleum Exporting Countries (OPEC). Oil has become the life blood of the industrial process, and without it, the developed world would come to a standstill. The transformation of the Saudi Arabian economy since it acquired oil wealth has been one of the most spectacular cases recorded in the annals of economic history. A steady production of 10 million barrels of oil a day, which sells for $34 per barrel (1982 price), is an asset producing $340 million per day. And costs of extraction are low. Oil has also been a vitally important asset to the economies of Algeria, Iran, Iraq, Kuwait, Libya, Indonesia, Nigeria, the United Arab Emirates, and Venezuela.

In the second group of developing countries are those that have a commodity or commodities sought by developed countries, but in which conditions do not favor creation of cartels. Such commodities would include natural rubber (Malaysia, Indonesia, Thailand), tea (India, Sri Lanka), coffee (Brazil, Colombia, Ivory Coast), cacao (Ghana, Nigeria, Brazil, Ivory Coast), bananas (Brazil, Ecuador, India), jute (India, Pakistan, Bangladesh), peanuts (India, Nigeria), chromium (Zimbabwe, Philippines, Iran), copper (Zambia, Chile, Zaire), and bauxite (Jamaica, Suriname, Guyana). These commodities enjoy a demand that is both widespread and increasing. Price fluctuations for the most part are not significant. Copper is a notable exception, however. They are commodities in which developing countries can afford to invest.

In the third group of developing countries are those that seem to lack resources capable of development. Given present knowledge, and the present state of technology, countries such as the Somali Republic, Chad, and Burundi belong in this group. Naturalistic subsistence ways are likely to persist in these countries, and new ways are not likely to make a strong impress.

In each of these three groups, however, are common problems and concerns that have led to common responses. For example, during the 1960s and 1970s some states (especially in Central and South America) attempted land reform, reducing the vast holdings of a few landowners and making these areas available to poorer citizens for agricultural purposes. In other countries, which are arid or semiarid, governments attempted to settle nomadic populations by providing water at fixed points in the territory. This would encourage settlement of humans and livestock as a prelude to further development—perhaps ranching. Other states attempted to improve transportation and communication. Road building, especially, received attention. Hard-surface, all-weather roads began to replace dirt roads, which became rivers of mud in the wet season and clouds of dust in the dry season.

Attempts have been made to improve educational facilities and to assault the problem of illiteracy, and with the rise in literacy come newspapers. Attempts are also being made to improve the health of populations. Advances have been made by the spread of the principles of hygiene, but many other health problems remain. Medical facilities and medical practitioners are in short supply. Banking is emerging, especially in the larger urban areas—a product of economic growth. Urbanization is also taking place. Although black Africa, for example, still has only three cities of one million or more, it has a number of towns numbering in the hundreds of thousands.

Essentially, some of the major problems could be overcome by the application of sufficient amounts of capital. But it takes capital to produce capital, and the problem is where to begin capital formation. During the 1950s and 1960s in particular, the OECD countries, and to a far lesser extent the Communist bloc, extended aid for a variety of projects. Other sources of capital include the World Bank and private investment from the multinational corporations of developed countries. Corporate capital is driven away by political instability, erratic activity (for example, Idi Amin's in Uganda), and the possibility of nationalization or freezing of foreign resources.

A solution to the energy needs of the developing countries would be a major stimulus to growth. Some believe that in the long run solar energy will provide the answer. The developing countries may then find themselves with an invaluable supply of sunshine that could initiate a new era in energy supply and cost. This, too, demands experimentation, which in turn demands capital. Many of the developing countries have substantial rivers flowing through them year-round, which would provide a cheap and clean source of energy. But it is clearly unwise to develop such a functioning source of power unless there is industry to feed. This in turn requires roads, railways, banking facilities, working population, and so on. Nevertheless, this sort of power has already been exploited in the developing world with considerable success, as, for example, on the Volta River, in Ghana, where bauxite is smelted cheaply.

Many of the developing countries are increasing the production of food and beverages for export, a pattern that was developed in colonial times. For many years this had been regarded as a class of production somehow less desirable than industrial production. This view is being reappraised since a burgeoning and ever more urbanized world population means that the price of food will rise sharply relative to other resources. Food-producing nations can anticipate a prosperous future.

The OPEC Revolution: A Turning Point

In the first three quarters of this century consumption of fossil fuels increased ten times in the United States. The growth of the United States, and indeed of the developed world, was predicated upon a cheap and easily available source and supply of energy. By 1973, each person each day in the United States used an average of more than 3 gallons of oil, 300 cubic feet of natural gas, 14 pounds of coal, and other forms of energy. This was close to six times the world average. Part of this was due to the fact that the United States is a very large and sparsely populated country, when compared to most other developed countries. One-quarter of the entire U.S. national energy budget is spent on transportation. This compares with 12 percent for the countries of Western Europe. Extravagance of energy use has become typical in the United States, as exemplified by the overheating of residences, schools, and places of work and the driving of fuel-inefficient cars.

The United States produces approximately 14 percent of the world's petroleum, and this percentage will decline once Iran and Iraq resume normal ouput. Half of the U.S. petroleum need is being imported. Western Europe confronts an even more serious situation. These countries constitute nearly 10 percent of the world population, consume 23 percent of world oil production, while contributing less than 3 percent of it. Japan finds itself in a particularly vulnerable position, consuming nearly 8 percent of world petroleum production, while producing virtually none. The USSR emerged as the world's leading producer of petroleum in 1974. It has very considerable known reserves and could increase production with time and investment. It satisfies its own needs and exports petroleum to Eastern Europe, hard-currency countries, and developing countries.

Historically, global consumption of petroleum has persistently increased. It is a commodity for which, in the short run (and perhaps a very substantial short run), there is no adequate substitute. It is not, then, difficult to comprehend how a cartel has been formed by a group of major producing countries, which themselves are not substantial consumers of petroleum. Petroleum is virtually inelastic in demand for most industrial countries. Economic recession and self-imposed conservation practices may reduce demand a little, but normative increments of growth in industry and population continue to increase the demand for petroleum, both as a fuel and as a raw material. In the longer run it may be that nuclear energy will alter the supply-demand equation for petroleum. But environmental considerations, episodes such as that experienced at Three Mile Island, the possibility of acts of terrorism, nuclear attack, or earthquake have, to date, discouraged the advanced development that was anticipated in the 1970s.

The year 1973 marked a turning point in the world energy situation. Some 50 years of ever-growing dependence on cheap Middle East oil by the United States, Europe, and Japan came to a halt. The price of OPEC oil was raised by more than 350 percent, bringing on the world recession of 1974–75. Nevertheless, U.S. imports of oil continued to rise in the period 1973 to 1976. This created a serious balance-of-payments problem for the United States, and the value of the dollar reached new lows internationally. By 1977, U.S. oil imports had risen to nearly 9 million barrels per day—one-third more than in 1973. Alaskan production began to help, but the drop in Iranian production as a result of the revolution reduced any gains that had been made. Energy prices subsequently rose faster than the rate of inflation, and there were scattered brown-outs, dimmed lights, and slowed air conditioners across the country. Electric utilities urged conservation instead of consumption. Winter fuel oil supplies ran low, and schools were closed for lack of heat. Gas rationing was also threatened. Conservation of energy was urged both on financial and environmental grounds. Clearly a coherent national energy policy was needed. In 1976 came the natural gas shortage, and in the summer of 1979 gasoline lines formed once again.

As the United States continues to import oil, less wealthy countries find themselves at a disadvantage in competing for ever more costly supplies. The foreign policy consequences of this situation are significant. There has been a massive shift in international political power. Leaders of OPEC countries are now courted by the industrialized countries. Vast amounts of capital have been transferred from oil-importing to OPEC countries. OPEC countries did not reinvest the petrodollars swiftly enough, and consequently 1974 and 1975 were recession years for the world economy. Gross national products declined severely. Developing countries suddenly found that plans for expansion based on cheap petroleum had to be revised. Meanwhile OPEC accumulated capital at an astonishing rate.

These countries purchased modern armaments, and their military forces now represent substantial power. Oil-producing countries may exact political or other concessions from importers. Saudi Arabia clearly influenced U.S.-Israeli relations in the decade of the 1970s. Erratic oil supplies can mean erratic industrial production, interrupted business, and a slowdown in employment. Conflict, too, is not far from the surface. At the height of the Saudi-U.S. oil-related tension, there was talk of invading Saudi oil fields and retaliatory talk of blowing up the fields. The producers realize that oil is the food of Western industry.

The Arab oil embargo of 1973 affected not only the energy policy of the rich industrialized countries. Immediately after World War II, it may be recalled, the United States began seeking self-sufficiency in, or at least assured access to, all kinds of commodities in preparation for another period of danger such as World War II. This concern persisted through the cold war, but waned during the 1960s and early 1970s. The oil embargo came as a rude and jolting reminder that sources of commodities could be cut off by forces beyond the developed countries' control. The OECD members thereupon renewed their efforts to ensure continuous supplies not only of energy but also of strategic minerals, including the polymetallic nodules containing rich concentrations of copper, cobalt, nickel, manganese, and other minerals that lie in the deep seabed.

Strategic and economic interests had once more combined to reinforce the old "colonial economy"—the exchange of commodities from tropical and semitropical countries (mostly former colonies) for the manufactured goods of industrialized countries in the middle latitudes. This has come to be known as the "North-South" division of the world's peoples. At the same time, the rich countries acquired a new reason to break this old pattern and lessen their own dependence on commodities imported from the poor countries. But no one has yet discovered how to do this, and it is very likely both impossible and unwise.

In the long run it is thought that research and development will lead to the use of sustainable energy sources, including nuclear fusion, solar energy, geothermal energy, and perhaps ocean thermal energy conversion (OTEC). Much will depend on public perception of the hazards associated with the production of nuclear energy and on the need to preserve environmental quality. In the future it may be that the developing countries will develop (and export) solar energy much as the temperate latitudes developed the coal resource pursuant to development of the steam engine.

DEVELOPMENT OF A WORLDWIDE ENVIRONMENTAL CONSCIOUSNESS

The countries of the developed world face a set of problems that may require modification of the very system and the way in which their people live. These problems have been reduced to four dilemmas. The first of these has been called the growth dilemma: We need continued economic growth but cannot endure the consequences of this growth. The second is the control dilemma: We need more advice and shared knowledge over technological advance, yet are reluctant to agree to central management. Third is the distribution dilemma: Wealthy nations find it too expensive to share wealth with poor nations, even though failure to share can lead to disaster. And the fourth is the work role dilemma: Industrialized societies cannot provide the young with the jobs that youth has learned to expect from the system.

All of this means that we may be facing new scarcities and may be approaching planetary limits to growth. A multitude of writings have appeared on the twin themes "limits to growth" and "the end of progress." A vast and ever-growing world population vies for what is ultimately a fixed nonrenewable resource base. Conflict over resources only rallocates these scarce goods. And, as the years pass, more of these nonrenewable resources are used in a way that threatens still further the ecological niche that man has created for himself on the planet.

Careful planning is essential to the maintenance of a sustainable world. One of the largest difficulties confronting meaningful planning is that jobs are harnessed to industry, and industry, in all its diversity, contributes to polluted air, polluted water, and polluted earth. Jobs and industries are very tangible. Pollution is less immediate and less threatening. And so in most of the world the immediate priority of jobs very much outweighs the significance of long-run environmental damage.

The United States, with some 6 percent of the world's population, consumes one-third of the world's energy and raw material output. This is a form of ecological imperialism, which is repeated to a greater or lesser degree throughout the developed world, wherein the metropolitan centers consume a disproportionately large share of the irreplaceable natural resources.

All this is vastly complicated when an act in one country leads to environmental degradation in another. In that case the problem is regional and international. In some cases, however, the problem is global, and resolution would almost certainly require international agreement. The global problems include the following: (1) There is a possibility that ever-increasing carbon dioxide in the atmosphere will increase the temperature, leading to ice melt. This could lead to a eustatic change of sea level and would cover low-lying land throughout the world (just where so many of the world's largest cities are located). (2) Ever-increasing particulate matter in the atmosphere increases the earth's albedo (ability to reflect incoming solar radiation). (3) All fuel and energy conversion on earth expresses itself in the form of heat, which is absorbed by the atmosphere. (4) Persistent toxins have now spread across the world's surface (for example, DDT has been found in Antarctic animals). By poisoning phytoplankton, these toxins could affect the oxygen-carbon dioxide balance.

These are only some of the global problems confronting humanity. They have not been approached in a manner that suggests control of the situation or even an understanding of priorities. It is an appalling fact that military defense draws twice as much budget support in the world as food growing and five times as much as housing. Even such fundamental regional problems as airborne and waterborne residuals have not been satisfactorily resolved. More particularly, in the United States more than 700 million tons of waste particles are released into the air. The fact that little effectively is done about this derives in part from the greed for profit, or the desire to remain employed as previously, or the belief that nothing can be done about it anyway, living as we are in a technocracy where machine is king. Economic imperialism mixes with ignorance, apathy, and bureaucratic ossification, producing a flight from reason into ecological degradation.

In the developing world, mankind enjoys propinquity and heightened communion with the physical environment. Man is more nearly recognized as a part of nature, and not apart from nature. However, to the developing world, pollution means factories, transportation, and a higher material standard of living. All this seems attractive. The developing world needs economic growth in a most urgent manner, and environmental issues are of secondary concern. The developed world, having achieved economic well-being, now pays ever-increasing attention to environmental matters. It is possible to increase the national product without generating a deterioration in the physical environment; for example, in Britain, following the Clean Air Act of 1956, smoke emissions were reduced by 80 percent and sulfur dioxide by 40 percent. The excessive fogs have disappeared and death from bronchitis and emphysema has been reduced. And, too, with more rigorous water management, numerous rivers are cleaner, and fish are returning to what was once considered "dead water." The point is that economic growth can coexist with a nondeteriorating environment, but study, care, and money are essential.

Additionally, developing countries can learn from the mistakes of those countries already developed. The lessons of history can be valuable. What has proved successful in the industrial experience can be emulated; what has proved to be ineffective in the industrialization process may be rejected. However, this presupposes that there are sufficient resources to be shared in a world in which population continues to increase at alarming rates. If all the poorer countries of the world were to achieve the same level of living as the developed countries, the claims on resources would outstrip availability. Unfortunately, countries in a hurry are less inclined to listen to richer countries that now show concern for the global environment.

In a world where conflict is still so frequently settled by resort to arms, it is hard to be optimistic about global agreements concerning environmental betterment. Such improvements as have been instituted are the product of individual or group effort and usually take place in one country at a time, and not in regional blocs. Those who comprehend facets of the problem of environmental degradation rarely speak with voices of power, and the politician with the voice of power is rarely able to comprehend the fragility of "spaceship earth."

Since the late 1960s, there have been meetings and conferences on environmental issues, national and international courses have been introduced in higher education, and even departments of environmental science have been instituted on many campuses. Books have been written on the problems, and science fiction has had a field day with possible and eventual scenarios. Yet ignorance remains the greatest barrier. Through a concerted attempt to educate people internationally, this issue will one day demand attention. We can only hope it will not be too late.

III
Contemporary Perspectives

This section contains a potpourri of broad perspectives on resources and their links with other important features of contemporary life. Together the selections form a background for the more detailed debates to come in subsequent sections. If the conflicting views seem confusing, it is only because the writers have different frames of reference. Many of the ideas presented here will appear later but in different contexts and perhaps with different twists. Each could generate a debate by itself.

The first selection, by the editors of the Foreign Policy Association, presents the basic dilemmas of resources today as objectively as possible and ends, appropriately, with questions but no answers. Harvard geologist Kirtley F. Mather, writing during World War II, exudes classic American (or Western Judeo-Christian) optimism about the abundance of the earth and totally rejects the gloomy projections of nineteenth-century English economist Thomas Malthus. But still he emphasizes the interdependence of all the world. The Brandt Commission (named for its chairman, former West German Chancellor Willy Brandt), a private group of leaders from both the North and South who investigated the growing divergence between the rich and poor countries of the world, is much less optimistic and concludes that the only way to avoid disaster is for everyone—rich and poor, Communist and capitalist, agricultural and industrialized—to cooperate. David Harvey, a leader of the Marxist geographers in the West, analyzes the relationship between population and resources and concludes that this complex relationship can only be managed properly in a society based on dialectical materialism.

A contemporary version of the traditional attitude of North American Indians toward their environment is forcefully put forward by Vine Deloria, Jr., a modern American Indian political leader. He decries the destruction of the land by whites and their creation of an artificial universe that cannot be sustained. M. C. B. Hotz recognizes the impulse of most peoples, not just whites, to create an artificial universe through industrialization and urges development based on conservation. Tanzanian President Julius K. Nyerere explains succinctly what developing countries mean by a New International Economic Order, including control over their own resources and preferential benefits from seabed mining. The legal aspects of the distribution of world resources and the benefits deriving therefrom are examined by Oscar Schachter, a noted international lawyer formerly with the United Nations, who in this extract is concerned more with values than with legalisms.

The population of the world is not only growing rapidly but is rapidly concentrating in urban areas. Virtually all prognosticators agree that the world of the future will be largely urban, and architect Richard L. Meier urges the application of the principles of ecology to cities.

In scouring the world for new resource pools, people have inevitably turned to Antarctica and the Southern Ocean. Barbara Mitchell, a British scholar with the International Institute for Environment and Development in London, was one of the first to examine the potential for both benefits and conflicts here. We should be prompted by her very early warning to ask whether, except for scientific research, this region is not one that simply should be left alone. Rice Odell of The Conservation Foundation in Washington, D.C., points out the likely social and political effects of resource scarcity in the context of preserving humanistic values and suggests a version of the "small is beautiful" approach. We end this section on a high note, with two chapters from J. Peter Vajk's exuberant description of human exploitation of outer space in the near future—his solution to earthly resource problems—which must surely raise some questions in the minds of his readers.

4

Protecting World Resources: Is Time Running Out?

Editors of the Foreign Policy Association

> If present trends continue, the world in 2000 will be more crowded, more polluted, less stable ecologically, and more vulnerable to disruption than the world we live in now.
>
> —***Global 2000 Report***
>
> What a big 'if' that is.
>
> —René Dubos, scientist and conservationist, of the ***Global 2000*** premise

Global 2000, a three-year study commissioned by President Jimmy Carter and released in 1980, opened with the words above. Its message was that the world's natural resources are being wasted, abused, and consumed at accelerating and often unsustainable rates. The report warned that "unless the nations of the world act decisively to alter current trends" by the year 2000, fewer than 20 years away . . .

- The world population will climb from about 4.5 billion to 6.35 billion—5 billion in the Third World; 90 percent of the growth will take place in the world's poorest countries. Although the rate of growth will have slowed, the number of children born each year will increase from 80 million in 1980 to 100 million in the year 2000.
- Although literacy rates, life expectancies, and income levels per capita will rise, the larger total number of human beings will include

Reprint of "Protecting World Resources: Is Time Running Out?" in *Great Decisions '82*. Copyright 1982 by the Foreign Policy Association, New York. Reprinted by permission of the publisher. Pp. 49–57.

more illiterate people and more people living in absolute poverty than now.

- The real price of food will double; the world requirement for water will also double. The real price of most minerals, including fossil fuels, will rise.
- Most accessible forests in many Third World nations will disappear. Firewood shortages will become more severe for the 25 percent of the world's people who depend on it for fuel.
- Desertification (turning fertile land into desert) and soil erosion will increasingly cause floods, famine, and migration, as well as permanently remove huge areas of arable land from productive use each year.
- The extinction of plant and animal species will continue to accelerate, leading by 2000 to the loss of perhaps one out of five of all species now on earth (mostly losses of tropical plants or insects).
- A reduction of the ozone layer of the stratosphere, if it occurs as some scientists suspect, would allow more ultraviolet radiation to reach the earth, causing thousands more cases of skin cancer each year.
- Acid rain, air and water pollution, radioactivity, and improper disposal of solid wastes and hazardous materials will endanger increasing numbers of people.
- While food production per capita will increase 15 percent, little of the increase will go to countries where food is in short supply now. In the Middle East and South Asia, conditions will remain poor; in sub-Saharan Africa, the amount of food per person is expected to decline as Africa's population doubles from the year 1975 to 2000.

The authors of *Global 2000* emphasize that the report is not a prediction but a warning of what *could* happen. They also acknowledge that the figures on which the projections are based were often incomplete or outdated. Critics of the report say it is too pessimistic and does not allow for human ingenuity or the power of science and technology to solve problems as they arise. " 'Present trends' involving people typically *don't* continue," remarked Ben Wattenberg of the American Enterprise Institute, a "think tank" in Washington, "particularly if the trends are unfavorable." Julian Simon, an economist at the University of Illinois at Urbana-Champaign, probably the most persistent critic of *Global 2000*, argues that the report was written by well-known "gloom and doom" members of the environmental movement and was carelessly researched and questionably analyzed. "For most or all the relevant matters I have checked," Simon charged, "the trends are positive rather than negative." Simon and other critics have pointed out that *Global 2000* itself projects increases in per capita income, food production, education, and life expectancy, and says that in many places rates of population growth, pollution, and deforestation show signs of declining. In fact, the critics say, historically mankind's lot has been improving, and it will continue to improve.

But both critics and defenders of *Global 2000*—perhaps the largest government survey ever done on world resource trends—agree that the issues it discusses are critical ones.

LINKS TO FOREIGN POLICY

As photographs from outer space vividly remind us, all of humanity shares one planet. In a real sense, the earth is one ecosystem. Significant change or deterioration of one part of any ecological system will affect the rest sooner or later. This "ripple effect" is amplified by modern trade, transportation, and telecommunications, which have made nations more dependent on each other than ever before.

The effects of environmental problems on politics are not obvious, but they are profound. When a country's physical base deteriorates, its economy will soon suffer. The first and most important result of environmental damage on a large scale is that it becomes harder and harder for a country to feed its own people and provide employment. This in turn affects other nations which may supply food to the poorer country or receive immigrants from it. The United States, which exports more grain than any other nation, is said by its own soil scientists to be suffering soil erosion and loss of farmland at an accelerated rate because of these exports. The exports also have the effect of raising food prices for U.S. consumers.

Long-term dependency on another country for food may also have dangerous consequences for a poor nation. Garrett Hardin, one well-known and controversial environmentalist, has suggested that it is inhumane in the long run for the United States and other food exporters to aid countries that cannot feed themselves. While lives may be saved immediately by such aid, Hardin argues, this guaranteed food supply from abroad allows the growth of a population larger than the country's own resources could ever support alone. When food aid stops sooner or later, there will be far more people to suffer starvation. Others have called Hardin's argument inhumane, and make the point that U.S. food supplements can tide a poor nation over till it can build up its own grain reserve—substantially what has happened in India over the past decade.

Almost every major environmental issue in the world has implications for the United States—as the world's largest food exporter; as an international leader in industry, technology, and military security; as a defender of democracy; as a magnet for immigrants; as the world's largest economy; as the home of one of the world's largest populations (only China, India, and the USSR have more people).

A LOOK AT THE PAST

Concern about the environment as a natural system that can be polluted or overburdened in many ways is a relatively recent phenomenon. Two closely related factors explain the rise of this concern in the second half of the twentieth century: the global industrial revolution after World War II and the worldwide population explosion. While in wealthy countries the impact of industry has been the main environmental concern, in poor countries the exponential growth of population has had a more important impact.

Pollution of the air or water is nothing new—complaints of filthy water or smoke in the air have come down to us from ancient times. But most of the pollution of early times was strictly local: wood smoke or coal "fog" over a city, for example. The Industrial Revolution increased the rate of pollution at the same time it helped people live better. But for many years pollution was considered a relatively unimportant side effect of development. After World War II, however, there were more and more incidents that gradually brought international attention to what are now called environmental problems. In 1952, a particularly bad London "fog" killed 3,000 people in a few days. Los Angeles smog was already famous, contributing a new word to the English language. People going back to visit their old "swimming holes" found them filled with scum and bubbles. In 1962, Rachel Carson's book *Silent Spring*, which described the inadvertent killing of birds by the insecticide DDT, focused public concern on the problems of pollution.

During the late 1960s, public support for environmentalism swelled. Along with Britain, West Germany, Japan, and other industrialized countries, the United States passed laws and set up agencies to try to clean up the air and water. In the relatively prosperous years of the late 1960s and early 1970s, the costs of environmental protection—estimated in 1970 at $3,500 per person per decade in the United States—were examined less critically than they would be later on. Environmental protection, especially for clean air and water, was overwhelmingly popular with the public, polls showed.

THE STOCKHOLM CONFERENCE

At the same time, support was growing for international cooperation on environmental issues. In 1968, the Swedish government proposed a United Nations conference on the human environment and offered Stockholm as a site. During the preparations for the conference, held in 1972, a special effort was made to interest less developed nations, many of which had previously considered the environment to be a concern only of industrialized countries. Before the conference, each country attending was to prepare, if it wished, a report on the state of its environment—forests, water, farmland, and other natural resources. For many nations, this was the first official acknowledgment that environmental problems existed within their borders. It has been said that this awareness alone would have made the Stockholm Conference a success.

When the delegates from 113 countries met in Stockholm, however, they quickly found that the common concern which all their countries shared for the environment did not mean they agreed on what the main issues were. The industrialized countries were primarily worried about pollution, overpopulation, and resource conservation. The less developed countries, on the other hand, considered environmental problems such as foul air or degraded soils and forests secondary to the more immediate problems of poverty—hunger, disease, illiteracy, and unemployment. Preventing pollution from factories, Third World countries said, was admirable. But for 80 percent of the people in the world, having sufficient food was far more important. Developing nations saw technology and industry, even with their accompanying pollution, as keys to improving their lives.

By the end of the two-week Stockholm Conference, however, the delegates had managed to agree that the human environment must be protected even as development continues. They adopted an action plan which proposed the establishment of the United Nations Environment Program. UNEP includes Earthwatch, a program to monitor and indicate changes in the physical earth and its biological resources, and other programs.

TEN YEARS LATER

In the decade since the landmark Stockholm Conference, most nations have come to the official recognition that wise management of their natural resources is necessary for long-term prosperity. More important than any single meeting or program that arose from the conference was the awareness it engendered of the earth's ecology as a whole. The environmental dilemmas of both rich and poor nations were for the first time placed in a global perspective. This awareness has meant that even some of the poorest countries that previously concentrated solely on economic development are now taking steps to protect their natural resources, to encourage family planning, and to guard against the worst side effects of industrialization.

During the 1970s, environmental disasters continued to warn the public that vigilance was necessary, even as in many places problems lessened after action was taken. In Seveso (Italy), Minamata (Japan), and

Love Canal (near Buffalo in the United States), chemicals poisoned inhabitants and made their towns' names bywords for contamination. At the same time, the river Thames in England came slowly back to life, supporting 95 species of fish, including salmon; air quality in New York and Los Angeles improved; many lakes and streams became safe for fishing and swimming after decades of abuse.

Perhaps the key event of the decade was the Organization of Petroleum Exporting Countries (OPEC) oil embargo of 1973. Although it was an artificial shortage, to many it foreshadowed an "era of limits," in which more and more people would be competing for fewer and fewer resources. During the 1970s, other trends reinforced this perception. The "energy crisis" of the developed world—in oil—was joined by a second energy crisis of the poor nations—in firewood. In many places in the Third World, firewood has become prohibitively expensive or is simply unavailable. Population growth rates—perhaps one of the most important factors affecting a country's living standard—began to slow in many countries in the 1970s, but the number of children born each year increased.

While environmentalists and others warn that conservation and resource protection, as well as possible drastic measures to curb population, may be necessary to avert the dire possibilities outlined in *Global 2000*, some analysts believe that the prospects are far from grim. In the early 1800s, it was feared that great cities would be left in darkness as the world ran out of whale oil for lamps. In 1864, Julian Simon points out, the famous English economist William Stanley Jevons predicted that England would soon cease to grow economically because of a lack of coal. This stagnation, Jevons wrote, would soon "render our population excessive." In these and other cases, the invention of new technologies made feared resource shortages irrelevant. Optimists believe that the current or predicted "era of limits" will similarly be averted. Simon, for example, believes that "human ingenuity, rather than nature, is limitlessly bountiful." In response to predictions of future scarcity, Simon uses historical trend data to show that prices for most commodities and resources have tended to go down relative to wages, largely as a result of new technologies which have evolved over the past 200 years. Moreover, statistical measures of resource reserves are misleading because typically no one searches for more reserves while supplies are adequate. When more reserves are needed they have historically been found.

Simon also argues in his book *The Ultimate Resource* that high population growth rates are not a problem, contrary to most current public perception. Wealth, according to Simon, is produced or created by people, not just collected by them. Therefore, the more people, the more wealth. As world population has increased in the last hundred years, he points out, indexes of health and prosperity have climbed.

The "no limits" message of Simon, Herman Kahn, and other analysts has readily received a hearing. In the late 1970s and early 1980s, public and government opinion has appeared to be swinging back from the "limits to growth" views of a decade earlier. Still, there is a consensus that continued development should include the wise management of resources and a concern for the environment.

ARE RESOURCES RENEWABLE?

The environmental questions facing the world today can be separated into two groups. The first concerns so-called renewable resources. If a forest is cut down, another forest can be planted in its place. If a river is polluted, the sources of pollution can be eliminated and natural rainfall will soon allow the river to run clean again. But in the second group, nonrenewable resources such as fossil fuels are consumed but not replaced. (Theoretically, fossil fuels are also renewable, but certainly not on a human time scale.) Animal and plant species are also "nonrenewable"; once they are extinct, they cannot be replaced.

The division between renewable and nonrenewable is not always distinct. For example, topsoil formation is slow, perhaps taking centuries for only a few inches, although it can be speeded with fertilizer. But if topsoil washes away faster than it is replaced, the area may become barren, and it may then take thousands of years before the topsoil returns. In the case of contamination by chemicals, radiation, metals, or other substances, whether or not the resource—air, earth, or water—is "renewable" on a human time scale depends on the duration of the contamination. Minerals are also nonrenewable in the sense that there is a finite amount of each mineral in the earth. However, many minerals can be recycled over and over, and the actual quantity of a mineral needed to accomplish a given task may well decrease with improved technology.

Water: Is the Tap Running Dry?

Water is the quintessential renewable resource. It is endlessly recycled through time; new water can also form occasionally in volcanic action. But most of the fresh water on earth is locked in the polar ice caps, and most of what is left is underground. The relatively small amount of surface water in streams, rivers, and lakes has traditionally been the main source of human water supplies.

Although water is the most abundant "resource" on earth, the amount of accessible, usable water is quite small. While the human population may increase greatly in an area, the local water supply does not grow to match it. The result may be that the community stops growing when the limits of water are reached. Or it may build long aqueducts to bring in more water. Los Angeles, for example, draws its water supply from rivers hundreds of miles away. The city's water officials are now looking covetously at rivers as distant as the Columbia in Oregon.

Groundwater is another solution for a thirsty community. Trapped between the surface and an impermeable layer of rock, large amounts of water may underlie even arid regions. But in an arid region, the formation of such a large aquifer may have taken thousands of years, as the water seeped through the soil and rock. In many parts of the world, the demands of a growing population are leading to the "mining" of this water—it is being drawn up so fast that the water table is plummeting. The high plains of Texas, Nebraska, Colorado, and Kansas are underlain by such a formation, the Ogallala aquifer. By the year 2000 most of the accessible water in the aquifer will be gone. Farmers in the region—which produces much of the nation's wheat, corn, cotton, and beef—will have to depend on another water source to keep up their present yields.

Many analysts have argued that it is unnatural for large cities and irrigated farms to sprout in the desert. But farmers in the Southwest point out that their region, if irrigated, can grow crops all year round, unlike the well-watered but cold East. Still, in recent years there has been more and more discussion of the limits imposed by nature on growth in the Southwest.

Another potential cause of water shortage is pollution. Most municipal water systems in developed countries can deal with biological pollution (that is, sewage), but they can often do little to remove chemicals. Towns that depend on groundwater, which purifies itself extremely slowly, may find out too late that industrial parks, fertilized potato fields, or cattle feed lots have contaminated their underground supplies for the indefinite future. Pollution in a water supply is harmful to people, of course, but even industry and agriculture, by far the main "consumers," need relatively pure water. Near some major cities, even in developing countries like Korea, rivers may be so polluted that no industrial use is possible.

While in wealthy countries industrial waste and agricultural chemicals are the greatest water polluters, in poor nations the main pollutant is untreated human sewage. Almost none of the rural people in poor countries have latrines or any kind of sewage system. Most of these people also lack the elementary education that would prevent them from using chamberpots to collect drinking water or putting contaminated fingers into their food. Less than half the world's people can get safe drinking water. Many have little chance to wash themselves, their food, their utensils, or their clothing—basic sanitation that could prevent disease and death. This lack of safe drinking water is probably the number one preventable cause of death in the world today.

Even if people have the knowledge to prevent contamination, it may be almost impossible to obtain decent sanitation and clean water. Women and children in many parts of the world spend up to eight hours a day walking to and from the well or stream, carrying huge pots of water on their heads. Fuel is often expensive, so boiling water to sterilize it may seem like a luxury, even to someone who knows better. On returning to the States, one American Peace Corps worker wrote,

> I used to turn on the water faucet and watch the water flow in disbelief. . . . I remembered how far the village women had to walk for it; how polluted it was when we got it; how expensive the wood was that was needed to purify it; and how we finally had to give that up because we couldn't afford it.

Where the water is contaminated with sewage, as it is in much of the Third World, people are inevitably in poor health. Cholera, typhoid, amebiasis, dysentery, hepatitis, schistosomiasis, and many other diseases are spread by people who use nearby water as both latrine and reservoir. While people who live in poor countries do eventually gain some immunity to the microbes in their food and drink, it is paid for in the loss of children's lives. Most deaths in poor countries are of children under five years old, most of whom die from diarrhea and other diseases caused by contaminated water. Perhaps no single step could improve the lives of the world's poor so much as access to safe drinking water for all. In recognition of this need, the UN has declared the 1980s the "International Drinking Water Supply and Sanitation Decade." The World Bank, the U.S. Agency for International Development (AID), and other organizations have allocated millions of dollars for water and sewage-treatment projects in the Third World.

Land Abuse by Rich and Poor

Land abuse includes uncontrolled deforestation, desertification, and their consequences: soil erosion, silting of rivers and reservoirs, flooding, loss of fuel, loss of fertilizer, even famine and drought. It also includes harm that may come from mishandled irrigation, which can waterlog the land or leave so much salt on it that it can no longer be farmed.

The problem of land abuse is global. In the United States, for example, the Department of Agriculture estimates that one-third of the nation's topsoil has eroded since farming began, in most places less than 200 years ago. But land abuse is generally more serious in densely populated developing countries. In these countries with fast-growing populations, the pressure to farm, graze livestock, and cut firewood and timber in new areas is intense. Unfortunately, in most countries that face this kind of pressure, the most suitable land was taken long ago. What is left is marginal land, too steep or wet or dry to be used except in desperate need. But, today, population pressure means that many people are in that desperate need. They have moved high on steep mountainsides in Nepal and onto silt islands miles out in the Indian Ocean off Bangladesh. They make a precarious living from subsistence farming—but they are often helping to destroy their own livelihood.

The uncontrolled deforestation of marginal or hilly land by people struggling to survive is one of the most serious problems the world environment faces today. Trees hold the soil in place, and when they are cut the soil begins to wash away—slowly when the land is flat and the rain is gentle (as in much of Western Europe); very quickly on steep land in the tropics, where many of the forests in developing countries are situated. When the tropical rainy season begins, torrents of soil pour into streams and rivers off deforested hillsides. Often farmers must move on after five or six years because not enough soil is left to grow crops. Terracing, planting hedges, or even contour plowing could help stop the erosion, but the peasant farmers who are now encroaching on forested hills around the world bring with them a tradition of flatland farming. They farm the hills as their fathers farmed the plains, with devastating consequences. In Nepal and Ethiopia, both highland nations, officials joke that their chief export is soil.

But soil erosion is not only destructive to land that loses soil. Almost everywhere in the less developed countries, flooding caused by upstream deforestation has increased drastically in this century. Silt from soil erosion builds up a river's bed and increases its volume so that it floods more often, bringing disaster to lowland farmers. Waterborne silt can make a new reservoir or hydroelectric dam useless within 25 years. The silting up of rivers can leave a port city stranded in a swamp unless the city can afford the expense of constant dredging; the newly created swamp may become infested with malarial mosquitoes. Thus, soil erosion leaves barren land behind it and brings destruction to new places. In much of the world, soil is disappearing too fast to be replaced for many human lifetimes.

A second effect of deforestation is that continued cutting of trees without replanting eventually means that people cannot find firewood. In the Third World, wood is used mainly for fuel to heat houses and to cook food. But the larger and larger populations of most poor countries are relying on fewer and fewer trees each year. In parts of Africa's Sahel Desert region, looking for firewood is a full-time, year-round occupation for at least one member of every family. In Katmandu, Nepal, a load of firewood may cost $125—while the gross national product per capita is only $120. In much of south and southwestern Asia, the Andes, and elsewhere, there are virtually no trees, and people can no longer buy firewood. Instead, they burn livestock dung and crop residues for fuel. Soil productivity then declines because the dung and residues are no longer spread on farmland as fertilizer.

The introduction of livestock to arid or steep land can also cause soil erosion and prevent regrowth of plants that would hold down the soil. Sheep and goats especially tend to crop young plants down to the roots. Livestock grazing is the single largest reason for the southward march of the Sahara, and has contributed greatly in the past and today to the barren condition of much of the Mediterranean region and the Middle East.

The governments of developing countries have become more interested in protecting their soil and forests as the gravity of the problem has become obvious in many places. China has doubled its forested land since 1949; South Korea and Israel have carried out major reforestation campaigns. Kenya, the Philippines, Mexico, Cuba, Thailand, and other nations officially promote the planting and protection of trees. The UN Food and Agriculture Organization is only one of a number of international organizations that are working to alleviate the problem. About half the world's much-needed forest grows in just three countries of the developed world: the USSR, Canada, and the United States.

A Change in the Air

Atmospheric pollution is the most universal of environmental problems, because air is constantly moving, respecting no national borders. When China conducts aboveground nuclear tests, the radioactivity may be detected above Seattle.

Smog is one of the oldest—and most visible—environmental problems. During the Middle Ages, coal burning was forbidden in London because of the smoke. The London fog that shrouded Sherlock Holmes was what we would now call heavy smog. In Belgium in the 1930s, after a smog disaster in the Meuse Valley, it was found for the first time that smog was capable of making people seriously ill and even of killing them. By the late 1960s, smog was a problem in large cities worldwide, caused as much by automobile exhaust as by industry. But because it was such an obvious health hazard, smog received early attention from lawmakers pressured by an angry public. In many industrial countries today, air pollution is less overwhelming than it was 10 or 20 years ago, although it has not ceased to be an important concern. As a result, the countries with the most extreme air pollution problems now tend to be less developed nations like Mexico—whose capital has perhaps the most smog of any large city in the world. Many of these countries, faced with a choice between development with accompanying pollution and no development, are willing to tolerate some pollution of the air and water.

Acid rain is a second problem, mainly affecting industrial nations. It appears when pollutants from a factory oxidize and fall as rain in areas often far from the smokestacks. The highly acidic rain can eventually eliminate all plant and fish life in lakes and streams. Acid rain has become a touchy issue between the United States and Canada; Canada alleges that most of the acid rain that has killed fish in its wilderness lakes comes from Ohio Valley pollution. The Scandinavian countries likewise complain that acid rain from West Germany, France, Britain, and the Low Countries is killing their fish. Since there is no obvious remedy for the condition of these lakes, and since the acid rain has been increasing for several decades, environmentalists have pressed for greater control over factory emissions. But businessmen and economists question the high costs, rigid standards, and soundness of scientific data on which the regulations governing clean air are based. They also question whether, particularly in a financial slump, the cost of expensive "scrubbers" for smokestacks is justified—especially since there is no way to prove that any one plant has damaged a particular body of water far away.

Another subject for concern has been the ozone layer, the crucial section of the stratosphere that screens life on earth from the sun's harmful ultraviolet rays. Recent research seems to indicate that chlorofluorocarbons, chemicals used as refrigerants, solvents, and propellants in spray cans, may be destroying ozone molecules as the chlorofluorocarbons float up through the stratosphere, over a period of from 10 to 200 years. The National Academy of Sciences has predicted a 16 percent increase in human exposure to ultraviolet rays over the next 20 years because of loss of ozone. The main result of increased exposure would be a rise in skin cancer rates. However, the effects of chlorofluorocarbons are still incompletely known. While the United States and Canada, among others, have banned their use except under certain restricted conditions, many nations continue to manufacture and use the chemicals, unconvinced that they may be dangerous.

Conspicuous Wastes: A Problem That Won't Go Away

As civilization has grown and become more sophisticated, so have the wastes it produces. Disposal of wastes—including biological, chemical, industrial, and nuclear—has become a major problem in modern societies.

The most serious disposal problem is that of nuclear wastes. Every year, the world's nuclear reactors produce millions of cubic feet of radioactive waste, including perhaps 140,000 cubic feet of high-level (that is, especially toxic) waste containing uranium and plutonium. So far, no permanent storage method for these wastes has been devised. A method that would keep the wastes secure for hundreds of years is not enough; plutonium, one of the most poisonous substances known, has a half-life of 25,000 years, about five times the length of recorded human history. (Half-life is the time it takes for half a radioactive substance to decay. For example, after 25,000 years half the original amount of plutonium would be left; after 50,000 years, one-quarter; and so on.) Any sizable amount of plutonium could therefore remain dangerous to human and other life for up to half a million years. Proposals that have been considered for the storage of these wastes include burial in containers deep in ocean-basin mud; encasing solidified waste in glass or ceramic and burying it in deep granite or salt formations; and sending it in rockets to outer space.

There are serious disposal problems with other kinds of toxic wastes, such as the 30,000 chemicals the United Nations International Register lists as possibly dangerous. Many modern chemicals are synthetic and do not easily decompose; they must be safely contained until they are no longer dangerous. In the United States, disposal of toxic wastes became a highly charged political issue after the publicity given the evacuation of Love Canal, a community built over a chemical dump that had been sold to the city. New laws require safe handling and disposal of toxic wastes in the United States, and most industrial countries now have fairly high standards.

Minerals and Fossil Fuels: A Burning Issue

Of all the potential "resource shortages," none has generated so much public discussion as the energy crisis. The world economy runs on fossil fuels, especially on oil, the leading world energy source. Fossil fuels, which form from organic matter over millions of years, are not as abundant as other minerals. While many minerals can be recycled over and over, fossil fuels can be burned for energy only once. Their relative scarcity and exhaustibility pose important questions for the future of the world economy. The present oil "glut" is undoubtedly temporary; it could last into the 1990s—or it could end sooner. When the reserves are exhausted and production ends, what will replace oil?

While coal and natural gas are more abundant than oil, they are also potentially exhaustible, in the sense that continued production at high rates would deplete known reserves within several human generations. While the same is theoretically true of other mineral reserves, in practice fossil fuels, since they can only be used once, are in more danger of disappearing. Also, the composition of the earth's core and mantle is still largely unknown and many scientists speculate that enormous amounts of minerals may eventually be mined from deep in the earth. But fossil fuels, because they come from ancient organic matter, are necessarily found near the earth's crust, and future deep-earth mining offers little hope of finding replacements for them.

The reaction to possible shortages of fossil fuels has been varied. Many environmentalists believe that conservation, solar energy, and other alternative power sources such as thermal and wind energy will provide enough energy for the world of the future. Some analysts believe that nuclear power offers the only hope to meet future energy needs. And some believe that market forces and new technology, as in the past, will lead to new, more efficient and cheaper energy sources. Under the pressure of rising oil prices since 1973, U.S. oil consumption has declined, supplies have become abundant again, and prices have flattened, they note, and the pessimistic projections of the past eight years proved wrong.

Most of the world's mineral production, like most of its fossil fuel, is consumed in the developed world. For example, Latin America, Asia, and Africa have about three-quarters of the world's people, but they consume less than a quarter of the world's minerals. As energy prices have risen, the cost of producing minerals has also gone up, since mining and processing are energy-intensive activities. This has meant that mineral supplies have not expanded as much as might have been expected from population and development figures. There is not likely to be a major shortage of minerals in the near future; however, some strategic minerals are found only in certain politically unstable nations, or nations unfriendly to the United States. Cobalt, essential in jet aircraft engines, for example, is found mainly in Zaire; chromium, used in stainless steel, is found primarily in South Africa, Zimbabwe, and the Soviet Union. Disruptions in trade with such nations could cause shortages.

Living Species and Wilderness: On the Endangered List?

Animals and plants may not often be thought of as natural resources, but they are so, today more than ever. While past arguments against species extinction—such as the right of nonhuman creatures to life, and their aesthetic and ecological value—are still valid, today there is the added consideration that the promising new technology of genetic engineering, as well as other sciences, depends on existing genes. Every species extinction impoverishes the science of the future by leaving it a smaller "gene pool" to draw on.

Most of the world's plant and animal species live in the tropics, especially in the tropical woodlands that are disappearing at high rates today. Only a small proportion of these tropical forest species (mostly insects and plants) has been classified, and an even smaller proportion has been explored for scientific value. Yet the discoveries made from them have already been immensely valuable. Many useful drugs, including quinine and treatments for various forms of cancer, hypertension, malaria, and other medical problems, originated in tropical plants. New strains of crops have also been found in the tropics and bred with "domesticated" varieties to produce hardier, more fertile plants. Sometimes, potentially valuable species are found in only one small place in the world, and that one place may be threatened with human activity that could destroy the species.

But at what cost to humans are species preserved? When the minuscule snail darter held up construction of the multimillion-dollar Tellico Dam in Tennessee for several years, many people were outraged; the dam was eventually completed. On the Serengeti Plain, in Tanzania, millions of animals roam across one of the world's largest game reserves. Tourists enrich the Tanzanian economy on their photographic safaris through the park. But the per capita income in Tanzania is $240 a year. A rhinoceros horn, or the skin of a leopard or cheetah, may bring a poacher enough money to feed his family for a year. Understandably, it has been difficult to halt poaching. How can the interests of people and other living species be reconciled?

Another kind of problem concerns the world fisheries. Fish for eating are in no danger of extinction. But since 1970, when it reached a high, the world fish catch has remained fairly steady. Fish are the only "wild animals" that are eaten in great numbers; it may be necessary to breed them on underwater "farms" to increase the catch, since even ultramodern trawling equipment has failed to bring in more fish over the past ten years. The leveling off of the catch seems to indicate that a natural limit of sorts has been reached. Barring some new development it seems likely that fish will provide a decreasing proportion of the world's protein in the coming years as the human population grows.

The resource and environmental problems discussed above serve to give some perspective on the scope of such problems. In many cases, the signs are alarming, and environmental damage seems to be increasing. But hopeful signs are also present, and human ingenuity has defeated many resource problems in the past.

LOOKING FOR ANSWERS

No one is "against" a healthy environment. When the environment is damaged, it is not because someone set out deliberately to harm it, but because the harm was a side effect of the pursuit of a goal. The goal may be simple survival, or it may be economic growth. The choices that must be made between the pursuit of these goals and environmental protection are seldom easy.

Is environmental protection compatible with economic growth, and if so, to what extent? Must there be a choice between environmental protection and the satisfaction of human needs? How will the growing world population affect these decisions? The answers to these questions may well be different in different parts of the world.

Environment vs. Economic Growth

"Are not poverty and need the greatest polluters?" asked India's Prime Minister Indira Gandhi at the Stockholm Conference. The countries of the Third World ask themselves if they can afford to set their environmental standards high, and for the most part their answer is no. Poor nations are usually willing to accept higher rates of industrial pollution both because they have less industry and because they have less money available for regulation than wealthy nations do. For their environmental problems, less developed nations also have little money. They must often depend on foreign aid for help in reforestation, agricultural extension work, drilling wells, and other projects that the national or local government would normally carry out.

Some believe that a higher standard of living is necessary before concern about the environment is warranted. In this argument, environmental advocacy is a luxury; this explains why environmentalism first arose in wealthy countries. After people's basic needs are supplied, they want a healthy and aesthetically pleasing environment. In a poor country, however, attention must be paid to economic development and social needs before environmental protection becomes relevant. Another argument, however, says that "prevention is better and cheaper than cure" and that without a healthy environment it is impossible to raise standards of living very far. Therefore it is necessary to protect and conserve in order to continue economic development.

In industrial nations, the environmental questions are of a different order. The money is available, and there are usually environmental regulations concerning air and water, but these alone do not necessarily guarantee a better environment. Industries complain that overregulation and rigid standards force them to spend enormous sums on measures that yield only marginal gains in health. The burden of making existing plants conform, they say, prevents them from building new facilities that would be less polluting and at the same time more profitable.

Some environmentalists in return say that regulation is essential and that the costs of regulation—to prevent health-damaging pollution and other problems—are part of doing business. Before regulation, these costs were "externalized"—not paid by industry or agriculture but by "civilians," in the form of higher medical bills, lost time at work, accidents, cleaning bills, and so on. Regulation, according to this argument, merely returns these externalized costs to their originators. For example, a Council on Environmental Quality (a government agency) study in 1978 estimated that while the United States spent $16.6 billion in 1977 to meet clean air standards, the savings in health care and air pollution damage to property came to $21.4 billion. Many supporters of environmental controls, however, also acknowledge that the present system in the United States is costly and in need of reform. The current laws, with permits and requirements, can lead to "analysis paralysis," in which nothing is done for years at a time, while reports are written and analyzed and lawyers argue in court. In the case of the multibillion-dollar federal sewage-treatment construction program authorized by the Clean Water Act of 1972, critics charge that the program (the second largest public works program in U.S. history) has contributed more to urban sprawl than to cleaning up streams. Communities have used federal funds to build sewage-treatment plants in anticipation of future growth.

In the Reagan administration, unlike the Carter administration, economic considerations are paramount as the White House emphasizes recovery from a decade or more of stagnation and inflation. President Ronald Reagan appointed as secretary of the interior the business-oriented—and controversial—James G. Watt. The Reagan administration has pushed for relaxation of some environmental standards, including the Clean Air Act of 1970, saying that the standards should be based on "sound" scientific data and "real" health risks. Current antipollution programs are too expensive for the benefits they provide, the administration believes, adding 0.4 percent a year to the consumer price index. The coal industry, for example, believes that the Clean Air Act, which mandates "scrubbers" to remove sulfur and solid particles in smoke, has been exorbitantly expensive to implement and has held up the development of coal—abundant in the United States—as an alternative to imported energy.

One proposal that some economists have suggested is for the government to tax polluters according to the monetary value it places on clean air and water. In the past, this argument goes, clean air and water were considered "free goods" that no one need account for, because they were so abundant. But it is now apparent that clean air and water are not unlimited and that they do have an economic value, although it is not clear what that value is. Should business have to pay for its consumptive use of clean air and water?

The conflict between full-scale environmental protection and full-scale economic development is a basic one. Has there been too much emphasis on protection and not enough on the wise utilization of resources? Should there be less or more "environmental protection" than now? The Reagan administration believes that existing laws are sufficient to protect the natural resources of the United States; when the United States must depend heavily on imported oil, in its view, it is neither right nor economical to keep fossil fuels "locked up" in protected wilderness, national forest, or national park areas. Are regulatory laws due for a reform, as many believe? Is there a risk that reforms would lead to a dismantling of present safeguards? Can environmental protection, as Secretary Watt contends, be compatible with increased development of natural resources? Can the United States afford, in a time of financial trouble, to insist on cleaning up air and water and on preserving the wilderness? Or, as U.S. population continues to increase, are clean air, clean water, and untouched nature more necessary than ever?

The United States and the World Environment

Does the United States have an economic or moral interest in the state of the environment in poorer nations? Or should the United States tend to the poor and unemployed of Detroit and New York and Los Angeles before it tries to right wrongs overseas? Many Americans believe foreign aid should be the nation's lowest priority, as many congressmen know from their mail; foreign aid heads the list of favorite budget cuts. Americans often believe that aid leads to dependency without gratitude. The administration is convinced that the solution to Third World development is freer trade, including low tariffs and opportunities for private investment with less regulation of foreign business. Private enterprise and the free market, in this view, brought high standards of living to Western countries and will do the same in the Third World. The administration plans to encourage continued high sales of food, especially grains, to other countries.

Another argument, however, says that foreign aid is necessary because such projects as the building of roads, railroads, and dams in the Third World do not draw foreign private investment. Without adequate ports, roads, and energy supplies, poor countries cannot attract the foreign corporations that can help their development. Although the proportion of the gross national product per capita that the United States spends on foreign aid has declined drastically over the past 20 years, the OPEC nations and Japan have begun sizable foreign aid programs in the past few years. They have done so, some observers claim, not because they are innately more altruistic but because they believe foreign aid to be in their own "enlightened self-interest," promoting a world in which more people are prosperous and therefore are better trade partners and are more interested in stability.

Is There Enough to Go Around?

The absolute problem of resource sufficiency concerns population more than any other factor. If the world population continues to increase at the rates of the past 20 years, it has been said, all causes are lost ones. While it is unlikely that such high growth rates will continue, and while they are already dropping even in many less developed countries, the world population will almost certainly continue to grow until well into the next century. Even if the relative problem of unequal distribution of resources were solved, such a continuously increasing population could put a tremendous strain on world institutions and supplies. The economic and political significance of an enormous national population is not yet completely understood. In China, the world's most populous nation, with over a billion people, newlywed couples are now urged to have only one child and are penalized if they go over the limit. While such measures may seem repugnant to people in democratic nations, many Chinese believe that this is the only realistic way to prevent the population from growing to disastrous proportions. What will happen when India, now a democratic nation of 650 million, reaches 1 billion, as projected by the year 2000? Some economists doubt that political freedom can survive in nations where the population reaches such vast numbers.

But population is not the only problem, as others are quick to point out. The distribution of resources is a major consideration. Would a reduction in U.S. consumption of resources, for example, help or hurt the less developed countries? Some say that it would benefit them in the long run, but others disagree. The United States, as consumer, is a major customer of the developing countries. Its economic growth and prosperity have a "ripple effect" that benefits the global economy. The United States and the other industrialized nations help raise the standard of living in less developed countries through aid, trade, industrialization, and shared technology.

In 1798, when the English economist Thomas Malthus published his famous *Essay on the Principle of Population*, which argued that population increased faster than food supply, he said, "There should be no more people in a country than could enjoy a glass of wine or a piece of beef with their dinner." Malthus believed that population was the key to world resource sufficiency, and that without control of population growth the world would face catastrophe. In his 1807 book, *Political and Philosophical Essays*, another noted Englishman, William Hazlitt, disagreed:

> Mr. Malthus wishes to confound the necessary limits of the earth with the arbitrary and artificial distribution of that produce according to the institutions of society or the caprice of individuals, the laws of God and nature with the laws of man.

In essence, this argument is still going on today. Are there by nature "limits to growth"? Or is there no limit to human ingenuity in overcoming limits?

5

The Age of Interdependence

Kirtley F. Mather

Thus far we have been appraising the resources of the whole earth in terms of the total demands of the entire human family. Data were drawn from many countries; sources of raw materials were considered without regard to national boundary lines. The gratifying conclusion that the bounties of the earth are adequate to supply all mankind with the means for comfortable existence was based upon world statistics. Our world, however, is divided into political units that exist not only on maps but also in the hearts and minds of men. National loyalties and racial instincts are deeply embedded in human nature. War revives the spirit of nationalism and gives it new strength, even as it breeds alliances and stimulates united action. It is therefore inevitable that we proceed next to a survey of the resources of the geographic regions occupied or controlled by separate nations. The question whether a great nation can live prosperously on its own resources must be answered before we can select intelligently the pattern for the future world organization.

It is conceivable that further advance of scientific research in the new directions sketched in the preceding chapter may some day make it possible for any community to organize its industries so that satisfactory subsistence is provided without drawing upon the resources of any foreign region. Such communities would have to possess considerable acreage of tillable soil, abundant supplies of iron ore and coal, adequate waterpower, and a frontage on the sea. Any desired product of the soil, whether for food or factory, would be cultivated in gigantic, air-conditioned greenhouses, regardless of the local climate. Aluminum would be secured from the ubiquitous clay deposits, magnesium and min-

An adaptation of "The Age of Interdependence," Chapter 4 in *Enough and to Spare* by Kirtley F. Mather. Copyright 1944 by Harper & Row, Publishers, Inc., New York. Reprinted by permission of the publisher. Pp. 71–83.

eral fertilizers from the ocean, nitrogen from the air. Plastics, gasoline, lubricating oils, and rubber would be synthesized from agricultural products and coal, possibly even from the former alone if coal were wanting. Let the modern alchemy of the metallurgical laboratory and the chemistry of the carbon compounds become just a bit more miraculous than they are today and an ersatz economy of self-sufficiency would be quite practicable for any fairly large fraction of a continent.

But all that is obviously a ghostly dream of the distant future. For the present, and presumably for many decades to come, no group of people can enjoy the benefits of modern science and technology unless they have access to a great variety of metalliferous ores, the mineral sources of a long list of elements and compounds, and the plants and animals that grow naturally in many different climatic environments. At the present moment, no satisfactory substitutes are known for tin, copper, antimony, platinum, jute, flax, camphor, and copra as they are now being used in certain essential ways, to mention only a few of the well-nigh insuperable barriers that prevent the realization of that dream in our time.

It is also a ghastly dream of a horrible future. The economic barrier thus artificially erected around our hypothetical community would segregate its inhabitants not only from the material resources of the rest of the world but from the intellectual and spiritual resources as well. Ideas and ideals, creative arts and ethical aspirations would be cramped and mutilated by the straitjacket of any such provincial economy. Jealousies and fears would be stimulated between rival political units and constant warfare would be the inevitable result. In short, no more certain and effective program for the suicide of the human species could be concocted.

There is, fortunately, no prospect that mankind in general will embark upon a course of action that would turn back the pages of history and restore the provincialism of bygone ages. All the compulsions of the environment provided by Mother Earth are operating in the opposite direction. Science cannot free man from his environmental controls; it merely helps man harmonize his life with the forces and factors of his environment.

The metallic ores, the nonmetallic deposits of economic value, and the mineral fuels that are the basic requisites for modern civilization occur under certain well-defined geological conditions. Their distribution is by no means haphazard or unpredictable. To assist in understanding their occurrence, the rocks of the earth's crust may be grouped in three categories. First there are the very old and generally much contorted or compressed rocks of the basement complex or Pre-Cambrian terrane. These include vast bodies of granite and other igneous rocks, many of them intensely metamorphosed, as well as sedimentary rocks that likewise have been greatly altered by heat and pressure during the many vicissitudes of crustal movement and volcanic eruption that have affected them throughout the long ages of geologic time. These ancient rocks contain many rich bodies of metallic ores, such as those yielding gold, silver, copper, nickel, and iron. Nowhere do they contain coal, petroleum, or the ores of such metals as aluminum and magnesium.

There are extensive areas of Pre-Cambrian rocks in every continent, and no large unit of these rocks, when adequately prospected, has thus far failed to yield essential metals. The Canadian Shield surrounding Hudson Bay in North America and extending southward into the United States in the Lake Superior region is matched by the Scandinavian Shield of northwestern Europe and the Angara Shield of north-central Siberia in Asia. In the southern hemisphere, the Brazilian Shield of South America is matched by the extensive bodies of Pre-Cambrian rock in south and central Africa and the basement complex of Australia.

The second group of rocks in this very loose classification includes the sedimentary formations of Cambrian and Post-Cambrian age. These may be flat-lying beds beneath the plains and in plateaus or they may be wrinkled into mountains like the Appalachians. It is from these that the world's resources of coal and petroleum are secured, as well as much of the potash and magnesium and some of the iron and nonferrous metals. Here, too, it is evident that every continent has its share. The widespread basin of the Mississippi Valley is matched by the extensive area of sedimentary rocks in central Europe between the Alps and the Scandinavian highlands. The vast lowland of the Amazon finds its structural counterpart in the interior basin of Australia and the broad plains of north-central Asia.

The third major type of geologic structure is that resulting from and associated with volcanic activity. Here the geologist has in mind not only the outpoured lavas and erupted cinders, ash, and bombs of volcanic cones and plateaus. He thinks also of the intruded masses of igneous rock that crystallized in the conduits leading to volcanic vents or spread out in sheets or dome-shaped bodies in the upper part of the earth's crust without ever breaking through to the surface. Some of the world's most important reserves of precious metals, of copper, lead and zinc, and of tungsten, vanadium, molybdenum, and manganese, essential in the production of modern steel alloys, are found in association with such rocks, especially those of Tertiary age. Here, again, we observe that nature plays no favorites where continents are concerned. The volcanic terranes of North America's western mountains have their equivalent in the Andes, the festooned arcs of the mountain systems in eastern and southern Asia, and the plateaus and cones of central Africa.

Every continent displays almost the entire gamut of possible geologic structures and therefore may be expected to contain extensive deposits of almost every kind of mineral resource that might be useful as a raw material of industry. Although the United States alone has produced nearly two-thirds of the world's entire production of petroleum, it is because Americans have been more successful than other people in finding and using this type of fuel. A century ago two-thirds of the world's supply of petroleum was not concentrated beneath the surface of the United States. On the contrary, with the exception of Australia and the possible exception of Africa, every continent probably contained petroleum resources roughly proportional to the entire total of the world's supply as the area of each continent is proportional to the total land of the earth.

Similarly, the fact that, to date, continental Europe, the United States, Great Britain, and Russia have produced over 80 percent of the earth's steel does not mean that the rest of the world contains only 20 percent of the earth's ores of iron. It means, instead, that the inhabitants of the regions mentioned have been most ingenious and efficient in discovering and utilizing the iron-ore deposits that they possessed. The iron ores of Asia, Africa, Australia, and South America for the most part await development. In other words, each continent has domestic sources of the majority of basically important minerals, adequate to supply most of the needs of its inhabitants even when their standards of living attain the characteristics of modern industrial civilization. Mother Earth provides equality of opportunity; man differs in response to opportunity.

This, however, does not mean that nature favors continental isolation or regional self-sufficiency as the pattern for world organization. There are many significant exceptions to this glittering generality of equalized continental distribution of mineral wealth. Even when we remember that, for many purposes, molybdenum may be substituted for tungsten, coal for petroleum, and magnesium for aluminum, we find that at present, and probably for a long time to come, the inhabitants of no continent and therefore of no one country can "live to themselves alone" without sacrificing many of the benefits of modern technology.

Tin is outstanding among these exceptions. Nature has played a strange trick in making tin ores scarce in the highly industrialized regions where the tin can is an essential item and tin must be used in the alloys that alone have proved satisfactory for the bearings of high-speed machines. There are almost no ores of tin in North America; the puny deposits of that metal in Europe are competent to meet only 5 percent of the needs of Europeans.

Much the same is true of nickel and radium. These are found only in a few rare localities in two or three of the six continents. To a slightly less degree, the ores of antimony, vanadium, and chromium are also scattered sparsely throughout the earth, with satisfactory concentrations only at a few places in three or four continents.

From the geologic point of view there is no basis for considering one continent inferior to another; each has mineral resources that are outstanding either in quantity or kind. But no one continent can provide sufficient amounts of every ingredient of modern civilization to satisfy all the needs of its inhabitants. Only as each contributes freely and without hindrance to the welfare of all mankind can the resources of any be utilized to the best advantage.

The case for interdependence becomes even stronger when the resources of the individual nations are considered. Not even the Soviet Union, Brazil, or the United States embraces within its political frontiers a sufficient variety of geologic structure to give it adequate supplies of all the metalliferous ores necessary as raw materials for modern industrial operations. Likewise, no nation enjoys a sufficient variety of climatic conditions to permit all kinds of foodstuffs to be grown on its farms or gathered from its forests, and to allow the growth of all the various plants contributing essential raw materials to industry.

The British Empire might perhaps be cited as an exception to these statements. With territory in every continent and climatic zone, it covers the entire range of geologic structure from the oldest to the youngest and from the least disturbed of sedimentary rocks to the most intensely metamorphosed of igneous bodies. It might therefore be expected that every possible requirement for raw materials would be met. But the British Empire is a commonwealth of nations joined physically by long and precarious routes of travel and transport over seas and through the air. No attempt has ever been made to establish economic independence for the empire, simply because such "splendid isolation" would inevitably lead to its prompt collapse. Only because its various self-governing units have been relatively free to capitalize their interdependence with other countries has the commonwealth persisted as a political unit. Only because Great Britain has maintained its import and export trade with nations ouside the empire have the citizens of that country been kept from insolvency.

Following the First World War, a strenuous attempt was made to discover and exploit resources within the empire that would make it self-sufficient in so far as raw materials are concerned. Oil fields were developed in the Middle and Far East; phosphate deposits on the mandated island of Nauru, formerly a German possession, were extensively worked. Even so, at the start of World War II the British Empire lacked sulfur, mercury, antimony, and molybdenum and was inadequately supplied from its own territory with petroleum and potash. This inability to attain mineral self-sufficiency by a group of associated countries so large and widely scattered as those in the British Empire is perhaps the strongest possible argument for acceptance of the fact that mineral interdependence is inescapable.

The Soviet Union is the largest compact political unit of the world today and is the only nation for which the geologist can hold out any hope of self-sufficiency in regard to mineral resources. For a score of years that has been one of the aims of its leaders; the search for mineral deposits, especially for those that would meet the union's deficiencies, has been prosecuted with high intelligence and great industry. Even so, the USSR is still totally lacking or seriously deficient in many minerals, such as nickel, tungsten, tin, vanadium, sulfur, antimony, and mercury. Further geologic exploration and prospecting may reveal adequate supplies of some of these, but the chances are not very favorable that all will be found in amounts great enough to meet the increasing needs of the nation's rapidly expanding industries. For certain agricultural resources, moreover, the Soviet Union is inescapably dependent upon foreign sources of supply. Almost all of its vast territory lies north of the fortieth parallel of latitude, and the most southerly point in Russia, east of the Caspian Sea, is in latitude thirty-five degrees. Consequently, none of the tropical plants and few of the subtropical can grow within its borders. If the citizens of the Soviet Union insist upon a policy of economic isolation, which at present they most certainly show no intention of doing, they would have to restrict their diet to the foodstuffs of northern latitudes and their industries to those that are not dependent upon the agricultural products of the tropics.

Brazil ranks next in area to the Soviet Union, but its annual production of minerals in recent years has been less than one-fortieth as great in value. Indeed, the mineral output of several of the smaller Latin American countries is far in excess of that of Brazil. This is due in part to geologic conditions; in spite of its great area, Brazil falls far short of encompassing all possible types of geologic structure. But in greater degree it is a result of the fact that until lately no really energetic attempt has been made to exploit its mineral resources, except in rare instances at a few localities. Although many parts of the country remain completely unexplored and still larger areas have never been adequately prospected, it is known that Brazilian iron-ore deposits are very rich and extensive, probably ranking first among the world's iron-ore reserves. Its bauxite deposits and manganese ores are also of great value. At present it produces nearly all of the world's supply of quartz crystals and a large fraction of the world's industrial diamonds. What is known concerning the general geology of the country, however, indicates unmistakably that when Brazil becomes a large consumer of industrial raw materials it must get many important mineral products from abroad.

The United States is third among the nations when ranked according to area but foremost both in the production and consumption of mineral wealth. Since it is among the most favored of nations because of its wide coverage of diversified geologic structure and its fortunate relation to climatic zones, it is not surprising that many Americans have toyed with the idea of building a fence around our country, organizing our economy on a completely self-sufficient basis, and letting the rest of the world go hang. That idea has of course been rather well demolished by the disruption of everyday life resulting from Japanese seizure of the sources of rubber and tin in the Far East. But it is likely to be revived as soon as synthetic rubber is available for everybody's automobile tires and Bolivian tin is smelted in sufficient quantity in Texas. It happens, however, that because of conditions over which man has no control the United States is inescapably dependent upon other nations for several essential raw materials of modern industry.

Our manufacturers must import nickel, tin, antimony, chromium, and platinum if they are to use these metals in the fabrication of articles essential to what we call the American way of life. For some of these uses satisfactory substitutes may be found among our domestic ores, but without these metals many of our tools and gadgets would be woefully and hopelessly defective. Similarly, because the southernmost point in the United States fails by several hundred miles to reach within the tropics, we are forced to import all the bananas, coffee, tea, camphor, tropical oils, jute, sisal, quinine, and rubber used in this country, either from foreign countries or from our own overseas possessions. It is possible that synthetic products may be made available within a few decades to replace all of these, or that substitutes of domestic origin may be found, as indeed they have already been for some. It is possible, too, that agrobiologists may some time find a practical way of extending into the United States the geographic limits of some of the plants whose products are included in this list. But for the present and probably for a long time in the future there is no escape from the fact that the United States is absolutely dependent upon foreign sources for many of the materials of life.

Indeed, American dependence upon foreign mineral resources may even increase during the next few decades. A "have" nation like ours in which a high standard of living is made possible by rapid consumption of nonrenewable materials must eventually become a "have-not" nation with respect to those materials. Nations that are tardy in their exploitation of such resources will then be looked upon as the wealthy possessors of earth's bounty. Already the pattern is fixed for petroleum. A dozen years hence it is more likely that we will be filling the gap between consumption and production of petroleum products by importing oil from Venezuela and other South American republics than by the more expensive process of manufacturing the required products from coal. Iron is probably next in line. Before the end of the century the extensive reserves of rich iron ore in Cuba and Brazil will begin to replace the dwindling stores of high-grade ore in the United States in spite of the presence here of a vast reserve of low-grade ore. In both instances, it will be a question of relative costs. The greater expense of treating leaner ores or using inherently costly processes of chemical alteration will be balanced against the cost of transportation from foreign sources. Unless tariff or other political barriers are raised too high, the foreign source will win. And this is as it should be, if there is anything valid in the idea of world community.

Surely, if American ingenuity and skill have failed to gain physical independence and lay a firm foundation for self-sufficiency in a region so richly and variously endowed as the United States, no country can hope to escape the bonds of interdependence forged for mankind during the geologic history of the earth. Enough is now known about the mineral resources of the world "to warrant the firm conclusion that, even though the nature, degree, and pattern of mineral interdependence will change, interdependence as such will continue."[1] Entirely apart from morals or ethics and without taking spiritual factors into account, the conclusion is based solely and crassly upon materialistic grounds that in an age of science and technology no nation can "live to itself alone."

Interdependence is the most important single principle affecting the life of man today. No nation, community, or individual can gain any lasting security without taking it into consideration. The resources man must utilize, if he wishes to make the most of the opportunity to gain life that is rich and full, are unevenly distributed and locally concentrated. The techniques of discovering and utilizing them are now fairly well known. The next item on the agenda of civilization is the invention and practice of satisfactory procedures for making them and their products available to all members of the human family. Fundamental to the consideration of those procedures is this geologic fact: the earth is far better adapted for occupation by men organized on a worldwide scale, with maximum opportunity for free exchange of raw materials and finished products the world around, than for occupation by men who insist upon building barriers between regions even so inclusive as a large nation or an entire continent.

NOTE

1. Charles Kenneth Leith, J. W. Furness, and Cleona Lewis, *World Minerals and World Peace*, (Washington, D.C.: The Brookings Institution, 1943).

6

North-South: The Setting

Independent Commission on International Development Issues

The crisis through which international relations and the world economy are now passing presents great dangers, and they appear to be growing more serious. We believe that the gap which separates rich and poor countries—a gap so wide that at the extremes people seem to live in different worlds—has not been sufficiently recognized as a major factor in this crisis. It is a great contradiction of our age that these disparities exist—and are in some respects widening—just when human society is beginning to have a clearer perception of how it is interrelated and of how North and South depend on each other in a single world economy. Yet all the efforts of international organizations and the meetings of the major powers have not been able to give hope to developing countries of escaping from poverty, or to reshape and revive the international economy to make it more responsive to the needs of both developing and industrialized countries. The dialogue between North and South will not by itself solve all the world's current problems, many of which are political rather than economic; but we are satisfied that the world community can have no real stability until it faces up to this basic challenge.

The North-South dialogue is not only an essential task in itself: it is also a wider call for action. It can make global action more probable by demonstrating that countries and continents can overcome their differences and resolve the contradictions between their self-interest and their joint interests. Now that both North and South are increasingly aware of their interdependence, they need to revitalize the dialogue to achieve specific goals, in a spirit of partnership and mutual interest rather than of inequality and charity. The dialogue must aim to give every society a full

From Chapter 1 of *North-South: A Program for Survival* by the Independent Commission on International Development Issues chaired by Willy Brandt. Reprinted by permission of The MIT Press, Cambridge, Massachusetts.

opportunity to develop as it wishes and satisfy the essential needs of its people at an acceptable pace; and to create a dynamic world in which every country can achieve its own development, each respecting the other and respecting also the imperatives of a shared planet. Leaders of public opinion everywhere must develop new insights into the historical forces which have for too long dominated and divided the international community; they must help the world to escape them and to break the vicious circle of shrill protest and mute response by tackling the causes rather than the symptoms of global problems.

We came to these problems separated widely by our experience and our positions on the political spectrum. But we have all come to agree that fundamental changes are essential, whether in trade, finance, energy, or other fields, if we are to avoid a serious breakdown of the world economy in the decades of the 1980s and the 1990s, and to give it instead a new stimulus to function in the interest of all the world's people.

THE NORTH-SOUTH DIVIDE

There are obvious objections to a simplified view of the world as being divided into two camps. The North includes two rich industrialized countries south of the equator, Australia and New Zealand. The South ranges from a booming half-industrial nation like Brazil to poor land-locked or island countries such as Chad or the Maldives. A few southern countries—mostly oil-exporters—have higher per capita incomes than some of the northern countries. But in general terms, and although neither is a uniform or permanent grouping, North and South are broadly synonymous with rich and poor, developed and developing.

Most of the North-South dialogue has been between the developing countries and the market-economy industrialized countries, which is how we will usually interpret the North in this report. But many of our observations also apply to the industrialized countries of Eastern Europe, which do not want to be lumped together with the West, or to be contrasted with the South in a division which they see as the consequences of colonial history. When we speak of the South we also usually exclude China, which has not formally joined the grouping of the developing countries, though it commonly identifies itself with them. But we attach great importance to the participation of the East European countries and China in the international economic system and institutions.

PREDICAMENT OF THE SOUTH

The nations of the South see themselves as sharing a common predicament. Their solidarity in global negotiations stems from the awareness of being dependent on the North and unequal with it; and a great many of them are bound together by their colonial experience. The North, including Eastern Europe, has a quarter of the world's population and four-fifths of its income; the South, including China, has three billion people—three-quarters of the world's population but living on one-fifth of the world's income. In the North, the average person can expect to live for more than 70 years; he or she will rarely be hungry, and will be educated at least up to secondary level. In the countries of the South the great majority of people have a life expectancy of closer to 50 years; in the poorest countries one out of every four children dies before the age of five; one-fifth or more of all the people in the South suffer from hunger and malnutrition; 50 percent have no chance to become literate.

Behind these differences lies the fundamental inequality of economic strength. It is not just that the North is so much richer than the South. Over 90 percent of the world's manufacturing industry is in the North. Most patents and new technology are the property of multinational corporations of the North, which conduct a large share of world investment and world trade in raw materials and manufactures. Because of this economic power northern countries dominate the international economic system—its rules and regulations and its international institutions of trade, money, and finance. Some developing countries have swum against this tide, taking the opportunities which exist and overcoming many obstacles; but most of them find the currents too strong for them. In the world as in nations, economic forces left entirely to themselves tend to produce growing inequality. Within nations public policy has to protect the weaker partners. The time has come to apply this precept to relations between nations within the world community.

FROM AID TO INTERDEPENDENCE

To help conquer poverty and hunger and to create a more just and a more effective international economic system, fundamental structural changes must be made in the markets in which developing countries are suppliers—of commodities, of manufactures, of labor—and in which they are customers—for capital and technology. Such changes are also required in the mechanisms and institutions which generate and distribute international finance, investment, and liquidity. The issue today is not only, or even mainly, one of aid; rather of basic changes in the world economy to help developing countries pay their own way. And the countries of the North, given their increasing interdependence with the South, themselves need international economic reform to ensure their own future prosperity.

The North-South debate is often described as if the rich were being asked to make sacrifices in response to the demands of the poor. We reject this view. The world is now a fragile and interlocking system, whether for its people, its ecology or its resources. Many individual societies have settled their inner conflicts by accommodation, to protect the weak and to promote principles of justice, becoming stronger as a result. The world too can become stronger by becoming a just and humane society. If it fails in this, it will move toward its own destruction.

MUTUAL INTERESTS IN GROWTH

While the international system has become much more complicated, with more independent nations, more institutions, and more centers of influence, it has also become much more interdependent. More and more local problems can only be solved through international solutions—including the environment, energy, and the coordination of economic activity, money, and trade. Above all, the achievement of economic growth in one country depends increasingly on the performance of others. The South cannot grow adequately without the North. The North cannot prosper or improve its situation unless there is greater progress in the South.

Many people in the North have questioned whether it is feasible, and even desirable, to maintain high rates of growth. It is undoubtedly true that past growth has been associated with heavy inroads on exhaustible resources and damage to the environment. But it can be argued that it is not growth, as such, but particular technologies, lifestyles, and industries which have made a heavy impact on environment and resources; and these can and should be controlled by selective intervention. Indeed, many forms of environmental protection are assisted by growth and the public resources which growth can provide. The quality of growth will command increasing attention; but it is unlikely that industrialized societies will reject growth itself, which since 1950 has permitted a reduction of about one-third in lifetime working hours and considerable improvements in standards of well-being.

THE SCOURGE OF UNEMPLOYMENT

Only economic growth can provide the means for more jobs and incomes, whether in North or South. All countries are troubled by rising unemployment. But for the South it is a question not just of stability but of survival. Raising employment levels in the South is acutely difficult. The numbers for whom jobs have to be provided are much greater than in the North, and resources for investment much more modest. It has been estimated that in India alone eight million jobs must be created every year between now and the year 2000 to cope with population growth—even though it is slowing down—and the past backlog of unemployment. With

600 million people, India has a GNP two-fifths the size of that of the United Kingdom, which has 55 million people. This story can be retold for many other countries, especially those of sub-Saharan Africa, where productive capacity is lower and labor force growth even faster than in South Asia. To increase employment at a reasonable rate, and to avoid social and economic disaster in the Third World, call for a tremendous effort both of national management and international collaboration.

Only with considerable increases in their resources for investment, and with more effective employment creation putting incomes in the hands of the poor, can these countries hope to increase the desperately slow pace of improvement of living conditions. Yet for the North to contribute to those resources—by expanding trade with the Third World, by changing the Third World's disadvantageous position in world markets, by increasing financial assistance—and also to solve its own problems, growth is a political necessity. Rising unemployment in the North is therefore from every point of view a cause for alarm. Part of it is due to technological change and new investment which substitutes capital for labor. But there are more important factors, primarily declining demand, and also more women workers and more jobs overseas, particularly through investments by multinational corporations. Imports from developing countries have not been a major factor—indeed [. . .], as many jobs have been created in recent years through selling to these countries as have been lost through competitive imports.

THE NECESSITY FOR RESTRUCTURING

Even though population is ceasing to grow in some northern countries, the labor force in most of them will continue to increase for some time. The growth in output required to absorb the labor force growth between 1980 and 1985, with productivity increasing, has been estimated at 3 to 5 percent. Virtually all countries will require active employment policies, to cope with the past backlog of the jobless, and because foreseeable economic growth will not generate full employment. Industrial countries face a major challenge: solving their own employment problems, including the "restructuring" of production to meet their domestic needs and the needs of the international economy.

Restructuring is a continuous process in efficient economies, through which more productive activities replace less productive ones—as in leather goods, shoes, textiles, or ships, whose production has increasingly moved to the Third World. The switch in the North to other activities is sometimes resisted and protection is demanded. In an expanding economy the call for protectionist measures, including subsidies, is less likely as economic growth provides many opportunities for alternatives employing labor and capital more efficiently. Restructuring is always needed as nations change their relative competitiveness, but it is also required for domestic economic efficiency. It should be a positive process. Future jobs in the North are thus related to both domestic and international policies to expand the northern economies. A significant proportion of jobs in the North depends on trade with the South. There will be difficult conflicts within the North between those who have to change their employment and those who do not. But if the North fails to adjust, it will be more difficult for everybody.

We are convinced that many of the world's problems can be solved in the mutual interest of North and South. The South has called for a new regime to protect the commodities which they export against price falls and fluctuations. The North has only slowly moved toward this, while being concerned about future supplies of raw materials and low investment in minerals, which cannot improve without remunerative and more stable prices. The South wants access to the markets of the North for its manufacturing, which raises problems for specific industries in the North—but overall the North can expand employment by a balanced increase in its trade with the South. The South needs to buy from the North, and to repay its debts, but for that it must earn foreign currency in the North by selling its goods there. The South wants a code to provide more harmonious relations with multinational corporations—but both sides can benefit if these corporations can invest confidently in the South, and if the South can have more confidence in the multinationals' behavior; future mineral investment in the South depends on such arrangements. Above all, we believe that a large-scale transfer of resources to the South can make a major impact on growth in both the South and the North and help to revive the flagging world economy.

AFTER THE SECOND WORLD WAR: A HISTORICAL NOTE

The current crisis can only be understood in the perspective of the postwar decades and in the context of the world institutions that grew up at that time. At the end of the Second World War, the United Nations was established with its headquarters in New York. It aimed to achieve universal membership and was built on the principle of one vote for each country—with a veto right for major powers in the Security Council. In 1946, the UN still had only 55 members. After 1947, when India gained independence, a succession of countries achieved nationhood in Africa, Asia, the Caribbean, and the Pacific until by 1979 the UN had 152 members, so that the South outnumbered both the West and the East.

When the war ended the United States emerged as the dominant Western power, and together with Britain took the lead in shaping the new institutions to provide the framework for world finance and trade. While the Western powers were committed to intervention in their home economies, they were determined to avoid the protectionism and "beggar thy neighbor" policies of the 1930s, by creating a strong free-trade system; it was a combination of Keynes at home and Adam Smith abroad. In 1944, when they met at Bretton Woods in New Hampshire, they established two central instruments for international financial and monetary cooperation: the International Bank for Reconstruction and Development (IBRD), known as the World Bank, to provide loans to assist the reconstruction of Europe and Japan and for the developing world, and the International Monetary Fund (IMF) to be the regulator of currencies, promoting stable exchange rates and providing liquidity for the freer flow of trade.

INTERNATIONAL INSTITUTIONS

The Bretton Woods system was originally intended to include an International Trade Organization which was negotiated and agreed upon in Havana in 1948; but the Havana charter was never ratified by the U.S. Congress. Some of its commercial provisions were incorporated in the less ambitious General Agreement on Tariffs and Trade (GATT) of 1948, which was intended as an interim arrangement, but became a mechanism which has served as the principal forum for multinational trade negotiation. The wider aims, including steps toward organizing commodity markets, were never implemented.

The World Bank and the IMF were established in Washington in 1945, where they have remained—working in adjoining buildings (though with separate staffs and different objectives). They were open to all countries, though the major industrial countries controlled them through votes weighted by contributions. The United States, which at first raised most of the bank's funds, retained a strong influence. India and Latin America were represented at Bretton Woods but most of the Third World were still dependencies in 1944, and the views and the needs of the South were not in the forefront of the negotiations. Both the Soviet Union and China took part in the Bretton Woods Conference. The Soviet Union chose not to join the institutions; and after the revolution of 1949, mainland China was not represented.

The West and the East soon established their own economic alliances. In 1947 the United States initiated the Marshall Plan for the economic recovery of Europe. It insisted that the European countries should cooperate in the allocation of U.S. funds, and the Organization for European Economic Cooperation (OEEC) was established for this purpose: in 1960 it became the Organization for Economic Cooperation and Development (OECD), with the United States, Canada, and eventually most Western industrialized countries as members. In 1949 a conference in

Moscow led to the Council for Mutual Economic Assistance, or CMEA—also known as Comecon—comprising Bulgaria, Czechoslovakia, Hungary, Poland, Romania, and the USSR, with the German Democratic Republic joining in the following year. They developed a separate international monetary system, and their trade was governed by long-term agreements related to five-year plans. As their economic system took shape, these countries had at first only modest relations with the rest of the world economy. Later on the Mongolian People's Republic, Cuba, and Vietnam joined the CMEA as developing country members, while Albania, which had joined later, left it.

THE UN AGENCIES AND THE BRETTON WOODS INSTITUTIONS

The United Nations became the principal forum for the South. The many new nations which emerged from the historic changes in the post-war years saw development issues as critical to their relations with the rest of the world, and their nation building, which was often turbulent, depended on economic and social development. As the UN and its related agencies expanded, including the World Health Organization (WHO), the International Labor Organization (ILO), the United Nations Development Program (UNDP), the Food and Agriculture Organization (FAO), and the United Nations Educational, Scientific and Cultural Organization (UNESCO), they became instruments of development which brought the issues of international poverty more prominently to the notice of the North. The World Bank and the IMF, though increasingly concerned with the problems of development, tended to follow a more conservative approach. Between the Bretton Woods and the United Nations institutions, each with their own language and assumptions, there remained a difference of orientation and of power. The South had majority votes in the General Assembly, which gave assurance of passing resolutions; but the North's position in the World Bank and IMF gave it control over key areas of money and finance.

In the two and a half decades following the Second World War the world economy was transformed. With a liberalized trading regime and relatively stable currencies, dominated by the American dollar, the industrialized world experienced economic growth and an expansion of trade without parallel in history, which contributed to growth in some parts of the Third World. The World Bank, the IMF, and GATT had to adapt themselves to the needs of developing countries. In 1960 the World Bank was augmented by the International Development Association (IDA), which provided a lending facility or "window" for loans on much easier concessional terms to developing countries; the IMF increased and broadened its financing to assist them; while GATT attracted more members from developing countries and partly exempted them, at least in principle, from its rule of reciprocity, by which a member country seeking concessions must offer equivalent concessions to other members.

CHANGING ATTITUDES TO AID

At first the Western governments saw development largely in terms of aid. The United States initiated its development aid program in 1949 and the UN began its program of technical assistance at the beginning of the 1950s. At first, aid grew very rapidly: by 1951 Western countries were lending $8 billion a year, almost 1 percent of their gross national product, though aid loans of the Eastern countries were much more restricted. In 1967 the World Bank suggested a grand assize which would "study the consequences of twenty years of development assistance, assess the results, clarify the errors and propose the policies which will work better in the future." This led to the formation in 1968 of a commission chaired by Lester B. Pearson, former prime minister of Canada. When in 1969 the Pearson Commission published its findings, aid questions occupied much of its attention, which reflected the prevailing philosophy in development circles, as well as the fact that its recommendations were mainly addressed to the Bretton Woods institutions and to aid-giving governments.

But there was also growing interest in the fundamental problems of development—many of them, such as land reform, of a domestic nature, others related to foreign trade and investment. In the 1950s many studies suggested that developing countries' trade with industrial countries was on unequal terms and that this seriously hindered their development. The nonaligned countries, which had been brought together by anticolonialism and a desire to stand apart from the cold war, began to press for fairer conditions of trade. And when the first UN Conference on Trade and Development (UNCTAD) was held in 1964, the Group of 77 (which now includes well over 100 members) was formed, by which the developing countries sought to promote their economic interests jointly. This group included a wide range, from semi-industrialized countries in Latin America to extremely poor countries in Africa and Asia, but they were determined to maintain a unified bargaining front in the face of the richer countries of the North, and this profoundly influenced the subsequent course of North-South relations.

NEW TRENDS IN THE 1970S

By the early 1970s the focus of debate had shifted away from aid to the structure of the world economic system. While the developing countries had benefited from the evolution of the international institutions, they wanted it to go much further. They maintained that the rules of the GATT were not sufficiently relevant to their special needs. They complained that the origins and initial power structure of the Bretton Woods institutions limited the capacity for change, and they asked for a restructuring of the international financial system. In trade, finance, and technology they were looking for reform and innovation.

But in UNCTAD and elsewhere, the Group of 77 faced an uphill task. At successive meetings they put forward proposals for international economic reform, but the North either did not like them or was not ready for them. The North has also argued that the South often makes inflexible demands which allow little room for negotiation. On the other hand, while some countries have made positive proposals, the North as a group has tended to react passively to those put forward by the South rather than present a constructive position of its own.

At the beginning of the 1970s the world economy suffered a modest recession; though it recovered rapidly in 1972 there was high inflation in several countries, and prices of grains and capital goods rose considerably. The monetary system had already weakened when the dollar was divorced from gold in August 1971; the postwar rules for the management of exchange rates were abandoned early in 1973. Major countries had to cope simultaneously with problems of inflation, unemployment, and the balance of payments, and their domestic restraints were holding back international trade. The Bretton Woods system had already begun to crumble.

A decisive change occurred with the increase in the price of oil in late 1973, which marked a major turning point in North-South relations. The oil-exporting countries, organized since 1960 in OPEC, the Organization of Petroleum Exporting Countries, announced a series of increases which quadrupled the price of crude oil in 1973–74. With hindsight it might seem inevitable, as the real price of oil had been falling for some time and did not reflect the future scarcity of energy resources. But the price change gave a substantial shock to the world economy in which the flows of oil were already playing a major part. A few oil-exporting countries found themselves with large financial surpluses, while oil-importing countries suffered sudden deterioration in their balance of payments. The results were serious in the industrialized countries, and—together with other price increases and the effects of global recession—even more so in parts of the developing world. For several countries there was substantial help from OPEC to offset the oil price increase; but many others were seriously affected.

The world economy has failed to return to its earlier buoyancy. The Western industrialized countries had grown at more than 4 percent a year from 1950 to 1960 and more than 5 percent from 1960 to 1973, but from 1973 to 1979 they grew at an average rate of only 2.5 percent a year. The

East European economies also grew more slowly, from over 9.5 percent a year in the 1950s and over 6.5 percent during 1960–73 to less than 5.5 percent during 1973–77—although figures for the East European countries are not strictly comparable with those for the West. Although some developing countries managed to maintain their growth momentum and their import demand—which helped to prevent an even worse recession in the industrialized countries—there was a marked slowdown after 1974 in Latin America and, most seriously, in the least developed countries, many of them in Africa. Their exports stagnated and their per capita incomes—little more than $100—increased by just over 1 percent, that is, by $1–$2 per year.

Where growth has slowed down in developing countries it has, of course, aggravated an already grave unemployment situation; in the Third World unemployment and underemployment are measured in hundreds of millions. And unemployment has been rising also in the industrialized world. By 1979 there were over 18 million unemployed in the OECD countries. Many sectors of their economies—especially older industries like steel, shipbuilding, or clothing—were in danger. Slow growth, inflation, the fluctuations of exchange rates, the rising costs of environmental protection, and the problematic future of energy all added to the uncertainty of businessmen who held back from new investment.

The oil price was not responsible for all these ills, but oil has obviously become critical to the world economy. And in the North-South context, the OPEC action has been of profound significance. For the first time a group of countries outside the circle of the industrialized world was able to exert its own powerful economic pressure. It belonged to the South and identified itself with the South's aspirations for fundamental reform of international economic relations. This gave the whole North-South dialogue a new impetus, though it still did not produce great progress in the 1970s.

As the decade drew to a close, the world economy was in serious difficulties, and the institutional framework which had served it since the war was inadequate to resolve them. Protectionism was on the increase, with no machinery strong enough to arrest it. In the monetary sphere arrangements for balance of payments adjustment or for an orderly pattern of exchange rates were not in sight. That there was a need for fundamental reform could hardly have been clearer.

CHANGING THE WORLD ECONOMY

The governments and people of the South have the primary responsibility for solving many of their own problems; they will have to continue to generate most of their resources by their own efforts, and to plan and manage their own economies. Only they can ensure that the fruits of development are fairly distributed inside their countries and that greater justice and equity in the world are matched by appropriate reforms at home.

The South needs and wants to be more self-reliant, to complete the process of political independence with economic independence. But that does not imply separation from the world economy. It means rather the ability to bargain on more equal terms with the richer countries, to obtain a fair return for what it produces, and to participate fairly in the control and running of international institutions. Many leaders in the South have complained that while the North may be prepared to spend money on alleviating southern poverty or distress, it is reluctant to surrender control over economic decisions. But this issue of sharing of power cannot be evaded.

[. . .] Commodity producers want to add more value to their products before they sell them: to export sawn planks or furniture instead of timber logs, instant coffee instead of coffee beans, refined metals instead of ores. But here the countries of the South run into tariff and other barriers in the major markets. An equally pressing need is for financial support to stabilize commodity prices and earnings. Most of the middle-income countries, and nearly all the poorer ones, depend very heavily on agricultural and mineral exports. Even Brazil or Malaysia, both middle-income countries which have moved into manufacturing, still rely heavily on coffee, rubber, or tin. All these producers depend on prices which fluctuate widely, and which can force them to sell on a falling market at less than the cost of production. Price stabilization would be helpful to the purchasing countries as well.

OBSTACLES TO THIRD WORLD INDUSTRIALIZATION

This in turn is part of the broader issue of access to markets. Exports of manufactures are important for developing countries' industrialization, but the North is raising obstacles against these too: including more "nontariff" barriers, such as formal or informal quotas, government subsidies, or purchases restricted to their own domestic companies. Within the internal trading system of the transnational corporations the prices of manufactures, commodities, or services can often be adjusted to the disadvantage of the developing countries. Further, a number of developing countries now count on the earnings of migrant workers as a critical source of foreign exchange. Pakistan, for example, receives almost as much from its workers abroad as from its total exports. But the migrants are often insecure and subject to discrimination; a recession can rapidly end their contracts, sending unemployment back to their home country. This labor market, like the market in commodities or manufactures, has weak sellers and powerful buyers.

In the international market for technology, the South faces other difficulties. Developing countries need to build up their own industry and research, and they are often in a weak position to bargain with the transnational corporations which control much of modern technology. They may benefit from direct investment, but the gains have not always been fully shared, which has caused political tension. They can buy technology through licenses, but only on terms set by foreign corporations. They do not wish to lose control over their economies; they want to be able to treat on fair terms and with equal expertise with the transnational corporations.

The South needs, above all, finance. Most rich countries have accepted the target of giving 0.7 percent of their GNP in the form of official development assistance, but few have lived up to it. Most aid goes to finance the foreign exchange costs of projects, but many of the poorer countries also need support for local expenditures and for imports of noncapital goods. Some of the more prosperous countries in the South have recently borrowed extensively from commercial banks, causing heavy problems in rolling over their loans, which by the end of the 1970s were causing anxiety to borrowers and lenders alike. And many developing countries will need much more finance over the next 20 years to produce any real improvement in health and nutrition, in mineral and industrial development, or in sustaining satisfactory growth.

Among monetary issues, there are a number of particular concern to the South, as well as many in which North and South alike have an interest. The mechanisms for creating and distributing international means of payment are strongly influenced by the national policies of a small number of major countries, and the South is calling for a greater influence in decision making.

LIMITED PROGRESS IN NEGOTIATIONS

On these and other issues the South has been negotiatiing with the North for many years. UNCTAD set an extensive agenda for reform at its meeting in Geneva in 1964, which was further elaborated in New Delhi in 1968, in Santiago in 1972, in Nairobi in 1976, and in Manila in 1979. The North has moved on some issues. They agreed to a Generalized System of Preferences in 1968 by which individual developed countries allow duty-free imports of some manufactures from developing countries, though this has been subject to many restrictions. The European Community has negotiated trade preferences with a large group of developing countries, most of which had earlier colonial connections, culminating in the second Lomé Convention of 1979; but their impact on development has so far been modest. Multilateral trade negotiations have taken place in GATT. North and South have had talks within other international institutions; thus monetary reform was studied in the Committee of Twenty within the IMF which by 1974 had reached some agreement on the objectives, although not the means, of reform.

There was a spate of intense activity in the first half of the 1970s. In 1973 a summit conference of the nonaligned countries in Algiers adopted an Action Program calling for "a new international economic order." This strategy of structural reforms was refined and adopted at the Sixth and Seventh Special Sessions of the UN General Assembly in 1974 and 1975. The 1974 General Assembly adopted the Charter of Economic Rights and Duties of States. The new importance of OPEC brought renewed world attention to the North-South dialogue and led to the Conference on International Economic Cooperation (CIEC), which opened in Paris in December 1975. These talks continued intermittently until mid-1977, but they ended without any substantial agreement, except one in principle on assisting the poorest countries.

There was some movement in other areas. UNCTAD had introduced in Nairobi an Integrated Program for Commodities whose centerpiece was the Common Fund, which would help to stabilize commodity prices. This proposal achieved partial agreement in 1979, which some regarded as a negotiating gain, others as a false start; but negotiations on the Common Fund continue. On the Law of the Sea there was complex and laborious work involving both North and South, resulting in 1979 in an agreement in principle to set up a Seabed Authority. There were also negotiations about new codes for the transfer of technology and for the conduct of transnational corporations. There were discussions about the burden of debt, and after the CIEC talks the debts of some of the poorest countries were canceled. But the main proposals for change have made little headway.

The most recent worldwide assembly was the fifth session of UNCTAD in Manila in 1979. While there was some concrete progress on a few secondary items, on the major questions of structural change which divide North and South there was virtually no movement toward any agreed measures which could be rapidly implemented. Did the delegations of the South perhaps not concentrate enough on the vital issues of mutual interests? Or were countries of the North simply lacking the political will to make major concessions?

EAST EUROPEAN INVOLVEMENT

Attitudes in the Third World toward the East European countries were also changing. They had long argued that they were not responsible for the colonial heritage of other powers. Developing countries appreciated that the Soviet Union had moved from great backwardness to a modern industrial power in a short time. Eastern Europe can often offer long-term trading agreements, and their support has sometimes provided an escape from exclusive dependence, both military and industrial, on Western countries.

In recent years Third World countries have expressed the wish for an increase in volumes of aid from and trade with Eastern countries and for their greater involvement in international economic discussions. The international links of the Eastern countries are growing; developing countries increasingly insist that their achievements and manifest influence in international affairs and the fact that many of them buy the Third World's commodities and sell manufactures to them on much the same terms—with significant exceptions—as everyone else, confer a responsibility to participate more fully in international aid and trade with developing countries. At their Arusha meeting in 1979 the Group of 77 called for "an increasingly more active role" to be played by the East European countries in bringing about the early establishment of a new international order.

The East European countries have expressed their willingness to cooperate further and they have also shared in international initiatives to solve global problems. Members of this commission have had contacts with East European leaders. The secretariat had a dialogue with Soviet experts of the Institute for World Economy in Moscow, who assured them that they were observing the problems of the Third World closely. They pointed out that they had undertaken great efforts for the development of the people within their own boundaries and also in a number of developing countries. They stressed the quality of Soviet aid and argued that necessary military expenditures limit their capacity to provide greater foreign assistance. They emphasized the need for improvement in East-West relations and progress towards disarmament. The Soviet experts were fully aware of the great needs of developing countries. They strongly favored changes in the international economic and financial system and institutions.

Many developing countries regard the Soviet Union as ranking in living standards among the industrialized countries. It is therefore hoped and expected that the Soviet Union and other Eastern industrialized countries will increase their participation in world trade and in economic, scientific, and technical cooperation, particularly with developing countries. Bolder political decisions in Eastern, as well as in Western and Third World countries, are needed to achieve a true international cooperation in the interest of development.

PARTICIPATION OF CHINA

China is the largest developing country, with nearly a quarter of the world's population, and its experience has many lessons for others.

While setting itself the long-term goal of industrialization, it gives the highest priority to agricultural production. It is strongly committed to population control. Even though China's annual income per head is less than $400, it has provided significant aid and technical assistance to other countries, both in quantity and quality.

The commission sent a small team to China as guests of the Chinese People's Institute for Foreign Affairs, who discussed policies and attitudes to international economic relations, and were also informed of China's own progress in modernization. China is interested in closer exchange with the international economy in trade, finance, and investment and is now considering membership of the Bretton Woods institutions and GATT. It is already receiving offers of large credits from many sources. We welcome this trend for the closer participation of China in the international economy, which will benefit China and the rest of the world.

UNITY TO AVERT CATASTROPHE

Current trends point to a somber future for the world economy and international relations. A painful outlook for the poorer countries with no end to poverty and hunger; continuing world stagnation combined with inflation; international monetary disorder; mounting debts and deficits; protectionism; major tensions between countries competing for energy, food, and raw materials; growing world population and more unemployment in North and South; increasing threats to the environment and the international commons through deforestation and desertification, overfishing, and overgrazing, the pollution of air and water. And overshadowing everything the menacing arms race.

For these trends to continue is dangerous enough, but they can easily worsen. A number of poor countries are threatened with the irreversible destruction of their ecological systems; many more face growing food deficits and possibly mass starvation. In the international economy there is the possibility of competitive trade restrictions or devaluations; a collapse of credit with defaults by major debtors, or bank failures; a deepening recession under possible energy shortages or further failures of international cooperation; an intensified struggle for spheres of interest and influence, or for control over resources, leading to military conflicts. The 1980s could witness even greater catastrophes than the 1930s.

Such developments are not improbable; but we do not believe them to be inevitable. Current trends do not have to continue, let alone worsen. We believe that nations, even on grounds of self-interest, can join in the common task of ensuring survival, to make the world more peaceful and less uncertain. A fundamental change in relations between North and South as well as between East and West is crucial to this task. The world is a unity, and we must begin to act as members of it who depend on each other. It is not enough, as one of our commissioners put it, to sit around tables talking like characters in Chekhov plays about insoluble problems. We have to lift ourselves above the immediate constrictions and offer the world a plan and a vision of hope, without which nothing substantial can be achieved.

7

Population, Resources, and the Ideology of Science

David Harvey

THE POLITICAL IMPLICATIONS OF POPULATION-RESOURCES THEORY

At the Stockholm Conference on the Environment in 1972, the Chinese delegation asserted that there was no such thing as a scarcity of resources and that it was meaningless to discuss environmental problems in such terms. Western commentators were mystified and some concluded that the Chinese must possess vast reserves of minerals and fossil fuels the discovery of which they had not yet communicated to the world. The Chinese view is, however, quite consistent with Marx's method and should be considered from such a perspective. To elucidate it we need to bring into our vocabulary three categories of thought:

1. *Subsistence.* Malthus appears to regard subsistence as something absolute, whereas Marx regards it as relative. For Marx, needs are not purely biological; they are also socially and culturally determined. Also, as both Malthus and Marx agree, needs can be created, which implies that the meaning of subsistence cannot be established independent of particular historical and cultural circumstances if, as Marx insisted, definitions of social wants and needs were produced under a given mode of production rather than immutably held down by the Malthusian laws of population. Subsistence is, then, defined internally to a mode of production and changes over time.

2. *Resources.* Resources are materials available "in nature" that are capable of being transformed into things of utility to man. It has long

Excerpt from "Population, Resources, and the Ideology of Science" by David Harvey in *Economic Geography* (Vol. 50, No. 3, July 1974). Reprinted by permission of the author and *Economic Geography*. Pp. 272–76.

been recognized that resources can be defined only with respect to a particular technical, cultural, and historical stage of development, and that they are, in effect, technical and cultural appraisals of nature.

3. *Scarcity.* It is often erroneously accepted that scarcity is something inherent in nature, when its definition is inextricably social and cultural in origin. Scarcity presupposes certain social ends, and it is these that define scarcity just as much as the lack of natural means to accomplish these ends. Furthermore, many of the scarcities we experience do not arise out of nature but are created by human activity and managed by social organization (the scarcity of building plots in central London is an example of the former; the scarcity of places at university is an example of the latter). Scarcity is in fact necessary to the survival of the capitalist mode of production, and it has to be carefully managed, otherwise the self-regulating aspect to the price mechanism will break down.

Armed with these definitions, let us consider a simple sentence: "Overpopulation arises because of the scarcity of resources available for meeting the subsistence needs of the mass of the population." If we substitute our definitions into this sentence we get: "There are too many people in the world because the particular ends we have in view (together with the form of social organization we have) and the materials available in nature, that we have the will and the way to use, are not sufficient to provide us with those things to which we are accustomed." Out of such a sentence all kinds of possibilities can be extracted:

1. We can change the ends we have in mind and alter the social organization of scarcity.
2. We can change our technical and cultural appraisals of nature.
3. We can change our views concerning the things to which we are accustomed.
4. We can seek to alter our numbers.

A real concern with environmental issues demands that all of these options be examined in relation to each other. To say that there are too many people in the world amounts to saying that we have not the imagination, will, or ability to do anything about propositions (1), (2), and (3). In fact (1) is very difficult to do anything about because it involves the replacement of the market exchange system as a working mode of economic integration; proposition (2) has always been the great hope for resolving our difficulties; and we have never thought too coherently about (3) particularly as it relates to the maintenance of an effective demand in capitalist economies (nobody appears to have calculated what the effects of much reduced personal consumption will have on capital accumulation and employment).

I will risk the generalization that nothing of consequence can be done about (1) and (3) without dismantling and replacing the capitalist market exchange economy. If we are reluctant to contemplate such an alternative and if (2) is not performing its function too well, then we have to go to (4). Much of the debate in the Western world focuses on (4), but in a society in which all four options can be integrated with each other, it must appear facile to discuss environmental problems in terms of naturally arising scarcities or overpopulation—this, presumably, is the point that the Chinese delegation to the Stockholm Conference was making.

The trouble with focusing exclusively on the control of population numbers is that it has certain political implications. Ideas about environment, population, and resources are not neutral. They are political in origin and have political effects. Historically it is depressing to look at the use made of the kind of sentence we have just analyzed. Once connotations of absolute limits come to surround the concepts of resource, scarcity, and subsistence, then an absolute limit is set for population. And what are the political implications (given these connotations) of saying there is "overpopulation" or a "scarcity of resources"? The meaning can all too quickly be established. Somebody, somewhere, is redundant, and there is not enough to go round. Am *I* redundant? Of course not. Are *you* redundant? Of course not. So who is redundant? Of course, it must be *them*. And if there is not enough to go round, then it is only right and proper that *they*, who contribute so little to society, ought to bear the brunt of the burden. And if we hold that there are certain of *us*, who, by virtue of our skills, abilities, and attainments, are capable of "conferring a signal benefit upon mankind" through our contributions to the common good and who, besides, are the purveyors of peace, freedom, culture, and civilization, then it would appear to be our bound duty to protect and preserve ourselves for the sake of all mankind.

Let me make an assertion. Whenever a theory of overpopulation seizes hold in a society dominated by an elite, then the nonelite invariably experience some form of political, economic, and social repression. Such an assertion can be justified by an appeal to the historical evidence. Britain shortly after the Napoleonic Wars, when Malthus was so influential, provides one example. The conservation movement in the United States at the turn of this century was based on a gospel of efficiency that embraced natural resource management and labor relations alike. The combination of the Aryan ethic and the need for increased lebensraum produced particularly evil results in Hitler's Germany. The policy prescriptions that frequently attach to essays on the problems of population and environment convey a similar warning. Jacks and Whyte, writing in the twilight years of the British Empire, could see only one way out of the scarcity of land resources in Africa:

> A feudal type of society in which the native cultivators would to some extent be tied to the lands of their European overlords seems most generally suited to meet the needs of the soil in the present state of African development. . . . It would enable the

> people who have been the prime cause of erosion [the Europeans] and who have the means and ability to control it to assume responsibility for the soil. At present, humanitarian considerations for the natives prevent Europeans from winning the attainable position of dominance over the soil.

Such direct apologetics for colonialism sound somewhat odd today.

Vogt, whose book *The Road to Survival* appeared in 1948, saw in Russian overpopulation a serious military and political threat. He argued that the Marshall Plan of aid to Europe was the result of an unenviable choice between allowing the spread of communism and providing international welfare, which would merely encourage population increase. He also points to the expendability of much of the world's population:

> There is little hope that the world will escape the horror of extensive famines in China within the next few years. But from the world point of view, these may be not only desirable but indispensable. A Chinese population that continued to increase at a geometric rate could only be a global calamity. The mission of General Marshall to this unhappy land was called a failure. Had it succeeded, it might well have been a disaster.

It is ironic indeed that this prediction was published in the very year that Mao Tse-tung came to power and sought, in true dialectical fashion, to transform China's problem into a solution through the mobilization of labor power to create resources where there had been none before. The resultant transformation of the Chinese earth (as Buchanan calls it) has eliminated famine, raised living standards, and effectively eliminated hunger and material misery.

It is easier to catch the political implications of overpopulation arguments in past eras than it is in our own. The lesson which these examples suggest is simply this: If we accept a theory of overpopulation and resource scarcity but insist upon keeping the capitalist mode of production intact, then the inevitable results are policies directed toward class or ethnic repression at home and policies of imperialism and neo-imperialism abroad. Unfortunately this relation can be structured in the other direction. If, for whatever reason, an elite group requires an argument to support policies of repression, then the overpopulation argument is most beautifully tailored to fit this purpose. Malthus and Ricardo provide us with one example of such apologetics. If a poverty class is necessary to the processes of capitalist accumulation or a subsistence wage essential to economic equilibrium, then what better way to explain it away than to appeal to a universal and supposedly "natural" law of population?

Malthus indicates another kind of apologetic use for the population principle. If an existing social order, an elite group of some sort, is under threat and is fighting to preserve its dominant position in society, then the overpopulation and shortage of resources arguments can be used as powerful ideological levers to persuade people into acceptance of the status quo and of authoritarian measures to maintain it. The English landed interest used Malthus's arguments thus in the early nineteenth century. And this kind of argument is, of course, even more effective if the elite group is in a position to create a scarcity to demonstrate the point.

The overpopulation argument is easily used as part of an elaborate apologetic through which class, ethnic, or (neo-) colonial repression may be justified. It is difficult to distinguish between arguments that have some real foundation and arguments fashioned for apologetic reasons. In general the two kinds of arguments get inextricably mixed up. Consequently, those who think there is a real problem of some sort may, unwittingly, contribute strength to the apologists, and individuals may contribute in good faith to a result which, as individuals, they might find abhorrent.

And what of the contemporary ecology and environmental movement? I believe it reflects all of the currents I have identified, but under the stress of contemporary events it is difficult to sort the arguments out clearly. There are deep structural problems to the capitalist growth process (epitomized by persistent "stagflation" and international monetary uncertainties). Adjustments seem necessary. The welfare population in America is being transformed from a tool for the manipulation of effective demand (which was its economic role in the 1960s) into a tool for attacking wage rates (through the work-fare provision)—and Malthus's arguments are all being used to do it. Wage rates have been under attack, and policies for depressing real earnings are emerging in both America and in Europe to compensate for falling rates of profit and a slowdown in the rate of capital accumulation. There can be no question that the existing social order perceived itself to be under some kind of threat in the late 1960s (particularly in France and the United States and now in Britain). Was it accidental that the environmentalist argument emerged so strongly in 1968 at the crest of campus disturbances? And what was the effect of replacing Marcuse by Ehrlich as campus hero? Conditions appear to be exactly right for the emergence of overpopulation arguments as part of a popular ideology to justify what had and what has to be done to stabilize a capitalist economic system that is under severe stress.

But at the same time there is mounting evidence (which has in fact been building up since the early 1950s) of certain ecological problems that now exist on a worldwide as opposed to on a purely local scale (the DDT example being the most spectacular). Such problems are real enough. The difficulty, of course, is to identify the underlying reason for the emergence of these difficulties. There has been some recognition that consumption patterns induced under capitalism may have something to do with it, and that the nature of private enterprise, with its predilection for shifting costs onto society in order to improve the competitive position of the firm, also plays a role. And there is no question that runaway rates of population growth (brought about to a large degree by the penetration of market and wage-labor relationships into traditional rural societies) have also played a role. But in their haste to lay the origin of these problems at the door of "overpopulation" (with all of its Malthusian connotations), many analysts have unwittingly invited the politics of repression that invariably seem to be attached to the Malthusian argument at a time when economic conditions are such as to make that argument extremely attractive to a ruling elite.

Ideas are social relations; they have their ultimate origin in the social concerns of mankind and have their ultimate impact upon the social life of mankind. Arguments concerning environmental degradation, population growth, resource scarcities, and the like can arise for quite disparate reasons and have quite diverse impacts. It is therefore crucial to establish the political and social origins and impacts of such arguments. The political consequences of injecting a strongly pessimistic view into a world structured hierarchically along class and ethnic lines and in which there is an ideological commitment to the preservation of the capitalist order are quite terrifying to contemplate. As Levi-Strauss warns in *Tristes Tropiques:*

> Once men begin to feel cramped in their geographical, social and mental habitat, they are in danger of being tempted by the simple solution of denying one section of the species the right to be considered human.

CONCLUSIONS

Twentieth-century science in the Western world is dominated by the tradition of Aristotelian materialism. Within that tradition, logical empiricism, backed by the philosophical strength of logical positivism, has provided a general paradigmatic basis for scientific enquiry. More recently the "model builders" and the "systems theorists" have come to play a larger role. All of these methods are destined to generate Malthusian or neo-Malthusian results when applied to the analysis of global problems in the population-resources relation. Individual scientists may express optimism or pessimism about the future, while the results of scientific investigation may indicate the inevitable stationary state to be far away or close at hand. But, given the nature of the methodology, all the indicators point in the same direction.

The political consequences that flow from these results can be serious. The projection of a neo-Malthusian view into the politics of the time appears to invite repression at home and neocolonial policies abroad. The neo-Malthusian view often functions to legitimate such policies and, thereby, to preserve the position of a ruling elite. Given the ethical neutrality assumption and the dominant conception of scientific method, all a ruling elite has to do to generate neo-Malthusian viewpoints is to ask the scientific community to consider the problems inherent in the population-resources relation. The scientific results are basically predetermined, although individual scientists may demur for personal "subjective" reasons.

It is, of course, the central argument of this paper that the only kind of method capable of dealing with the complexities of the population-resources relation in an integrated and truly dynamic way is that founded in a properly constituted version of dialectical materialism.

This conclusion will doubtless be unpalatable to many because it *sounds* ideological to a society of scholars nurtured in the belief that ideology is a dirty word. Such a belief is, as I have pointed out, ideological. Further, failure to make use of such a method in the face of a situation that all regard as problematic, and some regard as bordering on the catastrophic, is to court ignorance on a matter as serious as the survival of the human species. And if ignorance is the result of the ideological belief that science is and ought to be ideology free, then it is a hidden ideology that is the most serious barrier to enquiry. And if, out of ignorance, we participate in the politics of repression and the politics of fear, then we are doing so largely as a consequence of the ideological claim to be ideology free. But then, perhaps, it was precisely that participation that the claim to be ideology free was designed to elicit all along.

REFERENCES

Buchanan, K. *The Transformation of the Chinese Earth.* New York: Praeger, 1970.

Jacks, G. V. and R. O. Whyte. *Vanishing Lands.* New York: Doubleday, 1939.

Levi-Strauss, C. *Tristes Tropiques.* New York: Atheneum, 1973.

Vogt, W. *The Road to Survival.* New York: W. Sloane Associates, 1948.

8

The Artificial Universe

Vine Deloria, Jr.

The justification for taking lands from Indian people has always been that the needs and requirements of civilized people had to come first. Settlers arriving on these shores saw a virtual paradise untouched by the works of man. They drooled at the prospect of developing the land according to their own dictates. Thus a policy of genocide was advocated that would clear the land of the original inhabitants to make way for towns, cities, farms, factories, and highways. This was progress.

Even today Indian people hold their land at the sufferance of the non-Indian. The typical white attitude is that Indians can have land as long as whites have no use for it. When it becomes useful, then it naturally follows that the land must be taken by whites to put to a better use. I have often heard the remark "what happens to the Indian land base if we decide we need more land?" The fact that Indian rights to land are guaranteed by the Constitution of the United States, over 400 treaties, and some 6,000 statutes seems irrelevant to a people hungry for land and dedicated to law and order.

The major reason why whites have seen fit to steal Indian lands is that they feel that their method of using land is so much better than that of the Indian. It follows that God would want them to develop the land. During the Seneca fight against Kinzua Dam, sympathetic whites would raise the question of Indian legal rights and they would be shouted down by people who said that the Indians had had the land for 200 years and did *nothing* with it. It would be far better, they argued, to let whites take the land and develop something on it.

From the days of the earliest treaties, Indians were shocked at the white man's attitude toward land. The tribal elders laughed contemptuously at the idea that a man could sell land. "Why not sell the air we breathe, the water we drink, the animals we hunt?" some replied. It was ludicrous to Indians that people would consider land as commodity that could be owned by one man. The land, they would answer, supports all life. It is given to all people. No one has a superior claim to exclusive use of land, much less does anyone have the right to fence off a portion and deny others its use.

In the closing decades of the last century, Indian tribes fought fiercely for their lands. Reservations were agreed upon and tribes held a fragment of the once expansive hunting grounds they had roamed. But no sooner had Indians settled on the reservations, than the government, ably led by the churches, decided that the reservation areas should be divided into tiny plots of land for farming purposes. In many reservation areas it was virtually impossible to farm such lands. The situation in California was so desperate that a report was issued denouncing the government land policy for Indians. The report contained such detrimental material exposing the vast land swindles that it was pigeonholed in the Senate files and *has never been released and cannot be obtained today, nearly a century later!!!*

Tribe after tribe succumbed to the allotment process. After the little plots of land were passed out to individual Indians, the remainder, which should have been held in tribal hands, was declared surplus and opened to settlement. Millions of "excess" acres of lands were thus casually transferred to federal title and given to non-Indian settlers. Churches rushed in and grabbed the choice allotments for their chapels and cemeteries, and in some cases simply for income-producing purposes. They had been the chief advocates of allotment—on the basis that creating greed and selfishness among the Indians was the first step in civilizing them and making them Christians.

For years the development of the land did make it seem as if the whites had been correct in their theory of land use. Cities were built, productive farms were created, the wilderness was made safe, and superhighways were built linking one portion of the nation with the others. In some areas the very landscape was changed as massive earth-moving machines relocated mountains and streams, filled valleys, and created lakes out of wandering streams.

Where Indian people had had a reverence of the productiveness of the land, whites wanted to make the land support their way of life whether it was suited to do so or not. Much of San Francisco Bay was filled in and whole areas of the city were built upon the new land. Swamps were drained in the Chicago area and large portions of the city were built on them. A great portion of Ohio had been swamp and grassland and this was drained and farmed. Land was the great capital asset for speculation. People purchased apparently worthless desert land in Arizona, only to have the cities grow outward to their doorstep, raising land prices hundreds of percents. Land worth pennies an acre in the 1930s became worth thousands of dollars a front foot in the 1960s.

The rapid increase of population, technology, and capital has produced the present situation where the struggle for land will surpass anything that can be conceived. We are now on the verge of incredible development of certain areas into strip cities that will extend hundreds of miles along the coasts, major rivers, and mountain ranges. At the same time, many areas of the country are steadily losing population. Advanced farming techniques allow one man to do the work that several others formerly did, so that the total population needed in agricultural states continues to decline without a corresponding decline in productivity.

The result of rapid industrialization has been the creation of innumerable problems. Farm surpluses have lowered prices on agricultural products so that the federal government has had to enter the marketplace and support prices to ensure an adequate income for farmers. Farm subsidies are no longer a small business. In nine wheat and feed grain-producing counties in eastern Colorado in 1968, \$31.4 million was given in farm subsidies. In all of Colorado, \$62.8 million was given in 1968 to support farmers. This was a state with a declining farm population. Under the Agricultural Stabilization Conservation Service, some \$3.5 billion was paid out in 1968, \$675 million paid to 33,395 individual farmers as farm "income maintenance," some receiving amounts in excess of \$100,000.

For much of the rural farm areas the economy, the society, and the very structure of life is completely artificial. It depends wholly upon government welfare payments to landowners, a thinly disguised guaranteed annual income for the rich. If the payments were suddenly cut off, millions of acres would become idle because it would not pay to farm them and there would be no way to live on them without income. Our concern for the family farm and the rural area is thus a desperate effort to maintain the facade of a happy, peace-loving nation of farmers, tillers of the soil who stand as the bastion of rugged individualism.

If rural areas have an artificial economy, the urban areas surpass them in everything. Wilderness transformed into city streets, subways, giant buildings, and factories resulted in the complete substitution of the real world for the artificial world of the urban man. Instead of woods, large buildings rose. Instead of paths, avenues were built. Instead of lakes and streams, sewers and fountains were created. In short, urban man lives in a world of his own making and not in the world that his ancestors first encountered.

Surrounded by an artificial universe where the warning signals are not the shape of the sky, the cry of the animals, the changing of seasons, but simply the flashing of the traffic light and the wail of the ambulance and police car, urban people have no idea what the natural universe is like. They are devoured by the goddess of progress, and progress is defined solely in terms of convenience within the artificial technological universe with which they are familiar. Technological progress totally defines the outlook of most of America, so that as long as newer buildings and fancier roads can be built, additional lighting and electric appliances can be sold, and conveniences for modern living can be created there is not the slightest indication that urban man realizes that his artificial universe is dependent on the real world.

Milk comes in cartons, and cows are so strange an animal that hunters from large cities kill a substantial number of cattle every year on their annual hunting orgies. This despite the fact that in many areas farmers paint the word COW on the side of their animals to identify them. Food comes in plastic containers highly tinged with artificial sweeteners, colors, and preservatives. The very conception of plants, growing seasons, rainfall, and drought is foreign to city people. Artificial criteria of comfort define everything that urban areas need and therefore dominate the producing rural areas as to commercial products.

The total result of this strange social order is that there has been total disregard for the natural world. The earth is considered simply another commodity used to support additional suburbs and superhighways. Plant and animal life are subject to destruction at the whim of industrial development. Rivers are no more than wasted space separating areas of the large cities. In many areas they are open sewers carrying off the millions of tons of refuse discarded by the urban consumer.

The Indian lived with his land. He feared to destroy it by changing its natural shape because he realized that it was more than a useful tool for exploitation. It sustained all life, and without other forms of life, man himself could not survive. People used to laugh at the Indian respect for smaller animals. Indians called them little brother. The Plains Indians appeased the buffalo after they had slain them for food. They well understood that without all life respecting itself and each other no society could indefinitely maintain itself. All of this understanding was ruthlessly wiped out to make room for the white man so that civilization could progress according to God's divine plan.

In recent years we have come to understand what progress is. It is the total replacement of nature by an artificial technology. Progress is the absolute destruction of the real world in favor of a technology that creates a comfortable way of life for a few fortunately situated people. Within our lifetime the difference between the Indian use of land and the white use of land will become crystal clear. The Indian lived with his land. *The white destroyed his land. He destroyed the planet earth.* [. . .]

9

Resources and Development: Trying to Close the Gap Responsibly

M. C. B. Hotz

An old adage has it that death and taxes are the only certainties in this world, but it would be difficult to find anyone today who would dispute that change has become at least nearly as certain as the others. Over the last several years, many have written about the impacts of change on our societies and the problems posed when people are confronted by what appear to them to be unacceptably high rates of change in their surroundings.

Much of this has been negative in outlook. The destruction of life-styles resulting from lack of understanding in the transfer of technologies, or the introduction of foreign concepts alien to domestic cultures are among the most frequently cited when referring to developing countries. It is often forgotten, however, that the industrialized countries have passed through a succession of social, cultural, and economic shifts over the last few hundreds of years. These countries are now involved in a series of events whose socioeconomic dimensions not only pose problems for themselves that are akin to a second industrial revolution, but which could in many ways be disastrous for the developing countries that have chosen to follow the well-trodden path to prosperity through conventional industrialization.

This process is based on the principle of wealth generation through resource transformation, and the distribution of that wealth through participation of the entire active population in the economy. It implies that the services required by the distribution system are ancillary to the main thrust of wealth formation.

"Resources and Development: Trying to Close the Gap Responsibly" by M. C. B. Hotz reprinted from *Mazingira* (Vol. 5, No. 2, 1981). Reprinted by permission of *Mazingira* (published in Dublin, Ireland). Pp. 52–61.

To maintain productivity—a high flow of goods at the lowest possible cost—in the face of increasing labor costs, the industrial countries have tended to emphasize labor-saving technologies that are energy and capital intensive, and which are now being viewed in many quarters as being at least in part responsible for fundamental changes in their economies. It is a fact that, while much of the world aspires to achieving the benefits of industrialization, the industrialized countries themselves are confronted by a spate of economic and social problems that they seem powerless to resolve, and that threaten the continuation of the type of economic growth upon which they have come to depend.

Widespread unemployment, social and political unrest, inflation, the availability of resources, and many other concerns have given rise to the increasing opinion that structural changes are taking place, and that these symptoms represent alienation from the centers of decision making and the social institutions which they represent. If this is indeed so, the challenges represented by advances in electronic technology, coupled with the shifts in social and institutional thinking, imply that the outcome is likely to be new economic systems and sets of lifestyles and aspirations as radically different from those of today as ours are from those of preindustrial agrarianism.

As the industrial countries move ever closer to what has been variously termed an "information," "postindustrial," or even "leisure" society, it is clear that the aspirations and outlooks of their populations are changing in ways that are fundamentally different from those who are still struggling to turn themselves into industrial societies. Does it necessarily follow that the industrializing countries have to imitate those who have traveled the road before, and perforce make the same mistakes in their attempts to achieve more equitable lifestyles?

UNDERSTANDING THE PROBLEMS

A great deal has been written about the widening gap between the world's rich and poor. Originally focused on national situations that appeared to be simply distributive in nature, more recently attention has been directed to the disparities between what we are prone to call wealthy and poor countries. When we do this the imbalances that are responsible for these situations become clearer. Essentially, they relate to the possession of resources, demand for resources, and understanding of the technologies in which resources are used.

The technologically advanced countries, having developed their industrial bases by consuming their own resources, use a disproportionate share of the world's total resources in order to support the lifestyles to which they have become accustomed. These countries have the technological ability to use the resources available to them in processes resulting in high added value. The developing countries, many with resources currently surplus to their needs, have come to view rapid industrialization and the transfer of advanced technology as the key to their future well-being. However, inherent in these approaches are fundamental problems that relate to the management of mankind's use of its environment, as well as to the long-term benefits that accrue to these countries, benefits that will be of little value unless they make real inroads into the gap that separates the world's rich from its poor.

The labor intensity of technology remains a fundamental problem for many developing countries. Expanding populations, often underemployed, mean that their labor forces are among their most important resources, but the technologies transferred from industrial countries have been developed increasingly to minimize labor intensity.

The dependence on the extraction and export of bulk resources tends further to reduce the value-added component of their industrial activity. The energy intensity of new agricultural technologies, which are essential for food production, when coupled with increased rural populations, has contributed to the flow of work-seekers to urban centers. This has severely strained the urban infrastructures and led to demands for even more industrialization. It has also made apparent the need for the development of better rural infrastructures involving schools, social services, and education—a crucial component in the drive to prevent the wealth gap from widening even more.

A great deal has been done to improve the health of the populations of developing countries, and some endemic diseases have been almost wiped out. Agricultural research and water resource developments continue to increase their self-sufficiency for food, and these factors combine to raise national aspirations, leading inexorably to an increasing demand for a more equitable share of the world's energy and material resources. But even if the per capita consumption of resources was to fall in the industrialized countries, and if the rest of the world is successful in meeting the needs and only some of the desires of its population, total consumption will continue to rise. On the other hand, is it feasible to expect the populations of the industrial countries to restrain their demand, beyond an extent that can be achieved by personal choice guided by considerations of public policy, when they perceive their economic activity as playing a major role in sustaining the industrial and economic development of the rest of the world? Nevertheless, some shifts towards more reasonable consumption patterns are already discernible as the impact of rising prices, taxation, royalties, and increasing competition for available resources work their way through national economies and people become more conservation conscious.

But the questions of resources and development are more complex than one of haves and have-nots, or demands and numbers; what really matters is whether we understand our problems correctly, or even whether we are capable of understanding them in a rapidly changing world. If we do not understand these complex systems, the consequence becomes an inability to cope with them, and we tend to foreclose our options for the future in trying to deal with symptoms, rather than the illnesses. Unfortunately, we still do not have enough understanding to predict ways in which complex systems behave, but a great deal of research is currently under way into the ways in which apparently different problem areas interact with each other.

A fairly simple example of this is to be found in the construction of dams and impoundments in areas infested with sector-borne diseases. Fast flowing rivers provide the habitat for the blackfly *Simulium*, which is responsible for the spread of onchocerciasis, or river blindness. Damming the river destroys the habitat, but the still water is ideal for the malarial mosquito; building the dam has sometimes caused replacement of one disease by another. [. . .]

The most pressing problems that we have to resolve stem from the relationships between the economic and industrial activities of mankind and the biological and physical environment that sustains all life on this planet. We [first] have to consider the obvious problems of environmental pollution in this context, and the economic aspects of the systems that give rise to it: how low waste and recycling processes can at once reduce emissions and conserve resources; problems of health; nutrition; the impact of agriculture on climate; land use; resource management; human values; and many more. [We must then] attempt to integrate them in such ways as to help make sensible decisions. What is immediately evident is that the scientific and other information available tends to relate to specific concerns, and it is not easy to transform it into the synthesis needed for decisions that affect the totality of the human condition, the use of the biophysical environment and the world's energy and material resources.

ENVIRONMENTAL PERCEPTIONS

Mankind's perception of the environment has changed fundamentally during the evolution of most of our societies, and this change is basic to the attitudes that people have with respect to the interplay of environmental concerns with their personal aspirations and priorities.

Primitive man was very conscious of the limitations of his environment. He did not understand how or why it behaved as it did, but he knew well that he had to live within it, and the early societies that he developed reflect this dependence, being vitally concerned with the conservation and maximum possible use of available resources. He had no way of changing the vegetation of his surroundings even if he had wanted to, and until quite recent times, agriculture seems to have had comparatively little effect on the overall vegetative cover of the earth. Indeed, this vegetative cover, with everything that it implies regarding the habitat for wildlife, genetic diversity, and so on, has apparently been remarkably resilient to the indignities perpetrated on it over the last 3,000 years or so.

But where do we stand today? Modern man has come to believe that he can control his environment, and that he can invent the technology to solve all his problems. By striving to overcome the environment in pursuit of goals dictated by imperatives that he himself has devised, mankind has come dangerously close to forgetting that there are a number of basic needs that are dictated by the very nature of life for it to continue to exist in the forms in which we know it. Food, shelter, health—all are accepted as fundamental to the well-being of our species, but all are dependent on an even more fundamental "absolute"—the health of the life support systems of the biosphere, which we impair at our peril.

We have become aware of the danger that confronts us, perhaps in time to do something about it. But the problems posed by the activities of the human species are not solely concerned with its environment, and we often fail to see this environmental "absolute" in proper perspective. Perhaps because it has always been so faithful in serving our needs, we cannot believe that it can let us down. We turn our attentions to what are essentially problems of the societies that we have created, and fail to realize that the threatened environment is perhaps the most important of these societal problems. This failure is easy to understand—noticeable environmental changes usually become apparent over a longer time than that encompassed by our planning horizons, and we have not been conditioned to look far enough ahead in assessing the implications of our actions.

COMING TO TERMS WITH PROBLEMS

Becoming aware of industrial pollution and inadequate sewage treatment, the industrial countries were pressured by their populations to do something about it. They created institutions at national and international levels to study the situation, and started to regulate the most pressing problems. But at the same time, these very activities created a situation in which "environment" became equated with "pollution control" in the minds of millions of people, leading to a widespread view that all would be well if only we could develop and put in place the technology for clean-up. Until fairly recently, what had not entered into the picture was the collective impact of individual actions on the complex interactions of everything that forms part of the human environment.

The regulatory phase of environmental concern that came to the fore between the mid-1960s and 1970s concentrated on "end of pipe" alleviation—essentially clean-up technologies added on to existing processes to remove unwanted by-products. While such systems are not usually cost-effective, energy-effective, or resource-effective, the capital and development costs of totally new low waste and resource-conserving process technologies were unacceptable, given the time, capital, and technological constraints involved. The approach adopted made sense in a transient situation, but it ought to have given rise to national science and technology policies aimed at developing new industrial processes supportive of environmental policies that were aimed at succeeding generations of environmental concerns. Unfortunately, comparatively little was done to promote such thrusts in most industry sectors, and even the post-1973 pressures for energy conservation generally resulted in patchwork measures, although the realization that energy cost and supply problems are here to stay has recently been a strong incentive to industry to improve its research and development programs. But as we have developed the technology to more or less cope with pollution control, what are the other challenges that confront us?

Improved environmental monitoring systems, and particularly almost revolutionary changes in the techniques of chemical analysis that allow scientists to identify quantitatively substances in concentration of parts per billion and less, have led to the emergence of a host of potential problems, the interrelations of which are only starting to become apparent. At the same time, research in molecular biology is starting to make us aware of the genetic and physiological hazards, not only of many industrial products but also of some of our activities.

Let us look at just a few of these problems and try to imagine the linkages between each that could lead to reinforcement of undesirable effects, or impacts on our social, economic, or physical well-being. Waste disposal is a continuing problem. Suitable sites have to be found for solid wastes, and care taken to prevent contamination of the soil and groundwater by hazardous wastes from industrial processes. At the same time, prime agricultural land must be protected from the encroachment of urban areas, caused by industrial growth and population expansion. Continuing use of fossil fuels, both industrially and domestically, is causing a steady increase in the carbon dioxide content of the atmosphere, which, together with dusts from deserts, volcanoes, and industrial activities, threaten long-term climatic changes. Acid rains, resulting from long-range transportation of sulfur dioxide and nitrogen oxides, having their origins in fuel burning, industry, and agriculture, pose threats to life in lakes and streams and to crops; chlorofluorocarbons, widely used as refrigerants and spray propellants, react with ozone in the stratosphere, interfering with a complex series of chemical reactions that effectively shield the earth from harmful radiation and increase the risk of some forms of cancer. The expansion of agriculture, coupled with fuel shortages, has led to denuding forests and other changes in vegetative cover that involve destruction of habitat, might have climatic consequences, and also interfere to some extent with the oxygen balance of the atmosphere. Care must be taken with the introduction of fast-growing new strains of "miracle" grains not to interfere with genetic diversity, or to make agriculture more dependent on energy-intensive fertilizers and pesticides. Not to mention increasing desertification, and problems of the oceans and coastal zones. . . .

In trying to come to terms with these seeming clashes between our immediate requirements to satisfy the needs of an expanding global population, and our long-term interest in conserving our resources and environment for those who come after, we try to picture ourselves as stewards of the planet. But as stewards we are confronted with the aspirations of mankind for better life. The demands that these make upon the planet's resources, to which the biophysical environment is central, result in integrated sets of personal decisions on lifestyle. These are essentially based on economic, social, and institutional considerations, and in which environmental concerns as such fail to play a significant part. Are not the stewards rationalizing their behavior by a belief that everything will turn out for the best in the long run? If so this must surely be a far less honest philosophy than Madame de Pompadour's "après nous le déluge."

True, during national emergencies, people have responded to appeals to sort waste materials for recycling, only to revert to their former habits when the emergency was passed. Does it take a continuing emergency to convince people of the need to shift to a conservation ethic? Probably, but do we not have just such a situation?

ETHICS AND DEVELOPMENT

A great deal of political attention has been attached to the economic gap between the wealthier and the poorer countries, but in spite of the efforts to close it, the gap seems to be growing even wider. This is not to say that great strides have not been made—there is no doubt that many millions of people are significantly better off than before—but the disparities between the rates of change in the two groups are largely caused by the structural contrast between a low labor intensive, high energy and capital intensive, high value-added trend on the one hand, and a high energy, resource intensive, low value-added and insufficiently labor intensive trend on the other. Added to this is the difficulty in transferring sophisticated technologies that are often unsuited to the prevailing technical, managerial, social, and cultural infrastructures, because they are built around different conceptions of values from those held by the developers of the technologies.

Countries that show these trends run the risk of becoming locked into a type of exploitation resulting in ever greater dependency on external demands for bulk resources. The logical extension of this approach is the "branch plant economy," the problems of which are by no means restricted to the developing countries. In its ultimate form, no research and development is done locally to adapt technologies and products to national needs, and innovation outside the corporate headquarters is discouraged by restricting the export of products of high added value to the parent company. This approach is sometimes called "corporate colonialism," and it perhaps explains why the multinational corporation is so deeply resented, in spite of being one of the most effective instruments for technology transfer. Furthermore, the development of the resource industries mainly for export purposes imposes a greater burden of environmental stress than would otherwise be the case, and this is compounded by the cost of fuel and its implications for domestic and agricultural purposes.

The disadvantaged majority of the world's people, aware of the disparities between their lifestyles and those of the industrial nations, aver that they are quite prepared to accept some of the problems of environmental stress as part of the cost of the benefits of industrialization. Interestingly, this is much the same attitude of workers in "dangerous" industries in the wealthier countries, who are prepared to shoulder a greater risk in return for higher pay or, in the case of financially threatened industries, continued employment. But the acceptance of risk is only impersonal until one becomes personally affected.

Yet, implicit in the concept of an environmental "absolute"—that fundamental need to maintain the health of the life support systems of the biosphere—is the right to an environment that will sustain the reasonable aspirations of the people of the earth. To express this in human terms requires the acceptance by the entire population of this planet of an ethic of conservation with respect to resources: pollution control alone will not suffice. What needs to be done is to internalize concern for the environment in all decision making—from the highest level of government through the corporate and industrial structure down to the individual citizen's choices and actions. Surely the ultimate objective must be to make environmental concern as much a part of the decision process as consideration of economic or social factors.

This is not meant to imply that a conserver society is of necessity a nongrowth situation, or that appropriate technology is of necessity small scale. Indeed such a situation would be foredoomed to disaster. It is in the nature of mankind to pursue growth, but the growth patterns have to be reoriented away from resource and energy intensive industries and pursuits. Indeed, the industrialized countries have already started to do this by moving towards an information society. Some believe that the place at which these changes are occurring is straining at the limits of acceptable incrementalism—the extent to which people are conditioned to accept changes in their lifestyles and environments. This leads to the question whether it will be possible for the populations of the developing countries to industrialize themselves while at the same time orienting themselves towards the future and avoiding the dislocations that otherwise might ensue.

PARADIGMS AND EDUCATION

To do this will require building a new set of paradigms on traditional social and cultural norms and outlooks. Fortunately the base is sound; indigenous cultures that are essentially conserver societies have tended to favor the development of traditional technological bases that are well understood and are ready for sophistication. Interesting work has already been done in this regard, particularly with respect to traditional medicines and drugs. Some countries have undertaken surveys of traditional technologies with a view to incorporating well-understood concepts, that do not require expensive foreign expertise, into national development plans.

Central to ensuring that development and environmental conservation progress in harmony must be the establishment of national knowledge and understanding policies so that the right kind of science and technology can be developed. This, in turn, demands education policies that train people for the types of employment that are likely to be available in the societies in which they will live, and not those that are obsolescent. If the key to dealing with social and environmental problems does lie in education, it is not only children that have to be involved; perhaps the greater challenge is to ensure that adults are exposed to some form of continuing education. It is only in this way that people can become more aware of the significance of their individual actions, such as purchases, waste disposal habits, and consumption patterns, to the general collectivity, and accept the changes that are necessary as being in their own interests.

But there is a fundamental gap in our understanding of our environment that is imposed, in part, by urbanization. The increasing trend towards living in ever larger urban centers means that increasing numbers of people are being brought up without any real understanding of the natural environment and have less and less contact with it. This situation brings to mind the story of the psychologist who, developing an intelligence test for young children, asked where the milk came from. The rural child immediately said "From cows," but the ghetto-bred one equally correctly responded "From the supermarket." Predictable perhaps, even funny, but nevertheless a sobering and not particularly pleasant portent for the future. If people indeed become remote from the environment, how can they ever focus on the long-term need to maintain and support the life-support systems of the biological and physical environment in an understanding way?

Fortunately the ethic of conservation is deeply ingrained in many countries where waste is abhorrent and recycling is traditional. Indeed, the true conserver societies are probably to be found among the developing countries, and in the preservation of this outlook lies their possible shortcut to environmentally harmonious development. The strategy should not only be to preserve the conservation concept domestically, but to develop and export high value-added products and know-how that are based on the sophistication of indigenous technologies in ways consistent with this approach.

10

The Poor Speak Out

Julius K. Nyerere

My country, Tanzania, has the doubtful distinction of being included among the United Nations list of the 25 poorest countries of the world. Perhaps it is not surprising, therefore, that I am one of those people who complain bitterly about the present world economic system and loudly demand that it should be changed.

The complaint of the poor nations against the present system is not only that we are poor both in absolute terms and in comparison with the rich nations. It is also that within the existing structure of economic interaction we must remain poor, and get relatively poorer, whatever we do.

The present international economic and legal structure has developed gradually out of the interaction between the different nations of Europe and then the United States and the British dominions.

In this process the countries which are now known as the Third World were not involved. They were either colonies of one or the other major powers, or were so weak or so far away from the mainstream of economic intercourse that they could be—and were—ignored.

The dominant philosophy of international exchange which we met at independence—and which still prevails—is that of a "free market." Unfortunately the theory bears little relation to fact. The price of manufactured goods is fixed by the producers. Conversely, the price of primary products is fixed by the purchasers.

The primary producing countries which need to import manufactured goods are thus price-takers, not price-makers, both as seller and as buyer. We sell cheap and we buy dear, whether we like it or not. This is the position of most Third World countries—with the recent exception

Reprint of "The Poor Speak Out" by Julius K. Nyerere in *Ocean World* (Vol. 1, No. 1, January 1978). Reprinted by permission of *Ocean World* magazine. Pp. 13–14.

of the oil producers, who do now fix their own prices for the oil they sell. It is perhaps not surprising, therefore, that the terms of trade between the developing and developed countries have moved so steadily and consistently against the former; taking 1963 as a base the World Bank gives the Commodity Terms of Trade index as 87 for 1972—it was 122 in 1953!

To break out of this foreign exchange trap and at the same time to benefit from the multiplier effect of expanded economic activity, the poor countries endeavor to build up their industrial sector—to become price-makers, even in a small way. Naturally we start with the processing of our own primary products. But when we establish factories at enormous expense, we discover that processed commodities, and simple manufactured goods, are not so easy to export as raw products. They meet tariff barriers, quota regulations, or other devices intended to keep them out of the markets of the rich. The "free market" becomes less free!

Further, the poor nations have to ship both their imports and their exports in ships owned and managed in the developed countries. The freight rates are mostly fixed by a shipper's cartel—OPEC did not invent the idea of combining to fix the price of a vital commodity! This cartel has an apparently ineradicable bias against carrying processed goods away from East Africa: for a ton, it costs $41 to ship raw sisal and $73 to ship twine from and to the same port, with similar differentials between cotton lint and textiles, hides and leather, and so on.

There is no organized international mechanism designed to correct—or even ameliorate—the workings of the free market. On the contrary, such institutions and practices as do exist give further impetus to the growth of inequalities between nations—and to the misuse of the world's resources for high living by a few rather than their use for the basic needs of the masses. Let me give just a few examples.

The international financial system is regulated by the International Monetary Fund and the World Bank, helped or hindered by unilateral actions of major powers like the United States, the EEC nations, Japan, and a few other developed nations. Given that voting power in the governing bodies of the IMF and the World Bank is determined by the proportion of the capital contributed by different nations, the results are perhaps inevitable. The richer you are, and the more you trade in the world, the greater the support you can get in times of crises, and the greater will be your allocation of international credit when Special Drawing Rights are created.

Professor Triffin has estimated that the Third World, containing over 70 percent of the world's population, received less than 4 percent of the $126 billion of international liquidity created during the last two decades.

Yet the low international purchasing power of the poor is a factor in keeping poor countries locked in their poverty. Instead of facilitating growth in the world by enabling the poor to buy more—mostly capital goods from the rich—the created international credit has been used to promote trade between the rich themselves.

It is very difficult for Third World countries to obtain by more orthodox means the foreign exchange we need for development. International aid is certainly not the answer. The whole idea of aid is wrong because it is both ineffective in dealing with the problem of poverty and humiliating to the receiver. Within nations we no longer think it proper to deal with the problem of poverty through the personal charity of the rich. Yet voluntary charity by the rich nations is what is being advocated, as the method for dealing with the poverty of nations! The demand for a new International Economic Order is a way of saying that the poor nations must be enabled to develop themselves according to their own interests, and to benefit from the efforts which they make. The poor should not find themselves trying to run up the down-escalator while the rich sail upwards on their up-escalator, as now.

Very many economic experts and expert commissions have analyzed the international situation I am talking about here, and there is widespread intellectual agreement in principle—as well as agreement among the poor—about what needs doing.

First, and in some ways the most fundamental, is that the poor nations should have a greater voice in the world's economic decision making. Changes in the representation on major international economic institutions are not wanted for prestige purposes! The establishment of a link between development and the creation and distribution of international credit, and other actions to counteract the economic power of the wealthy, could be expected to follow. This demand for change should be considered in international councils as of right, and not simply out of charity or compassion.

It must be frankly admitted that we are seeking deliberate transfer of resources from the rich countries to the poor on reasonable terms. But this need not be the only method of fighting world poverty. The Conference on the Law of the Sea provides an opportunity for the world to direct the use of *new* wealth towards meeting the basic needs of the poor. For we are talking about who should own and benefit from untapped world resources which exist outside anyone's national jurisdiction. If we are really serious about the war on world poverty, therefore, the seabed and its resources will be used to benefit the 2 billion people in the world who are living in conditions of great poverty. The continued failure to reach agreement on this simple principle is not very encouraging.

On international trade there is need for measures to stabilize prices of primary commodities, in the short term by buffer stockpiles and in the longer term by assisting the poor to make long-term adjustments to changes in demand or supply.

It is important, however, that these measures should be linked with some advance along the road to the indexation of primary commodity prices in relation to the prices of manufactured goods. I do not believe that this admittedly difficult technical exercise is beyond the wit of man.

It is also necessary for the community of nations to agree on deliberate actions to hasten industrialization in the developing nations. The objective, that the share of Third World countries should be raised from its present 7 percent to 25 percent of world industrial production, will not happen through what are called the natural forces of the market!

Political freedom, social equality and respect, freedom of worship, freedom to live in peace and harmony with your fellows—all these things are very important to man. But the most basic human right of all is the right to life itself, and a life which is not made miserable by hunger, ignorance, or preventable disease.

For life is a whole: economic growth and economic exchange have a purpose. That purpose ought to be the service of man—all men—with priority for the basic needs of food, shelter, health, and education. The present economic order governing international production, development, and exchange does not in practice ensure progress towards meeting those basic needs for all people, all over the world. The plea of the poor is a New International Economic Order "which embraces for its objective the happiness of mankind."

11

International Equity and Its Dilemmas

Oscar Schachter

LEGITIMATE EXPECTATIONS AND HISTORIC ENTITLEMENT

Although in international bodies equity has been increasingly identified with meeting the needs of the disadvantaged, other notions of fairness and justice are also evidenced in regard to the distribution of resources. The most significant of these has an affinity to the idea of proportionate equality as used by Aristotle: that equality should be proportionate to what is due or deserved. Initially this idea appears to be little more than a tautology—"to each his due"—but it leads us to consider the basis of entitlement and the legitimate expectations which flow from it. In national societies such expectations usually derive from social norms and institutions, and this would seem to be true on the international level also. Principles of legitimacy and control, norms governing trade and exchange, and an extensive array of accepted practice relating to distribution all create the expectations that enable participants to recognize what is due and deserved.

You will note that these expectations are not usually based on any general valuational principle (such as need, or merit, or efficiency), nor are they dependent on a desired pattern of results. They are generated by the processes of acquisition and transfer, whether the results are considered good or bad. We need only remind ourselves that the great bulk of the world's resources has been divided among numerous sovereignties by a historic process, and that our conception of entitlement to those resources is largely determined by the legitimacy accorded that process.

When governments insist on their sovereign authority over their own natural resources and their rights to use and dispose of these resources freely (to determine who may exploit and purchase and at what price and conditions), they are basing their position on the legitimacy of their acquisition and on what they deem to be their just due. We can observe this in the disputes of governments with foreign enterprises, in their claims to adjacent ocean space, in their control over exports and access to their markets, and in various other manifestations of territorial jurisdiction. Their ideas of what is just and fair in their international relations are profoundly influenced by their conception of their sovereign rights. Nor is this influence limited to territorial sovereignty. Just entitlement may also include access to and use of natural resources outside of national jurisdiction, as, for example, historic fishery rights or customary transit rights over land or waters. Efforts to reduce or eliminate such acquired rights run counter to concepts of fairness and justice. The same holds true for entitlements arising from international agreements and the norms governing consensual transactions. These not only create expectations as to future behavior; they also condition attitudes about the equities involved. Holmes's "bad man" theory of contract does not quite fit international dealings; when states enter into treaties they are not simply buying an option to perform or pay damages. The commitment is itself a determinant of what is due and therefore of what is equitable, irrespective of the merits of the transaction. Of course there are exceptions, but we need not have a categorical rule to substantiate our conclusion about the general bearing of entitlement on ideas of equity.

In the light of these observations it may seem strange that in current discussions equity and distributive justice are identified almost entirely with the demands of the poor and disadvantaged for a larger share of resources, and that they are rarely used to refer to the kind of entitlements I have described. Perhaps one reason for this situation is that economists tend to employ the term equity (or distributive justice) as virtually a code word for wider income distribution and transfer payments to the poor. But this special meaning overlooks the significance of entitlements in actual disputes between nations in which strong feelings of injustice have been generated. Consider, for example, the dispute between Iceland and the United Kingdom over Iceland's claim to an extended, exclusive fishing zone, which came before the International Court of Justice in 1974; or the more general class of disputes between capital-exporting states and host countries over nationalization and contractual rights pertaining to foreign investment in natural resources; or the claims of lower riparians to a share of clean river water (as in the dispute between Mexico and the United States over the salination of the Colorado River). In these resource disputes, the equities asserted have been based on each side's conception of what was due to it and that, in turn, rested on historic and consensual processes and norms derived from them. Clearly, the idea of equity has a much wider meaning for governments than it does for economists and others who use it to refer to increasing the share of those less well-off. Nor should this be surprising. After all, the world's resources are distributed in accordance with entitlements based on territorial rights, custom, and consensual transactions, and it is only natural that ideas of equity should be significantly determined by that reality.

But how, it may be asked, can this idea be reconciled with the concept of equity as meeting the needs of the poor and disadvantaged? One way, evidenced in international debate, is to link demands based on needs to entitlements derived from accepted principles. For example, the claims of landlocked states and new states for access to and sharing of ocean resources have been advanced not so much on the basis of needs as on the basis that such access is due these states under the principle of the common heritage (the *res communis*) of the oceans. Similarly, in river disputes lower riparian countries assert not only their need for adequate supplies of water but also a customary or treaty right and on the latter basis may demand changes in the pattern of use and appropriation by the upper riparians. Even the broad and generalized demands of poor countries for preferences and grants are often advanced as entitlements owed to them because of past exploitation, oligopolistic restraints, or other allegedly illegitimate practices of the industrialized societies. Such demands illustrate a general tendency to utilize the two conceptions of equity in harness as mutually supportive rather than antagonistic principles of valuation. This is not merely a matter of "dialectics" or rhetoric. It reflects a political judgment that as an international criterion the maxim "to each according to his need" is too impractical and far-reaching in its implications to win acceptance as a general principle; but that when this maxim is conjoined with and limited by a principle of legitimacy, it becomes more acceptable because less threatening to the international order. In short, the Aristotelian principle of distributive justice may be seen as implicit in the normative assumptions of governments and as providing a counterpoint to competing egalitarian conceptions.

The interplay and linkage of the competing conceptions of equity are evidenced in two international principles which have received wide support in recent years. One is the principle of permanent sovereignty over natural resources. The other is the principle of rectification of past injustices. Later we shall have occasion to learn how both of these ideas have played roles in specific controversies over the distribution of resources. At this point, I should like only to indicate briefly how they are related to the two criteria of equity we have been discussing.

"Permanent sovereignty over natural resources" is linked to what I have called historic entitlement. Its normative premise is that territorial jurisdiction resulting from a historic process of acquisition is the paramount basis for rights over natural resources and that, in consequence, it is just and equitable to recognize the ascendancy of that principle in international decisions pertaining to resources. Each sovereignty has its "proportionate equality," however unequal its actual share may be. At the same time, the concept of permanent sovereignty is perceived by the less developed countries as a defense against alleged exploitation by the more advanced countries and their enterprises. They use it primarily to obtain a greater share for themselves, and it is therefore asserted to justify nationalization and other takeover measures directed against foreign enterprises, to limit profits and their repatriation, to remove foreign restraints on the transfer of technology, to override contractual arrangements on the grounds of public interest and need, and so on. Significantly, "permanent sovereignty" is rarely, if ever, advanced as an entitlement of the affluent countries in their relations with the less developed countries. Thus, decisions by the richer countries to restrict exports or to impose restraints on access to their markets are not justified by international bodies as proper exercise of "sovereignty over resources" but are regarded often as undesirable and unfair actions against the poorer countries. From one perspective this difference in attitude can be criticized as a double standard of sovereign rights, yet from another it may be seen as an indication of a single standard, namely, the principle of meeting the needs of the disadvantaged. We thus find in the concept of permanent sovereignty over resources a principle which is, so to speak, conservative in its stress on sovereign rights (based on historic acquisition) yet utilized by poor countries as a weapon of change.

In a somewhat analogous way, the idea of rectification of past wrongs has been advanced primarily as a right of disadvantaged countries with, again, the implication of a double standard in its application to developed and developing states. There is, of course, nothing new in the demand of governments and peoples for correction of historic injustices. In a sense that demand is the other side of the coin of historic entitlement. If entitlements are based on the legitimacy of the process of acquisition, they should also be open to attack on grounds of their illegitimacy and injustice; acts of fraud or the illegal use of force would vitiate an entitlement for reasons of equity, if not in law. We find this general notion of rectification reflected also in claims of unjust enrichment, advanced, for example, by governments which claim compensation for inordinate profits said to have been made by foreign concessions under conditions of political or economic domination. Even though such claims have received little support in judicial cases, they have been expressed in political bodies and in declarations of principle adopted in organs of the United Nations. For example, in 1974 the General Assembly declared that states and peoples which have been under "foreign occupation, alien and colonial domination" have the right to restitution and full compensation "for the exploitation and depletion of, and damages to, the natural and all other resources." One cannot but be struck by the breadth of this asserted principle when one thinks of the numerous countries in the developed areas of the world as well as in the Third World which have suffered even in the recent past from alien domination and foreign occupation. Almost certainly the proponents of the UN declaration had the poor countries primarily in mind as its beneficiaries, but the declaration's sweeping language and the grievances felt in many developed countries about foreign domination may presage its political use outside of the Third World. But even if the declaration is limited to the claims of developing countries, its scope is so wide and its meaning so uncertain as to cast doubt on the feasibility of its practical implementation.

These intrinsic difficulties do not mean that the notion of rectification will be ignored. It is too firmly grounded in widely held conceptions of justice to disappear from political and juridical claims. More specifically, it is a consequence of accepting entitlements based on the process of acquisition rather than on end results, for, as we noted, if there are historic rights, there will inevitably be historic wrongs. One could say that the principle of rectification is the natural and radical offspring of the conservative concept of acquired rights. Just how far this principle will be carried in international affairs and in what specific forms remain to be seen, but it seems likely that it will be utilized as still another conceptual weapon by dissatisfied governments seeking to change existing patterns of distribution.

My observations on the role of entitlements and need have, I hope, clarified my earlier reference to the dialectical interplay of competing notions of equity. I have sought to show how these two opposing criteria of distributive justice have been applied as mutually supportive grounds for new principles of equity asserted in international bodies and indeed how difficult it would be, in a political sense, to apply either one without the other. This analysis, as I have said, is essentially empirical; it is not based on moral theory or philosophical premises but rather on the actual positions taken by governments in their claims and responses regarding the world's resources. These positions are a product of existing tensions and conflicts. They are not ideal constructions, and they naturally manifest ambivalences and indeterminacies. But, as I have tried to show, they also reveal certain basic normative concepts which influence evaluative behavior and which give some determinate meaning and political force to the ideal of distributive justice. [. . .]

12

Redefining Urban Ecosystems

Richard L. Meier

Cities are destined to become the normal habitat for man. When human populations are numbered in the multiple billions, the metropolis must become home for all but a minor fraction. Only in the highly organized, carefully designed, and globally interconnected metropolis does any hope exist for coping successfully with prospective resource scarcities. Cities must diversify activities, acquire new competencies, preserve knowledge, and accumulate structure in dimensions and directions that are only now becoming evident. In the long run they should be able to provide the stable, natural environment within which the further evolution of living species, including man, will be accelerated.

The prospect is quite contrary to the widely circulated and commonly believed reports that our modern metropolises are about to die. Actually our great cities appear to be undergoing natural changes due to maturation, since after a long period of growth starting from insignificant origins the rates of increase of the first of them to be established appear to be leveling off. Many associations and institutions in such cities are feeling the emotional storms and uncertainties that accompany adolescence. The most highly developed of the great cities of the world—London, New York, Paris, Boston, Toronto, Chicago, Stockholm, and others—must now anticipate a "middle-aged spread," with rates of increase in the range of 0 to 2 percent per year in biomass and physical supports instead of the 3 to 10 percent rates previously experienced. With maturity comes a willingness to engage in the creation of enduring organizations so that growth is transferred to a nonphysical realm. Preservation, renewal, and

Excerpt from "Redefining Urban Ecosystems" in *Planning for an Urban World: The Design of Resource-Conserving Cities* by Richard L. Meier. Copyright 1974 by The MIT Press, Cambridge, Mass. Reprinted by permission of the publisher. Pp. 9–19.

conservation of scarce local resources then become the central issues for such cities, though elsewhere in the world the urgencies are more elemental. Newer metropolises must still learn how to overcome the grave threats to survival that arise from an increasing scarcity of natural resources and the consequent rates of social change.

Critics of cities usually repress facts embarrassing to their theses. They should be encouraged to explore in depth the recent histories of a few representative metropolises and compare their series of formal reports and statistics with others. Selecting any of the commonly used definitions of welfare they like, they should judge the shifts in such welfare generated in these cities over time. Those who have already done so cannot find a single city that is not a significantly better place to live for a majority of the population than it was a generation or so ago. The "bads" that have been recently recognized as potentially debilitating, such as the deterioration of atmospheric quality, traffic congestion, and crowding, are strongly outpointed by improvements in education, communications, most aspects of health, and in spatial mobility. More impressive yet is the performance in meeting emergencies, because an ability to detect threats in advance and to mobilize resources to counter them is evidence for the viability of a community in the environment with which it must interact. Reduced typical reaction times, which can be used as sensitive indicators of improved capability to overcome crises, prevail all over the world.

The great fault in the standard intellectual opinion about cities is that judgments are reached by comparing current urban conditions with concepts of what should be, and not at all with what has existed in the recent past. Such specifications of ideal conditions are not invariant, but as information about best examples is acquired, and the technical possibilities that allow further improvement are explored, they are strengthened over time and made more demanding. It is not unexpected then that the gap that separates the present situation from the utopian ideal continues to grow larger, nor is it unanticipated that shortcomings will excite a litany of pessimistic predictions that cities will become unlivable. The objective data that point to improving conditions are ignored, because they are not relevant to programs for action that, one hopes, will bring about truly substantial amelioration. Past gains, it is commonly believed, have been far from good enough—because felt deficiencies have increased still more.

Having contested current "doomsday" doctrine by indications of the existence of strong contrary evidence, an alternative concept for visualizing future society is required. Simply stated, it is the following: *The fundamental problem for most people presently living and soon to be born is still that of survival, preferably at a state noticeably above bare subsistence*. The fundamental problem is *not* how to achieve affluence for everyone. Moreover, the emergence of levels above subsistence must be achieved with increasing equity. Since resources are limited, how might a secure existence be achieved, which also allows hope for improvement? What are the principles connecting scarce resources with the functioning of cities? It is possible to take them up in order: first the significance of resources for cities, and then the city as ecosystem in a synthetic (designed?) environment.

THE METROPOLIS AS A RESOURCE TRANSFORMER

A living system is characterized by a set of inputs (or resources) and a set of outputs, with multiple, cybernetically stabilized pathways inside the system that effect the transformation. The metropolis therefore converts resources into something else; resources, together with the internal institutional environment, are used to grow *people*. The function of cities for generations to come will be to "create human capital" from inputs of unskilled immigrants and their newborn cohorts. The metropolis must gather in commodities won from the earth's crust and convert them into civilized, whole people able to make their way in an increasingly interdependent world. Neither waste, nor rubble, nor pollution should be allowed to accumulate, nor should instabilities in the internal pathways be permitted to develop to the point where they affect the survival and competence of the next generations.

As yet metropolises have achieved very little coordinated control over their resource supply or their own organization. The national state still jealously retains formal responsibility for constructing modern environments and programming the development of human resources. Thus far national states have done little to increase the efficiency of the consumption process (although they have on occasion instituted effective procedures for equitable rationing), and they tend to intervene in production schemes that draw directly upon natural resources in the hinterlands, insisting upon a more orderly exploitation. Nationalism is losing its hold upon loyalties, however, and, with the spread of television, its control over character development. Multinational organizations are inventing ways of moving knowledge, cash, people, commodities, and organizational forms across national boundaries faster than new controls are being devised. Therefore the future opportunities for great cities are more diverse than at present.

What is a resource? Everyone has a generalized idea of what resources are and the ways in which they may be identified. Each of us puts minerals and forests and waterfalls into this category almost automatically. Any person living near the sea will add fisheries to the list. Those who are in food enterprises recognize the significance of the living soil—microorganisms, worms, moisture, and humus—as a fundamental resource. More recently, highly unusual environments, the kinds that excite wonder in man, have been marked as a scenic resource. The common meaning of the word is based upon these agreements between people with quite different personal experiences.

It is important to examine further the implications of the *idea* of a resource. It starts with some unusual quality found in a locale that makes the area appear different from the typical physical environment. This difference is great enough to assign a functional name (for example, clay banks, oil pools, pine woods, fishing reefs, fruit belts, waterfalls, and natural harbors, to name a few) to the type of locale. Each is a resource, however, only when the information about it can be passed along from one place to another and one generation to the next. Only then can the locale produce something of value to man and become a resource. The knowledge embodied in a technology is, by definition, general enough to be diffusible across cultural boundaries; it can also evolve or develop over time, accumulating small-scale improvements as it is applied. Normally a technology is made up of a sequence of operations or processes that can be spelled out as a series of directions or recipes for what should be done with one or more resources in order to accomplish the conversion to a desired commodity or service.

The knowledge component of resource use has been increasing in quantity and significance over time. It is recorded in images—diagrams, blueprints, laboratory analyses, mathematical equations, sets of specifications, technical terminology, and so on. The resource has real value only if the effort invested in its use is more than compensated for by the returns to people. Most of the so-called natural resources in the world are not worth the expense involved in extracting or making use of them, and are therefore relegated to the submarginal class. They become true resources only when the scarcity of the primary commodities or services produced from such resources has increased, and price rises have occurred, or when a significant improvement in technological efficiency has been established. Of the two, advances in applied science have been more effective recently in creating resources worthy of development than has a rise in prices brought on by the exhaustion of deposits of richer concentration.

Most of the common mistakes in future-oriented public policy can be easily avoided when thinking about resources as grounded in this information-based formulation, rather than upon depletion-obsessed doctrines. According to the teaching of a past generation, we could look forward to a day when resources essential to civilization would be universally depleted; this would be a time when our great-grandchildren would be doomed to a way of life sustained only by the renewable resources of soils, vegetation, and waterpower. Feature stories in magazines and newspapers and university lectures on conservation have dwelt upon the hard times in the future brought about by the accelerated exhaustion and waste of our richest resources. These early projections were inadequate because they did not consider the specific effects of the steady growth of knowledge about technology; nevertheless this mode of thinking has continued up to the present.

The acquisition, storage, and transmission of knowledge are all uniquely human activities. Some individuals have greater aptitude for this work than others, but almost everyone can improve his mastery of such knowledge by the expenditure of time and attention. As natural resources are depleted, the knowledge about substitutes and alternatives that specific people possess or can quickly obtain may be drawn upon to prevent deprivation in the population as a whole. As far as society is concerned, the possessors of knowledge are a resource—the human resource produced by cities—and as valuable and dependable as any options on a new discovery of oil or the mapping of a new fishery.

These recent insights are a revelation; they greatly broaden the development strategy for a modern society. The planning horizon was once limited by the expected depletion time of energy sources, but now it can be extended by building up knowledge of substitutes that are more plentiful, just as nuclear fuels can replace coal and fuel oil by advancing the technology of nuclear reactors. Having dispensed with the misconceptions of the extreme pessimists, however, we should not make the mistake of extreme optimism. Energy and most other basic nonrenewable natural resources will become relatively more scarce and expensive over time; their price is likely to rise as rapidly as that of skilled, organized attention by permanent employees.

THE INTERDEPENDENT CONSTITUENT POPULATIONS

Continuing this analysis of the urban ecosystem, we must consider the *interactions* of populations—the relations of men, machines, animals, and plants with each other and with the supporting environment. Knowledge about environment is acquired by men, but embedded and stored as information and pattern in the other populations. When existing together as a community, the location, appearance, and responses of each of these populations are chosen so that it becomes better adapted to the others. Interdependencies can become very strong as the community matures and approaches the climax stage. These interdependencies are not merely day-to-day relationships but of a kind that can heal wounds and redress insults as long as the injuries are normal for the community and have been sustained several times before. All the principles by which we have come to understand living systems apply, as well as others barely glimpsed as yet.

Human populations are significant forces in a wilderness and controlling agents in the countryside, but in the city they became clearly *dominant*. Note that the plural of population has been used; the biologists' assignment of a single species to *Homo sapiens* is based upon the same criterion that is applied to animals—the capacity to maintain a common gene pool—but the peculiar properties of men allow them to transmit much more information from one generation to the next through nurture of the young and through highly organized social institutions than through gene recombination, so subspeciation is exceedingly important. Cities have always had markedly plural human societies, and the tendency is toward increased pluralism rather than homogenization. When urban locales dominated by a single ethnic, religious, occupational, or avocational group (now often referred to as ghettos, quarters, or districts) are dissolved, several new subcommunities find a place in mosaic structure; in them a significant number of individuals study and discipline themselves voluntarily to a distinct set of traditions that maintain the community against forces of assimilation. Cosmopolitan groups do not demand the total commitment of their members, and a single individual may belong to several different subspecies, dividing his time according to the requirements of the separate roles to be filled. The boundaries of the territories maintained by respective populations are marked in ways knowable only to initiated members of the communities, because they are increasingly overlapping and interpenetrating each other in the multistoried metropolis. An observer of the cityscape sees nothing but a jumble of partially decipherable patterns, but because he is an acknowledged member of some of the groups he will see the phenomenon of dominance in the urban system with a personal interest not available to the field biologist observing a community of plants and animals.

The populations that men most dominate and control in the urban communities are *machines*. They are slave populations, imported mostly from other cities, that come in all sizes, appearances, and many specializations. In the workshops of cities that still operate close to subsistence, the transition from tools to machines is still incomplete, and the supply of the actuating juice of electrical power is not drawn upon universally as yet. The growth and elaboration of these electrical machines require a huge expansion of the segment of the human population specializing in their maintenance. More potent self-propelled species of machines, which range in dimensions from diesel locomotives and jet aircraft to wristwatches and battery radios, consume refined or predigested energy sources instead of electricity, consuming up to 20 percent of all energy in the urban community. [. . .] An even greater proportion of humans addresses itself to their direction and maintenance as a full-time income-producing occupation, and the population of the self-propelled species expands even more rapidly than their masters.

Just as the first wave of machines in the nineteenth century relieved humans of most of the backbreaking labor required for civilized existence, the *automata*, a prolific new breed of machines possessing complex cybernetic capabilities, are now relieving humans, in turn, of mind-deadening routines and similar drudgery. Automata entered the most advanced cities in the 1950s and penetrated the poorest before the end of the 1960s. The basic input for these new machines is *information*, which may come from the physical environment through a sensor type instrument from records of human transactions, or, to an increasing extent, from the action of other machines. The automata of our era rarely locomote because they need minor but very steady sources of electrical power, but they are now going through a process of microminiaturization, reducing size for a given capability by a factor of a hundred, so that the 1980s will bring a huge variety of peripatetic automata. Normally, automata affect situations and conditions at a distance through the networks and switching gear of a telephone system which was originally designed to meet human communication needs. Computing centers, which provide the physical supports for most of the automata, are coming into continuous contact with each other and most of the information-based transactions among metropolises are carried out through them with the aid of microwave beams that reinforce the coaxial cables.

This new population of actors does not seem to have affected the numbers of animals living in cities. The urbanized wild animal species are primarily parasitic upon man, living off the surplus and inadvertent waste from his household. Rats, mice, birds, and insects are the most common, although they stay out of sight most of the time. Almost as numerous are the domesticated species of animals, which have been bred into diverse strains and have extraordinarily little resemblance to the original wild type. Their associations with humans are very close and their presence is especially evident in the less densely populated portions of the metropolitan area, where individually they often serve as human companions. Carefully bred populations reappear as delicacies providing variety in the diet. Populations of the parasitic species are usually kept down to convenient levels through indirect controls over habitat and food supplies, while reproduction in the domesticated species is generally controlled directly by men. The biomass of these tamed species tends to range between 5 percent and 20 percent of the human, depending heavily upon the subcultural values attached to associations with them, since dog lovers, cat owners, equestrians, and bird keepers are usually quite different kinds of people. Some city dwellers are beef eaters, some consume pork, many like chicken, but quite a few are vegetarians. Some modern cities maintain, in addition, large populations of domesticated animals at a distance, on ranches and market farms, from which they import milk, carcasses, and packaged flesh. Other cities are hosts for communities of fishermen who engage in organized predation on marine life.

Very few of the plant species native to the territory occupied by the city can continue to live in an urban community. Even weeds, the wild species springing up untended in the less trafficked interstices, most often belong to the introduced category. In the parts of the city where activity is most incessant, domesticated trees, shrubs, flowers, and grasses predominate. Their function is purely ornamental since the fruits, if any at all, are rarely harvested. Edible plants begin to be numerous out toward the edges of the metropolis; the ornamentals still hold sway in the land facing the roads, but patches and rows of fruit and vegetable monoculture are found very often behind the houses.

A metropolis consumes huge quantities of vegetable materials, many of which are imported from great distances, but almost all of them have been preprocessed before arrival into commodities like flour, sugar, lumber, paper, cloth, and soap, and have been rendered sterile so that they can be safely stockpiled. Once introduced and digested, most of these plant substances also sustain life among the animal species and the microorganisms.

Invisible plants in the soils and water bodies of the urban community are less modified from the natural state. Even the quantity of such life, considered as biomass, is not greatly changed, because the huge volume of imported organic substances needs to be decomposed. Thus ponds, streams, and tidal pools are likely to have more bacteria, and the soils have at least as much litter for them to decompose as elsewhere; the wild species of microorganisms present are very much the same as those before urbanization. Civilization intervenes to the extent of introducing pure cultures for a few purposes—domesticated strains of yeast for breweries, distilleries, and breadmaking, molds for cheesemaking, and varieties of bacteria for commodities like vinegar or yogurt. Close inspection of the city also reveals that special cultures of aerobic and anaerobic microorganisms are maintained in large stirred tanks in sanitary facilities that have been explicitly designed to expedite the decomposition of waste organic matter. The domestication of the various microbiological species has proceeded further in Japanese cities than in Occidental metropolises. These populations, with all their relationships and transformations, are not as simple as suggested by the foregoing generalizations, but actually constitute the most complex ecosystem ever evolved. It must be further emphasized that they form total communities which are not in equilibrium. Many are invading new territory and expanding their dimensions by as much as 10 percent per year. Quite a few observers regard the growth as "cancerous"; Ian McHarg has called it a "brown fungus" attacking earth. In North America the chief populations in the front lines of the invasion seem to be made up of a variety of piloted automotive vehicles, while in tropical Asia and Africa the frontiers of the metropolis are usually extended by human squatters, often accompanied by vehicles and domesticated animals.

Taken together, urban ecology is a fascinating subject. It is a pity that it is not studied as such, but only as a series of limited specializations. The term itself was appropriated by a subspecialty of sociology; bioecological investigators drew upon relatively undisturbed natural distributions to inspire their theories. Though ignored by the systems scientists, maintenance of the urban ecosystem has become a series of interrelated arts that are improved and transmitted from one generation of practitioners to the next. Thus, while we have not been conscious of it, the web of life in cities has become ever more intricate, and the overall system can more consistently restore conditions to the viable range than in earlier times. Neglect of this newly synthesized system cannot continue for long, however, because a huge pressure of human population is building up in the countryside, and it requires life supports regardless of where individual persons decide to live. The crucial life supports can be put together only with the semimanufactures and machines produced within an urban framework. [. . .]

13

Resources in Antarctica: Potential for Conflict

Barbara Mitchell

It was no accident that resource management was omitted from the 1959 Antarctic Treaty. The conflicts that the issue arouses would have prevented the conclusion of that agreement. Under today's changed circumstances, the controversy is greater still and this time the issue cannot be shelved.

RESOURCES AT STAKE

Interest in the economic potential of Antarctica is not new: whales and seals have been hunted in the area, and over the years there has been intermittent speculation about the minerals that might be found under the ice cap. Of late, however, this interest has acquired a new and more urgent dimension.

It is the marine resources of the area, those found in the shelf and waters surrounding the continent, that are attracting immediate attention. In the first place, there are signs that the western continental shelf may contain oil and gas. The work of Eltanin and Glomar Challenger has indicated the presence of sediments, mostly of Tertiary age, in places as thick as 2000 meters. The finding of traces of ethane and methane in three of the four holes drilled in 1972–73 by Glomar Challenger has lent further support to this theory.

Inevitably, there has been speculation as to the amounts involved. In 1973, on the basis of the geological histories of the surrounding conti-

Reprint of "Resources in Antarctica: Potential for Conflict" by Barbara Mitchell in *Marine Policy* (Vol. 1, No. 2, April 1977). Reprinted by permission of *Marine Policy* (published in Surrey, England). Pp. 91–100.

nents and exploration for oil and gas elsewhere, the U.S. Geological Survey produced an estimate of the *discoverable* petroleum and natural gas resources of the continental margin of western Antarctica. The total for the Bellinghausen, Ross, and Weddell Sea was put at 45 billion barrels of oil and 115 trillion cubic feet of natural gas. There has been serious questioning of the basis on which these figures were calculated, but 1976 U.S. estimates, though less precise, are no more conservative. They suggest that the shelf could contain tens of billions of barrels of *recoverable* oil. (One-third of discoverable oil is held to be recoverable.)

Offshore Antarctic exploitation will have to contend with the unique and extremely hazardous combination of icebergs and pack ice, but the technology required may not be very different from that being developed elsewhere. There is an increasing worldwide need for deep-water technology and subsurface completion systems. Several governments have already been approached by companies with preliminary enquiries about the possibilities of offshore exploration in Antarctica. Even if Antarctic oil is never exploited, more exploration will raise many of the same problems. Furthermore, in other areas, oil companies have sought exclusive rights well before they wished to begin exploration.

The waters of the Southern Ocean contain a number of potentially important and currently underexploited food resources such as krill, squid, and fish. The nutritional value, shoaling characteristics, and abundance of krill single it out as a potentially valuable resource. It has a high protein content and is comparatively easy to harvest, although subsequently difficult to handle. The estimates of standing stocks and potential yield of krill to man vary greatly, but it is generally agreed that these are high in comparison to the stocks and yield of conventional fisheries. Recent Soviet papers quoted in a 1975 FAO report on krill consider the potential yield of stocks to be at least 100 million tons per year. The second report of the U.K. Fisheries Research and Development Board suggests that an annual fishery of 50 million tons could be sustained. Compared to a total world marine catch of 59.9 million tons in 1974 these figures are striking.[1]

Growing world food requirements and the encroachment of coastal-state jurisdiction on traditional fishing grounds will increase the pressure on governments, particularly those with distant-water fleets, to exploit krill. The Soviets have been active in this field for about ten years: both they and the Japanese are now marketing krill-based products. Experimental work was carried out by the West Germans, Chileans, and Poles in 1975–76, and the Norwegians and Taiwanese have plans for a similar expedition in 1977.

Finally, reference should be made to a recent revival of the idea of harvesting icebergs. In October 1976, Saudi Arabia announced that it had commissioned a study by a French engineering concern on the feasibility of towing icebergs over a distance of 5,000 miles through the Indian Ocean and Red Sea. The Cicero Company hopes that this study will lead to a contract to begin the actual work very soon.

ROOTS OF DISSENSION

Between 1908 and 1942, claims to parts of Antarctica were made by Argentina, Chile, Norway, the United Kingdom, Australia, France, and New Zealand. Three of these overlap, although 15 percent of the area has never been claimed. None of these claims has ever received wide recognition and, indeed, they are all vigorously contested by several countries with long-standing interests in the area; in 1924 the United States asserted that it neither recognized nor claimed sovereignty in Antarctica, an example which was later followed by the Soviet Union. Japan, South Africa, and Belgium do not possess and have not formally recognized any claims. In 1959 all 12 of these countries signed the Antarctic Treaty, which skilfully avoids the question of ownership and simply sets the area aside as a peaceful scientific preserve. Although seven new members have joined the treaty since 1959, only the original 12 have full consultative rights.[2] These countries are now discussing resource management in two separate but connected forums: the Antarctic Treaty Consultative arrangements and the Scientific Committee on Antarctic Research (SCAR).

The prospect of resource exploitation presents a challenge to the existing framework. First and foremost, it may detract from the four objectives of the present arrangements: the prohibition of military conflict, the promotion of scientific research, the encouragement of worldwide cooperation, and the protection of the Antarctic environment. These objectives are important and should be considered in more detail.

The treaty begins with a recognition that "it is in the interest of all mankind that Antarctica shall continue to be used exclusively for peaceful purposes and shall not become the scene or object of international discord." Article 1 prohibits inter alia "any measure of the military nature such as the establishment of military bases and fortifications, the carrying out of military manoeuvres, as well as the testing of any type of weapons." In 1959 there was apprehension that Antarctica might be used for the launching of ICBMs and the presence of the Soviets on the continent was viewed with alarm by the surrounding countries. Although one should not overestimate the potential military role of Antarctica today, as long as the continent has any conceivable strategic value there are strong arguments for it to remain demilitarized. An important underpinning of this objective is the right of inspection enshrined in the treaty. All installations and equipment as well as ships and planes discharging or embarking cargoes or personnel are open to inspection by any of the consultative parties.

A second rationale for the treaty was the "substantial contributions to scientific knowledge resulting from international cooperation in scientific investigation in Antarctica." Indeed, the treaty was in large part an offshoot of the work of the International Geophysical Year (IGY) in which Antarctica was selected as a special focus. Testifying before the U.S. Senate Foreign Relations Committee conducting hearings on the Antarctica Treaty in 1960, the geologist Laurence Gould was convinced that "The most important export of Antarctica is going to be scientific data. And that is terribly important indeed. There is no single field of geophysics which does not demand for its completion data which can come only from Antarctica." Although some would dispute this as being the overriding value of Antarctica today, and others feel that the science policy involved can never be easily isolated from economics and politics, Antarctica still has an important role to play in scientific research.

The real significance of the present regime may be far less tangible. A product of the twin objectives of demilitarization and scientific research, it was hinted at by the signatories when they declared their conviction that "a treaty ensuring the use of Antarctica for peaceful purposes only and the continuance of international harmony in Antarctica will further the purposes and principles embodied in the Charter of the United Nations." It is, of course, impossible to assess the part played by the present Antarctic framework in alleviating world tensions. This would have been greatest in 1959 at the height of the cold war when any rapprochement between the Soviets and the United States was an achievement. Although one can exaggerate its value as a precedent or model for agreements in such areas as outer space and the seabed, Antarctic cooperation does seem to have had significant spin-off effects on joint scientific efforts in the Arctic and elsewhere.

Environmental protection has also been a central feature of the biennial Antarctic Treaty Consultative meetings since 1959. A number of recommendations have been passed dealing with specific aspects of the environment.[3]

Reassessment of Objectives

Scientific research, demilitarization, peaceful coexistence, and environmental protection are complementary goals. Exploitation, particularly of minerals, will not fit easily into this framework. One can hardly imagine companies welcoming inspection; the introduction of commercial interests into the area will almost certainly lead to restrictions on the freedom of movement and information, one of the mainstays of the existing arrangements. Exploitation and all it entails could also seriously impair Antarctica's role as a relatively undisturbed scientific laboratory. In general, the environmental implications of resource exploitation may be very serious indeed: it would be rash to tamper lightly with an ecosystem as delicately balanced and as important to the rest of the world as that of the Antarctic. There will have to be a reassessment of goals in Antarctica.

There is, however, little agreement as to who should be making this reassessment. Neither claimants nor nonclaimants abandoned their original stands on sovereignty when signing the treaty. Furthermore, the treaty itself adds a new layer of disputed jurisdiction, by effectively limiting the number of consultative parties. Consultative membership is only open to an acceding state "during such time as . . . (it) . . . demonstrates its interest in Antarctica by conducting substantial scientific research activity there, such as the establishment of a scientific station or the dispatch of a scientific expedition." Isolated elements of the international community have never been very happy about this exclusion; the resource question threatens to make their discontent an international issue.

In short, the conflicts raised by the discovery of resources revolve around two main issues: first, how the area should be used and second, who should decide who is to use it. It should be noted that there is a limit to the extent to which these questions can be separated.[4]

EXPLOITATION OR MORATORIUM?

As a decision on the future use of Antarctica is dependent on national priorities in the area, it is hardly surprising that the 12 have different views on the matter. As yet, this debate is confined to their ranks, although one might speculate, extrapolating from the Law of the Sea negotiations, that, should the developing countries become involved, they would favor strict regulation of any exploitation.

Of the 12, the United States is markedly the most interested in mineral exploitation. The United States is the key player in Antarctic negotiations and in the best position to develop the technology to recover the oil and gas. To a certain extent the situation within the U.S. Government bureaucracy reflects in microcosm the conflicts among the 12 over the future of the area.

Although the United States has consistently maintained that there is nothing in the treaty forbidding exploitation, there have been some significant fluctuations in its policy in the past few years. A National Security Council Decision Memorandum (NSDM) of 1973 suggested that no country, including the United States, should exploit Antarctica's minerals unilaterally. It further recommended that the United States discourage any exploitation and exploitation-linked exploration in the near future, until treaty nations had developed an approach. The State Department, fearful that exploitation would end an era of peaceful cooperation, was reported to be advocating a moratorium. However, the opposition of the resource-oriented agencies, Interior, Treasury, and the Federal Energy Administration, which wanted the United States to retain the option of unilateral exploitation, did much to neutralize the effect of the NSDM. Statements made by the U.S. delegation in the June 1975 Antarctic Treaty meeting indicate that the resource-oriented agencies have had considerable impact.[5] The United States held out the very real threat of unilateral action: "In the absence of a shared understanding, those countries who do not recognise claims to sovereignty would surely have to assert the right to commence mineral resource activities at their will, subject only to applicable provisions of the Antarctic Treaty."

As the energy crisis intensifies the pressures for unilateral exploitation will increase, but there are indications that the United States will continue to stress the importance of strict environmental control in the event of mineral exploration and exploitation. It recently commissioned an environmental impact statement on the effects of mineral extraction from the Institute of Polar Studies at Ohio State University.

There could not be greater contrast between this position and that taken by the Soviet Union and Japan. Such is the vehemence of the Soviet Union's opposition to offshore oil exploitation that the agenda of a meeting convened in Paris in June 1976 to consider the subject "Antarctic Resources—The Question of Mineral Resource Exploration and Exploitation in all its aspects in relation to the Treaty" had to be peppered with qualifications and reservations, and it proved impossible to convene another formal meeting to discuss the subject. The Soviet Union is proposing a renewable moratorium of 10 to 15 years on the "industrial" exploration and exploitation of mineral resources.

Both the Soviet Union and Japan are stressing the environmental argument. Noting that the USSR has the largest and most explicitly resource-oriented geological research program in Antarctica, observers put forward other explanations for its position. According to one school of thought, the USSR is simply anxious to gain time in which to develop the technology to compete on an equal footing with the United States for the prime mineral sites. Another possibility is that the USSR might be seeking to discard the treaty and curry favor with the Third World. Alternatively, those responsible for the Soviet scientific research effort in Antarctica may be anxious not to lose their large research budget.

As mentioned above, the opposition of Argentina and Chile to exploitation can be traced, in large part, to apprehension about losing control over their territorial claims. Chile, which imports 60 percent of its oil, has stated that it will favor exploitation when its claims are recognized. There are, however, signs of a new environmental awareness in these two Latin American countries, and as the nearest treaty parties to the Antarctic continent they have every reason to be sincere in this matter.

Until recently, New Zealand was also adamantly opposed to any mineral exploitation. In June 1975 it proposed that the area be declared an international park. Whether for reasons of its own economy or the need to find a realistic solution to the problems of the 12, it is now prepared to face the eventuality of exploitation. Every emphasis, however, is given to environmental control. The French, in spite of a difference of views between the various departments concerned, are also in favor of going ahead.

Within the 12 virtually every shade of opinion on mineral recovery, from firm advocacy of a moratorium to assertion of the right to exploit, is to be heard. In comparison, the krill debate is a quiet one. Krill exploitation is not felt to present such a threat to the environment and the treaty regime, and besides, a considerable number of treaty powers consider living resources to be high-seas resources. The Soviet Union, Japan, and possibly Chile have already made substantial investments in krill exploitation. A difference seems to have emerged, however, between the Soviet Union and the rest of the group. The USSR appears to have been boycotting the meetings of the SCAR Group of Specialists on the Living Resources of the Southern Ocean as though it were reluctant to be bound by any management decisions that might be reached in that forum. The remaining 11 might decide to tackle this resource on an entrepreneurial basis. In this case it would be a good idea if each country undertook to exchange catch statistics and limit annual increases in fishing effort.

Solidarity over living resources has probably been increased by a "threat" from outside. The FAO, in conjunction with UNDP, is considering a project to assist in the exploration, exploitation, and utilization of the living resources of the Southern Ocean for the benefit of developing countries as well as Antarctic Treaty parties.

CLAIMANTS VS. NONCLAIMANTS

Perhaps the most immediate problem facing the 12 is the old jurisdictional one from within their own ranks. This tangle has remained unchanged since 1959. The resource issue has undermined the consensus which existed among the 12 that the questions it raised could be left unanswered. The clash over mineral-resource exploitation is really one between concepts of sovereignty and freedom of access. Claimants claim ownership of resources in their sectors and the adjacent shelves, and nonclaimants would like freedom of access to the resources of the entire area.

The position of Argentina and Chile has changed little over the years. Their claims are inextricably bound up with national pride and prestige. According to their national legislation, and perhaps more importantly, according to domestic public opinion, the Antarctic sectors are part of metropolitan territory. As Argentina said at the opening of the Washington meeting at which the 1959 treaty was signed, ". . . Antarctica has taken root and established an awareness in the soul of the Argentine Nation." The demonstrations of ownership have been endless: maps have been drawn, churches built, and once the Argentine cabinet went so far as to hold a session on the ice.

Refusal to concede sovereignty has always been a basic condition of any agreement by the two Latin American states to participate in Antarctic negotiations. Proposals made by the United States in 1948 that the small group of countries involved in Antarctica should merge their claims and interests were unacceptable to Argentina and Chile. At the time their idea of cooperation was limited; Chile stated that it was only interested in international cooperation in scientific studies, the possibility of concluding an agreement providing for the exchange of information, and a formula to avoid incidents of an international character which might affect cordial relations. Several authors indicate that the Latin Americans were reluctantly dragged into the treaty: ". . . faced with a widely popular, concrete proposal, and the likelihood that the conference would be held in any event, Chile and Argentina agreed to participate." The Latin Americans are showing signs of a greater willingness to compromise. Words and concepts such as "regime" and "Antarctic Treaty system," formerly anathema to them, are becoming more acceptable. It has even been suggested that they might be prepared to contemplate exploitation by others in "their" areas in return for payment of royalties.

In contrast to the Latin Americans, Australia supported the U.S. initiative which resulted in the 1959 treaty, although it felt that the whole project could be better approached on a minimum essential basis. In recent talks Australia seems, however, to have retreated to a more territorialist position and has virtually joined ranks with Argentina and Chile.

The fight against the claims is led by the United States. Despite the protests of writers, private citizens, and senators, it has consistently refused to make a claim. This may not be unconnected with the fact that after the war the places to which the United States might have asserted rights were claimed by the United Kingdom, New Zealand, Argentina, and Chile, countries with which it was undesirable to have a clash of interests. The largest and most interesting parts had gone. The United States has, however, always reserved the right to make claims, but, despite renewed speculation, there seems little likelihood of this happening. A predictable corollary of this position is the refusal to recognize claims. Less predictable are the lengths to which the United States is prepared to take this view. Over mineral-resource exploitation it steadfastly refuses to make any concessions to the territorial claimants. Thus in 1975 it said: "Non-discriminatory guaranteed access by the USA and others for exploitation purposes to any part of the Antarctic Treaty area except specially protected areas is critical to avoid prejudicing our underlying juridical position."

Less extreme are the positions taken by Belgium, New Zealand, Norway, the United Kingdom, and France. Belgium, itself a nonclaimant, is prepared to go some way towards meeting the aspirations of claimants and particularly those of the southern hemisphere. New Zealand and Norway are probably the least committed of the claimants. Under Prime Minister Walter Nash, New Zealand told its partners at the Washington Conference that it was prepared to forego its claim. Although it accepted the final compromise it was disappointed that a more imaginative and adventurous solution had not been adopted. This was very much Nash's personal view, but traces of it are to be found in New Zealand's policy today. Norway has taken a similar, if somewhat lower-profile stand. In 1948 it was prepared to accept proposals to amalgamate claims in the area. According to one commentator, Norway's claim, made only in 1939, was essentially designed to forestall a move on the part of the Germans, and "to be on the safe side" in the case of an eventual settlement. The maintenance of this claim might well prove an embarrassment to Norway with its limited resources and manpower.

The United Kingdom has been a firm advocate of the merging of claims and interests in the area and in 1958 launched an initiative designed to bring this about. It has always maintained the need to ensure that knowledge of the Antarctic and freedom of access to it should not be limited by political considerations, and would have preferred an organization vested with effective and comprehensive powers to the arrangements that were agreed upon at the 1959 Washington Conference. But in recent years the United Kingdom's internationalist approach, particularly to the minerals issue, has been muted.

Perhaps some of this spirit will reemerge today. France with severe energy problems at home and the smallest claim (well under a twelfth of the continent) might also be persuaded to compromise.

In spite of these moderating influences, the outlook is not promising. Although most claimant states are willing to compromise they would be unable to move as far as the U.S. position requires. In this respect perhaps it is the United States and not the traditional villains of the piece, the claimants, who should be chastised for holding up agreement.

For the time being it is unclear whether the ownership of living resources will give rise to such dispute among the 12. The present state of flux of the Law of the Sea and particularly of coastal-state jurisdiction is reflected in the Antarctic. Most of the claimant states claim territorial seas and the Latin Americans have already proclaimed 200-mile zones off their territories, an example which other claimants may well follow. It is uncertain whether such declarations would be accompanied by attempts to maintain exclusive control over the living resources within the zone. The nonclaimants, of course, consider all these waters to be high seas.

INTERNATIONAL COMMUNITY VS. THE 12

In 1975 the subject of Antarctica was raised at the UN Economic and Social Council and General Assembly by the representative from Sri Lanka. In May 1976 Guinea insisted that control over the proposed FAO/UNDP Southern Fisheries Program be shared equally by developed and developing countries, pointing out the need for a new Antarctic Treaty. The Chinese are also showing signs of interest, while some Arab countries are proposing that the future Seabed Authority take Antarctica under its wing, and manage the offshore oil reserves. It may be only a matter of time before a coordinated protest movement gets under way.

How serious is this conflict likely to be? How adamant are the 12 about excluding the international community?

In the past a number of the 12 spoke of the need to open treaty membership to the international community. In an article in *Soviet News* in 1958 the USSR suggested that the projected international treaty would be much more effective if all states wishing to do so were to take part in discussion of the question. The matter was of interest not only to those states already carrying out work but to those which would like to undertake work in the future. The article gave as an example the interest of India. Walter Nash consistently promoted the idea of an international regime.[6] After the Washington Conference, New Zealand stressed its view that the settlement did not set up a monopolistic regime for the 12. Although the United Kingdom envisaged that administration would remain in the hands of the 12, it also wanted the widest possible range of countries to be included in the agreement. It was, furthermore, its understanding that the treaty would be "almost entirely a self-denying ordinance on the part of the signatories, who will derive from it virtually no privileges but only obligations."

Perhaps the possibility of resource exploitation has altered the picture. Certainly, informal talks held at the Nansen Foundation in 1973 revealed very little interest in widening the debate. The only new countries that are likely to be admitted to consultative membership are West Germany and Poland, and this on the strength of their activities in the area.

While it appears that there will be no move to prevent nontreaty countries from enjoying the living resources, no attempt will be made to assist in this process. Thus most Antarctic Treaty Consultative Parties are apprehensive about the expensive FAO/UNDP proposals mentioned above. There is a marked preference for a regulated version of the principle of freedom of access.

With regard to minerals, the same freedom of access is advocated by nonclaimants but opposed by the claimants. It is, besides, a particularly illusory freedom in the case of offshore oil and gas extraction which will be open only to the technologically powerful. However, the idea elaborated in the Law of the Sea negotiations, that the minerals of the deep seabed are to be shared by mankind, has done much to persuade the 12 of the necessity of sharing revenue from mineral exploitation in Antarctica with the international community.

NOTES

1. The estimated catch from all marine areas was 59,997,279 metric tons.

2. Brazil, Czechoslovakia, Denmark, the German Democratic Republic, the Netherlands, Poland, and Romania have acceded to the treaty.

3. Of these, the Agreed Measures for the Conservation of Antarctic Fauna and Flora are generally considered to represent one of the most advanced conservation regimes in the world.

4. For example, support provided by Argentina and Chile for a moratorium on exploration and exploitation is at least in part a move to prevent inroads being made into their sovereignty.

5. D. Shapley believes the resource agencies lost that round of the battle. D. Shapley, "North Pole, South Pole Resources Eyed," *Science* 189 (August 1975), 365.

6. Walter Nash proposed the establishment of Antarctica as a world territory under the control of the UN.

14

Values

Rice Odell

PRESERVING VALUES IN AN AGE OF SCARCITY

As environmental limitations and resource scarcities continue to take their toll of society, the way we deal with them will determine, in large measure, the very nature of our political and economic systems, and the kind of civilization we leave to future generations.

For two centuries, philosophers and politicians have warned of the many dangers that jeopardize the freedoms rooted in the United States' democratic system. And the nation seems to have survived—without a crippling, permanent erosion of these freedoms—such internal and external threats as the Civil War, the Great Depression, Hitlerian fascism, commmunism, racism, the Vietnam War, and Watergate.

But there is a new and lingering menace. It is not inherently political; it is not caused chiefly by people and their malevolent behavior. It is ecological and economic. It is caused by escalating demands on land, air, water, energy, and other natural resources that support the political and economic systems.

The result of environmental limitations is an increasing constriction of those systems and of the governmental, individual, and corporate freedoms that derive from them and that compose our way of life.

Scarcities can be caused, and their effects exacerbated, not only by growth in demand and population, but by manipulations and distribution and prices. The most obvious and serious examples so far, of course, are the world food problem and the Arab oil embargo and price-fixing agree-

---

From *Environmental Awakening: The New Revolution to Protect the Earth* by Rice Odell. Copyright 1980, The Conservation Foundation. Reprinted with permission from the Ballinger Publishing Company, Cambridge, Mass. Pp. 264–73.

ments, with their dire economic effects in the United States and elsewhere.

There are many other less blatant, or more localized, manifestations of a long-term dilemma—the land and housing crunch, the transportation mess, the large array of pollution and other chemical hazards. These are thorny to deal with politically. For the laws of ecology and economics cannot be amended. And the race to forestall their effects by applying more and more technology may be counterproductive.

There is a Greek chorus of warnings from many of our most perceptive thinkers about the insidious nature of this new dilemma. Their theme is distressingly consistent:

- "The future austerity will be perennial," says historian Arnold Toynbee, "and it will become progressively more severe. What then? . . . Within each of the beleaguered 'developed' countries there will be a bitter struggle for the control of their diminished resources." The struggle will have to be stopped, he says; therefore "a new way of life—a severely regimented way—will have to be imposed by a ruthless authoritarian government."

In a siege economy, Toynbee adds, such a government will have to impose a scale of subsistence payments, and most private property might have to be nationalized.

- A healthful and attractive urban environment "might have to be sustained to a considerable degree by coercion," write Martin and Margy Meyerson, both experts on urban planning. Most qualitative improvements in the environment—including pollution control, better transportation, more open space and recreation, decent housing—depend on public, collective actions, including not only taxation and funding support, but "regulation of behavior," or "requiring individuals or firms or agencies to refrain from previous practices—practices they have come to regard from habitual usage as freedoms."
- Says William Ophuls, a political scientist and writer:

> The problem that the tragedy of the commons forces us to confront is, in fact, the core issue of political philosophy: How to protect or advance the interests of the collectivity as a whole when the individuals that make it up . . . behave in a selfish, greedy and quarrelsome fashion. The only answer is a sufficient measure of coercion.
>
> In a situation of ecological scarcity . . . the individualistic basis of society, the concept of inalienable rights, the purely self-defined pursuit of happiness, liberty as maximum freedom of action, and laissez-faire itself all require abandonment or major modification if we wish to avoid inexorable environmental degradation and perhaps extinction as a civilization. We must thus question whether democracy as we know it can survive.

Ophuls notes that the historic responses to scarcity have been war, oppression, and "great inequality of wealth and the political measures needed to maintain it."

Nor is Ophuls sanguine about the potential for technological answers:

> If the optimists are right in supposing that we can adjust to ecological scarcity with economics and technology, this effort will have, as we say, "side effects." For the collision with physical limits can be forestalled only by moving toward some kind of steady-state economy—characterized by the most scrupulous husbanding of resources, by extreme vigilance against the ever-present possibility of disaster should breakdown occur, and therefore, by tight controls on human behavior.

• In his book *An Inquiry Into the Human Prospect*, Robert L. Heilbroner repeatedly sounds a similar theme, and speculates on the probably inadequate responses of both capitalist and socialist societies. He suggests that we must be prepared to face the fact that "values and beliefs precious to us may be assaulted by overriding claims of human survival."

Heilbroner, an economics professor, wonders whether the "exigencies of the future . . . point to the conclusion that only an authoritarian, or possibly only a revolutionary, regime will be capable of mounting the immense task of social reorganization needed to escape catastrophe."

He speaks of enormous inflationary pressures that could "require the imposition of much stronger control measures than any that capitalism has yet succeeded in introducing," and of "intolerable strains on the representative democratic political apparatus." He warns of "the need to exercise a much wider and deeper administration of both production and consumption," of "psychological insecurity," of sharpened feelings of nationalism, of "wars of redistribution."

WHAT'S AT STAKE

One could cite many other such warnings about the dangers of conflict, and of increasingly autocratic, overbearing government. For there can be no doubt that man's needs—not to mention his expectations—are outrunning the environment's ability to satisfy them. Individuals, nations, and other entities are likely to be fighting more and more over the division of shrinking natural resources, incomes, and gross national products and over competing values, freedoms, and amenities.

In fact, visible portents seem to be confirming the pessimistic prognoses. At the international level, we have seen cartels, embargoes, restrictions on immigration, fishing wars, disputes over access to the oceans—as well as increasing talk of coercive trade barriers and even the war over Middle Eastern oil. Many nations are pushing exports hard to cover their outlays for oil and reduce their trade deficits. The United States has furiously sold military equipment, with Middle East oil countries among the major buyers. The nation's surplus foods have sometimes been used for international economic and political leverage. "To a far greater degree than many Americans realize," notes Dan Morgan of the *Washington Post*, "the U.S. now depends on massive commercial exports of agricultural commodities in seeking a trade balance." Five international economists have wondered whether oil-importing countries, "as they reach desperately for each other's markets, will also erect more menacing barriers against each other's exports." They speak of the possibilities of currency devaluations, defaults by business and banking firms, debt moratoria—and political revolution and debt repudiation.

In this country, in addition to serious economic ills, we are witness to fuel allocations, disputes over the construction and location of energy facilities and waste disposal sites, efforts to restrain community growth, and many other confrontations over jobs, growth, and the protection of health and the environment.

In all these cases, someone's freedoms and privileges are at stake. But if the ecological-economic noose continues to tighten as expected, and we must brace ourselves for new restrictions on individual and corporate activity, then it will be useful to keep in mind that there are many ***kinds*** of freedoms and rights involved. Some are more critical to the welfare of the democratic system, and to the people, than others. Some, in fact, could more accurately be described as *privileges* that have come to be regarded as rights.

Consider a rough and perhaps arbitrary categorization of those rights and privileges that reflect the range of human values:

1. *Civil liberties*. Under this heading are the various political rights that are essential to democracy—the rights of free speech, assembly, due process of law, privacy, and security. One might add the right to play a role in political decision making, not just by voting but through direct participation in open government.

2. *Human rights*. The right to have enough to eat; the right to health and safety through sufficient protection from unsafe drinking water, polluted air, radioactivity, and hazardous chemicals in consumer products and in the workplace; and the right to reasonable space and quiet.

3. *Social rights*. Some of these might also be considered privileges or amenities. But the category could include the right to procreate; the right to have a job; the right to travel freely (to foreign lands? in a big car without expensive pollution controls? for unlimited mileage?); the right to own one's own home (a detached dwelling? with plenty of yard space?

a second home, too?); the right to have access to an aesthetic environment, open space, and recreation opportunities.

4. *Economic freedoms or privileges*. For the individual, there is the right to earn a decent living, or the right to a guaranteed minimum income; the right to profit in business or in the sale or development of land; and the right to indulge one's material wants, what Heilbroner calls the "freedom of acquisition."

For corporations, there is the right to earn a profit; to use, and possibly pollute, common air, water, or land resources; to be free of price controls, export controls, burdensome taxes, and other governmental interference with the marketplace; to withhold certain information from the public and the government; to obtain government subsidies; and to protect property from unfair confiscation.

5. *National rights*. A nation can be seen as entitled to freedom from unreasonable political, economic, or environmental aggression by other nations.

What is the status of environmental "rights" or "privileges"? René Dubos, the microbiologist and Pulitzer Prize–winning author has said: "The fact is that the right to a good environment has come to be regarded as a natural right of man for which the community is responsible." And he adds that "there has never been a lasting retreat from the recognition of a natural right of man."

Nevertheless, the many rights and privileges at work in society are frequently antagonistic, and there are many conflicting perceptions of which are most important, as a few examples serve to illustrate:

- René Dubos said, "Privacy, space and quietness may not be essential for survival, but they are needs deeply rooted in human nature, and the demand for them increases with prosperity." (He added that with labor, energy, and open land becoming more and more scarce and expensive, "the isolated freestanding house will become an economic burden too heavy for the average person, as well as becoming socially unacceptable."
- Citing examples of Environmental Protection Agency (EPA) interference with development projects and with efforts to increase energy supplies, Irving Kristol, professor of urban values at New York University and co-editor of *The Public Interest*, says that Congress and the public

> . . . certainly never intended to give a handful of bureaucrats such immense powers. If the EPA's conception of its mission is permitted to stand, it will be the single most powerful branch of government, having far greater direct control over our individual lives than Congress, or the Executive, or state and local government. . . . [N]or are the American people, likely to permit it

> to endure. Clean air is a good thing—but so is liberty, and so is democracy, and so are many other things.

• Edmund K. Faltermayer, an editor of *Fortune* magazine, has written that it is important to keep free enterprise as unfettered as possible, but added this:

> Only in one area—in the determination of land-use patterns—need there be any curtailment of laissez-faire. But land use has never been determined solely by the market mechanism anyway; government has always intervened to some extent, in order to prevent a state of total anarchy.

• In a 1974 attack on gasoline rationing, increased gasoline taxes, and wage-price controls, the *Dallas Morning News* said it is disturbing to hear officials "talk so blandly of coercive, totalitarian economic measures." It said that, "with more equanimity than is advisable, the American people are listening to a host of politicians demand that they be stripped of some basic liberties."

• Paul W. McCracken, former chairman of the Council of Economic Advisers, wrote that it's logical to encourage people to save energy by switching to smaller cars, but added:

> On the other hand, availability of personal transportation will continue to be a jealously-prized freedom in the American setting and an energy policy which involves a drastic curtailment of that freedom is not apt to have staying power.

ON SHIFTING GEARS

The relationships between people and automobiles are particularly illuminating when it comes to a discussion of values. While industry and government scratch for answers to the automobile problem, the people are out there doing their own motorized thing. Is the public passion for cars on the wane? Can American drivers be weaned from their cars? Should they be?

There is no agreement on the answers, of course, just as there is none between the sociologists and economists who extol cars and those who excoriate them. At least some observers believe the nation is growing out of the "American Graffiti" stage. But there is enough contrary evidence to deduce that cars will still be running around after all their drivers have expired.

There may be less reliance on the car as a status symbol. The conspicuousness of the automobile played a part in its early development, notes Joseph F. Coates, of the Office of Technology Assessment, U.S. Congress:

> It was good to have the first, or have the best, or the only, of an outstanding machine. This is a traditional characterization of American behavior in regard to gadgets, at least until a gadget becomes fully integrated in society.
>
> One still sees conspicuous consumption via the automobile, particularly among the nouveaux riches and in the ghettos.

But, he told an annual meeting of the American Association for the Advancement of Science, its importance diminishes as one moves up the socioeconomic ladder. "This may be an important long-term trend."

In fact, says Coates, there is an "anti-conspicuous consumption attitude on the part of the middle class," what with the adoption of blue jeans and other "marks of calculated informality." And there are many new routes to conspicuous consumption—travel, electronic equipment, cameras, etc.

Similarly, Coates thinks the automobile is needed less for another kind of psychic support: "the manliness and independence" associated with wheels and power and other factors with a "juvenile orientation." He sees "less association between machismo, manliness and the car." Besides, adds Coates, "For those with the machismo hang-up there is a far better instrument—the motorcycle."

Related to this are the effects on automobile usage of the change in sexual mores. The car "seems to be of declining popularity as a portable bedroom. The openness of sex now makes other facilities more readily available and convenient." Coates further thinks the emphasis on cars may diminish as Americans lean more on individuality, health, and self-sufficiency, and as they take more to walking, bicycling, and other active pursuits.

But there are many reasons to suspect that automobiles in some form will continue to hold the nation in their clutches, shaping both its economy and its whole culture, for decades. As of 1979, the number of cars on the road was estimated to be more than 120 million. It is not hard to imagine that this number will climb significantly—considering (1) the steadily growing population, (2) the likelihood of increasing affluence, (3) the new recreational and other uses to which cars and other vehicles are put, and (4) the potential market for more cars per family.

The following Census Bureau figures for 1970 indicate the nature of this potential, assuming that those families with one or more cars are happy to have them:

Percentage of Households With

No car—17.5	Two cars—29.3
One car—47.7	Three or more cars—5.5

Of course, many people without cars are unable to drive for various reasons.

The automobile's staying power in our society is partly explained by its functional values—its convenience, flexibility, and privacy. It is a source of mobility not only in the narrower sense, says Coates, but "in a larger sense of carrying us out of our neighborhoods, out of our milieu, out of our environment. . . . [I]t gives us choices and options regarding employment and recreation which go beyond the short-term immediate flexibilities of a day-to-day, work-a-day world."

Ironically, as people take up more outdoor activities such as boating, camping, and skiing, they become more dependent on cars to get them there, beyond urbanization. And so there are mounting sales of both cars and recreational vehicles. Author Edward Ayres says this indicates that "even people who love the outdoors are growing to like the idea of rolling through the wilderness on wheels." Ayres added that, "in all this automania, there lurks the danger of a slowly diminishing quality of existence, of a fading appreciation of the experiences cars have usurped from the bodies and senses of men." In a similar vein, San Diego columnist Neil Morgan has written that the freeway driving experience is "chillingly impersonal, suicidally frenetic, and so vacuous as to make [Los Angeles] inhabitants appear as the robots of a city that has become a puppet of technology."

Yet for all the putdowns of the driving experience, there are many who sing its praises. And they seem to voice a sort of public consensus when they note that driving, in addition to its obvious convenience, induces euphoric feelings of motion and control, of purpose, of peace, of liberation. This peace, which derives from the privacy of the car, is otherwise hard for many people to find.

"It's the only time we're really disengaged," says one driver. Another says he gets into his car when he has trouble working. "My whole mind opens up, I'm so aware of things. It's a strange kind of highway narcosis."

Even in the madding maze of city rush-hour traffic, these feelings may be at work. Speaking of privacy in mass society, sociologist Edward McDonagh said: "You find it driving to work, alongside all those other people, but alone with your thoughts. The car has become a secular sanctuary for the individual, his shrine to the self, his mobile Walden Pond."

CONFLICTING INTERESTS

In a time of tightening scarcities, private and public decisions can have a magnified effect on the distribution of resources, of economic benefits, and of freedoms and privileges. The recurring question will be: Who has the political or economic power to sustain their preferences? "The future," says Leonard J. Duhl, of the University of California's College of Environmental Design, "will be shaped by the outcome of the struggle of competing values."

In that struggle, the conflicts and compromises—the trade-offs of rights and privileges—will be between various interests, broken down somewhat arbitrarily as follows:

1. *Individual vs. individual.* One person wants his property rezoned to allow development; his neighbor wants to protect his environmental advantages. Everyone wants to have wastes dumped, or an oil refinery located, in someone else's state or community.

A person living on a fixed income wants to see government brake inflation; another, laid off from his job, wants an antidote to recession. "Inflation makes spending decisions for us that we once were free to make ouselves," said the magazine *Skeptic*. "Inflation has narrowed our choices and options. In the end, it threatens to eliminate them entirely." But the person out of a job is similarly without options.

The dilemma was put another way by Maurice Barbash in a letter to the *New York Times*: "A limitation on growth as our society is currently structured would impose a crushing sentence on the presently disadvantaged. We still operate under the terms of a 'trickle down' philosophy, where the poor get a little something only when the rich get richer."

2. *Individual vs. community.* A builder and a would-be homeowner are stymied by a community-imposed sewer moratorium. Or the government insists on purchase of an automobile pollution control device to safeguard the community's air resource.

3. *Individual, or community, vs. corporation.* The public wants a company to stop polluting a stream; but the company is anxious to avoid the high cost. To put it another way, a corporate activity that benefits stockholders and company managers may be in conflict with the interests of residents, workers, or consumers, or a government acting in their behalf, or vice versa.

4. *Corporation vs. corporation.* With shortages of oil and natural gas, companies clash over their allocations. The same goes for places in the West where water is in limited supply.

5. *Nation vs. nation.* Export controls and other trade barriers are obvious examples of friction between developed and less developed countries. These are unlikely to diminish with greater scarcity and greater conflict between environmental and development goals. "Mankind has still found no organized system for reconciling the driving demands and ambitions of national statehood with the wider unities of a shared planet," wrote Barbara Ward and René Dubos.

Richard H. Gardner, law professor at Columbia University and a former State Department official, has suggested a "mutual survival pact," with developed nations agreeing to conserve energy, food, and other resources, and to provide needed access to markets, technology, and capital, while undeveloped countries agree to change some of their "suicidal" population, food, and environmental practices.

6. *Present vs. future generations.* To what extent shall today's population husband its natural resources in the interests of tomorrow's, which has no say in the decisions? Heilbroner suggests that if we can acquiesce in the destruction of those contemporaries who rot in prison or starve to death, we are not likely to take the "painful actions" needed to protect future generations:

> Worse yet, will [we] not curse these future generations whose claims to life can be honored only by sacrificing present enjoyments; and will [we] not, if it comes to a choice, condemn them to nonexistence by choosing the present over the future.

Allen V. Kneese, of Resources For the Future, notes that one of the questions is whether society should strike what Alvin M. Weinberg called the Faustian bargain with atomic scientists and engineers.

> If so unforgiving a technology as large-scale nuclear fission energy production is adopted, it will impose a burden of continuous monitoring and sophisticated management of a dangerous material, essentially forever.

Columnist Anthony Lewis writes that one of society's greatest problems is the absence of

> . . . adequate mechanisms for weighing long-term interests against the immediate. Our system grew on the principle of the market. . . . The market ideal has given us wealth and much freedom. But its emphasis is necessarily on immediate gain. . . . We look to government to weigh the immediate against the distant, but our government is desperately short of people with the training and the vision to make such judgments.

The absence of such vision has been most starkly revealed in the energy crisis of the 1970s. Fortunately, however, there are many reasons to believe that the energy problem can be turned into a substantial, albeit disguised, blessing. For it offers an unprecedented opportunity to examine some questionable traditions, and to plan for the future with a deeper economic, social, and ecological understanding. Suddenly the nation can no longer afford the luxury of leisurely, ivory-tower discussion. The current state of urgency can force the country and the world to face key issues squarely and with new awareness. For the first time, every move a corporation or government agency makes, everything a consumer buys, is being assessed almost instinctively in terms of energy consumption. We have a sharpened perception of many issues, from economic growth to foreign affairs, from transportation and city planning to individual and community lifestyles.

The energy crisis, perhaps more than anything else in all of history, should engrave certain facts onto the world's generally numbed consciousness. These are: that vital resources are unevenly distributed; that because they are vital, they can be manipulated in politically dangerous ways; that as shortages become more binding, resources will be shared only through unprecedented multinational cooperation; and, most importantly, that all nations are in the same rather leaky, overloaded boat. [. . .]

15

Doomsday Has Been Cancelled

J. Peter Vajk

THE UNIVERSAL LABORATORY

Permanent habitation in space will result from the requirements of space industries for large numbers of workers in orbit. The largest number of space colony residents in the early years will be foundry workers and skilled construction workers involved in the extraction of useful materials from nonterrestrial ores and in the construction of solar power satellites. A modest number of people will be needed to support the space communities themselves, providing basic goods and services for the colonists. These will include maintenance workers, farmers, physicians, nurses, and medical technicians, administrators, teachers, and clergy.

The opportunities for scientific research and development will not be overlooked in the new environment of space. Areas of research which will obviously benefit from these new opportunities include astronomy, low-temperature physics, meteorology and climatology, and fusion-energy research. Another area of enormous potential is *genetic engineering*, which may become a powerful tool for the development of new strains of plants and animals, for understanding and perhaps reversing the aging process, and for the breeding of new strains of special-purpose microorganisms. Such microbes might be developed to digest specific chemical pollutants, to synthesize insulin and other pharmaceutical products, and, perhaps, to cure metabolic diseases due to errors in the genetic code.

Reprint of "The Universal Laboratory" and "The Endless Horizon," Chapters 28 and 29 in *Doomsday Has Been Cancelled* by J. Peter Vajk. Copyright 1978 by Peace Press, Inc., Culver City, Calif. Reprinted by permission of the publisher. Pp. 161–69.

One of the principal methods available for research on genetic engineering is recombinant DNA experimentation, in which fragments of genes from one type of organism are "spliced" into the genes of a recipient organism, perhaps of an entirely different species. The differences in the biochemical repertoire of an altered cell culture then provide information on the roles various pieces of the genes play in controlling the biochemical factory inside those cells.

During the 1970s considerable controversy has been raised over the safety of this line of research. One of the favorite recipient organisms used in these experiments is *Escherichia coli*, a bacterium which normally inhabits the human intestinal tract, and does no harm to us under normal conditions. The reason *E. coli* is so popular is because it is a very simple biochemical factory, having a total repertoire of only a thousand or so chemical processes, all of which have been cataloged. A great many of these reactions have been correlated with specific pieces of the single chromosome of *E. coli*, making it an almost ideal organism for such experiments.

The controversy over these experiments arises from the possibility that gene fragments, inserted into *E. coli* and other benign host organisms, might change them into virulent pathogens, producing serious epidemics if any of them were to escape from the laboratory, into the human intestinal tract or other habitats where these organisms are able to flourish. In the face of an unknowable risk potential, many critics have questioned whether laboratory procedures are adequate to prevent such an escape. Some have argued that such experiments should be performed only in a few laboratories, where very stringent confinement measures can be rigorously applied (such as the army's bacteriological research laboratories). Others have insisted that all such research should be postponed until we somehow learn enough to gauge the risks involved in this kind of research. A few have urged the use of alternative, recipient microorganisms, which are not adapted to living in humans, instead of *E. coli*. Whatever the interim decisions are, it is clear that recombinant DNA research could be carried on more safely in orbiting laboratories which could guarantee *total* quarantine from the general human population.

One area of astronomical research deserves special mention here—the search for planets of other stars and intelligent life elsewhere in the universe. Large telescopes on the surface of the earth or moon are not feasible because of gravity. On the earth, atmospheric turbulence limits the resolution achievable even with large telescopes. In free space, however, it is not necessary to support a telescope against its own weight. Instead of building telescopes only 200 inches in diameter (like the instrument at Mount Palomar, which has produced such profound changes in our perceptions and understanding of the cosmos), it will be practical to build telescopes 200 meters in diameter. Such a telescope could detect earth-sized planets, orbiting stars ten light-years away; directed at objects within our own solar system, such a telescope would provide resolution of surface details, only 20 kilometers in size, on Pluto.

Still larger telescopes up to two kilometers in diameter (about the presently foreseeable limit due to the necessity of keeping different parts of the mirror precisely aligned within a fraction of a wavelength of the light gathered) could also be built by space industrial facilities. Capable of detecting earth-sized planets up to 100 light-years distant, such an instrument would simplify the task of searching for technological civilizations about other stars, allowing us to concentrate our radio listening efforts on such planetary systems. Whether such distant civilizations would have anything to say to us (or we to them) remains, as yet, a matter for speculation.

Perhaps the biggest winners in research opportunities will be the "soft sciences." Once the number of space colonies has increased sufficiently to permit real cultural diversification, sociologists, anthropologists, psychologists, political scientists, and economists will have a field day. Some communities in space may decide to eliminate money completely in internal transactions; others may decide to try pure communism. One community may choose near-total isolationism; while others will maintain completely unrestricted, free trade among themselves. Even Plato's philosopher-kings may appear someday. The parameters of human interactions may thus be explored in ways which have never really been possible here on earth. But I think one thing can be stated with a high degree of certainty: although many space communities may be organized along utopian lines, none is more likely to achieve the desired utopian goals than any such attempts here on earth.

THE ENDLESS HORIZON

Once the first self-sufficient and self-reproducing human settlement in space has been established, every economic consideration will favor rapid growth of the human population living in the earth's atmosphere. Most of the increase in numbers will be due to emigration for better jobs, just as in the early history of the Americas and Australia, when the European population grew more by immigration than by births. In previous chapters, I have discussed the types of activities in space which are likely to be profitable in the next few decades; now I would like to indulge in some longer range speculations about the next few centuries.

Once asteroid mining begins in earnest, one or more space colonies of a few thousand people each are likely to be equipped with low-thrust propulsion systems (such as mass drivers, ion engines, or solar sails) to wander among the near-earth asteroids as prospecting and mining bases. These early wandering cities, dipping as close to the sun as the orbit of

Venus, soaring as far out as the orbit of Mars, would significantly reduce the costs of nonterrestrial mining.

Not long after that, other human settlements of several thousands of people would fan out to orbit around several or all of the planets of the solar system, providing bases for the systematic long-term scientific study and exploration of these alien worlds. In the past plans for the human exploration of Mars assumed the launch from the earth's surface: a handful of astronauts crowded into cramped spaceships barely larger than *Apollo* for two to three years, with only a few months spent on the surface of Mars, unable to explore more than a tiny vicinity of a single landing spot.

From an orbiting space colony, with access to abundant and inexpensive hydrogen and oxygen from asteroid mining, small expeditions could venture down to the surface of Mars, the polar regions of Mercury, or the surfaces of the moons of Jupiter, Saturn, Uranus, and Neptune as desired. Small, chemically powered rockets would allow numerous expeditions over a period of many years, at a far less total cost than for a single earth-based expedition to Mars.

Small-sized cities may ply the solar system like ocean liners, cruising tropical seas. With advanced propulsion systems (such as high-energy lasers on the ground, or in orbit around the earth, beaming energy to heat a gas aboard a rocket to provide high-performance propulsion), one or two year cruises to see Jupiter's Red Spot or to view the rings of Saturn and Uranus from close-up, would become feasible, without being prohibitively expensive, especially if these cruising cities provided university-level educational programs en route.

(A friend who is actively involved in laser propulsion concepts turned forty in December of 1977. Just a few weeks later, while we exchanged notes over a few beers, he told me he was really motivated by the desire to visit Saturn's rings for his sixtieth birthday—he just might make it!)

Early in the next century, several instrumented probes are likely to be built in space using nonterrestrial raw materials and launched toward the nearer stars. Equipped with sensors and computers, of a sophistication unbelievable to us today, such probes will be capable of searching the vicinity of another star for planets, for signs of life, and for indications of civilization, including space industries. Travel times for such probes destined to the nearest stars would be a few decades to a few centuries.

As the human population of the solar system grows, and as the total economy of the space communities expands and becomes more intricate and complex, small groups of people will have the opportunity to set out on their own, homesteading the asteroid belt or various orbits around other planets, to pursue whatever visions of lifestyles they may choose. In less than a hundred years human settlements will be found in most parts of the solar system with no possibility of crowding—after all, more than just a little bit of space is available out there.

Propulsion systems we can consider for use in space are based on chemical energy, solar energy, or nuclear energy. None of these is really adequate for efficient travel to interstellar distances. Until the discovery of radioactivity by Henri Becquerel in 1895, the most concentrated energy sources known were chemical. Chemical energy is associated with the molecular level of physical structure, in the electromagnetic interactions between two or more atoms. Typically, the chemical bond between two atoms in a molecule involves a few electron volts. (An electron volt is a very tiny unit of energy. It is the energy acquired by an electron, freely accelerated between two metallic plates hooked up with batteries, providing one volt of potential difference between the plates. The chemical energy released in metabolizing one day's food—about 3,000 calories—is 7.8×10^{25} electron volts.)

In contrast to chemical energy, the release of nuclear energy is far more concentrated, since it involves rearrangements in the structure of the atomic nucleus, some 10,000 times smaller in dimensions than the atom. The interactions between the protons and the neutrons of a nucleus involve a few million electron volts for each nucleus involved in a nuclear reaction of some kind. Because of this factor of a million greater concentration in energy release per atom involved, a pound of uranium used in a nuclear reactor is equivalent in energy content to hundreds of tons of coal.

During the twentieth century, advances in the study of radioactivity, nuclear physics, cosmic rays, and elementary particles have shown that atomic nuclei consist of protons and neutrons. But besides these two types of particles and electrons—which had been recognized as distinct entities late in the last century—an enormous bestiary of subnuclear particles have been identified and studied. Reactions and transmutations among these particles involve the release of a few thousand million electron volts, a thousand times greater than energies involved in nuclear reactions.

It is unlikely that we have reached the deepest levels of physical structure. A great deal of effort has been expended since the 1920s in attempting to gain a unified understanding of physics from the very smallest scale to the very largest. The most thorough understanding of small-scale structures and phenomena has come in this century through the development of quantum mechanics; while the most comprehensive understanding of the large scale behavior of the universe and the behavior of very massive objects has been attained through the theory of general relativity. These two branches of modern theoretical physics have transformed science and technology, with drastic revisions in our world-view. At first sight, the underlying philosophical foundations of these two branches of physics appear drastically different from each other and from the foundations of the classical physics of the nineteenth century. Attempts to merge these two theories into a single, unified theory have thus far had limited success, and results to date have been very primitive. Yet these results already suggest that several more layers of physical structure remain to be discovered below the level of structure of elementary particles—each level having energy concentrations a factor of a thousand or a million greater than the level above.

Should these speculations prove to be correct, and if we learn how to tap these far more concentrated energies, to provide new flows of entropy, then at some time in the future—perhaps only decades, but more likely a few centuries away—the possibility of a few thousand people and their supporting ecosystem leaving the solar system aboard a large space colony bound for other solar systems will become real, and Gaian life will have become galactic.

Why is outer space so fascinating and so attractive to so many people? Is this merely a Western-Aristotelian-expansionist infatuation, thoroughly opposed to human spiritual values? Is it just an adolescent, escapist fantasy?

Long before Western science and technology began, a fascination with the heavens above could be found in almost every human culture. The Roman poet Ovid, nearly 2,000 years ago, described the emergence of human consciousness in an image based on this fascination with the heavens:

> God elevated the forehead of Man
> And ordered him to contemplate the stars

Among some of the peoples of Gambia in West Africa, an infant was given its name under the starry sky, as the father held the naked newborn in his uplifted arms, facing the heavens, to whisper in the infant's ear, "Behold the only thing greater than yourself!"

Even if the desire to go into space is an adolescent escapist fantasy, we might do well not to dismiss it lightly, for a society which cannot participate in the dreams and fantasies of children and adolescents is surely a sad and melancholy place.

Oceanographer Jacques-Yves Cousteau argues persuasively that our curiosity and outward movement, wherever we are capable of going, is biological in origin:

> The more time I spend in observing nature, the more I believe that man's motivation for exploration is but the sophistication of a universal, instinctive drive deeply ingrained in all living creatures.
>
> Life is growth: individuals and species grow in size, number, in territorial appetite. The peripheral manifestation of growing is exploring the outside world.

> Plants develop in the most favorable direction, which implies that they have explored the others and found them less adequate. Some plants send shoots—that is, feelers—great distances before they claim the space that has been acknowledged propitious.
>
> For individual animals the world is to be explored and discovered from birth on, and for them, until they die, the wilderness is infinite; and infinity, for a tuna, is the vast ocean. In the animal world the physical need for exploration develops in collectivities as well: tribes, schools, packs—all reach out for new horizons . . .
>
> When the *impulse to explore*, built into each individual human being, is confined or antagonized by a rigid social or familial structure, it may be bent into unnatural drives—alcoholism, drug abuse, or sexual perversions.

We can certainly survive indefinitely into the future with just the material resources of the earth, but I think we would be crippled in our spirit, perhaps fatally damaged, if we were to be arbitrarily confined on this planet long after we have achieved the capability of transcending its gravitational hold on us. The step into space, which will happen in the next few decades, inevitably leads to an endless horizon. Our descendants—and many of us now living—will have limitless possibilities for living, learning, exploring, and loving freely and joyously. Life will have taken another step toward transforming more of the mute, lifeless matter of the universe into sentience and intelligent consciousness; more and more of the substance of the universe will come awake to see and appreciate itself, participating ever more fully in the never-ending process of creation.

IV
Terrestrial Resources: Food

As energy was the dominant resource problem in most of the world in the 1970s, so food is likely to be in the 1980s. The Brazilian scientist Josué de Castro, writing more than 30 years ago, scientifically but not dispassionately analyzed hunger in the modern world and the tendency to ignore or deny its existence rather than prevent or reduce it. The neo-Malthusian view is eloquently expressed by Lester R. Brown, head of the Worldwatch Institute, in Washington, D.C., and the opposite view is stated by sociologist Julian L. Simon, both of whom have access to the same information. Political science professor Robert L. Paarlberg, in a special issue of International Organization *devoted to the global political economy of food, examines the rarely discussed fact that most surplus food flows to the rich countries that can afford it rather than to the poor countries that need it.*

In a journal published in Cairo by the Afro-Asian Peoples' Solidarity Organization, Jacques Choncho considers the world food situation in the aftermath of the UN's World Food Conference, held in Rome in 1974, and advocates a rational program of self-sufficiency for developing countries. Attacking the widely held view that science and technology can solve all of the world's food problems, economist Frank Peacock describes the failure of the "Green Revolution" in Asia. Is it possible that a future "green revolution" will avoid previous mistakes and be successful? Perhaps, but it is by no means certain. The pivotal relationship between food and energy is the subject of the final selection from a speech by Soedjatmoko, the Indonesian rector of United Nations University.

16

The Taboo of Hunger

Josué de Castro

HUNGER A TABOO SUBJECT

The history of man from the beginning has been the history of his struggle for daily bread. It is very difficult to understand how this pretentiously superior animal, this lord and master of the universe who has won so many battles against the forces of nature, should have failed to obtain a decisive victory in his struggle for subsistence. For we know from scientific observation that even today, after some hundreds of thousands of years of striving, two-thirds of the world's population live in a permanent state of hunger. A billion and a half human beings can still not find the means of escaping this most terrible affliction of society.

Is it possible to consider hunger as a phenomenon inherent to life itself, a natural and inevitable contingency like death, or should it be regarded as a social evil, a plague of man's own making? It is with this dangerous and delicate question that [we] . . . will deal. Because of its explosive political and social implications, the subject until very recently has been one of the taboos of our civilization. It has been our highly vulnerable Achilles' heel, a subject which could not safely be discussed in public. Like sex, hunger was shameful, indecent, unclean. It was made untouchable, taboo.

Buddha, in antiquity, said that "hunger and love constitute the germ of all human history," and much later Schiller observed that "hunger and love rule the world." Nevertheless, very little has ever been written about the phenomenon of hunger. The number of books on the subject in any language is shockingly scanty—especially in view of the abundant litera-

---

ture on matters of obviously secondary social importance. What are the hidden motives that have led our culture to abstain from dealing with the problem of hunger, from trying to get at the root of it? It is strange to find that its narrow aspects of sensation, what Spinoza called the impulse and instinct that has served as the motive force of human evolution, have been ignored; but it is even more curious to observe the oppressive silence that has surrounded its broader influence as a universal calamity.

The disparity is most surprising when we compare the case of hunger with the other calamities that have repeatedly devastated the world—with, for example, wars and epidemics. It then becomes painfully clear that it is hunger which is least studied and discussed, least understood in its causes and effects. For each study of the problems of hunger there are over a thousand publications on the problems of war. A ratio of more than a thousand to one! Yet, as this [piece] . . . will abundantly demonstrate, the human waste resulting from hunger is considerably greater than that from wars and epidemics put together. The damage has been more extensive in the number of victims, and a great deal more serious in its biological and social consequences. In the last century the Swiss scientist Waser pointed out that the loss of life brought about by the plague or by war was usually made up in an average period of ten years, while the survivors of great famines were broken for the rest of their lives. But to dissipate any remaining doubts as to the unquestionable leadership of hunger's destructive powers, it is sufficient to emphasize the universally recognized fact that hunger has been the most common and effective cause of war and that it has been the advance agent which prepared the ground for the outbreak of the great epidemics.

Hunger, then, has unquestionably been the most potent source of social misfortunes, but our civilization has kept its eyes averted, afraid to face the sad reality. War has always been loudly discussed. Hymns and poems have been written to celebrate its glorious virtues as an agent of selection. In this civilization of ours, which began mercantilist and ended militarist, an attempt was even made to demonstrate by scientific theory that the existence of war was necessary and in accord with the natural law of life. Thus, while war became a leitmotiv of Western thought, hunger remained only a vulgar sensation, the repercussions of which were not supposed to emerge from the realm of the subconscious. The conscious mind, with ostentatious disdain, denied its existence.

THE PREJUDICES OF WESTERN CIVILIZATION

There were several motives for this conspiracy of silence. First, there was the question of morality; the phenomenon of hunger, whether hunger for food or sexual hunger, is a primary instinct, and there was something shocking about this to a rationalist culture which tried by all possible means to make reason dominate instinct in human conduct. Instinct was held to be animal, while reason alone had social value, and our civilization attempted systematically, though unsuccessfully, to deny the creative power of instinct, treating it as low and indecent.

Since the end of the eighteenth century Western culture, with its Encyclopedists and idealist philosophers, has put forward a concept of man and his behavior which renders him virtually angelic—a being who, from cannibal beginnings, soared on wings of culture to the purest intellectualism, free of animal impulses. But in reality each arrogant optimist of that infatuated nineteenth century, as he spoke of man's magnificent rise and his perfection, felt the indiscreet needling, in his most intimate being, of hunger and sexual desire, the remnants of his primitive bestiality. These cultural idealists thought that they could master the impulses by hiding and smothering them; European civilization made it a point not to mention these subjects. "And for a whole century, an extremely long century," said Stefan Zweig, "this cowardly moral conspiracy of silence dominated Europe." Until one day a genius, inconveniently and providentially, broke the oppressive quiet.

To the pretended astonishment of official science and contemporary morality, Sigmund Freud declared sex to be a force so intense that it extends to, and indeed dominates, the consciousness. Man, before everything else, is sex. This view of mankind was not entirely surprising, but it was inconvenient. Each of Freud's learned colleagues had felt the conflict of sexual instincts in himself, like a hidden abscess he dared not lance publicly for fear of revealing the pus. Freud broke open the abscess. Singlehanded, with opposition and disapproval on all sides, he carried out the lifesaving operation. Since then, it has been possible to speak of sex in a voice above a whisper.

HUNGER AND ECONOMIC IMPERIALISM

There were reasons even stronger than prejudice, reasons rooted in the shrouded world of economic interest, for suppressing discussion of hunger. Dominant and privileged minorities used their deftest sleight of hand to keep the question of hunger from the attention of the modern spirit. It was to the advantage of economic imperialism and international commerce, both controlled by profit-seeking minorities, that the production, distribution, and consumption of food products be regarded as purely business matters rather than as phenomena of the highest importance to society as a whole.

The world's geography expanded in the sixteenth century, and colonial economies followed the extending horizon, raising European civilization toward its zenith of splendor. In the seemingly fine world of imperial Europe there was no place for ugly revelations of starvation, particularly since hunger, too, was a product of the colonial system. Hunger has been chiefly created by the inhuman exploitation of colonial riches, by the latifundia and one-crop culture which lay waste the colony, so that the exploiting country can take too cheaply the raw materials its prosperous industrial economy requires. For economic reasons misery was hidden from the world's eyes; tragedies like that of China, where in the nineteenth century some 100 million individuals starved to death, or like that of India, where 20 million people died of hunger in the last 30 years of the century, were glossed over.

Western literature, inheriting Western culture, bent to its interests and blinded by its splendor, was an accomplice in its silence. A very few authors dared break the taboo and communicate their dark visions of the subterranean world of starvation and suffering: Knut Hamsun in his masterly novel *Hunger,* a detailed report of the confused and contradictory sensations produced by his own hunger; Panait Istrati, wandering famished across the glimmering plains of Rumania; Felekov and Alexander Neverov, describing dramatically the intense black hunger of Russia in convulsion; George Fink, starving in the gray and sordid suburbs of Berlin; and John Steinbeck telling, in *The Grapes of Wrath,* the story of the Joad family's epic journey of hunger across the richest lands of the richest country in the world. These and a few others were voices crying in the wilderness of indifference.

Western science and technique, brilliantly victorious over the forces of nature, failed almost entirely to do battle with hunger. The scientists kept a pointed silence about the living conditions of the world's hungry masses; consciously or unconsciously, they became accomplices in the conspiracy. The social reality of hunger stayed outside their laboratory walls.

Science, then, was catastrophically unprepared for the Allied liberation of the Nazi concentration camps. On April 12, 1945, Allied medical men and Red Cross technicians entered the horror camp of Bergen Belsen to find thousands of people in the last stages of starvation. They did not know what to do for them. They began medical treatment by feeding, orally, predigested foods, or, in the graver cases, by giving intravenous injections. The results were disastrous. Ingestion by mouth was very poorly tolerated, and injections increased the edemas which had come from starvation. Doctors and nurses had to watch the horrible reactions of their patients, who thought that this was a new form of torture. It took time and the sacrifice of many lives to learn that the best nourishment for such cases is skim milk.

Sir Jack Drummond, the great English specialist on nutrition, published an account of the Bergen Belsen episode three years ago. In spite of the enormous progress that has been made in the science of nutrition, he said, and "although in our lifetimes millions have died from starvation in Russia, China, India and elsewhere, it was not possible to find clear-cut advice how to resuscitate people who are near death from this cause. That fact," he commented, "is a terrible reflection on our lack of concern for the human race as a whole."

The story of Bergen Belsen's liberation constitutes a tremendous accusation against our Western civilization. It was necessary for famine to return and ravish Europe itself before Western science took an interest in combating it. Two terrible world wars were necessary, as well as a great social revolution—the Russian Revolution, in which 17 million people perished, 12 million of them from starvation—before Western civilization was persuaded that trying to conceal the reality of hunger was like trying to shut out the sun with a sieve.

The force of inexorable circumstance finally began to overcome the taboo on hunger. Scientists became interested, and they were permitted to study the subject objectively. Nations were urged to publish statistics on the real living conditions of their populations, and there was a move to stimulate publication of reports and essays on the forbidden subject.

THE WORLD AND THE SOCIAL REVOLUTION

The underlying reason for such a radical change of attitude is that the world is now passing through a revolutionary phase in its history. The two world wars and the Russian Revolution were no more than visible symptoms of the developing world revolution, cataclysmic manifestations of the impact of social forces seeking to remove obstacles from their path. But in order to make the dangerous statement, We are living in a world revolution, it is necessary to define "revolution."

The word "revolution" is used here not in the sense of violent overthrow of constituted authority and the seizure of power, but as meaning a process of transformation of the whole, a historical transmutation which replaces one world of social beliefs by another in which the former social values no longer have meaning. I use the term "revolutionary phase of history" to refer to what Ortega y Gasset calls the "historical crisis." The Spanish philosopher explains the historical process as taking place in two ways: by the successive change of things within our world, or by a change in the world as a whole. The former is a question of "historical evolution," while the latter represents a "crisis" or "historical revolution." In our times we are witnessing a complete overhauling of the social systems and ways of life that were in effect at the beginning of the century; we are passing from one social era to another.

Julian Huxley attempted to characterize the two eras of our age by calling that which is past the "era of economic man," and that of the future the "era of social man." And, indeed, the most noticeable feature of the violent contrast between these two worlds (both embraced by the life of one generation) is a shift of the center of interest. Until the First World

War, Western civilization, with its exaggerated economism, was exclusively preoccupied with the technical domination of the forces of nature. And while it was thus engaged with the problems of economic exploitation and the creation of wealth, man and his problems were almost entirely forgotten. In the postwar world, however, what we see on all sides—in both the capitalist West and the sovietized East—is a concentrated interest in biological man as a concrete entity, a sort of priority conceded to human problems over strictly economic problems. This does not mean that in the "era of social man" economics will be relegated to a secondary level, but rather that it will be oriented to function in the interest of human welfare. The democracies in our day have shown themselves to be deeply concerned with the protection and biological revalorization of man, while the USSR has developed its five-year plans in accordance with the principle of so-called Communist humanism. Present-day economic activity has ceased to be the art of establishing lucrative enterprises alone; economics is today a science that has been said to teach methods of promoting "a greater quantity of economic welfare." There are good prospects in this new era of making money serve man, instead of making man the slave of money; of organizing production to satisfy the fundamental needs of various groups of human beings, rather than letting men go on killing each other in an attempt to slake their insatiable thirst for the profits of production.

An interest in man and in the rehumanization of culture is the common denominator of both the great economic systems that are now struggling for universal supremacy. It seems to me that capitalist democracy and Russian "democracy" do not represent two worlds in irreconcilable struggle, but rather two poles of a single world. As social poles they have their differences and peculiarities, but the growing interest of man in man himself and the anxious search for means of collective betterment mark an area where the two systems must converge. As they come closer together they must necessarily resolve their conflicts, since they must both face the circumstance that men who live together have to get along with each other.

As our taboos were broken, and our social goals started to change, interesting studies of hunger began to appear. In 1928 the League of Nations put the problem of alimentation of populations on its permanent agenda; the League's Organization on Hygiene sponsored investigations in several countries and a series of valuable reports was published. The very first inquiries, carried on with strictly scientific method in the most varied regions of the world, revealed the alarming fact that more than two-thirds of humanity live in a permanent state of hunger.

This shocking situation, at a crucial moment of history when our only hope of finding the way to survival is to recognize the great errors of our civilization, has led the conscience of mankind to a radical change of attitude toward the problem. We have set out to face it with courage, and to solve it with energy.

Evidence of this new spirit was the first postwar conference on world reconstruction, the Food Conference called by the United Nations at Hot Springs in 1943. There the experts of 44 nations frankly confessed the nutritional facts of their countries' lives, and planned the joint steps necessary to fulfill their needs. They proposed to erase, or at least to lighten, those black areas which represent, on maps of qualitative demography, the nuclei of undernourished and starving populations. These groups, in their physical and cultural inferiority, in their alarming death rates and their incidence of deficiency diseases like beriberi, pellagra, scurvy, xerophthalmia, rickets, osteomalacia, endemic goiter, and anemias, show their organic lacks, their total or specific hungers for one, for several, sometimes for all the elements indispensable to human nourishment.

Hunger is the most degrading of adversities; it demonstrates the inability of existing culture to satisfy the most fundamental human necessities, and it always implies society's guilt. To combat and exterminate it as the Food Conference hoped to do, it will be necessary to have broader and more intense studies of nutrition throughout the world. Every student's observations ought to be published, as contributions to the preparation of a universal plan.

One great obstacle to adequate planning is our lack of knowledge of the problem as a whole. The question of feeding the peoples of the world involves a complex of manifestations, biological, economic, and social. Most scientific studies of nutrition limit themselves to one or another of its aspects and give only a unilateral view of its problems. They are almost always written by physiologists, chemists, or economists, specialists whose professional lives are limited to one field.

THE CIVILIZATION OF THE SPECIALISTS

Such narrowness of outlook is characteristic of Western civilization. Since the middle of the nineteenth century a kind of university instruction has developed which is no longer interested in transmitting a unified image of the world, but rather in isolating, and mutilating, facets of reality, in the supposed interest of science. The tremendous impact of scientific progress produced a fragmentation of culture and pulverized it into little grains of learning. Each scientific specialist seized his granule and turned it over and over beneath the powerful lens of his microscope, striving to penetrate its microcosm, with a marvelous indifference to and a towering ignorance of everything around him. Recently in Europe and the United States an extreme development of this type of university education has created within the culture a sort of civilization *sui generis*—a specialists' civilization—directed by men whose scientific outlook is rigorous but who suffer from a deplorable cultural and political myopia. Ortega y Gasset has called them the "new barbarians—men ever more and more learned, and less and less cultured." Worst of all, such men are the dominant type of our cultural elite, representatives of the social dynamic which has brought us to what Rathenau so aptly called "the vertical invasion of the barbarians." The narrow specialists, "men who know more and more about less and less," are one of the most dangerous elements in our cultural life.

As a consequence of the specialists' techniques, we find that even after the cultural barriers were broken few students faced the problem of hunger in its worldwide perspective, its multiple and correlated aspects. Some serious researchers, trying to explain and solve the problem of famine, did direct attention to our classic dilemma of food production in relation to population. The works of Lord Boyd-Orr, Imre Ferenczi, Frank Boudreau, and a few others can be considered to have a broad outlook and to be genuinely scientific. Some of the reports of the Food and Agriculture Organization of the United Nations, such as the *World Food Survey* published in 1946, have the same objectivity. Unfortunately, the problem of hunger constitutes such a pointed social question that most of the speculative works dealing with it are not free of current political prejudices and superstitions.

17

Global Food Prospects: Shadow of Malthus

Lester R. Brown

We are still in the early part of the new decade, but it is already clear that the worldwide effort to expand food production is losing momentum. The grain surpluses accumulated in food-exporting countries during the 1950s and 1960s have disappeared. Even though idled U.S. cropland recently has been returned to production, world food supplies are tightening and the slim margin between food production and population growth continues to narrow.

As the oil outlook changes, so too does the food prospect. The era of cheap oil that helped underwrite the explosive growth in world food output during the century's third quarter is now history. The depletion of oil reserves makes it more difficult to expand food production, even as the need to shift to alternative energy sources is setting up a new competition between the energy and food sectors for agricultural resources.

THE LOSS OF MOMENTUM

The middle of the twentieth century was a watershed in the evolution of world agriculture. From the beginning of agriculture until 1950, most increases in food output came from expanding the area under cultivation. Since then, most have come from raising yields on existing cropland. This drive to raise yields has made agriculture increasingly energy-intensive. Chemical fertilizers, irrigation, and mechanization—the primary means of expanding production—are all energy-intensive. In

Reprint of "Global Food Prospects: Shadow of Malthus" by Lester R. Brown in *Challenge* (January/February 1982). Based on *Building A Sustainable Society* (W. W. Norton, 1981). Pp. 14–21.

effect, as the frontiers disappeared, farmers learned to substitute energy for land.

The disappearance of frontiers notwithstanding, midcentury also marked the beginning of an unprecedented growth in food production. Between 1950 and 1971, the world's farmers increased grain production from 631 million tons to 1,237 million tons (see Table 1). In just 21 years, they nearly doubled output. In per capita terms, this period was also one of impressive progress. World cereal production per person climbed from 251 kilograms in 1950 to 330 kilograms in 1971, a gain of 31 percent. Diets improved measurably in many Third World countries, and consumption of livestock products climbed steadily throughout the industrial world.

Since 1971, gains in output have barely kept pace with population growth; production per person has fluctuated widely but shown little real increase. Indeed, per capita grain production of 324 kilograms in 1980, an unusually poor harvest, was actually lower than the 330 kilograms of 1971. As food prices have climbed, diets have deteriorated in some Third World countries, especially among landless laborers and the urban poor. In some industrial societies, tightening grain supplies have led to a drop in per capita consumption of beef and other livestock products.

The long postwar period of food-price stability came to an end with the massive Soviet wheat purchase in 1972. The largest food-import deal in history, it signaled the beginning of a new era. Within months, the

TABLE 1 World Grain Production, Total and Per Capita, 1950–80

Year	Population (billions)	Grain Production (million metric tons)	Grain Production per Capita (kilograms)
1950	2.51	631	251
1960	3.03	863	285
1970	3.68	1137	309
1971	3.75	1237	330
1972	3.82	1197	314
1973	3.88	1290	332
1974	3.96	1256	317
1975	4.03	1275	316
1976	4.11	1384	337
1977	4.18	1378	330
1978	4.26	1494	351
1979	4.34	1437	331
1980 (prel.)	4.42	1432	324

Source: U.S. Department of Agriculture and United Nations.

world price of wheat had doubled and famine had returned to the Indian subcontinent, Africa, and elsewhere after a quarter-century absence.

Until 1976 shortfalls in harvests prevented a rebuilding of the world food reserves depleted in 1972. With some uncommonly good harvests in the late 1970s, the food situation then stabilized temporarily. But in 1980, a poor harvest in the Soviet Union and a mediocre one in the United States resulted in a drawdown of world food reserves to a near-record low. Inefficient agrarian structures, soil erosion, the conversion of prime cropland to nonfarm uses, the falling yield response to chemical fertilizers in the agriculturally advanced countries, and rising energy costs—all contributed to the slower growth in food output.

THE NORTH AMERICAN BREADBASKET

More and more countries in which grain production has not kept pace with demand have come to rely on North America's exportable surplus (see Table 2). Prior to World War II, Western Europe was the only grain-importing region. North America was not the only exporter nor even the leading one. During the late 1930s, Latin American grain exports were nearly double those of North America, and Eastern Europe (including the Soviet Union) was exporting 5 million tons annually, the same amount as North America. All this has now changed beyond recognition. Asia has developed a massive deficit. Africa, Latin America, and Eastern Europe all import food. Western Europe, consistently importing 15 to 30 million tons, has been the most stable element throughout the period. North America's emergence as the world's breadbasket began in the 1940s. The scale of exports expanded gradually during the 1950s and 1960s, but then more than doubled during the 1970s as scores of countries began to lose the capacity to feed themselves.

TABLE 2 The Changing Pattern of World Grain Trade*

Region	1934–38	1948–52	1960	1970	1980
		(million metric tons)			
North America	+ 5	+ 23	+ 39	+ 56	+ 131
Latin America	+ 9	+ 1	0	+ 4	− 10
Western Europe	− 24	− 22	− 25	− 30	− 16
Eastern Europe and USSR	+ 5	0	0	0	− 46
Africa	+ 1	0	− 2	− 5	− 15
Asia	+ 2	− 6	− 17	− 37	− 63
Australia and New Zealand	+ 3	+ 3	+ 6	+ 12	+ 19

*Plus sign indicates net exports; minus sign, net imports.

Source: Food and Agriculture Organization, U.S. Department of Agriculture, and author's estimates.

This dramatic transformation of intercontinental food flows reflects wide differences in population growth, widely varying levels of agricultural management, and, in many countries, a rate of soil erosion that is draining cropland of its fertility. As recently as 1950, for example, North America and Latin America had roughly equal populations—163 and 168 million, respectively. But while North America's population growth has tapered off substantially since then, Latin America's has escalated. Mexico, Venezuela, Peru, and Brazil all have population growth rates of close to 3 percent per year. Had North America's 1950 population expanded at 3 percent per year, it would have reached 395 million in 1980 (rather than the actual 248 million) and absorbed virtually all the region's exportable surplus, leaving it struggling to maintain self-sufficiency.

Today, over 100 countries rely on North American grain. The worldwide movement of countries from export to import status is a much traveled one-way street. The reasons vary, but the tide is strong: no country has gone against it since World War II. Literally scores of countries have become food importers, but not one significant new exporter has emerged.

Not only are more countries joining the legions of importers, but the degree of reliance on outside supplies is growing. More and more nations, both industrial and developing, are importing more food than they produce. Among the countries that now import over half of their grain supply are Algeria, Belgium, Japan, Lebanon, Libya, Saudi Arabia, Senegal, Switzerland, and Venezuela. Other countries rapidly approaching primary dependence on imported foodstuffs include Costa Rica, Egypt, Portugal, South Korea, and Sri Lanka.

For most countries, the need for imported food is more likely to increase than decrease. Agricultural mismanagement and inefficiency have taken their toll on food production, particularly in the Third World and the centrally planned economies of Eastern Europe. It is difficult, for example, to see how the Soviet Union can avoid importing even more grain in the near future. In the late 1930s, the Soviet Union and Eastern Europe still had a regional export surplus of several million tons of grain yearly. But since then, the food balance has slowly shifted. Throughout the 1960s, the Soviet Union teetered on the brink of food self-sufficiency, sometimes as exporter, sometimes as importer. But with Moscow's decision in 1972 to offset crop shortfalls by importing grain rather than by slaughtering the livestock herds, the Soviet Union emerged as a chronically food-deficit country. During the mid-1970s, grain imports averaged 9 million tons per year. Late in the decade, they were averaging some 20 million tons per year. Even though U.S. grain shipments to the Soviet Union were restricted in January 1980 following the Soviet invasion of Afghanistan, the Soviets began the new decade by importing 31 million tons of grain in its first year, more than any country in history.

Although the Soviet Union has the largest cropland area of any country, the inefficiency of its agricultural system represents a problem Moscow planners seem unable to solve. The factory-style organization of agriculture on the state farms and the size of the collectives weaken the key link between effort and reward for those who work the land. Consequently, production on Soviet agricultural collectives and giant state farms cannot approach that of the family-farm system that dominates West European and North American agriculture.

Other countries also face rapidly growing deficits. Egypt has little opportunity for expanding its agricultural base and yet its population is growing rapidly. According to the International Food Policy Research Institute projections, Nigeria will have a food deficit of at least 17 million tons of grain in 1990 if recent trends continue. Mexican grain imports are growing by leaps and bounds, and unless Mexico loses an even larger fraction of its population through illegal migration to the United States, this trend is likely to continue. The story is fundamentally the same in scores of countries.

Although the need for imported grain is projected to continue growing, the capacity of North America to respond to these demands may ultimately be overwhelmed. The disappearance of idled cropland, the growing use of U.S. grain in alcohol fuel distilleries, and the projected decline in irrigated acreage in key farm states will all make it more difficult to sustain the rapid growth in North American exports on which the world has none too wisely come to rely.

Behind this trade issue, a philosophical debate is beginning to emerge on the wisdom of mining soils in order to meet the ever growing world demand. Many agricultural analysts and environmentalists now argue that it makes little sense to sacrifice a resource that has been a source of economic strength since colonial days merely to buy a few billion barrels of oil. Others contend that the current generation of farmers has no right to engage in the agronomic equivalent of deficit financing and thus mortgage the future of generations to come. The current trend is fraught with risks both for those whose livelihoods depend on land being productive and for those in countries dependent on food imports that will dry up if the mining of soil continues. Even for the importers, lower imports and a reduction in pressure on North American soil resources in the short term would be better than losing the region's export capacity over the long run.

GROWING FOOD INSECURITY

From the late 1940s through the early 1970s, the world enjoyed an unprecedented period of food security. Carryover stocks of grain, held largely by the principal exporters, and cropland idled under farm programs in the United States accounted for that security. Grain carryover stocks—the grain in bins when the new harvest begins—were available for use when needed. Idled U.S. cropland could be brought back into production within a year. Together, these two reserves provided security for all mankind, a cushion against any imaginable disaster.

As recently as 1969, the amount of grain that either was held in storage or that could be produced within a season on idled U.S. cropland amounted to 91 days of world consumption. Following poor harvests in key producing countries in 1972 and 1974, world reserves fell to only 40 days (see Table 3). At this level, grain stocks constituted little more than pipeline supplies, barely enough to fill the supply line between the farmer and the ultimate consumer.

The world enters the 1980s with only one of the two traditional reserves—carryover stocks of grain. For the first time in a generation, there is no cropland idled under U.S. farm programs. The loss of this reserve, which provided security for the entire world, may be permanent. Carryover stocks of grain in 1980 amounted to 40 days of consumption. In 1981, they [were] . . . expected to fall further. Except for 1974 and 1975, when reserves fell to 40 days of consumption after bad weather reduced the harvest, food supplies have not been this low since World War II.

World food insecurity was exacerbated by the extension of agriculture onto marginal lands. While climate has changed little in recent years, the vulnerability to climatic anomalies is undoubtedly increasing. Meteorologist Kenneth Hare observes that "the Sahelian drought in Africa, for example, had several predecessors over the previous 500 years. What has changed is the vulnerability of the human economy."

TABLE 3 Index of World Food Security, 1960–80

Year	Reserve Stocks of Grain	Grain Equivalent of Idled U.S. Cropland (million metric tons)	Total Reserves	Reserves as Days of World Consumption (days)
1960	198	36	234	102
1965	143	70	213	80
1970	165	71	236	77
1971	183	46	229	73
1972	142	78	220	66
1973	147	25	172	51
1974	132	4	136	40
1975	138	3	141	40
1976	192	3	195	55
1977	191	1	192	51
1978	218	21	239	62
1979	191	15	206	51
1980	151	0	151	40

Source: Worldwatch Institute derived from U.S. Department of Agriculture data.

Global food insecurity mounts inexorably as agriculture is extended into marginal areas because the food economy is now global. Although the Soviet "virgin lands" are a major source of bread for Soviet tables, they are in an area of light and highly variable rainfall, subject to crop failure in one year of every three or four. When the decision was made in Moscow to offset these periodic shortfalls by increasing imports, the instability that had been confined to the Soviet food economy began to affect the supply and price of food for the entire world.

Soil erosion also contributes to food supply instability. When the organic matter in soil is reduced as a result of erosion, the soil's water-retention capacity declines so that the land becomes more vulnerable to short-term dry spells. A study by the U.S. Center for Environmental Assessment Services showed that eroded soils that had a yield 30 percent less than a noneroded control plot also had a yield that was four times more variable. Too often, efforts to expand output by extending cultivation onto marginal land increase harvest variability and global food insecurity.

Another source of world food insecurity is the dependence of the entire world on North America for food supplies. This unhealthy dependence has both meteorological and political dimensions, since both the United States and Canada are affected by the same climatic cycles and since heavy dependence on any two countries for grain vests these countries with extraordinary political power. Both the United States and Canada already embargo the export of grain under certain conditions. The United States halted grain shipments to both the Soviet Union and Poland in the fall of 1975 because grain prices at home were rising too fast, while Canada refused to license wheat exports in 1975 until it could more precisely determine the size of its harvest.

Stripped of its reserves, the international community can no longer be counted on to respond effectively to crop shortages in poor countries. During the 1950s and 1960s, the story was quite different. Then the United States intervened unilaterally with food-aid shipments wherever famine threatened. For example, after consecutive monsoon failures in India in 1965 and 1966, the United States shipped a fifth of its wheat crop to that country two years in a row to avert famine.

The food scarcities and oscillating grain prices of the 1970s affected all countries, but the poorest ones suffered most. One of the hardest hit was Bangladesh. With two poor harvests during the 1970s, Bangladesh saw death rates climb sharply twice. An estimated 427,000 lives were lost in 1971–72 and another 330,000 in 1974–75.

India, too, was hard hit during the 1970s. After a weak monsoon and a poor harvest in 1972, the Indian government discovered that the Soviet Union had tied up most of the world's exportable wheat supplies, leaving little for India to use to offset its poor harvest. Thus, the Indian government sat by helplessly while food consumption fell and death rates climbed. The increase in death rates above the previous year in the three poorest states of Uttar Pradesh, Bihar, and Orissa claimed an estimated 829,000 lives. This loss of life in India alone far exceeded the total combat fatalities suffered in any war since World War II.

During the 1970s, hunger also took a heavy toll in Africa, where a prolonged drought in the Sahel brought the deteriorating food situation into sharp focus. Senegal, Mauritania, Niger, Upper Volta, Chad, and Mali—all lost lives. No one knows exactly how many died of starvation and hunger-related disease, though Cornell nutritionist Michael Latham testified before the U.S. Congress that the number may have been in excess of 100,000. Further east in Africa, the ecological deterioration of Ethiopia's food system was also made all too apparent by a drought that claimed an estimated 200,000 lives and brought Haile Selassie's 47-year reign to an end. In Somalia, too, thousands died of severe malnutrition and disease in 1975; many of them perished after they reached relief camps.

Although grain stocks were partially rebuilt in the late 1970s, after these calamities occurred in Africa and Asia, the global supply-demand balance has remained delicate, as the sensitivity of commodity prices to weather reports indicates. Now a poor harvest in a major producing country can set off a wave of global inflation. In poor countries, where rising food prices can push death rates upward, reduced harvests can have a demographic, as well as an economic, impact.

Following the grim experiences of the early 1970s, the United Nations convened a World Food Conference in Rome in November 1974. In addition to the general agreement on a greater effort to expand world food output, there was also agreement on the need to create an international food reserve. After years of negotiation, little progress has been made. In late 1980 the United States passed the Food Security Act which finally establishes a modest food reserve with an initial input of four million tons, to assist countries experiencing severe food shortages. This aside, the international community has made little progress in building an effective international food reserve.

LAND PRODUCTIVITY TRENDS

In a world where 70 million new residents are added each year and where little fertile land awaits the plow, land productivity is the key to the food prospect. From the beginning of agriculture until World War II, productivity edged upward only slowly, sometimes remaining static for long stretches. Rice yields in nineteenth-century Japan, for instance, were only marginally higher than those obtained during the fourteenth century. U.S. corn yields during the 1930s were no higher than those during the 1860s, the first decade for which reliable yields estimates are available.

Following World War II, however, crop yields began to rise in a sustained, systematic fashion in virtually every industrial country. During the 1960s, the introduction of the fertilizer-responsive varieties of wheat and rice enabled many Third World countries to raise food output per hectare too. Between midcentury and the early 1970s the steady rise in cereal yield per hectare was one of the most predictable trends in the world economy, increasing at an average of 2.2 percent annually. Since 1970, however, the rate has fallen to 1.5 percent per year (see Table 4).

Numerous factors appear responsible for the slower rate of yield increase. In the great majority of situations, the new cropland being brought under the plow is of lower quality than the land already in use. Often the marginal land added replaces the prime land that is continually being withdrawn for nonfarm uses, leading to a reduction in land quality that is not evident from data on overall cropland area.

Also sapping farmland productivity is the reduction of fallow area in dryland farming regions. As world wheat prices rose between 1969 and 1974, U.S. summer fallow land dropped from 17 million hectares to 13 million. This shrinkage led Kenneth Grant, then head of the Soil Conservation Service, to warn farmers that the other side of the lure of record wheat prices and short-term gains is the sacrifice of the land's long-term productivity. The stresses are evident in other dryland farming regions as well. The U.S. agricultural attaché in Moscow reported a strikingly similar reduction in fallow land in the Soviet Union from 17 million hectares to 12 million after the massive crop shortfall and heavy imports of 1972.

In tropical and subtropical regions, where fallowing has evolved as a method of restoring fertility, mounting population pressures are forcing shifting cultivators to shorten rotation cycles and thus to undermine the land's productivity. For example, in Nigeria, where farming has been expanded onto marginal land and fallow cycles shortened, cereal yields have been falling since the early 1960s. A World Bank study of Nigeria

TABLE 4 World Production, Harvested Area, and Yield of Cereals, 1950–80

Year	Production (million metric tons)	Area (million hectares)	Yield (metric tons per hectare)
1950	631	601	1.05
1960	863	682	1.26
1970	1137	704	1.62
1980	1432	758	1.89

Source: U.S. Department of Agriculture.

reports that "fallow periods under shifting cultivation have become too short to restore fertility in some areas." In some locales, the original cropping cycle of 10 to 15 years has already been reduced to 5.

While the shortening of fallow cycles is reducing land productivity in some countries, soil erosion is reducing it in others. One of the big unknowns facing agricultural analysts is how rapidly excessive soil erosion will reduce land productivity. If this erosion continues in the U.S. Corn Belt, the U.S. Department of Agriculture estimates that "potential corn and soybean yields would probably be reduced by 15 to 30 percent on some soils by the year 2030." A study of the erosion of Piedmont soils in Georgia showed a six-inch loss of topsoil reducing average yields 41 percent. A similar degree of erosion in west Tennessee led to a 42 percent drop in corn yields.

While enormous opportunities for raising cropland productivity exist in some countries, the outlook for further dramatic worldwide increases appears less hopeful now than at midcentury. Soil erosion is lowering the inherent fertility of perhaps one-fifth of the world's cropland, while the backlog of new agricultural technologies in the agriculturally advanced countries is dwindling. Together, these two factors cast a formidable shadow over the prospect of a continuing rapid rise in land productivity.

THE NEW FOOD-FUEL COMPETITION

As the 1980s begin, the long-standing competition between food and feed is expanding to include fuel. In the past, the energy sector has supported the food sector, providing fuel for fertilizer and pesticide production, tillage, harvesting, crop drying, and numerous other farm-related processes. With energy subsidizing agriculture, the earth's population-sustaining capacity increased dramatically. But now, as the shortage of liquid fuels grows, energy producers are beginning to compete with food producers for limited agricultural resources.

In the rush to develop indigenous liquid fuels to replace imported oil, alcohol distilled from farm commodities has emerged as a short-run alternative. Several countries have already launched agriculturally based alcohol-fuel programs. Brazil, the United States, and the Philippines have major programs to convert agricultural commodities into alcohol for use as an automotive fuel, while Australia, New Zealand, and South Africa have programs either in operation or on the drawing board. For countries buffeted by soaring oil prices and fearful of supply disruptions, the prospect of an indigenous substitute for some of the imported oil is reassuring, but it means that automobiles now compete with people and livestock for the harvest.

Until recently, the claims of the poor and the affluent on the earth's agricultural resources have not diverged by more than a factor of five, the difference between an affluent diet rich in livestock products and a grain-based subsistence diet. If energy crops are figured in, however, the ratio increases dramatically, since an automobile run on alcohol requires far more grain than a person does. Satisfying the annual food needs of a typical Third World consumer requires roughly one quarter of an acre of cropland, whereas the more affluent diet in an industrial society requires nearly an acre. By contrast, a typical American car fueled entirely by ethanol would require processing over seven tons of grain per year—the output from nine acres of average grain land. In Western Europe, where cars are more fuel-efficient and are driven less, the typical automobile could be run on a little over three tons of grain per year. These numbers are in a sense hypothetical because no country except Brazil is running automobiles exclusively on alcohol and because grain is by no means the only commodity from which alcohol can be made. Nonetheless, the figures do indicate how quickly alcohol fuel programs could absorb vast amounts of grain.

Providing gasohol (a 10 percent alcohol blend) for the typical U.S. car would each year require 1,460 pounds of grain, or slightly less grain than the average American annually consumes directly or indirectly as food. Accordingly, the cropland requirements of an American car owner who switches to grain-based gasohol would nearly double—rising from .9 to 1.7 acres. To the degree that the protein-rich by-product of the distillation process, distiller's dried grain, can be used successfully as livestock feed, the land requirement could be reduced. But if liquid fuel is used to produce and distill the grain, more land will be required to produce sufficient net amounts of liquid fuel. In the second case, headway toward reducing oil imports will be made two steps forward, one back.

For food-exporting countries, the immediate appeal of converting exportable food surpluses into alcohol fuel is undeniable. But in a world that has little if any excess food production capacity, channeling foodstuffs into automotive fuel production will inevitably drive food prices upward. For the world's affluent, such rises in food prices may lead to belt tightening; but for the several hundred million people who are already spending most of their meager incomes on food, rising food prices will further narrow the thin margin of survival.

THE FOOD PRICE PROSPECT

As the demand for food continues to press against the supply, inevitably real food prices will rise. The question no longer seems to be whether they will rise but how much. Since midcentury the growth in world grain production has unmistakably lost momentum. Expanding at well over 3 percent per year during the 1950s, growth fell to just over 2 percent annually during the 1970s.

In efforts to eliminate hunger, this loss of momentum is aggravated by the heavily skewed distribution of income both within and among countries. Incomes among the wealthier one-fifth of humanity are easily 20 times those of the poorest one-fifth. Similar ratios exist between the wealthiest and poorest fifths within societies where wealth is concentrated in a few hands, such as Iraq, Senegal, Brazil, Ecuador, and Mexico. Without effective efforts to redistribute income, meaningful progress in the eradication of hunger is unlikely.

The worldwide loss of agricultural momentum is serious in itself. But more serious are the gathering forces behind this loss. It is becoming ever more difficult to expand the cropland base, and soil erosion's toll on productivity is continuing unabated. Returns on the use of chemical fertilizer at the margin are also diminishing. Each of these forces promises to become an even stronger drag on the growth of food production during the 1980s.

It is tempting to look to science and technology for help. But at the moment new agricultural technologies provide only small comfort. Hopes run high for increasing the photosynthetic efficiency of major crops and for developing cereals that can fix nitrogen. But these advances represent major feats of biological engineering, feats that cannot be taken for granted. If commercial nitrogen-fixing cereals become a reality, they will reduce energy requirements in agriculture but not necessarily increase output. Moreover, beyond these two possibilities there does not appear to be anything on the technological drawing board that could lead to quantum jumps in world food output. We cannot expect gains such as those made possible in postwar agriculture by the use of chemical fertilizer, improved seeds, and irrigation.

Perhaps more than anything else, the price of food will be influenced by oil price rises. After the price of oil began its rapid climb in late 1973, it left the comparatively stable price of food far behind. But there are signs that food prices are beginning a long-term climb as well. Even as the price of liquid fuels required for farming rises, agriculture is being seen by more and more governments as a source of liquid fuels. With hundreds of large distilleries newly on line, under construction, or in the planning stage, the diversion of agricultural resources to automotive fuel production could escalate rapidly. In 1980, Brazil devoted nearly 1 million hectares of cropland to the production of sugarcane for automotive fuel; the United States used some 80,000 hectares to produce grain that was converted into alcohol fuel; and the Philippines started marketing "alcogas" made from sugarcane.

The sharp shift in the terms of trade between oil and grain tempts populous, oil-exporting countries that are having problems in agriculture to import more food. For these countries, which include the Soviet Union, Nigeria, Mexico, and China, the terms of exchange between oil and grain are exceedingly attractive, and they are rapidly expanding their food imports as the 1980s begin. This extraordinary leverage in the world grain market is driving food prices upward far more rapidly than was possible when a barrel of oil and a bushel of wheat had the same value. The effect is clear: the price of oil is gradually pulling the price of food upward in its wake.

This new relationship between the food and energy sectors makes food projections more complicated than ever before. The principal cushion now remaining in the world food economy is the grain that is fed to livestock. This grain could easily be made available for human consumption in times of shortage, though so far it has been diverted from livestock only when the price climbs to a level that induces widespread starvation.

The food price prospect inspires concern, not optimism. Just as the 1970s dramatically underscored the new energy realities, the 1980s promise to do the same for food. Indeed, rising food prices may become a more or less permanent feature of the economic landscape in the years ahead. Few, if any, economic indicators are as politically sensitive as food prices.

18

World Food Supplies

Julian L. Simon

The prediction that food production cannot keep up with population growth has been made repeatedly for more than a decade. For example, in 1968, Paul Ehrlich declared in his best-selling book *The Population Bomb* that "the battle to feed all humanity is over. In the 1970's the world will undergo famines—hundreds of millions of people are going to starve to death." In 1975, the United Nations Economic and Social Commission for Asia and the Pacific predicted "500 million starvation deaths in Asia between 1980 and 2025." The following year, the head of the United Nations Food and Agriculture Organization (UNFAO), Edouard Saoma, described the long-term prospects for food production in developing countries as "alarmingly inadequate." In 1975, a full-page advertisement sponsored by the Environmental Fund appeared in leading newspapers. It stated:

> The world as we know it will likely be ruined before the year 2000 and the reason for this will be its inhabitants' failure to comprehend two facts. These facts are:
>
> 1. World food production cannot keep pace with the galloping growth of population.
>
> 2. "Family planning" cannot and will not, in the foreseeable future, check this runaway growth.

Reprint of "World Food Supplies," Julian L. Simon, *Atlantic*,(Vol. 247, No. 7 July 1981).Copyright©1981 by Princeton University Press. Revised from Chapter 4 of *The Ultimate Resource*, Copyright©1981 by Princeton University Press. Reprinted by permission of Atlantic Monthly Company and Princeton University Press. Pp. 72–76.

The ad was signed by Isaac Asimov, Zbigniew Brzezinski, Malcolm Cowley, Paul Ehrlich, Clifton Fadiman, J. Paul Getty, Henry Luce III, Archibald MacLeish, Albert Szent-Gyorgyi, DeWitt Wallace, and Leonard Woodcock, among others.

Over the past ten years, such pronouncements have multiplied; they seem now to be regarded as facts of life rather than as conjectures. Some people see in these assertions a warrant for triage: the policy of abandoning the least fit in order to concentrate on victims who have a decent chance of surviving. A book by William and Paul Paddock, *Famine—1975!,* applied this wartime medical concept to food aid and produced the following judgments:

Haiti	Can't-be-saved
Egypt	Can't-be-saved
The Gambia	Walking wounded
Tunisia	Should receive food
Libya	Walking wounded
India	Can't-be-saved
Pakistan	Should receive food

A more severe version of triage is the "lifeboat ethic," proposed by the biologist Garrett Hardin (see "A Conversation with Garrett Hardin," by Harold Hayes, May 1981, *Atlantic*). Hardin argues against giving food to starving people, on the grounds that such aid abets population growth, which will leave future generations worse off.

Despite the popular consensus, buttressed by scientists of various disciplines, that the world is heading toward agricultural ruin, the view of mainstream agricultural economists is quite the contrary. It is an accepted idea among agricultural economists that the trend—as revealed in recent decades by statistics and in the more distant past by historical evidence—has been toward improvement in the food supplies of almost every main population group. For example, in 1973, even before the recent years of bumper harvests, D. Gale Johnson, who teaches agricultural economics at the University of Chicago, told the American Statistical Association that food supply had increased at least enough to match population growth in developing countries for four decades. He discerned a gradual improvement in per capita food consumption for the past two centuries.

The principal evidence for optimism is the record of food production, as represented by data collected by the UNFAO from member countries and by the U.S. Department of Agriculture [USDA] from 104 countries and from American agricultural attachés.

Production of food (as measured by food's adjusted value on the market in a given year, divided by the world population) was either 28 percent or 37 percent higher in 1979 than in the 1948–52 base period, according to the UNFAO and the USDA, respectively. The difference arises partly from the inclusion of China in the UNFAO figures, and in any case does not qualify the direction of the trend.

Although the two statistical indexes are far less reliable than one would like (economic data usually are), they are all that we have. Numbers that show a worsening trend in recent decades simply do not exist. Nevertheless, people resolutely ignore this silver lining and instead try to find the cloud. Consider, for example, this statement from an article by two demographers in the journal *Population and Development Review*: "During the last 25 years or so the average annual rate of increase of world food production has steadily deteriorated. . . . it fell from 3.1 percent in the 1950s to 2.8 percent in the 1960s and 2.2 percent in the first half of the 1970's." I shall leave aside the large question of whether such apparent changes are statistically meaningful. What is interesting for now is the word "deteriorated," which suggests that the world food situation is getting worse. But the data tell us only that the gain—the *improvement* was greater in the 1950s than it was later; they *don't* say that food production is not increasing.

Similarly, *Business Week* ran an article on food and illustrated it with a bar graph, comparing population with food per capita from 1954 to 1974. It seems at first glance to show population growing faster than food. That would mean a fall in food per capita, which would be a bad sign. But on close inspection we see that food per capita has increased—a good sign. It makes no sense to put a total figure (population) next to a per capita figure (food per capita). Why is it done? People apparently want to believe and to tell others that world food supplies are running out even though—statistically, at least—they are improving.

The incidence of famine is a useful clue to changes in the world's food supply over the years. Famine is hard to define and measure, however, because when nutrition is poor many people die of diseases and not directly of starvation. Historical studies therefore count as a famine any event that people living in a particular time referred to as such.

According to Johnson, who has surveyed the documentary history of famine and reports the result in his monograph *World Food Problems and Prospects* (1973), "It is highly unlikely that the famine-caused deaths [in the third quarter of the twentieth century] equal a tenth of [those for] the period 75 years earlier." He says that "there has not been a major famine, such as visited China and India in the past, during the past quarter century," and he considers the food supply "far more secure for poor people during the past quarter century than at any other comparable period in the last two or three centuries." Johnson states that many, if not most, of the 12 to 15 million famine deaths that have occurred in this century "were due to deliberate governmental policy, official mismanagement, or war and not to serious crop failure."

Accounts such as this by Johnson are not often mentioned in newspapers or in conversation. Instead, one hears the claim that "a lifetime of malnutrition and actual hunger is the lot of at least two thirds of mankind," first made by the director of the UNFAO in 1950. Unlike Johnson's assertions, this claim is not based on any data. The UN later reduced its estimate of people in "actual hunger" to between 10 and 15 percent of mankind. Even though the original UNFAO estimate was a guess, a great deal of research into minimum, or satisfactory, dietary needs, and the diets customary in various countries, has now been done, and disproves it. But the statement comes back again and again in popular discussion as evidence that food is not becoming more plentiful.

People say that "the death of a single human being from starvation is an unspeakable human tragedy." This sentiment implies that even if the food supply is improving, the world's population should be reduced so that no person will die from starvation. But, paradoxically, a greater population density seems to diminish the chance of famine. The concentration of population encourages improvements in roads and transportation, and transportation is the key to preventing starvation when crops fail.

The Sahel in Africa is a good example. A reporter for *Newsweek* posted this dispatch in 1972, during the severe drought:

> "Sure, the food is pouring in," observed British Red Cross liaison officer George Bolton, "but how the hell are we going to get it to the people who need it? There isn't a tarred road within a thousand miles of Juba." Bolton wasn't exaggerating. While I was in Juba, I witnessed the arrival of 5,000 gallons of cooking oil, which had been diverted from the nearby state of Rwanda. Since the rickety old ferry was not strong enough to carry the oil shipment across the White Nile so it could be distributed to the needy in the interior, the oil was promptly unloaded on the riverbank and stored in Juba.
>
> And this was not an isolated incident. I saw warehouses in Juba overflowing with millet, dried fish, cooking utensils, agricultural tools and medical supplies—all useless because nothing could be delivered to the people who needed it.

The Sahel is a case study of food, population, and public relations. Later we read in *Newsweek* (September 19, 1977) that "more than 100,000 West Africans perished of hunger" in the Sahel between 1968 and 1973 because of drought. Peter Gwynne, a *Newsweek* editor, informed me that the estimate came from Kurt Waldheim's message to the

UN Desertification Conference, in 1977. Waldheim had said, "Who can forget the horror of millions of men, women, and children starving, with more than 100,000 dying, because of an ecological calamity that turned grazing land and farms into bleak desert?" When I queried Waldheim for his source, I received a two-page excerpt from a memo by the UN Sahelian Office, dated November 8, 1974, saying, "It is not possible to calculate the present and future impact of this tragedy, on the populations. . . . Although precise figures are not available, indeed unobtainable . . . certainly there has been an extensive and tragic loss of life. . . ." Also enclosed was a one-page memo written specifically for the UN in 1975, by Helen Ware, an Australian specialist in African demography who was at that time a visiting fellow at the University of Ibadan. Ware calculated the normal death rate for the area, together with "the highest death rate in any group of nomads" during the drought. She figured that "at an absolute, and most improbable, upper limit a hundred thousand people who would not otherwise have died, succumbed to the effects of famine. . . . Even as a maximum [this estimate] represents an unreal limit."

Ware's figures, which cast considerable doubt on Waldheim's confident assertion, were on the first page of a document written for and sent out by the UN before the Desertification Conference was held and Waldheim's message was publicized. It seems to have been the only calculation the UN had. In a letter to me, Ware said: "The problem with deaths in the Sahel is precisely that there was so little evidence of them. . . ." A recent summary of the scientific evidence on the drought's effects by John Caldwell, a demographer who was familiar with the area prior to the drought and who lived there in 1973, echoes Ware's skepticism. Caldwell reports, "One cannot certainly identify the existence of the drought in the vital statistics. . . . nutritional levels, although poor, were similar to those found before the drought in other parts of Africa. The only possible exception was that of very young children."

The UN retreated in 1978 to the more modest but still unprovable assertion that "tens of thousands" died. But last July, the estimate was revised upward again when the UN announced (as reported by the Associated Press) that a forthcoming "permanent food crisis . . . will be deeper than the 1972–74 drought, when 300,000 or more died in Ethiopia and the Sahel belt south of the Sahara."

To question the accuracy of the number of dead people in the Sahel may seem heartless, but the number is important: if it exaggerates the magnitude of the problem, we may despair of any solution. Undoubtedly a drought did occur in the Sahel, crops failed, people suffered, and some died. But to suggest that one crop failure was more severe than it was, and that another will be permanent, as the UN has done, is likely to convince us that there is no hope.

Since global trends of food production can mask exceptions, let us consider two countries where food has been short: India and Bangladesh.

Net food grain availability—the amount available for human consumption—in kilograms per capita per year has been rising in India since at least 1950–51. Throughout the 1970s, food production increased at a faster rate than population. Why has India's food supply improved so dramatically? The cause is not an agronomic miracle but an expectable economic event. Most price controls on food were lifted, and price supports were substituted for the controls. Indian farmers had a greater incentive to produce more, so they did. They increased production by planting more crops a year, on more land, and by improving the land they had. They also introduced higher yield strains and improved fertilizers.

Some people are surprised that Indian farmers could find more land to cultivate. But in fact the total area of Indian cultivated land increased by about 20 percent between 1951 and 1971. In addition, there was a 25 percent increase in irrigated land between 1949–50 and 1960–61, and another 39 percent increase between 1961–65 and 1978.

When Bangladesh became independent, in late 1971, after a devastating war, [National Security Advisor] Henry Kissinger called the country "an international basket case." Since then, the food supply has at times been so low that some writers have advocated "letting Bangladesh go down the drain," whatever that means. Other people organized emergency relief operations. But production began to improve in 1975 and has continued to improve steadily over the years. From 1975 to 1980, Bangladesh's population increased at a rate of 2.7 percent; its food-grain production increased at a rate of 4 percent.

Nevertheless, even though half of the cultivated 22 million acres are suitable for two crops at a time, and some for three, yields per acre remain low. Only 3.4 million acres are irrigated, and there is no strong incentive to increase that amount. Storage capacity in Bangladesh is limited, and about 75 percent of the farms produce for subsistence rather than for the market.

Why would a subsistence farmer grow more than his family can eat? An urban housewife does not buy so many vegetables for the week that they spoil. Malthus spoke of a "natural want of will on the part of mankind to make efforts for the increase of food beyond what they could possibly consume." Food is produced to meet demand, either of subsistence-farming families or of the market. When demand increases, farmers are encouraged to find ways to produce more crops and improve the land.

Food, like other resources, is a market commodity. Wherever it is bought and sold, the most sensible measure of scarcity is price (and the cost of production, which is close to price over the long term). But we must keep in mind that price does not tell us everything about scarcity and social welfare. A product may be readily available, as measured by its low price, and there may still be social damage. For example, a daily ration of vitamin A may be cheap, but if people can't find a store that sells vitamin A, or if they don't believe they need it, then their health is nonetheless jeopardized. On the other hand, caviar may be expensive and scarce, but the lack of caviar has no effect on society's well-being. The price of a week's groceries may be higher now than in a previous year, but there is no harm to society if income also increases. Therefore, though the price of food and the social welfare are often connected, they are not identical.

In this country, the sharp rise in food prices in 1972–73 was interpreted by many consumers as the harbinger of an increasing scarcity of food. But the trend in food prices over the long term justifies a more cheerful attitude. Because wheat is important in the diets of so many countries, and because its price tends to move in concert with the prices of other grains, it is an important indicator of world food supplies generally. And U.S. export prices for food grains are reasonably representative of world-market prices. Since 1800, the price of wheat relative to wages has fallen sixfold. Relative to an estimated Consumer Price Index over the same period, it has fallen by more than a third. From this point of view, the abrupt price jump that took place in the 1970s is seen to be one of many fluctuations that have occurred in the midst of steady decline.

The decline in wheat prices is hard to believe, especially when one considers the great increase in demand resulting from world population increases and world income increases. But production increased even more—enough to overcome these pressures and keep the price down. There is no reason to assume that the future will not be continuous with the past. Thus, from the historical trend toward cheaper and more plentiful food, it is reasonable to conclude that real prices for food will continue to drop as food becomes more abundant.

Population growth has raised the specter of increased pressure on the land. More people, it is said, make for smaller farms per farmer, and hence a harder struggle to produce enough to eat, until each of us is scratching out three skimpy meals from 18 hours' work a day, on a plot the size of a window box. "More people, less land," the Environmental Fund says.

More people, it is further said, will ruin land, especially in arid areas. *Smithsonian* magazine has editorialized that in the desert, "traditional, more primitive agricutural techniques using natural ecological cycles are all that will work . . . and *that means small populations.*" The head of the Population/Food Fund, Charles M. Cargille, M.D., writes that "overpopulation contributes to . . . deforestation and agricultural practices damaging to soil fertility."

Yet the world now eats as well as, or better than, it did in earlier centuries—even in poor countries. This paradox is explained as follows: Reduction in the amount of land available to the farmer causes little hardship if previously he did not need to farm all the land that was available to him. (However, he may have to change his methods so as to cultivate the land more intensively.) Furthermore, when farmers need more land they make more land. They build land for cultivation by investing their energy, blood, money, and ingenuity in it. The increase in agricultural output as population rises (with or without an accompanying rise in income) has been accomplished, in most countries, largely by increases in the amount of land farmed.

The late Joginder Kumar, a demographer, did an enormous amount of hard work to collect and standardize data on land supply and use throughout the world. The results are reported in his book *Population and Land in World Agriculture* (1973). Kumar's finding: There was 9 percent more arable land in 1960 than in 1950 in the 87 countries for which he could find data; these countries account for 73 percent of the world's total land area. Some of the places where the quantity of cultivated land is increasing are surprising—India, for example, where the amount of cultivated land rose from 1,261,001 to 1,379,190 square kilometers between 1951 and 1960.

The trend that Kumar found from 1950 to 1960 continues. The UN-FAO has collected data back to the 1960s showing that there was a rise in "arable and permanent cropland" from 1,394 to 1,506 million hectares in the world as a whole between 1961–65 and 1975, an increase of 8 percent. In the developing countries the gain is particulary significant and encouraging.

The fact that the amount of arable land in the world is increasing does not forebode diminishing returns in the long run, with successively poorer land being brought into use, because it is also a fact that average yields per acre are increasing. Improvements in yield per acre and total production can be so great that farmers cultivate less land. Such was the case in the United States, for example, until the 1970s.

In this country, surplus production has been the problem. The high output has been obtained in large part with huge farm machines that require flat land for efficiency. This combination of increased productivity per acre of good land and increased use of equipment adapted to flat land has made it unprofitable to farm some land that formerly was cultivated. For example, between 1860 and 1974, the tillable area in New Hampshire declined from 2,367,000 acres to 172,000 acres. Although yields have continued to increase in the United States, world demand and changes in government agricultural policies were incentives for farmers to increase their acreage over the last decade. Not only is more pasture and fallow land being cropped now but also new cropland is being created at the rate of 1.25 (or, according to another estimate, 1.7) million acres a year, by irrigation, swamp drainage, and other means. This is a much larger quantity of land than the amount converted to cities and highways each year.

There are places where, for unhappy reasons—usually wars or fights about land tenure—good land that was once cultivated is fallow: Mexico, for example. In the mid-1970s, Mexican peasants, frustrated by the slow pace of agrarian reform, began seizing land. The big estates then cut their investments in fear of more seizures.

The potential for creating new land has increased as knowledge, machinery, and power sources have improved. At one time, most of Europe could not be planted, because the soils were "too heavy." When a plow that could farm the heavy soil was invented, much of Europe suddenly became arable in the eyes of the people who lived there. Most of Ireland and New England were once too hilly and stony for farming, but with effort the stones were removed and the land became "suitable for crops." Now this land is again not worth cropping and has been turned to other uses. In the twentieth century, bulldozers and dynamite have cleared out stumps that kept land from being plowed. And in the future, cheap transportation and desalination may transform what are now deserts into arable lands. The definition of "arable" changes as technology develops and the demand for land rises. Hence any calculation of "arable" land should be seen for what it is—a rough estimate without permanent force.

Experts and laymen alike continue to state the "obvious" (though incorrect) view that there is a limit on the amount of food in the world, and that if some countries consume more, others in need will have less. What I have tried to demonstrate here is that food has no long-run, physical limit. This does not mean that complacency about the food supply is in order. Droughts and famines occur; in some countries, even under ordinary circumstances, some people don't have enough to eat. But these conditions are not inevitable; they are rarely permanent. I believe that, with effort and with confidence, they can be reversed.

19

Shifting and Sharing Adjustment Burdens: The Role of the Industrial Food-Importing Nations

Robert L. Paarlberg

THE INDUSTRIAL FOOD-IMPORTING NATIONS: APPARENT SIMILARITIES AND CRITICAL DIFFERENCES

The European Community [EEC], Japan, and the USSR are all wealthy industrial regions which import very large quantities of food. Over the period 1973–75, the net grain imports of each of these three regions averaged between 10–20 million metric tons per year (see Table 1). Together, they import more grain on the average than the entire developing world.

These industrial food customers also import grain for a less urgent purpose than most of the developing world. The vast majority of these rich nation grain imports, close to 85 percent, come in the form of coarse grains such as corn, to supply feed for livestock. By contrast, the developing world imports almost all of its grain to supply human needs directly—an average of 96 percent consists of wheat. Moreover, rich nation imports show continuing potential for growth. While human caloric intake does tend to "flatten out" at high income levels, primary cereal consumption in all forms, including animal products, does not. Between 1964 and 1974, *per capita* cereal use in all forms increased 11 percent in the EEC, 17 percent in Japan, and 29 percent in the USSR, compared to a *per capita* increase of less than 5 percent in most poor countries. As these wealthy food customers continue to develop a taste for animal protein, their claim on world supplies will continue to increase.

Reprint of "Shifting and Sharing Adjustment Burdens: The Role of the Industrial Food-Importing Nations" by Robert L. Paarlberg in *International Organization* (Vol. 32, No. 3, Summer 1978), Special Issue: "The Global Political Economy of Food," edited by Raymond F. Hopkins and Donald J. Puchala. Reprinted by permission of The MIT Press, Cambridge, Mass. Pp. 657–77.

TABLE 1 Industrial Nation Net Grain Imports, 1973/74–1975/76 (million metric tons)

	1973/74	1974/75	1975/76	1973/74–1975/76 Average
European Community Nine	13.3	11.1	13.1	12.5
Japan	19.2	18.5	19.2	19.0
USSR	5.6	.3	26.4	10.8
Total	38.1	29.9	58.7	42.2
Developing World Total	26.6	35.9	30.6	31.0

Source: U.S. Department of Agriculture, "World Agricultural Situation," WAS-10 (July 1976), Table 10, p. 15.

As all three of these wealthy regions import large quantities of food, largely to support livestock production, they may appear to place parallel demands upon today's world food system. But trends over time show that the import needs of these three regions have been highly dissimilar. Only a dozen years ago the EEC imported *more* food from abroad than today, Japan imported much *less*, and the USSR was consistently a *net exporter* of food. So when the world food system entered its recent period of relative scarcity and insecurity, the import claims of Japan, and particularly the USSR, were rapidly increasing, while those of the EEC were actually in some decline (see Table 2).

Second, the response of these three wealthy food-importing regions to the tightened world supply of recent years also showed considerable variation (see Table 3). The EEC did encourage a very modest reduction in the use of grain to feed livestock soon after the 1972/73 decline in world food production. But in Japan, livestock feeding continued to increase (from its very low level) until 1975/76. And in the USSR livestock feeding also continued to increase until 1975/76, to surpass even the U.S. level in 1974/75, a year of very tight world supplies. Not until its own disastrous harvest of 1975, and only in the face of physical barriers to further feed grain imports, did the USSR finally reduce the feeding of grain to animals.

TABLE 2 Industrial Nation Net Grain Imports (million metric tons)

	1960/61–62/63 Average	1973/74–74/75 Average	Net Change
European Community Nine	21.5	12.5	− 9.0
Japan	5.3	19.0	+ 13.7
USSR	− 7.3	10.8	+ 18.1

Source: U.S. Department of Agriculture, "World Agricultural Situation," WAS-10 (July 1976), Table 10, p. 15.

TABLE 3 Industrial Nation Grain Fed to Livestock (million metric tons)

	1969/70–71/72 Average	1972/73	1973/74	1974/75	1975/76
European Community Nine	68.8	72.2	72.3	70.9	70.0
Japan	9.3	10.4	12.1	13.1	11.8
USSR	89.0	98.0	105.0	107.0	85.0
United States	136.5	148.5	143.2	106.4	120.2

Source: U.S. Department of Agriculture, "World Agricultural Situation," WAS-10 (July 1976), Table 14, p. 21.

So the EEC has steadily reduced its claims upon the world food market, by subsidizing its own domestic production and by moderating its livestock feeding in times of short supply. By contrast, Japan and the USSR have rapidly increased their food imports. And the Soviet Union, in particular, was slow to moderate its use of imported grain for animal feed during the world food emergency of 1973–75. These are gross distinctions, however. A closer look at the domestic and foreign agricultural policies of each of these three industrial importing regions is necessary to clarify and to qualify the role of each in the world food system.

THE EUROPEAN COMMUNITY

The enlarged European Community relies upon the world market to provide for roughly 20 percent of its very large coarse grain consumption.[1] In protein-rich animal feed concentrates the EEC is 80 percent dependent upon external supplies. Yet the Community would be far more dependent upon external food supplies today had it not invested so heavily in farm policies which protect and promote its own agricultural production.

Domestic Farm Policies

European agriculture has long been an industry in relative decline. Over the past two decades the agricultural work force has been decreasing by nearly 5 percent per year. And many of those who remain on farms face difficult commercial circumstances. Two-thirds of the farms within the Community are smaller than 25 acres, and half of those individuals running farms are 57 years of age or older, poorly educated, and ill-prepared to adopt mechanized farming techniques.

It is the announced policy of the EEC to protect this endangered farm population from the prospect of an even more rapid and painful economic decline. Individual governments had undertaken programs to support farm prices and to protect domestic producers from external competition for many years before the 1957 Rome Treaty. In some countries, especially France, farmers have long demanded such protection, in their role as a powerful political interest group. Over the period 1962–67, however, these separate national farm policies were strengthened and joined into one. This Common Agricultural Policy (CAP) did not eliminate entirely the separate role of national governments. But under the CAP, a common market organization does now extend to cover more than 91 percent of all EEC farm produce, and common support prices are offered for more than 70 percent of all farm production. Prices of individual agricultural commodities are established annually by the EEC Council of Ministers (in terms of "units of account") and are maintained by variable levies on low-priced imports from abroad and by official purchases of excess supplies at home.

The CAP has neither reversed the decline nor increased the efficiency of European agriculture. Farm incomes have grown, but at a rate sometimes slower than in other sectors of the economy. And the largest benefits of the CAP price support system fall where farm size and production are already large, so income gaps between the rich and poor farming regions of the Community have actually widened. Meanwhile, the structural weakness of European farming remains essentially uncorrected. Average farm size has grown by only 7.4 acres since 1958, and with 10 percent of its population still in agriculture the EEC is still far from approaching former Commission President Sicco L. Mansholt's vision of a 6 percent farm population by 1980.

Meanwhile, the costs of the CAP to consumer and taxpayer have been very high. Separate estimates (in the years 1966/67 and 1967/68) placed annual combined consumer and taxpayer costs of all EEC farm programs at a hefty $12 to $14 billion. Furthermore, these costs are not equally borne within the Community. Those member states with small farm populations and large food imports, such as Germany, carry the heaviest cost. Germany's burden is magnified by a cumbersome system of fixed "green exchange rates," which was designed to protect CAP prices from the instability of the current "floating" exchange rate system. Disparities which have developed between "market" and "green" exchange rates work to the disadvantage of nations, such as Germany, which have enjoyed appreciating currency values. Even Italy, a relatively poor member state with a depreciating currency, finds itself disadvantaged, by having to pay to support the surplus production of prosperous farmers in France and Holland. France, a food-exporting nation with a large farming population, and in recent years a depreciating currency, enjoys the strongest relative advantage under the CAP pricing system. The French have insisted upon this relative advantage in agriculture, since the inception of the Common Market, to compensate for the advantage which they consider West Germany to have received in a wider market for manufactured goods.

The effects of the CAP upon Europe were considerably altered when world food prices increased sharply after 1972. When these prices grew to surpass even the high support prices maintained within the EEC, the protective machinery of the CAP suddenly became an instrument for keeping consumer prices lower and limiting incentives for producers. In the summer of 1973 the EEC levies changed from tariffs on food imports to taxes on exports. This discouraged sales on the world market and moderated domestic food price inflation. In Great Britain this timely reversal helped also to moderate adverse views toward Community membership, which was then under reconsideration. Government ministers explained to Parliament in 1974 that the CAP was actually keeping down the cost of British food, rather than increasing that cost. But by protecting internal price levels in this fashion, the CAP severely distorts the free flow of international agricultural trade.

Food Trade Policies

Support and stabilization for farm prices within the Community require protection from more efficient foreign producers and from price fluctuation overseas. Separate European states had long protected themselves from North American competition by placing fixed tariffs against food imports. But today the CAP protects the Community as a whole by means of its variable levy system. During periods of global market surplus, as during the late 1960s and early 1970s, when the total charges of this levy system are converted into ad valorem equivalents, it becomes clear that the common policy has in effect increased average protection levels from the pre-CAP period. Comparison between 1959 and 1968 shows a protection level increase from 19 percent to 137 percent in dairy produce, from 14 percent to 52 percent in meat, and from 14 percent to 72 percent in cereals. Not surprisingly, Europe has become a declining market for exporters, as noted earlier.

In addition to restricting imports, the EEC has also subsidized exports during most of its operation. The high domestic target prices of the CAP, when unaccompanied by acreage restrictions, tend to generate surplus production. Disposal of these surpluses has been accomplished, in part, by offering export subsidies which permit the sale of food abroad at or below the world price. These subsidy payments, mostly to promote export of grains, dairy products, and sugar, totaled over $1 billion in 1969. In 1970 the Community subsidy for soft wheat exports was actually larger than the world price to which it was being added.

Such very large export subsidies have seriously disrupted patterns of international trade and production. They have often forced efficient producers in North America to store grain in large quantities, and even to withdraw land from production to avoid downward pressures on price, while allowing less efficient European producers to continue to export their own grain surplus with little regard to the effect on world prices.

Scarcity does not eliminate the disruptive effect of these EEC food trade policies. When world food supplies tightened, from 1972 to 1976, EEC export subsidies were discontinued and replaced by export taxes. Prices within the EEC were to be held down by reducing exports. Export taxes on wheat eventually grew to equal more than two-thirds of the already high domestic price. Having earlier dumped Europe's surplus onto a saturated world market, the CAP was now holding European produce away from a tight world market, in hopes of containing runaway food price inflation at home. All the while, the EEC continued to import substantial quantities of food. These trade practices raise questions about the overall contribution which European food policy makes to the security and stability of the larger world food system.

The Contribution of the European Community to World Food Security and Adjustment

In certain respects the EEC takes a "free ride" on the world food system. In times of oversupply, the EEC made things worse by restricting imports and subsidizing exports; in times of shortage, the CAP has reduced EEC exports even while the EEC has continued to bid against less wealthy food deficit nations for a high volume of imports. Such policies show considerable disregard for the goals of stability and security in external food markets.

The contribution of the EEC to global food security, however, has not been entirely negative. First, even while the EEC introduced its 1973 export tax on cereals, it continued to honor its considerable obligations with respect to Third World food aid. EEC financial contributions for food aid increased from less than $7 million in 1965 to nearly $450 million by 1974, or roughly 30 percent of the OECD total.[2] Second, to complement these food aid policies, the EEC has recognized a special obligation to provide access to exchange-earning agricultural exports from the Third World. The Community's Mediterranean Policy, its Generalized Preference Scheme (GSP), and the 1975 Lomé Convention offer privileged access to the European market for a growing number of poor-nation exports. The Lomé Convention dramatically expanded trade concessions earlier offered to 46 underdeveloped African, Caribbean, and Pacific (ACP) states, 18 of which are listed by the UN as among the world's poorest. These countries now enjoy duty free access to the Community for 96 percent of their agricultural production. The Lomé Convention may only bring a limited increase in trade, since most ACP products, apart from sugar, do not compete with major EEC commodities. Further, the EEC has various nontariff barriers to trade, including quality controls and previous bilateral agreements; these cancel some access provisions of the convention. But Lomé does provide a new export stabilization agreement (Stabex) to guarantee the monetary value of many Third World exports to the Community.

Yet the EEC makes its most important contribution to world food security simply by maintaining an indigenous capacity to produce a significant proportion of its own food. The EEC is by no means self-sufficient in food, but since full implementation of the CAP, annual grain imports have fallen from above 20 million tons in the early 1960s to an average 12.5 million tons by 1975. By 1973, owing in part to the CAP, the Community was 100 percent self-sufficient in wheat, barley, cheese, poultry, eggs, potatoes, pork, beef, and veal. The Community was more than 90 percent self-sufficient in oats, butter, rye, sugar, and fresh vegetables. When the sudden scarcity crisis burst upon international food markets in 1972, it was fortunate that EEC food import needs were in decline. If the "more efficient" farm regions of North America had been permitted to take over the feeding of Western Europe earlier during the 1960s, then the U.S. grain surplus would have been depleted much sooner. U.S. cropland would have already been in full production in 1972, and so there would have been a smaller excess capacity available after 1972 to meet the unexpected explosion in overseas demand. In short, a measure of European self-sufficiency in food supplies, even with the loss of some production efficiency, can be beneficial to world food security.

European self-sufficiency in agriculture remains a controversial policy, however. The recent FAO director general, A. H. Boerma, presented a draft strategy for international agricultural adjustment in 1975 which conceded that "a substantial degree of self-sufficiency" was an appropriate goal for those less developed countries with "limited opportunities for earning foreign exchange." But he warned: "Any general tendency for developed importing countries to adopt policies aiming at further increases in their self-sufficiency would represent a less effective use of resources available for agricultural production." Limited self-sufficiency and increasing "interdependence" in the world food trading system is naturally favored by net exporting regions, such as North America, but it is understandably troublesome to some net importers. In the absence of a global food regime which guarantees market access, and in the absence of predictable weather to guarantee high levels of production, interdependence will at times endanger the security of food importing states. As long as North American production remains vulnerable to unpredictable weather, as long as the global food distribution system remains vulnerable to technical limitations or to political uncertainties, and as long as food itself remains scarce in relation to nutritional needs, some of the less efficient producing regions, including Western Europe, may do well to maintain a "redundant" production capability.

Of course, the CAP has not been the most efficient means to promote European production capabilities. Its original motive was not to increase world food security, but rather to support very narrow domestic political constituencies. In its support for these powerful domestic farming interests, the CAP has placed heavy reliance upon price policy instruments alone; these do little to improve income distribution or to promote structural reform. If more CAP funds had been directed originally toward farm modernization, high European production could have been attained at higher political cost but at lower economic cost and with less external disruption.

Still, if we must face recurring food scarcities, any policy which promotes the production of more food deserves to be measured by a less rigid standard. The CAP may perpetuate an inefficient division of international agricultural labor, but its direct costs are largely borne by Europeans, and over time it has worked to reduce the total quantity of EEC food imports. By comparison, the agricultural policies of some other wealthy food-importing nations have had less favorable effects.

JAPAN

Japan's 110 million people (slightly over half the U.S. population) live in a land area smaller than the size of the state of Montana. Only 15 percent of this land can be brought under cultivation. Yet Japan still provides for nearly 73 percent (by value) of its own food needs. By any standard this is a remarkable performance, particularly since per capita intake of meat in Japan has tripled since 1960.

Japan's agricultural position, however, unlike that of the EEC, is one of increasing import dependence. Precisely at a time of uncertain international supply, Japan has emerged as the world's largest consistent importer of food. Japan's net grain imports increased from an average 5.3 million tons in the early 1960s to 14.4 million tons in 1969–72, and to the present level of nearly 20 million tons by 1973/74. In times of scarcity, this rapidly growing Japanese claim on the world food market can constitute a danger to less wealthy food deficit nations. It is also cause for some apprehension within Japan, where farm policies that once encouraged a high degree of food trade interdependence have now come under critical review.

Japanese Farm Policies

Modernization of Japanese agriculture dates from the Meiji Restoration, which abolished feudal land tenure in 1868. A further reform enacted under U.S. military occupation after World War II released nearly 30 percent of Japan's cultivated area from landlord ownership. But small average farm size and incomplete mechanization left Japan's agriculture ill-prepared for the high rate of economic growth which was to follow. In

1961 new farm legislation was enacted to support declining farm incomes during the transition to full industrial development. These Japanese support programs bear some resemblance to those enacted at roughly the same time by the EEC, and like the farm policies of the EEC, they have produced mixed results.

First, Japan's support policies have encouraged vast quantities of surplus rice production. Roughly 40 percent of the annual budget of the Ministry of Agriculture and Forestry has been devoted to supporting domestic rice prices, often at levels two or three times above the world price. Even in 1973, when the world price of rice had increased by 300 percent to an astonishing $636 per ton, Japan's domestic producers were being offered more, out of public funds. The generosity of these farm support policies reflects the political leverage which rural constituencies enjoy within the ruling Liberal Democratic party. The rice program produces an unmanageable surplus, some of which can be sold abroad under export subsidy. Yet to control surplus rice accumulation, farmers must also be paid not to produce. In 1970 almost 10 percent of the country's precious fields were actually left uncultivated. Despite the enormous public expense of these farm support policies ($3.1 billion for farm subsidies in 1975), agricultural incomes in Japan have continued to lag behind industry.[3]

Most important for the global food system, Japan's farm policies do not provide needed supplies of feed grain for livestock, to satisfy growing consumer tastes for animal protein. Between 1961 and 1971, while Japan produced an enormous rice surplus, its grain production actually *decreased* by 2.2 percent annually. Over the same period, grain consumption was increasing every year by 3.3 percent, spurred on by the growing dietary expectations which seem to accompany affluence throughout the world. Rice still provides for about one-third of Japan's caloric intake, but since 1960 per capita consumption of animal products has nearly tripled. This dietary revolution has brought with it an increased requirement for feed grain imports, which have grown since 1960 by a factor of five. Japanese wheat imports simultaneously doubled in volume, while soybean imports increased by a factor of three. Because of these rapidly increasing imports, Japan's "self-sufficiency" in wheat declined from 39 percent in 1960 to a mere 4 percent today, while self-sufficiency in coarse grain declined from 49 percent to 2 percent. When the world food market suddenly tightened in 1972, Japan had to reassess this drift toward a growing reliance on food imports.

Japan's Food Trade Policy

Before 1972, Japan's heavy dependence on overseas grain supplies had not been cause for anxiety. Japan recognized its own comparative disadvantage in wheat and soybean production, and made a conscious decision to buy from abroad. The world market was in a condition of oversupply, prices were low, and Japan's own trade balance was particularly strong with the United States, its primary source of food imports.

But following the market reversals of 1972, and then the oil shock and the brief U.S. imposition of export controls on soybeans in 1973, Japan began to reassess its growing food trade dependence. Public concern was aroused by a government study which indicated that if Japan's food and animal feed imports were halted, and if every available acre of land were farmed (for example, if the nation's golf courses were given over to sweet potato cultivation), levels of nutrition would still fall back to the very low standard of the immediate postwar period.

In response to such apparent dangers, the Ministry of Agriculture and Forestry adjusted its budget after 1973 to cut expenditures for rice and to provide increased support for wheat, barley, and soybeans. And in 1975, in a watershed report to the cabinet, Japan's Advisory Council on Agricultural Policy set a ten-year target of 75 percent (by value) self-sufficiency in aggregate food supplies. This meant reversing the decline in self-sufficiency (from 90 to 73 percent) that had been recorded since 1960. The report first called for expanding domestic production of all crops and livestock. "Whatever we can produce in Japan we should," ministry officials proclaimed. Secondarily, the plan projected reduced growth in per capita animal protein consumption. In combination, these measures were designed to hold the annual increase in import demand for feedstuffs to about .4 million tons per year, versus the .65 million tons per year noted over the past decade. In April 1976, as a further means to reduce food import dependence, a movement began to resubstitute rice for bread in school lunch diets.

In addition to increasing its agricultural self-sufficiency, Japan has also been seeking to diversify its overseas sources of food supply. Following the 1973 embargo, soybean imports were increased from Brazil and from the PRC [People's Republic of China], and the U.S. market share of Japan's feed grain imports fell from 71 percent to 59 percent. To secure this remaining share, Japan reached an informal agreement with the United States, in August 1975, recognizing Japan's intention to buy 3 million tons of wheat, 3 million tons of soybeans, and 8 million tons of feed grains in each of the coming three years, and also recognizing the intention of the United States to make these amounts available. Japan continues to seek such long-term import agreements, and has now initiated a modest food stockpiling program, to ease its near total dependence upon "pipeline" supplies.

It is too early to judge the absolute impact of these recent shifts in Japan's food trade policy, away from unguarded dependence upon overseas supplies. Despite high support prices and incentive payments to soybean producers, total Japanese oilseed production decreased in 1976, while the dollar value of agricultural imports from the United States increased by 16 percent. It will certainly not be easy, moreover, for Japan to curb the dietary expectations of its large and affluent population. Even while wheat output declines, bread consumption continues to rise at the expense of noodles and rice. Nor will Japan's economy find it easy to absorb the budgetary and inflationary costs of increasing agricultural self-sufficiency. Official estimates put the cost of reaching optimal 1985 self-sufficiency goals at $86 billion, which is roughly twice the total cost of all of Japan's food imports over the entire period 1960–72. As a world food surplus returns, as food prices come down, and as the memory of the 1973 soybean embargo continues to fade, it seems likely that Japan will lose interest in agricultural independence.

Japan's Contribution to World Food Security and Adjustment

Japan's position in the world food system is not so burdensome as its increasing dependence on food imports alone would imply. Against great odds, Japan has remained self-sufficient in many foods, particularly rice, and it now hopes to slow the increase in its purchase of grain from abroad. Further, it has made efforts to adjust its imports, when necessary, to reduce pressure on supply. Together with the EEC, Japan honored a U.S. request in 1974 to cut its purchase of corn by 10 percent in that very tight crop year.

Also, despite its difficulties at home, Japan has shown some increased interest in providing food aid and in promoting international agricultural development. In 1965 Japan's food aid contributions made up less than 1 percent of the OECD total, but by 1974 this figure had increased to 5 percent, and Japan had funded more than 100 aid projects for Third World agricultural development. In 1975 Japan established a new International Cooperation Corporation to further encourage food production in poor Asian countries. A dominant purpose behind these projects is clearly to develop new sources of overseas supply. But such new sources nonetheless add to worldwide food security.

All things considered, however, Japan remains something of a burden on the world food system. Its dubious contribution to food security actually extends beyond its growing reliance on feed grain imports. Notably, Japan is the nation with the world's largest fish catch. For the past 50 years Japan has consistently taken more fish from the ocean than any other nation in the world. In the years after 1964, Japan's annual fish catch grew at an annual rate of more than 5 percent, nearly doubling by 1972 to reach 10 million tons, or roughly 15 percent of the world total. Japan has continued to supply nearly half of its domestic animal protein consumption with fish products. By doing so it tries to moderate its dependence on feed grain imports. Until recently this seemed a responsible food supply strategy.

But after 1970 the world fish catch for all nations reversed its historical trend of steady growth and went into decline, prompting speculation that the global catch of table grade fish had finally approached a maximum sustainable yield. Japan's own distant water fish catch subsequently declined as well, by 7 percent in 1974, reflecting not only Japan's economic recession and increased marine fuel costs, but a genuine strain on world supplies. Specifically, Japan's take of endangered Alaskan pollock in 1974 dropped to one-third of the amount taken during the previous year. This declining distant water fish posed a clear threat to Japan's own food security. But it also posed a threat to the future food supply of other nations, including those developing nations which have yet to enter the competitive marine fishing industry.[4]

Finally, it must be observed that Japan's own continued rate of growth of population also places considerable pressure on global food supplies. Japan was generally credited with having done well to reduce its rate of growth of population to just above 1 percent soon after World War II. But this progress in reducing population growth has not continued. Japan's population continues to grow at 1.2 percent every year, roughly double the annual rate in Europe and North America. For a nation of 110 million, poorly endowed with resources to produce food for such numbers, and already the largest customer on the world food market, continued population growth can only promise a growing reliance upon overseas and ocean food supplies.

So Japan, for all that it has done, is likely to turn to the world market for ever larger quantities of food. In the event of renewed market scarcities, Japan's very large imports will place something of a burden on the world food system. Among the wealthy food-importing nations, however, its contribution to food security is not so burdensome as that of the Soviet Union.

THE SOVIET UNION

The Soviet Union imports, on average, less food than either the EEC or Japan. Yet its domestic and foreign agricultural policies made a much greater contribution to the recent destabilization of the world food system. During most of the postwar period, the Soviets were only marginal participants in the world food system. Their dramatic entry into the world market in 1972 was the direct result of changes in food trading policy. But beneath this event lies the enduring constraint of Soviet farm policy, the underperformance of Soviet agriculture itself.

Soviet Farm Policy

Much of the Soviet Union is either too cold or too dry to support agriculture. The USSR has rich soil and a land area nearly three times the size of the United States. But more than half of this area lacks adequate and reliable moisture, and much of the remaining half, the well-watered half, is unsuitable to farming because the growing season is too short and too cold. Odessa, in the southern Ukraine, falls on the same northern latitude as Duluth, in the state of Minnesota.

Together with a harsh climate, serfdom and tsarist oppression had constrained Russia's agricultural development long before the October 1917 revolution. But following that revolution, the Soviet leadership managed to perpetuate Russian agricultural underdevelopment by draining resources from the rural sector to speed industrial growth. The small landowning peasantry in Russia was viewed as a potential breeding ground for capitalist counterrevolution, so its sacrifice was scarcely mourned by the early Bolsheviks.[5] The sacrifice of the rural sector was most visible during the early Stalinist period, when a campaign to "eliminate" the kulaks (prosperous farmers), forced collectivization, and state confiscation of farm produce actually reduced food production. A rural famine in 1932–33 cost an estimated 5 million lives. And even 20 years later, in 1953, at the time of Stalin's death, the Soviet Union had yet to produce as much food annually as it had produced before the revolution, in 1913.

Under the more concerned leadership of the Khrushchev-Brezhnev era, Soviet farming has vastly improved. The proportion of state investment devoted to agriculture has increased in every one of the post-Stalin five-year plans. In the two plans covering the period 1966–75, the state invested twice as much in agriculture as in the preceding 50 years combined. And in the upcoming plan period (1976–80), proposed investments in agriculture will increase an additional 31 percent, while the rest of the economy will get an increase of only 24 percent. These massive investments have had a strong impact. Over the decade prior to the 1975 harvest setback (when crops fell 75 million tons or 33 percent below the production target), Soviet cereal production had increased at a respectable average annual rate of 3 percent.

Increases occurred despite the state and collective farming system of the Soviet Union which remains a barrier to flexible and efficient food production. Because the Soviet Union is so large, because its agricultural conditions are so various, and because its weather is so unsteady, it suffers more than otherwise from a farming system founded upon inflexible central direction. Central direction stifles farm level management, while collateral requirements for "uninterrupted" plan fulfillment discourage innovation and transition to new farming techniques.

These problems of Soviet agriculture have not gone unnoticed, and the current Soviet leadership does take a considerable interest in the availability of domestic food supplies. Following the 1970 Christmas food riots in Poland, which brought down the Gomulka regime, the Soviet party leadership determined that it must maintain a selection of cheap food products, including an increased variety of meat products, on its own retail shelves at home. Unfortunately, this intense political interest in cheap food only compounds the plight of Soviet agriculture. The requirement to hold down retail prices makes more difficult the task of expanding production. State retail store prices for both bread and beef in the USSR have not increased since 1962. In 1974 they were actually lower than prices in Europe and in North America. Despite the growth of costly government subsidies which help to compensate for these low retail prices, the rural sector has received little added incentive to increase its production. Prices actually received by state and collective farm producers in the USSR have not increased since 1970.

Effective reform of Soviet agriculture is blocked by a widespread leadership preference for very large operations run by central production command.[6] Those who advocate the alternative of decentralized management techniques may endanger their political future. In the months following the 1975 harvest failure, the Soviet minister of agriculture, Dmitri Polyansky, who opposed excessive centralization, was disgraced and removed from his post and from the Politburo, while those responsible for farm policy within the party secretariat were untouched.[7] In June 1976, the Central Committee then endorsed a policy of "agroindustrial integration," yet another step away from the alternative of decentralization.

It is unlikely that this vicious circle can soon be broken. Consumer demands in the USSR are expected to continue to grow faster than plans or incentives for domestic production. "Consumption norms" have been established by the Institute of Nutrition at the Soviet Academy of Sciences which indicate continued hopes for dietary improvement. Per capita meat consumption will have to increase by more than 40 percent from its 1975 level to reach the academy's "norm." But plan guidelines for the 1976–80 period allow for only a 3 percent growth in per capita meat consumption during a protracted recovery from the distress slaughter of 1975–76. This is a dramatic retreat from the 21 percent growth rate of the previous plan period.

In the meantime, the Soviet Union is left with only one politically acceptable response to a production shortfall: it must import food. Even the scaled-down goals of the 1976–80 plan will require the availability of an average 215–220 million tons of grain every year. Until 1976 the USSR has managed only one crop in excess of 200 million tons. If the Soviet Union continues to enjoy good weather and manages an average annual production of 200–210 million tons, it will still have to import an average 10–15 million tons of grain every year if it hopes to reach planned consumption goals.

Soviet Food Trade Policy

It was once the policy of the USSR to hide its agricultural setbacks from the outside world by refusing to import food during times of domestic shortage. Indeed, the Soviet Union often continued to *export* food during times of short supply. Food exports were continued during the famine of 1932–33, and [Premier Nikita S.] Khrushchev himself described widespread starvation, accompanied by instances of cannibalism, which occurred in the Ukraine during the poor harvest year of 1946, while [Premier Joseph] Stalin insisted upon continuing food exports to Poland and East Germany.

Today it is Soviet policy to import food in times of production shortfall and to hide agricultural failure from its own population. In the four years following the bad harvest of 1972, the USSR imported more than 53 million tons of grain from abroad. It has yet to disclose the magnitude of this new import dependence to its own citizens.

But the Soviet Union has also hidden its import needs, before the fact, from the world market, and in so doing it becomes more than just another wealthy customer in that market. By concealing its total needs and by dealing simultaneously and in great secrecy with a half dozen private exporting firms, the Soviet Union was able to complete its 1972 grain purchase from the United States within a few weeks time, at very low prices. This purchase, a record 19 million tons, contributed to a dramatic market price increase, up from $1.65 to more than $5 per bushel. By then the Soviets were safely out of the market, and other nations were left to meet their customary import needs at a prohibitive price. India, for example, purchased 1.5 million tons of wheat in January 1973, at nearly twice the price paid by Russia during the previous summer. This single purchase cost India, an "ally" of the USSR, nearly one-fifth of its depleted hard currency reserves.

Significantly, not even the private U.S. grain export companies were able to escape the bite of these Soviet purchasing tactics. None had fully anticipated the timing or the size of the 1972 purchase, and by GAO estimates three of the five companies dealing with the Soviets actually sustained losses on the sale of .9 to 1.9 cents per bushel. Cargill claims to have lost more than $600,000 in the Soviet deal, by selling too soon and buying too late.

Over the entire period 1960–73, the USSR alone was responsible for 80 percent of all deviation from trend in world wheat imports. This uneven and unpredictable food trading style reflects more than the considerable variability of Soviet harvest conditions. Buying when the price is low, the Soviets speculate against future world needs. The large 21 million ton net increase in Soviet grain imports noted in 1972/73 followed only a 13 million ton production shortfall. And while this purchase was still in the process of being delivered, the Soviet Union offered a 2 million ton "loan" of wheat to India, and even suggested a "resale" to the United States, at the much higher market price. Little wonder that after 1972, the United States eventually acted to contain the disruptive effect of these Soviet food trade policies. The five-year grain agreement of October

1975 stabilizes sales by setting a 6–8 million ton lower and upper limit on annual Soviet purchase of wheat and corn from the United States. The possibility of another Soviet "grain robbery," of the kind which upset the world food market in 1972, is now greatly reduced. But, unfortunately, the burden which the USSR places on world food security has not been entirely eliminated.

The Soviet Contribution to World Food Security and Adjustment

While facing new constraints on entry into the world food market, the USSR continues to take something of a "free ride" on the world food system. While others, including the EEC and Japan, discuss new means to exchange information, to promote Third World agricultural development, to increase food aid to hungry poor countries, and to rebuild world food stocks, the USSR prefers to stand aside.

The Soviet Union did send representatives to the 1974 Rome World Food Conference. But it still refuses to join the international agency most directly concerned with ongoing food issues, the Food and Agriculture Organization (FAO). The Soviets remain outside the FAO at least partly to escape the information-sharing obligations of that organization. For example, they have refused to participate in the new Global Information and Early Warning System established in November 1974 under the aegis of the FAO. The Soviet Union sends observers to FAO conferences to learn what they can about the agricultural policies and prospects of others, but they decline to participate themselves.

The Soviet Union has also refused to join other common food management efforts which grew out of the Rome Conference. The most important of these, and so far the most tangible result of that conference, is the $1 billion International Fund for Agricultural Development (IFAD). The Fund has so far received a pledge of financial support from both the OECD and from the OPEC nations, but it receives no support at all from the USSR which has acceded only to those World Food Council proposals which have no budgetary implications.

The Soviet Union is a member of the London International Wheat Council. But Soviet participation in the council, especially in its discussion of a proposed international grain reserve system, begun in 1975, is quite limited. It has enjoyed opportunities, however, to exacerbate U.S.-European Community differences over the uncertain jurisdiction of the council, as opposed to the GATT, over grain reserve schemes. All the while, the Soviets refuse to discuss their own grain reserve policy. They consider that policy to be an element of their strategic posture, and not a matter subject to international discussion or inspection, let alone control.[8]

Unfortunately, efforts to create world food reserves without Soviet participation are less likely to provide adequate security. As the world's largest and most irregular producer of wheat, and as the world's most disruptive grain trading nation, the Soviet Union has a special obligation to share in the financial burden of carrying an international grain reserve. Further, as a developed nation second in wealth and industrial capacity only to the United States, the Soviet Union surely has some obligation to contribute to Third World agricultural development. At the very least, the Soviet Union should be expected to share adequate "early warning" information on its own agricultural performance and import needs. But the Soviet Union has denied having such obligations. By refusing to participate in common global efforts at food policy management, the Soviet Union narrows the range for cooperation among those who do participate.

The USSR, among the wealthy food-importing nations, has introduced the greatest disruption into the international grain market, and has also made the smallest contribution to collective efforts to recover food security and to restore price stability. The Soviet Union, as a very large industrial nation unblessed with adequate natural agricultural resources, is reluctant to modify its own farm policies, and is ill-disposed to join international efforts at food policy cooperation. Yet it is equally impatient to achieve dietary affluence, and just wealthy enough to do so by disruptive entry into the world food market, frequently at the expense of more needy and more reliable customers. In different measure, the EEC and Japan have also added to world food problems by taking something of a free ride on the world's food system, through protective policies which force trade and production adjustments onto others. But during the recent period of food scarcity, these nations did seek to moderate import needs, they did extend assistance to poor food deficit nations, they did share information on their own agricultural performance, and they have joined in efforts at multilateral food policy management. By contrast, the USSR sought to increase its commercial access to the food supplies of others while contributing little to the maintenance of those supplies.

CONCLUSION AND RECOMMENDATIONS

Any conclusion which looks to the immediate future must be hedged against the enormous changeability of the world food market. Several years of good weather have restored that market to its traditional state of oversupply. Still, the more critical danger of scarcity can reemerge with only one or two years of bad weather. Under such changeable conditions, the policies of the wealthy food-importing nations must be judged along several dimensions at once. Policies which contribute the most to the world food "security" in times of scarcity may be incompatible with those which guarantee efficient production and harmonious trade in times of abundance. Alternatively, the politically motivated policies of some wealthy food-importing nations may contribute neither to food security, nor to efficiency, nor to harmonious trade. Under such various circumstances, three different kinds of remedial action can be imagined: multilateral, bilateral, and unilateral action.

Multilateral Measures: A Global Grain Reserve

A majority of the 134 nations at the 1974 World Food Conference accepted a resolution which called for creation of nationally held world grain reserves, to restore security and stability to the world food market. The creation of such reserves was to require participation from all of those wealthy food-importing nations that held a strong interest in market stability and security. The United States underlined this requirement in September 1975 by proposing to the International Wheat Council in London a reserve plan with shares calculated from trade volume, GNP [Gross National Product], and production variability. This was a formula clearly designed to require heavy participation from the EEC, Japan, and the USSR. This U.S. plan did not meet with wide or immediate approval. World carryover stocks were increased in 1976 and 1977 in the absence of any specific multilateral commitments.

Of course, a multilateral commitment to share the burden of reserve accumulation does not have to await the unlikely approval of all wealthy food-importing nations. An agreement could be reached with limited participation, prohibiting release of stocks to "nonmembers" in times of shortage. But such a restriction would immediately require multiple pricing systems, complicated control over end use of grain shipments, and extraordinary membership discipline. In times of tight supply, participating nations would be heavily pressured by domestic farm interests to release some of their stocks for lucrative commercial sale to a wealthy paying customer such as the USSR. In practice, a restrictive system might discriminate against the USSR just enough to create diplomatic problems for the United States, which would be the principal "enforcing" state, but not enough to protect reserve stocks from Soviet purchasing power—the worst of both worlds.

In the face of such difficulties, major participants in the world food system have not yet placed full reliance upon any system of multilateral grain reserve management. For that matter, they have made little or no progress toward the multilateral reduction of barriers to harmonious food trade. Seeking a second best solution, greater reliance has been placed upon "bilateral" food security, food trade, and even food aid agreements. The most dramatic example is the previously mentioned 1975 Moscow agreement.

Bilateral Measures: A Second Look at the Moscow Agreement

The October 1975 United States-Soviet agreement, and also the August 1975 food trade understanding reached between the United States and Japan, seem to provide an alternative model for dealing with wealthy food-importing nations. The understanding with Japan was intended to reassure that nation of its access to the U.S. market, and to underscore what has long been Japan's policy, as well as the policy of the EEC, to signal food import needs well in advance. Since 1975 the United States has extended similar bilateral assurances to Rumania, Poland, and Israel. The U.S.-Soviet agreement is a more ambitious measure. Its purpose is not merely to stabilize trade, or to restrict Soviet access to U.S. supplies in times of scarcity. By placing a 6 million ton *lower limit* on annual Soviet purchases, it also seeks to pressure the Soviet Union into carrying a larger share of the world's food reserves in times of abundance. That is, it seeks to accomplish through bilateral restriction precisely what has so far defied multilateral management.

In this respect, the success of the 1975 Moscow agreement is by no means assured. In their 1976–80 five-year plan, the Soviets have budgeted 3.5 billion rubles to construct 34 million tons of new off-farm grain elevator storage capacity. This is a promising sign. Yet the bilateral agreement does not control Soviet grain exports, which could be increased in times of abundance in lieu of still greater grain storage efforts at home. Subsidized exports to Eastern Europe or to other overseas customers could throw the stockpiling burden back upon the United States.

Moreover, it is not clear that the hasty negotiation of the Moscow agreement (partially undertaken in vain hope that Russia might offer low priced petroleum in return for a lifting of the temporary U.S. grain embargo) fits neatly into any larger vision of a viable international food-trading regime. With the further proliferation of bilateral trade agreements, the world food system might lose a valuable degree of its own internal freedom. Larger price and supply fluctuations would be forced onto those states not protected by agreements of their own. It is not for nothing that the United States, for example, sought to avoid such agreements over most of the past 30 years.

In truth, it is hard to imagine any low cost means, bilateral or otherwise, to pressure the USSR into a stronger contribution to global food security. Despite its recent high volume of imports, the USSR remains largely self-sufficient in food supplies. Even before the record harvest of 1976, over the four-year period of scarcity which included the massive import years of 1972 and 1975, Soviet *domestic* grain production was sufficient to satisfy 92 percent of all national requirements. External food supplies are convenient to Soviet planners, particularly when they can be purchased on U.S. credit at prices held low by export subsidies, as in

1972. But the USSR, the world's largest producer of wheat, is scarcely vulnerable to a bilateral or multilateral "food weapon."

Unilateral Measures: Burdens and Blessings of Self-Reliance

Multilateral and bilateral policy measures are those which enjoy greatest favor among today's outward looking architects of a new global food regime. Yet outward looking policies are not generally favored by the wealthy food-importing members of such a regime. The EEC, for example, considers its own inward-looking agricultural policies to be nonnegotiable. The Japanese also pay close attention to the domestic political aspects of farm policy, and have acquired certain suspicions concerning food-trade interdependence. The Soviet Union remains aloof from all multilateral food management schemes. In different measure, each of these wealthy food customers prefers to tend to its own internal needs, and to force most adjustment burdens onto others.

These introverted and "unilateral" industrial nation food policies may distress those with global perspectives. But they are at the same time a predictable feature of today's world food regime. The world food system, after all, is not yet characterized by the same advanced degree of interdependence that exists, for example, in the world energy system. Over the period 1970–75, despite high absolute volumes of international food trade, only about one-eighth of the world's grain production entered the world food market. The rest was grown, harvested, stored, marketed, and consumed, entirely within national or community borders, not across borders. Since most states, including wealthy importing states, are largely self-reliant in basic food supplies, it is easier for them to give priority to unilateral, self-directed food policies.

Fortunately, unilateral and self-directed food policies are not always destructive of world food security. In the case of the EEC, concern for the political and economic interests of farming populations at home did contribute to increased production, and in times of scarcity, to food security abroad. The protective policies of the EEC have built a sometimes useful redundancy into the world's food production system. In similar fashion, Japan's rice support program has prevented that nation from becoming excessively dependent upon overseas supply in times of scarcity. Of course, the USSR has not demonstrated a similar concern for the security of its own farming population. The Soviet political system is much less responsive to the needs of its own rural sector. In part for this reason, its unilateral policies are much less compatible with a secure international food regime.

Looking to the future, it is likely that progress toward global food security will continue to be made largely through unilateral (national or regional) food policy initiatives. These must include stockpiling initiatives in North America and production initiatives in the Third World. The EEC, Japan, and the USSR may neither join nor challenge these initiatives; they have emerged from the recent experience of food shortages convinced, as always, in the logic of self-protection and self-help. This introverted policy perspective undoubtedly continues to diminish prospects for free and perfectly harmonious world food trade. But it can scarcely be otherwise. Global food policy adjustment will not soon replace domestic political adjustment as the most cherished policy objective of most national policy leaders. Thankfully, these domestic policy objectives remain tolerably compatible, in most instances, with the security and stability of a somewhat compartmentalized world food system.

NOTES

1. The enlarged Community imports twice as much food as all of the nonmember states of the Western European region combined. Western European nations outside of the EEC, such as Spain, Portugal, and Greece, are increasing their food imports more rapidly, but the EEC itself still dominates the import trade of the region.

2. While the United States failed to negotiate a reduction of barriers to agricultural trade in the Kennedy Round of the GATT negotiations, the United States at least did persuade the EEC to enter into the 1967 Food Aid Convention, which pledged the EEC to contribute more than 20 percent to a 5 million ton food aid program for developing countries.

3. Average farm size has increased since World War II by only .2 acres, and 74 percent of the Japanese agricultural labor force now consists of women or of males over 60 years of age. Farm households survive, typically, by seeking more than half of their income from employment beyond agriculture. The Japanese government has recently emphasized the need to contain this situation by developing more farming operations by "full time male farmers."

4. Japan's distant water fishing activities are now coming under the restriction of national coastal fishing waters which extend out to 200 miles. Nearly half of Japan's distant water catch has been taken within 200 miles of other nations' shores, most conspicuously the United States and the USSR.

5. As early as 1901, Lenin set forth the orthodox view of agrarian questions: "To attempt to save the peasantry would mean a useless hindrance to social development."

6. Politburo member Gennadi Voronov saw his career come to a premature close in 1973, for having championed the agricultural reform policies of Ivan Khudenko, who had actually demonstrated that decentralization could increase productivity. Khudenko himself was accused of embezzlement in a rigged trial and died in a prison hospital in 1974.

7. Following the demise of Polyansky, the People's Republic of China taunted the Soviets with the observation that "During the 23 year period admin-

istered by Khrushchev and Brezhnev, a total of 8 ministers of agriculture have been dismissed from office—one scapegoat in less than every three years."

8. It is widely assumed that the USSR holds large underground "war reserves" of grain which may not be drawn down in peacetime.

20

World Food: Failure of Productivist Solutions

Jacques Choncho

THE FOOD SITUATION IN THE THIRD WORLD BEFORE THE ROME CONFERENCE

In 1972, a serious food crisis was revealed before international public opinion: for the first time since the 1950s, there was a shortfall in food output. Production of cereals had fallen by 33 million tons, while needs were growing at an annual rate of 25 million tons. This abrupt drop created an acute deficit at the same time that large cereal-exporting countries like the United States were pursuing production-control policies to avoid a slump in world market prices.

Reserve stocks of wheat, rice, and secondary cereals shrank to a critical low, triggering a rapid rise in prices through 1973 and 1974 despite bumper harvests in 1973. During the same period, prices of other food products rose steeply. This created grave problems for many Third World countries, several of which were heavily dependent on food imports to cover their needs and which, in addition, suffered balance of payments difficulties. It should be remembered that 1973 was also the year of the sudden hike in prices of oil and fertilizers. And finally, because of rising food prices and dwindling reserves, multilateral and bilateral aid to the poorest countries was cut back.

All these developments together led the international community to reexamine the world food situation, especially with respect to Third World countries. This examination brought to light a set of facts which

---

Reprint of "World Food: Failure of Productivist Solutions," Jacques Choncho, *Development & Socio-Economic Progress* (Afro-Asian Peoples' Solidarity Organisation, Issue No. 15, April–June 1981). Pp. 58–69.

made for a grim food outlook for their population, particularly the economically less-favored groups among them.

For example, it was found that while between 1952 and 1962 the average annual rate of increase in food output per person was 0.7 percent in Third World countries as a whole, between 1962 and 1972 the rate dropped to 0.3 percent.[1]

Of 97 Third World countries whose food situation was studied in 1970, 61 had an overall deficit in relation to their needs. In those following a capitalist economy, undernourishment—calculated in terms of very modest criteria—affected more than 400 million people. If more rigorous criteria were used, this figure would be considerably higher.[2]

A very important factor which contributed to the increase in the price of cereals was that they had become more and more in demand to serve the meat consumption needs of industrialized countries. These countries, whose populations represent 30 percent of the world population, consumed 51 percent of all cereals consumed by the world between 1969 and 1971. The 370 million tons of cereal used by these countries as fodder exceeded the consumption of the populations of China and India combined, i.e., 1.5 billion people representing 40 percent of the world population.

This situation, plus the gravity of the crisis of 1972–73, led the international community to try and define a new food policy. To this end, the World Food Conference was held in Rome, under UN auspices, from 5 to 16 November 1974.

THE ROME CONFERENCE AND ITS MAIN RESOLUTIONS

The objectives of the conference can be said to have focused on four main sets of measures:

- Measures to increase food production in so-called "developing" countries
- Policies and programs to improve the food situation of their populations
- Actions to enhance world food security
- Policies of trade, stabilization, and readjustment.

The results of the conference are expressed in a declaration for "the final elimination of hunger and malnutrition," followed by 22 resolutions. The declaration is very general, a statement of intent, as it were, that no one can refuse but which does not contain any firm commitments.

About a dozen of the resolutions deal with actions on the national and international levels to raise food production in the Third World and to upgrade the nutritional standard of its populations. They define objectives and strategies of food production, the priorities to be accorded to agriculture and rural development, the need to step up aid and increase production of fertilizers, programs of food and agricultural research and popularization, the need to draw up an agrological map of the world showing soil nature and output potential, expansion of irrigation systems and scientific distribution of water, facilities for the obtaining of insecticides and seeds, etc.

In addition, the conference agreed to establish a number of institutions and to reinforce existing ones which would assure action in the area of food security, better food aid, and more agricultural investments in the Third World. Eight such institutions were established or reinforced:

1. **The World Food Council**—to integrate and coordinate follow-up of conference resolutions.
2. **The International Fund for Agricultural Developments**—to help finance projects for agricultural development and food production in the Third World.
3. **The Committee for World Food Security**—to evaluate perspectives of demand, supply, and reserves of principal food products and to propose solutions to potential critical situations.
4. **The Committee for Food Aid and Programs**—for intergovernmental consultations in connection with bilateral or multilateral food aid programs.
5. **The Advisory Group on Food Production and Investment**—to encourage a greater inflow of external resources to reinforce food production.
6. **The International Information and Warning System on Food and Agriculture**—to supervise the activities of different national and international agencies and to facilitate the establishment of an information system on climatic conditions which can affect the international food situation.
7. **The Advisory Group for International Agriculture Research**—to support research activities of agricultural research centers in the Third World.
8. **The International Commitment for World Food Security**—to establish cooperation in building up reserve stocks of staple food products, especially cereals, in order to counter potential problems of supply and to reduce fluctuation in production and prices.

POSTCONFERENCE DEVELOPMENTS AND EVOLUTION OF THE WORLD FOOD SITUATION BETWEEN 1975 AND 1978

The successful implementation of this plan of action to improve the world food situation and security obviously depended on the political will of governments: those of the Third World, on the one hand, to embark on the steps required to increase food production and raise the nutritional standard of the poorest groups of their populations; those of the industrialized countries, on the other, to help them realize these objectives through investments and the transfer of technology. It was evident that the real problem was not so much one of technology as it was one of the political will to implement the recommendations and resolutions issued by the conference.

This paper will not attempt to give a detailed assessment of postconference developments, which can be found in a number of documents. Rather, it will set out to trace and analyze the broad lines of the world food situation as it evolved between 1975 and 1978 and to ascertain how far its evolution was influenced by the conference resolutions.

At first glance, the food situation in Third World countries would appear to have improved greatly after 1974. Indeed, the FAO [Food and Agriculture Organization] index of fluctuation in food production for the Third World as a whole rose from minus 0.8 percent per capita (the annual average in the years 1970–1974) to plus 0.6 percent (between 1974 and 1978). The increase in food production was particularly marked in the Far East (from − 1.0 to + 1.5) and in Latin America (from − 0.3 to + 0.7). Only a moderate increase was recorded for Africa (from − 1.8 to − 1.4), while in the Middle East food production figures actually fell (from + 0.2 to − 0.4). In the socialist countries of Asia, too, food output per person declined (from + 1.1 to + 0.9).

On the other hand, thanks to a number of bumper harvests, food stocks were replenished, rising from 107 million tons in 1973–74 to 178 million tons in 1977–78, equivalent to nearly 20 percent of world consumption. These figures do not include food reserves held by the Soviet Union and China.

Finally, the inflow of investments to support greater agricultural production in the Third World grew considerably, rising from a total of 2.5 billion dollars in 1973 to nearly 4.3 billion in 1977, thanks mainly to initiatives by international financial organizations.

However, these positive signs were accompanied by a number of negative signs. On the one hand, Third World countries had to go on increasing imports at a very rapid pace to meet their food needs. To take their wheat and secondary cereal imports, for example, these rose from 28 million tons a year (the average in 1969 to 1971) to 48 million tons in 1974 to 68 million tons in 1977–78, of which food aid amounted to no more than 9 million tons.

On the other hand, despite the exceptionally good harvests of the last few years and increased imports, the food situation of the poorest groups among Third World populations continues to deteriorate. According to FAO, even with the use of very modest criteria to measure malnutrition, the number of undernourished people in these countries swelled from 400 million in 1969–71 to 455 million in 1972–74. These figures represent nearly 30 percent of the total population in Africa and the Far East and over 15 percent in Latin America and the Middle East.

Using different criteria, the World Bank places the number of malnutrition victims in the Third World at over 1 billion.

Thus while granting that the recent bumper harvest boosted food production in the Third World and that food imports increased, the fact remains that the goal which the Rome Conference had set itself, namely, to liberate the world from hunger and malnutrition in ten years (i.e., by 1985), has not only drawn no closer but, if anything, seems to have receded still further.

Nor does the prospect of attaining an annual average growth rate of 4 percent in food production seem to be any closer. Between 1974 and 1978 food production in the Third World rose by 3.1 percent on the global level and by an average 0.6 percent per capita.

In attempting to assess postconference developments, therefore, it would be safe to conclude that despite some progress in the area of food production[3] and agricultural investments, the world food situation has not improved. For a substantial portion of Third World populations, namely, the poorest urban and rural inhabitants, the situation has steadily worsened, leading one to question whether the resolutions passed by the conference were in fact the best possible and if they were sufficient to attain their objective: the suppression of hunger and malnutrition in the world.

CONDITIONS FOR A FOOD POLICY

The answer to the above question can only be a negative one. The resolutions, which focused exclusively on raising production, increasing agricultural investments, stepping up food aid, and adjusting marked supply and demand, failed to take into sufficient account problems of food consumption which depend on many other factors, perhaps even more important than those of production or trade. This raises a fundamental question, namely, What do food systems depend on and what are the factors which determine these systems? What are the components of a food system in a given country? It is only on the basis of such an analysis that a sound food policy can be defined.

To begin with, taking each country as a comprehensive whole does not seem to be the best approach to such an analysis as it would tend to blur the sharp disparities which exist between the various groups making up the population of the same country. This is all the more true for Third World countries, where the food situation varies considerably from one income bracket to another and between urban and rural localities, than it is for industrialized countries, where food systems tend to be much more homogeneous for the population as a whole.

An analysis of this kind should depart, rather, from the premise of a given population, either on a national, regional or local level. This would make for a better grasp of the components of that population's food system.

Looking at things from this angle would entail taking two sets of factors into account: those which influence the food availability of the population on the one hand and those which influence its food consumption on the other.

Among the factors influencing availability are food production of the territory on which the population lives, storage and conservation of food products throughout the year, exports and imports of food products from and to the region, and distribution systems not only of imported food products but also of regional produce.

As for the factors which, over and above availability of food, determine the pattern of its consumption, these constitute a mesh of complex elements which must be taken into account. They include the rate of population growth, levels and distribution of income (by social class and by urban or rural zone), nutritional practice and changes in eating habits induced by the cultural, economic, and commercial influence of dominant countries, and, finally, the relationship between differences in food costs on the one hand and differences in income levels of the majority of the population on the other.

It is only by considering all these factors with respect to a given population and not by simply increasing availability of types of food products favored by the populations of rich Western countries that the problem of undernourishment and hunger can be effectively resolved.

In light of the above, then, a look at the specific reality prevailing in most Third World countries would show that a set of factors operates to impede the satisfaction of food needs for the poorest groups of the population. Thus in order to solve the food problems of these populations, it is necessary to act on these factors, which are the real obstacles to be overcome.

Obstacles in the Way of Food Availability

The four most formidable obstacles having a negative impact on food availability for the populations of these countries are:

First, the production system established under colonial domination and largely maintained, if not actually reinforced, in the postcolonial period, gives **priority to export agricultural products** rather than to traditional food products consumed by the majority of the indigenous population. Within this system, the best land, irrigation systems, the bulk of available capital, technological resources, and state support are mobilized to serve export products at the expense of cultivating food crops.

Even those governments stressing national autonomy and adopting firm stands against big-power imperialism strive for development in terms of world market demand; in other words, being competitive means exporting as much as possible as cheaply as possible, whether in the way of traditional export agricultural products cultivated during the colonial period or new agricultural products promoted today by the agro-industry of the industrialized countries.

As a result, internal food production lags behind growing needs and food imports are stepped up to cover the shortfall. This places an increasingly heavy burden on the balance of trade and renders global food systems still more fragile.

A second obstacle can be found in those countries dominated by capitalist economic systems, i.e., where the determining factor is the purchasing power of minority groups weighing most heavily on the market. This obstacle is **the lack of support for internal food production** except when it relates to an urban market important in terms of the monetary weight of its privileged middle class. In this case food is produced for the internal market, using modern techniques imported from the West which are very costly from the point of view of any combination of available resources. At the same time, food costs climb steeply because the transformation process was effected by an agro-food industry modelled on that of industrialized countries, whose main objective is to increase the industrial and service added value in relation to the agricultural value of these products. The types of food products thus processed are sold on the market at prices which place them beyond the reach of the poorest groups at a time when these groups see their quota of food shrinking.

A third obstacle is the considerable **postharvest loss** sustained because of inadequate storage and conservation facilities and an inefficient distribution system. According to experts, these losses range from a minimum of 10 percent for the cereal and vegetable harvest to a minimum of 20 percent for other basic crops and perishable foodstuffs. A modest estimate places the losses incurred by the Third World as a whole at 107 million tons of food products in 1976. The loss in cereals and vegetables alone is enough to cover the food needs of 163 million people.

And, finally, the fourth obstacle limiting the availability of food in most Third World countries is the shortage of **distribution facilities.** Even where no financial difficulties stand in the way of covering food deficits through importation (as in the case of OPEC members), a marked deficiency in harbor, storage, and transportation systems severely inhibits its distribution to the whole population, particularly rural communities living furthest from the ports.

Influence on Consumption

Among the factors affecting consumption and preventing the generalized satisfaction of minimal food requirements, particularly as relates to the poorest groups of the population, the following must be cited:

In the first place, there is the **insufficiency of income and the very sharp inequalities in its distribution.** This is organically linked to the problem of underdevelopment and weak productivity of the jobs available to the great majority of the active population. **There is no question but that it is here that the main obstacle to improving the world food situation lies, and not in the insufficiency of food production.**

The underemployment and underproductivity of the bulk of active populations in Third World countries derive in turn from the expansion and penetration into these countries' economies of the model of capitalist growth, which is developing today in a very different socioeconomic context from that which characterized industrialized capitalist countries at similar stages in the process of capitalist accumulation. The main differences lie in a greatly accelerated pace of population and work force growth, in the technology-intensive use of capital and in the trend to [employ] fewer, more highly skilled, workers.

This means that only a small portion of the active population is absorbed into the modern productive sector, while the rest remain on the fringe, working either as landless farmers in impermanent and insecure jobs, as agricultural producers cultivating tiny parcels of land incapable of meeting their minimal needs, as urban subproletariat working when they can in what is sometimes called the "informal urban sector,"[4] in domestic service or as small tradesmen. Because of the low level and insecurity of their incomes, these poor sections of the population are unable to satisfy their basic food needs, and it is among them and their families that malnutrition and undernourishment are found.

A case in point is India. A country which can boast the tenth national product in the world, where 100 million fundamentally urban men live at levels of productivity as advanced as the most industrialized in the world, India is also the country where 540 million poor live in conditions which have changed little over the centuries. True, Indian agriculture has made enormous progress in recent years, producing a record cereal harvest in 1978 of 125 million tons, more than adequate for the food needs of its population. The country has quadrupled its production of fertilizers in ten years and expanded the area of irrigated land by 50 percent. But despite all this progress, millions of Indians remain victims of malnutrition.

In 1971–72, 15 percent of urban and rural family units consumed less than 2,000 calories per person per day because of insufficient incomes. Food consumption within the same country can vary considerably **according to the level of development of the different regions and between rural and urban localities.**

In the case of Brazil, for example, a comparison between the food situation prevailing among the inhabitants of the northeast and that prevailing in the south shows that 48 percent of the family units in the urban northeast consume an average of less than 2,000 calories per person per day, while in the rural northeast 57 percent consume less than 2,140 calories.[5] In the south, on the other hand, only 15 percent of family units consume less than 2,000 calories per person per day and, according to statistics, all rural family units in the south consume more than 2,000. Again, this is linked to the level and distribution of income among the populations of these regions. It would thus be wrong to suppose that a simple increase in food production even of the annual rate of 4 percent recommended by the Rome Conference can solve the problem of malnutrition among the poor of the Third World countries adopting a market economy if development policies do not face up to this vital problem.

Another fundamental factor affecting food consumption and consolidating still further the effects analyzed above is the **penetration and extension of the food system or model of the industrialized countries into Third World countries,** thanks to which the agro-industrial multinational companies occupy a choice position. As demonstrated in a well-documented study by Susan George, the food system propagated by these companies, which has attained its most advanced form in the United States, has infiltrated the food systems of the Third World where it is developing with varying degrees of success. In its bid to become the system in universal usage, it brings all its financial, ideological, and technical power to bear. To this end it employs various complementary means, such as the propagation of certain cultural practices like those of the "Green Revolution." Linked to this is the creation of new markets to absorb the technologies produced directly by the transnationals or under their control. Another means is to change the food habits of peripheral countries through the use of publicity and food aid. This is related in turn to the elaboration of ever more sophisticated food production as a way to increase the industrial and service added value, where the bulk of profits is made. More and more expensive types of food are thus produced at prices way beyond the purchasing power of the popular masses. As this type of food develops in the Third World, the situation of the poor masses is deteriorating instead of improving. Many examples can be cited here but perhaps the most notorious is that involving the promotion of powdered milk formulas as a substitute for breast-feeding. Many too are the examples where replacing traditional foods or beverages by so-called "modern" products has led to a drop in the food situation of Third World populations. It can be maintained then that with the penetration of these food habits, the poor are paying more to eat less. This represents a grave problem for people whose incomes force them to live at a bare subsistence level and today constitutes one of the main reasons why the number of malnourished people in the world is increasing.

The foregoing analysis serves as an indicator of what actions should be taken in the Third World if it is to become self-sufficient in food.

A POLICY OF SELF-SUFFICIENCY IN FOOD

This does not imply, as some people might think, producing on a national, regional, or local level all the food needs of the population living on that territory. To confine oneself thus within given boundaries would be too costly and is conceivable only in exceptional circumstances (as during wars or when it is physically impossible to transact with the outside world) or for isolated communities living in completely self-contained systems.

What a policy of self-sufficiency in food does entail, on the contrary, is to strike a harmonious balance between several variables which must be integrated and coordinated in terms of the specific situation of each population.

These variables are the following:

1. A system of food production and rural development that would not involve a further marginalization of the peasant masses as producers and consumers. That is to say, a system capable of producing food while at the same time creating the productive jobs required to assure adequate incomes for the population as a whole. This would lead to a complete reexamination of the relations which now prevail in the Third World between available land—jobs to be provided—technologies to be used—types of productivity to promote.
2. A system of food production that would optimize the use of resources available for food production. To this end, it must take into account the nature of the soil, its suitability for different crops, the influence of climatic factors, and existing facilities (e.g., irrigation). A study should be undertaken to determine which food products can provide maximum calories and proteins for a given population, keeping in mind the different options possible, the food habits of that population, and the average income of the majority of the popular masses. Thus the types of food produced in the industrialized and temperate countries of the West would not be sought after per se because it is considered modern, especially with respect to populations living in tropical zones.
3. A system of food consumption and distribution which would try to minimize postharvest losses through the use of methods which are economically compatible with the country's economic development and which would assure control of harvests by the producers themselves and

by consumers' associations and not by powerful middlemen who exploit both producers and consumers.

4. A system of relations between variations in income levels on the one hand and in production and distribution costs on the other, to make satisfaction of basic food needs possible in terms of levels of income enjoyable by the majority of the population.

NOTES

1. In Third World countries following a capitalist economy the rate went down to 0.2 percent.

2. [. . .], according to Professor Joseph Klatzmann, the number of undernourished people in the world from the point of view of inadequate intake of calories and proteins comes to about 2 billion, most of whom are found in Asia.

3. Due mainly to natural and transient factors independent of human volition, like favorable climatic conditions.

4. Enterprises created by independent workers, of limited size and capital, using traditional technologies, etc.

5. Although these maxima are not strictly comparable given the manner in which the statistics are presented, they are nevertheless quite close.

21

Asian Agriculture: A Decade of Failure

Frank Peacock

The past few years have seen a food surplus in parts of Asia, a sharp contrast to the earlier part of this decade. To many, this might appear to be the promise of the "Green Revolution" coming true at last. A recent study by the Asian Development Bank, now published as *Rural Asia: Challenge and Opportunity,* shows how far from the truth this is. Examining the decade 1967–77 the survey finds that food production has barely kept pace with population growth in the area surveyed,[1] on top of which the poor in these countries are getting poorer and nutritional levels are falling. Looking at the past ten years the report states: "Overall, the most optimistic view which can be taken of the food situation is that the region is not much worse off now than at the time of the first Asian Agricultural Survey."

The extent of the failure is indicated by Table 1; looking at the first three columns of figures we can see that in aggregate, food production increased between 1953–57 and 1970–74, but if we look at the other three columns, which relate the increased food production to increased population, the picture is not nearly as clear. In some countries production has increased on a per capita basis, in some it has been close to static, while in yet others it has actually declined. This obviously brings into question the success or otherwise of the Green Revolution, but before this can be examined, it is worth determining what the objectives of the Green Revolution are.

Looking through the Asian Development Bank Study one is able to determine four quite separate objectives that the Green Revolution is supposed to achieve. These are:

Reprint of "Asian Agriculture: A Decade of Failure" by Frank Peacock in *Asian Profile* (Vol. 8, No. 5, October 1980). Reprinted by permission of the Asian Research Service, Hong Kong.

TABLE 1 Indices of Food Production and Per Capita Food Production for Selected DMCs, 1953–57 to 1970–74

Country	Food Production			Per Capita Food Production		
	1953–57[a]	1963–67	1970–74	1953–57	1963–67	1970–74
South Asia						
Afghanistan	100[b]	125	135	104[b]	104	94
India	103	125	152	104	99	103
Nepal	100[b]	96	105	96[b]	79	74
Pakistan[c]	102	133	n.a.	100	97	n.a.
Sri Lanka	100	149	169	98	114	109
Southeast Asia						
Burma	99	133	145	97	108	100
Cambodia	112[a]	155	137	105[b]	116	91
Indonesia	103	122	159	101	95	102
Malaysia (West)	105	158	252	102	113	150
Philippines	104	145	183	101	102	102
Thailand	100	161	202	97	116	116
East Asia						
China, Republic of	105	153	180[d]	102	105	103
Korea	110	168	198	108	126	125

[a]Annual average for the period shown.

[b]Average of 1956–57.

[c]Includes Bangladesh.

[d]Estimated on the assumption that the rate of increase in food production between 1969 and 1974 was the same as the change in the agricultural production index reported in *Taiwan Statistical Yearbook, 1975.*

Source: Asian Development Bank, *Rural Asia: Challenge and Opportunity* (New York: Praeger, 1978), Table 1.2.2. (p. 39). DMCs are developing member (of the Asian Development Bank) countries.

1. To increase the output of cereal grains. This is the first and most obvious objective, indeed at the time of the first Asian Agricultural Survey (1967) this was seen as the explicit objective, with all other problems somehow being solved by this increased output.
2. To increase the income of poor farmers, through the increase in output. This is an objective that has become increasingly important in this decade as the extent of rural poverty has at last been realized.
3. To increase the calorific intake of the population in the countries of Asia. An objective of major importance in view of the fact that the Asian region has the highest percentage of people with inadequate protein/energy in the world.
4. To save the foreign exchange that is at present going to buy imported food grains.

A number of assumptions are implicit in these above objectives, the first of these is that hunger in the poorer countries of Asia is a supply problem, i.e., people are hungry because insufficient food is produced. The second is that increased farm output will lead to increased farm incomes and the third assumption is that all of the above four objectives are compatible.

The Green Revolution itself is essentially the imposition of modern farming technology and methods onto the existing traditional structure. A traditional structure consists largely of subsistence farming with the owner or tenant growing food primarily for the use of himself and his family. This subsistence farming is very small-scale; in Bangladesh, India, Indonesia, Korea, and Sri Lanka, more than half of the land holdings are 1 hectare or less in size. Throughout Asia another feature of agriculture is share tenancy with from one-half to two-thirds of the crop being paid in rent to the owner of land. To this traditional agriculture the Green Revolution brings the use of selected, high yielding seeds, careful tilling and planting, fertilizers, pesticides, and herbicides, and properly controlled irrigation. All of these are inputs into the farming process that have been used in the developed countries for years. The Green Revolution attempts to adopt them to Asian conditions. For the Asian farmer to change to this new technology requires some major changes, one of the most important being the use of cash inputs.

Traditional agriculture requires few, if any, purchased inputs. It tends to rely on the use of land, labor, seeds retained from the previous harvest, and the inputs provided by nature: sun and water. The new techniques are, by comparison, costly in cash terms requiring the purchase of fertilizers, herbicides, selected seeds, and irrigation water. In many cases mechanical tillage has also been used. Governments in most of the Asian countries have realized the difficulty of the changes involved together with the costs faced by the farmers if they are to convert to the new technology, and, often with the help of funds from the multilateral lending agencies, have sought to subsidize the inputs and provide credit through government institutions. In dispensing these resources to agriculture, the governments appear to have favored the larger, rather than the small farmer.

The authors of the survey claim that Green Revolution technology is scale neutral, and, in the strict sense of measuring inputs and outputs in terms of a production function, it probably is. Therefore the size of the area farmed has no bearing on the adoption of the new technology nor on the benefits that accrue from that technology. However, farming does not operate in a vacuum, it takes place within a social structure, and one where, in most Asian countries, the ownership of land is of major importance. The large landowner holds a position of great social status within most rural communities and stemming from that social position often comes a great deal of local political power.[2] As a result of his position it is the large landowner who preempts much of the government resources that are directed toward rural development. This is reinforced by what one could perhaps refer to as "bureaucratic economies of scale." For example, the extension worker may find it far easier to persuade one large farmer to plant 40 acres of high yielding grain than to persuade 40 small farmers to plant 1 acre each. The same sort of scale economy will be equally applicable to other government agencies. Government provision of rural credit has become of increasing importance over the past decade. There is clearly some administrative cost to making this credit available, and this cost will increase for each loan that has to be administered. In fact, the administrative cost of very small loans may be as large as the actual loan. In such a situation there is some sense in restricting the minimum amount lent, and indeed, in favoring larger loans over smaller loans as, for any fixed total of lending, the administrative cost will tend to be lower for a smaller number of large loans, than for a larger number of small loans.

When government credit agencies have made a deliberate effort to lend to the small farmer the result has, in any case, invariably been a very high default rate. A large part of the reason for this is that the small farmer is a subsistence farmer. If credit is made available to him to enable him to adopt new seeds and methods of cultivation, the resulting increased output is likely to be used to increase the food consumption of his family. He therefore generates no cash flows and is in no position to repay the loan. Without the government-provided credit he would not have been able to adopt the new technology at all because of its requirement of cash inputs, but the credit has gone to improve his consumption level, an improvement that will only be maintained with a continuous flow of nonrepayable credit!

What one observes over the past decade is the reinforcement of the position of the large landowner as the result of an increased flow of government and aid funds into the rural sector. Together with this has gone a fundamental change in the pattern of farming in much of Asia. Traditionally, farming in many parts of Asia has consisted of using large inputs of labor to fairly small areas of land. For the large landowner the most efficient way of doing this was generally to parcel his land into small blocks and allow sharecropping. Large government subsidies and the provision of cheap credit, together with the adoption of modern farming technology, have all combined to change this. Commercial farming has become more profitable, and, of more importance, mechanization of farming has been encouraged.

The survey finds that the use of tractors does not increase crop yields, yet in spite of this the use of tractors has increased. The reason for this would appear to be that the price of tractors in many countries has been reduced relative to the price of labor. This is the result of the subsidized credit advanced by government agencies, and the implicit subsidy involved in allowing agricultural machinery into a country duty free or at a preferential exchange rate. The result of such mechanization has been the consolidation of landholdings and a replacement of labor by mechanical cultivation. Consequent to this has been a growth of the landless labor force (by 80 percent in India between 1961 and 1971).

It is worth noting that not only does mechanization not increase the output per hectare but it is, in economic terms, an inefficient production technique. Most of the farming areas of Asia have a scarcity of fertile land, an abundance of labor, and, being in a poor country, a shortage of capital. The production technique that uses the fixed and scarce resource (land) most efficiently is the one that combines it with the large quantities of the most plentiful resource (labor); that is, the traditional labor-intensive method of farming. To replace the labor with the scarce resource of capital, which is what is happening with mechanization, makes no economic sense at all; but such is the implementation of government rural development efforts that this is what is happening.

In terms of the previously identified objectives it is clear that the first of these, increased output, has not been achieved. Looking at the table we can treat the decade prior to 1963–67 as "pre-Green Revolution" and after 1963–67 as "post-Green Revolution." When we look at it this way we see that, with one exception,[3] gains in food output in Asian countries were greater prior to the Green Revolution than after it. In aggregate, the adoption of new technology in Asian farming has not led to a rise in per capita food output. The second objective, that of increasing the income of poor farmers, has clearly not been realized. Insofar as the poorer farmers tend to be tenants rather than landowners, the increasing adoption of mechanized methods of agriculture is causing them to be forced off the land. The increased incomes where they do occur are benefiting the large, already relatively affluent farmers, not the small, poor farmer. The survey finds that rural poverty has worsened over the past decade.

The third objective identified in the report is that of increasing the nutritional level of the population. The survey finds that over the past ten years consumption has remained fairly constant and below requirements in most countries. Within the Asian area 300 million people suffer from food deficiencies. It is fairly obvious that an increased food consumption resulting from increased food output cannot eventuate given the situation where food output per capita has remained static or fallen. However, even in years where, due to a combination of climatic and environmental factors, there have been unusually large harvests, there is little evidence that food intakes improved for the section of the population not directly employed in farming. The reason is that we are not looking at a supply problem at all. We are looking at a problem of effective demand. Many poor people in Asia ". . . simply (are) unable to find an occupation which will bring in enough income to feed themselves or their families."

Regardless of the level of food output, the very poor, the unemployed, the sick, lame, and aged, who do not command sufficient income are unable to buy food. This situation will not alter as long as food is bought and sold. It might be felt that increasing supply would reduce the price of many foods, thus bringing them within the reach of poorer people, but this ignores the cost of production. To increase the output of food using the new technology tends to be expensive. If the result of increasing output is that the price falls, then the technology is likely to be abandoned. Recognizing this, many governments have price support schemes for the farmer. They help in bolstering farm gate prices, but this is at the expense of the consumer. The twin objectives of maintaining farm incomes and increasing nutritional levels (by increasing the supply of food and reducing prices) are basically incompatible. They require the maintenance of farm support alongside food subsidy programs and, regardless of the desirability or otherwise of such a large-scale intervention in the marketplace, to run both schemes is too costly for the governments of poorer countries.

The final objective, that of reducing food imports, could only have been attained if food output had risen dramatically; but it has not. Making the most optimistic assumptions, the survey finds that the food-grain deficit for Asia will be 16.5 million tons by 1985. Less optimistic assumptions give a figure of 35 million tons.

The survey identifies a number of areas in which efforts should be directed over the coming decade if improvements are to be made, but it avoids asking the difficult questions. It recommends land reform but does not address the problem of how this is to come about when most Asian governments have already paid lip service to the idea during a period when the position and wealth of the large landowner has actually been consolidated. The large landowner is today the modern commercial farmer in Asia; he is in receipt of subsidies from government and the multilateral agencies, and where agencies can point to success in the adoption of new technology, it is the large landowner who has visibly achieved this success. He is almost certainly much better off than he was ten years ago, and his position of political importance has, if anything, been consolidated rather than reduced. Having achieved a flow of resources from government that has improved his financial position, he is unlikely to acquiesce to any change in the status quo.

The provision of rural jobs is emphasized in the survey because of its importance in reducing both the growing unemployment and growing poverty among the landless rural labor force. However, the cost of rural public works necessary to absorb such a large part of the work force would not appear to be forthcoming in most Asian countries.

Fundamental to the entire question of rural development and rural poverty however would appear to be whether there is any possibility of a small farmer gaining an income above poverty level by using his land to grow grain. The whole thrust of the Green Revolution was into grain crops, but however high the yield, 1 hectare of land under rice, wheat, or other grain would appear to be a recipe for continuing poverty. The survey, with its emphasis on food grains, tends to skate over this, and never puts the question of whether land-short countries should be producing grains at all or concentrating on higher value crops. Yet the fact that a subsistence economy grows its own food is not evidence that an economy which is aiming to increase the income of its population should be also trying for self–sufficiency in food.

In spite of deficiencies, the survey is possibly one of the most important documents on contemporary development in Asia to be published in this decade. The countries of Asia have, for the most part, agricultural based economies; the social, political, and economic structures of the countries result from this fact. The survey shows that in terms of the objectives set for it the Green Revolution has clearly been a failure. However, in the implementation of modern technology to Asian agriculture, major changes have been wrought, changes that are as radical as anything that has happened in Asia in the recent past. Age-old patterns of agriculture and employment have been destroyed as tractors have replaced labor, and share tenants have been moved from their land to join the army of landless labor. The implications of these changes will be felt way beyond the agricultural sector of the economy. What we have witnessed over the past decade is the start of a change that could be as socially disruptive as the enclosure movement was in England.

NOTES

1. Afghanistan, India, Nepal, Pakistan, Bangladesh, Burma, Cambodia, Laos, Indonesia, Malaysia, the Philippines, Thailand, South Korea, Republic of China (Taiwan).

2. That the ownership of large farms is still of major consequence in Asia is shown by figures given in the survey which show that 31 percent of the land in India is cultivated by 4 percent of the farmers, in the Philippines it is 5 percent of the farmers who cultivate 34 percent of the land, in Pakistan 11 percent who cultivate 43 percent.

3. Malaysia, which using the new technologies has increased grain output considerably.

22

Turning Point in Development: The Food-Energy Pivot

Soedjatmoko

The energy crisis that we now face is not so much one of absolute shortage but one of rising prices, of the struggle for access to and control of energy sources, and of the negative ecological and social impacts resulting from people's response to higher energy costs, especially in the large, populous, low-income countries in the region. It is already quite obvious that those who need energy most will be increasingly marginalized by these higher prices.

The food crisis is above all one of maldistribution and the incapacity of millions of poor people to either produce or buy their staple food. The rising energy prices will have a fourfold negative effect on the food situation:

- Fertilizer and other oil-based inputs will become more expensive; as a result, food prices would become highly sensitive to changes in oil prices.
- Poor people will be forced to resort even more to the predatory exploitation of fuel wood with the accompanying adverse ecological effects for agriculture because of deforestation and destabilization of water supplies.
- Cropland is likely to be shifted to the production of biomass energy, making not only food, but also fiber, more scarce.
- The economic advantages of substituting energy plantations for food crops, which could include new employment opportunities and incomes of many rural people, may also start an inflationary spiral of

---

"Turning Point in Development: The Food-Energy Pivot." Statement by Soedjatmoko to the Inter-Governmental Meeting of Development Assistance Coordinators in Asia and the Pacific, February 23–28, 1981, New Delhi (United Nations Development Program, 1981).

food prices to the extent that mounting oil prices will push biomass energy prices well above the value of food.

Beyond these generalities, the exact impact of rising energy cost on the production and price of food will be different for each country, and remains to be determined through careful research. Also our understanding of the exact social and economic connections between hunger and poverty is generally quite inadequate. We know, to take just one instance, very little about the flow of food through urban centers and the role of cash in it. Also, except if the liquid fuels were made from nonfood crops, or if the energy crops can be produced in addition to meeting consumptive needs in the food and fiber areas, the poor could be adversely affected by energy cropping in several ways—rising food prices due to decreased supplies, less food aid, rising fiber prices (because of reduced production of fiber crops), and possibly decreased security or stability of food supplies (depending upon whether or not priority was given to stability of liquid fuel production).

Neither do we know how higher prices will affect relative prices of different foodstuffs, and their differential impact in terms of nutritional intake on different income groups, especially of the poor in many countries, in both rural and urban areas. A major country-level research effort is therefore required before effective policy instruments can be developed and before the strategic points of policy intervention can be identified with a view to mitigate the negative effects of rising energy cost on food prices and production levels.

Pulling together the various studies that are available regarding the interrelationships between demographic, energy, ecological, and socioeconomic magnitudes, it is possible to draw the outline of a disturbing, emerging scenario that will reach its most critical stage in the coming two decades. This will, I hope, help us in discussing in a larger societal framework of constraints and opportunities the policy and planning dilemmas that we will have to confront during that period.

The fact that world food production in total has so far kept half a step ahead of population growth is a remarkable achievement. But looking ahead to the end of the century the outlook for continuing a sufficient overall supply of food is anything but assured. Using only present modern agricultural methods, our planet could theoretically produce enough food for the 6 billion people who will inhabit the earth in the year 2000. A sustained rate of agricultural growth of 2.7 percent, which is a reasonable extrapolation from present trends, would result in a global output of food grains of 2 billion metric tons by the end of the century. This would meet the projected commercial demand for food, even if high income growth raises the aggregate consumer demand for more and higher quality foods. In other words those who will be able to pay for food will not go hungry. The real problem remains, as it has been since time immemorial, the elimination of hunger caused by poverty, which places commercially available food beyond the reach of hundreds of millions of people. The Food and Agriculture Organization (FAO) considers it both desirable and feasible for the agricultural production of the developing nations (excluding China) to be increased by 107 percent between 1980 and 2000, which implies a considerable acceleration to an annual rate of increase of 3.7 percent. But such an expansion of production requires a total increase of commercial energy use by 380 percent, or about 8 percent annually, and the World Bank has concluded that if this high-growth scenario becomes real there would still be 470 million people living in absolute poverty by the year 2000. Their number could be as high as 710 million if the World Bank's low-growth scenarios materialize.

In this regard it should be pointed out that the global community's dependence on international trade in food grains and petroleum products has not led to food security. Although only about 10 percent of the world's total grain output enters international trade, crop failures in one country can jack up the price of food for all other countries. An American presidential commission on world hunger reported in March 1980 that a global production shortfall of 10 percent could increase the price of rice and wheat 200 percent or more on the world market. The developing countries import currently about 50 million metric tons of food grains. By 1988 their annual deficit of wheat, rice, and coarse grains could reach 85 million metric tons from 50 million at present, and by the year 2000, according to the FAO, developing countries will require imports of 175 million metric tons of food grains.

Such extrapolations do not address either the question of whether foreign exchange earnings, international credits, and food aid will be able to secure such quantities of food for the importing countries, or of the logistics of timely transportation and distribution of food grains around the globe in such unprecedented amounts. Even more disturbing is the likelihood that in the case of a major global shortfall of food grains, the richer and more successful newly industrialized nations, which are able to pay the highest prices, will take the food grains out of reach of the poorest countries through higher bidding. Much of the additional food that is required will therefore have to be produced in the developing countries themselves, even though these countries may continue sharply to increase their imports.

Efforts to increase agricultural production in the face of escalating energy prices place increasing strain on the natural resource base, i.e., land, water, and forests. Assured water supplies for crop growth increase the effectiveness with which the energy inputs (human, solar, and chemical) are used. We are truly privileged to meet in a country that has shown how the production of food grains in a developing country can be increased. No country offers a more impressive example of what the

"Green Revolution" of the 1960s and 1970s could achieve than India, whose stunning successes in crop increases deserve our admiration and respect. Still the Green Revolution with its reliance on energy-intensive inputs appears to be reaching its peak, as the price of petroleum limits the capacity of developing countries to provide fertilizers, pesticides, and equipment for their agriculture, and as their irrigation systems are nearing capacity.

Besides these inherent problems of energy-intensive agriculture, an even more pernicious negative synergism is threatening the developing countries. Crop failures, driving up the price of food grains on the world market, would have an even more severe impact on their vulnerable economies, if they happen to coincide with further increases in the price of crude oil. Although the energy consumption of the poorest developing countries accounts for only a small part of the world total, they are becoming rapidly unable to obtain the foreign exchange they require. Neither their major export earnings, nor foreign credits and grants will be able to provide indefinitely the means needed to import food, energy, and the capital and consumer goods on which their economic development depends. The developing countries will not be able to solve their food problem without solving their energy problem and, without a satisfactory solution to both, their economic growth will be severely constrained. The centrality of this food and energy nexus therefore makes any uncoordinated sectoral approach to a developing country's food and energy problem inadequate, and calls for a comprehensive policy approach.

In addition serious constraints are bound to confront, in different ways and degrees in each country, the effort to increase food production through the more intensive use of high-energy inputs such as fertilizers, pesticides, herbicides, and irrigation. There are already important indications of diminishing returns in this respect. The possibilities of extensive increase have all but vanished. Land under cultivation is, even by optimistic projections, not likely to increase more than 4 percent by the year 2000 because most good land is already being cultivated and even this may be upset by the fast growth of cities which in most cases is at the cost of agricultural land. In some regions it may be possible to bring additional land under cultivation through a large program of soil fertilization using irrigation and fertilizers. Elsewhere, given the decline in land availability, increases in food production to meet rising demands may make agriculture even more dependent on oil-based inputs than has been the case thus far.

All this has obvious and staggering implications for the cost of food production. Present projections indicate a 95 percent increase in the real price of food by the year 2000, but we may be in for much larger jumps in the price of oil than these projections assumed, in which case the effect on food prices could be still more marked. As mentioned earlier, world food production is projected to increase slightly above population increases. However, increase in per capita consumption will largely be confined to industrialized nations (most markedly in Eastern Europe, the USSR, and Japan) and, in the developing world, to Latin America and East Asia. In the populous countries of South Asia (accounting for 1.3 billion people by the year 2000) consumption will improve hardly at all, whereas the pressure on Southeast Asian countries like Thailand to export their grain and feed to meet balance of payments difficulties arising largely out of a greatly increased oil bill is likely to keep the poor of these societies continuously deprived. The outlook for improved diets for the poorest people in the poorer developing countries is grim indeed. As of now, consumption of calories, even on the average, continues to remain below the "minimum requirements" laid down by FAO, while evidence is beginning to emerge that these "minimum requirements" may have been set too low for people in developing countries. Moreover, income and food distribution within most LDCs [Less Developed Countries] is so skewed that the national average caloric consumption must be 20 to 40 percent above minimum levels before the poorest are likely to meet minimum standards of diet. All this will get accentuated with the steep rise in the cost of food production that lies ahead. In South, East, and Southeast Asia (as well as poor areas of North and Central Africa and the Middle East), the quantity of food available to the poorest groups of people will be so insufficient that their children will not be able to reach normal physical levels (height, body weight, etc.), not to speak of psychic energy and intelligence and good health, which are all so heavily dependent on nutrition. The World Bank has estimated that the number of malnourished people in the developing countries could rise from 400 to 600 million in the mid-1970s to 1.3 billion in the year 2000.

All this does not take into account the accelerating chances of ecological erosion under stringent production conditions, incidents of severe drought, floods, which have become a recurring feature in this part of the world, and climate instability, which is also in the cards. Nor does it take into account the very large increases that are bound to take place in the cost of fertilizers and the transportation of food, the latter often the largest component of food prices. Also, as more arid and marginal and weather-sensitive lands are brought under cultivation and as these are subjected to energy-intensive cultivation, there will be greatly increased pressure on the agro-resource base, producing low quality yields at very high costs of production. The costs of energy and energy-based inputs have already risen rapidly and are already bringing diminishing returns in many parts of the world, especially where these inputs have only now begun to be heavily used.

Meanwhile, there are taking place significant shifts in food and agricultural policy in the industrialized countries with the growing concern with protecting their agricultural resources, especially soils, and with growing realization of the resource implications of higher and higher production of food to meet world demands. Yet another source of pressure on their resource base can be expected to come from rising industrial demand for grain, especially for fermentation into alcohol-based fuels. These and other domestic pressures in the industrialized countries, the rapid increases in fossil fuel prices, and the growing inclination to use "resource diplomacy" could severely disrupt food production, raise food prices beyond manageable limits, and deprive millions of people—already suffering from extremes of disparity and grinding poverty—of even minimum nutrition for survival. All of this will force the LDCs as a whole, and especially their poor, which constitute a majority, to fend for themselves, a demand for which many of them seem to be unprepared.

The same dilemma also obtains for oil-based fertilizers, namely, the increasing dependence on them for the production of more food on the one hand and the steeply rising costs and growing dangers from their excessive use on the other. This applies to other inputs like pesticides, new strains of grain, and large irrigation systems as well. The accelerated use of pesticides is expected to raise crop yields quickly and substantially, especially in the developing countries. Yet many of these chemicals produce a wide range of serious environmental consequences and in turn adversely affect agricultural production. Indiscriminate use of pesticides (which is expected to increase six times over the 1975–2000 period if present rates of increase continue) itself causes severe pollution of irrigation canals, ponds, and rice paddies. But large-scale irrigation also adversely affects the quality of water and the stability of both freshwater and coastal ecosystems, not to speak of its high social cost, especially for the poorer and underprivileged people affected by it. Similarly, crop yields are expected to be increased significantly by much wider use of high-yield strains of grains. Unfortunately large monocultures of genetically identical crops pose increased risks of excessive depletion of nutrients leading to soil degradation and of catastrophic loss from insect attacks or crop epidemics.

In the meantime, many developing countries already have great difficulties in meeting their present energy needs, and the prospects for meeting their future needs are even worse. Eighty-five developing countries are net importers of oil or another form of commercial energy; one-fifth of these depend on oil for 90 percent or more of their commercial energy. The others depend on oil for between 50 and 90 percent of their energy use, with the exception of a few countries, particularly India. The result of the continuing rapid price increase of oil is that the trade deficits of the oil-importing developing countries keep growing. The possibility of a collapse of the world financial system as a result of a future oil crisis is no longer unthinkable. If the oil-importing countries cannot find means of payment to service their growing debts, they might be forced to default, request national debt moratoria or repudiate their debts. The world's financial organizations have done little to cope with this problem, although the International Monetary Fund has created an oil facility and the World Bank has started lending for energy development.

However, the industrialized countries of the OECD [Organization of Economic Cooperation and Development] group appear to be concerned primarily with their own vulnerability to the loss of oil imports. It would be excessively optimistic to assume that in crisis situations the OECD countries would come to the assistance of the poorer and most vulnerable oil-importing developing countries which are not included in the International Energy Agency's plans. OPEC aid programs have been the oil-importing developing countries. Worse may still be in store for these oil-importing developing countries. A World Bank study released in August 1980 concluded that if the oil-importing developing countries were not able to increase their domestic energy production faster than in recent years, to about 7 percent annually, their oil import bill in constant 1980 U.S. dollars would rise in 1990 to $110 billion. This study concluded that by maximizing domestic energy production from oil, gas, coal, hydropower, and biomass resources, and by a vigorous program of energy conservation, these countries could cut their oil import bill in 1990 by $25 to $30 billion (in 1980 dollars). This could be done without reducing overall economic growth. But the total investment needed for an expanded energy program by the oil-importing developing countries would be $450 to $500 billion (in 1980 dollars) over the next decade, to be obtained from both domestic savings and external sources, including assistance from the World Bank. At the end of the fiscal years 1979 and 1980, the World Bank had committed $4.5 billion for projects in the energy field and it plans to lend $13 billion more over the five-year period from 1981 to 1986, a shortfall of $12 billion less than what the World Bank considers desirable and feasible.

It is clear that the international community is not yet committed to helping the developing countries solve their energy problems. We can only hope that the inclination to use "resource diplomacy," through withholding food, energy, or technology, can be resisted by those countries so tempted, and that the concerted political and diplomatic efforts toward a comprehensive global solution will be continued despite all the obvious difficulties. Collapse of the international order into chaos appears to be the only alternative at a tremendous cost to hundreds of millions of people.

Terrestrial Resources: Energy

The oil crisis of 1973–74 reminded us once again that an industrial society is based on inanimate energy, most commonly from petroleum and generally imported. Since then a veritable flood of literature on the subject of energy has poured forth. The readings that follow have been selected because they treat some of the less publicized facts and viewpoints. We are assuming that the reader has some knowledge of the current debates about coal versus oil, for example, and the future of nuclear fission. The materials in this section must be incorporated in these debates if we are to develop responsible energy policies in the future.

Salah Al-Shaikhly, director of the Centre for Research on the New International Economic Order, Oxford, England, leads off with a defense of OPEC and a hardheaded interpretation of the "energy crisis." Donald Mills, former Jamaican ambassador to the United Nations, and the Venezuelan Francisco Parra, former secretary-general of OPEC and executive director of the International Energy Development Corporation, then engage in a friendly dialogue from two different starting points and agree more than they disagree. Anthony Pearce-Batten, former press officer of the Overseas Development Council in Washington, D.C., surveys the alternatives to our present reliance on fossil fuels and fission and urges us to master them before the oil runs out. An excerpt from a detailed report of the National Academy of Sciences' National Research Council, however, points out the risks of these same alternative energy sources, most of which are widely ignored. A small group of scholars and environmentalists meeting in 1976 under the auspices of The Georgia Conservancy produced "The Wolfcreek Statement," excerpted here, which argues for both conservation of energy and conversion to sunlight as our primary energy source. Thomas Hoffmann and Brian Johnson of the International Institute for Environment and Development, however, stress the need for worldwide cooperation in adopting and applying new energy policies as a vital element of economic development. No one today seriously advocates wasting energy or a total reliance on fossil fuels, but beyond that there is no agreement on how the world should be powered. Can there be?

23

Some Popular Myths About Energy

Salah Al-Shaikhly

So many fascinating myths have grown up around the energy issue that it is impossible to proceed toward a reasoned policy dialogue without first discussing them. The attempt here is not to be polemical but to place the energy issue in its appropriate historical and development perspective.

One of the major misrepresentations in popular literature is the equation of energy with oil. Oil, in fact, supplies less than 40 percent of the present world energy demands, and is likely to decline in relative importance as alternative sources of energy are developed. Furthermore, OPEC supplies only one-third of the world's oil.

There is also a popular belief that the "energy crisis" (i.e., the rising real cost of energy) has "caused" the world economic crisis. This, in reality, reverses the sequence of events. The rising real cost of energy is the *result* of the overload of the world economic system, not its cause. The rapid rate of increase in oil consumption has led to a rapid depletion of nonrenewable resources. This was the result of international oil companies, over a long period of time, keeping the price of oil artificially cheap and thereby effectively stimulating demand. If oil prices had been set, not in relation to the cost of production, which was irrelevant, but in relation to the cost of alternatives, the adjustment process would not have been so abrupt and traumatic.

It is interesting to note that most OECD [Organization of Economic Cooperation and Development] countries regard the reason for inflation and lower industrial output as the "huge oil price increases" since 1973/74. Although the rise of oil prices may have contributed to international

Reprint of "Some Popular Myths About Energy," by Salah Al-Shaikhly in *Development: Seeds of Change—Village Through Global Order*, 1981:2. Published by Society for International Development, Palazzo Civilta del Lavoro 00144 Roma, Italy. Pp. 11–14.

inflation, the magnitude is greatly exaggerated. Historical data show that during the 1960s, world import and export prices increased less than 1 percent per annum, while during the 12-month period preceding the oil price increases of 1974, they increased by 30 percent. Some economists attribute this to the sharp rise in the world's monetary reserves, which doubled between 1962 and 1972. Understandably, world inflation increased after the 1974 rise in oil prices, but by 1978 it dropped back to about 7 percent, the same level as 1973. Furthermore, West Germany and Switzerland were able to reduce inflation between 1973 and 1978 from 6.9 percent to 2.6 percent and from 8.8 percent to 1.1 percent, respectively. Their success provides strong evidence of the crucial roles of both budgetary deficits and domestic economic policies of the industrial countries in fueling inflation.

It is also widely believed that the price of oil is being kept artificially high at present through OPEC cartel-like action and that with the dismantling of OPEC this price will fall. This is a fallacy.

The current price of oil is determined by the forces of demand and supply as well as by the cost of alternative sources. Production decisions are usually made unilaterally by OPEC members, and not collectively, much the same way as the United States decides to curtail its wheat production to limit excessive supply. In fact, many OPEC members are producing more oil because of various international considerations than would be required by their own national needs. If OPEC did not exist today, the oil price would probably stay at the same level or even rise. Each oil producing and exporting nation would possibly decide to eliminate unneeded financial surpluses and instead try to protect the real value of its depleting assets by keeping more of its oil in the ground.

Moreover, there is no cheaper substitute for oil on the horizon. In fact, oil importing nations which are making costly and long-term investments in finding alternative sources of energy now have a major interest in a relatively high price of oil in order to justify these investments. Finally, and most importantly, the real determining factor for the future price of energy may well turn out to be on the demand side: that is the extent to which conservation policies are pursued and are effective. Thus, price of energy is being determined today like the price of any other commodity.

OPEC actions, far from manipulating market forces, often lag behind them. An understanding of this seems to be slowly penetrating popular perceptions. Thus, a recent *Washington Post* editorial, in a burst of candor, suggested that ". . . It wasn't a plot that raised the price of oil. In the early 1970s the world's demand for oil, rising very fast, outran the supply. Neither was flexible in the short term. The result was an explosion of prices. Brooding about cartels and sticking pins in images of OPEC won't help. There is only one way to stabilize the prices of oil and that's to reduce the consumption of it, steadily and rapidly."

It is sometimes argued that energy is the most important single input in the overall process of development and, by inference, that the solution to all other development problems depends on a solution to this problem. This is factually incorrect. According to standardized input-output tables, energy consumption varies widely from one sector to another. The latest analysis for EEC [European Economic Community] countries shows the range to be from 1 percent in low energy sectors to 10 percent in high energy sectors. It is patterns of development and consumption styles which determine, or ought to determine, the importance of energy in a given sector or in an entire economy—and not the other way around.

There is also widespread belief that OPEC nations are extremely rich; that they "create" enormous financial surpluses which they cannot use themselves and which put considerable pressure on the world economy; and that they are responsible, through higher oil import bills, for the financial difficulties of developing countries, but are as yet providing inadequate financial assistance to them.

Such claims only attempt to put OPEC nations on the defensive. They lack objectivity and offer few positive alternatives. To begin with, most OPEC nations are not rich. They are liquid but not wealthy, though liquidity and wealth are being freely confused these days. Even including the capital-surplus nations of Saudi Arabia, Kuwait, United Arab Emirates, Qatar, Libya, and Iraq, the 13 OPEC members had an average per capita income of less than $1,000 in 1978, only one-eighth of that in industrialized nations. In capital-surplus OPEC nations, the average per capita income was $3,340, only about 40 percent of that in industrialized nations. In addition, most OPEC nations are underdeveloped, with low literacy rates, short life expectancies, unskilled labor forces, low levels of technology and research, and little diversified development outside the oil sector. They suffer also from all the problems of a single-resource economy. Their recent financial liquidity has not yet been translated into lasting sources of real wealth.

Furthermore, OPEC does not "create" financial surpluses; it is the appetite of the industrialized nations for energy which does. If OPEC were to cut production to eliminate or reduce their present surpluses, the world economy would experience a severe slump. For OPEC nations, the value of these surpluses is not very clear; it is an open question whether oil in the ground will appreciate more over time than the real value of the surpluses. Moreover these surpluses remain a problem only because the world monetary system has not yet discovered means by which they could be recycled to deficit countries on appropriate terms. This requires a reform of the monetary system, not of OPEC policies. Finally, the capital-surplus OPEC nations have already provided, on the average, over 4 percent of their GNP during 1974–79 for concessional assistance compared to 0.35 percent by industrialized nations. In other words, they have given 12 times as much as developed countries even when their own per capita income is less than one-half that of developed countries (see Table 1). This is truly remarkable when it is realized that OPEC assistance is being given not out of current income but out of the proceeds of a depleting capital asset, oil. Hardly any other nation in the world provides assistance by running down its capital. In fact, during 1974–79 OPEC nations [gave] . . . away 12 percent of their net financial surpluses in the form of official development assistance. This assistance has often not been given in forms which would maximize its mileage, leverage, and visibility. This is not to suggest that OPEC assistance policies are optimal nor to foreclose any further avenues of mutual collaboration between OPEC and the rest of the Third World, but only to restore some perspective on this issue. There is also a myth that OPEC has placed a burden of adjustment on the world economy which is simply unmanageable. This again confuses the real issue. Oil imports account for less than 4 percent of the GNP of the industrialized nations, certainly a proportion which can be matched by the productivity and exports from these nations. The real cost is to the latecomers in the game of economic development: the developing countries. They are faced with the prospect of developing their economies in an era when energy and other costs are rising, thanks largely to the unrestrained consumption by the industrialized nations. In fact, this situation constitutes a powerful argument for the early users of resources to compensate latecomers through liberal assistance policies, since the incremental cost of development has risen so high because of the rapid depletion of many nonrenewable resources.

RESTORING THE PERSPECTIVE

Simple common sense tells us that a shortage or an imbalance of supply of any of the factors of production would affect both the developing and the industrialized countries. The industrialized countries are, theoretically, in a much more favorable position to sustain sudden changes in the supply of basic inputs. In reality, however, the picture is quite different, as the events of the past decade have shown. The unprecedented growth of the North during the 1960s rendered it extremely vulnerable to any downward change in the existing world economy. Toward the end of the 1960s and early 1970s, the North's own economic structure was showing the signs of disorder.

On the other hand, inflationary trends in northern economies following the 1973 adjustment in oil prices rendered most of the justifiable increases in oil prices ineffective in real terms. Very few politicians, economists, or media experts in the North admitted this fact, and it was convenient to blame the ailments of the economy of the North on the increase in oil prices. Denis Healey, in his recent article in *Foreign Affairs*, has contradicted this prevalent view. He claims that the world infla-

TABLE 1 ODA (official development assistance) Flows from Capital-Surplus Oil Exporters to Developing Countries

	1973		1974		1975		1976		1977		1978		1979	
	$ m.	Percent of GNP	$ m.	Percent of GNP	$ m.	Percent of GNP	$ m.	Percent of GNP	$ m.	Percent of GNP	$ m.	Percent of GNP	$ m.	Percent of GNP
Saudi Arabia	305	4.0	1,029	4.5	1,997	5.4	2,407	5.7	2,410	4.3	1,470	2.8	1,970	3.1
Kuwait	345	5.7	622	5.7	976	8.1	615	4.4	1,518	10.6	1,268	6.4	1,099	5.1
Iraq	11	2	423	4.0	218	1.7	232	1.4	61	3	172	8	861	2.9
UAE	289	16.0	511	7.6	1,046	14.1	1,060	11.0	1,177	10.2	690	5.6	207	1.6
Libya	215	3.3	147	1.2	261	2.3	94	6	115	7	169	9	146	6
Qatar	94	15.6	185	9.3	339	15.6	195	8.0	197	7.9	106	3.7	251	5.6
Total	1,259	4.5	2,917	4.5	4,837	5.8	4,603	4.6	5,478	4.5	3,875	3.0	4,534	2.9

Data for 1978 and 1979 are provisional.

Source: Robert S. McNamara, Address to the Board of Governors, September 1980, p. 13.

tion of the early 1970s had nothing to do with oil, but rather was caused by the failure of successive American administrations to finance the war in Vietnam out of current revenue. Another factor was the exceptional increase in raw material prices because a larger number of countries achieved unusually high growth rates. There were also a series of bad crop harvests. World export and import prices measured in dollars and other "stable" currencies had risen less than 1 percent a year in the decade of the 1960s, but were already increasing at 30 percent during the year preceding the increase in oil prices.

The present energy "crisis" was not born in 1973, and it is to the credit of certain American administrations as far back as 1952 that a warning was sounded.

However, as late as 1972/73 the industrial societies chose to ignore completely the early signs of an "energy crisis." The industrial countries whose oil companies controlled most of the exploration and prospecting for oil must have been aware of the looming crisis long before 1973. This awareness, unfortunately, was not disseminated to the public at large. No effort was made, officially or through the media, to get across the idea of a gradual change in consumer habits and the need for conservation. It is curious that even after the problem was well defined at the end of 1973, the northern media focused its attention not on the energy crisis per se, but on OPEC. Finally it is necessary to demystify the energy issue in order to clear the way for a constructive global dialogue. Dialogue on the energy issue that has taken place so far has been bogged down in side issues and peripheral controversies. Our objective is not to defend OPEC. Nor is it our intention to create new myths as we bury old ones. To make OPEC nations feel guilty is hardly an effective strategy for soliciting their cooperation. It is just as unreasonable to ask the industrialized nations and developing countries to adjust to a new energy environment without having a clear idea of what forces are shaping this environment. A fresh start on this issue can be made only by restoring the correct perspective on energy and development issues, by putting aside the myths and controversies of yesterday, and by looking ahead to the possibilities for practical cooperation between the nations of the world.

The energy problem can be seen in its proper perspective only if it is viewed as one of the many structural transformations that the world is going through. The energy issue arose when the world was already confronting a profound transition: concern for protecting world environment; for eradicating absolute poverty; for developing new self-reliant styles of development in the South and a new value system in the North; for controlling the impending international monetary crisis; for the establishment of a new international economic order. The energy issue greatly sharpened the global perception of such transitions by demonstrating the essential interdependence and vulnerability of all nations. It is within this broad perspective that the energy issue, linked with other related issues, can be helpful as an engine of transition.

The Energy Issue and Negotiations for a New Economic Order

The 1974 UN declaration for the establishment of a New International Economic Order called for a just and equitable relationship between prices of raw materials, primary commodities, manufactured and semimanufactured goods exported by developing countries, and the prices of the raw materials, primary commodities, capital goods, and equipment imported by them. The aim was to bring about sustained improvement in the developing countries' unsatisfactory terms of trade. It further called for the intensification of development assistance to developing countries by the international community and reform in the international monetary system to allow for a more adequate flow of real resources under conditions favorable to developing countries.

The Plan of Action, also adopted at the Sixth Special Session of the General Assembly in 1974, outlined a number of issues for further negotiations. Among these issues, the North chose to single out "oil" as the only one whose price and security of supply should be negotiated. The South insisted on the totality of the issues and chose the UN General Assembly as the forum for discussion.

Yet, the world was already beginning to witness a structural change in the power equation of energy, price, and supply. For three decades, the dominance by the North (transnational oil companies and governments) of the up-and-down-stream oil operations and its power to determine production levels, prices, and concessionary terms went unchallenged. By 1974, following the sudden change in positions of power between oil producers and consumers, the North had proposed a number of meetings to discuss this issue. When, consequently, a meeting took place on April 7, 1975, the agenda had been widened to include other raw materials, development and international financial questions.

The final report of the Paris Conference on International Economic Cooperation of July 1977 contained areas of both agreements and conflicts in all the four commissions of the conference: raw materials and trade, development, finance, and energy. It is

interesting to note that, in the field of energy, the conference had agreed on (a) the depletable nature of oil and gas and the need for transition from an oil-based energy mix to more permanent and renewable sources of energy; (b) the need for conservation and more efficient utilization; and (c) the need to develop all forms of energy. They had disagreed, however, on more important issues such as (a) the price of energy and the purchasing power of energy export earnings; (b) the accumulated revenues from oil exports; (c) financial assistance to bridge external payments problems of oil-importing countries; (d) recommendations on resources within the context of the Law of the Sea Conference; and (e) continuing consultations on energy.

After a series of confrontations (UNCTAD IV Nairobi, UNCTAD V Manila, UNIDO III New Delhi), the final stroke in this process of official North-South dialogue came when the eleventh Special Session of the UN General Assembly in August 1980 failed to agree on the process of global negotiations, although it did in principle approve the third development decade strategy.

24

Consumer-Producer Potential for a Global Compact?

Donald Mills and Francisco Parra

DIALOGUE BETWEEN A PRODUCER AND A CONSUMER

PARRA: A dialogue between North and South would be extremely difficult right now. It's hard to see quite where the focus would be. One of the points on which we must rule out dialogue between the producing and the consuming countries is the question of price at the political level. Price can be negotiated at the commercial level, but I don't think any member country of OPEC is willing to talk about price in any meaningful negotiations with a group of countries from the North. If you eliminate price, then you can only talk about supply, and here it is very difficult for member countries of OPEC to talk about supply in terms of anything except investment. You cannot really give firm assurances on continuous supplies with the kind of disruptions that occur and with things which, by their very nature, are not within your control.

Yes, it is true that the producers' own self-interest is the biggest guarantee for maintenance of supply. I think we have seen this in the past, but the best way one can now give limited assurances on supply is through investing in surplus capacity. And there I don't think, once again, that any OPEC country would find it politically possible to make pledges to other countries. It's not realistic. So, I don't really see where the possibility for dialogue lies.

The question of indexation rose around 1974, and, if I remember correctly, in the context of an *agreement* with the industrialized countries

Reprint of "Consumer-Producer Potential for a Global Compact?" by Donald Mills and Francisco Parra in *Development: Seeds of Change—Village Through Global Order*, 1981:2. Published by Society for International Development, Palazzo Civilta del Lavoro, 00144 Roma, Italy. Pp. 31–34.

of the North. Now, today, we've been through a period in which OPEC has developed a long-term strategy which includes indexation of prices, but not as a result of an agreement with the North. It's simply a matter of their adopting a pricing policy which includes indexation, but purely for internal use rather than as part of a global compact between producers and consumers.

If we discuss the possibility of agreement strictly between developing countries we see that producing countries, specifically those in OPEC, have already officially adopted a policy which guarantees supplies to developing countries at the official government prices. So, in times of crisis when the spot prices rise above official government levels, the other developing countries have a guarantee that they will continue to receive enough for their domestic requirements at the official government prices. That's the first thing. I do not think it is possible to administer a two- or three-tier price system which would discriminate in favor of other developing countries. This has been considered and set aside.

What has been done, although it's not enough, is to extend grants and soft loans to a large array of developing countries, partly to alleviate balance-of-payments problems and partly to assist in development. This aid program was a subject discussed by the long-term strategy committee and will be discussed again, the proposal being to expand aid very substantially. Unfortunately, as you know, the war between Iran and Iraq intervened before the committee's report could get up to the OPEC summit, so the thing is still somewhat in limbo. It is, however, being taken up again. The committee will reconvene and reconsider some of the points in its report.

MILLS: Starting at the end of 1973, the whole question of any dialogue, whether between North and South or between countries in the South, became very difficult, very sensitive. One of the reasons was, of course, that the situation was virtually new to everyone, including the OPEC countries. The OPEC countries found themselves under severe pressure. If you take the experience of the Paris Conference and what was tried before we got into the Paris formation—an attempt at dialogue on development with energy included as a part of it—you can see how difficult the whole situation became. Some developing countries, like Jamaica, attempted to promote some sort of dialogue between oil-importing and oil-exporting developing countries and we persisted in that effort over the years, but we grew to recognize the sensitivities and concluded it was not possible then to have a dialogue.

I must say, though, that in Paris the element of solidarity which existed between countries like mine, represented at Paris, and the OPEC countries was, in the face of the pressures from the North, very firm. We have come nearer to the possibility of a dialogue. What happened in Belgrade at the Non-Aligned meeting and at the Havana summit showed that there is a prospect for such a dialogue, especially if we could get ahead with the Global Round, which is in difficulty. One of the problems I see with any attempt to establish a dialogue is the refusal of the industrialized countries to talk about money in the way that they want to talk about energy. I quite agree with you, Frank, that it is really impossible to see how you can have a compact on price between producers and consumers. On supply, you're faced with the fact that you have almost random occurrences, like the Iran-Iraq war, which just throw the issue out. Even now, on the issue of the prospects for oil supplies, you get totally different scenarios.

There are some people who now believe that you're running into a situation where the supply will be running below the demand as demand rises. There are others who feel that the situation will be dramatically reversed. Which scenario do you accept and how do you come to an accommodation if there are such deep differences in views? But I do believe that it is really very important for the developing countries, both oil-importing and oil-exporting, to persist, in spite of the obvious obstacles and difficulties, in an attempt to establish a dialogue. Frank points out that there have been a number of positive developments. One was the attempts made at establishing a two-tier price, even though that went down the drain a long time ago. From 1974 the reaction was that such a system would be unmanageable and therefore undesirable. Jamaica came forward, at that time, with a proposal for a rebate system which was considered, but not accepted. More recently, we've seen a number of schemes. I will mention only those from my region. Trinidad and Tobago, Venezuela, and Mexico have all proposed schemes intended to help some countries in the region to meet the costs of oil supplies through having some sort of extended loan agreement. Such proposals are very helpful and I believe that more of this sort of thing can be done. One has to examine these schemes very carefully to make sure that they are as good as they seem. Certainly, at least, they are a step in the right direction.

I have always believed that, for reasons that go even beyond the question of energy, it is very important for the oil-importing and oil-exporting developing countries to use whatever political devices are necessary to establish a greater understanding. There is still not sufficient understanding. We've cleared up some of the fears on both sides, but we need to press on with that dialogue. It is related also to the whole question of South-South cooperation, where I have clearly detected—and others have also, I think—some fears on the part of OPEC countries that South-South cooperation may mean transferring the burden to them. I think we should try to remove that feeling. Any South-South cooperation involving OPEC must take the concerns of OPEC and the benefits to OPEC equally into consideration. OPEC must share equally in the bargain. But, following on from the Caracas meeting earlier this year—and I haven't seen the details of that yet—I would hope that we are one step nearer to a better understanding and better cooperation between the countries of the South on this. *Then,* I think, not only will we be able to face the North-South negotiations with greater strength, but I believe that the prospect of any greater global understanding on energy and oil might be improved if we have a better understanding within the South.

In the final analysis, I don't think we can exclude the need for better understanding and some sort of compact with the rest of the global community. Our cooperation efforts cannot be reserved only for the countries of the South. The developing countries are going to need more and more oil. There's no doubt about that. If the industrialized countries exploited their potential for moving to new and renewable sources, this would open up greater supplies of oil for the countries of the Third World. But it would, of course, require some sort of political understanding on all sides and equitable management of the released oil supplies.

Indeed, any agreement between the developing countries should include support for oil exploration. The question is, what are we going to ask the OPEC countries to do in terms of investment in oil exploration? What would be the terms of the partnerships which would exist? We have lived through a history in which the investments that have been made have always been made for the benefit of the investor countries from the North. So now, if we're going to ask OPEC countries to invest in oil development, we must decide what sort of partnership this is going to be—and that is really a political question as much as an economic one.

We have to work out viable relationships, viable partnerships in which the investor will have benefits, but which will not place us at the same disadvantage which has always characterized our relationship with investors from outside. This is, in my view, one of the interesting areas that we have to explore. Guarantees, yes, and the OPEC countries are extracting guarantees where they make investments, even among themselves. One must respect their need for investment security. Apart from that, there's the question of interesting partnerships in terms of how you share the benefits of the investment. No one would hope, nor would it be in the interests of the OPEC countries, merely to substitute themselves for the traditional investors from the West.

PARRA: If you look back over the past ten years, one of the most interesting phenomena has been the lack of increased exploration in the developing countries in response to the increases in price. You would have thought that, for instance, if the price of oil went up by a factor of five, the pace of exploration would also go up. Well, it didn't. If you take out of the picture the giant countries—Brazil, Mexico, Argentina, India—and look at exploratory drilling, you'll see there's absolutely no difference in the level of exploration between 1970 and today. Almost the identical number of wells are being drilled. Now, there are lots of reasons for this, but I think that one of the main ones is the attractiveness and the size of energy projects in the OECD [Organization of Economic Cooperation and Development] areas. The companies which have the resources to explore in the Third World are simply not interested. Exploration of small fields in Third World countries requires a lot of management, a lot of time, a lot of effort, and some money. It means too much management effort for too small a reward in terms of the size of the fields that you can expect to find, even though those fields may mean the difference between prosperity and poverty for the small developing country concerned.

That's one part. The other part is that there are large numbers of small oil companies in North America which have the technology and the know-how to do exploration, but which are simply too poor to be able to spread the risk. If you're going to explore throughout the world, you've got to have at least ten projects going with the hope of being successful in one or two. These companies are just not big enough.

Something else has to happen if we're going to see a substantial increase in exploration in developing countries. I'm not sure what that is. I think a step in the right direction was the proposed funding of exploration by OPEC—preferably, I would say, with no direct participation in the project, but simply to do it through the national oil companies of the countries concerned. Nearly all the developing countries now have a national oil company. Jamaica set one up just about a year ago and Jamaica has some reasonable possibility in terms of acreage. The newer companies will need technical assistance. I'm not sure that OPEC countries can supply this, but they can certainly supply the funds. We're at rather an early stage in all this, I'm afraid.

MILLS: But there we have a classic example of the need for new institutions . . .

PARRA: Right.

MILLS: . . . which would be different from the usual ones. We've been told that the benefit of the multinational is that you can be sure it brings the technology, the money, the marketing capability, and the management needed. Now what is happening is that, as you rightly say, OPEC has the financial resources but the technology has to come from elsewhere and the management probably from somewhere else again. So it's a question of trying to arrange some sort of consortium which protects all the interests involved, including the national interests. This means political innovation. Judging from the present efforts to solve the Law of the Sea issue, efforts to establish an institution through a political process to take care of many different wide-ranging interests, it is innovation that we need to address this sort of problem. You cannot expect OPEC to just walk in and take hold of a problem which other people will not touch. So, here again, I would say that the onus is very much on the developing countries who would want to promote this sort of exploration and development. They must put the political energy into the business of trying to design the acceptable institutional devices required.

To return to the compact. Where do the oil-producing, industrialized countries such as Britain, Norway, Canada, the United States—yes, and the USSR—come in? One cannot continue to talk about this issue as though it were restricted to OPEC and the non-OPEC developing countries. What is the responsibility of those other countries in terms of a contribution to the search for understanding and, way down the road, a compact?

Where do we begin to answer that? Well, there's a very interesting development taking place, although it hasn't yet taken a tangible form as far as I know. This is that the national oil companies of both Canada and Britain are going abroad to explore for oil. Norway is also contributing cooperation programs and technical aid programs to exploratory drives in developing countries. Such efforts are worth continuing especially if we can't reach some global-level compact or a compact between South and South.

One thing is certain: the world needs energy; the world needs oil. There is oil as yet unfound—that is pretty certain. You have resources of all sorts, whether in technology or in management or in money—all looking for opportunity. The opportunities are there. The question is, how do they get linked up? If you can't put together some institution using the creative abilities of the UN [United Nations] system or if the market, for some reason, is hamstrung by fears, suspicions, and political interests, there is still a tendency—and this is what you're saying—for the thing to inch forward, nervously, and in a small way. This is what is happening. Hopefully, over time, these efforts will grow. It is very difficult to envision how they will emerge in terms of structures and relationships.

PARRA: Just to round off. I don't believe that the market will stimulate exploration sufficiently. If the World Bank's energy affiliate can possibly get off the ground, it could make a big contribution. If we can get OPEC to firm up and translate into action its recommendations on aid to developing countries for the development of energy, that will be another big contribution. I think that there is plenty of room for other initiatives, notably initiatives from national oil companies in industrialized countries and bilateral aid for exploration.

MILLS: I agree absolutely, Frank, with you on that. I don't believe we can leave it to the market—not out of philosophical reasons, but just that it simply will not happen that way.

25

The Future of Renewable Energy

Anthony Pearce-Batten

People need natural resources to live, and none of the resources of nature is more important to us than those that produce energy. Today the future of the world's sources of energy is in doubt. For the United States and other industrial nations, the question is whether they can go on consuming fuel at the present rapid rate. For the poorer nations, the question is whether the energy they need to expand production and reach a higher standard of living will be available at a price they can afford, or indeed at any price at all.

Energy sources are of two kinds: nonrenewable and renewable. Nonrenewable energy, on which the industrial nations depend, comes from the fossil fuels, oil, coal, natural gas, and, recently, from nuclear fission. As the name indicates, these energy sources will eventually be used up, though no one can say when that will happen. Renewable energy sources include the sun's rays, wind and flowing water, plants produced by photosynthesis, geothermal heat, and perhaps nuclear fusion. These sources constantly renew themselves and in theory could provide an almost limitless supply of energy. But is this a realistic prospect? Can renewable energy save us from our dependence on energy sources that must one day run out?

Not generally today, or at today's prices. Some forms of renewable energy, such as large-scale hydroelectric power, are major sources today. The United States, for one, has put to use all or almost all of its major hydro sites. In other cases, renewable energy techniques can provide power for some uses at today's prices. For example, direct sunlight is be-

Reprint of "The Future of Renewable Energy" by Anthony Pearce-Batten in *Focus* (Vol. 29, No. 3, January/February, 1979). Reprinted by permission of the American Geographical Society, New York. Pp. 1–16.

ing used increasingly to provide domestic heat and hot water, but on a tiny scale. According to the United States Office of Technology Assessment, the combined output of solar hot water and heating systems equalled just 1/200th of 1 percent of total U.S. energy consumption in 1977. Thus in the industrialized countries at least, while renewable sources of energy will be substituted for conventional fuels for more uses as time goes on, they seem unlikely to become the primary fuel source during the remaining years of this century.

At the same time, this prophecy can become self-fulfilling. The direction of research effort determines later energy uses. Therefore, if research on renewables is neglected, they will not be used up to their potential. In the past, renewable sources of energy were far more important to the industrialized nations than they are today. Some 50 years ago, half of Canada's energy came from wood, a renewable source. More recently, homes in Florida and California used solar water heaters and solar refrigerators, until cheap fossil fuels priced them out of the market.

One reason why renewable sources of energy play such a small role is the existence of cheaper alternatives prior to 1973, when the oil-producing nations imposed a great price increase. Research on perfecting renewable technologies was neglected. The other reason has to do with the amount and quality of energy needed in the industrialized countries. The cost per unit of renewable energy (except hydroelectricity and geothermal heat) tends to rise with the quantity and heat needed. In industry, which needs large amounts of energy and high temperatures, renewables are not now competitive in cost with conventional fuels.

But by maximizing the use of renewable resources wherever it is technologically possible and economically feasible, all countries can contribute to an orderly transition to a postpetroleum era, by stretching out the supply for essential sectors of energy demand for which there are few substitutes for petroleum. Renewables are not a panacea to the world's energy problems, but they seem assured of being an increasingly large part of the solution, for several reasons. World energy demand rises inexorably with the growth of population, economic growth, and with rising living standards. As demand increases, the price of conventional fuels will also rise, unless more energy is discovered than is consumed.

Higher prices permit both more extensive exploration for new sources of conventional fuels and more intensive recovery from existing known deposits. More techniques of using renewable energy become attractive alternatives as the price of conventional fuel increases. While much of the world's oil remains to be discovered, and while the reevaluation of the Mexican reserves, among other developments, has reduced the immediate prospect of a global oil shortage, the long-term price trend for oil and conventional substitutes seems certain to be upward. Therefore the long-term trend is for renewables to become increasingly important.

THE RENEWABLE POTENTIAL

The industrialized countries can look to renewable sources of energy to meet only a small part of their energy needs. The maximum contribution possible in the United States, it is projected, would be around 25 percent by the year 2000. Other estimates are lower.

The situation in the developing countries (other than the few that have abundant oil) is rather different. Most of these countries are located in the tropics or subtropics with an abundance of forest area and sunlight. Although sources such as the World Bank estimate that much of the world's undiscovered oil may be located in these countries, the present lack of conventional fuels forces many of these countries to spend more on imports, using scarce foreign exchange, than they would if the fuel were available domestically.

In many countries, also, the road system is inadequate, and the costs of transportation are high. Many countries have large rural populations which are widely dispersed. The cost of distributing energy from the centralized sources, such as national electric grid systems, that are typical in the industrialized countries, would be prohibitive in the circumstances.

In addition, much of the energy demand in the developing nations is for domestic and small-scale industrial use. These uses require the relatively small amounts and low temperatures for which renewable energy is most efficient. At the same time, the technologies are simple and the equipment typically needs little maintenance—two crucial assets in the successful introduction of new techniques to the rural areas of developing nations. For example, simple mechanisms can use direct sunlight to dry crops or distill water for drinking. At a somewhat higher technical level, gas for cooking and light can be produced from garbage and agricultural wastes.

While the present energy needs of the developing countries are small by comparison with the needs of the industrialized countries, their demand for fossil fuels such as petroleum is growing at half again the rate of the industrialized countries. The total demand for energy in many developing countries can only be guessed at, since much of the energy used comes from traditional sources, notably firewood, animal wastes, and crop residues, for which few statistics of consumption patterns are available. Today the capacity of engines is still measured in terms of horsepower in the industrialized countries, while in the developing countries, the real unit of measure is cattle power or oxen power, since cattle and oxen are still the principal vehicles for pulling and carrying. A third energy source is human muscle power.

None of this seems to have much to do with renewable sources of energy, except that two trends are resulting in changes in the energy profiles (what kinds of energy they use for what purposes) of the developing countries. First, traditional fuels are becoming increasingly scarce in some areas. Second, the nature of energy needs is changing as these countries progress, so that traditional fuels can provide neither the amounts nor the qualities needed. Renewable sources of energy can provide some of that energy at competitive prices, especially where the cost of conventional fuels is much higher due to unfavorable local conditions.

An additional reason for the greater potential of renewable sources of energy in the developing countries results from the relationship between the available supply of energy and the stage and rate of economic progress. The types of energy available both release human labor for other tasks, increasing the efficiency of human output, and facilitate or even permit certain key processes that are essential to economic progress. Without coal, the manufacture of heavy machinery using high-grade iron and steel—and the Industrial Revolution—might never have been possible. Without gasoline produced from oil, the transportation revolution might never have been possible. But today the cost of economic growth in terms of energy is much higher for the developing countries as they begin to industrialize, or to think about it, than it was for the industrialized countries themselves. So the developing countries cannot follow the same path at the same price.

If countries continue to become more and more reliant on nonrenewable sources of energy, the costs of economic growth seem destined to increase faster than they would if renewable sources could be utilized effectively.

The availability of a cheap and abundant fuel—oil—was a key factor in the industrial expansion of the United States. Today, with the price of oil much higher, it is difficult for the United States, and other industrial nations, to move away from their dependency on oil, because many sectors of their economies grew in response to cheap oil. Transportation systems based on gasoline-burning cars and trucks are perhaps the best example.

In the developing countries, by contrast, the patterns of energy use are still in transition. It is not too late to integrate the latest renewable technologies, where these are economically feasible, into developing patterns of energy consumption. For example, modes of transportation in developing countries are changing as oxen, carts, and even bicycles give way to more efficient ways of moving people and goods. In the cities at least, electric-powered mass transport is a likelier alternative to cars and buses in those countries than in the United States, where the existing transport system would have to be changed at great expense.

Note, however, that a major role for renewable sources of energy is strictly potential. If anything, the developing countries today are seeking to use oil more, not less. There are considerable risks in seeking to maximize the use of renewable energy techniques, many of which have yet to be perfected under conditions of everyday use. So the future role of renewable sources of energy remains unclear. Yet the potential of renewable energy, while not unlimited, is sufficient to merit a major effort both in the industrialized countries that have most of the technology, and in the developing countries that stand to be the most reliant on renewables to power the process of development.

THE ENERGY-GROWTH LINK

Between 1950 and 1974, the global economy tripled in size. Global energy consumption also increased threefold. Indeed, increased energy consumption is the inevitable companion of economic growth, although the amount by which consumption increases varies with the stage of economic development and with efforts to reduce energy waste.

While energy needs increase in absolute terms with economic growth, the use of certain kinds of energy tends to grow even faster. Today, five years after the unprecedented rise in oil prices, all countries continue to become increasingly reliant on oil. Indeed, over the quarter century in which the global economy tripled in size, petroleum use in the industrialized countries increased 4.3 times.

Consumption in the developing countries, while a mere fraction of industrial-country oil use, increased more than sixfold, or at twice the rate of economic growth. In 1950, the developing countries, with half the world's population, accounted for just 1 percent of global energy consumption; by 1974, with about 70 percent of the world's population, these countries accounted for 10 percent of the world's consumption of energy. If this trend continues, the price of a decent living standard in the poorer nations must be a much faster using up of the world's nonrenewable resources.

As these countries continue to progress, their need for higher quality fuel sources will increase. Some of these countries, like Brazil, Mexico, India, and various Asian nations, are in the process of rapid industrialization. It is unlikely that renewable resources, except for hydroelectric power where it is available, can provide fuel in the quantities, heat intensities, and with the reliability that the industrial sectors of these countries will require, at least within the next decade.

In many other developing countries, and in the rural areas of the rapidly industrializing countries, another energy transition is taking place which could also greatly increase demand for petroleum, unless energy substitutes are available—and here renewable sources offer great potential. The transition is from noncommercial, traditional fuel sources such as firewood and animal and crop wastes, to commercial ones like oil. Despite its high price, petroleum offers a unique set of characteristics which favor its use even in rural areas; it is relatively easy to transport and can be used for many purposes. Renewable sources of energy could become viable substitutes for petroleum for many rural energy needs, especially if the uncertainties which hamper use of these sources today were removed as the result of further research, testing, and design of technologies adapted to existing social and technical conditions in the rural areas of the developing countries.

Three Views of India

Little information is available about noncommercial energy consumption patterns in these rural areas. But the case of India, for which the data base is good, offers some indications of the importance of these noncommercial sources. A conventional analysis of commercial energy use in India looks like this:

	Millions of Tons of Coal Equivalent (mtce)	Percent
Coal	51.35	40
Oil	29.90	23
Electricity	48.65	37
Total	129.90	100

Only the commercial sources—fossil fuels and hydropower—are included. But in fact, noncommercial fuels, notably firewood and animal dung, still account for more than half of all the fuels consumed in India, changing the picture considerably:

	mtce	Percent
Commercial energy	129.9	42
Noncommercial fuels	179.4	58
Total	309.3	100

An even more accurate picture of India's actual energy situation is gained if we also consider the role of animal draft power. In 1972, India's 130,000 tractors provided less than 3 billion horsepower, while 86 million draft animals provided an estimated 34 billion horsepower. Now the picture looks like this:

	mtce	Percent
Commercial energy	129.9	34
Noncommercial energy	179.4	46
Animal draft energy	77.8	20
Total	387.1	100

If human labor as an energy source were included—but no figures exist—the picture would change still further. It is obvious from the dramatic difference between one set of figures and the next that, at least in the Third World, any statistics that do not include traditional sources cannot accurately show the true energy situation.

Dependence on noncommercial traditional sources of energy obviously varies from one developing country to another. Several African countries are 90 percent dependent on noncommercial sources. But if the transition from noncommercial to commercial energy sources continues at the current pace, as seems likely, then fully one-third of the world's consumption of commercial energy by the year 2000 would be attributable to demand in the developing countries, which would by then be consuming about as much commercial energy as the developed world consumes today.

Intensive use of renewable sources of energy could reduce the degree to which the developing countries become reliant on petroleum. This would have several beneficial results. Petroleum supplies would last longer, the costs of economic development would be reduced—since otherwise petroleum would be scarcer and its price would rise faster—and the likelihood that supply shortages might disrupt economic development would be reduced.

The potential for greatly expanding use of renewable energy sources in the developing countries seems all the greater when the distribution of commercial energy demand is analyzed. In 1975, for example, almost three-quarters of total commercial energy consumption in the developing countries was attributable to just 16 countries. Half the total amount of electricity consumed in the developing world was used by six countries—India, Mexico, Brazil, Argentina, South Korea, and Taiwan. This relative concentration tells us that most developing countries, plus in most cases the large rural sectors even of the six big users, have yet to make the transition from traditional to modern energy sources.

In making that transition, the developing countries can follow the oil-intensive path of the industrial nations, or they can whenever possible rely on renewables, using oil only when necessary. Renewable energy sources, except hydroelectricity, are most feasible where the population is dispersed and per capita energy demand is relatively small. Thus for countries with large rural populations intent on improving their agriculture, renewables make a lot of sense. How much sense depends on several factors: the world price of oil, its price in terms of the importing nation's currency, how fast the price rises—and the cost of the renewable alternatives. These costs will vary from country to country, according to climatic conditions, and among types of renewable energy. The potential of renewables will also vary according to the nature of energy demand—the end use for which it is needed.

SOLAR ENERGY

The term solar energy covers a far wider range of energy sources than direct sunlight alone. Wind is a form of solar energy, induced in part by the varying intensities of direct sunlight falling on land areas. Biomass—all forms of vegetation—is a form of stored solar energy converted into vegetative matter by photosynthesis. But in this section we will only analyze the potential of direct sunlight.

Theoretically, direct sunshine could supply energy to almost all of the developing countries far in excess of their needs, if just a small fraction of the total were used. Virtually all of the land area of the developing countries, covering some 79 million hectares, and a good part of the land area of the industrialized countries, lies between 40°North and 40°South. In this global sunbelt, the Overseas Development Council estimates, each square meter of land area receives at least about 4 kilowatt hours (kwh) per day, for a total of more than 600 times the 1.4 billion tons of coal equivalent of commercial energy that these countries presently consume.

If only 2 percent of this incoming solar radiation were converted at 20 percent efficiency, some 3.6 billion tons of coal equivalent of energy could be produced, or nearly three times more than those nations' present total commercial energy consumption. But to harness even this fraction of the sun's potential would be a stupendous achievement. To cover 2 percent of the land area of the developing countries with solar reflectors would in the United States be roughly equivalent to the area presently covered by highways and other transit routes.

Technically speaking, direct sunlight could be used as a substitute for most conventional energy uses today, with the notable exception of transportation. But the cost of "going solar" is often much higher than the cost of the conventional energy source it would replace. This is especially true as energy needs escalate, in terms both of quantity per unit provided and quality—the higher the heat, the greater the cost per unit provided.

A second problem is the variability of direct sunlight, especially on a seasonal basis. Countries located outside the world's sunbelt receive eight or more times as much direct sunlight in summer months as in winter months, necessitating either backup energy sources or conversion of direct sunlight into a storable form, such as electricity. But the costs of such conversion processes are very high. Also the original cost for equipment for solar is very high, while maintenance is low and the fuel source—the sun—is of course free. Costs must therefore be compared over the life of the solar equipment.

Most of the comparisons of such costs have focused on typical energy prices in the industrialized countries and especially in the United States. As has been stated above, energy costs of conventional fuels in the developing countries tend often to be much higher than in the industrialized countries, while traditional renewable fuels—firewood, charcoal, dung, and crop residues—are theoretically free in dollar and cent terms (though often costly to the environment). So solar technologies which are not yet competitive in the United States may well have much more potential in the developing countries.

Conversion Technologies

Today solar energy generally has the most importance where energy needs are lowest in terms both of energy volume and energy intensity. As energy requirements escalate, so do the costs of meeting such needs from solar sources by using increasingly complex technologies.

What follows is a survey of the conversion techniques available by which solar energy may be utilized, ranging from the simplest technologies to the most complicated.

The simplest way of using the sun is by so-called "passive" techniques. These techniques make maximum use of sunlight without machinery. Examples are drying crops or laundry. In the United States, the major potential for solar use may lie in such passive techniques as siting and building houses to minimize the need for heating and cooling.

For most low-heat energy needs (below 100°C.) the various techniques of solar collection described below are technologically adequate, although not all such techniques are commercially attractive at the present time.

Flat plate collectors are the simplest. Australia, Japan, and Israel have used such collectors for years. In Australia, annual sales of such collectors have reached 1.5 million annually. Collectors were also used extensively to provide heat and hot water in California and Florida between 1900 and 1940, before cheaper oil and natural gas priced them out of the market.

A flat plate collector works on a simple principle: solar heat is collected by a fluid (usually water) passed across an insulated surface covered with absorptive material that is exposed to the sun. Such collectors are usually installed on the roofs of houses, where they provide hot water, central heating, and, most commonly, the energy to heat swimming pools. The heated water is stored for use in well-insulated tanks.

Pond collectors apply the same principle on a much larger scale to provide water heated to relatively low temperatures for selected industrial purposes. The water is stored for later use in a well-insulated pond. The Office of Technology Assessment reports that such a pond system has been devised to process uranium, while in Virginia, reports the OTA, a pond collector is being used to provide the entire heating needs of a house.

Tubular collectors pass the liquid through a rod or tube surrounded by a vacuum, which cuts the heat losses typically associated with flat plate collectors. As with the flat plate collectors, the liquid is then stored for use in a well-insulated tank.

Solar Concentration

Stationary solar collection equipment, used by itself, typically converts only a fraction of the energy in the sun's rays into a usable form. The sun moves across the sky, its rays fall on stationary devices with varying intensity, and much of the solar energy is lost. However, there are a variety of conversion techniques which increase the efficiency of these stationary collectors. The simplest way is to mount mirrors which reflect the sun onto the stationary collector whenever it is not shining on it directly. Such mirror boosters can increase the conversion efficiency by up to 1.6 times.

Parabolic reflectors arc around the stationary collector—usually a tubular collector—concentrating the sun's rays on it. Looking somewhat like a radar scanner, this design is perhaps the most familiar to people.

Solar tracking. By moving the collecting machine to track the path of the sun, on both a daily (single axis) and a seasonal basis (double axis), direct sunshine can be converted into heat for higher temperature uses. Double axis trackers can meet needs for temperatures up to 850°C.

Some techniques will convert the sun's energy into electricity, either by using a heat engine or with the use of photovoltaic cells. Many of the techniques of producing a high-intensity heat or energy from the direct sunlight are very much in the testing and development stages.

Perhaps the most intriguing conversion technique of this type is the heliostat concept, combined with the power tower, which was recently developed in Italy. Heliostats are simply mirrors, which are aimed to reflect the sun's rays onto a steam turbine situated atop a tower several hundred feet from the ground. The heat that is reflected is of such intensity that it converts water almost instantaneously into steam, which in turn activates the turbine to generate electricity.

These plans, however, are still very much in the experimental stage, and the cost of electricity that is generated is nowhere near today's commercial rates.

Solar Cells

Conversion of direct sunlight into electricity can also be achieved with the use of photovoltaic cells, a simple technology which uses cheap materials, has no moving parts, requires little maintenance, but which is extremely expensive at the start. These solar cells are extremely dependable, and were in fact first developed to provide electric power for U.S. space vehicles. But the electricity provided cost half a million dollars per installed kilowatt, 500 times the going rate. "The exceedingly high costs of development and fabrication of spacecraft solar arrays," reports the Office of Technology Assessment, "have discouraged any serious thought of widespread terrestrial use of such a technology at the present time, in spite of the potentially attractive characteristics of such systems."

Photovoltaics are used today in locations where other sources of electricity, renewable or nonrenewable, are not available. Solar cells are used in the United States, Japan, and other countries for battery recharging in remote forestry stations, military installations, and offshore drilling rigs. Other uses include power transmitters, signals buoys, water purification, refrigeration, and communications systems. Isolated needs which solar cells can meet have helped to bring the cost per delivered kilowatt of solar cells down considerably from the days of the space program. Today commercial firms are marketing photovoltaic systems at quoted costs of around $10,000 per kilowatt, which, while still much higher than conventionally generated electricity in the United States, represents a fiftyfold decline in the price in just a few years.

If the goal set by the Department of Energy of $500 per kilowatt by 1986 is met, electricity from solar sources would be available at a price likely by then to be competitive with conventional power.

Assessing the potential of solar energy as an effective substitute for conventional energy systems is like taking aim at two moving targets. There is little doubt today that solar energy, when converted into electricity, is about as effective a fuel source as the conventional sources that we may expect it one day to replace. The crucial questions—the moving targets—concern costs: How fast will conventional energy costs increase, and how fast will renewable—in this case, solar—costs decline? The answers are not known, and so any attempt to predict beyond the present minor role of solar energy in the U.S. composite energy profile necessarily reaches into the realm of uncertainty.

Solar Energy in the United States

As stated earlier, the potential contribution that renewable energy sources can make to supplying any nation's total need for energy will depend very much on the nature of that country's energy demand. Perhaps the most ambitious attempt to assess solar's potential for the United States was published recently by the United States Office of Technology Assessment in a major report entitled "Application of Solar Technology to Today's Energy Needs." In that assessment, the OTA shows the contribution that solar can make in meeting the energy needs of each sector of the U.S. economy.

Here briefly are the report's major findings. Solar systems can provide domestic hot water—comprising 3.5 percent of total U.S. energy demand—at an average monthly price over the lifetime of these systems that is now competitive with hot water provided by electricity in much of the United States. Solar space heat—18 percent of total energy demand—either is, or soon could be, competitive with electric space heat in much of the United States. Solar systems providing heat and hot water are expected to be competitive with oil or gas for residential and commercial use by the mid-1980s. Electricity generated from solar sources could be cost competitive, for other uses providing 9 percent of energy demands, with conventionally produced electricity by the mid-1980s, delivering power at $0.04 to $.10 per kilowatt hour. In terms of production cost alone, solar energy could not compete with coal as a source of "agricultural or industrial process heat" below 100° C.—comprising from 2 to 7 percent of present energy demand. However, environmental factors and coal supply constraints might favor the use of solar for this purpose.

United States: Conspicuous Consumption

By any standard, energy consumption in the United States is extraordinarily high, which is one reason why the potential of renewable sources is limited by comparison. The following figures give some indication of how much more energy the United States consumes than other countries.

- **Measured in coal equivalent terms, almost 30 percent of the world's energy consumption in 1975 occurred in the United States.**
- **Although there is a link between economic growth and energy use, the United States consumes more energy than countries with higher income levels. In 1975, the United States used twice as much energy per capita as Sweden, and three times as much as Switzerland, both of which had higher per capita incomes. The United States used twice as much energy as West Germany, which had a comparable income level.**
- **In 1975, the United States accounted for 46 percent of all gasoline used to operate the world's motor vehicles. U.S. gasoline consumption alone accounted for 5.6 percent of total world commercial energy demand that year.**
- **In 1977, for every new American baby, over three new automobiles appeared on U.S. roads.**
- **In 1975, some 213 million Americans used 60 percent as much**

commercial energy—as gasoline—to drive motor vehicles as the 3 billion inhabitants of the developing countries used for their entire commercial energy needs.

- **In 1975, the United States consumed more commercial energy as jet fuel (measured in coal equivalent terms) than any developing country except India and China used to meet its entire commercial energy needs. Yet jet fuel consumption accounted for just 3 percent of total U.S. commercial energy consumption.**

The potential contribution that solar energy can make to each sector of U.S. energy demand, and the relative importance of that sector in this country's composite energy profile, is shown in [. . . a chart accompanying the report]. . . .

From the OTA figures it is apparent that, until cost breakthroughs are achieved in techniques of generating electricity from solar sources, direct sunlight is unlikely to have a major impact on today's profile of energy use in the United States, or probably in any of the other industrialized countries. It is also evident that generation of electricity for domestic purposes is a very different proposition from generating electricity in either the quantities or the voltages required for industry, which is the biggest single consumer of energy today.

Thus, in the United States and other industrialized countries, it is apparent that solar energy is no panacea for the problem of rising energy costs. It is equally apparent that for a few selected energy needs today, direct sunshine offers a viable alternative to conventionally produced, mostly nonrenewable energy. Within the next one to two decades, the role of solar energy is expected to expand sharply. But the dream of a modern industrial state like the United States completely dependent on renewable energy sources such as direct sunlight remains just that, a dream.

Solar in the Third World

As with the industrialized countries, solar technologies offer varying possibilities in the Third World according to the end use for which energy is needed. Many of these end uses are completely different from those in the industrialized countries. Although few developing countries have any need of home heating, some of their other energy needs lend themselves to the use of solar techniques. Yet, as shall be seen, there are institutional, cultural, and maintenance problems with the adoption of any new technology, and solar technology is no exception.

What follows focuses principally on solar usage in the developing countries. However, since many of these techniques were used first in the industrialized countries, or are being developed there, some examples from these countries are also included.

The general adage for adopting any new technology is the simpler the better. Solar cooking is the exception. Technologically, solar cookers consisting of small parabolic reflectors make a lot of sense; culturally, they are complete failures.

The solar cooker concentrates the sun's rays into a cooking surface, or grill, and the heat intensities are more than adequate for cooking needs. There are essentially two cultural problems with solar cookers which have labeled them practical failures. First, most cooking takes place before sunrise or after the sun goes down. Second, solar cooked food lacks the smoky flavor of wood or charcoal cooked food.

Solar Water

Where the water supply is contaminated, and no alternatives are readily available, solar distillation may well be the cheapest way to provide potable drinking water. First used in Chile in 1892, solar distillers have been used in the United States, the Soviet Union, Australia, the Caribbean, and around the Mediterranean to provide water for small island communities and towns.

Although there are numerous designs, a solar distiller at its simplest consists of a box in which sits a suspended black tray where the dirty water rests, covered by a clear sloping glass pane. Water is vaporized by sunlight and condenses on the glass, then trickles down the walls of the distiller into clean containers at its base. Such stills, which require little maintenance, can yield up to 4 liters (4.2 quarts) per square meter of glass pane per day. While such solar distillers do not compare to fossil fuel fired distillers for quantities of more than 200,000 liters per day, they compare favorably up to that level, especially when the economies of using local rather than imported materials to construct stills are included in the calculations.

Sunlight has been used to dry crops, fruits, and vegetables—and laundry—since time immemorial. For the last 20 years, flatplate solar collectors have been used in the United States, Turkey, Canada, and several other countries, to help the process along. Solar drying of tobacco, for example, has become increasingly attractive as the cost of conventional fuels has increased, and timber drying in Australia using solar energy has been found to be only marginally more expensive today than using fossil fuels.

WIND POWER

One of the most familiar features of the rural United States even today is the "wind-pumper," a small windmill on a steel tower that pumps water. A major source of power decades ago—some 6 million wind machines have been used in the United States over the course of the last 100 years—up to 150,000 such wind machines are still reported to be in use today. Another 250,000 machines are reportedly not in use but in repairable condition. As with many of the renewable sources of energy, there is a resurgence of interest in wind power as a result of the rise in fossil fuel prices, and research is underway in the United States, Canada, the Netherlands, and in India, Senegal, and Tanzania.

As with solar energy, there is a world "wind belt," in fact there are two, girdling the globe between 30° and 40° both north and south of the equator. However, wind is even more variable than direct sunlight, and within these global belts wind potential varies widely with the local topography. Trees, hills, and valleys all affect wind velocity. So do large bodies of water, where differential rates of heat absorption from the surrounding land area create alternating directions of wind-blowing toward land by day and toward water by night. Therefore, siting of wind machines is of crucial importance. In addition, wind power, like the intensity of direct sunlight, varies widely on a seasonal basis.

Speed affects the efficiency of harnessing wind power. Wind machines typically operate best within fixed ranges of wind speeds, and their efficiency tends to decline markedly when actual wind velocities do not fall within these ranges. The Electrical Power Research Institute, for example, estimates that a 200-foot tower fitted with rotors 200 feet in diameter could provide 1,600 kilowatts of electricity at wind speeds of 30 mph. At half that speed, however, the power output would fall eightfold to 200 kilowatts.

These features of wind make it even more variable than direct sunlight, and without storage of its energy as electricity, wind can only be used in situations where a constant supply of energy is not necessary. Thus wind power is typically used in agriculture, notably for irrigation and pumping water. Direct use of wind power holds much more potential for developing countries, whose economies remain largely agrarian, than for the industrialized countries, where agriculture plays a small if vital role in the national economy. Nevertheless, farmers in the industrialized countries are beginning to turn back to wind power, and American companies are manufacturing wind machines for both the export and home markets. Designs range from the familiar wind-pumper, and "sailmills" to more modern designs like the Darrieu, or egg beater design, which is used strictly for generation of electricity.

Measure for Measure

Any student of energy research quickly encounters a bewildering array of different energy measures. This article is no exception, although an effort has been made to standardize these measures. Here is a brief explanation of the energy measures used in this article, together with some additional measures which often appear in books and articles about energy.

Calorie. **A unit of heat energy, defined as the amount of heat energy required to raise the temperature of one gram of water by 1 °C. One calorie is equal to .00397 British thermal units, or .001 watt-hours, or 4.18 joules.**

British thermal unit **(Btu). The amount of heat energy required to heat one pound of water by 1 °F. One Btu is equal to 252 calories, .293 watt-hours, or 1,055 joules.**

Quad. **One quadrillion Btu's.**

Joule. **The basic unit of energy measurement. It equals .239 calorie.**

Watt. **The basic unit of electrical energy, defined as the consumption of one joule per second.**

Kilowatt **(kw). 1,000 watts.**

Megawatt **(mw). 1,000 kilowatts.**

Gigawatt **(gw). 1,000 megawatts.**

Terawatt **(tw). 1,000 gigawatts.**

Kilowatt-hour **(kwh). The amount of electricity generated by one kilowatt of electrical capacity in one hour. One kwh is equal to 3,415 Btu. One kilowatt of electrical capacity can generate up to 8,760 kwh annually.**

Watt-hour **(wh). The amount of electricity generated by one watt of capacity in one hour.**

Langley. **A unit of solar radiation, equivalent to one calorie of radiation energy per square centimeter, or to .21622 kwh per square foot.**

A *barrel* of oil is equivalent to 42 gallons, or 5.8 million Btu's.

One metric ton of coal equivalent **(MTCE) equals 8,000 kwh, 4.8 barrels of oil, or 27,800 cubic feet of natural gas.**

Electricity from Wind

Generation of electricity from wind is not a new technique. Between 1941 and 1945, when it collapsed in high winds, a 1.25 megawatt Smith-Putnam generator contributed power to the Central Vermont Public Service Corporation. But wind electricity is not economical today in the United States. Family-sized windmills would cost from $5–25,000, reports the Edison Electrical Institute, and would be usable only in those areas of the United States with sufficient wind speeds: the Central Plains and the East and West coasts.

Prototypes of models expected to be available in the near future—within five years—could provide wind-generated electricity at costs comparable to the $700–$1,000 per kilowatt that electricity today costs utilities to produce.

The record of wind use in the developing countries is rather mixed. Wind pumps have been used for irrigation in various places, though maintenance appears to have been a major problem. But in Tanzania and Uganda, at least, wind machines have been used with considerable success, as well as in Zambia and Argentina.

In both the industrialized countries and the developing countries, wind power seems to have some potential in direct applications where a constant supply of energy is not a necessity. Electrical applications may be feasible in the future, at market prices, but in general wind power has rather little potential when compared to direct sunlight, hydroelectricity, or biomass.

HYDROELECTRIC POWER

Unlike many of the other renewable energy sources, the technology to harness hydropower is widely used today. Waterpower has been important since antiquity, for such uses as grinding grains and pumping water. Following introduction of the water turbine in the early nineteenth century, water mills lined the creeks and streams of the northeastern United States and Europe, producing mechanical power for agriculture and for much of the industrial expansion of that era. But hydro did not become a major power source until the late nineteenth century, with the construction of large dams and, more important, the conversion of waterpower into electrical power.

Hydropower today accounts for almost 3 percent of the world's total commercial energy consumption, and almost one-quarter of the world's electricity output, some 1.6 billion gigawatt hours. Eighty percent of this electricity is produced and consumed in the industrialized countries, where most of the major hydro sites have been built.

Hydropower represents a much larger proportion of total electric capacity in the developing than in the industrialized countries, 39 to 22 percent, respectively, because relatively little electricity in the developing countries is generated from other sources, such as coal, nuclear fission, or oil. Moreover, there is ample room still for expansion. Only a fraction of the major hydro potential of these countries (an estimated 44 percent of the world total) has been put to use. This immense store of self-renewing energy could help fuel the process of industrialization which most of these countries hope eventually to undergo.

Hydropower depends on two factors: the volume of water flow and the "head," the distance that water falls before entering the turbine chamber. As a result, most major natural hydro sites are located on large streams in mountainous regions.

The technology of hydroelectricity has progressed in response to the power needs of the industrialized countries. As these needs increased, technological development kept pace. One consequence was that hydro facilities increased in scale. Another was that interest in "small" as opposed to "large" hydro technology, like so many other techniques of renewable energy use, lapsed as electricity generated from burning coal or oil provided cheaper power in greater volume.

The large-scale orientation of hydropower development to the energy needs of the industrialized countries is a major reason why so little of the hydro potential in the developing countries is producing electricity today. Large-scale hydroelectric facilities are capable of producing enormous quantities of electricity, and the more that is generated, the cheaper it becomes. The industrialized countries, which can use all the home-produced power they can get to replace imported oil, have capitalized on these characteristics, which is why most of the large-scale potential hydro sites in these countries are producing electricity today. The cost of transmission—getting the power from the dam to the user—is not an insuperable problem in these countries, where both industrial users and population are concentrated in relatively small areas.

Circumstances are different in most developing countries. Energy needs are simply too low to permit them to realize the economies of scale—and the cheap electricity—that large-scale hydropower can provide. Per capita energy use is low, in a population which is often highly dispersed, and is often located considerable distances from the mountainous terrain which is the natural source of hydropower. As a result, the cost of transmission to each user is a greater part of the total expense of hydroelectric projects. Furthermore the transmission costs themselves tend to be much higher in the developing than in the industrialized countries. The greater transmission costs and the very high initial capital costs put hydropower beyond the reach of many, though not all, developing countries, unless extended financing is available.

In a few developing countries, however, some of which are well into the process of rapid industrialization, hydropower is virtually the sole source of electricity. Brazil, for example, derives 92 percent of its electricity from hydropower, much of it installed on the Parana River and its tributaries. Brazil is now constructing the largest hydro facility in the world, in partnership with neighboring Paraguay, on the Parana River. When completed this site will have the potential of producing 12 billion watts of electricity, which means adding more than half again to the present electricity capacity of these two countries. In Zaire, the Inga project on the Zaire River has the potential to provide up to 200,000 gigawatt hours per year, enough to add almost 1.5 percent to the world's total installed capacity.

Mini Hydro Power

While the era of cheap oil led to reduced interest in hydropower for many uses, the end of that era has resulted in a resurgence of interest in water's potential. In fact, in parts of the world primitive uses of hydropower never went away, or perhaps more accurately, the era of cheap oil never arrived. Indigenous water wheels are still in wide use today in, for example, the mountainous areas of Afghanistan and in central and eastern Turkey.

In the United States, the Corps of Engineers recently reported, the installation of new generating equipment at existing but abandoned dams, of mostly small and medium scale, could contribute 54,000 megawatts to the nation's generating capacity, adding about 10 percent to that capacity. By partially developing just 10 percent of the 50,000 potential small dam sites located in the United States, estimates the Federal Power Commission, the nation could save half a million barrels of oil per day in imports, or at least 5 percent of the oil it imports at present.

But, based on the reported success of the People's Republic of China, the major potential of mini hydro appears to be in the developing countries, where it has several advantages over major hydro. First, many streams and rivers are good potential mini hydro sites, and these also tend to be the places where rural people live. Thus the major expense of transmission costs is avoided. In addition, mini hydro sites produce energy in relatively small amounts suited to village needs, thus avoiding the expense and waste of unused capacity.

The Chinese report that up to 15,000 mini hydro electric units of between 3 and 50 kilowatt capacity were in use in 1968. By 1974, this figure had increased more than threefold, and was contributing something like 7.5 billion kilowatt hours to national energy output. While this probably represented a fairly small percentage of China's total electricity output in that year, it did provide for the needs of a very substantial portion of the rural population in China.

In Tanzania, a recent workshop sponsored by the National Academy of Sciences concluded that mini hydro units in that country's rural areas would be cheaper than either electricity generated with oil or electricity generated from large-scale hydroelectric plants. These findings were particularly interesting given the prevailing view of Tanzania as a dry and arid country. In point of fact, population in Tanzania, which has actively pursued a policy of decentralized, rural development, settles mostly where water is available, and that is also where mini hydro potential is located.

In Nepal, site of one of the world's worst rates of deforestation and its attendant calamities, another workshop found that mini hydro could be used to provide energy in combination with a woodlot to produce nitrogen-based fertilizer essential in reforestation programs. The workshop found that "for a typical hill village of 250 persons, a 16–18 kilowatt hydropower plant and a 30–40 hectare managed woodlot can provide significant irrigation, fertilizer, domestic water supply, lighting, and small industry returns while having enormous social benefits."

Small-scale hydroelectricity, while still perhaps in its formative stages, seems, where the sites exist, to be a viable source of electricity for today's small scale energy needs in the developing countries.

BIOMASS

What is biomass? Simply put, it is solar energy that has been converted into organic matter through photosynthesis. The general heading of biomass includes trees and all other forms of vegetation, including aquatic varieties and human and animal wastes.

The term biomass is a new name for a wide variety of traditional fuels. Energy has been recovered from wood, though inefficiently through burning, from the earliest days of human existence. Indeed, less than a century ago firewood was America's major fuel source, providing fully half of its needs. Canada was just as dependent on firewood up to 50 years ago. And today, for the vast majority of the people of developing countries, firewood remains the principal energy source.

But the energy that biomass contains can be recovered in many ways, and much more effectively than by simple burning. Human and animal wastes can be converted into methane gas, by means of a process called anaerobic digestion, which provides cooking and even lighting fuel, while the residue makes a rich fertilizer, of particular value in areas where the need to increase agricultural output is critical. High-starch vegetable wastes—such as sugarcane—can be converted into alcohol, ethanol, or methanol, which can be used as supplements or even substitutes for gasoline. An ambitious project to do just that is under way in Brazil today.

When the president's Domestic Policy Staff Review on Solar Energy concluded that the United States could supply up to 20 percent of its energy needs from solar sources by the end of the century, biomass was a big reason why. In Sweden today, according to Allen Hammond, an expert on solar energy, the forestry products industry satisfies 60 percent of its energy needs from biomass in the form of its own waste products, and "the larger United States forestry industry expects to be even closer to energy self-sufficiency by 1990."

In fact, Hammond continues, theoretically the United States could derive the energy equivalent of 3 million barrels of oil per day from biomass sources by the end of the century, or the equivalent of about 15 percent of the oil that this country now imports. On a global basis, estimates Princeton physicist Ted Taylor, the energy content of biomass, if completely reclaimed, would be equal to one-quarter of the world's present energy consumption, although the practical rate of recovery would certainly be much lower.

Firewood

Even today, firewood remains the principal fuel source for the majority of the world's population. With proper forestry management and conservation techniques, the world's forests would be more than adequate to meet the world's wood needs in the foreseeable future. Experts at Canada's International Development Research Centre report that almost half of the world's total energy production from all sources in 1970 was in the form of wood being added every year to forests located in the developing countries alone.

There are other, more sobering statistics. Nearly a third of the world's original tropical forest area has been destroyed within recorded history, a victim of clearing land for farm use and for fuel needs. Between 1956 and 1966 alone, aerial photographs revealed that the Ivory Coast's dense rainforest declined by a similar amount. And in Indonesia large parts of the country now have less than one-eighth of their original forest cover. Furthermore, despite the cheery estimates noted above, an accurate estimate of the world's stock of wood fuels—simply a census of trees—does not exist today, so no one really knows how much wood there is, or in what condition the forests are.

Such information is critically important because if demands on wood exceed the capacity of forests to replace themselves, wood is no longer a renewable energy source. As this fuel base declines, the search for fuel takes up more time, energy, and money, and the demands on the declining forestry base become increasingly insupportable. As deforestation sets in, the valuable agricultural areas become susceptible to erosion and flooding, and crop outputs decline.

The Search for Alternatives

As firewood becomes increasingly scarce and more expensive in terms of gathering time or purchasing price, people are turning to available alternatives. The principal substitute for firewood in the developing countries is animal dung, which is widely used today in countries as diverse as India, Nepal, the Sahelian countries, Ethiopia, Iraq, and the Andean area. The problem is that, apart from the health hazards involved, the use of dung as fuel deprives people of its use as fertilizer, reducing in turn the potential agricultural output of the land.

The present alternative to burning dung, however, is further deforestation, which also has harmful effects on agricultural output.

Today, in most developing countries, firewood is burned in the open, in open fires. Wood or dung burns in open fires with about 5–11 percent efficiency. This is the traditional and least effective way of recovering the energy in wood. More effective ways include, first and most simple, the use of closed stoves. Use of closed stoves such as the familiar Franklin stove can increase efficiency to only around 12.5 percent for cooking, but for space heating efficiencies of up to 50 percent are possible in those few developing countries where climatic conditions require heating.

Conversion of wood—and as we shall see, other crop wastes—into charcoal can increase fuel efficiency to between 20 and 35 percent, while gasification can increase fuel efficiencies up to around 45 percent for cooking.

Pyrolysis

Wood and crop residues and wastes can be converted into more efficient fuels—charcoal and gas—by pyrolysis, a process of controlled partial burning. Charcoal, for example, has been produced by pyrolysis in the industrialized countries for centuries. During this century, technological advances have permitted the extraction from wood of valuable gases, including methanol and acetic acid, to supply industry. After the 1930s, however, interest in pyrolysis as a fuel source in the industrialized countries declined as more economical methods were discovered to produce these gases from petrochemicals. Interest in pyrolysis [. . . was] renewed during the 1970s, as a result of rising ecological and energy supply concerns. Several cities in the United States and in Europe today are experimenting with pyrolysis plants to process urban waste into combustible fuel.

In the developing countries, the story is rather different. Generally speaking, charcoal consumption in these countries is rising more quickly than wood consumption. It is more efficient, burns more clearly, and is easier to transport. In addition, charcoal can be produced from crop residues and fibers which would otherwise have little or no economic use. As a fuel, charcoal can be up to 7.5 times more efficient than comparable units by weight of either wood or crop residues. But traditional methods of producing charcoal in the developing countries, using primitive earthen pit kilns, do not even approach this figure.

Despite the hazards of adopting new technologies, if forestry resources are to be preserved by increasing the efficiency of fuel recovery from wood, improved techniques of charcoal production will have to be part of the solution. Modern kilns can bring the fuel recovery rate up to some 44 percent. The Nichols Research and Engineering Corporation of New Jersey has developed a furnace process, producing gas and charcoal, which can increase the rate of recovery by two-thirds. Scientists at Georgia Tech have developed a process which can recover up to 92 percent of the fuel potential of wood, by producing charcoal, oil, and gases, although recoveries in the range of 70 to 90 percent are more frequent. Costs are still very high, and the scale of production usually exceeds village needs.

Biogas

Some cities in North America and Europe have been experimenting with treating their sewage by anaerobic digestion, a form of fermentation, which yields carbon dioxide and methane gas. The operation is powered by the methane gas it produces, and any excess is piped into the municipal gas supply. However, the primary purpose of this process is to sterilize wastes.

In a number of developing countries today, small-scale anaerobic digesters are being used to produce methane gas as a cooking fuel, as a substitute for scarce woodfuels, or for animal dung or crop residues.

The production of biogas from animal wastes, where this is possible, has two big advantages over burning animal dung. It delivers a great deal more energy, of higher quality, and yet it preserves all of the dung's potential as fertilizer.

Efforts to convert dung into fuel and fertilizer in the developing countries date to the early 1950s. In India, where up to half the total cow dung produced every year is used for agriculture, some 46,000 anaerobic digesters are presently in operation on small farms, a number targeted to increase to 100,000 by 1980 (still not much for India's many millions of farms). China has apparently made more progress, and now reportedly has nearly 5 million units in operation. Other countries, notably Tanzania, Ethiopia, Ecuador, and Nepal, are experimenting with anaerobic digesters.

Biogasification is unlikely to become a major fuel source in the developing countries. But it is well suited to the scale of energy needs of those farmers and their families who keep livestock.

Bio-Alcohol

Alcohol produced from biomass by fermentation or distillation can be used, blended with gasoline, for most transportation needs. With some modification of auto engines, bio-alcohol could be used as a complete substitute for gasoline, although, quite apart from the costs, the land areas involved to produce sufficient bio-alcohol (since it is made from plants) would probably prohibit complete displacement of gasoline as the staple fuel of transportation. Nevertheless, bio-alcohol and its possibilities mean that renewable energy can be used not only to conserve oil for most nontransportation purposes, but can be used to supplement oil in the transportation sector as well.

In fact gasoline synthetics or additives are widely produced today, principally from natural gas. The technology to produce bio-alcohol from wood and high-starch and high-sugar crops and their residues has long been known. Indeed, methanol was widely produced from wood as a fuel in Europe before kerosene priced it out of the market. Efforts to refine this research and to bring the price down may well result in bio-alcohol that is price competitive with gasoline, especially in those developing nations which are critically short of the foreign exchange necessary to import oil.

Brazil has been the pioneer in manufacturing bio-alcohol from crops and their residues, having produced ethanol from surplus sugarcane for several years for use as a gasoline additive. Interest in the program escalated sharply with the 1973–1974 rises in the price of gasoline, and today up to one-fifth of every gallon of auto fuel sold in Brazil is bio-alcohol. In December 1977, Petrobras, Brazil's oil monopoly, opened the world's first large-scale commercial bio-alcohol plant, capable of producing 60,000 liters of ethanol per day. With gasoline prices among the highest in the world, Brazil's bio-alcohol, at 60 cents per liter, is apparently a good deal.

The Brazilian example indicates that while ethanol is not the complete answer to future shortage of oil in many developing countries, it could be used to reduce oil imports and save foreign exchange.

OTHER SOURCES OF RENEWABLE ENERGY

Geothermal Power

Yellowstone Park's geyser Old Faithful is more than a tourist attraction; it is a potential source of energy. Geothermal power—heat from the earth's core—is being tapped in several industrialized countries, as well as in Mexico, El Salvador, and the Philippines. At least 80 developing countries have some sort of geothermal power potential, according to the United Nations, and in 15 such countries exploration is either under way or planned.

Geothermal power can either be used directly, for hot water and space heat needs in agriculture, and for domestic purposes, or it can be converted into electricity. The generation of electricity from geothermal heat is very similar to generation from more conventional sources, in that steam or hot water is used to operate a turbine which produces electricity.

The cost of geothermal power varies widely, but in general it remains higher than conventional alternatives. However, in a number of countries, the generation costs alone are competitive with electricity from power, diesel fuel, or from coal or natural gas. These countries include Greece, Guatemala, Nicaragua, El Salvador, and the Philippines, as well as Ethiopia, India, and Kenya. But geothermal power, like large-scale hydroelectricity, is "site bound," that is, the generating eqiupment must be located close to the source of geothermal power. Therefore, if the population is dispersed, or is located some distance from the site, transmission costs could be much higher for geothermal power than for some alternative sources.

Nuclear Fusion

Today there is increasing concern that nuclear energy plants are environmental and security hazards, a concern that is intensifying as more developing countries show interest in investing in such sources of power. Today's atomic plants operate on the principle of nuclear fission, dependent on the limited supply of radioactive elements, and so are nonrenewable sources of energy. Nuclear fusion, on the other hand, is theoretically self-renewing; indeed it could operate on seawater. But the technology to put fusion to use does not exist at present. Most energy analysts are agreed that nuclear fusion is likely to remain beyond the realm of technological and economic feasibility for at least the remainder of this century—if not forever—although both the United States and the Soviet Union have active research programs.

Ocean Thermal Energy Conversion

Ocean thermal energy conversion, or OTEC, operates on the same thermodynamic principle as some conventional methods of generating electricity—temperature differences. But whereas conventional methods typically involve very high temperatures, ocean thermal energy conversion uses the solar energy contained in surface seawater to turn a turbine, and cooler, deeper seawater as a coolant. However, since surface seawater never reaches a temperature above 85°F., OTEC power plants either use liquids with lower vaporization points or pressurize seawater to reduce its boiling point way below 212°F. Unlike direct sunlight or tidal power, OTEC is a constant source of renewable energy, available 24 hours a day year-round.

The first OTEC power plant, designed by Georges Claude of France, went into operation in 1930 in Cuba's Matanza Bay. Although the power plant never produced as much energy as it needed to operate and was destroyed by a tropical storm shortly after commencing operation, it did prove the technical feasibility of reclaiming solar energy from seawater. By pressurizing ammonia, the Claude plant brought its vaporization point below the surface temperature of seawater. The resulting gas turned a turbine which operated an electrical generator. Cooler seawater was then pumped up from greater depths to convert the ammonia back into liquid form, and the process would begin again.

In addition to an updated version of Claude's ammonia-using pioneer effort, which is apparently the most efficient, there are at least two other contemporary OTEC power plant designs. One uses liquid propane, which requires no pressurization to reach vaporization point at surface sea temperatures. Its inventors claim that a 100-megawatt version of this power plant could be cost competitive with conventionally generated electricity. A second design uses seawater, which is brought to boil at low temperatures in a partial vacuum.

The best location for an OTEC power plant would be in a tropical climate where the surface seawater reaches its highest temperatures, although a much wider area of the world's oceans would provide the minimum temperatures required. However, there are other limitations. Ideal OTEC locations are too far from population concentrations. Cold water currents typically circulate at a depth of a half mile or more, requiring pipelines of considerable depth. The power plant would need to be located outside the world's hurricane and tropical storm zone—the ideal location is close to the equator.

The principal potential for OTEC seems to be for those tropical developing countries that are short of fossil fuels, and which presently export raw materials used in energy-intensive industries, such as aluminum. With OTEC, they could process those raw materials on the spot.

Tidal Power

Using the same principle as hydroelectric power, the power inherent in sea tides can be converted into usable energy by damming off an estuary, where tide and river meet. When the tide flows in, gates open up and the movement of water through the gates activates turbines, which in turn generate electricity. As soon as the tide begins to recede, the gates are closed off until the tide reaches its lowest ebb, when the gates are reopened, permitting the dammed water to flow back to the sea and reactivating the turbines.

Although all coastal areas are subject to some tidal changes, only those few areas with a large enough tidal range, of some 4–5 meters, are potential sites for tidal power plants. Those sites are located for the most part on both sides of the North Atlantic, the English Channel, and the Arctic coast of the Soviet Union. A few developing countries, such as Argentina and India, also have some tidal power potential. There are presently two tidal power pilot projects, in the Soviet Union and in France. The French project is capable of generating some 544 gigawatt hours.

Improved technology for harnessing the flow of tides in and out of estuaries has reduced somewhat the expense of tidal energy, although not even the recent increases in oil prices make it competitive with conventional sources of power.

Wave Power

In 1976, the British government concluded that, of all the renewable sources of energy available to Britain, ocean wave power was "intrinsically the most attractive." Much of that intrinsic appeal resulted from the fact that ocean wave power is most readily available in the winter, when domestic energy demand is at its highest. A number of designs to use the perpetual movement of ocean waves are being experimented with. Japan is also interested in wave power, which is best suited to island countries located in areas where the seasonal variation in direct sunlight is too great to permit year-round reliance on that renewable source of energy.

THE FUTURE

Renewables are a very diverse collection of resources: some, as major hydropower, are intensively used; others, such as tidal power or nuclear fusion, are used little or not at all. These supply constraints are a major issue that any analysis of the potential of renewable energy must consider. So too is the question: How fast can technological breakthroughs be achieved?

In the short term, on the supply side, the renewables with the greatest potential generally seem to be small-scale hydroelectricity and the various types of biomass. Direct sunlight also figures to be a major resource, but only if we assume that technological and cost breakthroughs can be achieved in converting solar energy into electricity. On the other hand, such renewables as wave power or nuclear fusion do not appear at this time to be major potential sources.

On the demand side, national energy needs vary widely depending on the level of economic development and on the local availability of energy resources. The developing countries have a definite advantage in this respect. Their energy needs are generally low scale, which makes it easier to use renewables. Many of these countries are just in the process of switching away from traditional fuels like firewood. Therefore they are not yet addicted to oil; they have not built an industrial and social structure on the unique qualities of oil or other fossil fuels. So they still have the opportunity to emphasize other, renewable energy sources when they make policy decisions about the pace and direction of economic development.

The industrialized countries, for their part, have the technical expertise and the capital to develop the techniques to harness renewable sources of energy. It is in their self-interest to do so. Industrialized countries can extend the lifetime of nonrenewables wherever possible, both at home and in the developing world, where local conditions may make renewables attractive when they would not be in the industrialized countries. This will help everyone by postponing the day when the world runs out of easily available fossil fuels.

Governments in industrialized countries can encourage development of renewable techniques and equipment with investment credits, subsidies, and an active government research program. Renewables today generally cost more than the nonrenewable alternatives. However, in many cases, today's renewable price does not reflect the future costs that shortages in finite resources such as petroleum will cause.

No one knows for sure when shortages might occur, because no one knows for sure how much petroleum there really is, or how quickly the demand for oil is likely to grow. But several observations can be made. First, global use of petroleum is growing. Second, new discoveries of oil will have to be bigger and bigger to delay the onset of major shortages. Third, such major discoveries are becoming less and less likely.

It is a certainty that oil will one day run out. But it is by no means certain that the end of the petroleum era need be a disaster. With the proper planning, societies can make the necessary transition to other sources of energy in time to avoid major dislocations. Such planning should include renewable sources of energy. It is a certainty that one day renewables will be—must be—the major source of the world's fuel. How much effort is made to reduce the cost of that fuel, and to multiply the ways in which the fuel can be used, will have crucial implications for the way in which humanity makes the transition to the "renewable age," and when it is made. The transition will at best be difficult. But if we do not master the new sources of energy *before* we run out of today's indispensable fuel, oil, humanity will face disaster on a scale that is hard even to imagine.

26

Energy in Transition 1985—2010

National Academy of Sciences

WATER AND CLIMATE

This section is concerned with the effects of energy systems on precipitation, climate, and water supply. As dealt with here, these tend to be very large-scale problems, affecting regions of the nation or even the entire world.

Acid Precipitation

The formation of acids in the atmosphere from combustion-generated sulfur dioxide (SO_2) and nitrogen dioxide (NO_2) acidifies rain and snow. It was estimated that about 60 percent of the effect 10 years ago was due to acid-sulfate aerosols, and 40 percent to acid-nitrate aerosols. During the past 10 years, however, the nitric acid moiety has become relatively more important, presumably because of the increased use of low-sulfur fuels. Best available control technology will continue for some years to reduce sulfur oxide emissions relative to those of nitrogen oxides.

The distribution pattern of acid rain, determined by meteorological conditions, may extend for many hundreds of miles from the source, as first dramatically demonstrated in Sweden and Norway, where the effects were attributed to emissions from central Europe and the United Kingdom. In the United States, the Northeast is the focal area, and the pH of

---

Excerpt from *Energy in Transition 1985–2010*. Final Report of the Committee on Nuclear and Alternative Energy Systems, National Research Council, National Academy of Sciences (San Francisco, W. H. Freeman and Company, 1980). Pp. 467–99.

precipitation now averages annually about 4–4.3, with values as low as 2–3 observed at particular locations during storms. To the west and northwest, the pH gradient rises (to fall eventually in certain restricted areas), and in the desert regions, the pH averages about 7 (neutrality). [There has been an] increasing spread of the low pH region over a period of some 15 years (1955–72). These trends were confirmed in 1978.

The ecological effects are greatest in waters that contain the least dissolved matter—waters that are poorly buffered. Thousands of lakes in southern Norway and Sweden have shown a decline in fish populations, associated with increased acidity of the water, in turn associated with acid precipitation. A similar trend has been reported for the Adirondack Mountain region. Effects on terrestrial systems have been more difficult to isolate unambiguously, perhaps because changes register less quickly. A recent report points out that as a result of acid precipitation, the forest-floor leaching mechanism in a New England coniferous ecosystem has changed from a carbonic-organic acid type to a mineral acid type, which may accelerate leaching and increase the concentrations of dissolved trace metals of potential toxicity. Damage to forests and sport fishing has been estimated at $100 million annually.

Comparing various fuel cycles, it appears that the use of all fossil fuels involves some risk owning to the production of NO_2, and the use of those containing sulfur (coal, oil) present an additional risk.

Global Climate

Energy systems can influence climate on a large scale by the production of heat and by the production of carbon dioxide, both discharged into the atmosphere.[1] Other less important factors include the discharge of particulate matter and water vapor, and the resulting changes in albedo. From a global point of view, heat production is trivial: It amounts to just 0.01 percent of the sun's input of 150 W/m^2, when averaged over the earth's surface. On a regional or local basis, however, the concentration of industrial and other energy systems may produce sufficient heat to change patterns of wind, precipitation, humidity, and cloudiness, and to elevate temperature. While of significant local interest, these effects—which can develop and disappear rapidly since they are reversible—are much less important than those of carbon dioxide. Carbon dioxide production could become the chief factor limiting the use of fossil fuels.

Although quantitatively a minor constituent of the atmosphere (330 parts per million by volume (ppmv) in 1979), carbon dioxide takes part in the control of temperature through the so-called "greenhouse effect." Virtually transparent to visible light, carbon dioxide strongly absorbs certain infrared wavelengths (heat) radiated from the earth's surface, to which other atmospheric gases are transparent. An increase in carbon dioxide in the troposphere, therefore, alters the path of the radiation of heat from earth into space, and thereby elevates the temperature of the lower troposphere—that portion of the atmosphere 5 miles from the earth's surface and below—in which variations in weather are largely determined.

The concentration of carbon dioxide in the atmosphere has been growing in parallel with increasing fossil fuel consumption throughout the world.[2] The future rate of increase will depend on the continuing availability of oil and natural gas and especially on the increasing use of coal. To the extent that coal is substituted for the other two fuels, the problem will be worsened: Coal produces some 200 pounds of carbon dioxide per million Btu (89 metric tons per trillion joules), oil produces 80 percent as much, and natural gas about 57 percent. Synthetic liquids from coal produce 140 percent as much. Nuclear power makes no contribution to this problem, nor do solar technologies.[3]

It is estimated that the atmospheric concentration of carbon dioxide has increased some 10 percent since the beginning of continuous measurements in 1958. At present rates of growth in the consumption of energy (according to one estimate), it could rise from the present level of 330 ppmv to 360–400 by the year 2000, and might double by 2040. Uncertainty about the quantitative role of the biosphere in the overall carbon dioxide cycle adds uncertainty to these estimates, but the Risk and Impact Panel and other experts consider the projected trend correct.

One set of gross estimates for additional increments of atmospheric carbon dioxide and resulting rise in temperature [indicates] the following:

1. For a doubling of atmospheric carbon dioxide concentration there is a 2°C–3°C rise in the average temperature of the lower atmosphere at middle latitudes, and a 7 percent increase in average precipitation.
2. The temperature rise is threefold to fourfold greater in the polar regions in this model.
3. For each 1°C rise in average temperature for the middle latitudes, there might be a 10-day average increase in the growing season. In the higher latitudes (40°C–50°C), the average growing season could be lengthened by two or three times this amount. (There could be wide local variations from the average.)
4. Extensive and complex changes in precipitation patterns might occur as a result of the diminution in the polar-equator temperature difference, and general enhancement of the hydrological cycle.

A doubling of the carbon dioxide level presumably would have no significant direct effect on human health.

The implications of the changes indicated above are potentially great. Increased temperature in the polar regions would lead to changes in precipitation patterns. Not only would the duration of the seasons be affected in other latitudes, but also humidity, cloudiness, and rainfall, which in turn would affect the extent and location of agricultural lands. Shifts in grazing, agricultural, and forest belts might occur, as well as increases or decreases in their extent. Such regional modulations might be much more important than the rise in temperature alone. Increased temperatures in the polar regions might lead to a "slow" melting of polar ice, in turn leading to a slowly rising water level and changing coastline.

It is important to emphasize, however, that while the trend of such a global picture may be generally correct, it has no degree of certainty today for particular times or places. Present models cannot project when and what will happen at Fargo, North Dakota, or Paris, France. Obviously, the regional effects might be good or bad. But even if the ultimate effects are good, the transitional period will presumably involve significant dislocations and inconvenience at the very least, if not problems that are far worse. Furthermore, the realization that major changes are anticipated is bound to cause distress and political tension.

The problem is a global one that should be analyzed and planned for at an international level. Further study is required to predict when major climatic changes might occur in relation to anticipated carbon dioxide levels, and to determine the influence of changes in carbon dioxide output now, or 15 years from now, on the course of climatic events. [. . .] Study is required to predict with greater certainty and precision if and where the changes will occur, to outline their varied distribution, and to indicate more precisely what their consequences will be. Areas of uncertainty as well as certainty in these predictions should be defined as precisely as possible. On the basis of such estimates, society will have to consider building sufficient flexibility into its economic and international organizations to have some chance of adjusting to the changes gradually—in advance of their occurrence, if possible. Such adjustments might well include reduction in dependence on fossil fuels. This is one important reason to increase the diversification in our energy supply system, and to have nonfossil energy sources available for rapid substitution in the future.

Water Supply

A detailed discussion of the risk that increased energy consumption will induce a shortage of water, or that the limitations in water supply may curtail the use of energy, is . . . largely based on the report of the Risk and Impact Panel. Here we note briefly that the water problem may become a major limiting factor of energy availability. The difficulties pertain to mining, to the increased production of electricity, and to the proposed production of synthetic fuels from coal.

Some water is consumed in the routine processes of coal mining. The mining of coal or oil shale can disrupt aquifers and contaminate local drainage systems with acidic wastes.

More dramatic, however, is the issue of land reclamation in the arid western regions containing large deposits of surface coal (the upper Colorado and Missouri hydrological regions). By law, the mined land must be reclaimed, but the report of the Risk and Impact Panel warns that the success of reclamation in the high arid plains of these regions will depend critically on the ability of the soil to redevelop its capacity for aeration, water retention, and biological nutrient regeneration. The amount of water required per year to assist this process, for how many years, and with what promise of success remains an open question. Adequate water supply depends on the particular conditions at specific sites, but in general, the outlook for satisfying additional demands for water from indigenous supplies in these regions is very poor.

On the other hand, large amounts of coal in the eastern production regions lie within the basins of the upper Mississippi, Ohio, and Tennessee rivers. Even though increased mining and reclamation may indeed be feasible in these and certain western areas, the use of that coal in the production of synthetic fuels or for the production of additional electricity could again raise the question whether local supplies of water are adequate. The generation of electricity consumes 15 times more water than mining the coal it burns.

Suppose the nation required an additional 18 quads of coal per year for the generation of electricity (11.5 quads) and the production of synthetic fuels (6.5 quads) for the next 20 years (a significant amount in national plans). Based on Samuels's criterion, the analysis indicates that it would be desirable (perhaps necessary) to shift a major part of the burden to hydrological regions outside the western states. The adequacy of Samuels's criterion may be questioned: By attempting to guarantee that water flow in the area of interest will not fall below the weekly minimum observed the past 10 years, it may be too restrictive. It may, however, serve as a goal for ecologically sound practices.

An equivalent problem has been studied in greater detail by the six national laboratories that analyzed the water requirements of the President's National Energy Plan of 1977. That plan called for an additional 18 quads of coal—13.5 for electricity and 4.5 for industrial use—and the findings were considered to apply by and large to the plans under the subsequent National Energy Act of 1978. Using a less demanding water shortage criterion (critical surface supply) than that employed by the Risk and Impact Panel, the laboratories' report concludes that such an increase is feasible, provided that particular attention is paid to the many siting problems that will occur.[4] The problem will not be in the mining of the coal, but in its use.

It is clear that regional and interregional as well as local hydrological analysis must become an integral part of national energy planning, both to prevent water-supply failure and especially to obtain optimal use of our hydrological resources. We recommend that the relatively unstudied hydrological regions be examined. Water resources are largely under the control of the states. Two different approaches in law have been used to control them (the Riparian Doctrine and the Appropriation Doctrine). Their utilization in national planning will not be a simple matter. The energy-water problem is, in fact, a part of a much broader one of water as a limiting factor in the activities of society.

ECOSYSTEMS

The following review offers brief summaries of the effects of the principal energy systems on ecosystems, based largely on the report of the Ecosystems Resource Group of the Risk and Impact Panel. The field of study is still young. Its magnitude and extreme diversity are added burdens to investigators who recognize the value of expressing their findings in simple, generally applicable, quantitative terms. The resource group set the following criteria for adverse effects: Loss of arable land and of water resources; loss of open space in or near urban areas; intrusion into wilderness areas and loss of beauty; and loss of habitat and loss of wild populations, particularly when leading to extinction of species. It is recognized that much more work should be done to translate qualitative descriptions or observations into quantitative assessments that can be related to energy system activity per unit of time. However, the National Environmental Policy Act explicitly states that unquantified environmental amenities and values must be given appropriate consideration in decision making, as well as economic and technical information.

Decisions on the expanded production and use of energy taken in the face of predicted effects on ecosystems may involve a difficult balancing of values that cannot be made comparable. Threats to ecosystems are generally speculative and subject to a high degree of uncertainty. The causal connections leading from the source to the ultimate (and long-term) consequences are long and complicated, and the consequences themselves are judged differently. To one group, the extinction of a few endangered species may seem a small price to pay for expanded consumer choice in material consumption, but to another group, the benefit of a few more material goods may seem frivolous—hardly worth the destruction of an endangered species.

Hydroelectric Power

The ecological effects of hydroelectric projects are difficult to quantify and are extremely variable from case to case. If hydroelectric capacity expands in the future, the total ecological damage is likely to increase more than proportionately as the more suitable sites are used. This could be temporarily offset by a major development such as the Canadian James Bay project, but few suitable sites remain in the United States.

Among the adverse ecological consequences of new dam construction are the loss of habitat in the immediate area of the reservoir, subtle effects on the biological productivity of the river below the dam, damage to scenic areas along the wild stretches of the river, damage to the ecological balance of estuaries due to alteration of freshwater flow patterns, accelerated siltation and eutrophication[5] in the artificial lakes behind dams, adverse effects on fish species (such as salmon) that swim up rivers to spawn, and excess evaporation of water from artifical lakes and the resulting increased salinity, particularly in arid regions.

Some of these effects can be reduced or mitigated by proper design measures, but in the opinion of the Ecosystems Resource Group of the Risk and Impact Panel, the ecological damage per unit of energy produced is probably greater for hydroelectricity than for any other energy source.[6] The social value assigned to these ecological losses varies. There is no question, however, that free-flowing rivers constitute a nonrenewable and rapidly disappearing feature of the American landscape. Their complete destruction would be too high a price for a small contribution to solving the energy problem.

Geothermal Energy

In considering the ecological effects of this source, it is necessary to distinguish existing technologies for sources of steam and hot water from future technologies for hot dry rock or geopressured brines. The existing technologies are limited in their capacity to supply a significant fraction of total energy needs. Their ecological effects are specific to location: Some sources could destroy habitats and release toxic emissions that would affect local flora and fauna. Hydrogen sulfide is a particular problem for some sites.

Hot dry rock may be cleaner, but its exploitation as a source of energy will require methods of fracturing the rock at depth to provide access for water over a sufficiently large volume. In some cases, the procedures used (such as high explosives) could contaminate groundwater or trigger seismic disturbances. Seismic effects could present significant hazards if large-scale exploitation of the normal thermal gradient in the earth's crust ever becomes feasible.

In the case of geopressured sources, the volume of brine that must be handled is enormous, and its removal could create ecological problems unless a satisfactory technique for reinjection is available: Land subsidence, for example, could be significant.

Too little is known about feasible methods of exploiting geopressured brines or hot dry rock to judge the ecological effects or techniques to avoid them.

Solar Power

The diversity of solar power systems is so great (photothermal, photoelectric, photochemical) that generalizations about the effects of these systems are difficult. The evaluation is complicated in the case of most solar power systems by a complete lack of practical experience. They appear to be no worse as a group than other energy systems, and in many forms, far superior. The caution must be voiced here (as for other alternative sources of energy) that the ecological effects depend on specific processes and siting plans.

In one respect, all solar systems may be expected to be benign. They do not directly contaminate the atmosphere, nor do they dig deep into the earth or strip its surface, particularly in areas that are difficult to reclaim. The centralized stations required for large-scale power production would affect land areas and even the ocean. Thermal stations would require about 6 acres/MWe; placed in the desert for optimal operation, their effect would be amplified by the ecological fragility of the location. On a per-GWe basis, solar central stations would require about 6,000 acres, or 15 times the area of a nuclear plant and 10 times the area of a coal plant of comparable capacity (not counting the land required to mine the coal over its life).[7]

Decentralized rooftop solar collectors represent a minor environmental risk compared to centralized solar collectors. They offer the possibility of generating electricity and space heat, thus using a greater fraction of incident solar energy. The main problems will result from the necessity of removing shade trees. With clustered buildings, this problem can be reduced by sharing the energy among the buildings: Each building does not have to be unshaded throughout the day.

Wind power would require 120,000 acres/GWe (about 20 times the land required for a solar thermal plant), but the land between towers could be used for other purposes, such as agriculture. Access roads would be required for maintenance, as well as transmission lines interconnecting the numerous towers. The environmental effects of these requirements would depend on competing demands for use of the land. Wind power would be most valuable in areas where it could be integrated into a grid supplied by hydroelectric power, which could be used to compensate for the fluctuations in wind. Besides presenting aesthetic problems in many areas, wind-turbine installations may endanger migratory birds and interfere with TV and other communications.

The development of ocean thermal [energy conversion] power (OTEC) is almost certain to affect marine ecosystems, particularly if this source of energy is eventually relied upon for a significant fraction of total energy. The mixing of surface and deep waters will bring nutrients to the surface and may also release carbon dioxide to the atmosphere, although in lesser amounts than would be released by producing an equivalent amount of energy through the combustion of fossil fuel. Large-scale deployment of ocean thermal power might ultimately modify ocean currents and temperature distributions, with significant effects on regional or global ecosystems. Very little attention has been given to any of these environmental questions. Most of the effects mentioned, however, would only be of concern with very large-scale deployment and cannot be regarded as major deterrents to the development of OTEC.

Large-scale bioconversion or "biomass" is a popular option advocated by proponents of solar energy. To the extent that biomass is derived from organic wastes or from materials grown on special areas of the ocean or unused lands, the ecological effects would be minimal. This source of energy could supply perhaps 5 quads of total demand by 2010. Bioconversion is estimated to become progressively less desirable above this level as more land is dedicated to the cultivation of energy crops. To obtain an economic harvest and avoid soil depletion, chemical fertilizers and large amounts of water would have to be used. The land requirements would be enormous. At 1 percent average photosynthetic efficiency, 1.5 percent of the land area of the United States—an area about the size of Arkansas—would be required to generate about 10 quads of primary energy. The development of especially hardy species to increase the yields and improve the overall economics of energy from biomass would run some risk of spreading these species where they would be undesirable.

Coal

One of the most disruptive energy sources is coal. Underground mining can affect underground water systems and their associated drainage patterns and lead to subsidence. The underground waters that drain through the mine carry off toxic substances, and the mine itself disturbs the pattern of underground drainage. Strip mining without suitable reclamation is ruinous to surface land, and in some areas the possibility of lasting reclamation must be doubted.

Reclamation does not imply restitution (return to original conditions), but its water requirements may be high in areas where water supply is low. Areas that are relatively flat and possess an abundant water supply with high humidity are the most suitable for reclamation. Much strippable coal exists in areas where it may be effectively impossible to return the land to its prestripped state, even with the abundant use of water transported from elsewhere. If the consumption of coal increases rapidly, pressures will mount to initiate production in areas where reclamation will be relatively ineffective.

Deep mining is less destructive of the surface environment but can lead to subsidence and toxic effects in associated aquatic systems. These latter problems, however, appear susceptible to proper management, especially with improved mining technology.

Large resources of coal can be neither mined nor stripped but could be recovered by underground gasification. Little is known about the environmental effects of this practice. It could have adverse effects on important groundwater resources and thus directly affect ecosystems. The potential problems need to be kept in mind as the technology is developed.

In combustion, coal emits air pollutants that affect plant growth and lead to acid precipitation, which affects freshwater aquatic systems and forests (as explained earlier). The accumulation of carbon dioxide released in all fossil fuel combustion could ultimately result in drastic alteration of both natural and agricultural ecosystems.

The conversion of coal to synthetic fuels (liquids or gas) produces wastes, including contaminated liquids (phenol is a major constituent), that are unsuitable for immediate discharge. Present regulations and experience with coking operations offer assurance that adequate control can be achieved, but this can only be established in practice. The combustion of these fuels should be a relatively clean process (less polluting than combustion of oil or coal), since many impurities are removed in the process of conversion.

Oil

Drilling for oil can lead to accidental discharges that are harmful to local ecosystems. Likewise, spills of oil in transit or from routine operations are a serious hazard that can have devastating effects on marine and freshwater systems. The delayed as well as the prompt effects vary. The refining of oil and the release of pollutants in its combustion may have widely dispersed effects. Pipelines may promote erosion and, when overland, may hinder species migration. That suitable planning can prevent such untoward effects is now being tested by the operation of the Alaska pipeline. The overall ecosystem effects of oil are less serious than those of coal for corresponding energy production levels. Automobile emissions affect not only human health and comfort but also agricultural and plant life systems.

Natural Gas

The extraction and delivery of natural gas can threaten natural habitats. Pipeline leaks, by blanketing with natural gas and thus excluding oxygen, may leave an area barren for several months after the leak has been stopped. Fires and leaks from receiving facilities in marine areas are particularly hard on estuary life. The combustion of natural gas is indirectly damaging to ecosystems through the accompanying oxidation of atmospheric nitrogen. The nitrogen oxides thus formed are an important factor in acid precipitation (discussed under "Water and Climate"). In association with the photochemical-oxidant system or sulfur dioxide, they can be toxic to plant life (as previously noted). In total, however, the effects are much less severe than those of coal.

Shale Oil and Coal-Derived Synthetic Fuels

The ecological effects of coal-derived fuels are much the same as those for coal itself. On the other hand, the production of oil from shale carries with it the threat of considerably more ecological damage than conventional production of oil. The attractive oil shale resources in the United States are located in limited areas of the western states that are ecologically fragile and that are short of water, of which large quantities would be needed. Solid-waste disposal is a problem. Experimentation has been initiated on conversion of oil shale in situ, a technique that might or might not be less damaging ecologically than retorting in aboveground plants but that may involve serious aquifer disruption.

Nuclear Power

The principal ecological effects of nuclear power result from uranium mining—effects similar to coal mining, but far less severe (only 3–4 percent as much ore is required today). Recycling uranium and plutonium in light water reactors and lowering enrichment tails could reduce the uranium ore required per gigawatt (electric) by as much as 40 percent and thereby reduce the ecological consequences of uranium mining and also of waste disposal. Light water reactors use about 50 percent more water than fossil-fueled generating plants. If breeders were widely adopted, the remaining ecological effects would be those from thermal pollution, similar to that accompanying the generation of electricity from other sources. The same would tend to be true for advanced converters. If the breeder option is foreclosed but dependence on nuclear power continues, the demand for uranium will lead to the mining of ever lower grade ores, gradually increasing the adverse ecological effects per gigawatt (electric) capacity. Use of the very lowest-grade sources, such as shales, would create environmental disruption comparable to that of strip-mined coal.

DISCUSSION

Before stating the conclusions drawn in this chapter, it may be useful to review some of the problems encountered in formulating them, as well as the concept of risk assessment itself.

Limitations in Risk Assessment

In assessing the risks of energy systems to health, biological systems, and the environment, we have been constrained by the limited data in certain important areas. The major factor here is the early age of this field. While it is true that public health considerations have been in the public view for many years, they have centered on infectious diseases. Our concerns today center on diseases induced by chemicals or radiation. They are more difficult to detect because they are not uniquely associated with their causative agents, and are more difficult to cure because in general they are not so precisely defined and understood.

Two other factors materially increase the difficulty of risk assessment—the no-threshold, dose-effect curve and the "late" effect. The latter, exemplified by cancer, may not be observed earlier than 20 years after exposure. The assumption of a no-threshold dose-effect curve is equivalent to the claim that any dose, no matter how small, has a finite chance of damaging someone in the exposed population. Together, both factors create a state of uncertainty in the public mind that leads to the setting of standards at progressively lower levels of dose and smaller probabilities of effect. Epidemiological investigation may not always be able to keep up with the pace of such standard setting, and the validation of a new standard—by scientific study and cost-benefit analysis—may be impossible.

In some cases that deal with very low levels of exposure, it may be asked if such validation could ever be achieved. Nonetheless, epidemiological and other related studies should be conducted, if only to establish the liminal value for risk that can be determined by research. No society can be free of risk, nor is the goal of a risk-free society necessarily worth striving for.

Somewhat analogously, the estimate of risks from rare nuclear accidents may never be precise enough to satisfy those taking a position against nuclear power. Two factors enter here. First, there is the analysis for mechanical failure, such as that reported in great detail in WASH-1400. Second, there is another risk that was recognized in that report but that could not be dealt with so extensively without a great deal more industrial experience—the risk of human error, that management may not be adequate under the stress of unforeseen and previously unexperienced circumstances. It is our impression that this second risk contributed to the damage in the Three Mile Island reactor accident.

Finally, we note the inherent difficulty of comparing one energy system with another, since some of their important risks may be different and thus not strictly comparable. Nor can such differences be reduced to the terms of one common measure. Value judgments must therefore be made in the final determination of the risks society may prefer, from which sources, and at what cost.

For perspective, it may be of interest to note some of the other risks that are current in our society. In 1974, the following annual accident death rates per 100,000 persons at risk applied to the United States: motor vehicle, 22.0; falls, 7.7; drowning, 3.1; burning, 2.9; and firearms, 1.2. A British investigator has summarized United Kingdom experience thus: A one-in-a-million risk of death has been attributed to 400 miles by air, 60 miles by car, three fourths of a cigarette, 1.5 min. of rock climbing, 1.5 weeks of typical factory work, and 20 min. of being a man 60 years old.

Perception of Risk

Society's tolerance of risks that have been lived with is greater than its tolerance of risks associated with new technologies. The personal evaluation of risks tends to be formed when a technology first becomes visible. At the time older technologies were introduced, risks were more readily accepted than they are today. An important question is how subjective evaluations should be taken into account along with the more objective measures, such as fatalities per GWe-plant-year of energy production. If the subjective values are ignored, energy policy may stalemate.

The recent incident at the Three Mile Island reactor bears on this point. From the dosimetry, it is clear that damage to public health was negligible, but the public's perception of the dangers of nuclear power (rightly or wrongly) has been greatly heightened. The uncertainty of management and the tenor of the information released in the early days after the accident no doubt played a role in this. It will be of interest to see how public perception is affected by the report of the presidential commission.

A point of difference between the objective quantification of risk and its sociopolitical assessment is the role of "*attitude* toward risk" in the latter. An energy system may be viewed as a hazard by a particular group of people (organized or unorganized) for reasons that may not reflect biological or ecological assessments of the risks. Nuclear power, for example, may be opposed as a symbol of big government, impersonal corporate business, or unrestrained economic growth. Gasoline shortages are viewed by many as tricks on the part of the big oil corporations rather than as a consequence of conditions of supply and demand on the world market.

One conclusion that may be drawn is that adequate information must continually be made easily available to the public, to inform the decision-making process, and to prevent the spread of false conclusions and impressions. We emphasize the continuous nature of the task, since energy policy in general and knowledge of its associated risks in particular will be developing for many years to come.

Regulation

From the point of view of practical governance, the foregoing considerations are encompassed by the regulatory process, a function that has been evolving rapidly and in a somewhat uncoordinated way (in the areas dealt with here). It should not occasion surprise that this is so. As we have noted, many congressional committees and many units of the executive branch are involved.

Steps should be taken to simplify the regulatory process, but the extent to which such improvements can actually be effected is a matter of conjecture. It would be unrealistic to suppose that the work of a very large number of departments and agencies could be rapidly coordinated and made efficient during a period of rapid expansion in governmental responsibility. The government today is still in the process of learning through its own experience how to regulate and control the risks of energy systems in ways that satisfy many diverse groups.

With respect to the evaluation of risk, it should be recognized as a matter of policy that energy plans require time for their implementation. The assessment of risk therefore can be advantageously made a sequential process. In moving forward, the goal might be set to control overall total risk: As one energy system expands, the risk per unit of product should decline. Ideally, the total risk would not rise and might even fall. Progress toward this goal will also occur whenever the expansion of one system replaces another that is riskier.

Social and Political Risks

The concerned citizen and policymaker will have to go beyond the scientific and technical comparisons we have made and consider sociological and political risk comparisons as well. An extreme example would be to compare the loss of unique natural beauty with the advantages of local business development. There are many less extreme but important examples. To change the activity of a fuel system, for example, in response to its health risks might be weighed against the risk of reduced employment or of forcing a change in established cultural patterns. Other major comparisons lie completely within the sociopolitical domain, such as the risk of an accelerating oil shortage compared to the economic inflation engendered by increasing the price of oil.

An important aspect of such sociopolitical considerations is the geographical dissociation of risks and benefits. For example, western states might bear more than their share of the adverse consequences of rapidly developed mining (e.g., the boomtown), but the economic benefits would not return to the affected communities in the same proportion.

Appalachia has already demonstrated such effects over the years. Likewise, air and water pollution generated at any stage of the fuel cycle are not necessarily borne by the users of the energy in proportion to use.

Traditional cost-benefit analysis, as applied to energy decisions, does not usually include these distributional effects. Extension of the analysis can in principle identify costs and benefits to particular groups or geographical regions, but the balancing of costs to one group against benefits to another, or to the general welfare, is inherently a political judgment. There is a need for some kind of compensation to redress the imbalance in the distributed effects of energy systems.

Finally, we wish to mention four sociopolitical risks that may figure prominently in the deliberation of energy policy and that serve to place other sociopolitical risks in perspective.

1. In the minds of some, the greatest risk associated with the production of nuclear energy is that the associated technology and materials can assist in the proliferation of nuclear weapons. In comparison to nuclear war, all other risks are small. But the closeness of the connection between development and the threat of nuclear hostilities or war is uncertain. [. . .] CONAES is divided on this issue.

2. A related risk is that the protection of nuclear fuel cycles against sabotage and theft will lead to unacceptable security measures, incompatible with our standards for civil liberties.[8] Some argue that such measures will be necessary in a world of increasing violence and terrorism. Other energy sources, in particular, dams and storage facilities for liquefied natural gas, are subject to sabotage, as are such nonenergy facilities as supplies of drinking water. Nuclear facilities, in principle, may be easier to guard without intrusion into the rest of society by virtue of the small area involved and the limited number of personnel.

3. The third risk is associated with the further large-scale development of natural energy systems, whose operation and control become increasingly centralized and increasingly out of the reach of the ordinary citizen. It is argued that numerous self-sufficient energy systems at the household and neighborhood level would be more flexible and responsive to local needs. The development of such systems for the future is certainly desirable, if only to provide for greater diversity of energy alternatives.[9] Nevertheless, large-scale electrical and gas-distribution systems are working well today. Decentralized systems, to serve their intended purposes, would have to be mass produced, widely distributed, and maintained on a large scale. Without more experience, it is impossible to say how sturdy such decentralized systems could be.

4. The fourth risk is not having enough energy. CONAES has not considered the risks that could be faced by a society in which energy supplies fall short of the citizens' legitimate needs.[10]

CONCLUSION

Limits of Risk Control

The increasing interest in protecting public health and natural resources is of major historical significance, and no doubt will continue to increase in extent and influence. Regulations will always engender controversy. This is especially true today, owing to the tremendous expansion of regulatory activity and to the fact that we are still learning how to manage it. In dealing with these problems, we must recognize that there are practical limits to the refined ascertainment of risk and its control. Energy systems (or other systems) cannot be made risk-free, nor can all improvements be made as a matter of course without significant economic penalty or other adjustment. The public should be made aware of these limitations, and of the possibility that the absolute control of risk may not only be impossible, but undesirable.

Conservation

For the most part, conservation is the least risky strategy from the standpoint of direct effects on the environment and public health. (One potential problem is the possibility of indoor air pollution buildup in connection with certain conservation measures in buildings.) The main reason that conservation cannot be the only strategy is that at some level of application, it would give rise to indirect socioeconomic and political effects, mostly through economic adversity, that would predominate over its direct benefits. We cannot be sure where that point is, but all the CONAES technical analyses suggest that it is far from where we are now, possibly at an energy/GNP ratio of about half its present value, given several decades for adjustment. The maximum conservation achievable without adverse socioeconomic effects will likely have health and environmental benefits and therefore should have highest priority in policies to reduce the risks of energy systems.

Fossil Fuels

Among fossil fuels, natural gas presents the smallest health and environmental risks in both production and consumption, although there is the possibility of serious accidents in the transportation and storage of liquefied natural gas. Oil is next, and coal is much higher in risk. This ranking is likely to persist, although the gap may narrow with improvements in technology. Research is most urgently needed on the health effects of coal combustion by utilities and industry, and on the possible occupation and public health hazards of producing and using synthetic fuels.

We must be prepared for the possibility that adverse health effects, global CO_2 increase and associated climatic change, freshwater supply problems, and ecological considerations will eventually severely restrict continuing expansion of coal use. These problems are likely, though not certain, to become critical at about three times current coal output, or less.

Carbon Dioxide

The accelerating increase in the level of atmospheric carbon dioxide, paralleling the increase in combustion of fossil fuels worldwide, may affect global climate by elevating the mean global temperature. The substitution of coal for oil (or synthetic liquids for oil) and oil for gas will tend to hasten this process, but the combustion of any fossil fuel contributes CO_2 to the atmosphere. Assuming continued growth in the use of fossil fuels, a perceptible change has been projected by one model for the year 2000 and significant change by the year 2030. A serious concern is that climatic changes due to CO_2 would be practically irreversible by the time they were detected. It should be noted that the ultimate effects may be good as well as bad (or mixed), but the transitional period could be disruptive in its effects on agriculture and industry in some regions. Vigorous international efforts should be undertaken to predict the course of carbon dioxide buildup and to determine its climatic and consequent ecological effects. There is a parallel need for planning studies to mitigate possible economic and social disruption, including plans to curtail the use of fossil fuels.

Nuclear Power

The routine risks of nuclear power include the induction of cancer and genetic effects by ionizing radiation released throughout the nuclear energy cycle. These risks are very small in comparison to the overall incidence of cancer and genetic effects in the general population, and they could be significantly smaller yet if the most important source of radiation in the nuclear energy cycle—uranium mill tailings—were generally better protected.[11] There are also risks of severe accidents, whose probabilities have been estimated with a great deal of uncertainty, but whose severities could be comparable to those of large dam failures and liquefied natural gas storage system fires.[12] There are also risks from the disposal of radioactive waste; these are less than those of the other parts of the nuclear energy cycle, but only if appropriate action is taken to find suitable long-term disposal sites and methods.

It should be clear from the earlier general discussion of risk comparisons that any ranking of the risks of technologies as disparate as coal-fired and nuclear electricity generation is subject to very broad, and in some cases irreducible, uncertainties. However, if one takes all health effects into account (including mining and transportation accidents and the estimated expectations from nuclear accidents), the health effects of coal production and use appear to be a good deal greater than those of the nuclear energy cycle. If in this comparison, though, one takes the most optimistic view of the health effects of coal-derived air pollution and the most pessimistic view of the risk of nuclear accidents, coal might have a small advantage in such a comparison.[13]

Nuclear power is associated also with risks of nuclear weapons proliferation and terrorism, but the magnitude of these risks (and even whether nuclear power increases or decreases the risks) cannot be assessed in terms of probabilities and consequences.

Water Supply

The supply of water may constrain the continued growth of electrical power, the mining and the conversion of coal to synthetic fuels, the production of oil from shale, and the use of coal by industry. Water scarcity is greater in the West than the East, but affects particular localities in both parts of the country. The projection reported in this study shows that the constraint could indeed be significant when, for example, the amount of additional electricity and synthetic fuels that could be produced from 40 quads of coal is produced nationally. The projection assumes present technology (which could be improved) and does not allow for large-scale use of brackish water or seawater. We urge that regional and interregional hydrological analyses become an integral part of energy production planning, to prevent actual water shortage, and especially to distribute production to make optimal use of our hydrological resources. Such planning will probably be difficult. We note that the water-energy problem is a single manifestation of the broader problem of water as a limiting factor in the growth of society.

Solar Energy

Several solar energy technologies appear very promising from the standpoint of health and environmental risk. Hydroelectric power (classed by convention with solar energy), however, while benign with regard to air pollution, is quite destructive of ecosystems per unit of output. Terrestrial energy farms are also likely to be ecologically destructive if deployed on a scale large enough to provide more than a few percent of total energy needs. (Biomass production at sea could avoid this problem.)

For most solar technologies, the main risks are those associated with extracting and processing the requisite large amounts of construction materials.

Air Quality Standards and Research

The difficult tasks of setting standards for ambient air quality and emissions have been greatly complicated by a lack of precise knowledge of the levels at which epidemiological effects first appear and of the diversity of such effects. Pragmatic decisions must therefore be made in the face of uncertainty—uncertainty magnified by the periodic (and appropriate) review of these standards. Industrialists may claim that the standards are set too low, in order to make them safe regardless of cost and convenience; this inhibits industrial planning and has been a deterrent in the further use of coal. The situation calls for a major research effort into the effects of pollutants, including emissions from mobile sources (nitrogen oxides, ozone, nonmethane hydrocarbons), as well as from the stationary sources (nitrogen oxides, sulfur oxides, particulates) that this chapter considers at length.

The committee recommends that investigation center on the dose-effect curve (or exposure-effect curve) in the region near and below the present ambient air quality standards.

1. The quantitative assessment of exposure, and if possible, of dose per individual, is essential to advance knowledge in this field. One or two centrally located stations are insufficient to monitor an urban area for epidemiological research (they may be sufficient for other purposes). Measurements of indoor and outdoor, residential and occupational exposures are necessary.
2. Mortality is too gross an endpoint to be used alone. Others must be selected for specific types of morbidity and for physiological and biochemical response.
3. While immediate responses are important, late effects in specific individuals may be even more important.
4. The effects of emissions on plants and ecosystems should receive major attention.
5. The magnitude of the several problems to be investigated necessitates undertaking and maintaining long-term studies. Some will take decades to complete.
6. Much of the work cannot be planned from first to last detail, and none of it should be subject to political control. Coupled with the need for an effort adequate in scale to the problems under investigation, there is a need for flexibility and independence in pursuing the studies that suggests scientists outside the government should conduct much of the work.

7. We should realize that answers will come slowly and decisions will have to be made on an uncertain basis for some time in the future.

Public Appraisal of Energy Systems

There is a need for research that will contribute to better understanding of the factors that determine public perceptions of the health and environmental risks of energy systems, and their acceptance by different subgroups within the public. No strategy for risk reduction in energy systems can be fully acceptable if it does not take into account these public perceptions and judgments, even when they are seen as unfounded by experts.[14] It is unlikely that the appraisal of risk will ever be able to avoid difficult relative value judgments between different kinds of risks, as well as between risks and economic or other benefits of energy technologies. This is not to say that present methods of risk assessment cannot be improved. Nevertheless, the judgmental factor will continue to predominate in decisions among energy alternatives, and is unlikely ever to be superseded by formal analysis of risks and benefits. This underscores the importance of an informed and open public debate.

NOTES

1. In addition, dust and nitrogen oxides have the potential to make a quantitative contribution.

2. And possibly also widespread deforestation, although the role of the biosphere is not clear. Reforestation has been recommended.

3. Statement by H. Brooks: The harvesting of wood on a large scale would reduce the average amount of carbon stored as biomass in forests and would thus contribute some CO_2 to the atmosphere. OTEC would also release CO_2 to the atmosphere from the deep oceans. However, per unit of energy produced, these effects would probably be less than a third those from fossil fuels.

4. Statement by H. Brooks: However, the President's Energy Plan does not go beyond 1990 in projecting coal use. Unless energy growth leveled off after that date, there would be a growing problem.

5. Eutrophication refers to the enhancement of the basic nutritional level of lakes and other bodies of water that eventually disrupt the natural ecological relationships between species, permitting "undesirable" ones to outgrow and inhibit the rest and leading to profound changes in the entire habitat.

6. Statement by H. Brooks: However, hydroelectricity may be attractive on other grounds. It generates no air pollution and has a low accident rate, although accidents in the construction of dams, as well as the threat of catastrophic dam failure, are significant risks.

7. Statement by H. Brooks: Depending on the source of coal, if one includes the land area necessary for mining enough for the full lifetime of a plant, solar and coal-fired electricity are comparable.

8. Statement by B. I. Spinrad and H. Brooks: [As noted in previous discussion of this topic] where it is pointed out that the civil liberties argument is an unprovable allegation. We see no grounds for taking it as a basis for policy.

9. Statement by B. I. Spinrad and H. Brooks: We would replace "if only" by "but only" in this sentence. This is because centralized energy systems serve population centers more efficiently than decentralized ones do, and serve interregional equity better.

10. Statement by J. P. Holdren: The Demand and Conservation Panel found very low growth in energy use compatible with high prosperity. Only *sudden* shortfalls were not considered.

11. Statement by H. I. Kohn: [. . .] This may contradict Table 5. Presumably, it assumes that the improper and now illegal practices of the past will be continued.

12. Statement by H. I. Kohn: Note the *non*comparability of some of the risks in this comparison. For nonradiation systems, there are property losses and immediate injury. For radiation accidents, in addition and usually more importantly, there are cancer and genetic effects.

13. Statement by J. P. Holdren: The situation is even more ambiguous than the text suggests because it is not actually possible to do what is implied by the words, "if one takes all health effects into account." Specifically, the statement that coal's health effects "appear to be a good deal greater" than nuclear's requires either that one ignore the million-year accumulation of excess cancer deaths plausibly attributable to uranium-mill tailings if the linear hypothesis is accepted (an excess that could amount to 30–400 deaths per GWe-year of electricity, according to the Academy's own recent report, *Risks Associated with Nuclear Power: A Critical Review of the Literature*, Committee on Science and Public Policy, Committee on Literature Survey of Risks Associated with Nuclear Power (Washington, D.C.: National Academy of Sciences, April 1979)), or that one assume without any quantitative support that the health effects of today's coal use over the next million years will be as large or larger. Suppose this troublesome issue, which is completely unresolvable at present, is neglected. Suppose one also neglects genetic illness from nontailings routine emissions, for which there is an uncertainty range spanning at least a factor of 20 on the nuclear side (extending on the high end to consequences about equal to those of the excess cancers) and for which no quantitative estimates at all are available on the coal side. Suppose one neglects, further, the health effects of emissions of oxides of nitrogen, hydrocarbons, and trace metals from coal combustion, which are generally presumed (but not proved) to be smaller than those of the sulfur oxides and generalized particulates that existing dose-response relations include. In the restricted comparison that remains after all these troublesome factors are excluded, the widespread view that coal comes out "a good deal" worse than nuclear rests on various combinations of the following three errors: (1) attribution to coal of practices in mine health and safety, power plant siting, and pollution control that are illegal or inconceivable (and usually both) in the new, large facilities relevant to comparisons with nuclear power; (2) failure to note that the "excess deaths" attributed to air pollution from coal typically deprive the victims of far less life expectancy than the cancers attributed to nuclear power (the ratio is almost certainly more than 10:1); (3) refusal to take seriously the upper end of the range of responsible opinion on conceivable nuclear accident risk, while taking completely seriously the upper-limit estimates of excess deaths from air pol-

lution. When these errors are avoided, the "best estimates" of the years of life lost per GWe-year of electricity from coal and nuclear differ by an amount small compared to the uncertainties associated with each.

14. Statement by H. Brooks, D. J. Rose, and B. I. Spinrad: Although we agree with the statement, we fear it might be interpreted as implying that government planning should accept the most irrational appraisals of risk put forward by politically active minorities.

27

The Wolfcreek Statement: Toward a Sustainable Energy Society

The Georgia Conservancy

The United States urgently needs a rational energy policy. Without a comprehensive and farsighted approach to energy, we cannot implement sound foreign, economic, agricultural, or urban policies. The time has come for a new policy based on new realities. Clinging instead to outmoded ideas and extending past trends of exponential energy growth will seriously damage our social and economic health and will soon put our best alternatives out of reach. If we chose now, however, we can expand our options for the future while strengthening our economy and society.

The keystone of a rational energy policy must be a national commitment to energy conservation. Such a commitment will provide the time we need to develop and deploy energy technologies that are safe and sustainable, appropriately scaled, and economically sound. To achieve these objectives we recommend (1) removing all subsidies for nonrenewable fuels; (2) placing a royalty on nonrenewable fuels in a manner that is equitable to all and beneficial to the economy; and (3) eliminating all institutional barriers to efficient energy use.

The advantages of this course are overwhelming: Employment can be increased; inflation can be more easily controlled; pollution can be reduced; scarce resources can be conserved; social equity and the quality of life can be improved; dependence on foreign energy sources can be reduced; and the pressure toward nuclear proliferation can be relieved. But time is short. More than half of our recoverable domestic supply of our two choicest fuels has been exhausted.

The future holds inevitable conflicts between habits and prices, between convenience and vulnerability, between the broad public good and narrow private interests. To solve these conflicts our approach requires active leadership by the president and by those in all levels of government—leadership that encourages new attitudes about people, resources, and the economy. We make no pretense that such a course will be easy, but we believe that, given strong leadership, the people of this nation will join in the search for a viable future.

CONVENTIONAL ENERGY FORECASTS

Present energy forecasts describe the United States as caught in the iron grip of inexorably rising demand. According to such forecasts population will increase by less than one-fifth in the next few decades, total energy demand will double, and demand for electricity will triple. The advertisements paid for by U.S. energy companies and their financial supporters threaten that any reduction in energy use means cold homes and rising unemployment. Not surprisingly their forecasts show the necessity of unlimited energy growth. But such self-fulfilling predictions elevate energy from a means to an end on the assumption that the more energy we use the higher will be our quality of life. We suggest, on the contrary, that unlimited energy growth leads to increased unemployment, persistent inflation, serious capital shortages, and social instability.

The physical realities of the conventional energy approach are becoming all too familiar: thousands of giant power stations, both coal fired and nuclear; ubiquitous transmission towers; vast strip mines; thousands of arctic and offshore oil and gas wells; and huge refineries. We are promised even more: a massive new synthetic fuels industry; oil shale development with even more strip mining; coal slurry lines; and the emergence of a plutonium economy and its attendant transport and support facilities.

The economic realities of the conventional course are equally dismal. Synthetic fuels are many times more capital and energy intensive than are traditional direct fuel technologies, and electrification is even more capital demanding. The costs of a high energy growth program are responsibly estimated to be as much as two-thirds of all net new capital investment between now and 1985. Such vast expenditures would, among other things, foster rising prices and deprive industry of the funds it needs to invest in more energy-efficient technologies. Moreover, such an investment pattern would push unemployment upward since investments in energy facilities produce fewer jobs per dollar than any other investment we can make.

The environmental risks of the proposed giant energy technologies are forbidding. Drilling for oil in arctic and offshore areas would introduce unprecedented technical risks to fragile regions. Coal, shale, and uranium mining would devastate hundreds of communities and millions of acres, often irrevocably. The predicted doubling of the amount of carbon dioxide in the atmosphere from the burning of fossil fuels will jeopardize climatic stability and world agriculture. Energy growth increases the likelihood that catastrophic events—including nuclear accidents, oil spills, natural gas explosions, and dam failures—would undermine both natural and social systems.

Ecological risks would be joined by social and political risks. Centralized energy systems would have to be protected against the terrorist attacks to which they are vulnerable, and against the legitimate dissent they are likely to arouse. The powers of the state would have to expand to try to divert needed resources into the energy sector to override local siting objections, to substitute elitist technocracy for democratic processes, and to regulate energy through bureaucracies far removed from the people they supposedly serve. The resultant changes in a democratic society ought not to be taken lightly in view of our recent experience of abuses of police power by the CIA and the FBI. Moreover, the conventional path of energy growth could lead to the creation of "zones of national sacrifice" and to divisive interregional conflicts.

Similar divisions and conflicts could occur internationally. Expanded use of complex and expensive technologies developed by the wealthy states could in poorer countries create technological dependencies and commercial monopolies while simultaneously imposing inappropriate cultural patterns and values upon the new users. Even more important, American reliance upon nuclear power both directly and indirectly promotes the international spread of nuclear power and its inevitable companion: nuclear weapons capability.

The United States is now at an historic crossroad in its national life. Before us is the unprecedented task of moving from dependence upon a rapidly declining nonrenewable energy base to dependence upon a new base that is as yet undetermined. Our present drift can only lead us into unresolvable conflicts between energy production and food production, between democratic ideals and emerging technological imperatives, and between safety and our seemingly relentless addiction to energy. History offers few, if any, examples of equivalent challenges. To a large extent the ultimate success of the incoming administration will depend upon its ability to create a rational, farsighted energy policy to guide the nation through this transition.

THE CASE FOR CONSERVATION

We reject the conventional approach to the energy problem and with it any notion that we must be compelled by the force of uncontrollable energy demands. But if, as we argue, our present course is unacceptable, is there a plausible, realistic alternative? We believe there is. A growing body of evidence suggests that an energy conservation program that would allow us time to create a sustainable energy posture is possible in the immediate future. But while desirable, such a program is not inevitable, and is indeed improbable without a major national commitment and a transition policy extending over a period of several decades.

The largest source of energy available to the United States is the energy we currently waste. Our country ranks only fourteenth among the 18 members of the International Energy Agency in terms of effective energy conservation efforts. Sweden, West Germany, and Switzerland, at comparable standards of living, consume only 60 percent as much energy per capita. In 1976 Americans wasted more fossil fuel than was used by two-thirds of the world's population. This excess, which currently comprises one-half of our energy budget, represents our nation's largest, cheapest, cleanest, and safest near-term source of new energy.

It is feasible for the United States to sharply increase its energy efficiency by the year 2000 and in the process greatly extend its energy supply. Energy consumption can be made more efficient by carefully matching the quality of fuel with the quality of work desired. Such matching would eliminate, for example, the burning of high quality natural gas and oil at temperatures in excess of 1,000° to obtain room temperatures of 70°. Energy consumption can also be reduced by changing the patterns of consumption to favor efficiency through the use of mass transit, bikeways, cluster housing, district heating, and recycling.

The list of good ways to conserve energy is long. For example, ceiling insulation in a typical home costs about $300 but will save about seven barrels of oil each year for the lifetime of the house. These seven barrels, which are as valuable as new oil pumped out of the ground, can then be employed more productively elsewhere. The energy saved in just 10 years would amount to 70 barrels, which means that we are "producing" oil at $4.30/barrel. When heating oil costs $3 per barrel, insulation was no bargain. But today, heating oil often costs $16 per barrel, and insulation has become a cheap source of new energy.

Industry currently consumes 40 percent of this country's fuel. Recent studies by the Conference Board and the Ford Foundation's Energy Policy Project suggest that enormous energy savings can be made with existing technology without denting industrial productivity. The primary metals industries use about one-fifth of all industrial fuel. By adopting technologies now widely employed in other countries, the steel industry can reduce its inordinate fuel demands by about 50 percent by 1995. Using the new chloride process instead of the traditional Hall method to refine aluminum yields energy savings of about one-third. Recycled scrap aluminum requires only 5 percent as much energy as aluminum refined from virgin ore.

Forty-five percent of all industrial fuel is used to generate process steam. If this steam were first used to generate electricity and then used as process steam, considerably more electricity would be produced than the entire industrial sector now purchases from utilities. The additional fuel and capital needed per kilowatt-hour of industrial "co-generation" is only half that required by the most efficient new centralized power-plants.

From 30 to 50 percent of the operating energy in most buildings can be economically conserved now. Moreover, the American Institute of Architects estimates that the use of advanced conservation technologies, including solar devices, heat pumps, and total energy systems, can conserve up to 80 percent of energy consumption in new buildings. A national commitment to upgrading the energy efficiency of buildings would, by 1990, save the equivalent of 12.5 million barrels of oil a day.

Equally dramatic energy savings are within practical reach in the transportation sector. The use of manual transmissions would save one-tenth of all automotive fuel consumed. Switching to radial tires would save another tenth. Reducing the average vehicle size from 3,600 pounds to 2,700 pounds would save the nation one quarter of its present gasoline use. Carpooling, the use of mass transit, and greater use of railroads could further cut energy waste.

Aside from the intrinsic merit of saving scarce fuels, the case for energy conservation rests on at least four additional points. First, conserving energy by substituting labor for energy can help to reduce unemployment. A carefully designed program of energy conservation can create up to 930,000 jobs per quad (quadrillion Btu's; total U.S. energy use in 1974 was 73 quads) of energy saved. The return to a more labor intensive economy can also encourage meaningful employment and worker participation, both of which are conducive to personal development. Second, by increasing employment while encouraging energy thrift, we can reduce the rate of inflation. Third, conservation will reduce the environmental damage implicit in the acquisition, transport, and consumption of energy. Fourth, energy conservation allows us to reduce our reliance on foreign sources of fossil fuels, which has steadily increased despite a stated policy of "energy independence."

THE LONG-TERM GOAL: A SUSTAINABLE ENERGY SOCIETY

Energy conservation will give us the time we need to make a transition from an energy base consisting of geologic capital (oil, coal, natural gas, and uranium) to one based on renewable, safe, and direct and indirect solar income. This time provides a reprieve in which we can examine alternative energy technologies. If our present knowledge advances even modestly over the next several decades, we may confidently expect a rising level of energy derived from the renewable income sources.

In most respects solar power is an ideal energy source: It is free, abundant, and safe; it implies no social or political regimentation; and it can either be used in its low temperature form or concentrated to high temperatures. Solar energy can be used directly as a source of low grade heat (which constitutes over one-half of our energy needs), and indirectly in the form of wind and bioconversion for industrial processes. Moreover, there is reason to expect that the direct conversion of sunlight into electricity will be commercially feasible within the next two decades.

Because sunlight is compatible with decentralized applications, many solar proposals dispense entirely with the expensive transportation and distribution networks that encumber conventional energy sources. But this savings must be weighed against the additional costs of collecting and storing a form of energy that is dilute, intermittent, and seasonally variable.

Objections to solar energy on grounds that it is more expensive than its alternatives are based on the practices of discounting the value of energy resources *in situ* and of granting of depletion allowances to encourage resource exploitation. The illusion of cheap energy based on this kind of thinking has led to extravagant use and rapid exhaustion of scarce supplies. Pricing nonrenewable fuel at its renewable replacement cost, which is at least as logical and a good deal wiser, would make the price of renewable energy technologies competitive immediately.

A sustainable energy posture would also offer the advantages of greater political stability and immunity to disruption through sabotage. The vulnerability of decentralized technology systems to terrorism and the likelihood that they will be misused as weapons is negligible. Political stability would also be enhanced by the movement toward decentralized, small-scale, and adaptable energy production systems that reduce the need for distant, high technology experts and large regulatory bureaucracies. The positive implications for the conservation and expansion of civil liberties in such a society are considerable.

Internationally, the transition to a sustainable energy society would be the most significant contribution the United States could make to world peace. An alternative to present forms of modernization that are economically and ecologically unsustainable is obviously necessary. Modern states have climbed the ladder of prosperity only to find the upper rungs are loose. To those clamoring to make the same ascent, our protestations that the ladder cannot support our combined weight are inevitably and, properly, interpreted as self-serving. In these circumstances the creation of an alternative that would ease our weight on the ladder and demonstrate an alternative model of sustainable energy development would mean more than all the foreign aid we could conceivably muster. Initially such a course would, by freeing resources needed elsewhere, signal our serious interest in global equity and would reestablish American moral influence in the world.

Equally important would be the effect of sustainable energy goals in lessening the prospect of energy wars and in arresting the steady slide toward nuclear proliferation. To remain on the current path with a sizable U.S. commitment to nuclear energy can only encourage the spread of nuclear energy technology and, eventually, of nuclear weapons. To expect others to abstain where we have indulged lacks both prudence and wit.

28

Breaking the Logjam

Thomas Hoffmann and Brian Johnson

Two fundamental economic assumptions have recently been overthrown. Their abandonment is having a worldwide effect that is likely to be much greater than we can now envision.

The first assumption was that cheap commercial energy would be available indefinitely as a principal foundation of economic growth. The second was that *free* fuel would serve the heating and cooking needs of the world's poor (and largely rural) inhabitants. Now, firewood and oil race to outstrip one another in rates of depletion and spiraling cost. As a result, the world does not face a problem of tinkering with the old energy order; it must radically alter and indeed replace that order. So far governments and the international institutions that serve them have been unwilling or unable to meet this challenge, even though massive pressure for change is building against old inertias and resistances. Nowhere is this logjam more perplexing than in the response of Western governments toward the energy problems of the developing world, even though the logical steps that might be taken would, in most cases, serve mutual interests. It is difficult to respond technologically, because most new energy sources are still being researched and tested. It seems impossible to respond financially on an adequate scale, because "aid"—even programs instituted principally by donor self-interest—almost always lacks broad domestic political support. And it is thought naïve to respond with political creativity, if the polarized North-South dialogue is a sound indicator of the willingness to compromise. This impasse is not, of course, exclu-

Reprint of "Breaking the Logjam," Chapter 6 in *The World Energy Triangle: A Strategy for Cooperation* by Thomas Hoffmann and Brian Johnson. Copyright 1981 by the International Institute for Environment and Development. Reprinted with permission from Ballinger Publishing Company, Cambridge, Mass. Pp. 107–22.

sively or even primarily a result of Western inaction; rather it is perpetuated by [a] "suspicious triangle." [. . .]

But where does this impasse leave the West in its energy relations with the Third World? The Brandt Commission has recently highlighted the common concerns of North and South in their overall economic relations. With respect to energy, both developed and less developed countries need secure oil supplies now and for the foreseeable future. Both have a profound stake in hastening the advent of renewable energy sources, and both depend upon the security of the international financial system. The need to cooperate is becoming overwhelming. And indeed, many comparatively small practical measures have been taken or are contemplated. But their magnitude does not compare favorably to the scale of the problems they are meant to solve. They are not the product of fundamental rethinking of old assumptions about resource availability, capital flows, technological innovation, and development aid. In short, with one or two important exceptions, the recent Western response to the developing world's energy plight up to now looks too much like rearranging deck chairs on the Titanic.

GOALS FOR MUTUAL BENEFIT

[. . .] Energy aid and cooperation programs have lacked strategic focus. It is not therefore surprising that the objectives of specific programs are often ill-defined and rarely reflect any effort at setting priorities. In the first chapter we emphasized some essential elements of a strategy for energy aid and cooperation. Here we suggest five objectives to be emphasized in the new energy programs of the 1980s. We believe these objectives will be politically acceptable to each side of the energy triangle. They also seek to balance efforts to alleviate immediate crises against the need to pursue longer term readjustments, and they can be designed so as to mobilize the necessary capital, technology, and organizational effort.

First, it is in the North's own interest to help finance and carry out exploration for, and production of, oil in developing countries that now import oil. The major oil exporters need have no fears as to the impact of such activity on the price of their oil. Demand for oil is such that their economic interests cannot be threatened by this kind of assistance. Indeed, to the extent that oil-importing poor countries can meet their own needs, the political solidarity of the Third World is less likely to be shattered by OPEC pricing policies. This last argument might work against Western willingness to cooperate, of course, to the extent that the Western industrialized nations feel threatened by Third World alliances. But Western governments are far more interested in improving their own energy positions than in devising problematic ways of disrupting Third World solidarity.

Second, the rash of governmental programs to promote the export of solar energy technology to developing countries must be designed to avoid the pitfalls of other kinds of technology transfer and to be mutually beneficial for both solar exporters and importers. Remarkably little creativity in this regard has so far been shown by the four or five Western governments (and the European Community) who are eager to subsidize their solar industries' marketing in the Third World. New approaches are supposed to be a matter of Western self-interest because, put simply, sharing solar technology could be the West's political compensation for consuming the lion's share of the world's oil. But technology transfer programs that pay only lip service to developing country participation and indigenous capability have rarely, if ever, taken firm root. There is, therefore, a more abiding Western self-interest in encouraging genuine partnership in energy innovation.

The third objective for the 1980s is closely related to the opportunities for cooperation on solar energy. Many OPEC (particularly Arab) countries have recently shown great interest in solar energy. Joint solar energy programs with oil-exporting countries not only can create new markets in those countries, but can also lead to a broadening and strengthening of support for the renewable energy effort in the poorer developing countries. Arab aid donors, in particular, recognize that they too will benefit from efforts to tap renewable energy resources in developing countries. It should therefore be a major objective of Western energy aid to work increasingly closely with the aid programs of oil-exporting countries, both to ensure that OPEC as well as Western capital is reinvested in energy and to achieve the broader political benefits of increasing cooperation with some of the OPEC members.

As a fourth objective, the disastrous depletion of world firewood supplies must be slowed, if possible halted, and indeed reversed. This may appear at first sight to require more altruism than some of the other priorities we have listed. But for those who see degradation of natural resources—and the resulting competition for those that remain—as remote from present political crises, we would point out that at least one regional war fought in the last ten years (between Ethiopia and Somalia) had as a principal cause competition for disappearing rangeland. The prospects for the poorest countries seem even more disquieting when one adds competition between use of land for food and fuel to the equation.

A fifth and final objective covers every energy aid project: Such programs have to increase their emphasis on helping developing countries to solve their own energy problems. Third World universities, research facilities, and even government agencies need financial support and technical assistance. Practically speaking, there is no alternative to such an effort: If Western donors simply descend with their own solutions, local suspicion and resistance will be insurmountable.

THE DIPLOMATIC CHALLENGES

It is relatively easy to offer objectives. It is less easy to devise a realistic path toward them. Is it possible to move toward cooperation with the major oil exporters for the benefit (in the first instance) of the poor developing countries, without simultaneously negotiating with the members of OPEC on other issues of direct Western self-interest? Former British chancellor of the exchequer, Denis Healey, saw the first building blocks of Western-Arab cooperation in terms of fixed oil-price agreements:

> International economic diplomacy is like rowing a boat through treacle. I think the most hopeful area of agreement to aim at would probably involve the consumers' accepting regular small increases in price—at least indexed to inflation in the countries that provide OPEC with manufactured goods—in return for some guarantee of output from the producers. If we could create even one precedent for such cooperation between producers and consumers, wider agreements might flow from it. If we do not try, the situation is certain to deteriorate.

It is now so difficult to negotiate directly with most members of OPEC—indeed, "negotiations" no longer occur—that the best development strategy may be to emphasize the plight of oil-importing Third World countries as the ground of common concern and to work progressively toward the issues where there now seems to be no starting point at all.

Certainly it seems that it would be easier to make progress on producer-consumer relations in an atmosphere lightened by success in other arenas. And even if most diplomatic negotiations fail to bear fruit, we would argue that three-cornered progress can still be made through quiet, unpublicized technical cooperation within Western and Arab aid programs, and among energy organizations like the IEA, OLADE, and others.

A second challenge is to ensure that new initiatives are not undermined by the mixture of motives that bring them into being. In an attempt to make sense of very large issues, we have discussed energy cooperation questions under five separate headings involving matters of foreign policy, technology, institutional programs, selected private investment, and policymaking in Third World countries. But it ought also to be clear that every energy decision faced by an aid donor will encounter some conflict between these viewpoints. For example, cooperating with OPEC donors on the development of renewable energy technologies seems sound enough from a foreign policy perspective. But so far, solar energy companies seem to believe that such cooperation would deny them some of the benefits of their investments to date by giving away trade secrets for diplomatic advantage, and they therefore remain skeptical.

Shifting combinations of special interests and conflicting motives have so far produced hybrid Third World energy policies in almost every aid-giving country. We would not argue that it is necessarily a bad thing that policies differ among aid donors, or even within different agencies of particular governments. But this situation does make for complicated selection and structuring of energy programs. The differences in approach between U.S. AID and the European Development Fund, both working in Mali, illustrated the international dimension of this problem. But its impact is more directly felt *within* aid-giving national governments, as they try to reconcile competing policy objectives. Certainly this is the case in the United States, where different government agencies are planning programs in the Third World that seem to share little in the way of common objectives.

The U.S. Department of Energy's plan to promote photovoltaic cells internationally, for example, ignores many of U.S. AID's objectives. DOE plans almost no effort to ensure that developmental and marketing objectives are matched to local circumstances in the purchasing countries. But is it really sensible to initiate a major U.S. international effort that ignores the issues of technology transfer that have plagued international aid and trade discussions for more than five years? The Department of Energy (or indeed any promotional mechanism in almost any Western country) would answer that the photovoltaic program is essentially designed to reduce the cost of solar energy, coincidentally selling American products, and that the program should not be judged by developmental or foreign policy standards. There is logic in this response, but it entirely begs the question of whether the U.S. government as a whole has decided what it can accomplish on energy cooperation with Third World countries, and how best to go about it.

One should not expect that any amount of careful thought or planning can eliminate these kinds of conflicts among diverse interests. They are surely endemic to systems that mix governmental programs and private investment spurred by governmental incentives. But these conflicts could be better understood, and disparate programs reconciled, if the overriding objectives of energy policy toward the Third World were clarified and, where possible, agreed upon.

OLD INERTIA AND NEW IDEAS

It is still widely assumed in aid agencies and even in developing country governments that new energy solutions are a distant promise, still five or ten years over the horizon, but not a solution to today's problems. This assumption perhaps reflects the tendency of well-established biases to linger tenaciously, even when their economic justifications are collapsing. It is still difficult, for example, to locate many Third World energy specialists who pay much attention to the efficiency with which energy is used. They were trained simply to worry about increasing energy supplies.

The present dilemma is that while new energy sources appear to catch on and spread rapidly in use once they are boldly and widely introduced, they can only be introduced by development planners who have not until now grasped their advantages and are not therefore inclined to back them to the necessary degree. This is not to say that aid agency and government officials hold out any hope for the return of cheap conventional energy. They do not. But many of these officials remain unmoved by the myriad possibilities for energy conservation in agriculture and industry, for diversification of fossil fuel supplies, for replenishment of fuel wood stocks, and for a range of small but promising remote solar applications, which could all be acted on today. In short, concerted action has been impeded as much by a lag in planning and innovation as by any shortage of technical options.

On the other hand, blinkered idealism can equally frustrate its own objectives. Uncompromising efforts to achieve only the ideal arrangements and the perfect solutions can make it impossible to achieve quite modest steps forward. The time when reality conforms to the models of energy planners will never come. Developing countries are making new energy investment decisions every day (and falling further in debt). Time to formulate perfect programs is an unaffordable luxury because action is needed so urgently.

At both ends of the spectrum, the challenge is to break out of the inertia that has gripped energy planners and agencies. Despite many promising new initiatives, these institutions generally admit the inadequacy of measures taken to date. We will not at this stage attempt to recapitulate all of the positive steps that governments might take. Throughout this book we have indicated general directions and lines of approach. Here, our aim is to specify the type of major initiative that is needed: to assure adequate financing of aid programs, to adapt private investment in new energy sources to the circumstances of developing countries, and to achieve greater international cooperation on energy. Some of the needed actions can only be taken by governments, others could be initiated by aid programs or international institutions.

The Challenge to Governments

Proposals for increased development aid are not popular in the Western political climate of 1980. Efforts to locate and use new sources of energy have, however, an altogether better chance to capture the public imagination. Energy cooperation can help relieve the overall strain on global energy supplies and hasten the transition away from extreme fossil fuel dependence. The United States in particular among the Western aid donors can ill afford any further political isolation on energy, because its proportionate consumption of oil alienates both its Western allies and many of the Third World countries whose political stability is critical to world peace.

There is the danger that focusing funds on one aspect of development may imbalance development programs. Special funds or pledges are also sometimes resisted on the grounds that financial resources should not be mobilized until their dedication is carefully planned and committed. In the case of energy, it need hardly be said that the same logic was never applied to the development of nuclear power, which received vast subsidies in its developmental stages. But a better parallel is surely the commitment made by aid-giving nations in the 1960s to transfer 1 percent of their GNPs to the developing world on concessional terms. Many nations, including the United States, fail year after year to keep this particular promise. But it stands as a solid reminder of the agreed level of effort that development assistance, as a whole, requires. In the same way, it is politically essential to begin now to subscribe funds on the scale that will be needed, three or five years from now, for strong and successful energy programs during the coming decade. Without major new financial pledges, new programs will tend to be designed solely to fit the level of support that is anticipated. In this era of increasing unpopularity of aid programs, that kind of planning may seem pragmatic but in fact tends to set off a self-limiting cycle of caution and inadequate funding. Worse, it leads to programs that may be "successful" by their own terms of reference, but that are wholly inadequate if measured by the scale of the problem they are meant to address.

At least three important activities are currently inadequately financed and should get priority attention. First, assured funding is needed for oil and gas development programs like the World Bank's, including the work of other institutions such as the UNDP.[1] Jointly financed projects with Arab aid agencies, some of which have already been agreed to, offer one important source of increased funding in this regard. International institutions in addition to the World Bank need supplementing money both to encourage oil and gas exploration and to provide an additional source of international "risk insurance." Second, widespread testing and demonstration projects are needed to encourage commercial development of new—particularly solar—technology. And finally, further concessional aid must be made available to create credit facilities for the purchase of small-scale renewable energy-using and energy-saving devices such as wood-burning stoves. (Without these greatly expanded credit operations, it will be difficult for poor energy *users* to become energy *purchasers*.)

We advocate the establishment of an international energy development fund, not as an autonomous new international organization but as a joint facility to receive payments by governments. Member governments' subscribing to the fund should ask the World Bank to establish it jointly with the reconstituted OPEC Fund, and the United Nations Development Program.

The fund would not itself need the technical capacity to finance projects. It would provide loans on highly concessional terms, drawing upon the technical capabilities of the sponsoring institutions. Among other purposes, those loans could finance the payment of interest charges on ordinary development bank loans, for example, those of the regional development banks. In the case of renewable energy technology projects, for example, this type of arrangement would enable the World Bank and the regional development banks to finance renewable energy projects sooner than would otherwise be the case (by supporting financially higher risk work on adaptation and application). The involvement of these institutions would, in turn, ensure that the development of renewable energy projects is not left exclusively in the hands of export-minded bilateral aid programs.

Apart from overcoming suspicion that an international energy fund would be a new guise for foreign aid, two complicated political issues would have to be resolved. First, Western resistance to special funding for energy often is based on the argument that Western governments should not raise money to counterbalance the effects on developing countries of OPEC price increases. That argument ignores the widespread Third World perception that oil price rises are caused by the intense bidding of Western consumers: That the cartel now follows the price rather than pushes it. More important to Western politicians, their resistance also ignores the direct benefits the West can expect from energy cooperation *regardless* of who "causes" oil price increases.

The second political hurdle poses more of a diplomatic challenge: Equitable fund raising among OECD countries would be difficult to accomplish. One approach might be for each OECD nation to contribute 1 percent of the value of its net petroleum imports. Under this formula, for instance, the U.S. contribution would be between $400 and $500 million annually. The difficulty with this system would be the burden it placed on countries like Japan and West Germany, heavily dependent on imported oil. The United States, as the dominant consumer, might become a disproportionately small contributor in the eyes of its allies. Another formula would tie payments to GNP, weighted by oil consumption and oil imports. This would obviously be more complicated, but leaves room for negotiation. The critical concern, which should never be allowed off center stage, is the need for the OECD countries to persuade OPEC nations to make a matching pledge. A high-visibility effort for the benefit of the developing countries who are most badly hurt by oil price increases would be difficult for OPEC to ignore. The return on this investment, through diversified world oil supply and a hastened transition to renewable energy sources, would be immense.

Firewood: The Top Priority

Of all the measures urgently needed in the poorest developing countries, firewood emerges as the first priority. Many of these countries face environmental and human catastrophe unless their exhaustion of firewood supplies is slowed and eventually reversed. It is surprising that only the American and Dutch aid agencies are so far ready to commit themselves to large firewood replenishment programs. The World Bank intends to incorporate wood plantation components in many of its forestry projects. But reforestation should also be a priority concern of very concessional bilateral aid, because the short-term economic return of afforestation projects makes them problematic for the conventional cost-benefit lending criteria of development banking institutions.

Development of oil and renewable energy resources is so clearly in direct Western self-interest that we have considered it separately from the firewood problem. Whether or not an international energy fund is launched to address those problems, we believe that every OECD bilateral aid program should commit itself in the Development Assistance Committee (DAC) of the OECD to participate in firewood projects and should confirm this commitment at the ministerial level of the OECD's Council. The Sahel has received considerable attention because of the work of the Committee on Interstate Drought Control in the Sahel and the Club du Sahel, and also due to the worldwide publicity generated by the famine of the early 1970s, but other areas of the world are neglected. Agencies that lack sufficient forestry and agricultural staff could offer support through cofinancing with World Bank and regional development bank projects. The effort called for is daunting, and it is for this reason that we feel governmental leadership at the highest levels is essential.

Innovation in Technology Transfer

The third type of action that can only be expected to succeed if there is governmental support would perhaps be, eventually, the most far-reaching energy initiative that northern countries could undertake. Private industrial investments in new sources of energy that are being attracted to Third World markets need not only to be stimulated, but also to be shaped innovatively. To transfer technology on terms more profitable politically and commercially than has been the case in other fields will require innovative consultation between buyers and sellers of the new energy technologies. The first steps can best be initiated under the leadership of the companies' home governments, particularly where those governments are using public funds to support the new energy industries, because the companies are clearly unlikely to cooperate on their own initiative. The vehicle might be a solar industry advisory service, for example, sponsored by a national government and consortium of industries within the OECD or the donor-coordinating mechanisms that are emerging.

This type of advisory group would aim to make a modest beginning by encouraging an exchange of views among alternative energy industries and Third World planners, researchers, and manufacturers. These groups have rarely communicated with one another except on a secretive, commercially competitive, individual basis. It should not be excessively difficult, politically, to constitute such a group, because neither side has anything to lose by participating. Later on, increasingly practical functions could be taken on. For example, regional demonstration projects might be specified for competitive bidding, or opportunities for joint ventures could be identified and publicized.

At the outset, two types of participants should be involved. Representatives of a cross section of renewable energy industries (particularly the solar industry, given its export-mindedness) should participate. If necessary, national industrial associations could be asked to designate representatives. Third World representation should particularly include government development planners but should also embrace representatives of research facilities and private industry. If narrowing of Third World representatives proved difficult, the developing country directors of the World Bank might constitute themselves as an informal committee to make initial suggestions.

Aid Programs and International Organizations

So far in this chapter, we have been discussing the large energy issues, areas in which it seems certain that only governments can take the lead. And we have argued that Western governments should use these opportunities to identify new avenues of cooperation with willing members of OPEC. But there are also a number of very important steps that aid programs, international development banks, and U.N. agencies can take under the decision of their own leadership. Too much stress should not be laid here on formal coordination among aid programs. Donors generally work quite closely together on an informal basis, when the need is seen, and are unwilling to engage in excessive, structured exchange of information and ideas. Energy aid is changing rapidly, however, and for this reason, the informal consultative process started in June 1979 by the World Bank should be put on a regular basis. The aim should be to improve international cooperation on energy aid matters both between bilateral and multilateral agencies on the one hand, and between OPEC and Western aid funds on the other.

The World Bank's original interest was to explain and launch its oil and gas program. Now donors need to set up an ad hoc working group on energy assistance. It should emphatically not be designed to allocate aid money among developing countries (a function that would meet bitter resistance), but should concentrate on technical cooperation and exchange. For example, one immediate objective of the group could be to sponsor methodological exchange on national energy assessments and to assure that as many countries as possible receive this type of assistance as soon as possible.

Donors should also seek agreement on more-open exchange of energy data gathered by project teams and missions (particularly including the great quantities of data generated for projects that failed to be approved). This goal relates closely to the creation of a forward planning mechanism so that agencies have advance warning of energy projects planned elsewhere and can allocate their own resources accordingly. In theory this already happens on an ad hoc basis, particularly among field staff, but in fact the existing system is grossly inefficient.

Finally, but most important, frameworks are needed in which to place new energy cooperation ventures that might otherwise flounder for lack of a fertile planting ground. For example, an energy working group of aid donors could be one logical setting for multilateral efforts to influence the directions taken by the solar energy industry. More formal channels might be needed, but it is almost certainly better to avoid the UN system, which is mistrusted by industry. Both industry and developing country governments and institutions would be most comfortable meeting on the neutral territory that a consortium of aid donors might provide.

The International Energy Agency should be encouraged by its member governments to continue to sponsor regular technical workshops, such as it held in December 1978. Indeed, a general enlargement of the IEA's "service" role would be a sure indicator to developing countries that the major industrialized powers are now serious about cooperation on energy matters, since the IEA's established responsibility has been exclusively to protect the most direct self-interest of its members. The IEA's official mandate need not be formally broadened, since technical cooperation is already one of its primary functions. But the agency staff is likely to be so overburdened by present oil supply conditions that its Governing Council should act to establish a small staff with permanent responsibility for technical cooperation with developing countries. Such a group should also have the expertise and authority to explore developing country participation in other mainstream IEA work. For example, the international energy technology group requested by the Tokyo summit might make a very significant contribution, linking renewable energy promoters and developing country users. Similarly, the IEA could, without any revision in its procedures, enlarge its role as a center of North-South exchange on energy research programs.

Many of these activities, and others not mentioned here, will be debated at the August 1981 United Nations Conference on New and Renewable Sources of Energy. [. . .] It is impossible to evaluate the chances for a "successful" conference, but it ought to be recalled that the developing countries' definition of success will clearly differ from that of the OECD countries. The perception in the West of the United Nations system as an ineffective yet pretentious structure is not shared by developing countries, for whom it is important to their place in international diplomacy. Many Western countries may actually regard this latest United Nations conference as successful if it simply avoids blatant public failure. But these same governments accept the importance of emphasizing serious technical discussion, which is most likely to occur if there is already evidence of political progress elsewhere. In short, a United Nations conference is not a good place to launch new ideas, but it is the inevitable forum for gathering support behind them.

Action Today: Practical Measures

The large portrait of improved financing and major political initiative is likely to remain clouded for a long time. But even while new energy debates occur, aid agencies and institutions should press forward with practical changes in policy and programs. We have spoken of the need for a great deal more planning assistance, training, and institutional strengthening in developing country energy departments to enable them to determine their own energy strategies. In fact, a major new effort behind this type of energy aid could be the vital link between diplomatic initiative and practical action. This type of help is necessary for two reasons. First, developing countries have little reason to take energy advice from the great energy consumers and many reasons to suspect it. So the new technologies and the new sources of energy that the North will be promoting are more likely to prove acceptable if understood and planned for by the poor countries themselves. Donor countries will also find this approach advantageous in that it will help to protect them from blame and resentment that may arise when investments fail or experiments go awry. There will be mistakes—in North and South—as new energy programs are sifted and implemented. Aid donors will not want to be fully responsible for those that occur in the South.

National energy assessments are needed immediately where these have not been conducted. The urgency of the need for them arises from the fact that energy investment decisions are being made every day. Alternative approaches and procedures need to be tested, and a major effort is needed to enlarge their credibility in the eyes of host governments, perhaps by financing multidonor assessments. National assessments should include significant participation by nationals of the host country and should always be backed by training programs geared to establishing an energy planning capability in the host country.

A second step for aid programs is a much larger concentration of effort to train developing country energy experts at every level of sophistication. Some training work can be done in Europe or North America. For example, the French government brings Third World nationals to petroleum development programs in France, and U.S. AID sponsors a six-week course at the Brookhaven National Laboratory to develop skills needed for energy development and management. But a great deal more training is also needed in the developing countries to prepare maintenance and installation technicians (both for the introduction of new energy technologies and for better upkeep and utilization of existing or traditional systems). In particular, to build up the indigenous capability of those developing country institutions that have energy responsibilities, aid programs should seek out experts in national scientific research institutions, help them upgrade their knowledge, and encourage their involvement in the various stages of project development. This will help raise the standing of these scientists with their governments and also help them acquire the confidence and experience needed to share the task of energy planning and project implementation with development aid institutions.

It has become almost commonplace to suggest that more research is needed on developing country energy needs and resources. While this is true, we would emphasize the great need for concentrating research efforts in a few key areas whose neglect has the potential to cause serious misdirection of investment. The full costs and benefits of choices among energy systems (marginal investments in centralized versus decentralized and renewable versus nonrenewable electrification, and electrification versus primary energy applications in any particular setting) have, so far as can be ascertained, remained largely uncompared. The World Bank has apparently reevaluated the economics of central station rural electrification. This research should be shared with other donors and made public. Likewise, hydroelectric power projects seem to be enjoying a resurgence, and there appears to be a widespread renewal of interest in large dams as part of major regional development schemes. It is essential here to ensure that many of the flagrant mistakes of the past are not repeated.

Joint research efforts between developing country researchers and northern institutions (aid programs *and* technical or energy ministries) are also an important new initiative. Too often, developing country research institutions lack adequate facilities and staff and cannot find sufficient support in their own governments. Increased aid agency support for, and cooperation with, these institutions may catalyze national efforts. Donor involvement may also reduce the incidence of "pure" research that is essentially wasted by being swamped by parallel efforts elsewhere. Applied research—the type of work that can only be done well on a local basis—should receive the highest priority support of aid programs.

A different type of aid agency involvement is needed to finance "low technology" energy projects such as biogas digesters, windmills made of local materials, and small nonturbine hydroelectric generators. These projects have low foreign-exchange requirements and limited technology transfer components. Many badly needed energy projects—biogas, for example—require almost *no* foreign-exchange component and *no* transfer of northern technology. To facilitate financing of this type of project as well as to encourage the adaptation of solar and other technologies, several innovations are badly needed.

There are at least three opportunities for aid agencies to increase their prospects for financing very small energy projects on a local scale. First, the authority of local aid officers to authorize small loans and grants should be increased. Regulations in this area are ordinarily excessively complex, but despite significant bureaucratic barriers, this could be one area of significant, quick change. Second, industrial development banks and national development banks in the developing countries could be mobilized for these purposes. These institutions can make small loans at very concessional interest rates and this could be done on a sectoral basis. Naturally, Third World governments prefer funds that are not earmarked for a sector, but loans could be advanced for institutions that indicate an interest in the energy area. It seems clear that a special effort is needed to cut red tape and make funds available to local manufacturers and users of the new energy technologies. Third, multilateral agencies should try to establish better links with private voluntary organizations. This has for some time been seen as a critical area for encouraging new initiatives with alternative energy, because these small groups almost always work with local populace in developing countries and so have a unique position from which to advise on the social and cultural problems that new energy systems are likely to encounter. Grants to these agencies for project purposes are ordinarily quite small, but all of the major bilateral agencies have funds for this type of activity. (The World Bank and most regional development banks have not.)

BEYOND STALEMATE?

This book is written at a time when hopes for progress in its two main areas of concern, energy and development, seem dim if not forbidding. Development assistance is politically unpopular in the West, both because it lacks powerful domestic constituencies and because we face a time of economic retrenchment. Economic "independence" seems to be gaining popularity as a political banner just as economic interdependence becomes increasingly unavoidable. Energy policies encompass problems of a different character, due to their entanglement with intense domestic politics in every Western country. It seems certain that the energy crisis of the West will tax our human and financial resources for years to come.

Those who believe that today's policies toward the Third World should simply be tougher, boiled down versions of yesterday's are not looking carefully at the world about them. To begin with, control of the world's capital resources has shifted dramatically. It is more dispersed than ever before. And the developing nations themselves, after learning that "development" does not automatically follow the drafting of successive five-year plans, are politically and economically more volatile than at any time since independence. Their instability cannot be confined to the southern continents; it shows every sign of affecting Western interests in immeasurable ways in the coming decade.

Against all of this, we have put forward some rather modest suggestions for working toward one idea: that it is possible to cooperate with the less developed countries and the members of OPEC, working together to improve the energy position of all. We have argued that new institutional creations are not likely to break existing logjams, but would only complicate them. The cumulative effect of the measures proposed here would, of course, not alone solve any of the Third World's energy problems. Our hope was not to set forth specific solutions in great detail, but to contribute to a changing climate in which new types of measures are considered and negotiated.

Failure to take decisive action now and at every future opportunity will turn a worsening situation into a virtually hopeless one in some parts of the world, and help to aggravate political confrontations regionally, and perhaps internationally, at incalculable cost. The development plans of many Third World nations—along with their belief that a better life is possible—hang in the balance. So, too, do hopes for a new energy order based on anything other than the starkest political and perhaps military confrontation. The energy problems of the Third World are at least as challenging as those faced by the industrialized countries, which, it seems, have only one sensible choice: to join with far greater effort in the search for practical solutions.

NOTE

1. It is particularly important that this type of program not be jeopardized by the uncertainties of donor (particularly American) appropriations. World Bank lending for oil/gas projects in middle-income countries would not be directly endangered by restraint in the aid appropriations process. The Bank loans to these countries are financed by the international sale of bonds, whose creditworthiness is underwritten by callable capital provided by donor governments. However, the poorest countries receive World Bank loans from the International Development Association (IDA) on highly concessional terms that cannot be underwritten by the international money market. IDA funds are replenished directly by governments. And the contributions of all other governments are tied by informal agreement to the U.S. contribution to IDA. If the U.S. replenishment of IDA is withheld, therefore, it affects *all* IDA funding and all projects.

Terrestrial Resources: Minerals

The "energy crisis" made American policymakers acutely aware of our dependence on imported minerals for the very existence of our modern industries, and this realization triggered a frantic search for ways of reducing this dependence. The term "strategic mineral" came into common use but is not generally understood. Bohdan O. Szuprowicz, an aeronautical engineer and president of 21st Century Research in New Jersey, presents a very different picture of the distribution of minerals in the world than Kirtley Mather did in 1944, only partly because we now have more information than Mather did. Chapter 1 of Szuprowicz' book is essentially a useful inventory of strategic materials today; the rest of the book is a chauvinistic plea for an "America first" policy on such materials. The AFL-CIO, while speaking for organized labor rather than for the "military-industrial complex," reaches essentially the same conclusions in its report, Raw Materials for America. *This should not be surprising, since both are products of the same environment and culture and have the same frame of reference.*

The late Walter Rodney, intellectual, labor leader, and political activist in Guyana, has a very different perspective. He analyzes colonialism and expresses the now respectable view that the industrialization of Europe and North America was possible only because of their exploitation of the resources and peoples of Africa, Asia, and Latin America, and that this exploitation continues today, even after formal decolonization. World Bank economists Rex Bosson and Bension Varon also focus on the so-called Third World, but emphasize the interdependence of minerals' producers and consumers. Finally, F. E. Trainer of the University of New South Wales, Australia, dissects the doctrine of limitless growth of industrial society and arrives at distinctly pessimistic conclusions about mineral supplies in the intermediate future.

29

What Are Strategic Materials?

Bohdan O. Szuprowicz

Raw materials such as oil, iron ore, copper, aluminum, chromium, rubber, and many others are the lifeblood of modern industries. Most occur in the form of minerals or natural resources in practically every part of the world. Theoretically the earth's crust and the seas are believed to contain enormous reserves sufficient to satisfy the needs of the whole world for centuries to come.

In practice, however, mineral deposits that are economically exploitable with currently existing technologies are often concentrated in only a few regions of the world. Moreover many of the highly industrialized countries that are primary consumers of those raw materials often do not possess sufficient deposits of all the necessary minerals within their territorial boundaries. Japan is a good example of an economy with rapidly growing needs that must rely almost entirely on the imports of most of its raw materials from overseas.

When basic industries of a country become significantly dependent on supplies of such raw materials from foreign sources these become strategically important to the economies of those countries. Conversely an industrialized nation that possesses all the necessary raw materials within its own borders can consider itself truly self-sufficent. The United States until the late 1950s and the Soviet Union at present are two rare examples of such self-sufficient superpowers. China, Brazil, and southern Africa as a region are possible future groupings where such conditions may develop.

Not all the raw materials are of equal strategic importance to all the countries at all times. Even when a particular mineral is critical to one

---

industry it may not be of importance to another unless it in turn depends on the output of the other industry. As a result the definition of what is truly strategic and critical material will vary not only from country to country but also among industries and even enterprises within each country.

The concentration of global oil resources in the Middle East and the OPEC cartel focus the world's attention on oil as the most strategic and critical material in the world. But oil is only one form of energy, and although up to a point it is indispensable to all countries and all modern industries, it is not necessarily the most strategic or critical of them all.

Other minerals, less known than oil, are of immense strategic importance. These include chromium, cobalt, gold, titanium, tungsten, platinum, diamonds, and uranium. In recent years most of those minerals have been the subject of violent price and supply fluctuations often more unstable than the oil markets.

A QUESTION OF ACCESS AND PRICE

Among the 194 countries of the world there are three basic groups of nations that have differing vital interests in the supply and consumption of raw materials. These include the industrialized free market economies, the centrally planned economies dominated by the Soviet Union, and the developing countries of the Third World.

The industrialized free market economies are the largest users of all raw materials and account for about 70 percent of global consumption by volume. Those countries are also the largest producers of raw materials, accounting for about 45 percent of all such output in the world. This means that already 25 percent of the world's consumption of all raw materials must be imported by the industrialized free market economies from sources outside the territories under their political control.

As a result access to sources of raw materials and secure means of transportation to end users is of paramount importance to industrialized free market economies. The price of raw materials under certain conditions may not be the decisive factor, particularly in the case of minerals whose sources are relatively few and for which substitute materials are not readily available. Such conditions are conducive to the formation of cartels that can unilaterally dictate the prices in full knowledge that continuing supplies even at escalating prices are of the utmost importance to the end users.

By comparison the Third World countries produce about 30 percent of the world's raw materials. This is in fact somewhat less than the total production in the industrialized free market economies. However, the Third World countries consume only 6 percent of all the raw materials used in the world. In effect most Third World countries are large exporters of raw materials, and of paramount importance to them is their ability to obtain the best price for their exports. This objective is often coupled with a desire to obtain financing and technology to establish more advanced minerals processing and end-user industries within their own countries. This objective becomes extremely important when one realizes that the world will need 1 billion new jobs before the year 2000, most of which must be created in Third World countries.

This basic imbalance between raw materials positions of industrialized free market economies and Third World countries is further aggravated by the fact that known world resources of raw materials are considerably larger in Third World countries than in the relatively more depleted industrialized free market economies. Developing countries are now believed to contain about 42 percent of all known resources. By contrast the market economies account for only 35 percent of such resources, but it must be kept in mind that these assessments are not static and continue to change, depending on political and economic factors at work.

Resources are discovered where exploration is taking place, and some observers believe that the relatively large known resources in developing countries resulted from anticipated low costs of their exploitation. If prices of raw materials in these countries were to increase to unreasonable levels it is believed that additional exploration in such vast industrialized countries as Australia and Canada would considerably increase the overall known resources of the free market economies.

Centrally planned economies present a more balanced picture of raw materials resources, production, and consumption and give the appearance of relative self-sufficiency and independence of external sources of raw materials. They account for 25 percent of global consumption and produce approximately the same percentage of the world's raw materials. Known resources of the centrally planned economies are believed to be about 23 percent of global resources, but further exploration of such vast territories as Siberia, Afghanistan, Mongolia, China, and Vietnam are likely to result in an increase of these countries' share of the world's resources.

As a result centrally planned economies, and the Soviet Union in particular, are practically self-sufficient in raw materials, which puts them in an advantageous position relative to the rest of the world. They do not have to be concerned about access to any foreign sources, and they centrally control their production levels to meet their internal demands. When world prices for a particular commodity are depressed because of slackening demand or recession the Soviets can benefit from cheap imports and can even reduce their domestic production if necessary. When prices escalate the Soviets are in a position to increase their own output and export raw materials in exchange for hard currencies and high-technology equipment and know-how.

More important, raw materials self-sufficiency and central control of production provide the Soviet Union with the means to exercise political and economic leverage in various countries of the world. This new-found political power may be increasingly coming into play in the future, particularly in disputes between industrialized free market economies and Third World countries about access and prices of raw materials.

NATIONAL ECONOMY AND SECURITY CONSIDERATIONS

On a national level each country has a different raw materials demand and supply framework, although fuels and the so-called basic materials such as steel, copper, aluminum, nickel, lead, zinc, and tin are universally consumed in varying quantities by all countries. On the other hand the economy's nature and its status as a political and military power will determine which materials are considered strategic to the nation as a whole and which are only critical to the existence of specific industries.

Several factors influence the supply and consumption of various raw materials in any particular country. These include the existence of mineral deposits, availability of capital and technology, sufficient energy supplies, transportation infrastructure, industrial and military demand, and export potential.

Political power is probably the most important factor influencing raw materials supply and demand in most countries, although it may not appear to be so at first glance. This is so because political power controls such other factors as exploratory rights, labor costs and availability, environmental restrictions, capital investment, energy supplies, rights of way, taxation, import and export duties, foreign trade organizations, and industrial development.

The degree of dependence and interaction between these various factors influencing the supplies of all raw materials vary, depending on the type of political control in a particular country. In the centrally planned economies this interaction and control are extreme, and politics dominates all other factors. In free market economies and particularly in the United States most factors come into play independently, and numerous alternatives may exist at any one time leading to various conflicts of interest and excessive foreign dependence.

In Third World countries politics plays a much greater role than in the free market economies. This is so because in many instances the mining and production of raw materials is a major industry in those countries that lack the diversity of industrialized economies. Exports of raw materials provide foreign exchange that is required to pay for imports of equipment and technology to keep the economy in operation and maintain political power.

National security in the case of the superpowers such as the United States and the Soviet Union is perceived to be dependent on a large military establishment and high-technology industries. These in turn depend on supplies of strategic materials that may or may not be the same as those required by the civilian economy.

Ideally a superpower should be self-sufficient in all the strategic materials or have assured sources of supply in foreign countries friendly or allied to its policies. Other industrialized economies, which are not self-sufficient in raw materials, must choose to become client states of either the superpowers or other geopolitical groupings such as OPEC to assure themselves of adequate supplies of all the strategic materials required to maintain the growth of their economies.

The economies of East European countries are closely linked to the availability of fuels and raw materials from the Soviet Union. Characteristically only Romania, which has its own significant oil resources, has been showing a modicum of independence from the Soviet Union. The same argument could be applied in the case of China, which broke its close relationshp with the Soviet Union and embarked on self-sufficiency policies of development only after it became clear that China possessed significant oil resources of its own.

Any Western political initiatives to "loosen" the Soviet grip on Eastern Europe would have to assure those countries the energy and raw materials supplies to run their economies. Following World War II when the United States was still a self-sufficient superpower and Western Europe had greater control over its raw materials supplies this may have been a more realistic proposition. Since then the free market economies have become increasingly dependent on imports of their raw materials from Third World countries whose political objectives are not only volatile but also may differ significantly from those of the West.

There is a very basic difference between raw materials policies of the centrally planned economies and those of free market economies. In the Soviet Union raw materials supplies are allocated according to centrally planned objectives for specific industries and the military establishment. It is basically a wartime measure designed to overcome shortages by establishing priorities.

By contrast free market economies in general and that of the United States in particular have developed in an environment of abundant natural and capital resources. Under those conditions government leaders, industrial end users, the military establishment, and raw materials suppliers all follow their own independent objectives with regard to raw materials supply and consumption. Materials managers and design engineers are primarily concerned with raw materials prices and physical characteristics. Now they are beginning to face the problems of shortages and availability as paramount in their planning and budgeting.

HOW TO IDENTIFY STRATEGIC AND CRITICAL MATERIALS

If there exists the possibility of a severe shortage or outright supply disruption of a material that cannot be readily substituted in an industry then it must be considered as being strategic or critical to the end users. This is particularly true if such a material originates from foreign sources outside the political control of the country in which end users and their industries are located. Oil is an obvious example, particularly in the case of countries that do not possess any domestic resources of this mineral.

Unexpected price escalations may also play havoc with production schedules in cases when the end product contains a large proportion of materials whose prices increase significantly. On the other hand even drastic price increases of materials that are used in very small quantities in some products may not be critical to end users. In such cases availability of such indispensable materials and unexpected shortages regardless of price may nevertheless create severe problems to the end-user industries.

Numerous danger points signal the criticality of each particular material to end users that can be determined in advance. These range from the number and location of supply sources to various characteristics of the material that may threaten excessive regulation of its production and its eventual disappearance from the market. Many of these danger points are listed in Table 1.[. . .]

The existence of several danger characteristics with regard to a particular material does not in itself imply that the material's supplies will be inadequate in the future. Whether these danger points will have a disruptive effect on the supplies depends on other events and conditions of a political, economic, and social nature. Most of these are completely beyond the control of the end user regardless of whether the materials originate from domestic or foreign sources. Many such events are also beyond the control of materials traders and distributors who are the intermediaries between the actual producers and the end users and whose business objectives are often at variance with those of the materials-consuming industries.

Those "trigger" events and conditions are often political in nature but are not necessarily unpredictable. Materials managers whose enterprises depend on strategic and critical materials that exhibit many danger characteristics would do well to become familiar with the sources of their materials and the political climates of those environments. They can protect their organizations from serious loss of revenues or work disruptions by assessing political risks involved well in advance and prepare alternative action plans. In a world of materials shortages this course of action is the sine qua non of survival.

The events and conditions that must be monitored for this purpose both on the domestic scene and in foreign countries include labor costs,

TABLE 1 Materials Availability Danger Points

1. Single supply source
2. Lack of domestic reserves
3. Lack of substitute materials
4. Inadequate world reserves
5. High import dependence
6. Supplies by allocation
7. Price controls
8. Excessive energy requirements
9. Irregular and infrequent supplies
10. Import and export controls
11. Environmental restrictions on use
12. Health and safety impacts on production
13. Very high military usage (over 95%)
14. Declining use of material
15. Technological development threat
16. Low volume of total sales
17. Low level of production
18. Poor usage visibility
19. Low recycling potential
20. High existing or potential taxation

strikes, civil unrest, wars, cartels, boycotts, embargoes, terrorist activities, revolutions, new legislation, taxation, as well as acts of God in distant places such as droughts, floods, fires, and earthquakes.

ENERGY RESOURCES

Energy resources are most often associated with oil, but in fact these exist in various alternate forms in different countries. They include oil, natural gas, coal, lignite, and biogas, as well as hydroelectric, nuclear, geothermal, solar, tidal, and wind power. Oil provides the most convenient source of energy, but there are many countries that to this day rely primarily on coal as their major energy source. These include China, South Africa, India, Czechoslovakia, Poland, and East Germany.

There are about 30 countries in the world that appear to have significant energy resources, although not necessarily in the form of oil. Among those are the major producers, consumers, and exporters of energy in the form of oil, natural gas, or coal. Besides OPEC members these countries include most of the industrialized powers and populous developing countries like China, India, Mexico, Brazil, Indonesia, and Nigeria (Table 2).

The more significant energy have-nots of the world are France, Japan, and Italy. At the same time these countries are big energy consumers.

TABLE 2 Proved Energy Reserves in Selected Countries Ranked by Crude Oil Reserves in 1978

Country	Crude Oil (billion barrels)	Natural Gas (trillion ft.^{3})	Coal (million metric tons)
Saudi Arabia	166 OPEC	94	0
Kuwait	66 OPEC	31	0
Iran	59 OPEC	500	200
Soviet Union	35 state owned	1,020	256,000
Iraq	32 OPEC	28	0
Abu Dhabi	30 OPEC	20	0
United States	28	205	178,600
Libya	24 OPEC	24	0
China	20 state owned	25	98,900
Nigeria	18 OPEC	42	100
Venezuela	18 OPEC	41	1,000
Mexico	16 state run	32	900
United Kingdom	16	27	45,000
Indonesia	10 OPEC	24	1,400
Canada	6	59	9,400
Norway	6	24	na
Algeria	6 OPEC	105	na
Qatar	4 OPEC	40	0
Egypt	3 state run	3	neg
India	3	4	33,700
Oman	2	2	0
Syria	2	2	0
Brazil	1	2	8,100
Ecuador	1 OPEC	4	0
Romania	1 state owned	9	400
West Germany	neg	6	34,400
South Africa	0	0	26,900
Poland	neg	5	21,800
Yugoslavia	neg	1	8,500
North Korea	0	0	8,500

Source: National Foreign Assessment Center, ER 79–10274, August 1979.

It is therefore not by accident that nuclear power development programs are well advanced in those countries. That, however, creates another dependence on sources of uranium for nuclear fuels, making that metal a strategic energy resource.

Over 50 countries are now in the process of developing nuclear power that has the added attraction of nuclear weapons development potential. This makes uranium doubly strategic as a raw material to most countries in the world.

Energy resources and related problems have been widely discussed for years as a result of the emergence of OPEC as a new form of an international economic and political power center. The main objective of this book is to explore the problems associated with possible shortages or supply disruptions of critical nonenergy resources such as metals and minerals that are also vital to the operation of modern economies.

Nevertheless availability of adequate energy supplies is also of great significance to the minerals and metals production cycle and must be taken into account. Energy in one form or another is indispensable in exploration, mining, processing, refining, and transportation of raw materials. The different metals in their finished form can indeed be rated according to the amount of energy that is required to produce a unit amount of each (Table 3).

High cost or shortages of energy in a particular country or region will increasingly play a role in determining which metals will substitute for others and where production may be discontinued. In the United States, for example, 4 percent of all the energy consumed is used to produce aluminum alone. But recovery of aluminum from scrap can be accomplished with only a fraction of that energy; therefore as prices of energy continue to escalate organizations that are heavy end users of aluminum may find it profitable to engage in large scrap recovery operations. By the same token any reduction of imports of bauxite or alumina from which aluminum is extracted may set into motion reciprocal actions of exporting countries.

Alternatively energy-rich countries such as Bahrain in the Persian Gulf have developed aluminum refining capacity in their own territory based on cheap and abundant local energy supplies. Such developments may further reduce domestic aluminum production capacity in other

TABLE 3 Relative Energy Requirements in Metals Production

Metal	Relative Requirements of Energy per Ton of Finished Metal
Iron	1.00
Copper	2.76
Steel	2.84
Aluminum	12.15
Magnesium	18.50
Titanium	25.80

Source: U.S. House of Representatives, Committee on Science and Technology, *Materials Policy Handbook*, June 1977.

countries where energy is much more expensive and may lead to strange new arrangements between countries that have the energy and those with deposits of strategic minerals.

There is a discernible trend among energy-rich states toward the development of energy intensive industries in their own territories. But if these countries do not possess sufficiently large markets to absorb the output of such industries there is the danger of disruption of existing markets in other countries through exports of products at significantly lower prices to capture market shares. Interestingly the centrally planned economies can protect themselves by strict foreign trade monopolies under central political control, but the free market economies are vulnerable to domestic output declines and unemployment in several threatened industries. Steel and textile industries are good examples of that type of industrial setback.

The Persian Gulf states provide about 70 percent of oil consumed in the industrialized countries of the West. There are some political analysts who now believe that revolutions similar to that which occurred in Iran in 1979 may change the political climate in such major oil-producing countries as Saudi Arabia or Kuwait in the near future. This could mean further reductions of oil exports from the Persian Gulf with a serious impact on the cost of the production of metals and minerals in Third World countries that rely on imports of energy.

BASIC METALS AND RAW MATERIALS

Over 70 percent of the total value of the world's production of the top 50 most valuable minerals is represented by energy resources, and at least 23 percent constitutes metallic minerals. The remainder are minerals such as diamonds, salt, phosphates, asbestos, sulfur, mica, fluorspar, graphite, and asphalt.

Several of the metallic minerals are produced in great quantities in the form of ores from which the basic metals in most common usage are extracted. These include iron ore, copper, aluminum, nickel, tin, zinc, and lead. Production of some of the metals, including iron, copper, aluminum, zinc, and lead, reaches millions of tons per year on a global basis. These basic metals are critical to many industries because they are used in such large quantities (Table 4).

Aluminum, in the form of bauxite, and iron ore are respectively the third and the fourth most abundant elements in the earth's crust. The other basic metals are considerably less abundant, and together with all other elements constitute only a few percent of the earth's crust. Nevertheless the volume of the earth is so huge that millions of tons of all those metals can be produced every year.

TABLE 4 Basic Metals Reserves of the World

Metal Ores	Rank of Relative Abundance	Largest Reserves Areas
Iron ore	4	Soviet Union, Brazil, Canada, Australia, India, United States
Copper	26	United States, Chile, Canada, Soviet Union, Peru, Zambia, Zaire
Aluminum	3	Australia, Guinea, Brazil, Jamaica
Nickel	23	New Caledonia, Canada, Australia, Indonesia, Cuba
Tin	54	China, Thailand, Malaysia, Bolivia
Zinc	24	United States, Canada
Lead	36	United States

Despite the fact that aluminum and iron ore are so abundant there still exists the possibility of a producer's cartel because these metals are very widely used and because their ore deposits are very uneven and the highest-grade areas are concentrated in only a few countries.

Iron Ore

This mineral is the primary source of iron and steel, basic to any industrial system. Major use in construction, shipbuilding, railroads, machine tools, automobiles, heavy equipment, agricultural machinery, and numerous consumer appliances makes this metal the most common in the world.

However, over 31 percent of high-grade iron ore reserves is believed to be located in the Soviet Union, which is by far also the largest producer of iron ore in the world, accounting for almost a third of the total. Another 45 percent of iron ore reserves is located in Brazil, Canada, Australia, and India. The United States is believed to contain only about 6 percent of global reserves and is a net importer of iron ore from abroad.

China is actually the second largest producer of iron ore in the world after the Soviet Union, but the quality of Chinese ores is low. China is also a major importer of some ores from Australia and steels from Japan, West Germany, and other countries.

The resulting steels that are produced from iron ores in the steelmaking process are widely used for industrial and military applications. High-quality steels are alloys that also require large quantities of manganese, chromium, nickel, molybdenum, vanadium, and smaller amounts of other metals. Any shortages of these alloy metals could pose very serious problems to many of the high technology industries that require the use of special quality steels.

Aluminum

The use of aluminum in the world now exceeds the use of any other metal except iron. Construction industries are the largest consumers of aluminum, and transportation, packaging, electrical, and telecommunications industries are also major users of the metal.

Transportation use includes aircraft manufacturing, for which aluminum is critical. Civilian jet transports and helicopters are also important in the export trade of major aircraft manufacturing countries, including the United States, France, the United Kingdom, Germany, and the Soviet Union. Military aircraft are major weapons systems and also contribute to the export trade of all major aircraft manufacturing countries. These applications make aluminum a very strategic material, particularly to those countries that do not possess bauxite deposits within their territories.

Geographically major high-grade bauxite reserves are located in Australia, Guinea, Brazil, and Jamaica that together account for 75 percent of all known reserves. The bauxites are subjected to hydrometallurgical processing to produce alumina that in turn is reduced to aluminum by an electrolytic process which consumes very large quantities of energy in the form of electric power. Although aluminum may be substituted by magnesium, production of that metal requires even larger quantities of energy.

The United States is the largest producer of primary aluminum metal from imported bauxite and alumina. The Soviet Union is the second largest aluminum producer from its own domestic bauxites, and it also imports some aluminum from other producers. Japan, Canada, West Germany, and Norway are the next largest aluminum-producing countries.

Copper

After oil, coal, and natural gas, copper production accounts for over 6 percent of the value of all the minerals produced in the world. Copper is one of the first metals known and used by mankind, and the importance of this metal lies in its excellent characteristics as a conductor of heat and electricity.

Copper is indispensable for use in electric power transmission, communications, generators, motors, transformers, switchgear, heat exchangers, condensers, air conditioning, refrigeration, tubing and piping, bearings, and military cartridge and shell casings. It is one of the most strategic materials and can substitute for many other metals, although it is itself hard to replace.

The United States and Chile are estimated to contain 40 percent of the world's copper reserves. Canada, the Soviet Union, Peru, and Zambia are believed to account for another 32 percent of the total. However four developing countries—namely, Chile, Peru, Zambia, and Zaire—account for over 80 percent of copper exports in the world. Poland is another country that recently developed its significant copper deposits. Copper is the third most important raw material moving in foreign trade after oil and wheat and accounts for about 3 percent of global exports of all primary products.

It is worth noting here that in the recent past Chile experienced a Marxist government, Zaire was the subject of the Katanga secession war in the 1960s and two subsequent Shaba province invasions of the copper-producing areas, Zambia received significant foreign aid from China, and Peru received economic aid from China and significant military and economic aid from the Soviet Union.

Nickel

This metal is one of the most versatile alloying materials used in the production of stainless steels and corrosion resistant superalloys capable of withstanding very high temperatures. Nickel can be substituted in almost every use but only at increased cost or loss of product performance.

The metal has numerous strategic applications and is essential in military uses, including nuclear applications, jet engines, aircraft frames, submarines, armor plating, gun barrels, and rocket motor casings. About 90 percent of nickel is consumed in the form of alloys; the remaining consumption consists of use in electroplating, electrical equipment, machinery, vehicles, catalysts, batteries, fuel cells, ceramics, and household appliances.

As much as 25 percent of known nickel reserves of the world are in New Caledonia, a French Overseas Territory located in the South Pacific northeast of Australia. Canada is believed to account for 15 percent and the Soviet Union for 14 percent of world reserves. Indonesia has 13 percent; the Philippines and Australia, about 9 percent each; and Cuba, 6 percent of the total.

The Soviet Union is now believed to be the largest producer of refined nickel, having surpassed Canada in the mid-1970s. Japan, Australia, New Caledonia (with France), and Cuba are the next largest refined nickel producers. The Soviet Union is financing a $600 million expansion program of Cuban nickel production that may make Cuba the third largest nickel producer by 1985. This would give the Soviet bloc control of 60 percent of the world's nickel production, and if the demand of the Council for Mutual Economic Assistance (COMECON) does not absorb this output attempts to export large quantities of nickel to the West could seriously affect the stability of nickel markets.

Tin

Tin is considered essential to an industrial society, and for many of this metal's applications there are no completely satisfactory substitutes. At least one-third of all the tin is used in the manufacture of cans and containers. Other important uses are in solders, babbits, and bearing metals, brass and bronze, tinning, foils, ceramics, pigments, and miscellaneous chemical uses. About 20 percent of the tin used in the United States is reclaimed from scrap.

Major tin reserves exist in Southeast Asian countries. Indonesia is estimated to contain 24 percent of world reserves; the People's Republic of China has 15 percent; Thailand, 12 percent; Bolivia, about 10 percent; Malaysia, over 8 percent; and the Soviet Union and Brazil, about 6 percent each. Nigeria, Australia, Zaire, and Burma also possess some tin.

Malaysia is the leading primary tin producer in the world, accounting for about 40 percent of the total, followed by the Soviet Union, which produces about 17 percent. Thailand, Indonesia, Bolivia, and China are the next largest tin producers, ranging from 16 to 8 percent of the world's tin output.

Tin is uniquely the only metal subject to an international agreement between producing and consuming countries. The International Tin Council (ITC) [has existed] since 1956, and in 1976 the United States joined the Fifth International Tin Agreement for the first time. The council seeks to secure long-term balance between production and consumption of tin by establishing a floor and a ceiling price. This is effected by maintenance of tin "buffer stocks" and by applying export controls on tin producers.

Zinc

Zinc is the third most commonly used nonferrous metal in the world after copper and aluminum. It is versatile and essential in modern living. Principal use is in automobile die castings, typewriter chassis, housings, galvanizing iron and steel products, as alloying element in brass, in rubber, and as paint pigment. No adequate substitute is known for zinc in its use in galvanizing steel. Brass sheet as cartridge brass is used in large quantities to manufacture small arms ammunition shell casings for sporting and military use.

Highest zinc reserves are in the United States and Canada, which are estimated to contain about 27 and 20 percent of global reserves, respectively. Other major zinc reserves are in Australia, Peru, Japan, and the Soviet Union, but zinc mining also is significant in Mexico, Zaire, Italy, Germany, and Poland.

The Soviet Union is the largest producer of refined zinc, followed by Japan, Canada, and the United States. Poland, West Germany, Australia,

Belgium, France, Italy, Spain, Finland, and Mexico are among the larger producers. In total at least 30 countries produce zinc, which means that many alternative sources of the metal exist.

Despite this wide occurrence and production zinc is only the twenty-fourth most abundant metal in the earth's crust, but it is being used in relatively large quantities. It is estimated that if current rates of consumption continue existing known reserves will not be sufficient to meet global demand during the 1990s. On the other hand it is also held that new and significant reserves of zinc may come into play in the future if the usage of zinc continues unabated.

Lead

The principal use of lead is in storage batteries, bearings, gasoline antiknock additives, and in the electrical industries. Lead is also used in paints, solder, type metal, and some brasses and bronzes. More strategic uses include ammunition and as shielding against nuclear radioactivity.

Nickel-cadmium batteries are now also in use and could substitute for lead, but the cost is high and the supply of nickel and cadmium in an emergency may be more critical than that of lead. However, in the United States 40 percent of lead is being recycled. In terms of the amount of nonferrous metals consumed, lead ranks fourth after aluminum, copper, and zinc (it is often coproduced with zinc).

The United States is estimated to contain 37 percent of global lead reserves, followed by Canada with 13 percent and Australia with 12 percent. Nevertheless in 1978 the Soviet Union was the largest smelter lead producer, having just surpassed the United States in 1977. Australia, Japan, Canada, Mexico, and Bulgaria are also major lead-producing countries. At least 22 countries are significant lead producers.

Environmental legislature such as the Clean Air Act Amendment of 1977 and the Occupational Safety and Health Administration regulations affect the use and price of lead through strikes and supply disruptions. These may lead to a further shift from use of lead in nonessential applications such as has already occurred in gasoline additives and paints. On the other hand increasing terrorism and the possibility of nuclear threats or even wars may result in a run on lead as one of the best nuclear radioactivity shielding materials.

HIGH-TECHNOLOGY MATERIALS

Since World War II many new materials have been introduced to develop high-technology industries that are new such as nuclear power, space vehicles, rockets, supersonic aircraft, jet engines, electronics, petrochemicals, telecommunications, lasers, cryogenics, solar systems, microwaves, and xerography.

Many of the metals on which those industries critically depend did not enter into commercial production until it became obvious that previously existing materials could not perform satisfactorily in extreme temperature, pressure, or corrosive environments. Large-scale use of titanium, for example, did not occur until the development of the aerospace industry. Similarly the use of zirconium is closely related to the development and mass production of nuclear reactors. For the same reason uranium became strategically important as a nuclear fuel, weapons material, and a source of plutonium (a manufactured element that does not occur in nature).

During the 1940s materials such as beryllium, cobalt, hafnium, selenium, silicon, and titanium went into production for the first time on a commercial basis. During the 1950s and 1960s technological advances demanded introduction on a commercial basis of such exotic new materials as bismuth, columbium, germanium, tantalum, tellurium, vanadium, and zirconium. The arms race of the cold war, the venturing of people into space and the development of satellites, and now the space race with man on the moon and interplanetary probes did much to fund and promote these developments.

Over 30 different metals besides the basic materials previously discussed can be identified with high-technology applications. In current research and development almost all the elements are being constantly evaluated either on their own or in combinations with other elements in search of cheaper or more effective substitutions. Because most of the high-technology products have more often than not specific military applications all the materials in this category automatically become strategic in nature. It is not by accident that most in fact can be found in the strategic stockpile maintained by the General Services Administration of the United States.

However, except in the case of gold, cobalt, magnesium, platinum metals, silver, titanium, tungsten, and uranium most of the high-technology metals are little known. This is so because relatively small quantities of these materials are used, and in most cases each represents only a fraction of a percent of the total value of all the minerals produced in the world. Similarly many of those very strategic materials are seldom visible in the international trade statistics. More often than not the exports and imports of these materials between producing and consuming countries are obscured under overall trade classifications such as "nonferrous metals" or "other minerals and ores."

Cobalt, for example, which is vital to the manufacture of jet turbine blades and high-performance magnetic alloys, was for many years readily available in world markets. It was not until repeated rebel invasions of the Shaba province in Zaire, which produces 60 percent of the world's cobalt, that end users of the metal began seriously considering political and technological alternatives to further threats of shortages and price escalations.

DEFENSE INDUSTRIES AND MILITARY MATERIALS

Various metals and minerals used specifically for military applications such as ammunition, armor plate, explosives, gun barrels, missiles, nuclear weapons, rocket motors, satellites, small arms, and submarines are strategic in the fullest meaning of the word. Some like aluminum and copper are also basic to the economy, but others like barite, opium, or shellac have very precise use in the military establishment without corresponding application in the civilian economy. On the whole most materials critical to the military equipment and its supporting industrial complex are the same as materials required by high-technology industries.

From the point of view of an industrial manager and an international politician it is important to realize which materials are critical to the military establishment. In times of crises or wartime emergencies those are the materials that will first come under government control, and shortages of such materials may develop rapidly.

At the same time selective price controls may be imposed on trade involving such materials, and supplies may be based on allocations or some other form of rationing to prevent hoarding and profiteering by private interests. This is particularly true in the case of those materials that must be imported from abroad as a result of limited or nonexistent domestic production because it is relatively easy to police the movement of such materials through government-controlled institutions such as customs and export controls. Chromium, cobalt, germanium, manganese, and natural rubber would be good examples of such critical materials.

THE MOST CRITICAL MATERIALS FOR THE UNITED STATES

For many decades until the 1950s the United States produced more raw materials than it consumed. This was true in the case of oil, of which the United States was a major exporter in the first half of this century, as well as in the case of other minerals. Although many minerals have also been imported in earlier decades, the low cost of foreign supplies was the main reason for that action.

Those conditions do not exist today anymore, and the United States has become a raw materials deficit nation. At present it is the largest producer in the world only of copper, molybdenum, and natural gas, among the major materials. It is the second largest world producer of coal and lead and the third largest producer of oil and zinc. On the other hand the United States continues to be the largest consumer of most raw materials and as such is increasingly being perceived by resource-rich Third World countries as a target for exploitation of their unique supply positions in one or more raw materials.

To be sure the United States continues to produce most basic and critical materials, but in many instances domestic consumption far outstrips domestic production, and the country must increasingly rely on imports from foreign sources.

At the beginning of 1980 the United States imported 50 percent or more of its apparent demand of about 20 of the most important basic and critical materials. These include natural rubber, manganese, diamonds, cobalt, chromium, tantalum, titanium, platinum, palladium, rhodium, ruthenium, aluminum, tin, fluorspar, nickel, gold, germanium, indium, mercury, beryllium, zirconium, tungsten, zinc, and oil.

It is clear that most of those materials are critical to the high-technology industries and to the military establishment. But a high import dependence in itself is not the best measure of the real criticality of those materials. What matters also are the number of foreign suppliers and their political ideology and stability, availability of alternative sources, potential domestic reserves, substitutes, and stockpile position. On the other hand the magnitude of import dependence is becoming a more important factor every day as OPEC continues to escalate the price of oil and as stability in many Third World countries is being undermined by nationalistic aspirations of various revolutionary leaders often assisted in their "liberations" struggles by the countries of the socialist camp.

Considering several such factors the U.S. Army War College Strategic Studies Group applied a quantitative test to a number of nonoil minerals that appeared vulnerable to political and nonmarket forces from foreign suppliers. This strategic materials vulnerability study showed that the United States is particularly vulnerable to potential supply disruptions of chromium, platinum metals, tungsten, manganese, cobalt, aluminum, titanium, tantalum, nickel, mercury, and tin. Simultaneous disruptions of supplies of several of those, particularly of chromium, platinum, cobalt, and nickel, could create an extremely serious economic situation for the United States. Because of a unique concentration of supplies of chromium, platinum, and cobalt in southern Africa and the Soviet Union and negligible reserves of those same materials in the United States, Western Europe, and Japan such a possibility should not be ruled out (Table 5).

GOLD, SILVER, AND PLATINUM METALS

Primarily known for its monetary and jewelry applications gold is also an essential industrial material. It is used in integrated circuits in electronics, for reliable connectors in computers, as shielding in spacecraft,

TABLE 5 The Most Strategic Materials for the United States

Material	U.S. Army War College Vulnerability Index	Major Supplier Countries
Chromium	34	Soviet Union, South Africa
Platinum metals	32	Sovet Union, South Africa
Tungsten	27	Canada, Peru
Manganese	23	Brazil, Gabon
Aluminum	22	Jamaica, Canada
Titanium	20	Australia, Canada
Cobalt	20	Zaire, Canada
Tantalum	16	Zaire, Brazil, Canada
Nickel	14	Canada, Norway
Mercury	11	Canada, Mexico, Spain
Tin	6	Malaysia, Thailand

and in brazing alloys for bonding turbine blades to rotors in aircraft jet engines.

The use of gold in electronics is the most important industrial use of the metal and in the United States is estimated to account for 6 to 7 percent of fabricated gold. Over a dozen countries consume gold in their electronics industries, notably Japan, Korea, and the Netherlands. It is also believed that the most important industrial use of gold in the Soviet Union and other centrally planned economies is in the production of electronic devices.

The importance of gold in electronics stems from the fact that modern solid state electronics devices operate on very low currents and voltages. These devices require reliable connectors, contacts, switches, and components that will remain uncontaminated and clean throughout the life of these devices. This is particularly important in the production of printed circuit boards, connectors, terminal keyboard contacts, and miniaturized circuitry. As a result of escalating gold prices in recent years platinum, palladium, silver, and other metals have been partially substituted in some products, but sometimes this is done at the risk of lower product performance and reliability.

Gold plays a strategic role in electronic equipment used for military applications. The U.S. Department of Defense operates a program to recover gold from military scrap, and other government agencies are free to participate in their own gold recovery programs.

Total industrial consumption of gold in 1977 in the United States amounted to 1.2 million troy ounces of which less than 1 million were considered to be critical applications. There is little threat of a shortage of gold for strategic use in a country like the United States because of the huge gold reserves held by the U.S. Department of the Treasury that in

1977 amounted to 278 million troy ounces. In addition several million ounces of gold are held in commercial and private bullion stocks.

Nearly half of all the gold that has been mined in the world is held in the form of reserves by governments of countries such as the United States, West Germany, Switzerland, France, Italy, the Netherlands, Japan, and the United Kingdom. The cumulative world production of gold at the end of 1977 was estimated at about 2.8 billion troy ounces. This can be visualized as a cube comparable in size to a five-story building 55 feet long and wide. Of this total South Africa supplied 40 percent and to this day remains by far the largest producer of gold in the world.

Another way to understand the scarcity of gold on earth is to imagine that all the existing gold were distributed in equal amounts to the 4 billion people in the world. In such a case every person would receive only 0.7 ounce of gold worth about $500 at early 1980 gold prices—not enough to buy even a single Krugerrand.

South Africa produces about 60 percent of the global gold output from the operation of 40 large underground mines controlled by seven large corporations that work very closely with each other. The second largest gold-producing country is the Soviet Union whose output is estimated to be in the order of 17 to 20 percent of the world's total gold supply and is controlled by a state monopoly. Canada and the United States are the next two largest producers of gold, accounting for about 6 and 4 percent of global production, respectively. Other significant gold-producing countries include Australia, Zimbabwe, the Philippines, Ghana, Colombia, Mexico, Japan, India, Zaire, and Nicaragua (Table 6).

Estimated reserves of gold depend on the price of gold. As the price increases this automatically reclassifies certain gold resources into reserves that could be economically exploited at predominating prices and costs of production. On that basis South Africa contains about 50 percent of global gold reserves or resources, whichever way one looks at it. The Soviet Union remains as the country with the second largest gold reserves and resources in the world.

As a result South Africa is expected to remain the dominant factor in world gold production, although industry observers feel that South Africa's gold production will trend downward in the future. Similarly the Soviet Union is playing an increasingly important role as a gold-producing and supplier country. In recent years the Soviet Union has been benefiting from the sales of gold for hard currencies, increasing its proceeds from $725 million in 1975 to $2.67 billion in 1978.

Silver

The major use of silver is in photography, electronics, silverware, and jewelry, but photography is by far the most important single silver-

TABLE 6 Major Gold-Producing Countries of the World and Their Estimated Gold Reserves and Resources

Country	Percentage of Global Reserves	Percentage of Global Resources	1978 Gold Production (troy ounces)
South Africa	48.0	52.0	22,900,000
Soviet Union	21.0	15.7	8,840,000
Canada	3.7	3.4	1,670,000
United States	9.0	12.6	970,000
Australia	3.0	2.9	660,000
Rhodesia	1.2	1.3	590,000
Philippines	1.5	1.3	590,000
Ghana	0.3	1.6	480,000
Colombia	na	na	280,000
Mexico	1.0	1.3	240,000
Japan	0.4	0.5	180,000
India	na	na	90,000
Zaire	na	na	80,000
Nicaragua	na	na	70,000

Source: U.S. Handbook of Economic Statistics, ER 79–10274, August 1979; and U.S. Bureau of Mines, *Gold*, Mineral Commodity Profile, MCP-25, October 1978.

consuming industry and accounts for about 35 percent of the total consumption of silver.

Because of its importance to photography and electronics silver is considered a strategic material, and the United States maintains a supply of silver in its strategic stockpile. On the other hand the United States is a major producer of silver often as a by-product of basic metals production such as copper, lead, and zinc. From that point of view there is little concern about any potential disruptions to the supply of silver.

This is not the case for the industrial countries of Western Europe, most of which depend on imports of silver from foreign sources. Japan, with its rapidly expanding electronics and photography industries, is also a large consumer, although it has only minor silver reserves.

The Soviet Union is believed to have the largest silver reserves in the world, amounting to 26 percent of the total, followed by almost equal reserves of the United States that are estimated at 25 percent. Mexico, Canada, and Peru are countries with the next largest silver reserves, amounting to 14, 12, and 10 percent, respectively. With over 60 percent of the silver reserves located in the western hemisphere, mostly in North America, there is little threat that a strategic shortage could develop; this is so because the reserves appear to be sufficient to supply the needs of all NATO countries.

Platinum Metals

Platinum group metals consist of platinum, palladium, iridium, rhodium, ruthenium, and osmium, all of which exhibit outstanding anticorrosive characteristics and are extremely rare. Iridium is the most corrosion-resistant element known and is usually alloyed with platinum to make high-temperature tools.

Platinum metals are important in several of the high technology applications, particularly as catalysts in petroleum cracking and refining processes. Platinum is also used in catalytic converters to reduce pollution from automobile exhausts. Platinum metals are used as electrical contacts, cathode emitters, and in electronic devices, as well as in high-reliability aircraft spark plugs.

The Soviet Union has been the largest producer of platinum group metals for years and has been a major exporter, supplying between 20 to 25 percent of international exports of platinum. Soviet production accounts for over 51 percent of total global output, whereas South Africa produces another 43 percent of the world's output of platinum metals. Canada is the third producing country, but its production accounts for less than 6 percent of the world's total.

Platinum metals are among the most strategic materials imported by the United States, Western Europe, and Japan because practically all the supplies must come from either the Soviet Union or South Africa. Platinum metals are used in only small quantities when compared with many other critical materials, but where their particular characteristics are critical there are no practical substitutions.

INDUSTRIAL DIAMONDS

Strategically important to industries that make tools for modern machines are industrial diamonds, which are particularly adaptable to automatic cutting and grinding processes. Such diamonds are used in many grinding wheels to shape and sharpen tungsten carbide cutting tools. Industrial diamonds are also used for turning, grinding, boring, and drilling hard metals, ceramics, and glass and for rock drilling bits. These in turn are quite indispensable in oil exploration.

Of strategic importance are also diamond dies that are required for drawing very fine wires of diameters smaller than 0.0008 inch. Such superfine wires are required for use in semiconductors, integrated circuit connectors, microammeters, timing devices, magnetic field coils, precision fuse elements, and ignition wire primers.

Industrial diamonds resources are concentrated in Zaire, which is estimated to contain 73 percent of all such resources in the world. South Africa and Botswana are each believed to have about 7 percent of the world's resources, and the Soviet Union and Ghana have 3.7 percent each.

Major producers of all types of diamonds measured by the number of karats per year include Zaire, the Soviet Union, South Africa, Botswana, and Namibia in that order. Other producers include Angola, Ghana, Sierra Leone, Lesotho, and Tanzania. Initial sales of over 50 percent of all the diamonds produced in the world every year are strictly controlled by De Beers and its consolidated companies. De Beers is considered to be a de facto cartel whose primary objective is to maintain a floor price on diamond in output sales.

Synthetic diamond grit and powder are also produced in great quantities by General Electric and Du Pont companies in the United States and in other countries, including Ireland, Sweden, South Africa, Japan, and the Soviet Union. In recent years China also announced capability to manufacture synthetic diamonds because it is not certain that natural diamonds are found in China in any significant quantities and it has been importing such diamonds from abroad.

However, synthetic manufacture of some diamonds requires the use of wonderstone, a raw material from South Africa that is used in the manufacture of synthetic diamonds in the United States.

Estimates of the Bureau of Mines suggest that world reserves of industrial stones are not sufficient to meet global demand by the year 2000 if current consumption trends continue. As a result it is expected that large-scale synthetic diamond production will increase both in the United States and abroad as the simplest and most cost-effective solution. Under such circumstances countries that control the supplies of wonderstone or other suitable raw materials required for the manufacture of synthetic diamonds will become important strategically to the consuming nations.

NUCLEAR MATERIALS

One of the most strategic and controversial raw materials in the world today is uranium, the nuclear fuels derived from uranium, and plutonium, a prime nuclear weapons material. Despite antinuclear sentiments, protests, and demonstrations a surprisingly large number of countries are constructing nuclear power plants to produce part of their energy requirements from the atom.

At least 55 countries of the world have a total of 775 nuclear reactors in operation, under construction, on order, or in planning stages to go into operation before 1985. In addition at least 18 countries are planning to operate their own uranium enrichment or plutonium separation plants. Governments and nuclear industries of many countries are committed to spending hundreds of billions of dollars to develop nuclear power.

One of the attractions of nuclear power plants and nuclear fuel-manufacturing capability is the political prestige suggestive of the potential for developing nuclear weapons. The very existence of a nonproliferation treaty only confirms this trend among governments big and small, and many political analysts are convinced that whereas nuclear weapons proliferation may be delayed by various political and economic measures it is unlikely that it can be halted unless the existing nuclear powers literally destroy their nuclear arsenals and nuclear weapons establishments. Needless to say such a development is not very likely to take place after the tremendous investments that have been made by several countries in nuclear weapons and nuclear power development.

At present China, France, India, the United Kingdom, the United States, and the Soviet Union are considered to have nuclear weapons capability by virtue of demonstrated ability to engineer nuclear explosions. Of those countries all except the United Kingdom possess some uranium resources within their own territories.

Standing in the wings of the nuclear stage are a group of Third World countries that are believed to be working toward the achievement of nuclear power status—often driven by political and energy incentives. Some of those countries are even believed to already possess the nuclear weapons capability or to be within grasp within a very short time. These include Argentina, Brazil, Egypt, Iran, Israel, South Korea, Pakistan, South Africa, Taiwan, and perhaps even Yugoslavia. Some African political and social scientists are also advocating nuclear power status for such key African countries as Nigeria and Zaire to give those important African states a voice in global politics to which Western powers will have to pay more attention.

There is yet a third group of countries that are industrialized and heavily dependent on imports of energy from abroad to whom nuclear power provides an immediate and important source of energy. These include Czechoslovakia, Japan, France, Germany, Italy, Spain, Sweden, and Switzerland. All could develop nuclear weapons without much trouble because each has an advanced scientific and technological establishment capable of that. So far all have chosen not to build their own nuclear weapons, but it is questionable how long this resolve will last if various Third World states become armed with nuclear weapons and start threatening vital interests of industrialized nations.

The two countries considered to already possess nuclear weapons are Israel and South Africa, which are rumored to have been collaborating in nuclear research for some time. In September 1979 a large explosion was registered by intelligence satellites off the coast of South Africa, and it was speculated that this was a South African test of a nuclear weapon. In February 1980 the Western media suggested that Israel and South Africa collaborated for some time in a joint nuclear weapons program and indeed tested their first nuclear bomb off the coast of South Africa.

Whereas these suggestions have been categorically denied by both countries the fact remains that each has a nuclear program and capabilities to build nuclear weapons. The collaboration of the two countries makes a lot of sense geopolitically for both, because each must develop independent energy sources and a national security apparatus. Israel has the technology and wide access to Western know-how, and South Africa controls more than adequate uranium resources and large areas of land and sea regions suitable for remote testing of nuclear weapons.

Among the industrialized nations all except Germany also have some uranium resources in their territories that give them additional incentives to develop nuclear industries of their own.

As a result of these dual politicoeconomic incentives many countries that possess uranium resources feel that the time will come when they will play an important role in global politics. Aside from the major nuclear powers uranium is already being produced in Argentina, Brazil, Australia, Canada, Czechoslovakia, Gabon, Italy, Japan, Mexico, Namibia, Niger, Portugal, South Africa, Spain, and Sweden. In addition countries with uranium resources include the Central African Republic, Greenland (Denmark), Finland, India, Angola, Turkey, Yugoslavia, and Zaire. Uranium will undoubtedly be found in other regions as its price rises and the importance of its existence increases because it is quite widely distributed in the world.

At present the United States is the largest uranium producer in the world, with a capacity to produce about 35 percent of the global uranium output. The Soviet Union is believed to be the second largest uranium-producing country with its output estimated at 28 percent of the world's total, although no official statistics about Soviet uranium mining are known. Canada, South Africa, and France are the next three largest uranium-producing countries. Niger, Namibia, Australia, and Gabon are the next significant uranium-producing countries. The new uranium mine at Rossing in Namibia is believed to be the largest single uranium mine in the world, and this gives a special strategic significance to the emerging country of Namibia.

Since the OPEC oil embargo in 1973 uranium mining and prices as well as nuclear power development received a shot in the arm following a prolonged decline in nuclear power development targets and much political opposition. Interestingly the Soviet Union, threatened with a declining oil production during the 1980s, is promoting nuclear power within the Soviet bloc countries without political opposition. Although the Soviet Union and Czechoslovakia both produce uranium the extent of their resources is unknown, and the Soviet bloc may be trying to secure for itself future uranium supplies to keep its nuclear power programs on stream. Soviet-Cuban penetration into southern Africa regions such as Angola and Mozambique, with the possible Marxist takeover of neighboring Namibia would be one possible solution for future COMECON uranium supplies.

Thorium Resources

Among nuclear materials thorium is another possibility as a nuclear fuel for the future. Thorium could come into importance as a fuel for high-temperature nuclear reactors, although developments in this area are in prototype design stages. Nevertheless it is important to keep in mind those countries that at present are known to possess thorium resources. The major producer of thorium at present is Brazil, but thorium reserves have been discovered in Canada, Egypt, India, South Africa, Sri Lanka, Turkey, and the United States.

NONMETALLIC STRATEGIC MATERIALS

Nonmetallic minerals other than the energy minerals such as coal and oil account for only between 5 to 6 percent of the total value among the top 50 most valuable minerals produced in the world. The most important of those are salt, potash, diamonds, phosphates, asbestos, sulfur, kaolin, fluorspar, pyrite, talc, boron, limestone, barytes, mica, feldspar, nitrates, soda, graphite, and asphalt.

Diamonds, already discussed earlier in this chapter, are the best known as having specific strategic value, but fertilizer materials that include potash, phosphates, and nitrates are also of crucial importance in the production of fertilizers in countries concerned about increasing the productivity of their agriculture. Limestone and fluorspar are important to the steelmaking process; asbestos is vital in high-temperature thermal insulation, in shipbuilding, and for electrical insulation; talc finds uses in electronics, precision insulators, and ultrahigh frequency transmitters.

Not all the materials are strategically important, since some are available from many sources and there are many natural and synthetic substitutes. Perhaps the best assessment of the most strategically critical can be made by an analysis of the U.S. strategic stockpile that includes among nonmetallic materials asbestos, diamonds, fluorspar, graphite, iodine, mica, opium, sapphire, ruby, talc, and sulfur.

NATURAL RUBBER

Natural rubber is the traditional strategic material even though since World War II synthetic rubber has substituted for natural rubber in most applications. Nevertheless natural rubber continues to be very important in about 10 to 15 percent of all rubber applications because it has a lower heat buildup under stress, greater resistance to cracking, and better adhesive qualities than synthetic rubber. Because of these properties natural rubber is much better suited for airplane tires, truck tires, radial tires, and surgical gloves and adhesives. All these applications are important in military uses, but in addition escalating prices of oil, which is the raw material for making synthetic rubber, may soon eliminate the price advantage that synthetic rubber has over natural rubber.

Malaysia is the leading producer of natural rubber, accounting for about 45 percent of the world's total. Indonesia is the second largest producing country, with about 27 percent, and Thailand is third, with about 14 percent. India and Sri Lanka are also significant producers, with small amounts coming from West Africa and South America.

As a result all the industrialized countries depend totally on imports of natural rubber primarily from the Southeast Asia region. Because of continued unrest in that area, even though supplies of natural rubber have been meeting world demand, the price has been going up. Another indication of this material's importance is the fact that the United States continues to maintain natural rubber in its strategic stockpile.

GRAINS AND FOOD AS STRATEGIC COMMODITIES

The most important agricultural commodities include wheat, corn, rice, soybeans, coffee, cotton, palm oil, sugar, tea, beef, and lumber. Fish and fishing rights may also play an important role in international relations and as a reciprocal concession between countries.

As a result of the grain trade embargo to the Soviet Union in 1980, imposed because of that country's invasion of Afghanistan, a lot of attention has been given to the use of grain as a weapon to achieve political objectives. These proposals stem from the fact that the Soviet Union, China, East Europe, the OPEC countries, and many Third World countries are all net importers of grain and food. It is believed by some political analysts that such grain and food embargos would influence the foreign policies of some of those countries.

Actually China and the Soviet Union are very large grain and food producers, comparable in total output levels of those of the United States. However, the loss of grain as a result of poor management of crops, lack of proper storage facilities, and less intensive use of fertilizers and mechanization contribute to creating demand deficits despite relatively large production levels. Imports of grains by such countries, although they appear massive because of central buying, represent only a few percent of their total consumption and will probably decline in the future with improved harvesting techniques and higher productivity.

In addition supplies and demand for grains depend on the weather, a very unpredictable factor. Grains and foodstuffs are also highly perishable commodities by comparison with minerals that can be stored in the ground by simply not being mined.

30

Recommendations for a National Materials Policy

AFL-CIO

For the Industrial Union Department, the need for a national materials policy stems from five sources, all interrelated. The five are as follows:

1. *The need to maintain a strong, stable industrial base.* Only with such a base can the United States maintain a healthy, prosperous, growing economy. As imports of manufactured goods continue to increase and as the shift of the economy from the production of goods to the provision of services continues its relentless pace, the U.S. industrial base is being steadily eroded. If these developments are allowed to continue unchecked, the implications are very serious, not only for U.S. workers whose jobs are at stake but for the economy as a whole.

2. *The need to assure a steady, secure, reasonably priced supply of raw materials to sustain our industrial base.* Since the health of the economy is dependent on maintenance of a strong industrial base, then it is equally dependent on a secure supply of the essential raw materials required to keep industry both going and growing.

3. *The increasing dependence of the United States on imported supplies of many essential raw materials.* Although the United States has many important materials resources within its borders and although U.S. dependence on imported materials is relatively limited compared to most other industrialized nations, there are still some essential commodities in which import dependence is significant and not easily overcome. In the case of manganese, nickel, chrome, tin, and bauxite, U.S. requirements must be met almost entirely from imports. This dependence makes the

Reprint of "Recommendations for a National Materials Policy," Part III, *Raw Materials: The Case for a Comprehensive National Policy* (Jocelyn Gutchess for The Industrial Union Department, AFL-CIO, December 1977).

economy vulnerable to supply disruptions, whether such disruptions are the result of natural causes or of political or economic forces beyond direct control. It is a relief to know that the worry so prevalent a few years ago—that the world was about to run out of everything it needs—has been laid to rest by a consensus of experts, and that in the long run, resource supply will prove adequate to demand. But the threat of temporary supply disruptions has not been removed. Indeed, if anything, that threat has increased in the past two years.

4. *The continuing growth of the multinational corporation as the dominant form for the conduct of business and commerce increases the vulnerability of materials supply to potential disruption.* To the extent that these large corporations are able to develop and exercise oligopoly control over the materials markets, the potential for market manipulation and supply disruption must be taken into account.

5. *The steady and determined movement of the Third World countries toward a "New International Economic Order."* While it does not appear likely at this time that OPEC-type cartels will develop among the producers of other raw materials, the Third World drive to gain for themselves a larger share of the world's wealth, and specifically to use their raw materials as leverage to force such a gain, represents a significant new facet of the materials problem.

These, then, are some of the principal forces that lie behind the U.S. materials problems. But until now, the United States has no unified, coherent policy to protect its interests and the interests of its labor force against the threats of either producing countries or producing corporations. There is no national materials policy or program. There are only bits and pieces. There is a defense stockpile that all too frequently has been used for both political and economic purposes; a tax system that encourages the exploitation of virgin materials resources; other tax policies that favor the growth of the MNCs; spotty support and inadequate direction of materials research and development; lax enforcement of antitrust laws; in and out government regulation, compounded by duplication and overlap of responsibility among government agencies; a foreign policy that blows cold and hot vis-a-vis the Third World goals and objectives; and, above all, a lack of systematic planning to assure that materials supplies will, in fact, be available when we need them, and at a price consistent with economic stability.

No comprehensive contingency plan for use in the event of foreign initiated supply restraints has been articulated or adopted. Neither is there a policy to encourage U.S. fabricators and manufacturers to produce at home. National policy on recycling is nonexistent. No clear decisions have yet been made on developing seabed resources. And the efforts to coordinate these very important elements into an overall materials strategy are at best tenuous, timid, and uncertain.

In order to deal with these shortcomings, the U.S. needs a comprehensive materials policy that includes three kinds of policy instruments.

- It must include policies to stabilize or increase the supply of essential raw materials that the United States must import from foreign sources,
- It should include policies and programs which will increase U.S. domestic supplies,
- It should include policies and programs involving direct governmental intervention in the materials markets in order to counter wild fluctuations in price and supply or market manipulation either by foreign governments or multinational corporations.

The tendency in some influential circles is to think that the market itself will take care of all but the most serious emergency situations. But, as has been demonstrated, the materials market is far from perfect. The concentration of control of the materials industries among a few companies, the conflicting interests of have and have-not nations, the uneven distribution of the physical resources of materials, even the presence of the speculative materials markets—all together mean that reliance on a free market mechanism for protection against supply disruptions is a poor substitute for a materials policy.

Two years ago, the IUD proposed a ten-point raw materials strategy to assure a stable, secure supply of essential raw materials. For the most part, that program is still valid today, although the course of events over the past two years has made necessary the modification of some of the recommendations and the addition of others. The policies that should be adopted in order to increase or stabilize the supply of materials for which the United States depends on foreign sources include the following:

- The United States should enter into long-term commodity agreements with the nations that supply us with raw materials. Agreements guaranteeing a specific quantity of the raw materials in exchange for a U.S. guaranteed floor price are recommended. Two years ago it was recommended that such commodity agreements be on a bilateral basis. This was primarily in recognition of the practical problems involved in negotiating multilateral agreements. However, if multilateral agreements can be worked out expeditiously, the United States should support that approach. Such agreements should be on a commodity-by-commodity basis.
- A multicommodity agreement, financed through a common internationally supported fund, is not workable, and will not provide the materials supply security that the United States needs. It should be recognized that raw materials producers and consumers approach the commodity agreement issue from different standpoints. The raw materials

producers naturally want agreements on the commodities that they produce and export. These, of course, are the commodities on which their economies generally depend.

The consumers—and particularly the United States—are interested only in agreements for those commodities on which they are import-dependent. In some cases, the interests of the two groups will be coincidental—for example, for chrome or manganese. But for some commodities, most notably copper, interests are not coincidental. The major copper producers—Zaire, Zambia, Chile, and Peru, for example—would like an agreement on copper. But for the United States, which is the world's largest copper producer, a copper agreement does not hold the same advantage. This is not to say that we should not work toward such agreements, only that it will not be easy.

- In exchange for some kind of guaranteed access to materials supplies, whether in the form of bilateral commodity agreements or international buffer stock schemes, the United States could make available to the developing countries that are the producers of raw materials the capital and technical assistance they need to better their standard of living. However, in providing such assistance, full consideration must be given to the impact of any resulting shifts or expansion of foreign production capability on the U.S. industry and the U.S. economy. Since the world's economy is to such a large extent dependent on the U.S. economy, no country gains for long if the gain is made at the expense of the U.S. economy.
- The United States should pursue the potential for active participation in producer-consumer arrangements such as the International Tin Agreement. The decision of the United States to join the Fifth International Tin Agreement is a welcome one. Further, President Carter's recommendation that the United States back up its participation by making a voluntary contribution to the buffer stock is to be commended.
- Long-term purchasing agreements should be encouraged and, if necessary, backed by government guarantees. What is involved here are agreements involving the private sector rather than government-to-government agreements. But in both instances the purpose would be to introduce some element of concern for the public interest, which heretofore has been notably absent from the materials scene.

At the same time that the United States is stabilizing the security of foreign supply sources, it should also be developing new and better domestic sources as well as new techniques of increasing the use of raw materials:

- There must be increased and systematically planned government support of materials research and development. Until recently supplies of raw materials have been relatively cheap and reasonably accessible, so there has been little incentive for the development of new materials technology that might provide for more efficient and less costly methods of extraction and primary processing. High energy costs, the need to tap lower grade ores, as well as the necessity to safeguard the environment, all require the development of new methods, new technologies, the invention of economic substitutes, and the opening up of new resources. This R&D effort should not be left entirely to private initiative and private risk.

- There must be greater efforts to encourage the use of recycled materials. Not only should the government support additional technological research in this area, but the present incentives that encourage the use of virgin materials should be eliminated.
- Among the materials resources that should be explored and developed further are the deep seabed resources. The United States is one of only a few nations that presently has the technology, and the ability, to pursue development in this important area. The United States has not proceeded as fast as it might, in part because the development work has been left entirely to private interest and in part because of the inability of the nations of the world to get together on a common Law of the Sea. Even if the present stalemate on the proposed International Law of the Sea is not broken, the United States should go ahead without further delay to support seabed resource development.
- Another way to strengthen U.S. ability to protect itself from potentially crippling supply disruption is to establish domestic economic stockpiles, particularly of some sensitive commodities. Such stockpiles should be managed as a buffer to protect both the accessibility and price of U.S. supply sources. Domestic economic buffer stocks are, of course, a form of long-term commodity agreement. And in both instances the objectives are the same—to ensure a reliable supply of critical industrial materials and to stabilize the materials market. Judicially managed, they could also increase U.S. leverage in world markets. In this connection, some would argue that price stabilization is not a valid purpose for economic stockpiling, that the market is a better arbiter of prices. In our view, however, stabilization of price fluctuations is not a no-no as far as stockpiles are concerned and indeed is a justifiable purpose for government intervention. Obviously, if the United States is going to move toward the development of internationally controlled stockpiles—as currently seems likely—that will affect the need for unilaterally held stockpiles. However, to make certain that the United States does not give up more than it gets, we believe that, at the very least, such stockpiles should be on a commodity-by-commodity basis, not lumped together under a common fund.

The current copper situation provides a good example. U.S. copper producers cannot produce copper at a price that is competitive in the world market, not because they are inefficient but because foreign producers, faced with the necessity to maintain both export earnings and employment, apparently are selling below cost. If the U.S. government were to buy copper, at the U.S. producer price, the world price would rise and U.S. producers could again be competitive. If later either the foreign producers or the corporations attempt to set prices above market value, which could happen as copper stocks are drawn down, the U.S. buffer stock would serve as a stabilizer. The effectiveness of a U.S.-held buffer is demonstrated in tin, where just the rumor that the U.S. government was considering disposal of some of its tin stocks resulted in a sharp drop in the London Metals Exchange tin price.

- Additional protection would be afforded by the building or maintaining of special standby plants and other facilities. Mines and metals processing plants take a long time (two to five years) to develop, construct, and put into operation. Also, once closed, they cannot quickly be put back into operation. The United States must be prepared to bring additional materials capacity onstream within a relatively short time in order to counter foreign threats of supply disruption.

The final group of policies involves certain government actions that will impact on the materials market as it presently operates, so that some of the existing market flaws are removed or at least counteracted. These policies include the following:

- Strict enforcement of the antitrust laws is necessary to reduce the domination and control of the materials industries by a few corporations and to bring about more competition. In this connection, it should be noted that encouragement of recycling, and increased use of secondary sources of materials, i.e., scrap, will also help to increase competition in the materials industries, since typically the secondary industry is not nearly as concentrated as the primary industry.
- The raw materials strategy must protect and strengthen the U.S. industrial base. This can be done by eliminating the tax incentives that encourage the growth of the MNCs and help to make them unresponsive and unresponsible to both host and home governments, and by providing for representation of the U.S. public interest in decisions as to location of fabricating and manufacturing plants in essential basic industries. In addition, more research is needed into the question of the balance between the service-oriented and goods production-oriented sectors of the economy. If there is a "proper" balance—and we suspect there is—policymakers need to know what it is, and they need to know it now.
- Recognizing that U.S. dependency on imports of many essential raw materials will continue, and indeed probably increase, in the years ahead, the United States must develop a strong maritime industry. To the extent that the United States must depend on foreign-flag ships to transport these foreign-source materials, vulnerability to cartel-like actions and contrived shortages increases. That cannot be allowed to happen.

The machinery to implement all of these policies must be put into place. A Commission on National Resources should be established to be the principal policymaking body within the executive department on materials questions. This body should have direct responsibility for the development of a materials policy as well as the oversight and management of much of the policy program. Long-range resource planning is also essential to policy development. This function should be performed at the top levels of government and integrated with other aspects of a national planning effort.

With millions of jobs, billions of dollars, and the stability of the U.S. economy at stake, the United States must adopt a unified, coherent, and comprehensive set of policies to assure that the continued supply and price of raw materials be both reasonable and reliable. The machinery to implement these policies is equally essential.

In developing the mechanisms needed to establish and implement a comprehensive materials policy, there are two important points to be made: First, there is the need to plan ahead. Resources problems *can* be dealt with if we plan on a systematic and regular basis. Planning is not dreaming. Nor is it rigid regulation. There is an important middle ground—some call it indicative planning. Such planning, to be effective, requires the establishment of numerical goals or guideposts; it cannot be done in a vacuum. But unless we move quickly toward some form of national indicative planning, we will find ourselves confronted—again and again—with materials and resource problems, which can only become increasingly severe as time goes by. Second, there is a need for focus within the government on the materials issues. It is not that we need more government agencies, but squarely fixed responsibility—at a level high enough to count.

Finally, the record of the past few years indicates that lack of sustained public concern may play an important, perhaps the most important, part in explaining the continuing policy vacuum in the materials field. There cannot be effective resource planning, nor can there be a coordinated comprehensive national materials policy and program without broad public concern and support. Hopefully, this paper will help to stimulate the concern and generate the necessary support.

31

Africa's Contribution to the Capitalist Development of Europe—The Colonial Period

Walter Rodney

The colonies have been created for the metropole by the metropole.

—French saying

Sales operations in the United States and management of the fourteen (Unilever) plants are directed from Lever House on New York's fashionable Park Avenue. You look at this tall, striking, glass-and-steel structure and you wonder how many hours of underpaid black labour and how many thousands of tons of underpriced palm oil and peanuts and cocoa it cost to build it.

—W. Alpheus Hunton

EXPATRIATION OF AFRICAN SURPLUS UNDER COLONIALISM

Capital and African Wage Labor

Colonial Africa fell within that part of the international capitalist economy from which surplus was drawn to feed the metropolitan sector. As seen earlier, exploitation of land and labor is essential for human social advance, but only on the assumption that the product is made available within the area where the exploitation takes place. Colonialism was not merely a system of exploitation, but one whose essential purpose was to repatriate the profits to the so-called mother country. From an African

Excerpt from "Africa's Contribution to the Capitalist Development of Europe—The Colonial Period" in *How Europe Underdeveloped Africa* by Walter Rodney. Reprinted by permission of Howard University Press, Washington, D.C., copyright 1972 by Walter Rodney. Pp. 149–61.

viewpoint, that amounted to consistent expatriation of surplus produced by African labor out of African resources. It meant the development of Europe as part of the same dialectical process in which Africa was underdeveloped.

By any standards, labor was cheap in Africa, and the amount of surplus extracted from the African laborer was great. The employer under colonialism paid an extremely small wage—a wage usually insufficient to keep the worker physically alive—and, therefore, he had to grow food to survive. This applied in particular to farm labor of the plantation type, to work in mines, and to certain forms of urban employment. At the time of the imposition of European colonial rule, Africans were able to gain a livelihood from the land. Many retained some contact with the land in the years ahead, and they worked away from their *shambas* in order to pay taxes or because they were forced to do so. After feudalism in Europe had ended, the worker had absolutely no means of sustenance other than through the sale of his labor to capitalists. Therefore, to some extent the employer was responsible for insuring the physical survival of the worker by giving him a "living wage." In Africa, this was not the case. Europeans offered the lowest possible wages and relied on legislation backed by force to do the rest.

There were several reasons why the African worker was more crudely exploited than his European counterpart in the present century. Firstly, the alien colonial state had a monopoly of political power, after crushing all opposition by superior armed force. Secondly, the African working class was small, very dispersed, and very unstable owing to migratory practices. Thirdly, while capitalism was willing to exploit all workers everywhere, European capitalists in Africa had additional racial justifications for dealing unjustly with the African worker. The racist theory that the black man was inferior led to the conclusion that he deserved lower wages; and interestingly enough, the light-skinned Arab and Berber populations of North Africa were treated as "blacks" by the white racist French. The combination of the above factors in turn made it extremely difficult for African workers to organize themselves. It is only the organization and resoluteness of the working class which protects it from the natural tendency of the capitalist to exploit to the utmost. That is why in all colonial territories, when African workers realized the necessity for trade union solidarity, numerous obstacles were placed in their paths by the colonial regimes.

Wages paid to workers in Europe and North America were much higher than wages paid to African workers in comparable categories. The Nigerian coal miner at Enugu earned one shilling per day for working underground and nine pence per day for jobs on the surface. Such a miserable wage would be beyond the comprehension of a Scottish or German coal miner, who could virtually earn in an hour what the Enugu miner was paid for a six-day week. The same disparity existed with port workers. The records of the large American shipping company, Farrell Lines, show that in 1955, of the total amount spent on loading and discharging cargo moving between Africa and America, five-sixths went to American workers and one-sixth to Africans. Yet, it was the same amount of cargo loaded and unloaded at both ends. The wages paid to the American stevedore and the European coal miners were still such as to insure that the capitalists made a profit. The point here is merely to illustrate how much greater was the rate of exploitation of African workers.

When discrepancies such as the above were pointed out during the colonial period and subsequently, those who justified colonialism were quick to reply that the standard and cost of living was higher in capitalist countries. The fact is that the higher standard was made possible by the exploitation of colonies, and there was no justification for keeping African living standards so depressed in an age where better was possible and in a situation where a higher standard was possible because of the work output of Africans themselves. The kind of living standard supportable by African labor within the continent is readily illustrated by the salaries and the lifestyle of the whites inside Africa.

Colonial governments discriminated against the employment of Africans in senior categories; and, whenever it happened that a white and a black filled the same post, the white man was sure to be paid considerably more. This was true at all levels, ranging from civil service posts to mine workers. African salaried workers in the British colonies of Gold Coast and Nigeria were better off than their brothers in many other parts of the continent, but they were restricted to the "junior staff" level in the civil service. In the period before the last world war, European civil servants in the Gold Coast received an average of 40 pounds per month, with quarters and other privileges. Africans got an average salary of 4 pounds. There were instances where one European in an establishment earned as much as his 25 African assistants put together. Outside the civil service, Africans obtained work in building projects, in mines, and as domestics—all low-paying jobs. It was exploitation without responsibility and without redress. In 1934, 41 Africans were killed in a gold mine disaster in the Gold Coast, and the capitalist company offered only 3 pounds to the dependents of each of these men as compensation.

Where European settlers were found in considerable numbers, the wage differential was readily perceived. In North Africa, the wages of Moroccans and Algerians were from 16 percent to 25 percent those of Europeans. In East Africa, the position was much worse, notably in Kenya and Tanganyika. A comparison with white settler earnings and standards brings out by sharp contrast how incredibly low African wages were. While Lord Delamere controlled 100,000 acres of Kenya's land, the Kenyan had to carry a *kipande* pass in his own country to beg for a wage of 15 to 20 shillings per month. The absolute limit of brutal exploitation was found in the southern parts of the continent; and in Southern Rhodesia, for example, agricultural laborers rarely received more than 15 shillings per month. Workers in mines got a little more if they were semiskilled, but they also had more intolerable working conditions. Unskilled laborers in the mines of Northern Rhodesia often got as little as 7 shillings per month. A truck driver on the famous copper belt was in a semiskilled grade. In one mine, Europeans performed that job for 30 pounds per month, while in another, Africans did it for 3 pounds per month.

In all colonial territories, wages were reduced during the period of crisis which shook the capitalist world during the 1930s, and they were not restored or increased until after the last capitalist world war. In Southern Rhodesia in 1949, Africans employed in municipal areas were awarded minimum wages from 35 to 75 shillings per month. That was a considerable improvement over previous years, but white workers (on the job for 8 hours per day compared to the Africans' 10 or 14 hours) received a minimum wage of 20 shillings *per day* plus free quarters and other benefits.

The Rhodesians offered a miniature version of South Africa's apartheid system, which oppressed the largest industrial working class on the continent. In the Union of South Africa, African laborers worked deep underground, under inhuman conditions which would not have been tolerated by miners in Europe. Consequently, black South African workers recovered gold from deposits which elsewhere would be regarded as noncommercial. And yet it is the white section of the working class which received whatever benefits were available in terms of wages and salaries. Officials have admitted that the mining companies could pay whites higher than miners in any other part of the world because of the superprofits made by paying black workers a mere pittance.*

In the final analysis, the shareholders of the mining companies were the ones who benefited most of all. They remained in Europe and North America and collected fabulous dividends every year from the gold, diamonds, manganese, uranium, etc., which were brought out of the South African subsoil by African labor. For years, the capitalist press itself praised Southern Africa as an investment outlet returning superprofits on capital invested. From the very beginning of the "Scramble for Africa," huge fortunes were made from gold and diamonds in Southern Africa by people like Cecil Rhodes. In the present century, both the investment and the outflow of surplus have increased. Investment was mainly concentrated in mining and finance where the profits were greatest. In the mid-1950's, British investments in South Africa were estimated at 860 million pounds and yielded a stable profit of 15 percent, or 129 million pounds every year. Most mining companies had returns well above that average. De Beers Consolidated Mines made a profit that was both phenomenal

---

*As is well known, those conditions still operate. However, this chapter presents matters in the past tense to picture the colonial epoch.

and consistently high—between $26 million and $29 million throughout the 1950s.

The complex of Southern African mining concerns operated not just in South Africa itself, but also in South-West Africa, Angola, Mozambique, Northern Rhodesia, Southern Rhodesia, and the Congo. Congo was consistently a source of immense wealth for Europe, because from the time of colonization until 1906, King Leopold II of Belgium made at least $20 million from rubber and ivory. The period of mineral exploitation started quite early, and then gained momentum after political control passed from King Leopold to the Belgium state in 1908. Total foreign capital inflow into the Congo between 1887 and 1953 was estimated by the Belgians to have been 5,700 million pounds. The value of the outflow in the same period was said to have been 4,300 million pounds, exclusive of profits retained within the Congo. As was true everywhere else on the continent, the expatriation of surplus from the Congo increased as the colonial period wore on. In the five years preceding independence the net outflow of capital from Congo to Belgium reached massive proportions. Most of the expatriation of surplus was handled by a major European finance monopoly, the Société Générale. The Société Générale had as its most important subsidiary the Union Minière de Haute-Katanga, which has monopolized Congolese copper production since 1889 (when it was known as the Compagnie de Katanga): Union Minière has been known to make a profit of 27 million pounds in a single year.

It is no wonder that of the total wealth produced in Congo in any given year during the colonial period, more than one-third went out in the form of profits for big business and salaries for their expatriate staffs. But the comparable figure for Northern Rhodesia under the British was one-half. In Katanga, Union Minière at least had a reputation for leaving some of the profits behind in the form of things like housing and maternity services for African workers. The Rhodesian Copper Belt Companies expatriated profits without compunction.

It should not be forgotten that outside Southern Africa there were also significant mining operations during the colonial period. In North Africa, foreign capital exploited natural resources of phosphates, oil, lead, zinc, manganese, and iron ore. In Guinea, Sierra Leone, and Liberia, there were important workings of gold, diamonds, iron ore, and bauxite. To all that should be added the tin of Nigeria, the gold and manganese of Ghana, the gold and diamonds of Tanganyika, and the copper of Uganda and Congo Brazzaville. In each case, an understanding of the situation must begin with an inquiry into the degree of exploitation of African resources and labor, and then must proceed to follow the surplus to its destination outside Africa—into the bank accounts of the capitalists who control the majority shares in the huge multinational mining combines.

The African working class produced a less spectacular surplus for export with regard to companies engaged in agriculture. Agricultural plantations were widespread in North, East, and South Africa; and they also appeared in West Africa to a lesser extent. Their profits depended on the incredibly low wages and harsh working conditions imposed on African agricultural laborers and on the fact that they invested very little capital in obtaining the land, which was robbed wholesale from Africans by colonial powers and they sold to whites at nominal prices. For instance, after the Kenya highlands had been declared "crown land," the British handed over to Lord Delamere 100,000 acres of the best land at a cost of a penny per acre. Lord Francis Scott purchased 350,000 acres, the East African Estates Ltd. got another 350,000 acres, and the East African Syndicate took 100,000 acres adjoining Lord Delamere's estate—all at giveaway prices. Needless to say, such plantations made huge profits, even if the rate was lower than in a South African gold mine or an Angolan diamond mine.

During the colonial era, Liberia was supposedly independent; but to all intents and purposes, it was a colony of the United States. In 1926, the Firestone Rubber Company of the United States was able to acquire 1 million acres of forest land in Liberia at a cost of 6 cents per acre and 1 percent of the value of the exported rubber. Because of the demand for and the strategic importance of rubber, Firestone's profits from Liberia's land and labor carried them to twenty-fifth position among the giant companies of the United States.

European Trading Companies versus the African Peasant

So far, this section has been dealing with that part of the surplus produced by African wage earners in mines and plantations. But the African working class under colonialism was extremely small and the vast majority of Africans engaged in the colonial money economy were independent peasants. How then can it be said that these self-employed peasants were contributing to the expatriation of African surplus? Apologists for colonialism argue that it was a positive benefit for such farmers to have been given the opportunity to create surplus by growing or collecting produce such as cocoa, coffee, palm oil. It is essential that this misrepresentation be clarified.

A peasant growing a cash crop or collecting produce had his labor exploited by a long chain of individuals, starting with local businessmen. Sometimes, those local businessmen were Europeans. Very rarely were they Africans, and more usually they were a minority group brought in from outside and serving as intermediaries between the white colonialists and the exploited African peasant. In West Africa, the Lebanese and Syrians played this role; while in East Africa the Indians rose to this position. Arabs were also in the middleman category in Zanzibar and a few other places on the East African coast.

Cash-crop peasants never had any capital of their own. They existed from one crop to another, depending on good harvests and good prices. Any bad harvest or fall of prices caused the peasants to borrow in order to find money to pay taxes and buy certain necessities. As security, they mortgaged their future crops to moneylenders in the middleman category. Nonpayment of debts could and did lead to their farms' being taken away by the moneylenders. The rate of interest on the loans was always fantastically high, amounting to what is known as "usury." In East Africa, things were so bad that even the British colonial government had to step in and enact a "Native Credit Ordinance" to protect Africans from Asian businessmen.

However, in spite of some minor clashes between the colonialists and the middlemen, the two were part and parcel of the same apparatus of exploitation. On the whole, the Lebanese and Indians did the smaller jobs which Europeans could not be bothered with. They owned things such as cotton gins which separated the seed from the lint; while of course Europeans concentrated on the cotton mills in Europe. The middlemen also went out to the villages, while Europeans liked to stay in towns. In the villages, the Indians and Lebanese took over virtually all buying and selling, channeling most of the profits back to Europeans in the towns and those overseas.

The share of profits which went to middlemen was insignificant in comparison to those profits reaped by big European business interests and by the European governments themselves. The capitalist institution which came into most direct contact with African peasants was the colonial trading company: that is to say, a company specializing in moving goods to and from the colonies. The most notorious were the French concerns Compagnie Française d'Afrique Occidentale (CFAO) and Société Commerciale Ouest Africaine (SCOA) and the British-controlled United Africa Company (UAC). These were responsible for expatriating a great proportion of Africa's wealth produced by peasant toil.

Several of the colonial trading companies already had African blood on their hands from participation in the slave trade. Thus, after French merchants in Bordeaux made fortunes from the European slave trade, they transferred that capital to the trade in groundnuts from Senegal and Gambia in the middle of the nineteenth century. The firms concerned continued to operate in the colonial period, although they changed hands and there were a lot of mergers. In Senegal, Mauritania, and Mali, the names of Maurel & Prom, Maurel Brothers, Buhan & Teyssere, Delmas & Clastre, were all well known. Several of them were eventually incorporated into SCOA, which was dominated by a consortium of French and Swiss financiers. A parallel process in the French port of Marseilles led to the transfer of slave-trade capital into direct trade between Africa and France. After the end of the First World War, most of the small Marseilles firms were absorbed into the massive CFAO, which imported into French

West Africa whatever European goods the market would take, and exported in turn the agricultural produce that was largely the consequence of peasant labor. CFAO also had British and Dutch capital, and its activities extended into Liberia and into British and Belgian colonies. It is said that SCOA and CFAO made a profit of up to 90 percent in good years and 25 percent in bad years.

In Britain, the notorious slave-trading port of Liverpool was the first to switch to palm oil early in the nineteenth century when the trade in slaves became difficult or impossible. This meant that Liverpool firms were no longer exploiting Africa by removing its labor physically to another part of the world. Instead, they were exploiting the labor and raw materials of Africa *inside* Africa. Throughout the nineteenth century and right into the colonial era, Liverpool concentrated largely on importing African peasant produce. Backed by the industrial districts of Manchester and Cheshire, this British port was in control of a great proportion of Britain's and Europe's trade with Africa in the colonial period—just as it had done in the slave-trade period. Glasgow also had a keen interest in the colonial trade, and so did the merchants and big business interests of London. By 1929, London replaced Liverpool as the chief port dealing with African import and export.

As indicated, the UAC was the British company which was best known among the commercial concerns. It was a subsidiary of the giant Anglo-Dutch monopoly Unilever; and its agencies were found in all the British colonies of West Africa and on a smaller scale in East Africa. Unilever also controlled the Compagnie du Niger Français, the Compagnie Française de la Côte d'Ivoire, SCKN in Chad, NOSOCO in Senegal, NSCA in Portuguese Guinea, and John Walken & Co. Ltd. in Dahomey. Certain other British and French firms were not found in every colony, but they did well in the particular area in which they were entrenched. For example, there was John Holt in Nigeria.

In East Africa, the import-export business tended to have smaller firms than in West Africa, but even so there were five or six which were much larger than the rest and appropriated the largest amounts. One of the oldest was Smith Mackenzie, which was an offshoot of the Scottish company of Mackinnon and Mackenzie, which had spearheaded British colonization in East Africa and which also had interests in India. Other notable commercial firms were those of A. Baumann, Wigglesworth and Company, Dalgetty, Leslie & Anderson, Ralli Bros., Michael Cotts, Jos. Hansen, the African Mercantile and Twentsche Overseas Trading Co. Some of them amalgamated before colonial rule was over, and they all had several other subsidiaries, as well as themselves being related to bigger companies in the metropoles. The UAC also had a slice of the East African import trade, having brought up the firm of Gailey and Roberts which was started by white settlers in 1904.

The pattern of appropriation of surplus in East Africa was easy to follow, in that there was centralization of the extractive mechanisms in Nairobi and the port of Mombasa. All the big firms operated from Nairobi, with important offices in Mombasa to deal with warehousing, shipping, insuring. Uganda and Tanganyika were then brought into the picture via their capital cities of Kampala and Dar es Salaam, where the big firms had branches. Up to the start of the last war, the volume of trade from East Africa was fairly small, but it jumped rapidly after that. For instance, the value of Kenya imports rose from 4 million pounds in 1938 to 34 million in 1950 and to 70 million in 1960. The value of exports was of course rising at the same time, and the commercial firms were among the principal beneficiaries of the growth in foreign trade.

Trading companies made huge fortunes on relatively small investments in those parts of Africa where peasant cash-crop farming was widespread. The companies did not have to spend a penny to grow the agricultural raw materials. The African peasant went in for cash-crop farming for many reasons. A minority eagerly took up the opportunity to continue to acquire European goods, which they had become accustomed to during the precolonial period. Many others in every section of the continent took to earning cash because they had to pay various taxes in money or because they were forced to work. Good examples of Africans literally being forced to grow cash crops by gun and whip were to be found in Tanganyika under German rule, in Portuguese colonies, and in French Equatorial Africa and the French Sudan in the 1930s.* In any event, there were very few cases where the peasant was wholly dependent on the cash for his actual sustenance. The trading companies took full advantage of that fact. Knowing that an African peasant and his family would keep alive by their own food *shambas*, the companies had no obligation to pay prices sufficient for the maintenance of a peasant and his family. In a way, the companies were simply receiving tribute from a conquered people, without even the necessity to trouble themselves as to how the tributary goods were produced.

Trading companies also had their own means of transport inside Africa, such as motor vessels and trucks. But, usually they transferred the burden of transport costs on to the peasant via the Lebanese or Indian middlemen. Those capitalist companies held the African farmer in a double squeeze, by controlling the price paid for the crop and by controlling the price of imported goods such as tools, clothing, and bicycles to which peasants aspired. For example, prices of palm products were severely re-

*These facts came most dramatically to the attention of the outside world when Africans resorted to violence. For example, forced cultivation of cotton was a major grievance behind the outbreak of Maji Maji wars in Tanganyika and behind the nationalist revolt in Angola as late as 1960.

duced by the UAC and other trading companies in Nigeria in 1929, while the cost of living was rising owing to increased charges for imported goods. In 1924, the price for palm oil had been 14 shillings per gallon. This fell to 7 in 1928 and to slightly over 1 shilling in the following year. Although the trading companies received less for every ton of palm oil during the depression years, their profit margin increased—showing how brazenly surplus was being pounded out of the peasant. In the midst of the depression the UAC was showing a handsome profit. The profits in 1934 were 6,302,875 pounds and a dividend of 15 percent was paid on ordinary shares.

In every part of colonial Africa, the depression years followed the same pattern. In Sukumaland (Tanganyika) the price of cotton dropped in 1930 from 50 cents to 10 cents per pound. The French colonies were hit a little later, because the depression did not make its impact on the French monetary zone until after 1931. Then, prices of Senegalese groundnuts were cut by more than half. Coffee and cocoa dropped even further, since they were relative luxuries to the European buyer. Again, it can be noted that French firms such as CFAO and SCOA faced lower prices when they sold the raw materials in Europe, but they never absorbed any losses. Instead, African peasants and workers bore the pressure, even if it meant forced labor. African peasants in French territories were forced to join so-called cooperative societies which made them grow certain crops like cotton and made them accept whatever price was offered.

Hardly had the depression ended when Europe was at war. The Western powers dragged in the African people to fight for freedom! The trading firms stepped up the rate of plunder in the name of God and country. On the Gold Coast, they paid 10 pounds per ton for cocoa beans as compared to 50 pounds before the war. At the same time, the price of imported goods doubled or trebled. Many necessities passed beyond the reach of the ordinary man. On the Gold Coast, a piece of cotton print which had sold before the war for 12½ shillings was 90 shillings in 1945. In Nigeria a yard of khaki which was 3 shillings in prewar days went up to 16; a bundle of iron sheets formerly costing 30 went up to 100.

Urban workers were hardest hit by rising prices, since they had to purchase everyday necessities with money, and part of their food was imported. Worker dissatisfaction highlighted this exploitative postwar situation. There were several strikes, and in the Gold Coast, the boycott of imported goods in 1948 is famous as the prelude to self-government under Nkrumah. However, peasants were also restless under low prices and expensive imports. In Uganda, the cotton-growing peasants could stand things no longer by 1947. They could not get their hands on the big British import-export firms, but they could at least deal with the Indian and African middlemen. So they marched against the Indian-owned cotton gins and demonstrated outside the palace of the Kabaka—the hereditary ruler who often functioned as a British agent in Uganda.

To insure that at all times the profit margin was kept as high as possible, the trading firms found it convenient to form "pools." The pools fixed the price to be paid to the African cultivator, and kept the prices down to the minimum. In addition, the trading companies spread into several other aspects of the economic life of the colonies, in such a way as to introduce several straws for the sucking out of surplus. In Morocco, to give one example, the Compagnie Générale du Maroc owned large estates, livestock farms, timber workings, mines, fisheries, railways, ports, and power stations. The giants like CFAO and UAC also had their fingers in everything. CFAO's interests ranged from groundnut plantations to shares in the Fabre & Frassinet shipping line. The people of Ghana and Nigeria met the UAC everywhere they turned. It controlled wholesale and retail trade, owned butter factories, sawmills, soap factories, singlet factories, cold storage plants, engineering and motor repair shops, tugs, coastal boats. Some of those businesses directly exploited African wage labor, while in one way or another all operations skimmed the cream produced by peasant efforts in the cash-crop sector.

Sometimes, the firms which purchased agricultural products in Africa were the same concerns which manufactured goods based on those agricultural raw materials. For instance, Cadbury and Fry, the two foremost English manufacturers of cocoa and chocolate, were buyers on the West African coast, while in East Africa the tea manufacturing concern of Brooke Bond both grew and exported tea. Many of the Marseilles, Bordeaux, and Liverpool trading companies were also engaged in manufacturing items such as soap and margarine in their home territories. This applied fully to the UAC, while the powerful Lesieur group processing oils and fats in France had commercial buyers in Africa. However, it is possible to separate the trading operations from the industrial ones. The latter represented the final stage in the long process of exploiting the labor of African peasants—in some ways the most damaging stage.

Peasants worked for large numbers of hours to produce a given cash crop, and the price of the product was the price of those long hours of labor. Since primary produce from Africa has always received low prices, it follows that the buyer and user of the raw material was engaging in massive exploitation of the peasants.

The above generalization can be illustrated with reference to cotton, which is one of the most widely encountered cash crops in Africa. The Ugandan farmer grew cotton which ultimately made its way into an English factory in Lancashire or a British-owned factory in India. The Lancashire factory owner paid his workers as little as possible, but his exploitation of their labor was limited by several factors. His exploitation of the labor of the Ugandan peasant was unlimited because of his power in the colonial state, which insured that Ugandans worked long hours for very little. Besides, the price of the finished cotton shirt was so high that when reimported into Uganda, cotton in the form of a shirt was beyond the purchasing power of the peasant who grew the cotton.

The differences between the prices of African exports of raw materials and their importation of manufactured goods constituted a form of unequal exchange. Throughout the colonial period, this inequality in exchange got worse. Economists refer to the process as one of deteriorating terms of trade. In 1939, with the same quality of primary goods colonies could buy only 60 percent of manufactured goods which they bought in the decade 1870–80 before colonial rule. By 1960, the amount of European manufactured goods purchasable by the same quantity of African raw materials had fallen still further. There was no objective economic law which determined that primary produce should be worth so little. Indeed, the developed countries sold certain raw materials like timber and wheat at much higher prices than a colony could command. The explanation is that the unequal exchange was forced upon Africa by the political and military supremacy of the colonizers, just as in the sphere of international relations unequal treaties were forced upon small states in the dependencies, like those in Latin America.

The unequal nature of the trade between the metropole and the colonies was emphasized by the concept of the "protected market," which meant even an inefficient metropolitan producer could find a guaranteed market in the colony where his class had political control. Furthermore, as in the preceding era of precolonial trade, European manufacturers built up useful sidelines of goods which would have been substandard in their own markets, especially in textiles. The European farmer also gained in the same way by selling cheap butter, while the Scandinavian fisherman came into his own through the export of salted cod. Africa was not a large market for European products, compared to other continents, but both buying prices and selling prices were set by European capitalists. That certainly allowed their manufacturers and traders more easy access to the surplus of wealth produced in Africa than they would have had if Africans were in a position to raise the price of their own exports. [. . .]

32

Problems of Mineral Development in Developing Countries

Rex Bosson and Bension Varon

The most controversial problems of mineral development in the developing countries have to do with their relation to the developed countries as providers of capital and technology and as consumers of the minerals produced. [Here] we consider the growing interdependence of developed and developing countries and the problems and conflicts to which this gives rise.

INTERDEPENDENCE OF DEVELOPING AND DEVELOPED COUNTRIES

We have suggested that during the next decade developed economies may rely increasingly on the supply of minerals from developing economies and, [. . .] this may make an important contribution to the future foreign exchange earnings of the developing economies. Modern mining and processing methods have become so capital intensive, however, and the capital requirements of modern mines and their attendant infrastructure so large that few of the developing countries can expect to bring a sizable project into operation on their own. Up to now, the large mining companies have provided most of the funds, technical know-how, and marketing outlets, although with the recent trend toward national autonomy, the situation has been changing. Some developing countries have already managed to produce a cadre of experts in this field, working through the public and private sectors. Nevertheless, the

Excerpts from "Problems of Mineral Development in Developing Countries," Chapter 5 in *The Mining Industry and the Developing Countries* by Rex Bosson and Bension Varon. Copyright 1977 by Oxford University Press, New York. Reprinted by permission of the publisher. Pp. 132–43, 147–50.

remaining gap in skills, finance, and technology will require continued participation of the large integrated producers in mining development in the developing countries. Whatever the form of future cooperative arrangements, if they are to be workable, they must be acceptable to both importing and supplying nations, reflecting their common interest in an expanded flow of resources to the world markets.

In the long run the stake of the developing nations in resource development may be greater than that of developed countries, since for a number of important minerals technology is providing a broad array of options in the form of synthetics, abundant natural substitutes, and processes for extracting minerals from internationally available raw materials. The past advantages of suppliers with rich ore reserves have been further reduced because even low-grade ores can now be made competitive through advanced technology and large-scale extraction. Despite increased reliance on mineral supplies from developing countries, industrialized nations do not face an immediately critical supply situation. Over the long run, however, developing countries will be able to negotiate their more abundant supply situation into better leverage over, and larger benefits from, joint exploration and production ventures. While the position of the industrialized nations may weaken, developing countries' revolution of expectations and growing absorptive capacity will intensify the pressure on the development of their resources. Thus, the interests of the two parties will again interlock, intersect, and interrelate.

DIVERGENT OBJECTIVES OF INVESTORS AND HOST GOVERNMENTS

Because of the major role the large multinational mining companies have played and must continue to play in the development of mineral resources in the developing countries—though under different rules—their conditions of operation, position in the developing countries, and relationship with the various parties in the host countries warrant brief review.

It is unlikely that the objectives established for the exploitation of any particular mineral deposit by a multinational firm will coincide with those of the host government; in fact, these objectives may diverge considerably. The multinational company will act to maximize profits and spread the risks of the company as a whole, not necessarily those of the affiliate in a particular producing country alone. In determining the distribution of production between subsidiaries located in different countries, a mining company will take into account the relative costs (including taxes) of the different subsidiaries, the preferential access to some markets of various suppliers, the need to maintain minimum production levels as specified by contracts, and the degree of political risk in each country. Furthermore, intrafirm transfer prices may not be based on world prices (often a world price does not exist), but may reflect a concentration of profit in a particular affiliate in order to minimize taxes or avoid restrictions on transfer of profits.

On the marketing side, companies tend to specialize in commodities experiencing high growth rates and to shift incremental resources from a commodity whose growth rate has fallen off to one with a higher growth rate. In the copper industry, for example, the shift has been to a competing commodity, aluminum (as with Anaconda, Revere, and Kennecott). Countries with marginal deposits and an uncertain investment climate may not fare as well as those with better mineral resources and more favorable investment conditions. Moreover, the companies themselves are deeply involved in influencing the growth and displacement of commodities through their large research and development establishments, which are constantly putting forward new products and promoting product uses based on their mineral resources. Perhaps most notable is the demand for aluminum, which has been very significantly influenced by the aluminum companies themselves.

A government, on the other hand, is concerned with maximizing total revenues of the subsidiaries operating within its territory, and especially its share of revenues, with little interest in overall corporate profits. Governments also seek to influence the level and geographic pattern of resource development; encourage backward and forward linkages in the economy; and expand the processing, refining, and fabrication of raw materials, both for domestic use and for export.

THE SOURCES OF CONFLICT

The divergence of objectives can lead to serious conflict and some form of nationalization or confiscation, as evidenced in the recent past in Algeria, Bolivia, Burma, Chile, Ghana, Guyana, Tunisia, Peru, Zaire, and Zambia. In his recent investigation of two copper mining projects, Raymond F. Mikesell concluded: "The two case studies confirm the generalization that conflicts between the host government and the foreign investor tend to be more or less continuous, and the greater the profitability of the mine the more intense will be the demand for renegotiation of the contract on the part of the host government."[1]

A vast confidence gap characterizes the relations between host government and foreign company from the very beginning. Alun G. Davies of the Overseas Mining Association, London, described the problem as follows:

> From the point of view of the host country, the mining company negotiators represent a hard-faced, profit-dominated negotiator entirely motivated by the capitalistic urge to maximize advantages and ignore whatever arguments may appeal to the other party. To the third world, moreover, these negotiators appear as diabolically clever, fully apprised about all the technicalities of the subject, and prepared to take the other side for a ride at any time. . . . From the point of the negotiating mining company, the other side often seems so suspicious of motive that it is unable to make up its mind on most subjects, and unable to comprehend the factors which govern competitive business in this world. Moreover, there is a difference in time factors, and the important significance which is attached to prompt decision making. Above all, there is sometimes lack of mutual confidence, or even of a recognition that Western world mining companies have a capacity for objective consideration and a conscientious regard for the rights of others. . . . Given the desperate needs of developing countries for outside capital for resource development, the existence of a psychological abyss between the two parties is a tragedy, both from the point of view of development in the third world, and from the point of view of encouragement of international trade in essential raw materials.[2]

John Carman of the United Nations lists among the "inhibitors of investment" in mining, especially in the developing countries, "suspicion on the part of governments of the motives, ethics and methods of the large international mining houses; a suspicion, incidentally which is more than amply reciprocated when said houses size up governments." He then adds, "Neither party lacks justification."[3]

The power and spread of the multinational allow it to influence, directly or indirectly, the policies and actions of home and host countries, and can at times place countries in the interdependent or dependent positions. Multinational corporations have been known to cause jurisdictional disputes among governments and sometimes—when they succeed in drawing their home countries into their own disputes with host countries—bring about political confrontations. Traditionally, host countries, and recently some home countries also, have found that the global context in which corporations operate and the many options open to them can restrict the effectiveness of government policies. Social and cultural conflict can also arise when nationalistic or reformist forces in the host country perceive the operations of the corporation as a threat to the country's traditions and heritage.

Foreign companies sometimes enter the host country under a concession agreement covering ownership and control of the project, including production levels, marketing and export pricing, exploration requirements, and degree of processing. Alternatively, they may acquire the mineral rights of domestic enterprises. Conflict may arise if either party violates the terms of the concession or if the government changes legislation, fails to acknowledge agreements of previous governments, or imposes additional taxes and conditions.

On an even broader plane, the multinational mining company, together with the nonmining multinationals, can have a disruptive influence on the functioning of the international monetary and trade system. The recent currency crises have focused attention on hot money movements; the predominance of intracorporation transactions in trade may, at the very least, render adjustment mechanisms less sensitive and limit free market operations. In addition to raising questions relating to the prospects and implications of nationalization, taxation of multinational corporations creates a number of difficult problems. The complexities of intercountry differences in tax rates, definitions of taxable income, and taxation principles regarding income accruing abroad are compounded by transfer pricing practices which affect income allocation and government schemes of compensation for taxes paid abroad. Bilateral tax treaties, mainly among developed market economies, have provided a partial solution, but alternatives need to be explored, especially with respect to operations in the developing countries.

An issue central to the conflict between the host country and the foreign investor is the split of revenues. The arrangements agreed upon will depend largely on the bargaining strengths of the two parties at the time of establishing the frame of reference for the foreign company's activities. The configuration of bargaining power can vary considerably depending upon the level of development of the mineral sector, the extent to which the existence and economic value of mineral resources are known, the alternative economic opportunities available to the country, and the changing relationship between the foreign investor and the host country from exploration through exploitation. Following is a brief description of the relative negotiating positions of the parties at different stages of mineral resource development, preexploration, preexploitation, and postimplementation.

Preexploration

At the preexploration stage, there is frequently little or no geological information available on the basis of which to evaluate the mineral potential of a region. Investment must therefore be made strictly with risk capital. Governments of developing countries have little or no surplus resources available for such investment. Because of the worldwide scarcity of exploration capital and the number of different areas competing for it, the private firm, particularly the large multinational firm, enjoys a strong bargaining position. This position is further strengthened by the firm's ability to offer scarce exploration know-how.

The major strengths of the host government in this situation lie in its power to solicit bids from different firms and in the attractiveness of its terms and conditions relative to other countries. The exploration booms of Canada, Australia, South Africa, and Ireland in the past are attributable not only to the terms and conditions available there but to the unfavorable terms and conditions of other countries. The recent hardening of the terms imposed by some of the provincial governments in Canada has already caused a flight of exploration capital, a slowdown of the exploration effort, and the cancellation of several concessions. A similar slowdown was experienced in Australia around 1974 and 1975 with the hardening of investment laws, and the cancellation of the 20-year tax-exempt period in Ireland has stemmed the flow of risk capital into that country.

As there is no return on exploration activities alone, the multinational firms will invariably try to negotiate as many of the exploitation terms as possible before exploration. Given the high-risk element of exploration, they must, under the basic rules of corporate survival, negotiate terms which provide returns sufficiently high to cover not only the successful exploration expenditure, but also unsuccessful exploration activities in the same country and elsewhere. Most host governments are reluctant to accept the argument that successful mineral operations within their territories should subsidize exploration in another country. At the same time, they fail to recognize that the very exploration expenditures which located their mineral reserves were subsidized by other successful operations, possibly in other countries.

Preexploitation

The bargaining position of the government becomes stronger if exploration conducted by or for it has succeeded in finding and delineating economic mineral reserves. Although the multinational firm is still needed for its expertise, marketing outlets and in most cases capital, its bargaining position is weaker, for the government will be in a position to invite competitive bidding for the project by a number of firms. It is even possible (though only in a few countries) that the government might proceed without foreign participation. On the other hand, since the risk of investment at this stage is considerably lower, the cost of capital is also significantly lower; consequently, foreign firms may be willing to soften their negotiating position and agree to enter into joint ventures with nationals.

This raises the question of whether the economic and social benefits which may be realized by a country through a better bargaining position are greater than the cost of upgrading the country's knowledge of its mineral potential and, if so, the extent to which it should itself undertake exploration, and by what method. The spread and hardening of nationalistic sentiments over the past decade will force the mining firms to soften their terms. (Many companies have already become more cautious in the exercise of their power and more sensitive to their social responsibilities.) But it may also stem the flow of exploration funds and make firms more selective in their choice of areas. This trend has already been apparent over the past decade, as evidenced by the concentration of exploration in countries such as Canada and Australia, although these countries are now following the developing countries in demanding greater national control over the exploitation of their natural resources. The reduction in exploration funds also means that the developing countries, particularly those in which there has been little development of the mineral sector, will have to participate more actively in exploration if they expect to improve their position in the world mineral markets.

Of perhaps greater importance than physical (geological) risk is political risk. The high returns sought by foreign companies coming in at a low level of geological information increase the risk of potential confiscation and of legislative action designed to reduce their share of benefits at some later stage. Where, because of better geological knowledge, a lower return is acceptable to the foreign corporation, political risk is reduced and the development of the mineral sector is facilitated. On these grounds alone, therefore, it seems desirable for a country to increase the level of its geological information.

Postimplementation

After investment has been made and a mine is in production the bargaining power of the foreign investor diminishes considerably. Some governments become oblivious to the risks under which the capital was first invested, may ignore expenditures on unsuccessful ventures, and are prone to look only at the level of company earnings from successful operations. Often they request renegotiation without taking into account the potential adverse effects of such action over the long term—for example, the possibility that it may discourage new foreign investment. The position of the government is strengthened with the growth of the mining sector, its increased geological and marketing knowledge, and its expanding cadre of trained local personnel. The options open to the foreign investors in the event of conflict at this stage are to refuse to provide capital or managerial, technical, and marketing services; to withdraw; or to call for support from their own government in the form of guarantees or economic pressure. A number of governments in developed countries insure their private investors against political risks. The United States, Japan, and the Federal Republic of Germany have offered such insurance for some years. Eleven other countries (Australia, Belgium, Canada, Denmark, France, Japan, the Netherlands, Norway, Sweden, Switzerland, and the United Kingdom) have recently established insurance systems. Austria and Portugal have limited schemes. With the increasing tension between host governments and foreign investors, there has been a surge of interest in such problems. Perhaps the strongest weapon is the control of foreign corporations over markets. For some minerals, this control is absolute, giving the country no alternative outlet for its product, although this situation is rapidly changing. Because nearly all developing countries are heavily dependent on external aid, however, their governments operate within severe constraints, though the widespread sensitivity to accusations of political or economic imperialism has made the threat of reprisals less significant than previously. The new sources of finance from the recently enlarged oil revenues may significantly move the balance of power in the direction of the developing countries and away from the multinationals.

THE DIVISION OF BENEFITS

The division of benefits between the host nation and the foreign investor varies widely from country to country, mineral to mineral, and project to project. The arrangements in any given case depend on the relative bargaining strength of the two parties at the time of negotiation, subsequent changes, and the attitude of the host government towards private, particularly foreign, investment within its territory. The early investors in mining in the developing countries managed to secure very favorable terms and conditions because investment opportunities were plentiful and pressure to develop resources was low, so that the foreign investor could be attracted only by very high potential returns. Consequently, a large portion of the profits and revenues went to the foreign companies and little to the host government. In the 1920s, for example, the Chilean government's share of pretax profits was only 16 percent. Furthermore, virtually all supplies were purchased from foreign sources; a high proportion of the employees were foreign and received salaries paid in foreign currency; and much of the output was shipped as low value-added concentrate.

Over time, countries have sought to increase their revenues. The first step has often been a change in tax laws, which could frequently be achieved without violating the original concession agreement. Increased taxes and retroactive taxation tend to create a climate of uncertainty, however, which reduces the level of production and the volume of investment. The copper industry in Chile offers a good example: the government share of pretax profits increased from 16 percent in 1930 to 28 percent in 1940, 58 percent in 1950, and 69 percent in 1965. During the period 1944–55, Chilean copper production dropped from 540,000 tons per year to 400,000 tons per year, while over the same period world copper production increased by 20 percent. In constant prices, government receipts declined, although they rose in current values because of the increase in copper prices. Virtually all profits from the U.S. affiliates in Chile and other Latin American countries were repatriated in the late 1960s, whereas in Canada, where a high degree of tax certainty and political stability prevailed, almost 50 percent of earnings were reinvested. Greater tax certainty is frequently a condition for increased investment, as illustrated in Chile by the Frei government agreement with the copper companies in the 1960s which provided a 20-year guarantee on tax rates as one of the conditions for considerable additional investment by the companies. Long-term tax agreements (later abrogated) in Ireland resulted in a major influx of mineral exploration and investment capital.

There is a limit to how far a government can use taxes to increase its share of revenues without becoming involved in the control of heretofore corporate prerogatives, since the variables determining the net profits to which the tax is applied are largely under the control of the corporation itself. The corporation normally starts out with considerable leeway over the size of depreciation, depletion, and amortization allowances; the option of either expensing or capitalizing exploration and development expenditures; and significant control over the price used to value the production, which is often an accounting item used for tax manipulation purposes.

GOVERNMENT INTERVENTION IN FOREIGN-OWNED COMPANIES

Most governments are aware that changes in accounting procedures and prices have a significant impact on tax receipts. Hence, they seek to participate in decisions on production levels, accounting practices, pricing, and marketing. In some cases governments have established an artificial exchange rate for the mineral sector, which has the effect of imposing an additional tax on the companies. Furthermore, governments may insist on posted prices for valuing exports and taxes, and require that additional processing of the raw material be carried out within their territory. Added to these restrictions on the companies' freedom of operation (as they perceive it) has been the increasing frequency of labor disruption, sometimes political in nature.

To reduce investment risks in the developing countries and sometimes to comply with legislation requiring varying degrees of domestic participation in resource projects, an increasing number of mining companies have been promoting private domestic participation or joint ventures with the government or government agencies. The object is to facilitate the conclusion of agreements with governments and to help assure their continued effectiveness over the long run. An even more recent approach—one that is particularly designed to minimize friction and disputes over the split of benefits—is the phaseout investment under which ownership and control by the foreign partner are phased out or substantially reduced in accordance with an agreed timetable. Mining companies are adapting to the situation and have recently indicated their willingness to provide technical and managerial assistance, principally in return for assured supplies.

The long-term contract approach pioneered by Japan has already gained wide acceptance; it is attractive to both sides, since it provides both security of supply and security of demand. Though seductive in its simplicity, however, the approach delivers less than it promises, for the security is neither long term nor of equal value to the partners. It is unlikely that in a dynamic world the terms and conditions agreed upon at the time of signature will remain satisfactory to both sides for the duration of the contract—which, in Japanese contracts, can run up to 20 years. For this reason, long-term contracts have been described as "no more than gentlemen's agreements to do business together;"[4] both sides must understand that renegotiation of terms cannot be avoided. Furthermore, experience with such arrangements is limited; although the current recession has put them to a severe test,[5] the big test is still to come. It remains to be seen how changed secular trends or structural adjustments —for instance, a significant downward revision of the growth rate of the Japanese economy, or the urgent desire to increase processing in the producing countries—will be reflected in renegotiation of existing contracts. Finally, while the security provided by long-term contracts goes a long way to reduce conflict and to accelerate the flow of technology and funds (as governments are more willing to make or guarantee loans), it does not address the problem of finding equity participation fully and directly. This problem and the attendant questions of, for example, equitable return on investment, security of investment, and transfer of earnings have to be addressed and solved simultaneously. Even achieving the limited objectives of long-term contracts requires prior and explicit agreement on a schedule for renegotiation and the areas open to renegotiation. It requires, above all, the narrowing of the confidence gap and the psychological abyss referred to earlier in the chapter.

In the longer run, joint venture and phaseout agreements and management contracts may become more common as the only effective and feasible solutions acceptable to both sides. However, they require that developing countries accept a much greater share of the responsibility and risks and contribute more of their own resources than they have in the past. A substantial degree of caution will also be required if the benefits hoped for are to outweigh the additional economic costs. Additional funds must be made available to host countries for private and public mineral investment, and the host country must know well in advance that it can count on these funds when it needs them. The source of these funds can be multilateral or bilateral aid agencies; the oil revenues of the OPEC countries could be used to this end if suitable channels can be established; and the banking and financial institutions may be willing to provide funds given satisfactory returns and guarantees. The policies of all these parties are not yet clear and need to be ascertained. Some compromises definitely need to be worked out in altering past policies, which attached greater importance to the financial strength of the multinational sponsor than to the viability of the project or the creditworthiness of the host government. This would strengthen the domestic bargaining position of developing countries and should result in agreements fair to both parties, not only at the time of negotiation but over the life of the agreement.[. . .]

THE PITFALLS OF FOREIGN AID

Expanded aid programs are clearly required because of the major exploration gap in the developing countries. While there are many examples of excellent past or ongoing aid programs by multilateral and bilateral agencies, however, some of the aid now provided is inefficient and ineffective. Some of it is poorly designed and planned and even more poorly implemented; lack of coordination between the various aid agencies is common, duplication of effort noticeable, and cost frequently unnecessarily high.

The shortcomings of aid programs have been the subject of regular attention by the UN Committee on Natural Resources which has had "the coordination of programs within the United Nations system in the field of natural resource development" as a permanent item on its agenda for several sessions. While considerable progress in this area is reported, "drawing a comprehensive plan of action" for this purpose—a long-standing objective—has eluded the committee so far.[6] There are encouraging signs that the problems are becoming widely recognized by technical experts from both donor and recipient countries and, equally important, that the experts are willing to talk about them candidly. A recent example is provided by the International Workshop on Earth Science Aid to Developing Countries held at Memorial University, St. John's, Newfoundland, in May 1974.[7]

Many experts at the workshop pointed out that response to requests for assistance is generally not as rapid as it should be because of red tape in donor and recipient organizations. Delays of several years between initial requests and inception of programs are far too common. Many of the aid programs are being handled by agencies "locked into the format of their own paperwork." The earth scientists who work with them should be constantly trying to adapt to new changes in Third World conditions "otherwise we are trying to solve what are really tomorrow's problems with yesterday's tools, and worse yet with yesterday's paperwork!"[8]

Effectiveness of the aid is sometimes diluted by actions of the recipient. The use of counterparts to supplement the foreign experts, frequently required for external or internal reasons, can have a major influence. Equipment may be badly treated and operated, geologists may introduce ploys to avoid going to the field, misinterpret data, and do substandard work. The reason generally is not laziness, as is often claimed, but lack of motivation (because of inadequate pay which forces professionals to hold down two or more jobs), lack of opportunity to gain experience and competence, lack of equipment and facilities, and especially the social norms of some host countries. A clean hands attitude in many countries makes the job of sweating up a ladder as a shift boss or braving the elements as a field geologist unattractive. This is a major problem, since efficient exploration requires highly qualified and experienced geologists in the field; a good geologist can make the difference between a discovery and an unsuccessful exploration program. Furthermore, the selection of counterpart staff may be based more on political than technical grounds.

The training part of the aid is often overplayed and misdirected. Too often it provides fellowships for graduate study by professionals, most of whom would be better served with practical on-the-job training. Many fellows do not return home, and those countries with the greatest need for a cadre of experts have no candidates qualified for the fellowship programs as designed. Restructuring the training to serve the long-term needs of the sector rather than the immediate project requirements would ensure better use of the funds. Practical training of skilled labor and subprofessionals can have immense long-term benefits.

The unavailability of counterpart financing and contribution in kind causes significant delays in aid programs. This touches on the real objectives of some of the aid programs as perceived by the donor. In many cases aid has been provided without regard to the benefits to, or the aspirations of, the recipient. The construction of uneconomic, small-scale smelters, the development of underground deposits in place of more competitive surface deposits, and exploration programs geared to specific minerals (often those needed by the bilateral donor) rather than a broader program more useful to host governments are all examples of less than honest aid programs.

By and large, insufficient care is given to adapting the aid program, particularly the technology, to local conditions. To illustrate, in many of the developed countries the large-scale geological map has often provided the takeoff for detailed exploration. For the poorer nations, however, such maps are a luxury they cannot afford and accelerators have to be sought which, though perhaps not technically as satisfactory, can develop sufficient data to attract the needed capital fairly quickly. Similarly, making airborne geophysical measurements over very large areas is entirely reasonable in a developed country with plentiful capital, but to do so over tropical rainforest burdens the government with the impossible and expensive task of follow-up work on the ground, without which the airborne data cannot be interpreted and would go to waste. Groups often promote major regional geophysical surveys without mention of the time-consuming and costly follow-up work required.

Under most ot the aid programs the cost of expertise is very high, sometimes up to three times what the expert earns at home. Hence, since most programs are financed by loan, even though on soft terms, the developing country often does not get a bargain. In fact, exploration costs in the developing countries are often considerably higher than in the developed ones. Many programs also seem more geared to providing the expert with data for a doctoral thesis than to mineral development.

This raises the question whether some of the aid agencies are as deficient as the multinationals in social consciousness. As emphasized above, many of the former's aid programs are ill conceived and designed for phases so preliminary that the end product cannot support economic development decisions. The multinationals are much more investment oriented. The aid agencies, bilateral and multilateral, are often too rigid in their approach and their procedures too bureaucratic to service the needs of the developing country.

Vast improvements in aid to the developing countries for mineral sector development can be realized by coordinating the activities of the various parties, the bilateral and multilateral agencies, the multinationals, the national agencies, and local mining industry. This requires preparation of a sector development strategy, a conscious determination by the host government to implement this strategy, and good administration. Many developing countries unfortunately do not have the expertise or resources to prepare, implement, or administer such strategy. One of the other parties therefore has to take the lead in a professional, unbiased manner.

Mineral sector development, especially the promotion of exploration by the host government, requires funds from sources other than the traditional multinationals. Most developing countries can ill afford to supply these funds from their own coffers—which leaves the multilateral and bilateral aid agencies as possible sources. The use of these sources, however, can have many pitfalls; developing countries should be cognizant of them and incorporate appropriate safeguards. Nevertheless, in our opinion, a major increase in multilateral and bilateral aid is needed to promote mineral exploration and development in the developing countries.

It is also of paramount importance not to overlook the already significant opportunities for cooperation among the developing countries, not only in training and research and development, where joint facilities may be established, but in all areas, including processing, where economies of scale and similarity of problems or community of interests may make them logical long-term partners. Other opportunities for such cooperation will be cited in the next chapter. Here, too, aid agencies and the UN regional commissions can play a useful role as catalysts.

Finally, both bilateral and multilateral programs have a role to play, and each has its different advantages. As noted in the proceedings of St. John's Workshop, bilateral programs often give more control over projects to the recipient country and are thus especially useful in aiding institutions. On the other hand, they are more subject to the political views of the donor's country; tied to the donor's products, equipment, or personnel; and too little concerned with the follow-up stage. Multilateral programs are bound to be relatively apolitical and thus perhaps best suited to large mineral exploration projects, but a common criticism is that they are often less precise and well-planned than bilateral projects and suffer from the differences in background of the team members. Obviously, "there can be no single blueprint for aid to developing countries."[9]

NOTES

1. *Foreign Investment in Copper Mining* (Baltimore and London: Johns Hopkins University Press, 1975) p. xxii. See also Mikesell's earlier, authoritative work on the subject, *Foreign Investment in the Petroleum and Mineral Industries* (Baltimore and London: Johns Hopkins University Press for Resources for the Future, 1971). With regard to the Bougainville project in Papua New Guinea, the remarkably high profitability of the early years which brought about this pressure was largely due to the outstanding engineering and administrative performance of the company. A less satisfactory or even average performance by the company would have resulted in the mine's coming on stream with a long delay, missing the abnormally high copper prices of recent years, turning in average returns, and reducing government reaction.

2. Alun G. Davies, *Taxation and Incentives* (paper prepared for the UN Interregional Workshop on Negotiation and Drafting of Mining Development Agreements, Buenos Aires, November 2–18, 1973) (ESA/RT/AC.7/9) (New York, September 27, 1973), p. 2.

3. John S. Carman, "Notes on Impediments to Mining Investments in the Developing World" (prepared for the Meeting of the Association of Geoscientists for International Development, Bagauda, Nigeria, September 1975; processed), p. 18.

4. Bension Varon, "Coke and Coking Coal Availabilities: A Potential Problem or Not?" World Bank Staff Working Paper, no. 124 (Washington D.C., January 1972), p. 21.

5. Japan's difficulty in taking delivery of contracted quantities, especially of copper, in the recessionary conditions of 1974–75—despite its sincerity and vested interest in respecting the agreement—led it to renege on its iron ore contracts with Australia and to sanction the export of copper metal, which depressed world copper prices even further.

6. See United Nations, Committee on Natural Resources, *Report on the Fourth Session* (March 24–April 4, 1975) (E/5663, E/C.7/56) (ESCOR, 59th sess., supp. no. 3), p. 32.

7. For the proceedings, see A. R. Berger (ed.), *Geoscientists and the Third World: A Collective Critique of Existing Aid Programs*, Geological Survey of Canada, Paper 34–57, 1975.

8. Ibid., p. 7.

9. Ibid., p. 4.

33

Potentially Recoverable Resources: How Recoverable?

F. E. Trainer

The sudden price rises of oil and other commodities in the early 1970s fueled an extensive literature on world resource depletions. However, by the later 1970s earlier worries were generally regarded to have been unfounded. In part this reaction was justifiably strengthened by attention to the initially neglected distinction between reserves and resources. For instance, the discussion in *The Limits to Growth* by Meadows et al. was carried out only in terms of reserves, and critics were quick to point out that reserve figures give little or no clue to the quantity of potentially recoverable resources. It was also argued that since the earth is largely made up of minerals there is a sense in which we shall never run out of them, and this argument seemed to convert the problem into a challenge that technical advance might continue to meet.

This paper argues that the recent optimistic climate is seen to be challengeable when attention is focused on estimates of potentially recoverable resources, trends in energy costs, discovery rates and investment in mineral industries, and on the prospects for extending the high material living standards of the developed countries to the underdeveloped world.

ESTIMATES OF POTENTIALLY RECOVERABLE RESOURCES

Estimates of quantities of potentially recoverable resources of commonly used minerals became available in the 1970s (Table 1). The figures must be regarded as imprecise at the current stage of geological knowl-

Reprint of "Potentially Recoverable Resources: How Recoverable?" by F. E. Trainer in *Resources Policy* (Vol. 8, No. 1, March 1982). Reprinted by permission of the author and Butterworth Scientific Ltd., Guildford, UK. Pp. 41–42.

TABLE 1 Estimates of Potentially Recoverable Mineral Resources

Minerals	Estimates (tons)				
	Rajaraman	MIMIC	USGS	CDS	Skinner
Aluminum		24×10^{12}	3.5×10^{12}		
Antimony		150×10^{6}	19×10^{6}	5×10^{6}	
Barium		12×10^{10}	1.7×10^{10}	1.8×10^{9}	
Bauxite				38×10^{9}	
Beryllium		6×10^{8}	64×10^{6}		
Bismuth		9×10^{5}	0.12×10^{6}		
Chrome	$2{,}001 \times 10^{6}$	24×10^{9}	3.3×10^{9}	8.1×10^{9}	
Cobalt		6×10^{9}	760×10^{6}	4.5×10^{6}	
Copper	$1{,}323 \times 10^{6}$	15×10^{9}	$2{,}100 \times 10^{6}$	$1{,}456 \times 10^{6}$	$1{,}000 \times 10^{6}$
Fluorine	368×10^{6}	15×10^{10}	2×10^{10}		
Gold		12×10^{5}	0.15×10^{6}		34,000
Iron		15×10^{12}	2×10^{12}	720×10^{9}	
Lead	$1{,}668 \times 10^{6}$	3×10^{9}	5.5×10^{6}	1.35×10^{9}	170×10^{6}
Lithium		6×10^{9}	930×10^{6}	7.8×10^{6}	
Manganese		3×10^{11}	4.2×10^{10}		
Mercury		24×10^{6}	3.4×10^{6}		340,000
Molybdenum		3×10^{8}	47×10^{6}	107×10^{9}	20×10^{6}
Nickel		18×10^{9}	$2{,}600 \times 10^{6}$	129×10^{6}	$1{,}200 \times 10^{6}$
Niobium		6×10^{9}	850×10^{6}		340×10^{6}
Phosphorus		3×10^{11}	5.1×10^{10}		
Platinum		6×10^{6}	1.2×10^{6}	44,950	84,000
Selenium		18×10^{6}	2.5×10^{6}		
Silver		21×10^{6}	2.8×10^{6}		1.3×10^{6}
Tantalum		6×10^{6}	97×10^{6}		40×10^{6}
Tellurium		0.12×10^{6}	0.015×10^{6}		
Tin		6×10^{8}	68×10^{6}		25×10^{6}
Titanium		15×10^{11}	2.3×10^{11}		
Tungsten		3×10^{8}	51×10^{6}		17×10^{6}
Vanadium		3×10^{10}	$5{,}100 \times 10^{6}$		
Zinc	$5{,}045 \times 10^{6}$	24×10^{9}	$3{,}400 \times 10^{6}$	$4{,}500 \times 10^{6}$	

Sources: I. Rajaraman, "Non-renewable resources; a review of long-term projections," *Futures*, Vol 8, No 3, June 1976, pp. 228–242. MIMIC high and low estimates are given in D. Gabor, *Beyond the Age of Waste*, Pergamon, Oxford, 1978. The MIMIC estimates were originally stated in terms of a range with a low figure and a high figure 10 times as great. For convenience of comparison the geometric means of these ranges have been given here. (A depth of 2.5 km and three times present extraction costs are assumed.) USGS estimates are from R. L. Erikson, "Crustal abundance of elements and mineral reserves and resources," in D. A. Bobst and W. P. Pratt, eds, *United States Mineral Resources*, Geological Survey Professional Paper 820, US Government Printing Office, Washington, DC, 1973. (A depth of 1 km and present extraction costs are assumed.) *Commodity Data Summaries* of the U.S. Bureau of Mines, 1976. B. J. Skinner, "A second iron age ahead?" *American Scientist*, May/June 1976, pp. 258–269 (a depth of 10 km under continents is assumed).

edge. They are derived from estimates of the abundance of the various minerals in the earth's crust and in general they reflect the assumption that 0.01–0.1 percent of the quantity of a mineral in the top kilometer of the crust has been concentrated to form an ore that could be refined economically assuming present costs. B. J. Skinner argues for a figure of 0.001–0.01 percent on the basis of the analysis put forward by the American National Academy of Science's Committee on Mineral Resources and the Environment. (This is the main reason why his estimates in Table 1 are lower than the others.) The U.S. Geological Survey's (USGS) figures take into account all recoverable material to a depth of 1 kilometer in the crust, the MIMIC figures assume a depth of 2.5 kilometers, and Skinner assumes 10 kilometers under the continental crust. Some estimates include materials up to three times present extraction costs per unit, and others assume only present costs. On average the highest figures in Table 1 (MIMIC) are about 30 times the lowest figures (Skinner). For the purpose of the following discussion, reference is made primarily to the USGS estimates, which are the most frequently quoted resource figures.

WHAT PROPORTION OF RESOURCES ARE LIKELY TO BE RETRIEVED?

There are three main reasons why recoverable resource figures state quantities that are probably much greater than those ever likely to be obtained. These figures refer to the probable quantities of minerals existing in deposits of ores that are sufficiently rich to process; they do not take into account the probability of finding these deposits. The USGS figures include all deposits anywhere in the crust to a depth of 1 kilometer, including those parts of the crust under the oceans (70 percent of the earth's surface), under the poles, under mountain ranges, under cities, and in other regions where discovery would be very difficult and costly. There is at present no way of estimating what fraction of these totals we shall find, since this depends on unpredictable factors such as technical advance. However, when one reflects on the task of locating all mineable deposits up to 1 kilometer below oceans, poles, mountains, etc., the prospects of finding more than a small proportion of the quantities that exist seem remote.

> It is difficult to convey to someone who is not a geologist the magnitude of the problem of finding a mineral deposit, even in a favourable region. To find near-surface deposits beneath the cover of glacial debris and the endless coniferous forests of Canada or beneath twenty metres of lateritic soil in tropical Africa is an awe-inspiring task. To expect to be able to find a deposit . . .

> located hundreds of metres below bedrock surfaces, implies an extraordinary faith in exploration methods.[1]

Similarly, total recoverable resource figures must be tempered to take into account the fact that many of the deposits that might be found will be in locations where it will be extremely difficult or impossible to mine.

The third limiting factor is that many deposits are of ores rich enough to refine but too small in total quantity of mineral contained in the deposit to warrant the digging of a mine at that site. For instance, it would not pay to dig up pure gold golf balls if they were located 1 kilometer apart at a depth of 1 kilometer. The potential significance of this factor can be seen in the way it drastically reduces probable yields from seafloor deposits of manganese nodules. Although there could be hundreds of billions of tons of copper, manganese, nickel, and cobalt in these deposits, it might not be economic to gather them from sites where the distribution is such that less than 1 to 3 million tons can be collected each year. According to the Canadian Department of Energy, Mines and Resources, there might be only five sites with a higher annual yield than this. If so, the yield would be about 1 percent of the 400 million tons per year some have anticipated on the basis of World Bank predictions. Similarly, oil deposits discovered within the Eromanga Basin in the center of Australia will not be economic to develop unless they are large enough to yield at least 13 million barrels.

Unfortunately, there is as yet no way of predicting much about the geographical distribution of deposits containing various quantities of minerals. It is generally assumed that the distribution of deposits according to size is lognormal, i.e., that most deposits are relatively small in quantity and only a few are large. It is therefore likely that a considerable proportion of the recoverable deposits that will be found and that are of ore grades rich enough to process economically will remain unavailable to us because they contain too little material to warrant constructing a mine at the site.

These three factors indicate that the quantities of minerals we retrieve could end up being only a small fraction of the quantities that exist in ores of grades that are rich enough to process; i.e., the quantities represented in Table 1.

HOW MUCH GREATER THAN RESERVES ARE RESOURCES?

The three factors noted above indicate that reserves plus past use will never approach a high proportion of the total recoverable resource base. This would not be disturbing if the total recoverable resource figures were vastly greater than reserve figures, but in most cases this is not so. For 11 of the 29 items for which information is available, USGS figures on recoverable resources are less than 10 times reserve figures. For only seven of the items are estimated resources more than 50 times presently known and economic reserves. Should the difficulty of finding resources and of mining them economically effectively prohibit access to 50 percent of the total recoverable resources that exist, then in the case of one-third of commonly used minerals we can not expect to increase present reserves more than five-fold. However, as Meadows et al. show, if reserves were increased to five times their present quantities in most cases this would only add a few decades to their lifetimes, assuming use of resources continues to increase at rates characteristic of the recent past. Meadows et al. present information on seven of the 11 minerals for which reserves are more than one-tenth of USGS resource figures, and they show that, on average, five times present reserves of these minerals would last 77 years.

If on average we can retrieve no more than 20 percent of the potentially recoverable resources, then for 16 of the 27 items under discussion the ration of reserves to "actually recoverable" resources is higher than 1:5 (and for another eight it is between 1:5 and 1:10). In other words, if 20 percent of potentially recoverable resources is the attainable limit, then for most of the commonly used minerals reserves cannot be increased more than fivefold and effective exhaustion will occur well within a century at present rates of increase in use.

PAY A LITTLE MORE AND GET A LOT MORE?

The foregoing discussion has been about quantities of minerals that might be obtained economically assuming current costs. Greater quantities will be accessible if higher costs are accepted. The MIMIC figures in Table 1 assume extraction costs of up to three times present costs, and if these figures are divided by 2.5 (to take into account the fact that they refer to a 2.5 km depth in the crust), we arrive at the rough approximation that accepting a trebling of costs might treble recoverable resources. The fact that minerals now account for a relatively small proportion of the GNP of developed nations might be taken to mean that we could afford large increases in minerals costs and therefore that potentially recoverable resources can be greatly increased without much difficulty. Unfortunately this conclusion could be quite mistaken.

It is commonly assumed that all we have to do at any point in time to increase supplies of any mineral is to move to slightly poorer grades of ore. There are a number of factors making the situation more complicated and difficult than this suggests. What is often not realized is that movement towards poorer ores will reach a point where catastrophic increases in energy costs start to occur. Just having to mine the greater quantity of ore produces [a very steep] energy cost curve of the sort represented in Figure 1. In addition, poorer ores require finer grinding to release minerals, and a higher percentage of contained minerals remain unreleased. Both of these factors mean that more energy is required per ton of mineral eventually retrieved.

With most minerals we are not close to the point where energy costs start to rise [exponentially], but current increases in costs are anything but negligible. In fact, the evidence outlined below indicates that in general the energy cost per ton for minerals produced in the United States might be increasing at well in excess of 2 percent per annum. Continuation of even a 2 percent per annum rate of increase would mean that energy costs per ton of minerals would treble by early in the twenty-first century. If this happened, the MIMIC resource figures might have to be thought of as being associated with around a ninefold increase in real costs rather than a threefold increase.[2]

The idea of continually moving to poorer ores also assumes that the high-grade ores which are currently being mined are comparatively rare. Unfortunately that distribution is probably typical of only a few geochemically abundant minerals such as iron, aluminum, magnesium, and titanium [which are represented in figure 2]. As Skinner and others have pointed out, present geochemical knowledge indicates that for the many

FIGURE 1 Relationship Between Ore Grade and Ore Tonnage Required to Produce One Ton of Metal.

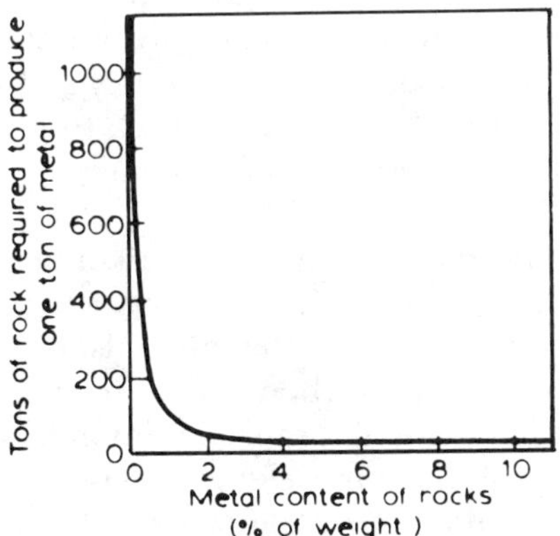

Source: N. J. Page and S. C. Creasey, "Ore grade, metal production and energy", *Journal of Research*, US Geological Survey, Vol 3, No 1, January/February 1975, p. 10.

FIGURE 2 Amount of Mineral Contained in Different Ore Grades (abundant minerals).

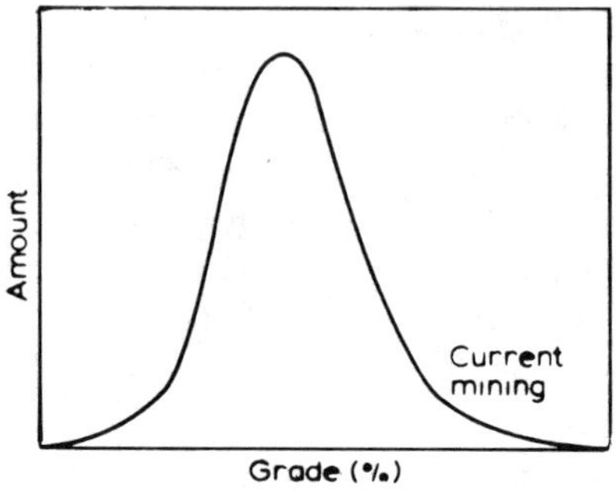

Source: B. J. Skinner, "A second iron age ahead", *American Scientist*, Vol 64, No 3, May/June 1976, pp. 258–269.

geochemically scarce minerals, the quantities at different ore grades are distributed as in Figure 3.

This means that the small proportion of the earth's minerals existing in deposits tends to be in concentrations well above the concentrations of these minerals in common rock, and that when these deposits have been worked out there will be few others richer than the extremely low concentrations in common rock. For example, the concentrations of copper, nickel, zinc, and tin now worked are, respectively, at least 56, 100, 370, and 2,000 times greater than the concentrations of these metals in common rock. To mine and refine common rock to retrieve these minerals would require many times the amounts of energy presently required per unit of mineral.

Unfortunately there are other factors likely to increase the energy cost of obtaining minerals after the relatively small quantities in ore deposits have been used up. Most of the minerals in the crust exist in common rock in a quite different chemical state to those that have been concentrated in ore deposits. The most common form of occurrence is as silicates, which require much more enegy to process than oxides or sulphides (the forms in which more concentrated ore deposits tend to occur). For these two reasons releasing a given quantity of metal from these sources can take 100 to 1,000 times as much energy as it takes to release them from ores now worked.[3]

These considerations indicate that reserves cannot be continually increased simply by accepting slightly higher costs. If we use up the relatively small proportion of most minerals that have been concentrated

FIGURE 3 Amount of Mineral Contained in Different Ore Grades (scarce minerals).

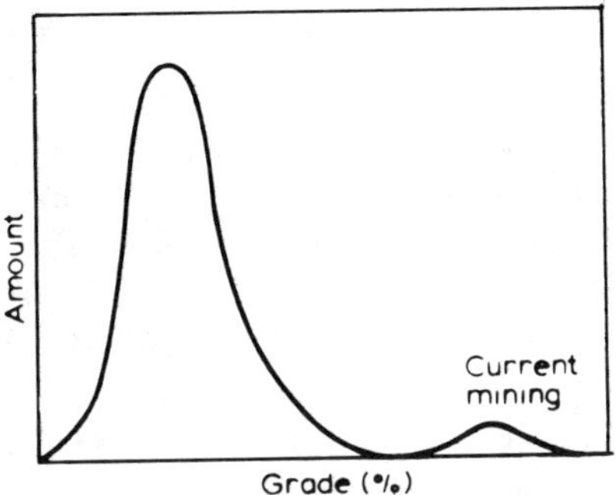

Source: B. J. Skinner, "A second iron age ahead", *American Scientist*, Vol 64, No 3, May/June 1976, pp. 258–269.

into ore deposits, it will become far too costly in terms of energy to produce them for most purposes. The key question is how long it will take to exhaust these deposits. Clear answers cannot be given because we have no confident idea of the shapes of the various distributions of quantities of minerals at different grades below those now being worked; i.e., we do not know how big the small humps represented in Figure 3 might be. Skinner believes that we will have exhausted these deposits for all but the few geochemically abundant minerals within 100 years and possibly within 50 years.

Skinner's solution is to recommend that we develop ways of relying mainly on the few abundant minerals. He does not discuss whether an industrial society could do this easily. Each year we now use around 35 million tons of the geochemically scarce minerals (i.e., excluding iron, aluminum, phosphates, oil, and coal) and many of these have properties and functions that make substitution difficult, costly, and in some cases impossible. Serious energy problems might still have to be faced even if we can make do with the abundant minerals. First, many of the substitutes adopted will involve increased energy costs. For example, aluminum is an effective replacement for many electrical uses of copper, but the energy cost per ton is higher than for copper. Even steel involves about a 50 percent higher energy cost than lead, zinc, and tin. Plastics can replace many nonferrous metal functions, e.g., plastic-coated iron plate can substitute for galvanized iron, but the energy cost of plastics is around 50 percent higher than steel and 100 percent higher than zinc.

More importantly, the energy costs of producing even the geochemically abundant minerals are rising and there are reasons for concern about the levels these trends will reach in coming years.

RECENT TRENDS IN ENERGY COSTS OF MINERAL PRODUCTION

Although most of the discontinuous factors mentioned in the previous section will not be fully encountered for some time, marked rises in energy costs of various aspects of mineral production in the United States seem to be occurring. According to Chapman: "Over the past 50 years the annual output tonnage of all U.S. mines has increased by about 50% whereas the annual fuel consumption has increased by 600% in the past 25 years."

Available Census of Mineral Industries figures show that between 1940 and 1963 the installed horsepower in U.S. mines increased by 280 percent, but the quantities of bauxite, nonferrous metals, and coal produced increased by only 153 percent, 6 percent, and 20 percent, respectively, and iron ore production fell by 2.5 percent.

Analysis of figures given in the Census of Manufacturers shows that from 1939 to 1972 energy used in U.S. metal mining increased by 240 percent. Yet the production of iron ore, the item which carries by far the most weight, fell 0.7 percent. Bauxite production rose 230 percent in the period, but it totalled only one-fortieth of iron ore production. Energy used in all mineral industries increased by 250 percent in the period, but increases in the output of the two dominant items, iron and coal, were only 120 percent and 17 percent.[4] Nonferrous metal production increased 82 percent (28 percent excluding aluminum).

Census of Manufacturers figures from 1954 to 1967 show that energy consumed in primary mineral industries over the period rose by 35 percent. *Mineral Yearbook* and *Commodity Data Summaries* data show that corresponding changes in output were as follows: steel increased 15 percent; iron ore fell 10 percent; aluminum increased 92 percent; and other nonferrous metal production increased 24 percent. It should be noted that imports of iron ore and bauxite were high, and that had U.S. ores been used energy consumption in the production of aluminum and steel would have been higher. Figures for the period 1972 to 1976 showed a 42 percent rise in energy used in primary mineral industries associated with the following changes in production: a 3.4 percent rise in iron ore; a 4 percent fall in raw steel; a 3 percent rise in aluminum; and a 4 percent fall in nonferrous metals excluding aluminum.[5]

Information on energy costs associated with the production of particular items is more difficult to come by and to interpret, especially since it is not easy to separate the effects of the use of large proportions of imported ores. These ores tend to be of higher grades than ores mined in the United States and hence energy cost trends in the more heavily mined countries are obscured. Information on metal production given in U.S. Department of Commerce publications yields conflicting and ambiguous impressions. Information in these publications on ore production in the United States is much more meaningful. Between 1963 and 1972, expenditure of energy per ton of copper ore produced in the United States rose by 33 percent. For iron ore the rise was 57 percent. For bauxite there was a fall of 9 percent. Gelb has published figures indicating that energy costs per ton for copper, iron, and bauxite produced in the United States between 1954 and 1972 increased 85 percent, 113 percent, and 78 percent, respectively.[6]

These figures yield six clear estimates of rates of increase in energy costs of particular minerals, averaging 3.95 percent per annum. They yield another 17 indirect estimates—i.e., those derived by comparing overall energy use in mineral production with production of specific minerals—and these average 4.4 percent per annum. These are all average annual increases; estimated exponential rates of increase would be lower. Even an exponential increase as low as 2 percent per annum would generate serious energy problems in a few decades, given that in the mid-1970s about 16 percent of U.S. energy use could be attributed to minerals production.[7]

Brown expects the fraction of U.S. energy consumption accounted for by mineral industries to rise to one-third by the end of this century, and Govett and Govett point out that rising energy and capital costs are now reducing reserves by making some known deposits too costly to mine: ". . . a few years ago ores with less than 0.4% copper were mineable but this is no longer true at today's copper prices due to the recent escalation of capital and energy costs." Admittedly these figures refer to the United States where ore grades are now likely to be much lower than in many areas in the relatively unexplored Third World. It does not follow that we can look forward to inevitably lower energy costs associated with the latter sources. Much depends on problems of infrastructure development, transport difficulties and costs, political instability, and other factors which may outweigh advantages due to higher ore grades.

Interpretation of these rising trends in energy costs is complicated by the fact that U.S. mineral industries have been replacing labor with machines. It is difficult to determine the extent to which rising energy costs are due to the need to search harder for minerals and to deal with deteriorating ore grades and the extent to which energy costs have risen with mechanization. Although it does not throw unambiguous light on the question, it is interesting that a 20 percent increase in output of iron ore per employee over the period 1946–72 has been associated with approximately five times as big an increase in energy use per ton of ore produced in the United States.

Some reference should be made here to the argument that the overall energy cost of minerals is not likely to rise much because 85 percent of the world's mineral production by weight is accounted for by a few geochemically abundant items such as iron, cement, and aluminum. In 1976 world iron production was 887 million tons, aluminum 12.8 million tons, and all other nonferrous minerals about 35 million tons. Goeller and Weinberg argue that we shall have access to virtually inexhaustible reserves of iron, aluminum, titanium, and magnesium at grades that do not require much more energy than those now worked. This argument assumes that the distribution of quantities of the abundant minerals at different grades will be found to bulge to virtually inexhaustible amounts at grades slightly below those now being worked. Unfortunately the distribution of quantities at grades between those now worked and crustal abundance is largely unknown. Admittedly the concentrations of iron and aluminum in the crust are high relative to the ores now used. The multiples are one-half to one-quarter in the case of iron, and one-third to one-sixth in the case of aluminum, which suggests that we should always be able to obtain large quantities of these minerals if we can afford up to four or six times the energy per ton that we now pay.[8] However, in the case of titanium and magnesium the ratio between concentrations in the crust and present cut-off ore grades are 1:16 and 1:350, respectively, leaving considerable scope for the existence of grade/tonnage distributions which could produce energy costs per ton many times present levels.

Roberts puts forward a similar argument to the effect that dollar costs of minerals are unlikely to multiply by more than a factor of 2. The heavy weighting that a few items like iron, cement, and aluminum have in the total energy cost sum means that the cost of all the nonferrous metals could actually increase by a factor of 17 (not just 5 to 10 as Roberts states) before the average price of metals would double. Neither Roberts nor Goeller and Weinberg confront the argument that there are good reasons for expecting the prices of a number of minerals to multiply many times before long, and that this could make these particular items too expensive to use, regardless of the small effects these rises might have on the total cost of minerals. For example, copper at $6 per kg can be used for guttering at present, but if its price multiplied 17 times to $102 per kg it would in effect have ceased to be available for this purpose and it would be no consolation to know that the price of minerals as a whole had barely doubled.

DISCOVERY COSTS

Worsening trends are also evident with respect to discovery rates and the costs of discovery. Govett and Govett point out that: "In the more carefully prospected areas of the world the discovery rate has already fallen drastically," and they have noted elsewhere that there has been "an alarming escalation in the cost of finding a new economic metallic deposit." These generalizations can be illustrated by evidence from Canada and the United States, both resource-rich countries. Over the period 1951–70 discovery costs rose from 0.6 percent to 2 percent of the value of minerals discovered in Canada. The corresponding figure for the western United States rose from 1 percent to 2.2 percent between 1955 and 1969.

Despite a fivefold increase in expenditure on exploration in Canada between 1946 and 1971, the value of discoveries per year has not increased since 1955 and reserves have only been increased by 50 percent. The cost per deposit discovered rose by a factor of 13 and costs per unit of ore discovered doubled. Connolly and Perlman have stated Canadian discovery costs to be 4 percent of the value of production and growing at 4 percent per year. Although this is still a small percentage of mineral costs, the rate of increase is quite high, with costs doubling every 18 years.[9]

The U.S. National Academy of Science's publication *Mineral Resources and the Environment* concludes that ten- to twentyfold increases in present discovery costs are probable as we move from the present "second phase" of mineral discovery into a "third phase" which will have to use sophisticated techniques capable of much more searching exploration than is now carried out.

Much less exploratory activity has been carried out in the Third World than in the industrialized countries and this is sometimes taken to imply that large discoveries can be expected when activity is eventually increased. Geologists tend not to be so enthusiastic about this possibility. For instance, Govett and Govett say that, even assuming large exploratory efforts in the relatively unexplored Third World, the possibility of discovering major metallogenic provinces is limited. The USGS claims that ". . . for *conventional* types of deposits there are only a limited number of important minerals—titanium, phosphorus, copper and nickel—for which there is a very strong probability of finding totally new unknown mineralised districts."

INVESTMENT TRENDS

Similar worrying trends can be seen in recent figures on mining investment and capital costs. When figures for 1963 and 1977 are compared, annual investment in U.S. mining can be seen to have increased by 130 percent (in constant dollars), but output measured by tonnage increased by only 38 percent (33 percent if coal is omitted). In the same period U.S. gross private domestic investment increased by 100 percent and GNP increased by 75 percent in real terms. Investment in iron and steel production rose 48 percent, but production of pig iron increased 11.3 percent, production of steel increased 6.6 percent, and production of iron ore increased only 5 percent.[10] The rate of increase in investment in nonferrous metals over the period 1963–76 was five times the rate for all U.S. investment, yet production (excluding aluminum) increased to only 1.28 times 1963 production. Aluminum production increased 1.8 times. Nonferrous metal investment actually increased at a rate 50 percent faster than petroleum investment.[11]

These figures indicate that mining investment is yielding sharply diminishing returns in terms of quantities produced. Unfortunately interpretation is again complicated by the fact that some proportion of the increase in investment will have been due to the replacement of labor by machines.

"BUSINESS AS USUAL"

It can be argued that the early 1970s marked a point of change from an era of cheap and abundant resources to an era of scarcity. The real prices of many minerals and raw materials showed long-term reductions until the 1960s, but since then significant rises have occurred. For instance, between 1960 and 1975 the real costs of chrome, tin, platinum, and zinc rose by 200–300 percent, and the prices of aluminum, copper, and nickel rose by 52 percent, 100 percent, and 174 percent, respectively. Writing in 1979, Peterson and Maxwell commented that: "Practically all major mineral commodities have reached or passed their price trough; their real price is therefore likely to rise in the future." From here on technical advances are not expected to keep up with increasing energy costs. The Worldwatch Institute argues that the rise in mineral prices must be among the basic causes of the high rates of inflation that have set in over the last decade.

The evidence summarized above indicates that early in the twenty-first century these rising trends in real costs could reach levels at which supplies are in effect seriously curtailed, despite the fact that vast quantities of potentially recoverable resources remain within the crust. In other words, primarily because of the disposition of minerals within the crust and rising energy costs, it is quite possible that a large proportion of potentially recoverable resources will not be recovered. Prospects are even more problematic when one takes into account factors not dealt with in this paper, especially the environmental costs of mineral industries, potential difficulties surrounding total energy supply, continued growth in per capita demand in developed countries, and the possibility of more restricted access to Third World minerals.

The Significance of the Third World

Almost all discussions of mineral resource availability have concerned themselves only with the question of whether "business as usual" can continue for the foreseeable future. "Business as usual" is a situation in which the few developed countries account for most of the world's annual resource consumption and in which their per capita resource use is 10 to 20 times that of most countries in the Third World. In the case of energy, the U.S. per capita use is approximately 62 times that of India and 331 times that of Ethiopia. The developed countries now import one-third to one-half of their minerals from underdeveloped countries (up to 70 percent of their raw materials when agricultural produce is included). This percentage is increasing and it is likely to go on increasing.

In some cases current consumption and production figures obscure the fact that the developed countries have considerable quantities of resources left at lower grades than it is economic to import, but the general trends are ominous. The developed countries have used up their deposits of the richest and most accessible ores and are now using increasing quantities of the reserves in the Third World. For instance, the world average grade of copper ores currently mined is in the region of 1.5 percent copper, but the average grade being processed in the United States is approximately 0.53 percent copper, having fallen from 4 percent in 1900.

The political future of South Africa is especially important in the discussion of resource access for the developed nations. South Africa now supplies 42 percent of world manganese, 74 percent of chrome, 47 percent of platinum metals, 60 percent of vanadium, 12 percent of diamonds, 56 percent of gold, 14 percent of arsenic, 45 percent of gemstones, 10 percent of germanium, 33 percent of kyanite (excluding U.S. contribution, not published), 14 percent of lithium (excluding U.S. contribution), and 40 percent of vermiculate (excluding communist countries). South Africa's proportion of world reserves of platinum, chrome, vanadium, and manganese is higher than the above proportions for its share of production.

If South Africa's apartheid problem leads to either a Soviet-aligned black revolutionary government or to a collapse of industrial and mining output, the above quantities might have to be transferred from the developed to the underdeveloped list of nations and serious reductions might occur in supplies of these minerals to the industrialized economies.

Perhaps the most sobering theme in this area concerns the virtual impossibility of everyone in the Third World ever sharing the per capita material living standards typical of the developed countries. UN and other population projections made in the early 1970s indicated that world population will probably stabilize after 2050 at about 12 billion (more recent estimates point to a somewhat lower figure). The UN's high projection was 15.8 billion. If mineral production was increased to the point where 12 billion people each consumed as much as each American did in the 1970s, the recoverable resources of 11 of the 24 most common minerals (as estimated by the USGS) would be exhausted before 2050. For instance, U.S. per capita consumption of lead in the 1970s was approximately 6 kg per annum; to supply 12 billion people with this quantity would require annual production of 72 million tons per annum. At this rate the recoverable resources estimated by the USGS, 550 million tons, would last only 7.6 years (this assumes that 100 percent of recoverable resources will be secured, despite the difficulties in finding and mining discussed above). If used by 12 billion people at 1970s U.S. per capita rates, coal resources (assumed at 7×10^{12} tons, a high estimate)[12] would last 193 years, petroleum (assumed at 2,000 billion barrels) would last about 5.7 years, and uranium (assumed at 4 million tons, not used in breeder reactors) would last 8.3 years. These figures ignore the proportion of the ultimately recoverable resource figure already consumed, approximately one-third in the case of petroleum. All these energy sources, plus shale oil (assumed at 6×10^{12} barrels), would last 34 to 74 years unless breeder reactors were used.

Another approach that comes to much the same conclusion is to ask what quantity of each mineral would have to be discovered each year to supply 12 billion people with mid-1970s per capita use year after year. If we take the discovery rate of 18 minerals over the period 1950–74 we find that for only one of them, chrome, would the required rate of discovery be less than it was in recent decades. Over the 27 most commonly used minerals the discovery rate would have to average 9.4 times what it was in the period 1950–74. The discovery rate seems to have risen in the 1970s, but for the 11 cases for which recent information was available the discovery rate for this period was still no more than one-seventh of what it would have to be. This means that if the standard of living of the West is to be extended to the anticipated world population of the mid-twenty-first century something like seven or nine times as much of each mineral would have to be discovered each year as has been found in the last few decades, and this would have to be repeated for as long as an affluent world society is to be kept running.

The foregoing exercises do not take into account the fact that the Western way of life is dedicated to endless growth in material living standards. What would the magnitude of the resource problem be if it is assumed that American per capita use of resources will increase over the period to 2050, and that in that year there will be 12 billion people each using as much as each American is then using? American per capita rates of consumption for items in Table 1 appear to have risen on average by more than 2 percent per year over the period 1963 to 1976. If this rate were to continue to 2050, American consumption per person would then be about four to six times what it was in 1976.[13] To supply 12 billion people with these levels of resource use would exhaust the total recoverable resource base for all but eight of the 27 items in the USGS estimates within 100 years (again assuming 100 percent recovery).

CONCLUSIONS

This analysis seems to show that there is no chance of everyone being able to live at anywhere near the material living standards that Americans had in the mid-1970s. In order to sustain the way of life of the developed countries as a model that all can aspire to, one must assume that the quantities taken into the above exercises are grossly in error. In particular, one must assume that recoverable resources are many times greater than the USGS figures and that we will find and be able to mine a high percentage of recoverable resources.

The question of whether we will run out of resources can, therefore, be seen to depend primarily on whether one envisages mere "business as usual" for the few developed nations, or whether everyone is to be raised to the material living standards taken for granted by people in the developed world. Even if any question of growth in the material living standards of the developed countries is ignored, and if it is assumed that a high proportion of the potentially recoverable resources will be recovered, there is little doubt that we will run out of accessible resources very quickly if the goal is to be the extension of Western living standards to the less developed countries. If this conclusion is correct, then the values and structures of the developed countries face fundamental moral challenges. In particular this conclusion reinforces the claim that pressing global problems such as the poverty and unsatisfactory development of the Third World, and especially the chances of serious international conflict, can only be ultimately resolved if affluence and growth are abandoned as basic values.

NOTES

1. G. J. S. Govett and M. H. Govett, *World Mineral Supplies*, Elsevier, Amsterdam, The Netherlands, 1976, p. 4.

2. The multiple would be lower to the extent that nonenergy costs per ton rose slower than energy costs. Many apparent nonenergy costs involve indirect energy costs; e.g., in the machinery produced by energy.

3. Skinner considers that this theory has a high probability of being correct.

4. The apparent discrepancy between this figure and the above figure for iron may be largely accounted for by the fact that the former figure is for ore as distinct from metal. The latter figure involves large imports of ore.

5. Apparent discontinuities between the figures for 1954 to 1976 and those from 1972 to 1976 suggest that different definitions or categories were involved. Hence the data have not been combined to yield conclusions for the period 1954 to 1976.

6. . . . Gelb's figures are in terms of Btu/dollar of production. The conclusions stated here have been derived from Gelb's data using additional information on the inflation rate and mineral prices for the relevant dates. The copper and iron conclusions align with those drawn above, but there is a major discrepancy regarding bauxite.

7. . . . A thorough analysis of the situation would also have to take into account the fact that considerable quantities of energy are used overseas in the production of minerals imported into the United States. For iron and aluminum (metal plus ores), among the largest items in terms of total energy consumed in mineral production, 30 percent and 85 percent used in the United States is imported.

8. . . . Cook believes that iron and aluminum are the only items for which energy costs would not become prohibitively high well before grades approaching energy abundance have to be used.

9. These figures derive from the period before the effects of the 1970s oil price increases had been felt on exploration costs.

10. Investment rose smoothly throughout the period; the conclusions arrived at here do not result from the selection of atypical years.

11. Mining investment rose at about the same pace as all investment and blast furnace equipment rose at half the pace.

12. Hubbert quotes 7.6×10^{12} as a high estimate and 2×10^{12} as a low estimate.

13. Figures from 1977 and 1968, on the 25 items on which information was available yield an average annual rate of increase of 2.35 percent. These figures were arrived at by dividing total consumption by population; i.e., they are not exponential rates. The exponential growth rates given by Rockefeller for U.S. use of 14 basic nonfuel minerals average 3.4 percent per annum, which represents a per capita increase in excess of 2 percent. The U.S. Bureau of Mines projected U.S. demand rates for these items in the period 1972 to 2000 quoted by Rockefeller.

Terrestrial Resources: Forests

We who live in forested lands tend to take them for granted, along with their products that are so much a part of our everyday lives. But our current concern with resources in general, coupled with the massive devastation of tropical and subtropical forests in the past three decades, has made us more aware of this remarkable but beleaguered feature of the landscape. In the opening selection, the American land-use authority Marion Clawson surveys American forests in their ecological and cultural contexts and, while generally optimistic, emphasizes the need for trade-offs in resource policy in general. The World Bank, while taking a broader view of forests and their role in the economic development of the poor countries that have them, arrives at similar conclusions. The excerpt from "Where Have All the Flowers Gone? Deforestation in the Third World," however, spotlights a major problem which threatens to obliterate the very resource which the World Bank considers so important for development. Since forests are renewable, reforestation could theoretically more than balance deforestation. Environmentalist Erik P. Eckholm of the Worldwatch Institute, however, is not so sanguine about our will to bring this about. Who is right? Will humanity rise to the challenge and sustain the world's forests at relatively little cost in cash and manpower? Or will we ignore the lesson of the denudation of the Mediterranean Basin not so very long ago?

34

Forests for Whom and for What?

Marion Clawson

Forests are important in the total American landscape, in the natural resource base of our economy, and in the economic and social life of the people. The importance of forests tends generally to be underestimated in the United States, but is better understood in the Pacific Northwest than almost anywhere else in the country.

Forests of one kind or another today occupy one-third of the land in the 50 states. About a third of the total forest area is classed as "noncommercial" in the usual forest statistics, because its timber stand per acre is too low, or its potential for growing wood annually is too small, or for some other reason. Much of the noncommercial forest is in the interior of Alaska where annual wood growth per acre is low. In my judgment, repeatedly expressed, about one-fourth of the forest area classified as commercial is actually incapable of continued economic wood production. By any reasonable accounting, however, there remains a substantial acreage of commercial forest.

The United States has many kinds of forests and, in my estimate, some 4,000 significantly different forest management situations. There are about a score of major forest types, well over 100 important commercial tree species, a dozen important regionally distinct forest situations, and at least four major kinds of forest ownerships. In addition, forest sites differ greatly in productivity, and present forest stands differ in degree of stocking, age of trees, freedom from disease, and other factors.

One can generalize about forests in the same sense that one can generalize about farms, lakes, cities, or schools. But for many purposes, it is highly important to specify the kind of forest under discussion because

---

what is true of one forest may not be true of another. In this chapter, I speak about forests as a whole.

The forested acreage in the United States today is considerably smaller than it was when the first colonists arrived from Europe. But in recent years forests have become reestablished on millions of acres that were once cleared, as they had to be if cultivated crops were to be grown and if towns and roads were to be built. To the first settlers the forests were often a nuisance, something to be gotten rid of. For over 100 years, and especially in the past 50 years, trees have been invading abandoned cropland, notably along the Atlantic Coast, especially in hilly and mountainous areas, but also in parts of the coastal plain and Piedmont.

Trees grow "naturally" in much of the United States. That is, in the absence of man's efforts to prevent tree growth by such means as annual plowing or mowing, trees of some species will invade the land. Many tree species are aggressive and persistent invaders on any land where they are not firmly suppressed. The resultant growth may not be productive forest, and the initial invading species may be replaced in a few years by other species, but the land surface quickly becomes covered with trees in these extensive naturally forested regions.

The capacity of trees to grow, in spite of man's efforts to keep them out or in the face of his neglect of the land, has been grossly and repeatedly underestimated. Cries of timber famine have been heard over the years when someone noted that timber harvest had removed tree cover, and then projected that rate of removal some years ahead without considering probable tree growth. Gifford Pinchot and T. R. Roosevelt did this shortly after the turn of the century. Others foresaw economic decline as old-growth timber was harvested in the 1920s and 1930s, and modern "conservationists" have been greatly disturbed at timber harvest. All of them grossly underestimated the capacity of trees to become reestablished. I do not mean to say that timber harvest and forest management practices have been fully satisfactory. On the contrary, there was much waste and little forethought for the future. But no one should underestimate the recuperative capacity of any ecosystem, especially of forests on sites well suited for tree growth.

FORESTS PRODUCE MANY OUTPUTS

Foresters have long emphasized that forests produce many kinds of outputs. First and most obvious, of course, is wood. Trees, like all living matter, have a finite life cycle. The tree starts with a seed that sprouts to become a seedling, and then passes through the sapling and pole stages into adulthood, and, if unharvested, ultimately declines and dies. The casual observer seeing a forest annually or at other relatively short intervals may be unaware of the life-cycle changes that are typically spread over several decades. No tree can be kept alive and growing forever; even those antiquarians, the *Sequoia gigantea* and the bristle cone pine, ultimately die. Forests, like cultivated crops, grow at widely varying rates on different sites.

Forests also serve as rather special watersheds. Every area that supports a commercial forest has at least a fair amount of annual precipitation. The trees protect the surface of the land from erosion; intercept some of the rain or snow, which evaporates before it hits ground; and consume large amounts of soil moisture from both deep and shallow layers of the soil. In general, forests are an excellent kind of watershed, and their extensive area makes them especially important in the United States.

Wildlife is also a forest output. The edges of the forest and the forest clearings, in particular, offer food, shelter, and breeding areas for many kinds of wildlife.

Many people seek outdoor recreation in a forest setting. A dense forest is often unattractive for outdoor recreation, but trees enhance the attractiveness of camping and picnicking recreation areas. The recreationist is often unaware and unconcerned about annual growth as long as the trees seem relatively healthy and attractive. He is also unlikely to be aware of how his activities can affect the forest. Overuse for outdoor recreation will produce adverse environmental impacts, just as will overuse for any other forest product.

A special form of recreation that has aroused much interest and controversy in recent years is wilderness use. Wilderness is a term of many meanings. In the broadest sense it refers to a kind of area and a kind of personal experience, although complete agreement exists on neither. Must each wilderness area be 100,000 acres in extent, as in the original Forest Service definition, or 5,000 acres as in the roadless areas now under consideration for wilderness classification, or may it be no more than 20 acres, as a private "mini-wilderness"? Must the wilderness user encounter no other persons, or are a few other wilderness visitors tolerable, or does the "wilderness" begin when the user steps off the edge of a blacktop road? Regardless of definition, a wilderness need not be a commercial forest. Indeed, about half the acreage of wilderness areas within national forests do not have commercial forests as these are conventionally defined. Some wilderness areas are above timber line or have very sparse stands of trees; some are lakes or swamps.

Another important, yet hard to describe, output of forests may best be called "a general forest environment." Even persons uninformed about forests and generally unappreciative of them will find a green forest a more pleasant site than bare land, burned-over areas, or weedy and brushy fields. Many people, of course, are well informed and concerned about forests and are able to recognize and appreciate healthy, vigorous ones. Walking, riding, or driving through forests is satisfying to many people. Forests in this general environmental sense are as important as lawns, shrubs, and flowers in towns and cities on land never occupied by the observer.

WHO USES FORESTS?

Most people are unaware of how much they depend on forests for important everyday needs. Everyone uses wood, for instance, every day in some form. I have tried to imagine someone who used no wood. He or she would have to live in a cave, for all buildings use wood in some way, whether during the construction process or as part of the building. He or she would have to use stone furniture, for all other furniture is either made of wood or wood is used in the construction process. Coal picked up from the surface of the ground would have to constitute the sole fuel, for any other source of fuel requires wood at some point in the production process.

Most people, as they shop for foods or other items packaged (at least at some stage) in paper, or as they buy newspapers or magazines, or use any of the scores of other items common to ordinary day-to-day living, are unaware of their dependence on wood and wood fiber. They may be acutely conscious of the cost of these products, and would be greatly upset if such products were unavailable in stores, yet they do not make the connection between their needs and the forest.

Everyone uses water, of course, and the probabilities are very high that at least part of the water consumed fell to earth on a forested area. Again, the connection between the water flowing from the tap and the forested watershed from which it came is not apparent to the average urban dweller.

Perhaps half of the total population each year enjoys outdoor recreation in a forest setting. Some people do not participate in outdoor recreation because they are too old, too young, ill, or cannot afford to travel to recreation sites. Others could participate but choose not to. Most of the outdoor recreation in a forest setting is in publicly owned forests or parks, but much is on forest-industry forests, and many people own forested properties for their own enjoyment.

Forested wilderness areas are used by a relatively small part of the total population. Visitors to formally designated forested wilderness areas each year are less than 2 percent of the total population, and perhaps no more than 10 percent of the population ever visit such areas. A higher percentage of the population endorses the idea of wilderness and gets a certain satisfaction simply from knowing that such areas are there, but it is very difficult to estimate just how many people fall in this category.

Likewise, it is difficult to know how many people enjoy the general forest environment, or just how important this enjoyment may be to them, but intuitively one judges that their numbers are larger.

FORESTS ARE A RENEWABLE RESOURCE

Forests are a renewable resource. Plants growing within forests capture solar energy and transform it into products that man can use. Only a small part of the total solar energy is transformed into products, it is true but no process other than photosynthesis utilizes so much of this energy so economically.

The renewability of forests is most often emphasized in connection with wood production. Even if forests are managed with no more than a minimum of competence, wood can be grown indefinitely on each forest area. All the substitutes for wood in construction, packaging, and other wood-fiber use are nonrenewable. In general, wood requires less energy for processing than do alternative materials. These important values of wood must, of course, be balanced against other factors in using wood and alternative materials.

Water is equally a renewable resource. From evaporation to precipitation to flow, the hydrologic cycle is powered by solar energy. An unforested area of land might yield as much or even more water than a forested area, but the water quality is likely to be inferior.

Forest services such as outdoor recreation, wilderness experiences, and wildlife production are all renewable resources too. Forests can produce these services indefinitely also.

Although forest outputs are renewable, they are also perishable. The wood grown one year may be harvested in any one of many future years, depending in part upon the species and the age of the tree. Once harvested, the wood will normally last for decades, although in the end it rots and decays. Most other forest outputs lie at the opposite end of the perishability scale. An outdoor recreation or wilderness opportunity not used this year—indeed, not used this day—cannot be stored for later use but is lost forever. Likewise, the stream flow unused by man one year (or day) may be lost for later use. Economic management of these "perishable" forest outputs requires some means for using them at the rate they are produced.

FOREST OWNERSHIP AND FOREST USES

Four major categories of forest ownership are recognized in much of the data about forests: national forests, other public forests, forest-industry forests, and "other" forests. Some of these major categories are often divided further. For instance, some of the other public forests are federally owned and managed by various federal agencies such as the Bureau of Land Management, the Tennessee Valley Authority, the Department of Defense, and others; and some are owned by states and counties. The "other" forests are owned by a mixed lot of private parties—some as parts of farms, some as incidental to other businesses, some for hobbies or personal recreation, and some primarily for speculative gains in price. To some extent, each kind of owner faces problems peculiar to his ownership class. But all forest owners, public and private, face certain problems more or less to the same extent.

One problem common to all forest ownership is how the owner can secure some economic return for valuable forest outputs that are generally not marketed for cash. Outdoor recreation, wilderness use, water, wildlife, and the general forest environment each has economic value, but in the American society those who enjoy these forest outputs rarely pay much or anything for them. Millions of people enjoy outdoor recreation activities on both publicly and privately owned forests, paying little or nothing for the privilege. The man who owns a tract of forest for his own enjoyment does indeed bear the costs of ownership, but often he is unable to prevent others from using his property without payment. Wilderness exists mostly on public land, and wilderness users pay little for their enjoyment of such areas. Except for a few municipal watersheds, water flowing from forested areas is free to users who have established water rights under applicable law. Only rarely does a forest owner collect anything for protecting wildlife.

The legal right of the forest owner to exclude those who do not pay for these forest outputs or to charge user fees is too complex an issue to be explored here. But the practical, social, and political obstacles to collecting any significant revenues at any reasonable administrative cost are well-nigh insurmountable. The average American seems to think he should enjoy many forests outputs without paying for them, and he shows little concern for the problems his use creates for the forest owner.

A few of the problems peculiar to each particular class of forest owners may be mentioned briefly. Public forests as a whole seem to suffer from two major problems: (1) a notable lack of clear legislative directives on how to manage these forests; and (2) tardy and inadequate annual appropriations for competent management. The "other" forests, mostly relatively small units the owners of which are technically untrained in forestry, often will not repay the time and effort needed for careful management. The owners cannot afford to own equipment or to maintain a permanent labor force, and often they find it difficult or impossible to carry out the forest practices they would like to employ.

COMPATIBLE AND INCOMPATIBLE FOREST USES

Three of the many uses or outputs of forests are basically incompatible with one another: wood production, wilderness, and outdoor recreation other than wilderness. Three other uses, however, are reasonably compatible with one another and with each of the three incompatibles. These are watershed, wildlife, and general forest environment.

Timber harvest destroys wilderness areas, and wilderness reservation makes timber harvest impossible. If one relaxes the standards of wilderness, something akin to the old wilderness may be recreated in 50 to 100 years after timber harvest, if roads are closed and other uses are prohibited. But if one insists on virginity in his wilderness, then timber harvest is impossible forever.

Wilderness is equally incompatible with outdoor recreation of moderately intensive types. An access road, a picnic area, a campground, an intensive fishing area, and other recreation developments are fully as incompatible with a wilderness as are chain saws and logging trucks.

Moderately intensive outdoor recreation and wood production are primarily incompatible but not entirely so. Some forms of outdoor recreation, such as hunting, are facilitated by timber harvest, because game animals and birds increase on the cutover areas. Timber can be harvested on campgrounds on a selective basis or on a long rotation. Roads for timber harvest open up areas for outdoor recreation. Other compatibilities might be cited, but, on the whole, timber harvest and active outdoor recreation are largely incompatible.

In contrast, watershed, wildlife, and general forest environment are generally compatible with one another and with each of the three incompatibles. A properly planned and executed timber harvest will preserve the watershed and the forest environment and favor some wildlife while disadvantaging other kinds. Wilderness is generally favorable to each of these three compatible uses. Outdoor recreation can damage any of the three if it is too intensive, but when properly controlled it is not inimical to them.

The degree of compatibility or incompatibility is often affected by the forest type, the site classification of the land, and the stage in the tree-growing cycle. The general relationships suggested above may need modification for particular forest situations. In many instances, trade-offs are possible—a little less timber harvest for much more outdoor recreation, for instance. The important trade-off may not be between outputs, but between one input and another output—a little more money spent on timber access roads to reduce damage to the watershed, for instance.

A compatibility-incompatibility analysis is, in my judgment, vastly more useful than sloganeering about multiple use. If one interprets multiple use to mean that every output is sought on every acre every year, then the idea is absurd. If one interprets multiple use as a variable combination of outputs on different tracts, so that the larger area is managed for all feasible combinations of outputs, then multiple use acquires a larger and more practical meaning. In any case, the trade-offs between one use and another are critical, and it is here that the compatibility-incompatibility analysis is particularly useful.

POTENTIAL OF FORESTS TO SERVE PEOPLE

The gap between actual and potential output is greater for forests than for any other natural resource of the United States with which I am at all familiar. This statement is generally true for each major kind of forest ownership and for most specific forest situations. There are exceptions, of course, and some forests are producing at or close to their economic potential. While forests now contribute greatly to American life, they are capable of contributing much more. These general statements apply to all forest outputs—wood, outdoor recreation, wilderness, wildlife, water, and others; but the data are best for wood, and the quantitative relationships can most easily be expressed for wood production. In 1970 (the last year for which reasonably good data are available) the forests of the United States were growing just half as much wood as fully stocked and reasonably well-managed natural stands of timber would grow. The forest-industry forests achieved 59 percent of their potential, but the national forests achieved only 39 percent of their potential. Intensive forest management, if applied to all forests, could produce twice as much wood annually as reasonably good natural stand management does.

Intensive forest management for wood production will not pay on all forest sites or for some forest types. On the less productive sites, the more remote sites, and the sites where road building and other harvest costs are high, intensive management will return less than it costs. Indeed, on some of these sites, even good natural stand management may not pay. In addition to the economic considerations, environmental concerns should eliminate wood harvest, and hence wood growing, on excessively steep slopes, easily erodable soils, sites where tree reproduction is uncertain or slow, and on the edge of some water courses and water bodies. But, after full allowance for limiting production on such sites, annual wood production from American forests could still be fully double the current level.

I have not mentioned the limitation that wilderness reservation would impose upon wood growing, because much depends on how wilderness is defined. If a forest wilderness continues to be defined as an area of at least 5,000 roadless acres and no permanent human occupancy, then wilderness offers little threat to wood growing. About half of the areas that meet these standards have no commercial forest, and considerable parts of the others should not be used for continued wood production for economic and environmental reasons.

The threat that wilderness advocates pose for wood production lies in two different directions. The first derives from the definition of wilderness. When the Forest Service first established wilderness areas by administrative action in the 1920s, 100,000 acres was considered the minimum unit; since the Wilderness Act was passed in 1964, areas of 5,000 roadless acres have been studied for possible wilderness designation, and some much smaller areas have in fact been designated as wilderness. A further drastic lowering of minimum area would involve far larger acreages and far more valuable timber lands. It would also drastically lower the quality of the wilderness experience. The second threat to wood production, posed by the wilderness advocates as a group rather than by wilderness use as such, lies in the attempts to prescribe timber rotations, harvest methods, rates of cutting, and the like on areas fully capable of economic timber production. This latter type of activity is vastly more of a threat to wood growing than is any probable reservation of wilderness areas.

The acreage of land (some not forested) within national forests which meets present wilderness standards is three times, possibly more, the area presently so designated. In addition, the resource potential exists for the establishment of some "restored wildernesses" or some "quasi-wildernesses" on lands not federally owned, if wilderness users are prepared to pay the costs. Still further, the capacity of wilderness areas to accommodate visitors without significant loss in the quality of the wilderness experience could be increased greatly by the building of more trails into presently unused areas and by more careful scheduling of visitors on the trails.

The capacity of forests to provide outdoor recreation, to serve as a home for wildlife to yield water, and to be an attractive part of the total natural environment far exceeds current production of each of these outputs. Through the application of modern technology, the investment of more capital and labor, and, above all, a higher level of management skills, the output of each of these forest services could be increased. The physical or biological potential for each service is greater than the economic potential, but even the latter is well above the present output.

The dominant, indeed, the dramatic, fact about forest potential is that the American people can have more of *everything* from the forests, if they but apply enough thought and effort. Over the past 50 years forests have indeed yielded more of everything—more wilderness use, more outdoor recreation of other kinds, more wildlife, and more wood. In particular situations and at particular times, more wood has meant less recreation, or other conflicts, and trade-offs have occurred. But for the forest system as a whole and over a significant period of time, all outputs can be increased.

ANALYSIS OF FOREST POLICY ISSUES

The management and the use of forests, both private and public, frequently pose important issues of policy. For the public forests, the public policy issues are inescapable, a necessary consequence of public ownership. But privately owned forests also pose issues of public policy because private forestry has always had a substantial public input of one kind or another. Privately owned forests also pose issues of private policy for their owners.

Many kinds of policy issues arise for such forests: how much land to use for forests; how to manage old growth forests during their conversion to regular rotations; how much forest to reserve from cutting for wilderness, environmental, or other reasons; how much to invest and to expend in production of those forest outputs that produce no cash income; how to protect environmental values on forest land; and what policy to follow with respect to exports of forest commodities. These and numerous other issues have arisen in the past and are likely to reappear in the future.

Policy issues are nearly always complex. If they were simple, they would be resolved easily and quickly. A policy issue always involves several contending parties or forces, since there would be no issue over policy if there were only one viewpoint. It is generally difficult to reach an agreement on any issue that satisfies everyone equally. The position of some people is often made worse by a particular policy decision, and some people usually gain more than others. Sometimes, policies are arrived at by sheer political or economic force and sometimes in ways that seem dubiously rational.

Nevertheless, and in spite of the limitations of the policy-making process, a rational and comprehensive framework for analyzing policy issues is highly desirable. If unanimous agreement on policy is not possible, the contestants may at least be able to agree on what the disagreement is all about. Arriving at a wise policy decision that will stand the test of time is facilitated by agreement on "facts." But this is far from easy to attain. There may be disagreement on what kinds of information or opinion are relevant facts. One old definition describes a "fact" as: "an opinion not now in dispute." On this basis, the existence of the dispute throws the fact into challenge. The problem is exacerbated because the relevant facts are those related to the future, which is in considerable measure unknown and unknowable.

In the analysis of all natural resource policy issues, I think it necessary to consider five different kinds of facts and to make five different kinds of analyses: (1) physical and biological feasibility and consequences; (2) economic efficiency; (3) economic equity, or who gains and who pays; (4) cultural acceptability; and (5) administrative or operational practicality.

Every use of natural resources has some physical or biological aspects. Some uses of a particular resource are technically easy, others are difficult but possible, and still others are impossible or nearly so. These statements are true for forests as for many other kinds of natural resource situations. Some species of trees may be easily grown in a particular location, others can be grown only poorly or with considerable risk of failure, and still others cannot be grown at all. Soils, climate in all its manifold respects, elevation, position on earth's surface, and many other factors affect forest growth. Here in the Pacific Northwest we are surrounded by Douglas fir, hemlock, pines, and associated species; we do not encounter natural stands of oak, cypress, hickory, maple, beech, and birch and would find it difficult to grow them here.

In addition to considerations of physical and biological feasibility, there are physical and biological consequences of every resource management action. Whether a forest is cut partially by selective cutting, totally by clearcutting, or to an intermediate degree by another method, the ecosystem will be modified to some extent. Removal of the best trees of some desired species may greatly change the future forest, for instance. This has happened on millions of acres of mixed hardwoods in the South and East, which have been severely degraded by this type of selective removal. If one removes some or all of the trees, in situations where forest regeneration is slow and uncertain, severe physical and biological consequences will follow. It is often less well understood that doing nothing will have physical and biological consequences too. The mature forest, which seems so timeless, permanent, and indestructible to the casual observer, is in fact constantly changing, and some day those old trees will all be blown down, or die and fall, or be killed by fire, disease, or insects.

Just as physical and biological feasibility limit what can be done in resource management, so economic efficiency determines what can be done profitably. Many resource actions are technically feasible but economically impractical. Trees can be planted on poor sites but the costs will exceed the values of the resultant growth. Or old growth trees can be harvested from remote sites, possibly by balloon or helicopter methods, but at costs that far exceed the values. A cutover forested area could be nursed back to a reasonable facsimile of a wilderness in 100 years or so by careful management and exclusion of nonconforming uses, but would the cost be worth it?

Economic efficiency is typically measured by benefit/cost ratios. More properly, it is the absolute margin of benefit in excess of cost which should be maximized, rather than the ratio between them. Since costs are incurred and benefits are received on different time patterns, it is necessary to compare them on a present value basis by a process of discounting. The choice of interest rate may affect economic feasibility as much as any other single factor that enters into the benefit/cost calculation.

Although benefit/cost calculations are unavoidably only approximate, in part because they deal with an unknown future, and although the benefit/cost analysis has frequently been prostituted by those who distort it to produce their predetermined "answers," a calculation of probable benefits and probable costs is the most powerful tool yet devised for economically sound resource management. The technique is fully usable for forest outputs not marketed for cash. For instance, the forest wildlife specialist with a limited budget must decide where to spend it and for what purposes, and he makes a benefit/cost analysis—even when he protests that he does not.

But economic equity is as important as economic efficiency. Every natural resource management action and every resource policy produce some gains and involve some costs. Frequently, the persons or the groups who secure the gains do not bear the costs, or at least do not bear all of them. Sometimes society as a whole (or general government) bears part of the cost, as for research, fire prevention, roads, and other aspects of forest management. But, of course, government is merely the totality of its citizens, and governmental revenues are simply taxes paid by individuals. Profitable forest management is enormously more difficult because of its "freeloaders," the people who enjoy forest outputs such as water, wildlife, recreation, and wilderness without paying much or anything for them. At the same time, forest owners sometimes impose costs upon other persons—when the quality of water flowing off their land is degraded, for example.

There is no neat test to determine optimum economic equity, analogous to the benefit/cost criterion for economic efficiency. In the American society we reject complete equality of income as both unattainable and undesirable; we are unwilling to reduce everyone to the same level. We talk about reducing great disparities in income, but have achieved relatively little toward this end. From time to time we are outraged because some individual or some small group reaps a large and undeserved income at public expense. In forestry, we argue that users of wood from public and private forests should pay for the wood they get at as near a fair price as we can estimate. But users of other forest outputs rarely pay for what they receive, and only slowly do we, as a nation, seem to be moving to a policy of making forest users pay for what they get.

Cultural acceptability is my fourth criterion of forest policy. It is not enough that we know how to do something, that it is economically efficient, and that the gains and costs are fairly distributed. The result of our policy must be one that we, as a people, want or at least will accept. For instance, the outcry over some timber harvests arose from dissatisfaction with the appearance of the harvested area. Outrage at slash and defective wood left on the side, at rectangular and unattractive lines bounding harvested areas, and at raw exposed soil was primarily a sociological or cultural phenomenon. If beauty is in the eye of the beholder, so is ugliness. Considerations of biological, economic, and environmental efficiency were dwarfed by rejection of unaesthetic results. Public and private forestry will be more influenced by human attitudes in the future than they have been in the past.

Finally, every resource policy must be capable of being carried out in practice; otherwise it is useless or worse. Nothing is gained and a good deal may be lost by adopting a policy that cannot be, or is unlikely to be, put into effective operation. If policy requires information that does not exist, or calls for a level of competence in personnel that is unavailable, or for some other reason cannot be or will not be put into operation, it is unproductive of good results and may discredit ideas or organizations that under other conditions might be effective. There is no use urging a small private forest owner to undertake a management program that in fact he cannot carry out, for instance. I have always felt that any attempt at public regulation of private forestry practices would founder on administrative detail, even if it were strongly supported, which I doubt it would be.

The formation of natural resource policy for forests or for any other resource requires a consideration of these five kinds of information and of these five approaches—physical and biological feasibility and consequences, economic efficiency, economic equity, cultural acceptability, and operational or administrative practicality. This is extremely difficult. Because five different kinds of factors are involved, the simple comparison of one with another is impossible. It is impossible to simultaneously maximize each of the five variables, were some complex formula for policy decisions possible.

Because it is so difficult to use five different kinds of data and five different methods of analysis, some persons have argued that a simpler approach must be found. One could, of course, maximize economic efficiency by disregarding economic equity and cultural acceptability. The result would appear neat and decisive but would probably be rejected if an effort were made to apply the proposed policy. Life is complex, not simple; models can abstract part of reality and thereby throw some light on a problem, but their apparent "answer" is nearly always unacceptable or unusable in practice. The problem lies not in the complexity of any method of analysis but in the inherent complexity of natural resource situations in general.

The solution to the complexities of resource policy formation must lie in pragmatic compromises among viewpoints and among forms of analysis. Trade-offs between economic efficiency and economic equity, for example, may not be simple, yet some compromise should be possible. Likewise, trade-offs between other pairs of considerations are necessary. A viable policy rarely involves complete dominance of one viewpoint and complete subservience of all others. An explicit consideration of all relevant factors, with the best pragmatic compromise among divergent approaches, is more likely to produce a good or at least a tolerable solution to complex policy issues than will any superficially simpler but deficient approach.

35

Forestry and Development

The World Bank

Forests cover one-third of the land area of the world and over half the land of developing countries. Annual world production of forest products exceeds $115,000 million; global trade amounts to more than $30,000 million. Forests play a significant role in economic development; they provide subsistence, shelter, and employment, as well as resources for the development of other sectors. In addition to being a readily convertible and largely self-regenerating store of wealth, forests have a beneficial impact on the natural environment and provide innumerable products of vital use to man.

ROLE OF FORESTRY IN DEVELOPMENT

Ecological effects. Forests are outwardly grand but fragile ecosystems. They have pronounced microclimatic effects, for they reduce the range of daily temperature variation, help retain a layer of cool moist air, and enhance the local climate. Their overall impact—with consequent widespread benefits to mankind—is to soften the interaction of elements that comprise the ecological system.

The ecological impact of forests is most easily recognized in their effect on water catchments and the role they play in regulating stream flows. Forests in catchment areas act as porous reservoirs by retaining water in the roots and humus layers and releasing it as a sustained flow over a long period of time. In this way, forests protect the land beneath them from erosion, reduce flooding and erosion in adjacent areas, and, in turn, minimize the silting of rivers, canals, and dams. The absorbed water

Reprint of "Forestry and Development," Chapter 1 in *Forestry,* Sector Policy Paper (The World Bank, February 1978). Pp. 13–24.

feeds streams and underground aquifers and thus contributes to a stable hydrology essential to irrigated agriculture.

In the form of shelter belts, and by modifying the microclimate, forests can reduce wind erosion and slow the expansion of deserts. These effects can be achieved either by manmade plantations and planted shelter belts or by natural forests.

Forest areas provide a habitat for wildlife, many species of which cannot survive in an unforested environment. They also provide recreational outlets for city dwellers, as well as places to live for those whose livelihood comes from forests.

Indigenous consumption. Where large trees give way to settled agriculture and, indeed, throughout the countryside, forest products are extensively used. In varying degrees, forests provide food, fuel, fiber, and building materials. Some tribal groups live in forests and are totally dependent on them. Others find, in forest products, part of their consumption needs, plus some items for processing and for trading with neighboring groups. For the latter, forest products are generally supplemented by a degree of settled agriculture.

The major use of the forest in developing countries is as a source of fuel—as firewood or as charcoal. Roughly 90 percent of annual wood consumption in developing countries is used for fuel. In most societies, wood provides the cheapest form of fuel, since, compared with most other fuels, it requires less complex equipment for its use and distribution.

There is a substantial, positive interaction between forests and food production. Forests provide food through the gathering of fruits, nuts, berries, tubers, and mushrooms, as well as through hunting of wildlife. Trees indirectly improve soil fertility by fixing nitrogen (e.g., certain acacias) and by adding organic matter—a fundamental factor in the widespread practice of shifting cultivation.

More generally recognized is the role of forests in providing wood for building poles, sawn boards, and furniture. Wood is a common building material in most rural societies, and is frequently preferred even when other materials are available. In addition, the forest provides materials for weaving, a habitat for food and materials produced by insects (such as honey, silk, and waxes), and is a source of special woods and ashes used in the manufacture of ornaments and artwork. Through these products, forests contribute in varying degrees to the livelihood and well-being of vast numbers of people in rural societies, and through trading, to many more in urban areas.

Industrial uses. More developed economies and the modern sectors of developing countries make extensive use of wood and forest by-products in the production, through industrial processes, of a vast array of wood and paper products. Wood enters more activities in a modern industrial economy than any other single commodity. Though processed wood products are, quantitatively, the most significant and best known, leather goods, paint, glues, and caulking materials, and even cough medicines are dependent upon various gums, resins, waxes, and oils taken from forests as essential ingredients.

The least processed wood products are poles, pitprops, and railway ties. These have traditionally been hewn where felled, and transported to where they are to be used. Only slightly more processed is sawn lumber, which is used for all kinds of construction, joinery, furniture, shipbuilding, and other purposes. To some extent, "solid" lumber is being displaced by plywood and wood-based panels in these industries.

Another category, the demand for which grows rapidly with rising incomes, is composed of the products of pulpwood—newsprint, paperboard, writing paper, domestic tissues, containers, packaging, textiles, and clothing. These are the products of the most complex and most capital-intensive industrial processing of all forest products. The final product, in most cases, is not recognizable as a forest product due to extensive transformations that have taken place.

These numerous end products, their intermediates, and the mode in which they are used [. . .] reveal the extent to which forests and forest products contribute to human well-being. Apart from obtaining the advantages from direct consumption, as summarized in the chart, countries with forest stocks in excess of their domestic needs may obtain economic benefits in the form of increased employment and the generation of foreign exchange through the export of both rough wood and finished products. These can, in turn, be exchanged in international markets for the foreign manufactured goods required for economic development. Depending on a country's state of development, exports may range from round wood, sawn timber board, and plywood veneer to pulp and paper and manufactured goods of all kinds.

FOREST UTILIZATION IN PRACTICE

The existing forest stock in developing countries (estimated at 1,200 million hectares of mature forest) is currently being consumed at the rate of 15 million to 20 million hectares a year. At this rate, assuming no growth in demand, the remaining tropical forests will be consumed in about 60 to 80 years. Allowing for population growth in developing countries, with no growth in exports, the current forest stock is likely to be consumed in less than 40 years. This alarming prospect takes no account of the fact that forests can be a self-regenerating resource—but neither does it convey the far-reaching implications of too-rapid forest exploitation without proper management.

Environmental disruption. Large-scale removal of the forest cover, if not accompanied by reforestation for catchment protection (or sound agricultural practices), may lead to rapid runoff, soil erosion, silting, and flooding in the rainy season, followed by reduced downstream flows in dry weather. In extreme cases, removal of the forest cover has led to the cessation of dry weather stream flow, with the subsequent disruption of agriculture. Studies have shown, for instance, that the incidence of flooding in the Indus River system in Pakistan has been far higher in the last 25 years than during the previous 60 years. Increased flooding, which is attributed to the denudation of catchment areas, has been accompanied by serious silting of the dams and canals of Pakistan's irrigation system.

The undesirable effects of uncontrolled forest exploitation have been widely publicized in the present century. "Dust bowls," flash floods, landslides, gulley erosion, and similar phenomena have all been at least partly caused by uncontrolled forest exploitation in widespread areas, such as the Tennessee Valley of the United States, the Peruvian Sierra in Latin America, the Ethiopian highlands of Africa, and large parts of Indonesia and the Philippines in Asia. The rate at which forests are destroyed is a cause for widespread concern. The Food and Agriculture Organization of the United Nations (FAO) estimates that some 5 million to 10 million hectares of forest are "lost" each year in Latin America; in Africa, some 2 million hectares, and in Asia, some 5 million hectares, are "lost" yearly.

Just how long this process has been recognized and the degree to which the human race resists the lessons of its environment are brought home sharply by the following quotation from Plato (*Criteas*, about 400 B.C.):

> There are mountains in Attica which can now keep nothing more than bees, but which were clothed not so very long ago with fine trees, producing timber suitable for roofing the largest buildings; the roofs hewn from this timber are still in existence. There were also many lofty cultivated trees, while the country produced bountiful pastures for cattle. The annual supply of rainfall was not then lost, as it is at present, through being allowed to flow over a denuded surface to the sea. It was received by the country in all its abundance, stored in impervious potter's earth, and so was able to discharge the drainage of the hills into the hollows in the form of springs or rivers with an abundant volume and a wide distribution. The shrines that survive to the present day on the sites of extinct water supplies are evidence for the correctness of my present hypothesis.

This desolation persists to the present day in the overgrazed regions of the Peloponnesus and Mesopotamia, although remedial action, through reforestation, is slowly progressing. The penalties, paid over the centuries, are lowlands, flooded by torrents from the bare mountains, and seaports, left far inland by the advancing deposits of soil and rubble washed down from the hills.

It is humbling to realize that so clear an analysis was possible by observation and deduction four centuries before the birth of Christ, and it is alarming that 2,000 years later, at least half the human race lives in rapidly growing communities that make no effective provision for the protection of watersheds.

Population growth and encroachment. Humans are—out of perceived necessity—destroying the basis of their own livelihood as they violate the limits of natural systems. Those most vulnerable to these trends are the poor of the world. Their search for the basic requirements of food and fuel often forces them to hasten the destruction of their own productive environment. Some 10 percent of the world's population live in mountain areas, but another 40 percent live in adjacent lowlands; fully half of mankind, therefore, is intimately affected by trends in watershed environments. A further 5 percent pursue a livelihood in the drier zones of poor countries, where they are subject to the vagaries of cyclical climatic effects and long-term movements of deserts, along the southern and northern edges of the Sahara and the deserts of the Middle East and India.

Unfortunately, these abstractions are rarely visualized in terms of the actual effects they have on the land and people: increasing population pressure forces the cultivation of ever steeper mountain slopes, where crops and topsoil quickly wash away; forest resources, which are vital for flood control and soil stabilization, are used for fuel; dust bowls replace once-fertile pastures. These effects result from increasing population pressure on existing land, intensified by static farming technology and iniquitous land tenure systems that prevent access to, and fuller use of, the better croplands. Despite the insight provided by past abuses, and the advanced technological skills of present society, there is a striking disparity in the quality of diets among the peoples of the world, indicating mankind's failure to utilize lands best suited for agriculture and to halt trends that are ecologically destructive.

One manifestation of population pressure is seen in the growing demand for fuel wood. In the Sahelian zone, for example, an average family requires more than 1 cubic meter of stacked firewood a year, or wood equal to the average growth from 2 hectares of natural forest. Until recently, Bamako, the capital of Mali, with a population of 300,000 persons, could be supplied with firewood for domestic use gathered from forests less than 50 kilometers away from the capital; in 1975, the distance was 100 kilometers. By 1990, Bamako will need (annually) wood produced from over 100,000 hectares of forest plantations, or an amount well beyond the current resources of the government of that West African nation to plant in the time available.

Uncontrolled Commercial Extraction

Many developing countries with extensive natural forest stocks allow commercial extraction of wood, especially hardwood, for industrial processing, which generates useful economic activity and valuable foreign exchange. Using sensible cutting plans, such that sufficient time is allowed for regeneration—say, 25 to 30 years for natural regeneration, or less, if a replanting program follows the cutting—commercial cutting can take place without reducing the total area or sustainable yield of standing forest, and with minimal damage to watershed cover. Many countries, including the Philippines and Brazil, have failed to introduce or enforce controlled cutting plans, and extensive loss of forest area and a devastating destruction of watershed environments have ensued. The failure to adopt a controlled forestry policy is attributable to a lack of political will, reflecting both a shortsighted view and a long-established primitive attitude toward forests. This situation has usually been exacerbated by a lack of appropriate institutions through which controlled extraction programs and orderly forest management can be implemented and introduced.

Historically, much of the world's forest area has been in public ownership because of the long-term nature of forest development and the divergence of private and social benefits that makes private investment often unattractive. Government forestry institutions have, as a result, played a major role in forestry preservation and development programs. In most developing countries, however, these institutions are often of recent origin and are relatively weak due to the lack of experience, unrestricted funds, and adequate training programs. Institutional weakness is reflected in poor planning and regulation of forest management and the consequent accelerated rundown of forest resources.

These problems are often accompanied by distorted pricing policies for forest products (particularly exports)—including tariff and trade terms that encourage log exports rather than domestic processing and manufacture of wood products. Because funds are lacking, reforestation and afforestation have lapsed in many countries below the level needed to ensure an adequate supply of wood—for both fuel wood and other forest products.

The divergence of economic and social objectives so often observed in developing countries tends to be more accentuated in the forestry sector than in others. The operators of privately owned sawmills, for example, are primarily interested in maximizing current profits from lumber sales, and are less concerned with the long-term management of the forests from which they cut their logs. Similarly, upland people often exploit the fodder and grazing potential of forest areas and give little thought to ensuring adequate regeneration of tree seedlings or soil protection. Because of this divergence of objectives, there is often little political advantage to be found by diverting funds and staff resources to forestry and forest development. In very many developing countries, afforestation programs are currently running at less than half the rate recommended by the expert panels of the World Forestry Congress.*

TOWARD A STRATEGY FOR FOREST DEVELOPMENT

An obvious disparity exists between the perceived role of forests in development and observable experience in developing countries. In almost every country, the environmental benefits from forestry are ignored and, to varying degrees, the subtle balances of ecology are upset. In many countries, due largely to population pressure, the acceptable limits to the rate of forest exploitation are being breached. Further, in a great many cases, the tenets of good forest management are disregarded. Yet, while these circumstances prevail widely and, in places, tend to worsen, there is an awakening interest in managing forests for development. This awakening is manifest in a reorientation of perceptions about the ways in which forests can be used to further the goals of development, and in the number of modified approaches being tried in practice.

Changing perceptions. The new interest in forestry development is largely a response to current economic realities. Overall, the growth of population and of individual wealth creates a growing demand for forest products. Although some wood products are displaced by manmade materials (such as plastics for furniture and concrete for railway ties and telegraph poles), the emergence of new products, especially pulp and paper items, continually expands the demand for wood. Increased demand, in turn, has led to higher wood prices in world markets, has enhanced values of standing forests, and has brought greater returns to private investment in forestry. These changes in price signals have caused both wood-exporting and wood-importing nations to examine their potential for export earnings and import substitution, respectively, through domestic forestry development.

The growth of population in developing countries is adding pressure to the existing land base and is creating a growing demand for fuel wood, as well as wood for other purposes. The expansion of demand for fuel wood has been reinforced by the "energy crisis" that has increased the cost of alternative fuels such as kerosene and heating oil. Lack of adequate fuel-wood supplies is a cause of social hardship; in many areas of the world, the use of animal dung and agricultural residues as fuel affects soil fertility and reduces potential agricultural crop yields. In India, for

---

*The World Forestry Congress is a body that meets every six years under the auspices of the FAO for intergovernmental consultation on forestry policies and issues. The Congess last met in 1972 in Buenos Aires, Argentina.

example, lack of fuel wood has forced many rural householders to use cattle dung as an alternative fuel. Dung used as fuel is equivalent to over 6 million tons of nitrogenous fertilizer—a figure slightly more than current total annual fertilizer consumption in India.

The adverse impact of a growing world population and increased industrial usage of natural resources, especially forests, have led to renewed attention to environmental protection and the emergence of a worldwide movement to protect the environment. Individuals and groups within society have reviewed their attitudes and policies toward natural resources; in turn, governments are now giving more attention to the management of their resource stocks, including forests.

As the social benefits associated with forests—in terms of modifying local climates, protecting watersheds, and providing recreation—have been assessed more accurately, the value placed by governments on forest reserves and management programs has increased. New legislation has been passed, and new institutions with multiple aims, and charged with implementing legislation aimed at improving the management of forests for the benefit of society as a whole, have been created and funded. This movement is observable in Malaysia and Thailand, for example, as well as in most developed countries.

The impact of population pressure and the extent and intractable nature of poverty in developing countries have also led to increased attention being given to strategies and programs for rural development that emphasize the necessity of meeting the needs of growing numbers of rural people from the existing resource base. Recognition of the contribution of forests in meeting this need, and growing awareness of the numbers of rural people who are, to varying degrees, dependent on forests for subsistence, have caused governments of developing countries to respond with concern to this additional aspect of forestry economics. While a positive response is neither ubiquitous nor uniform, it is observable—at least in some countries.

Selected experiences. Some of the best examples of recent official responses to forestry needs are found in programs relating to fuel wood. Wood is the preferred fuel of poor people for whom it has obvious advantages: it can be gathered by the family; it has little or no cost; and only the simplest equipment is needed. In the form of charcoal, wood has added advantages: it burns without smoke; it is light and easily transportable; and it keeps well in both rainy and dry seasons.

An obvious solution in some areas to the critical shortage of fuel wood is to grow new plantations. By using exotic species such as Australian eucalyptus, plantations can produce more than 20 times the annual growth of natural forest. One hectare of this kind of plantation can support the firewood needs of from 15 to 20 people. Eucalyptus plantings require little technical skill, and the costs can frequently be kept below $100 a hectare. Much of the economic cost of plantation establishment is labor. Provision of an adequate supply of seeds or seedlings and extension advice may be all that is needed to induce villagers to undertake tree planting on their own land, or, collectively, in village woodlots. The Republic of Korea has, for example, an annual program to plant 50,000 hectares of village woodlots, while India expects to establish over 500,000 hectares of fuel-wood plantations a year.

In the Zinder district of south-central Niger, farmers are growing forest trees as part of their farming operations. Since 1974, when forestry officials sat down with village councils, six villages have taken land out of farming to establish village woodlots to provide firewood for the whole community. Within five years, it is hoped that 70 villages will have such woodlots, which will save families long walks to gather firewood.

Pakistan's Forest Service is experimenting with various species of trees for intensive planting along the banks of irrigation canals in the central plains area. It hopes these plantations will provide not only wood for fuel but also windbreaks to shelter crops and livestock.

At M'Bidi in northern Senegal, the herds have grazed and stripped away the tree and ground cover surrounding village wells. A scheme of reforestation that is a model of integrated land use management, is now under way on a 200-hectare site. The trees will not only produce wood for fuel, but shelter for vegetable gardens and gum arabic (from acacia trees). Once it can be demonstrated that trees provide a multiple source of income, it is expected that herdsmen will be less prone to destroy the tree cover.

Numerous research projects are under way to develop new tree varieties and appropriate management practices. For instance, in the Philippines, there is a project concerned with propagating the fast growing *ipil-ipil (Leucaena leucocephala)* for production of fuel wood, charcoal, pitprops, animal fodder, and pulp and paper manufacture.

The way ahead. Recognition of the ecological and environmental implications of forestry development is growing. The impact of the global concern about the environmental effects of population growth, the example of China in remedying its earlier devastation, and the successes of other countries in pursuing programs of forest management all add to the current momentum for environmental protection. It is important that forestry development policies reflect these concerns.

Local needs for fuel and building wood, particularly on the part of poorer groups, are pressing and, partly as a reaction to increasing awareness of the plight of the rural poor and to the energy shortage, there has been a recent worldwide surge of interest in agroforestry and rural afforestation schemes. Forestry policy in the developing countries should reflect this change in direction.

Industrial demand for timber is also increasing. Consequently, there is a considerable number of interest groups in favor of controlled forestry development. The developing countries have a substantial advantage in the area of industrial forestry. They hold the main world reserves of tropical hardwood for which market demand is buoyant. During the coming decade, a significant increase in real prices for tropical hardwood is expected; the bargaining position of producing countries should, as a result, steadily improve.

Developing countries have a comparative advantage in fast-growing plantations. Because of their climatic and ecological conditions, shorter rotations are possible, resulting in wood production costs that are cheaper than those in countries located in the temperate zones. Because land prices in most of the developing world are relatively low, it is possible, in some places, to secure large areas of land close to suitable industrial mill sites for the establishment of concentrated blocks of industrial plantations. Because wood is heavy and costly to transport, domestic primary and secondary manufacture is likely to become more common and to increase at a faster rate as the value of tropical hardwood rises. The potential for production of cheap pulpwood supplies, and the fact that traditional world pulpwood resources are becoming scarcer and more costly, present to developing countries an opportunity to fill part of the rising world export demand for pulp and paper products, and to substitute for imports of finished products from abroad.

Adoption of technology that will favor the creation of employment and result in the expansion of domestic manufactures can be a viable economic alternative to capital-intensive industrial forest projects in some areas. Additional employment and income can be obtained, for example, by organizing reforestation and cutting and extraction through labor-intensive methods using suitable technology rather than tree-planting machines and bulldozers—with added benefits in terms of saving foreign exchange. Adoption of new manufacturing techniques, such as smaller-scale pulp mills, can significantly advance the time at which it becomes economically viable to establish a new industry.

The buoyant world demand for forest products could provide a substantial stimulus to economic development in those developing countries that have existing forest stocks, and also in those with land, climate, and human resources that make plantation forests feasible. It is important that forest policies take account of these possibilities with a view to promoting good forest management and maximizing the contribution of forestry to economic development.

Forestry programs are, in fact, proving increasingly acceptable to governments, since they provide many benefits and are relatively inexpensive to finance. There is increasing recognition, too, that environmental considerations, local requirements, and industrial uses and exports need not be mutually exclusive; rather, they are seen as three sequential and reinforcing reasons for the promotion of forest development.

36

Where Have All the Flowers Gone? Deforestation in the Third World

Editors, Studies in Third World Societies

SOME CONSEQUENCES OF DEFORESTATION IN THE HUMID TROPICS

The decline of TMFs [tropical moist forests] will have many and varied consequences.

First of all, the tropical countries in question will lose a source of potentially renewable foreign exchange earnings. Their hardwood exports are now worth U.S. $4.5 billion per year, and are growing at a rate far faster than that for international trade in all forest products. In fact, tropical wood exports now amount to about 4 percent of the value of all developing-world exports, excluding oil, making it one of the five most important export commodities produced by the developing world. At the same time, the main markets for tropical hardwood, affluent nations, will lose the prospect of sustainable supplies of specialist timbers.

Secondly, elimination of these forests can trigger an "ecological backlash," both at a local and global level. Especially important are watershed repercussions of deforestation. Forty percent of developing-world farmers live in valleylands, and so depend heavily on the "sponge effect" of forests in surrounding catchment areas. When forests disappear, rainy-season supplies of water tend to be released in floods, followed by months-long droughts. In parts of Southeast Asia, the Green Revolution is losing momentum as farmers find they can no longer look for regular supplies of irrigation water for their multiple crops of bumper-harvest rice each year.

Excerpt from "Where Have All the Flowers Gone? Deforestation in the Third World." Reprinted by permission of The Editors, *Studies in Third World Societies*, Department of Anthropology, The College of William and Mary, Williamsburg, Va., 1981. Pp. 12–16.

In addition, deforestation leads to soil erosion, causing sedimentation of water reservoirs and hydropower installations. Reservoirs in the Philippines, Pakistan, Ecuador, and Colombia are now estimated to be losing their capacity within half their projected life spans. Similarly, the Panama Canal is filling up with washed-off soil from eroded watersheds, making it less able to handle outsize cargo ships. In Thailand, waterways that once provided an energy-efficient transportation network have become too choked with silt debris to be navigable. Now that additional deforestation-caused troubles, notably disastrous floods, are spreading to broad sectors of Thailand, the government has decided to use extraordinary powers of summary judgment, even execution, to punish unauthorized cutting of forests.

Regrettable as these ecological repercussions are for the tropical countries concerned, they are far from the whole story. From the standpoint of interdependency within the global community, some further, and ultimately more important, issues arise. Were TMFs to be largely eliminated, the process could have a major impact on world climates.

These climatic consequences are scarcely more important than the impending loss of a large portion of the earth's stocks of species. Of the 5–10 million species that are believed to exist on earth, as many as 40–50 percent are thought to live in TMFs. The next few decades could see the elimination of at least 1 million species in these forests, conceivably many more. It is not unrealistic to suppose that we are losing at least one species per day right now. Aesthetic and ethical arguments aside, there are strong economic factors in favor of safeguarding species.

To consider agriculture first, TMFs have supplied the origins of many staple foods, notably rice, millet, cassava, pigeon pea, mung bean, yam, taro, banana, pineapple, and sugarcane, to name but the better known. A huge cornucopia of other foods waits to be investigated. In Indonesia alone, some 4,000 plant species are thought to have proved useful to native peoples as food of one sort or another, yet less than one-tenth have come into wide use. At least 1,650 plants of tropical forests offer highly nutritious leaves.

Moreover, TMFs contain many wild relatives of modern food crops—crops that, being the refined products of genetic engineering, require constant "topping up" with fresh germ plasm in order to resist new types of diseases and pests, environmental stresses, and the like, as well as to increase productivity and nutritive content. During this century, genetic resources from tropical forests have saved a number of important crops, including bananas, sugarcane, cocoa, and coffee. To give an idea of the economic values involved, groundnuts worldwide have suffered from leafspot diseases—a problem that proved surmountable through resistant varieties from wild forms in the rainforests of Amazonia, among other areas. The annual value of eliminating the diseases is estimated, by the International Crop Research Institute for the Semi-Arid Tropics (ICRISAT) at U.S. $500 million.

Forest animals can also assist modern agriculture. Within the forests of the Thailand/Kampuchea (Cambodia) border lives a secretive cow-like creature, the kouprey. This creature is believed to have been one of the wild ancestors of the humped zebu cattle of southern Asia. Fresh crossbreeding between the two bovids could boost cattle raising throughout an entire region. Regrettably, the kouprey's survival is doubtful because of military activities within its habitats during the past 15 years, and little prospect exists for secure living space in the foreseeable future.

TMFs can also help to keep down the numerous pests that reduce the amount of food already grown around the world. Despite an annual pesticide bill of several billion dollars, at least 40 percent of global crops are lost each year to insects and similar pests, both in the fields and in storage. A sound way to control pests is to utilize chemicals from plants that have developed mechanisms to repel insects. The main source of these plants is TMFs. Pest control can also be advanced through selective breeding of adapted species of insects—a method that could prove more effective and economic in the long run, and result in less environmental disruption than widespread application of persistent toxic chemicals.

In addition to providing a hefty boost to agriculture, TMFs are earth's main repository of drug-yielding plants. At least 70 percent of the 3,000 species of plants that are known to possess anticancer properties exist in the tropics, mainly in TMFs. The huge stock of tropical forest plants still to be investigated could well supply many more. In addition, recent research suggests that many insects, notably butterflies, offer potential anticancer compounds—and TMFs harbor between 1.5 and 3.5 million insect species. It is on these grounds that the National Cancer Institute of the United States believes that the widespread elimination of TMFs could represent a setback to the anticancer campaign.

Let us also look briefly at a category of drugs that is of growing importance—those that serve as contraceptives and abortifacients. The rhizomes of a forest zone vine, the Mexican yam *(Dioscorea composita)*, yield virtually the world's entire supply of diosgenin, from which a variety of sex hormone combinations are prepared, including the "pill." (Diosgenin is also used to manufacture cortisone and hydrocortisone, used against rheumatoid arthritis, rheumatic fever, sciatica, certain allergies, Addison's disease, and several skin diseases.) By the mid-1970s the world was using up to 180 tons of diosgenin per year; by 1985, the amount could reach 500 tons, and by 1995, 3,000 tons. Current sales of Mexican yam materials for contraceptive pills amount to U.S. $7 million per year; when chemical compounds have been made up, the figure rises to $70 million, and across-the-counter sales for final products total $700 million.

A third category of products is derived from TMFs—specialist materials for industrial use. From Southeast Asia's forests alone come latex, gums, camphor, dammar, resins, dyes, and ethereal oils. One group of industrial products is especially important, oils and lubricants. Many forest plants bear oil-rich seeds, such as the Babassu palm *(Orbignya martiana)*, the Seje palm *(Jessenia polycarpa)*, several species of the Garyocar genus, and a number of other trees that grow wild in Amazonia. The Babassu's fruit contain up to 72 percent oil, which can be used to produce fibers, cattlefeed, soap, detergents, starch, and general edibles, and can serve as a substitute for diesel oil. Similarly, the "petroleum nut" *(Pittosporum resiniferum)* of the Philippines produces a highly volatile oil, and was used by the Japanese as fuel during World War II.

Many other plants of TMFs could offer utilitarian benefits to man, if their economic potential can be investigated before their habitats are eliminated. One hundred years ago the value of the rubber tree was unknown. What new "rubber tree" now stands in the way of some settlement project in Borneo or a ranching enterprise in Amazonia? TMFs contain many thousands of local species, any of which could be forever lost in a single month's cutting for a fresh land development project. This is not an unduly pessimistic prognosis. A tree that was once a major source of timber in Ecuador's lowland forests swiftly lost its native habitats to plantations of bananas and oil palms after its wildland home was opened up by a road in 1960. It is now reduced to 12 reproducing individuals in half a square mile of forest at the Rio Palenque Biological Center—the center itself being the last surviving patch of lowland wet forest along the western base of the Andes in central Ecuador.

Another valuable "resource" is likewise headed for oblivion: the large number of forest-dwelling tribes who still pursue their traditional way of life. In 1900 there were 230 tribal groups living in Brazil's sector of Amazonia, totaling 1 million people. Now there are only 143 groups numbering 50,000 people. On humanitarian grounds alone, forest tribes should be permitted to adapt to the outside world at their own pace. The demise of forest peoples is all the more regrettable in that they represent a fund of experience whose value can hardly be estimated. Amerindians of Amazonia know of 750 plant species with medicinal properties. It was from Amazonian tribesmen who use curare—a muscle relaxant—on their arrow tips as a hunting poison that Western surgeons learned of the substance's potential for human operations. Indonesia's National Biological Institute tells of a tribe that utilizes a forest tree as a spermicide, while certain South Pacific islands feature a number of forest plants that are used as first-month abortifacients. The World Health Organization (WHO) is searching for safer and more effective materials from which to manufacture an improved "pill," and believes a likely source lies with tribal peoples who have used some 3,000 plant species for their antifertility properties.

All in all, it seems a statistical certainty that genetic reservoirs of TMFs contain source materials for many new foods, pesticides, medicines, and industrial goods. Provided the wild species in question survive, benefits could accrue to the whole of humanity in perpetuity. In the short run, however, many of the benefits will accrue to developed-world communities far outside tropical forest zones, these being the communities with the technological know-how to exploit genetic resources.

The elimination of TMFs affects not only the developing countries in question. It could precipitate severe if not critical consequences for countries of the temperate zones as well. We either all lose together, or, through sufficient conservation measures, we all gain together.

37

Planting for the Future: Forestry for Human Needs

Erik Eckholm

FORESTS AND HUMAN NEEDS

When surrounded by the synthetic materials of the modern age, people can easily forget their dependence on trees. In the rural areas of the Third World, the importance of forests, which provide essential cooking fuel and building materials, is obvious enough. But economic advancement does not reduce a society's reliance on forest products. As countries develop, wood remains a basic raw material for construction and also takes such useful forms as furniture, railroad ties, power poles, cellophane, rayon, and plastics. Transformed into paper, it serves as an essential tool for government, commerce, education, and communications. In the years to come, wood may also provide liquid fuels and a wide array of petrochemical substitutes. For urbanites, forests provide natural havens of inestimable value to mental health, while trees both in and out of cities help create a more pleasant and comfortable milieu.

Forests perform irreplaceable ecological services as well as provide economic products and recreation. They assist in the global cycling of water, oxygen, carbon, and nitrogen. They lend stability to hydrological systems, reducing the severity of floods and permitting the recharging of springs, streams, and underground waters. Trees keep soil from washing off mountainsides and sand from blowing off deserts; they keep sediment out of rivers and reservoirs and, properly placed, help hold topsoil on agricultural fields. Forests house millions of plant and animal species that will disappear if the woodlands are destroyed.

Recent writings about the "basic needs" of the world's poor have generally ignored the fundamental importance of forests to human well-being, an analytical blind spot reflected in the paucity of programs to reduce the forest deprivation now suffered by many. Describing conditions in the central Indian state of Madhya Pradesh, but with words applicable to much of the Third World, forester R. Chakravarti writes: "It is often said that the three basic human needs are food, clothing and shelter. One cannot think of food and shelter without wood, which is a more basic need. In fact it may be truthfully said of an average villager of the State that he is still in the 'wood age.' "

Cultivation in Madhya Pradesh, as in many underdeveloped areas, relies mainly on wooden plows, and produce is transported in wooden bullock carts. Houses are built of wood and mud or bamboo and thatch. Wood is required for a host of other purposes such as fencing, furniture, implements, and handicrafts. Above all, continues Chakravarti, "wood, a marvelous, God-given means of storing solar energy, is also required to cook food with. . . . In fact, the production of food-grains without the means to cook them and make them edible would appear to be a half-hearted attempt at achieving freedom from hunger."

Nonwood forest products are important as well. In many regions, tree leaves and forest grasses sustain cattle, which in turn pull plows and carts and supply milk and fertilizer. Leaves, fruits, nuts, honey, and wild animals provide a significant share of the food supply of hundreds of millions of people. Traditional medicines and useful barks are taken from forests. Commercially valuable products such as mushrooms, drugs, gums, and resins are extracted from forests as well. Forests are often evaluated by economists in terms of their ability to provide a dead product—wood; but for many of those residing in and around them, forests are a living, dynamic resource.

The global pattern of forest-product use and distribution mirrors the pattern of economic wealth and development. Eighty percent of the wood used in the Third World is burned for fuel, and much of it never passes through a commercial market. Though developing countries contain three-fourths of the world's people and more than half its forests, they account for just 13 percent of global consumption of "industrial wood"—marketed logs, sawn wood, panel products such as plywood and fiberboard, paper, and other manufactured products. Annual per capita paper use in developing countries is 6 kilograms, compared to 257 kilograms in North America. In fact, each year the average American consumes about as much wood—2 cubic meters—in the form of paper as the average resident in many Third World countries burns as cooking fuel.

About one-third of the world's industrial wood is traded internationally. Four-fifths of the trade originates and ends in developed countries, with North America and the Soviet Union having a surplus and Japan and Western Europe a deficit. Partly because of the plethora of specialized forest products used in modern economies, most countries both import and export them to some degree. Hence the United States sends lumber to Japan and pulp and paper to many destinations, but imports enough wood and paper, mainly from Canada, to be not only a net importer but in fact the world's largest single importer of forest products.

Many poorer tropical countries export timber, usually as unsawn hardwood logs, but these countries, like most other developing nations, must import much of their paper and manufactured wood products. Southeast Asia exports a large volume of timber to Japan in particular, while African tropical logs go mainly to Western Europe. With wood, as with other resources, buying power rather than need determines the global allocation of traded products.

According to demand projections by the Food and Agriculture Organization (FAO) based on expected rises in income and population, worldwide consumption of wood for all purposes will grow from 2.5 billion cubic meters in 1976 to 4 billion cubic meters in 1994. Commercial wood demand is rising particularly fast in less developed countries, most of which combine rapid population growth and relatively high economic growth rates with low current levels of industrial wood consumption. The FAO projects that Third World consumption of wood-panel products and paper will quadruple over the next two decades, and that consumption of sawn wood will rise by 50 percent a decade. These latter estimates cover commercial demand only; even if they are realized, many poor people will remain deprived of basic forest products.

Even as the demand for industrial wood soars, a large proportion of humanity will continue to rely on firewood for cooking and home heating. John Spears of the World Bank has assessed future firewood needs, based on optimistic assumptions about the spread of wood-conserving stoves and cooking alternatives such as biogas plants and solar cookers. According to his calculations, 20 to 25 million hectares of new plantations will have to be in place by the year 2000. At the current rate of planting for this purpose, only about 2 million hectares, one-tenth of what is needed, will be established. A recent analysis of energy prospects in the Sahelian zone of West Africa concluded that the planting rate must be multiplied 50-fold if regional firewood needs by the century's end are to be met.

Leaving questions of accessibility aside, there are currently about 75 cubic meters of wood in the world's dense forests for every person. By the end of the century, however, the per capita amount of potentially exploitable timber will be nearly cut in half if the current deforestation rate is maintained, if existing population projections materialize, and if the worldwide tree-planting effort is not pushed far above its current level. This "transition from a period of global forest wealth to a period of global forest poverty," as it is described in a forthcoming U.S. government study, would clearly have palpable and painful economic effects, particularly among the poorer groups within poorer countries. "Relative prices of industrial wood products, paper, sawn lumber, wood panels, wood-based chemicals, plastics, and many other products are sure to increase," the study concludes. If they occur, these price rises will choke off demand well before the projected consumption increases come about, fueling inflation everywhere and denying people in forest-poor countries many of the benefits, and even some of the necessities, that forest products provide. Meanwhile, the continued loss of forests will accentuate the environmental costs of denudation already apparent in many countries—erosion, desertification, siltation, flooding, and the extinction of species.

To some extent, as economists are quick to point out, market forces automatically help offset timber scarcity. Higher prices will induce technological innovation and new investments, spur the substitution of alternative materials, and encourage the conservation and recycling of forest products. But in the forest sector, as in others, these natural market tendencies alone will not provide an acceptable solution. In a world of extreme income disparities, the adjustments of the market take a heavy toll among those at the bottom, many of whom will have no good substitute for writing paper in school or for firewood on the hearth. Even in more affluent countries, rising forest-product prices will impose social burdens. Public policies that incorporate both the needed time horizon and the needed social vision into forestry planning are essential.

WORLD FOREST TRENDS

Important as forests are to human well-being, knowledge about their extent or the rate at which they are disappearing is surprisingly incomplete. Only about half the world's forests have been subjected to detailed surveys, and only a fraction of these have been surveyed more than once so that changes over time could be documented. The spreading use of satellite technologies is improving the situation: with the aid of remote sensing, Brazil's huge Amazonian forest has been mapped for the first time. Still, any discussion at present of global forest resources and trends must be based on a concoction of subjective observations and surveys of varied quality.

Definitional differences among surveys and misinformation, put out deliberately or otherwise, further bedevil forest statisticians. The last official UN World Forest Inventory, published in 1963, called 29 percent of the earth's land suface "forestland," but this figure included everything from thick rainforests to lightly wooded arctic tundra that would not fit many people's idea of forest at all. Government statistics on forest areas—which usually find their way into international statistics—are sometimes doctored outright and, in any case, frequently include large areas euphemistically labeled "unstocked." Clear-cut lands where natural regeneration is slow or impossible and even lands occupied by farmers are designated as forest in many Third World statistical books. For the economist, even a precise measure of densely wooded areas would be inadequate; accessibility, steepness, and mix of species affect the commercial potential of a given region.

At present, the best available global survey is that compiled by Swedish analyst Reidar Persson. In his data, he has usefully distinguished between "closed forests," where tree crowns cover 20 percent or more of the ground when viewed from above, and "open woodlands," where a scattering of trees provides a crown cover of 5 to 19 percent. In general, only the closed forests would be suitable for commercial timber operations. While the gaps in data remain huge, Persson has adjusted government statistics in keeping with available field observations and surveys wherever possible.

According to Persson's calculations, closed forests covered about one-fifth of the earth's land in the mid-seventies. (See Table 1.) The true proportion is quite likely to be even lower than that, for only outdated surveys exist for many regions, and areas recently cleared or severely degraded are almost certainly included in the totals. Open woodlands cover perhaps another 12 percent of the earth's land area; this estimate is even rougher than that for denser forests. Although firm comparisons with earlier global inventories are impossible, by one estimate the area of land covered with closed forests in 1950 amounted to about one-fourth of the earth's land surface, which gives some idea of the pace of change.

In terms of sheer tree-covered area, Latin America and the Soviet Union lead by far among regions, with 680 million hectares of closed for-

TABLE 1 The World's Forests By Region, Mid-1970s

Region	Closed Forest (million hectares)	Closed Forest as Share of Land Area (percent)	Open Woodlands (million hectares)	Open Woodlands as Share of Land Area (percent)
Latin America	680	33	280	14
USSR	680	30	240	11
North America	470	25	176	9
Asia	410	15	100	4
Africa	190	6	640	21
Europe	138	28	37	8
Oceania	89	10	105	12
World total	2,657	20	1,578	12

Source: North American data from *Global 2000 Report*; all other from Reidar Persson, "Need for a Continuous Assessment."

est in each. From an economic perspective, however, such totals can be misleading. While most of the Soviet Union's trees are conifers, whose soft woods are sought after for construction and papermaking, a good share of them stand in remote, cold areas where harvesting is commercially unfeasible and growth is extremely slow. While the Soviet Union does enjoy a wood surplus, the widespread notion that it will become a major supplier of forest products to a wood-short world is not grounded in economic reality.

The total for Latin America is so high largely because of the Amazon Basin, which is covered by the world's largest tropical moist forest.

But forest-product industries have not yet begun to make good use of many of the incredibly numerous species in rainforests. Much tropical timber exploitation to date has been, in the words of former FAO forestry chief K.F.S. King, "primitive, costly and wasteful," and of little lasting benefit to nearby residents. Although the Brazilian Government has recently unveiled controversial plans to expand Amazonian timber cutting and exports, the country has subsidized huge private tree plantations in its temperate south in order to meet its soaring domestic needs. Brazil is currently a net importer of forest products.

As of the mid-1970s, there were about 0.7 hectare of closed forest for each of the world's 4 billion people. (See Table 2.) The disparities among regions, and among countries within regions, in per capita forest area are huge. Two or more hectares of forest stood per person in the USSR, Latin America, North America, and Oceania; only half a hectare or less per person existed in Africa, Europe, and Asia. Again, though, aggregates can mislead. Many people in Latin America, especially in Central America and the Andean countries, live amidst barren hills and wood scarcity; the richness of rainforests elsewhere in the continent means lit-

TABLE 2 Forest Resources per Person, Mid-1970s

Region	Closed-Forest Area per Person (hectares)	Standing Wood Volume per Person* (cubic meters)
Oceania	4.2	238
USSR	2.7	329
Latin America	2.1	253
North America	2.0	179
Africa	0.5	107
Europe	0.3	31
Asia	0.2	15
World total	0.7	75

*Closed forests only. World total volume in open woodlands estimated to be about 12.5 cubic meters per person.

Source: North American data from *Global 2000 Report*; all other from Reidar Persson, "Need for a Continuous Assessment."

tle to them. Residents of a few countries in Central and West Africa are surrounded by dense tropical forests, though people throughout much of Africa suffer from an extreme paucity of trees. Asia's forest area per person, an abysmal 0.2 hectare, is only that high because the remaining thick stands of Southeast Asia are included in the calculation. These forests aside, most of Asia faces an extraordinary scarcity of trees. Looking at the other side of the coin, Europe's forests, many of which have been intensively managed for more than a century, produce far more harvestable timber—and on a sustainable basis—than the low per capita figure might imply.

Estimates of the rate at which closed forests are disappearing range from 10 to 20 million hectares each year, with the most recent surveys suggesting that a total near the lower end of that range is probably correct. Nearly all the shrinkage in closed-forest area is occurring in the humid tropics; in the best published analysis of tropical moist-forest trends, Adrian Sommer estimates that their total area is declining annually by about 1.2 percent, or 11 million hectares—an area the size of Bulgaria or Cuba. Covering 935 million hectares in the mid-1970s, tropical moist forests have already been reduced from their natural domain by more than 40 percent.

In North America and Europe, the forest area is roughly stable; in fact, the modernization of agriculture over the last half-century has allowed a considerable reversion of farm to forest. A slight increase in forest area is projected for Europe over coming decades, while a slight decrease may be in store in North America. In these regions, the challenge in the years ahead is less one of simply preserving forestlands than of balancing competing environmental, recreational, and industrial demands and of choosing appropriate timber-management techniques. Among less developed countries, China and South Korea stand out for having substantially increased their forested areas in recent times.

Throughout most of Africa, Asia, and Latin America, the forest area itself is shrinking and usually not according to any rational land-use plan. Areas that were densely settled long ago—such as the Middle East, parts of North Africa, the Andean region of South America, and most of China and South Asia—lost the bulk of their forests in ages past, so the absolute decline, if any, in closed-forest area today is not large even though the depletion of tree cover in and out of forests generally continues. But many developing countries, especially those in the humid tropical belt, are now experiencing rapid and massive forest destruction. According to one FAO estimate, the annual loss of forests in Latin America is 5 to 10 million hectares, in Africa about 2 million hectares, and in Asia about 5 million hectares. Even figures like these greatly understate the deforestation problem, for they reflect neither the massive degradation of timber and other biological resources occurring *within* many still-standing forests nor the severe depletion of open woodlands and countryside vegetation that currently blights most Third World countries.

In long denuded and more arid regions, the hardships imposed by a dearth of trees have long been felt. Now the combination of destructive logging practices and the ill-planned spread of cultivation is even pulling many seemingly timber-rich countries of the humid tropics toward forest-related economic and ecological crises. In late 1977, while pressing for the adoption of a new forestry policy, the deputy premier of peninsular Malaysia shocked his compatriots by projecting that the region's once-lush forests would be severely depleted in just 12 years. He predicted that by 1990 the rate of timber production would not be adequate to meet domestic, let alone foreign, demand. Stringent new logging controls are being imposed in Thailand following the National Forestry Department's estimate that the country's forests are shrinking by 250,000 hectares a year, and that they will be virtually gone in 25 years if present logging and farming practices continue. (Thailand has a special problem with poachers of valuable tropical hardwoods; each year 30 to 40 forest guards are killed in gun battles.)

Recent satellite pictures of the Philippines, traditionally a major timber exporter, indicate that forests now cover just 30 percent of the country, though the goverment feels a forest cover of 46 percent is desirable for economic and environmental reasons. If existing logging patterns prevail, a consortium of Philippine research organizations has concluded, all original old-growth forests will have been cut down by the year 2000 and projected timber supplies from second-growth forests and plantations will not suffice to meet even domestic needs. Destructive increases in flooding and sedimentation have already been registered.

Examining logging and agricultural trends in the timber-exporting zones of West and Central Africa, Reidar Persson believes it is "likely that all exploitable forests in West Africa and most of Central Africa (except Zaire) will be exploited a first time before the turn of the century with resulting impoverishment of the natural forests. In a number of countries future exploitation will have to decrease." Increasingly far from harbors and good roads, Africa's remaining virgin forests will be expensive to exploit. Existing planting programs and natural regeneration are not nearly offsetting the pace at which prime export species are depleted. Nor are plantations to meet the continent's own escalating needs for lumber, pulp and paper, and firewood being established at anything close to the needed rate.

On a worldwide basis, the extent to which tree planting is offsetting forest losses is impossible to ascertain. What data do exist on reforestation and plantation programs often do not distinguish the restocking of existing forestlands from the extension of plantations to new areas. In a 1978 report, the FAO estimated the "current world planting programme" to be "about 4 million hectares a year." China and developed countries undoubtedly account for most of the total. Persson has recently estimated the planting rate in the developing countries, excluding China and Korea, to be about 650,000 hectares a year. The FAO's 1976 review of forest trends in Asia assumed that new planting in the region's developing countries, again excluding China, would total only 1.5 million hectares during the decade of the 1970s.

Given the alarm about forest losses and firewood scarcity that has recently been voiced by many governments and aid agencies, and the flurry of reforestation programs now being initiated, the planting totals are probably rising fast. Still, the current pace of tree planting looks pitifully slow when compared with the pace of forest loss, and slower still when compared with the gargantuan demands that will be placed on the world's forests in the decades to come. [. . .]

Terrestrial Resources: Water

Water is still largely taken for granted in much of the world, even as wood is, but it seems likely that water will supplant food before very long as the world's dominant resource problem. This section highlights five aspects of water use, all of which are interrelated, not only with one another but with all other resources and elements of our physical environment. When we estimate, for example, the potential for increasing food production, we must realistically take into account the available and potential soil and water resources without which there can be little agriculture. This Jan van Schilfgaarde does very cogently in an article both optimistic and wary. M. Falkenmark of the Swedish Natural Science Research Council takes a broader view of the man-water relationship and is more cautionary, urging international cooperation in such things as development of international rivers and land- and water-use planning. The geographers Gilbert F. White, David J. Bradley, and Anne U. White bring the question of water use down to the household level, using East Africa as a study area and deriving therefrom important lessons and major recommendations for policymakers.

The foregoing pieces concentrate on water use in general and rural water use in particular. The next piece, by urban geographers Brian J. L. Berry and Frank E. Horton and based on a monograph by geographer James F. Johnson of Columbia, Maryland, calls attention to growing water problems and recommends recycling of urban water supplies. Finally, the roundup of the 1977 UN Conference on Desertification illuminates a problem that, combined with deforestation and soil erosion, is progressively reducing *the useful land area of the world very considerably at a time when our needs are increasing rapidly and dramatically.*

38

Earth and Water

Jan van Schilfgaarde

Whatever ingenuity man brings to bear, the resource base of land and water, together with solar energy, is finite; ultimately, it limits the potential for agricultural production. The potential production from the world's land resources has been estimated to be about 40 times the present level, based on a very high level of technological, capital, and energy-intensive inputs; however, considering a far lower "labor-oriented" level of technology, the potential production on the maximum land base would feed only 20 percent more than the current world population.

Such global estimates must be qualified since they do not account for distributional problems or weather variability. They do indicate that the potential for increasing food production is substantial. Also, they emphasize the importance of the basic resources, land and water, as well as the need for intensive technological intervention.

Agriculture does not exist in isolation. It is an integral part of an advancing society. Agricultural technology benefits directly from many developments in other fields—the space program, electronics, biochemistry—and suffers from others, such as automobile-caused air pollution. One aspect of this interaction was illustrated instructively by researchers who studied the returns to agriculture from investments in research. One of their findings was that science-oriented research per se did not seem to have a high payoff. Only when it was teamed with technology-oriented research was the payoff substantial.

In the broad and ill-defined field of soil and water management, the interaction between agriculture and other phases of society is evident.

Industry competes with irrigated farming for limited water resources; home builders and highway planners compete with farmers for prime land. More subtly, soil science tends to build and expand on principles derived in physics, chemistry, and biology.

Some recent developments in soil and water science augur for future advances in soundly based management strategies; and some technological innovations, based on principles established earlier, now enable us to make better use of our resources. These examples offer hope for the future, but several caveats are in order. Money and people tend to follow the trends of the moment. The spectacular new findings in genetics have caused a reorientation of research emphasis towards biochemistry. Justified as this enthusiasm may be, it also endangers the support for less glamorous areas of endeavor. Moreover, decisions—or the lack of them—that adversely affect soil and water resources in the United States, or improper development of extensive but difficult to manage soils of the tropics, can do damage that will take centuries to repair. Similarly, the mining of groundwater for irrigation, as is being done in western Texas, Arizona, and California, clearly cannot be continued indefinitely. To paraphrase Georgescu-Roegen, when we make our decisions on resource use and abuse, who bids for future generations? And what happens when groundwater supplies are exhausted? Sound exploitation of land and water resources, in a manner that leads to continuous productivity over time, may not excite the imagination of the science writer or maximize the immediate returns to the investor; yet it is of the highest priority if the future interests of mankind are to be served.

Soil science, as a recognized discipline, emerged around the turn of the century. It is fascinating to note, in perusing the literature, that many of the principles taught today were being enunciated around that time and that a number of the controversies receiving attention in today's laboratories were being argued in the early decades of this century. For example, a prime theme in soil physics is the movement of water and solutes through soils. As early as 1907, Buckingham laid the physical foundation for describing the flow of water through soils. Ignored for many years, his ideas were expanded and refined in the late 1920s, leading finally to a classic paper by Richards (1931) that still is quoted widely. After the Second World War, a veritable deluge of papers appeared, continuing into the 1970s. Aided by better experimental techniques and, especially, increased computer capability, we now are able to predict or describe the movement of water, salts, pesticides, and heavy metals with a reasonable degree of certainty. That movement is of paramount importance when dealing with irrigation and drainage, salinity management, and pollution control. We also have "discovered" a new problem: use of such mathematical models requires quantitative knowledge of the pertinent soil properties. Whereas these often can be measured adequately on soil samples, soils are notoriously unhomogeneous (as well as variable in time), and serious questions arise as to the extrapolation to field-scale situations. Significant progress has recently been made in defining the nature of the spatial variability by drawing on concepts from statistics and geology and in interpreting the consequences of this variability. Thus, in the next few years, we should witness a substantial increase in our capability to move from the laboratory to the field in making predictions, or to recommend with confidence management options that will optimize use of the soil and water resources while minimizing pollution hazards.

Another example may be taken from soil chemistry. In the 1920s and 1930s, Mattson published nearly 30 papers dealing with colloidal behavior, in which he argued that the electrical charge that binds anions and cations to soils varied both in magnitude and in sign depending on solute composition and pH. The introduction of X-ray techniques in that same time period established the crystalline nature of clay minerals and showed that a constant, negative surface-charge density could be deduced from isomorphic substitution within the clay lattice. The latter finding, with later elaboration and refinements, led to a theoretical base for describing exchange reactions in soils that was found generally satisfactory for temperate-zone soils, and Mattson was ignored by the majority of soil scientists. More recently, the failure of these theories to explain the behavior of tropical soils led to a revived interest in the question of the origin of charge. A series of recent papers have offered sophisticated theoretical models that give a far broader theoretical understanding of the behavior of soils. Aside from intellectual satisfaction, these developments provide the basis for rational management recommendations on tropical soils, the one huge frontier for expansion of the food production base, that have just refused to respond as temperate-zone soil scientists anticipated.

One other example seems appropriate. To some, soil morphology and genesis, often called pedology, is the essence of soil science. The problem of describing and classifying soils in a meaningful manner has faced the profession for generations. Hilgard, active around the turn of the century, can properly be credited with enumerating the principles of soil formation and classification upon which later work was based. After years of work by many scientists, punctuated by local as well as international controversy, the seventh approximation for soil classification culminated in soil taxonomy. Primarily the brain child of Guy Smith, this system provides a hierarchical description of soils in quantitative terms. No doubt revisions and refinements will continue to be made. However, for the first time we have a tool that can be used not only to inventory soil resources rationally but to transfer knowledge gained across the world from one place to the other where similar soils occur. Considering the number of field experiments that are conducted year after year—on crop response to fertilizer, need for liming, or what have you—it doesn't take great imagination to recognize the value of a universal system of classification. Unfortunately, however, soil taxonomy has yet to be accepted worldwide—not too surprising if we consider our reluctance to accept the international system of units. Also, although the framework exists, soil taxonomy will not meet its potential unless substantially more effort is expended on systems of interpretation for specific uses.

The science of soil and water management extends beyond the customary field of soil science. Soils and water are managed to grow crops and we need to understand the very intricate interaction among plants, soils, and climate, including the effect of environmental stresses on plant growth. One such stress is salinity. Although much empirical evidence permits us to describe the impact of salinity, we as yet don't understand the physiological mechanisms that make some crops more tolerant than others. Recent work supports the hypothesis that salinity tolerance is directly linked to the energy-transfer system: it requires energy to overcome stress. The details are not important here, but slowly we are reaching the level of understanding that may lead to a rational approach towards modifying the plant to withstand greater stress from salinity.

These few examples illustrate the often slow but continuing process of scientific discovery, field application, and feedback. At a given moment, it is sometimes difficult to see the forest for the trees and it may appear that research is often done to reinvent the wheel (some is). Yet in a broader perspective, existing trends, which give confidence in future advances, become clear. It serves our goal better, however, to change direction.

Much of the recent research effort in soil and water management has been directed towards environmental quality. Priorities, and hence funding sources, deemphasized agricultural production per se and stressed adverse effects of runoff and erosion and of fertilizer and pesticide applications on water quality. Yet, both because and in spite of these directives, there have been clear gains in our ability to at least sustain productivity without adverse effects.

Only 12 percent of the land in agriculture is irrigated, but its production represents about 25 percent of the total. Irrigation is a primary user of water. It also accounts for a high percentage of the fossil energy used in agricultural production. In Nebraska, 55 percent of the agricultural fossil energy is used for irrigation. Water of good quality is becoming a scarce commodity. Lindh, in reviewing global water resources, concluded that by the year 2000 limitations in available water will be a decisive factor in economic development on most continents; in much of the world we need not wait that long. The importance of water in irrigation agriculture is obvious and explicit. Although less obvious, in rain-fed agriculture the timely availability of water is very often the primary restraint to increasing production; water erosion is of overriding concern in maintaining productivity over time.

Until recently, irrigation water has been cheap and abundant, especially when it was supplied and subsidized by some central authority. For the farmer, labor saving often has been the primary criterion in choosing irrigation practices. Now, water and energy conservation have gained in importance.

To obtain the maximum agricultural product per unit of water applied, water must be provided to the crop in the right amounts at the proper times. The goal should be to maintain the soil water potential (or the soil water content) in the root zone uniformly high, recognizing that such a practice might need to be modified to permit soil storage of rainwater and use of stored soil water. In practice, water is supplied periodically, with the time between irrigations used for other farming operations. Good management, then, makes it critical to know when a crop needs irrigating. Many experiments, together with studies of the physics of evaporation, have provided extensive knowledge about the rate of water use by various crops as a function of stage of growth and weather variables, so that irrigation scheduling schemes could be developed to tell the farmer when to apply how much water. An accurate time span within which an irrigation must take place is important for good water use. Using computers, a number of private and public organizations currently provide such a service to help farmers improve their water management. Scheduling, which moved from research and demonstration to commercial application during the 1970s, is one effective way to improve water use. Scheduling, of course, cannot overcome system deficiencies.

Typically, in a gravity (surface) irrigation system, water is induced to flow across a gently sloping field surface in a manner that attempts to provide an equal "intake opportunity time." Some water is bound to run off the end of the field and the actual amount stored in the soil will vary from place to place because of variability in soil properties as well as hydraulic complications. In conventional sprinkler irrigation, wind distortion plus the geometric problems of overlapping circular spray patterns also lead to irregular water distribution. Irrigation efficiencies, in terms of water stored in the root zone compared to water applied, vary over a wide range but tend to be low. These low efficiencies do not necessarily waste water; excess water may be recaptured and used later. Still, the opportunities for conserving water (and energy if the water is pumped) are substantial.

In recent years, tremendous changes have taken place in irrigation. They have come about because of new technology based on old principles. The pivot sprinkler—a 400-meter pipe moved around a pivot on wheeled towers, with sprinklers mounted on the pipe—can supply water uniformly to a circular field. It permits unattended, efficient irrigation. The original designs required relatively high pressures and high water-application rates that could cause severe erosion unless they were restricted to sandy soils. Recently, lower-pressure units that use less energy have become available. In just the last two years, reliable systems have been developed that move laterally rather than in circles and thus are better adapted to rectangular fields. By replacing the regularly spaced, rotating sprinkler heads with leaky hoses that drag in the furrows behind the machine, they have been modified to operate at low pressures; both energy and water are conserved. Various machines that place temporary check dams in the long furrows prevent runoff and thus control erosion.

These systems are being adopted readily for several reasons other than water conservation. By irrigating frequently in small amounts, they permit development of sandy soils otherwise too costly to irrigate; fully automatic, they save labor; with careful control over water distribution, they result in high crop yields. The key to their success is that control over water distribution is obtained by confining the water to a closed conduit, thus avoiding the variability due to the nonhomogeneity of soils. Fly over Nebraska, or fly over Libya: the hundreds of green circles attest to the new technology.

Another new development using closed conduits is "trickle irrigation." An Israeli development, this consists of a low-pressure, small-diameter plastic pipe distribution system that lets water trickle out at controlled rates at numerous points across a field. So far, the cost limits the use of trickle irrigation to high-value row crops, such as melons, with the emitters placed as close as 30 centimeters apart along a crop row, or tree crops, where two or three emitters may be spaced around a tree. The slow, almost continuous, localized water application permits precise control of irrigation rates. It also makes it possible to wet only part of the soil surface, thus limiting evaporation losses. A variation on the theme is Rawlins's low-head bubbler system for tree crops; using inexpensive, shallowly buried, corrugated plastic tubing for distribution and a small-diameter (10-millimeter) overflow tube at each tree, this system fills a small basin around each tree as frequently as desired. It can be installed with simple tools and adjusted, with nothing more than a measuring tape, to control the volume of water delivered to each tree within 2 percent and it requires practically no pressure.

Thus a host of devices have become available to improve water utilization with closed-conduit irrigation systems. Substantial advances have also been made in gravity systems. For the uninitiated, it may be difficult to visualize the complications of moving relatively large streams of water from field to field and, in turn, spreading this water uniformly across the fields. Although the principle is the same, the irrigator does a bit more than opening and closing the garden hose faucet. Clock-operated devices that automatically open and close gates or ports in appropriate sequences are now reliable enough for routine use. Under development is a system that sequences water flows from field to field on the basis of volume of water passed, rather than time elapsed. With these devices, farmers now are able to "automate" irrigation with gravity-flow, open-ditch systems; that is, having decided in what order and with how much water they wish to irrigate a series of fields, they can program a central control panel, start the process, and walk away. Automation saves labor. In principle, it has no effect on water-use efficiency; in practice, however, it does. Water can be changed at the proper time without intefering with the irrigator's other activities.

Efficient gravity irrigation demands precise land preparation. The advent of the laser has made frequent, precision land-grading operations practical. Combined with automation, laser grading has the potential for dramatic increases in efficiency. A system called "dead level" divides a field into sections, their size depending on soils and topography, which are then leveled as smooth as a table top and surrounded by low levees. Water is applied in large streams to provide quick and uniform temporary flooding. Developed in Arizona, it is now spreading to other areas. Of course, it is a modern adaptation of a system that goes back millennia! In one study on a series of fields aggregating about 3,000 hectares, a comparison of on-farm irrigation before and after improvements were made showed an increased efficiency from about 60 to about 80 percent.

All irrigation waters contain at least some salts. Even pristine mountain streams dissolve salts from the minerals they contact. As pure water is returned to the atmosphere through the process of evapotranspiration, the dissolved salt is retained in the smaller volume of water remaining, thus increasing its concentration. Salinity problems are ubiquitous wherever irrigation is practiced.

Statistics are hard to come by, but it has been suggested that each year as much land is lost to salinity as is brought under new irrigation development. Whereas the principles of salinity management are simple and well established, the details are quite another matter. Conceptually, it generally suffices to apply enough irrigation water in excess of crop requirements to establish a downward flux through the soil profile that will wash out any accumulating salts and remove them with the drainage water.

In this area, also, a number of recent developments can lead to enhanced continuing use of natural resources. As a consequence of the ability to manage irrigation more effectively it also becomes possible to provide more effective salinity control. A key question reduces to how much is enough in applying excess water for salt removal—in the jargon: What is the leaching requirement? Work at our laboratory led to the conclusion that the leaching requirement is substantially less than previously estimated.

It would carry us too far afield to elaborate in detail on this finding, its limitations and consequences. Suffice it to note that one researcher verified that Valencia oranges could be irrigated without yield reduction with 10 percent leaching in an area where 50 percent was the norm. The practical consequences of implementing minimum leaching, however, are highly site-specific and frequently the benefits are greater off-site than on the field in question. In one valley in Arizona, it has been demonstrated that broad-scale application of practices to maximize irrigation efficiency in consonance with the new leaching requirement offers a technically sound alternative to a power-hungry desalting plant in meeting the objectives of downstream water quality prescribed by international obligations; a third alternative would be to discontinue irrigated agriculture in the valley. Considering that the annual cost of the desalting complex is likely to exceed $30 million and the power requirement is estimated at 35 megawatts, the potential impact of modern water and salinity management principles speaks for itself.

Water management, other than irrigation and erosion, also involves drainage: the timely removal of excess water. Here again, a centuries-old art has undergone drastic changes of late, involving theory of water flow, introduction of new materials, and new installation techniques. A body of theory has developed, primarily since World War II, that describes in detail the movement of water through saturated and unsaturated soils and the effect of a drainage system on such movement. Not until recently, however, has there been much success in effectively applying such theory to practical field design. A set of computer programs has been developed that are both simple enough and sufficiently realistic to enable relatively routine design that takes account of soil properties, weather variations, and anticipated crops to be grown. The last decade also has seen the virtually complete replacement of clay or concrete drain pipes with corrugated plastic tubing, resulting in substantial savings in materials and materials handling costs, and the development of laser-controlled machines for installation—either trenchers or trenchless types—that operate much faster and at lower unit costs. In short, the changes in drainage technology have been phenomenal, promising significantly better water management at acceptable costs, and thus contributing to increased food production.

A key concern of long standing has been soil fertility, or rather crop nutrition. Increased understanding of the dynamic interaction between soil chemistry and water movement has led to significant recent progress in methodology for testing both plants and soils to determine fertility status and fertilizer needs. Of special interest, however, are three rather different areas of inquiry, dealing with the elements selenium, nitrogen, and phosphorus. Much of this work may not yet have led to widespread applications, but it offers important future possibilities.

Selenium (Se) is an element that occurs in soils in various chemical forms and in varying concentrations. It seems it is not essential for plants, but it is for animals and man. Either too low or too high a concentration in the feed (within quite narrow limits) can cause a range of livestock diseases. Scientists have learned a great deal about the cycling of Se from soil to plant to animal and back to soil; one important product of this research has been a map of the United States showing areas where the Se level in crops is deficient, sufficient, or excessive for the health of livestock; Se supplements in livestock feeds from low Se areas have had significant impact on the economics of livestock production as well as on the nutritional value of the animal products. The link between soil and human health is more tenuous, in part because the movement of food stuffs through the markets makes assessment of dietary Se levels difficult. A recent report from China indicated that "Keshan disease," a congestive heart condition, is due to Se deficiency. In the region where this disease is prevalent, locally grown cereals contain extremely low Se levels. This report suggests that the export of U.S. and Canadian bread wheats (which tend to be relatively rich in Se) may unwittingly have aided in preventing more widespread human Se deficiency.

The next topic concerns the management of nitrogen in the soil. Nitrogen fertilizer, considered a necessity for efficient crop production, is generally applied in the ammonium or nitrate form. In general, less than one-half the nitrogen applied as fertilizer is taken up by plants; the rest is lost by leaching or volatilization. The introduction of biocidal compounds to reduce the rate of mineralization extends the residence time of applied ammonia fertilizer and thus makes more of it available to the crop over a longer period of time. Several such compounds have been identified and tested extensively. One, nitropyrin, has been approved for field use in the United States on a number of crops. Use of denitrification inhibitors tends to increase crop yield, even with lower fertilizer application rates, and saves energy in two ways: nitrogen fertilizer is made from natural gas; also, use of inhibitors makes it possible to apply the fertilizer less often, thus saving farming operations.

Finally, consider the rhizosphere, that highly complex, constantly changing region of the soil where plants' roots thrive and microorganisms abound. The subtle manifold interaction among organisms that, together, make up the system in which plants grow is still not fully understood. Of special interest are the endomycorrhizae, a special class of symbiotic associations between fungi and higher plants. Recent work has clearly established that mycorrhizae enhance the nutrition of many plant species, especially with respect to phosphorus. The largest proportion (about 40 percent) of the potentially arable but still virtually unused land in the world lies in the vast savanna areas of Latin America. Particularly in these regions, nutritional problems are prevalent. It has been amply demonstrated that, in principle, enhancement of appropriate mycorrhizae can be a major assist in solving these problems. The practical details still need to be resolved.

The tremendous damage from erosion on the cotton plantations of our South is legendary. Many will recall the coming of age of the conservation movement in the 1930s. Despite this long-standing recognition and the many decades of intensive activity, erosion continues to be a serious threat on much of the cropland in the United States; in many other parts of the world, the situation is worse.

As a college sophomore in the 1940s, in a beginning course on agricultural machinery, I recall being confronted with the question, "Why do farmers plow?" A satisfactory answer could not be given. Yet the moldboard plow has long been the primary tool of the farmer.

Much more recently, in response to the energy crisis, formal proposals were floated to collect all crop residues from the land as an alternative source of fuel, while at the same time removing the nuisance such trash posed to efficient farming.

These three apparently random observations are closely intertwined. They point to the interaction of the many components in a soil-crop management system; they illustrate the real and substantial dangers of monoculture and excessive tillage and remind us of the value of crop residues in reducing erosion, in conserving soil water, and in recycling plant nutrients. They also serve to introduce several separate lines of research that have paid substantial dividends in recent years.

Formal research on the mechanisms of erosion and on management practices for its control started in the 1930s. Strongly influenced by the demands imposed by environmental legislation, this work was consolidated and advanced in the last few years, so that we now have available reasonably reliable procedures for quantitative evaluation of the expected erosion rate from any given soil as a function of cropping pattern, management practices, and climate. We now can—with some trepidation—make explicit determinations to aid in decision making by landowners or, sign of the times, regulators. We also have used these same techniques, together with the findings from other studies, to determine, soil-by-soil and region-by-region, how much plant residue can safely be removed from the land without endangering its long-term productivity; or conversely, what residues must be left on the land for its protection.

Somewhat independently, but still closely related, we have witnessed drastic changes in crop management and in tillage practices. Grouped under the nonspecific term "conservation tillage," research, often spurred on by farmers' insistence, has led to numerous innovations of tillage practices called by many names. Conservation tillage may be described as any tillage system that reduces soil or water loss compared to clean tillage.

Conditions vary drastically from region to region, and from site to site within a region. Conservation tillage systems do not offer a panacea. On wet, "heavy" soils, some of these systems tend to reduce yields and increase weed-control problems; in some other cases, they reduce yields because of greater incidence of disease or damage from phytotoxic substances (poisons released by decomposing plant residues). Still, the widespread, profitable, and constructive shift in tillage practices reflects a significant application of research results, many of very recent vintage. New tillage and new crop-management systems that increase crop yields, reduce erosion, conserve energy, and save labor are being adopted (and continuously modified) on millions of hectares.

A few examples must suffice. On the rugged hills of Appalachia, the cultivation of a row crop like corn is precarious. A grass crop will control erosion but provides little cash income. Using a herbicide to stunt (but not kill) the grass, corn can be planted directly into the sod. By the time the corn is harvested, the grass has recovered from the herbicide. Thus two crops are grown in the place of one while erosion is controlled, and most tillage operations are eliminated. Soybeans planted without tillage in winter-wheat stubble provided a higher net income than other practices, such as continuous corn, in experiments in North Carolina. About 6 percent of the soybeans grown in the Piedmont of North Carolina were double-cropped in 1974. In the corn belt, also, various reduced-tillage systems have been found advantageous, often combined with double-cropping systems (such as soybeans following winter wheat); in this area, only the better-drained soils lend themselves to "no till" practices.

Similar examples could be cited from other regions. Although the rate at which these various sytems are being adopted is remarkable, a number of problems remain and practices continue to be modified. They all have in common that they work towards a reduction in the intensity or frequency of tillage operations, thus saving labor and energy; they are geared to reducing erosion and to maintaining a cover of either living plants or plant residue; and they tend to make more effective use of the precipitation that falls on the land.

In 1979 Collis-George opined, ". . . Most of the major conceptual advances in [the basic soil science] disciplines of relevance to agricultural production have been made." He added, however, that new developments in management techniques based on these concepts are still to come. Some might question this judgment. On the whole, however, it may well be close to the mark, in that the primary challenge facing those concerned with rational use of soil and water resources—for food production in harmony with other uses—lies in the imaginative application of existing concepts to the solution of problems.

In the United States, an era of apparently unlimited natural resources led to a remarkably effective food-production system that is capital intensive, energy intensive, and labor poor. Its development profited handsomely from developments in science; we can expect that this fertile relationship will continue. However, even in the United States, we now recognize that there are limits; most of the world wasn't so fortunate from the start. Thus the objectives must change from maximizing return on capital investment to maximizing return from the resource base. The path to this new objective, no less than for its predecessor, will profit from the existing store of scientific knowledge and its future treasures. Its attainment will demand imagination; it will require sophistication, technological innovation, and, importantly, a change in outlook.

With Collis-George, I propose that the greatest opportunities for research in soil science are now found in learning to characterize field situations. We basically understand the flow of water and solutes through soils and the chemical reactions that take place; we have learned to measure the pertinent parameters on a sample or in a laboratory column. We do not yet have the ability to make adequate measurements in the great outdoors, at a reasonable cost, to provide the feedback needed for the best management of the soil-water system. Furthermore, the higher demands of the future, together with the inherent interactions between competing uses for increasingly scarce resources, emphasize the need for total ecosystem management. The broad range of disciplines involved in such an endeavor points to the need for research workers with strong scientific expertise, but also broad interests and experience. Specialists in soil and water management have the advantage that their activity, historically, has encompassed a broad range of problems; still, future demands will be particularly severe.

Further progress in increasing food production does not depend solely on technical expertise. A major restraint is institutional. To illustrate, consider the system of water allocation and pricing in the western United States. Overcoming such restraints will require concerted efforts to effect appropriate socioeconomic adjustments.

Subtly related are the attitudes and perceptions of the scientific worker. Too often we still think in terms of bigness as an end in itself, of the eight-row machine rather than the back-toted, hand-operated herbicide sprayer powered by a solar cell; of correcting plant nutrition problems with imported fertilizer rather than enhancing the symbioses in the rhizosphere; of monoculture where multiple cropping could increase total yield and reduce the dependence on pesticides. Even organic farming—oh, horror—should be mentioned in this connection. The only "scientific study" of which I am aware came to conclusions, irrationally attacked in *Science* (10 October 1975), that tended to support many of the popular claims. And what about crop residues as a source for liquid fuels by fermentation, with the pulp returned to the land? Such innovations are needed here and abroad. They will come, but the more readily the more clearly this need is recognized explicitly.

Although the absolute potential for increased world food production is substantial, it behooves us to recognize the clear limits on the natural resource base. Notwithstanding a solid and constantly expanding base of knowledge and technology for its protection and responsible development, mismanagement is still all too prevalent. Some of the resulting damage, unfortunately, is irreversible.

Yet recent changes for the better, both in terms of recognition and of resolution of problems encountered, are indeed encouraging. Across the broad front of soil and water management, progress continues to be made in enlightened understanding, while new concepts find their way into practice through innovative technology.

It is especially in the introduction of new technology that progress has been remarkable of late. This also is the area of greatest urgency for the near future. No discipline can maintain itself or fulfill its mission without a continuing, sound base of fundamental inquiry; but the gap between conceptual understanding and practical application is particularly glaring.

I have sketched, by example, the spiral of increasing sophistication in scientific understanding over time; I have illustrated how recent technological breakthroughs have had a major impact on land and water use. I have also stressed the distance from where we are to where we ought to be.

The future is bright. The potential is there for significant advances towards the responsible and effective use of our precious soil and water resources in increased food production. The possibility also exists that we will fail to meet the challenge.

39

Main Problems of Water Use and Transfer of Technology

M. Falkenmark

INTRODUCTION

Man and water are closely related to each other in a dualistic manner. The mutual interactions between man, society, and water are extremely complex. On one hand, he is deeply dependent on water not only for his survival but for numerous functions of society. Making use of water and seeking protection from water are in fact prerequisites for all social development. On the other hand, this dependence forces man to intervene in numerous ways with the natural water circulation system, thereby causing modifications of water circulation, runoff process, as well as water quality.

Often local water conditions are inadequate for all water needs and this creates problems. When two simultaneous water demands cannot both be satisfied, competition is created, and competing demands can develop into conflicts either between individuals, between branches of society, or between countries sharing the same river basin. A new generation of problems is created by the measures taken to simplify the water use or counteract problems. Secondary conflicts are also created when measures taken to satisfy one water use are not compatible with another water use.

Reprint of "Main Problems of Water Use and Transfer of Technology," by M. Falkenmark, *GeoJournal* (Vol. 3, No. 5, 1979). Pp. 435-42. Reprinted by permission of *GeoJournal* (published in Wiesbaden, West Germany).

MAN'S WATER-RELATED NEEDS AND INTERESTS

Basic Functions of Water

Water has a few basic functions in social development. The primary one has to do with survival. Water is a basic condition for support of life but also for the hygiene basic for all health care. We all know that access to clean drinking water is in fact a necessary prerequisite for health. This simple fact caused the UN Water Conference to declare the next decade as the drinking water decade.

Another function of water is that it is an important **production factor** in society. Water is needed for agricultural production, where adequate soil water availability constitutes a basic condition for plant growth. Most industries depend on water for different functions all the way from process water to cooling water. The potential energy acquired by water in the hydrologic cycle can be used for energy production and this energy source constitutes a major natural resource in great parts of the developing world. Since prehistoric times rivers have constituted important transportation channels. Water also plays a central role for the modern service functions of urban life, which creates the headache of today's rapidly growing urban centers in water-scarce areas.

At the same time, water is an important ingredient of well-being and quality of life. Recreational and spare-time activities of different kinds are often closely related to water. Water bodies often also represent great aesthetic values, covered by the concept of water as an amenity.

Finally, water has a large imminent value as symbol, reflected in numerous expressions such as "water of life" and in multifarious religious rituals from everyday blessings to rituals in connection with death.

Water can be used both on-site (in channel) and off-site (off-channel). On-site uses are normally site-related, whereas off-site uses often imply that water is withdrawn from the water course and transferred to the site where it is to be used. Such off-site uses are often flow-related, exemplified by the water supply for settlements, industries, and irrigation schemes. For such uses the primary resource characteristic is constituted by the river flow or the groundwater flow, although the water quality is often quite important too. For most site-specific uses, on the other hand, the pure existence of the water body constitutes the main resource and its quality may be the basic characteristic, although some uses are dependent also on a certain through-flow of water.

Water-Related Needs Imply Demands on the Natural Water System

Man's water-related needs emanate from a number of basic needs. The biological needs include drinking water supply, fishing, drainage, irrigation, water for basic hygiene, and flood protection. Materially based needs include industrial water supply, hydropower production, irrigation, inland waterways, water supply for urban functions, etc. Psychological needs involve water aesthetics, preservation of natural environments and water landscapes, and water recreation activities such as swimming, fishing, boating, and shore life. In most primitive societies water needs are mainly biological. During subsequent phases of social and economic development, materially based needs add to the biological ones and gradually take on a character of real needs. Psychological needs turn up in modern society, often as a reaction against damages caused by a shortsighted exploitation of natural resources.

To satisfy these water-related needs, man raises different demands on the natural water circulation system, implying either the right to use water or to interfere with it. To start with, he claims the right to make use of the natural water system as a water source, as a recipient for wastewater, as a source for hydropower production, as a base for boating, swimming, fishing, etc. Many of these demands include claims as to the right to withdraw a certain quantity of water, or that water quality should hold a certain minimum standard. In order to make the use possible, man also claims the right to interfere in certain distinct ways with the natural water circulation system. He either tries to correct certain imperfections in water availability in time and space, or he carries out different land-based activities which at the same time modify the runoff formation process. Examples of the former kinds of interferences are withdrawals and transfers of water, construction of facilities for flow regulation, sluices, canals, etc. Examples of effects caused by the latter kinds of activities are altered seasonal flow fluctuations, increased high water, decreased low flow, changed water quality, etc. Man may also present claims of the opposite character, i.e., that water conditions should be preserved. Such preservational demands could in fact be seen as demands of "noninterfering."

In conclusion, we may operate with the following sequence of concepts:

↗ use water
basic needs → water-related needs → demands to
↘ interfere with water

It is evident from the above that man's interest in water has many different aspects that fall into three main categories:

- Beneficial use of water—either withdrawal uses for water supply or irrigation or on-site (nonwithdrawal) uses for hydropower production, inland water traffic, fishing, recreation, etc.
- Protection against excess water by building structures in low-lying

areas to prevent inundation during periods of floods or by drainage of water-logged lands to make possible housing, agricultural production, or forestry.

- Protection of water against pollution or other damage caused by human activities.

WATER AVAILABILITY VERSUS WATER NEEDS

Water Availability Is Governed by Hydrologic Conditions

In water management, water needs have to be matched against water availability. The primary water source being precipitation, one might argue that this element characterizes water availability in general. However, different water uses are dependent on different kinds of water. One should therefore distinguish water availability for plant production from water availability for satisfying human supply needs.

Water availability for plant production is characterized by the amount of water present in the root zone that can be taken up by the plants. This water is recharged by the amount of water infiltrated into the soil. The infiltration could therefore be taken as an index of this water availability.

Water for withdrawal can be taken either from the groundwater aquifers or from the surface-water bodies. In this case, water availability is constituted by the water flow in these environments; in the aquifers by the annual—or rather the long-term—recharge, in the rivers by the dependable flow, i.e., the base flow available in the river during the dry season.

The naturally available water can be augmented by different control measures. The soil moisture can be augmented by soil conservation measures or by irrigation. The groundwater availability can be enhanced by augmenting infiltration and percolation (for instance, by reforestation) or by artificial groundwater recharge. The dependable river flow can be increased by storing flood water in surface or subsurface reservoirs, by augmenting the recharge of groundwater aquifers drained by the river, or by importing water from an adjacent river basin. Also such measures as artificial production of water through desalination or rainmaking activities can be used to improve local water availability.

Water Need Is Governed by Population Density and Phase of Socioeconomic Development

As earlier noted, water needs usually develop more or less successively, following a rather typical pattern in most societies. In primitive societies, where household water has to be carried by women and children, the per capita water use may remain as low as 5–25 liters per day (l/d). Standpipes in the vicinity of the home make water more easily available and the per capita amount increases. In order to satisfy main hygienic purposes, preferably some 75 l/d are needed. The World Health Organization (WHO) [. . .] 15 years ago considered 150 l/d to be an adequate amount for planning urban supply in developing countries.

When industry develops, the needed amount increases. In regions with water surplus some branches of industries have developed technologies with relatively high water demands. At present, water-saving technology is being developed in many places in order to make industrial development less dependent on large amounts of good quality water. In some countries, industrial water use has lately declined considerably in response to more stringent antipollution legislation. The industrial development now taking place in numerous water-scarce areas will evidently be largely facilitated by the development of such water-saving technology. The importance of such a development was also heavily stressed by the UN Water Conference in Mar del Plata (United Nations 1977).

Already ahead of the substantial increase in water needs generated by industrial development, great water demands are often raised in arid and semiarid countries aiming at increased self-sufficiency in food production. In water-scarce areas, the amounts of water needed for irrigation may indeed be very large. In India, for example, most of the water that is technically handled [has been used for irrigation for a long time.] Today, agricultural water needs account for 94 percent of the total withdrawal uses.

Future Water Needs

In spite of society's diverse water dependence, water has in fact remained a forgotten item in many futuristic studies. This extraordinary fact is probably a conspicuous effect of climatic bias. However, a number of estimates have been made during the past decade of future flow-related water needs in different world regions. When studying these estimates [. . . more closely], one finds that they tend to converge in the neighborhood of 1,000 m^3/yr per capita both in the temperate regions and in tropical regions. In the former case industry constitutes a main water user, in the latter agriculture.

[. . .] Dependable water flow is assumed to constitute respectively 5, 10, 20, and 40 percent of the average water flow.

At present the total river water flow (which includes the main part of the groundwater flow) is estimated to be about 40,000 km^3/yr. This is equivalent to about 10,000 m^3yr per capita when equally distributed on the present world population. About 35 percent of this flow is dependable. This means that on an average basis there is at present no need for any concern about global water scarcity. Looking one generation ahead, however, we have to base our calculations on a nearly doubled world population. In such a situation the relative availability of water would decrease to 5,000 m^3/yr out of which about 1,800 m^3/yr would be available on a year-round basis. Even in this case, the amount of water is evidently large enough as long as we see it on a global scale.

Both water and people are, however, very unevenly distributed over the earth's land areas. In order to get a picture of potential problems it is necessary to consider future needs. [. . .] It is evident that as long as 20 percent of the average flow is available on a year-round basis, about 5,000 m^3/yr would be necessary to cover the "ultimate" water needs of a modern society of 1,000 m^3/yr.

[. . .] Already at present two regions (North Africa and the Middle East and Central Planned Asia) should be seen as potentially water scarce when taking into account the successively increasing water demands normally imminent in the socioeconomic development. If we allow also for the next generation of population increase, we have to include also Central America and South and Southeast Asia and possibly southern Africa as potentially water-scarce regions.

In this composite view two facts have to be considered. One is that even if the regional average looks uncomplicated, there of course exist intraregional differences. In fact water supply difficulties exist already today in numerous places in these areas. For instance, in spite of the fact that in Western Europe as a whole nearly 6,000 m^3/yr are available on a per capita basis, even a well-watered area as England and Wales has only 1,700 m^3/yr, and an intricate system of water transfers is already being planned to satisfy future water needs.

The other fact is that, in the subtropics, water availability is subject to considerable interannual variations. This simple fact substantially reduces the information value to be ascribed to the long-term average, especially as years with precipitation below average tend to repeat themselves, creating the well-known multiyear sequences of drought conditions, causing so much human suffering.

WATER PROBLEMS CREATED BY MAN'S ACTIVITIES

Impact of Man on the Natural Circulation of Water

Water is circulated through nature on a module basis with the river catchment (drainage basin) as the basic unit. The transient nature of water means that the different parts of the water circulation within the basin interact. Activities affecting earlier phases in the sequence of hydrologic processes thus also affect later phases. In this sequence of interactions, the soil cover and the vegetation act as key zones. All land-use changes which modify vegetational cover—foliage density, root depth, soil penetration characteristics, or roughness of ground surface—also cause changes in the water cycle processes. Human action causing modification of any of these factors therefore changes the water flow in different respects.

Therefore, man should be seen as **one of the factors** in the river basin influencing the water circulation. His interactions with the hydrologic processes result from three categories of activities affecting the water environment:

1. **Water withdrawal** from its natural course in rivers and groundwater aquifers for water supply of communities, industry, and for irrigation, whereafter water is returned either to the atmosphere by evaporation or to the drainage system as wastewater.
2. **In-stream structures** to facilitate on-site (nonwithdrawal) uses, such as fishing, hydropower production, and recreation, and regulate river flow to reduce stream flow fluctuations and allow navigation.
3. **Land-use changes** implying manipulations of the land-soil-vegetation system leading to alterations in the runoff-formation process.

A number of water-related disturbances, some of them natural and others man-caused, complicate man's use of water resources. The central role played by water in the ecosystem implies that practically all measures leading to modifications of the passage of water through soil, subsoil, and rivers cause ecological changes of one kind or another. These environmental impacts of water-related activities primarily affect the population living in the same river basin. Apart from the intended benefits therefore, human manipulations are usually associated with different kinds of disturbances attributable to secondary effects of the modifications.

Therefore, the question is not whether there will be any environmental impact from a water project, but rather how much of that impact is in fact acceptable. In other words, the benefits of a water scheme have to be purchased at the expenditure of certain natural assets.

Water Problems and Their Consequences

Water problems could be structured into a few main categories:

- **Natural water problems,** to which man has adapted himself, and caused by natural conditions such as seasonality, droughts or floods, waterlogging, erosion, and sedimentation. These water problems are to be attacked by different countermeasures: water conservation, water storage, irrigation, drainage, soil conservation measures, etc.

- Problems caused by either **changing needs** which do not comply with the existing resources or by **competing demands.**
- Problems caused by **secondary effects** of man's activities, e.g., overdraft of aquifers, water pollution, salinization and waterlogging of irrigated areas, water-related diseases caused by pollutants, man-generated floods and droughts, etc.

In order to avoid unforeseen negative impacts on water due to secondary effects of land and water development, all water-related projects should be evaluated for their consequences. In some countries it is now legally required that manipulations with the natural water circulation system be fully analyzed as to their environmental and social consequences in order to avoid any inadvertent effects. As far as natural sciences are concerned, such impact analysis to a certain degree seems to be more a question of applying existing knowledge than of developing a new one.

The close interaction between man and water also means however that social sciences have to be much more deeply involved in water planning than has yet been the case. Improved analysis of social consequences of water projects will make necessary a considerable development of the rather new field of **hydrosociology.** It should be observed, though, that cultural, religious, and social differences between regions introduce large difficulties in the transfer of knowledge and technology from one cultural and climatic region to another.

Water Problems Tend to Change with Time

Innumerable water problems have challenged man since the dawn of history. Many problems have been overcome by ingenious solutions of technical or administrative kind, the classical examples being the hydraulic societies of ancient time. In a society under continuous development, however, the problems tend to aggravate with time due to the appearance of new water demands and aspects. Increasing needs and increasing population can severely magnify the stress on the available water. Claims for improved quality of life and nature preservation make many classical technical approaches less self-evident and have developed into much more rigorous conditions to be met by new water projects.

Water problems originate from a combination of the resource situation and the demand situation. One might also say that water problems occur when a water situation to which man is adapted changes. Such a change may be caused by population increase which puts a new stress on the resource. More immediate problems are caused by natural phenomena such as droughts and floods. The reason why these phenomena, which are fully natural, cause problems is that man settles in areas that are from time to time exposed to droughts and floods. The problems are sometimes aggravated by the fact that short-lived events cause long-lasting secondary effects.

By applying a thorough water planning including water conservation measures, man has shown that it is possible to live both in drought-prone and flood-prone areas. Israel and the western United States constitute examples where advanced standard of living has been achieved in spite of severe water deficiency. In such cases, however, not only water planning but also land-use planning is necessary to retain the control over man-caused water impacts. Without land-use planning including soil conservation measures, newly created reservoirs are rapidly clogged with sediment. In the planning also sociocultural conditions have to be taken into account so that society can adapt to the new situation. Necessary infrastructures constitute an important aspect of water planning and management to guarantee the full value of the planned water use.

The water-problems profile of an area evidently changes with time. Countermeasures are taken against floods already at an early stage. Improved health is another important weapon to achieve social development. To this end water-related diseases have to be eliminated. This is why both the UN Conferences on Human Settlements 1976 and Water 1977 recommended that every human being should have access to clean drinking water and organized sanitation by 1990 at the latest.

Global Pattern of Dominating Water Problems

Differences in climatic conditions and thereby in basic natural water problems, on one hand, and differences in social and economic development and therefore in dominating water problems, on the other, combine to create certain regional differences in the global pattern of dominating water problems.

[. . .] Three groups [of countries] may be distinguished [in which urgent water problems are encountered.]

The first group is composed of North Africa and the Middle East, and is characterized by a very real shortage in combination with strong seasonality. The water resources are extremely scarce already as a regional average (less than 2,000 m^3/yr). Water conservation is of basic importance but has to be complemented by augmentation of water supplies with unconventional resources. Already in 1968, as a matter of fact, 75 percent of the world's total desalination capacity was installed in this region.

In the second group, we find the rest of Africa, North and South America, as well as Eastern Europe and the USSR. Here the water supply is acceptable or even good on an average (over 10,000 m^3/yr); and therefore quality problems are the dominating ones, whether it be due to industrial pollution in the northern regions or due to natural reasons or human pollution in the southern regions.

The third group is composed of south and southeastern Africa, Central Planned Asia, Central America, Australia, and South Africa, together with the rest of Europe. These regions combine a short supply (2,000–10,000 m^3/yr) partly with seasonality, partly with industrial pollution. Numerous problems appear side by side: definite water shortage, droughts, floods, water-related diseases, sedimentation, and problems related to natural water quality. Important management tools are both water conservation and quality improvement.

It might be added that in many of the industrialized countries a new generation of water-related diseases may be a hidden risk where river water is used as a source for drinking water. The unintentional reuse of polluted water involves the risk of oral intake of undetected toxic substances in the drinking water. WHO's present drinking water quality standards do not take such a risk into account.

The Special Case of International Rivers

The transient nature of water implies that upper parts of a river interact with lower parts, so that man's upstream activities affect the potential activities further downstream. This is a fact of larger importance than one might at all realize. In fact 40 percent of the present world population live in transnational river basins, which means that they are for their social development dependent on a water resource which has, by necessity, to be shared with one or several neighboring countries.

[. . .] The largest 52 rivers in the world (river basins larger than 100,000 km^2) are all international and pass between two and eight countries. Of the rivers with a basin smaller than 100,000 km^2, 148 flow through more than one country.

This simple fact constitutes an immense source of potential conflicts. All over the world great activity has to be put into international negotiations during the forthcoming decade. The international community has furthermore to cooperate to develop a practical international legislation. Such work is already on the move within the UN Environment Program and the International Law Commission.

EXCHANGE OF INFORMATION AND CLIMATIC BIAS

Even if the water-use profile and the emanating problem pattern vary from region to region, the basic ingredients are evidently the same. Therefore extensive exchange of experience between regions is of utmost importance in water development. The extensive documentation to the UN Water Conference in Mar del Plata was a clear demonstration of this fact.

However, the great differences in climatic, hydrologic, as well as cultural respect between countries, especially those industrialized countries situated in the temperate zone and those developing countries situated in the subtropical zone, introduce large difficulties into the process of transfer of knowledge and technology from industrialized countries to developing countries. According to the International Water Resources Association, one of the myths of development is that the transfer of advanced technology and institutional arrangements from the developed countries can solve many of the problems facing the developing world. Part of the background of the faith in this myth is probably what has already been referred to as "climatic bias."

Not only is the emitter in this transfer process trained under the conditions prevailing in the temperate zone, so that both his concepts and in fact the whole of infrastructures to which he is used (cultural, technical as well as administrative) are heavily influenced by the physical environment dominating in that zone. But also important representatives of the receiver part of the process, i.e., many politicians, as well as experts from developing countries, have also got their education at universities in the temperate zone. This is a coincidence to which much more attention has to be paid in the future in order to take adequate steps to speed up the process of transfer of knowledge and technology.

Furthermore, it is most important that the process of exchange of information is also run in the opposite direction, so that experience gained over the millennia under harsh social and environmental conditions is absorbed by the international scientific community, today contributing to much of the scientific knowledge necessary for continued global development. Only in this way will the present constraints to the applicability of the present pool of knowledge be fully revealed and a more reliable base created for future water development in water-scarce areas.

40

Water, Community Well-Being, and Public Policy

Gilbert F. White, David J. Bradley, and Anne U. White

One of the unwritten precepts of certain Western cultures is that if a little of something is good, more of it must be better. Surely this is the feeling about much water management. Municipal systems and price schedules were designed to promote larger use. To be sure, pure supplies are essential to reaching certain health standards and, up to a medium range, quantity of water also is important. However, if instead of asking how to provide more water the initial question is how water may best serve the well-being of the community, a different kind of analysis results.

In reporting the use and cost of water for household purposes in a variety of East African environments, we have emphasized aspects of water supply that do not figure in conventional studies of new projects. Proposals for construction of new or enlarged supplies commonly stress the projection of historical demand, the efficient design of needed works, and the financial feasibility of the required investment. All of these are important. The methods are well understood and we have not tried to restate them. Yet, if investment of scarce capital is to be weighed in a fashion appropriate to developing countries, still other evidence should be considered. The way people respond to present and improved supplies and the effect this has on community health and welfare should be examined for the whole range of theoretically possible improvements. Increased volume of use does not necessarily bring proportionate gains in health. Neither does the construction of additional safe supplies necessarily result in increased use by those people who most need them.

Reprint of "Water, Community Well-Being, and Public Policy," Chapter 9 in *Drawers of Water: Domestic Water Use in East Africa,* by Gilbert F. White, David J. Bradley, and Anne U. White (Chicago, Ill., The University of Illinois Press, 1972). Pp. 251–80.

Thus our analysis gives special attention to how much water people in fact use, to what accounts for their volume of use and choice of source, and to the only partly understood relationships between health costs and water quality and quantity. By dwelling on these points we seek to offset the imbalance of the customary demand projection and its accompanying plan to expand supplies. In doing so we may be guilty of placing undue weight on these considerations.

In the higher income communities of Europe and North America multiple-tap service is taken for granted. It is expected to be used by all, with resulting elimination of most health hazards linked to unclean or sparse water supplies. In a general way, multiple-tap use is known to increase as income and material wealth rise and to be curbed somewhat by metering and restrictive rates. The situation is far more complex and much less understood for water use by the majority of the earth's population who draw water from a single source either inside or outside the home. In the earlier stages of economic development, the variety of sources is large and the possible combinations of water quality, quantity, and use from both improved and unimproved sources is immense. Processes of individual and group decision are more subtle. Their consequences for the lives and well-being of people are more difficult to trace. We have tried to sum up the state of knowledge and ignorance concerning these aspects.

Although the general conclusions brought together in the following pages are drawn primarily from observations in the highly diverse environment provided by East Africa, they have been compared as far as practicable with experience in other areas, principally in India, highland Bolivia, parts of West Africa, and the United States, having markedly different cultural and physical environments. The details may differ, but there is reason to think from the data so far examined that the major generalizations will fit conditions in numerous other sectors of the tropical developing world. [. . .]

RANGE OF DOMESTIC WATER USE

In the most rigorous and extreme conditions of water supply and of gaining a living, men seem to use a minimum of about 2 liters of water daily per capita to meet their domestic requirements for drinking and washing, the limit depending on the water content of their food. In the sites investigated in East Africa, the reported minimum liters per capita daily ranged from 1.4 in a rural household with carried water to 116 in a very low density city environment with piped water.

When users are supplied with an abundant volume of water which is carried from a standpipe in the neighborhood, daily use commonly runs from 10 to 20 liters per capita. No matter how plentiful the water nearby, or how suitable its quality for health and culinary purposes, one person's use rarely exceeds 40 liters where the supply is carried.

Where water is less readily available because of either time or quality, the daily use per capita ordinarily ranges from 4 to 20 liters. For global purposes, a rough figure of about 12 liters may be taken as a conservative estimate of the daily use of those who are obliged to draw water from outside their households. This includes workers going to a crowded city standpipe as well as women making a daily walk of several kilometers across a parched plain.

Where engineering skill brings piped water into the family household, the daily use in virtually all cases exceeds 16 liters per capita, and 30 to 40 liters approaches a mean for buildings with only one tap per family group and without indoor waste disposal. In households with more than one tap and with indoor waste disposal, the use ranges from 25 to more than 600 liters daily. Mean use for modern cities is about 100 to 180 liters, but this average figure masks variations of as much as 60 to 600 liters among consumers within the same city.

It is estimated that approximately 70 percent of the world's population takes water from sources outside the home. Using a liberal figure of 20 liters per capita for those who must carry water and a mean figure of 80 liters for those who draw it from pipes in the household, we arrive at a global domestic water withdrawal for 4 billion inhabitants of 152 billion liters daily. This is the roughest estimate but it gives an order of magnitude. One stream having the average flow of the Nile at Aswan could, if properly regulated, provide more than the entire domestic needs of the human race. However, total urban needs include commercial, industrial, and public uses which may be two to five times the domestic uses. Inasmuch as a large part (60–90 percent) of urban water use is nonconsumptive, much of this flow could be returned for other uses if treated.

HOW USE VARIES

In many parts of the world the pattern of water use in households with piped supplies seems to differ basically from that of households that are required to carry their water. The East African investigations, as corroborated by a few observations elsewhere, indicate that factors associated with variations in water use operate in two different combinations.

In both piped and unpiped households, the per capita use is partly a function of number of people in the household. Generally, the larger the number of people the smaller the per capita use. The larger per capita uses are found in households of one or two working adults. At the other extreme, there may be a very small consumption in a household with only one elderly adult. Likewise, the greater the number of children, the smaller is per capita withdrawal.

Where supplies are carried from the source, the per capita use tends to be positively related to the material wealth of the household, with the absolute range of use differing according to ethnic groups. The size of the carrying container appears to be relatively uniform within each ethnic group and varies from one group to another so that, since the average number of trips a woman makes daily to the source varies between 2.5 and 3.5 in the areas studied, the per capita use is partly an expression of the conventional container size. Thus, one convenient way of classifying cultural groups according to water use is in terms of the volume of the common carrying vessel. Vessel size becomes a rough index to other relationships which hold more generally between ethnic groups.

The volume of use is lower, of course, where clothes are washed at the source, and there is some indication that those living farthest from the source are likely to carry clothes to the source rather than to wash at home. Those living nearest to the source also tend to perform more of the washing functions at the source rather than carrying water to the household. Those who live nearest and farthest from the source use it for washing more than those in the intermediate distances.

It is notable that volumes of use in the households studied is not strongly associated with either the distance water is carried or the energy expended to carry it. Up to distances of 1.6 kilometers, use tends to be uniform; beyond that distance the volume falls off.

Nor is there any clear association between level of formal education and the volume used: schooling by a household member does not necessarily lead to greater demand for water that is carried.

Where supplies are drawn from taps in the household, the daily use tends to be strongly associated with material wealth:* volumes of withdrawal can be predicted with a moderate degree of confidence according to the level of material possessions as reflected in the housing density and number of water connections, especially water heaters. Lacking accurate estimates of per capita income, housing density may be taken as a less satisfactory but roughly descriptive index of material wealth in city areas of East Africa. The level of formal schooling is closely correlated with material wealth in urban areas and accordingly varies with water use.

The domestic demand for water from piped supplies is not highly responsive to the price of the product. Factors of income, education, and

*Using very crude water consumption data for 31 countries, Lee was unable to either refute or confirm the hypothesis that there were differences in water consumption between countries with different levels of per capita gross national product.

physical environment remaining constant, a difference in price has only a modest effect upon daily consumption. But because of the prevailing price schedules which favor large users, the selling price per liter tends to be lower for the high income households than for the low income households, and so low charges per liter but high charges per capita are associated with high use.

As households gain piped connections in the process of urbanization, ethnic characteristics seem to lose their significance as dependent variables affecting water use. Africans of many tribes, Asians, and Europeans of all origins appear to use about the same amounts of water if they live in an area of low housing density.

Conditions of climate and terrain seem to affect piped water use, and this is very significant, chiefly to the extent that they impose needs for lawn and garden watering among the middle and upper income households. Wherever cultural preference encourages the use of water for maintenance of lawns and gardens during the dry seasons, as in the southwest United States, the consumption of water for lawn watering figures dominantly in household usage.

The relations among climate, terrain, and water use in areas without piped household connections are complex and do not include strong associations of aridity or temperature with volume of use. There is some association with average slope. However, as physical factors are associated with farming systems, and as farming systems, in turn, are involved in setting patterns of land use and daily work budgets, the physical conditions are significant in describing limits within which working women and other laborers in the family may use time and energy for drawing water. Thus, the Chiga woman is so pressed for time by the need to cultivate her small, scattered, and steep fields that she delegates water drawing to the children, who then carry very small amounts.

Seasonal fluctuations in water use were not recorded in unpiped areas, although they were measured for urban areas. The available data do not indicate that there are important variations in domestic demand within dry periods or hot periods except as lawn and garden watering requirements are affected in city areas. Because of the difficulty of finding comparable observations on carried water from other parts of the world, this must be put forward as tentative. Data from a few other areas are in disagreement on this point, and it may be that our observations are skewed by the season in which they were taken. Use may be curtailed by absolute shortage in available water supply, as where springs run dry or city water pressure is reduced in dry periods, but the demand does not seem to fluctuate markedly where gardens are not maintained. In some areas use is higher in the wet season than in the dry season because of increased washing.

DIRECT COSTS OF WATER

If water costs were to be regarded simply as direct cash payment, a very large proportion of people who carry water would have no cost. These are the people who go to the source, draw it themselves, and pay for neither supply nor transport. Only a minority of rural water users make any monetary payment.

When the household does pay a carrier, as do a substantial number of dwellers on urban peripheries who take water from public sources at which charges are made, or when the urbanite pays for transport from free standpipe supplies, the cash payments may run as high as $0.0025 ($9.46 per 1,000 gallons) per liter or $0.686 per capita daily ($25.04 per year). Contrary to the view that city workers are deprived of essential quantities of water by its high costs, the low income urban worker seems to use more water than his country cousins and to pay a proportionately larger share of his income for it.

A broader view of direct water costs includes the energy expended by those, usually girls and women, who carry water without payment as part of their domestic duties. The mean cost of those caloric inputs at each site is found to range from close to 0, where much of the water is captured from the roof, to $0.0003 per liter ($1.14 per 1,000 gallons) or $0.0021 per capita daily ($0.77 per capita per year).

The range of direct costs for households with piped supply is also great, with mean costs for various sectors of the urban community running from $0.0008 to $0.00031 ($0.30 to $1.17 per 1,000 gallons) and from $0.0042 to $0.0506 per capita daily ($1.53 to $18.47 per year).

One striking observation is that the daily direct costs for some users of unpiped supplies are higher than those for some users of piped supplies. This clearly is true in terms of cost per unit of water, and it holds in many instances when cost is expressed as a proportion of daily expenditures.

As might be expected from the economies of scale inherent in storing, treating, and distributing large volumes of water, the per liter cost of water in the piped units is generally less than when water is carried.

The higher the income of the city dweller with piped supplies, the smaller the proportion of his income he devotes to water. The class of users making the heaviest proportion of total cash and labor expenditures for water are the low income workers who carry water from public standpipes or who pay water carriers for transport. Where they carry their own water, the caloric expenditures are relatively low, but they may be obliged to pay for water at the source. Carriers' rates are high, and as much as 10 percent of income may go for water. This compares with as little as 4 percent of income for those in medium income brackets with piped supply, and less than 2 percent for those in upper income classes, with differential income effects.

COST TO HEALTH

If an attempt is made to gauge the full magnitude of effects of water quality and use on society, still a different set of values is called into play. It is impractical to assign precise monetary values to the debilitating effect of water-related diseases. The effects encompass the decrease in labor productivity, the increase in public costs of therapy, and the offsetting costs of public-health preventive measures. Rough measures of these can be made by estimating the degree to which water improvements reduce the disease incidence from the maximum which would prevail with scarce and heavily polluted water supplies.

The changes in health conditions vary according to the local environment. It is helpful to think of urban environment as either high density or low and medium density. Rural environment can be divided into the characteristic dispersed settlement pattern of East Africa and the nucleated pattern which prevails in so many parts of the world. In either case the distinction among hot arid, lowland humid, and highland humid climatic conditions recognizes major differences in water availability in nature.

Although in general terms better and more water leads to better health, the particular evidence supporting this conclusion is complex and not readily summarized. It is helpful to consider water-related diseases in four categories. Waterborne diseases in the strict sense are infections carried by polluted water, give rise to dramatic epidemics, and are removed by providing pure water. The well-known infections, such as typhoid and cholera, may be augmented by various other infections where pollution reaches very high levels. Another large group of diseases, which we have called water-washed, are reduced when ample water is available for hygiene even if that water is not completely pure. Many of these are superficial infections of the skin and eyes. The other large group in this second category is the diarrheal disorders. A group of tropical parasitic infections, which we may call water-based, depend on aquatic intermediate hosts for their development. The larval parasites may either bore in through the skin, as with schistosomes, or be ingested. The fourth category of infections related to water includes those with insect vectors that either breed in water or bite near surface water. All four categories should be considered in any alteration of water resources—it is not unusual for improvements in some aspects of supply to create additional health problems.

IMPLICATIONS FOR RESEARCH ON WATER-RELATED INFECTIONS

The construction of a conceptual model and the development of quantitative analyses at once show up deficiencies in the data available. If the pollution of a source is halved, or the quantity of water per person is doubled, what improvement of health will result? We can be confident that increasing supply by half a liter for those consuming 3 liters a day will have some effect, and we can also be sure that allowing another 100 liters of bath water for the rich man who already wallows in 100 liters will change health but little. There is a sector—we would guess somewhere in the 20 to 80 liters per person range—where health benefits of increasing water begin to level out. It is essential to find more precisely where this point lies, since it greatly affects social costing of water, and this can best be determined by field studies of the effects of varying levels of water improvement. It is remarkable that such studies have not yet been carried out.

A point of some theoretical interest concerns the epidemiology of sporadic waterborne infections, and here [. . .] traditional epidemiological methods are not much help. The precise etiology of many diarrheal episodes in the tropics, the effects of intermittent as compared with perpetual exposure to polluted water, and many other important matters are still unknown. The common delusion that everything useful or important is already known about infections and waterborne disease is clearly far from true, and many of the problems can well be studied in the tropics.

AGGREGATE SOCIAL COSTS

Along with measures of public health, account must be taken of the community cost of providing supplies of improved quality and reliability. Where a completely adequate supply is provided, the deleterious effects on health would approach zero and the total social cost would consist of improvement and conveyance costs. Where the improved supply is only partly adequate in quality or quantity, the residual health effects would need to be considered along with improvement costs. Per capita costs of piped systems run from $8 to $300 for construction. For rural systems the costs run from $1 to $30, $5 being a widely accepted estimate of the minimum cost of providing supplies for relatively nucleated rural communities. Obviously, the per capita costs in rural communities, unlike those in urban areas where there is relatively uniform density and distribution of settlement, depend on the overall density and spatial pattern of distribution of households. The East African pattern of dispersed settlements makes for maximum costs in rural areas, and represents an extreme of environmental conditions. A conventional diagram which shows health costs falling as water costs rise may be misleading.

There is little reason to think that once a point of minimum social cost has been reached national economic development gains substantially from expansion of the available quantity of good quality water for domestic purposes, as contrasted with agricultural uses. In particular, the relation of low unit price to development is questionable. The amenities of living for workers and managers are enhanced by increasing the supply, but their health is not notably improved. Their demand for water for the amenities appears to be more a function of income level than of price, although higher income groups may respond to price of water for lawn watering.

To the cost of new water supplies above a use of about 30 liters per capita must be added the costs of household plumbing facilities (often requiring use of foreign exchange for purchase), and of sewer and sewage disposal systems for waterborne waste. The latter run from one-quarter to more than three-quarters the percentage of costs for water supply, with cost of required waste treatment offsetting economies of scale as water use increases. The larger amount of water consumed in an urban system, the greater the public cost per capita of disposing of the waste. In the United States it is estimated that the annual per capita cost of collecting and treating sewage runs about one-half to two-thirds the costs of supplying water. The calculations of around $10 per capita include operation, maintenance, and amortization (U.S. Senate 1961). To offset these costs there are the gains in health which come from improved sanitary disposal, and here the difficulty of assigning quantitative value is great. In general it appears that, as with water supply, once a minimum service is provided the unit gain to health from units of improvement probably decreases sharply as refinements of treatment and disposal are adopted.

GOVERNMENT DECISIONS

In dealing with supplies pumped directly into households, it is common for public bodies to apply two general policies in towns such as Dar es Salaam or Tororo. First, it is assumed that the population which can afford to pay for house connections should be enabled to use as much water as it wishes at a cost sufficient to return the public outlay for construction, operation, and maintenance. Second, it is required that the cash revenues from either meter or flat rates pay off the total investment in construction and maintenance. This policy is not in force everywhere, and to the extent that less than the direct outlay is recovered, the difference represents a public subsidy. To the extent that revenues exceed costs, the water enterprise becomes a form of differential taxation.

Designers of new pipe systems in East African urban areas seek supplies that will be reliable in quantity, relatively pure in quality, and minimum in cost. The public scheme typically attempts to distribute potable water through whatever fixtures the consumer chooses, and the pricing schedules often favor larger use. Under prevailing price and repayment schedules, the higher income users pay relatively less per unit than do the low income users. For those who lack piped connections, standpipes are provided at convenient points: some municipal governments, such as Kampala and Nairobi, charge enough to repay estimated operating costs. Construction costs for standpipe connections are less because smaller pipes and storage are required than for multiple taps. Tanzania makes no charge and counts the costs as warranted public expenditures, but not at the loss of net returns from the system as a whole, thus spreading the cost to consumers having piped connections.

The public policies for providing supplies in rural areas are more diverse. Developing countries in their early years cannot expect to rival the comprehensive programs which have brought water to virtually all of Britain's farmers. In Argentina, a country with a per capita annual income of more than $700, a financing program concentrates on bringing potable water to residents of rural communities between 100 and 3,000 in population. In 1968 only 7 percent of the rural population and 72 percent of the urban population had potable water. In East Africa there has been a recognized obligation to aid in furnishing water where it is especially difficult to obtain, as with extraction of water from very deep formations in Karamoja or building storage or deep wells where surface sources are sparse on the central Tanzanian plateau. Until recently, schemes for further improvement were distributed chiefly in new settlement projects or where opportunities for gravity supply make it especially easy, as at Zaina, or where there has been special stimulation to local initiative in constructing or demanding better facilities. Although the national governments include rural water supply improvement as a goal, it is only since 1968 that they have launched programs to bring good quality water to specified proportions of the rural population. The tendency was to concentrate on a single technique of improvement or to deal with the areas where supplies are especially short and curb farming development. In 1968 Kenya moved toward a rural improvement plan which would outstrip population growth. In its five-year plan for 1969–74 Tanzania placed high priority on water supplies for rural areas, placing highest priority on low-cost projects providing benefits to maximum numbers of people. Special attention was given to development of Ujamaa villages, areas of acute scarcity, and areas of productive activities for agriculture and livestock.

National water improvement decisions inevitably are linked with other policy considerations. New domestic supplies in an arid area may stimulate increased livestock production and range deterioration. Improvements in rural districts may be viewed as stemming migration to the cities, whereas urban improvements may attract farm migrants. More intensive agricultural settlement may be contingent upon developing adequate supplies. Water supply and waste disposal are traditional alternatives to health service investments. Class 6 improvements in urban areas may require heavy expenditures for foreign materials and may also be dependent upon overseas aid for financing. In most instances the national decision is based upon assumptions as to how individual users will respond to new improvements and the effect those responses will have on public well-being.

INDIVIDUAL DECISIONS

For individual carriers of water the decision process is far more complex than in households having piped supplies where the individual exercises choice primarily about the volume of water withdrawn. Typically, the user seeks what she perceives as a healthful and technically accessible supply and is somewhat less influenced by cost or by convenience. Her perception of the available sources of water seems to emphasize their purity by her standards. Considerations of direct cost enter heavily into her discrimination among those sources which are perceived as healthful. She may then be disposed to select a source that avoids the irritations of conflicting users or of potentially abrasive encounters. Neither old nor new households in East Africa appear to be sited with primary regard for water. After the site is selected because of soil and land form qualities, water is sought from the nearest source that is regarded as meeting minimum requirements of quality, manageable technology, and social congeniality. However, in very dry areas domestic water improvement may be a necessary condition to new agricultural development, and the borehole or pipeline must precede the plow.

It would be a mistake to regard water users in rural areas as heavily bound by traditional views of water quality and source. The drawer of water usually appraises several alternatives. She may fail to go to a new borehole which has been established by the government, or she may walk a considerable distance to draw on a supply as contaminated as one nearer her home, but these choices, in many instances, may be traced to views of cleanliness, practicability, and interpersonal consequences which represent discerning choice on her part rather than blind conformity to the customary procedures of her cultural group. To the extent that this is true, a change in choice of source is not a matter of breaking habit or the hard cake of custom but involves cultivating new perceptions of health, convenience, and cost.

IMPLICATIONS FOR RESOURCES MANAGEMENT THEORY

The field observations in East Africa suggest that a descriptive model of resource decisions in which a household's elementary transaction with nature is defined in terms of individual perception of choice, resource, technology, economic efficiency, and linkages goes a long way toward explaining why particular water sources are used and why certain responses may be expected to public intervention in providing new sources of supply. The water user's perception of the choices available to her seems to run consistently less than the theoretical number of choices which the scientific observer might describe or that she could identify if pressed hard to do so. This is to be expected as a common method of coping with complexity in dealing with an intricate environment, and it is interesting that users rarely are able to specify a range of choice of more than four or five.

Perception of the quantity and quality of the water resource shows itself casual or unsophisticated in only a few instances. Water users characteristically look for qualities of healthfulness and cleanliness in supplies, placing heavy weight upon taste and visible characteristics of water. Although some households show little recognition of the importance of fecal contamination in water supplies, these same people may demonstrate a deep and persistent concern for avoiding supplies considered unhealthful because they alter the flavor of food, display an algal scum on the surface, or occasionally have slicks of oil, or because it is known that other humans have waded in them. In the field observations it was found that water users rarely were willing to sacrifice health to household convenience. They widely misjudged factors affecting health, but they gave them heavy weight as perceived.

The perception of available technology for improving water supplies is not closely associated with education, nor could it be readily described in terms of diffusion of innovations. We encountered no adequate way of explaining why tin roofs are not used more efficiently to catch rainfall: this is an example of an aspect of the decision process which needs vigorous explanation. Differentials in observation and information are likely explanations but are not clear. It also is likely that the different roles of man and woman in commanding household expenditures may explain the reluctance to invest in such improvements.

In perceiving the economic efficiency of alternative water sources, the water user tends to choose the most efficient source within limits established by quality of the resource, spatial linkages, and available technology. That is, economic efficiency appears to govern within a range set by some other factors rather than to be the primary consideration. The same relationship seems to hold with respect to cost of water and volume of use. The user essentially pursues a satisfying strategy in seeking to meet her perceived needs. Where the user is subject to severe limitations in available labor through circumstances or urban employment, this does not seem to influence the amount of water used or necessarily affect the choice of source. In the case of demanding farm employment for a woman there may be reductions in use.

Water users characteristically are sensitive to linkages of water use with other members of the community. Contrary to the view held in some quarters, it was found that users in East Africa prefer private to communal sources when they have the opportunity. They avoid situations where there is risk of irritating confrontation. They may enjoy sharing communal sources when this is required, but when presented with a genuinely viable choice between a communal source and one affording privacy, they seem to choose the latter except in certain special circumstances. These include water sources and containers which make it necessary for a woman to have the aid of another woman in hoisting the water to her head before carrying it home, as in parts of Lango. It was found that where the assignment of rights to land conveys with it control of access to water sources, even though the water sources are regarded under the customary law as being common property, individuals tend to avoid using sources that would imply a need for trespass or would interfere with what may be newly conveyed rights of ownership in the sources. Thus the trend toward assignment of propery rights in areas where formerly there had been no cadastral lines and no deeded rights to land reduces the range of choice in drawing upon water.

Although the median and mean usages for an area of homgeneous ethnic origins may be different from those in areas with other ethnic characteristics, the decision behavior of the users suggests that when presented with new sources and new technologies they will respond in relation to their perception of resource quality, available technology, and expected economic costs and will not be curbed rigidly by the conventional patterns.

There is no persuasive evidence that the location of individual households in nonarid areas of dispersed settlement is strongly associated with the availability of water. This is observable neither in the traditional patterns of settlement nor in the design of contemporary land settlement under government auspices in Kenya and in Tanzania.

From what has been found about the choice exercised among water users, it is likely that new improvements will be used to the extent that the potential users are convinced that water quality is suitable. Their perceptions of an improved source may differ markedly from those of the water chemist, although each has the aim of protecting human health. To plan delivery of better quality water without knowing what the users consider to be better water is to run the risk of its being ignored. Thus, improvement needs to go hand in hand with information. This, in turn, often may best be developed through participation in the canvass of water need and possible designs.

If water improvement were being planned in a rural area and the planner wanted to predict the response of local water users, the procedure most likely to yield accurate results would be to arrange for the users themselves to participate in designing, constructing, and operating the scheme. There is no more direct way of finding out their preferences and their willingness to contribute to building and using the improvement. Next best is to study their current habits of water use and the factors which seem to account for choice in present circumstances. The few generalizations drawn from our studies should not be applied elsewhere except with great caution, unless tested in practice.

The location of new improvements so that cost of transport is minimized is important where the users see the resulting water supply as satisfactory. Without such perception, considerations of distance and slope may count for little.

IMPLICATIONS FOR PUBLIC POLICY

A cross-sectional survey of the type we have carried out provides an essentially static picture of present water use. From the observed patterns, the way these patterns have evolved can only be inferred. It is even more uncertain to extrapolate from this to predict the effects of changes in public policy upon future communities. Although we may observe that in a community where all the members have an income of $4,000 the members are happy and contented, it does not follow that, in an adjacent community, transferring half the income of a member receiving $8,000 to his penniless neighbor will produce similar social benefits. Our comments on the nature of the problem therefore have a more solid basis than our suggestions on how it should be approached.

It is necessary first to define objectives and second to consider practical financial and administrative arrangements to achieve them. Objectives for rural and urban areas will be considered separately, as they involve different problems. Often our conclusions may resemble those already reached by guesswork or empirical means, but not always. In proposing possible alternatives to existing policies we wish to stimulate appraisal of still other alternatives which might serve the same general aims.

Rural Aims and Methods

The major social costs of poor rural water are disease and energy. Disease results from low volume usage, waterborne and water-washed diseases, water-based diseases, and diseases with water-related insect vectors. If common water sources cannot be protected from pollution, the stated preference for a private source is epidemiologically best, as shown above. For the helminths, source protection by concreting edges is the best answer to guinea worm. The simplest means of schistosome protection once water reaches the household is storing water for at least two days before use. One might speculate that a reasonably large household storage capacity combined with cheaper transport might also, by separating the acts of fetching and usage, lead to more flexibility in water usage. But much schistosome infection occurs in cultivating fields, swimming, and fishing. To the extent that time is claimed by domestic or other work, it would be as important a measure of cost as energy.

An idealized case of rural water supply might be one in which each household has ready and exclusive access to an adjacent spring or rainwater source yielding year-round supplies not subject to serious human pollution. Disease effects would be minimal, and energy costs also would be nominal. In these circumstances, the aggregate cost would be low and might even be below that for a household having low-cost piped supplies.

The steps toward this ideal to be taken first will depend on the area. No one technique of improvement would be best for all environments. In the hilly highlands of Kenya, gravity-fed piped systems concentrating on bringing water closer to the home should have priority. In schistosome-infected areas, storage facilities of two drums or tanks per household should come first; in guinea worm zones, it should be source protection. In places with high rainfall most of the year, emphasis should be on storage from the roof: this may call for linking guttering and storage to corrugated iron roofs as a status symbol. Where the sources are numerous, caution is required against improving only a few sources, since the resulting concentration of users—assuming that they perceive the improvement as beneficial—may outweigh the gains from using a larger number of slightly polluted supplies. This last point needs further field investigation.

Where sources are few, enhancement of water quality and its accessibility comes first and provision of boreholes is important. However, it is clear from the number of unused yet fairly functional boreholes to be found that boreholes are not the general panacea they are sometimes assumed to be, and that local assessment of the best measures is always required. Acceptance of improvements may be impeded by the procedures and conflicts of government agencies as well as by the perceptions of local users.

National policy should therefore be in terms of concrete goals, not methods. We would suggest that the rural aspect of a national policy which sought to minimize the social cost of water supply might have these features:

1. For all rural communities, efforts would be made to provide all inhabitants with improved supplies offering up to 20 liters per capita

with moderate contamination hazard at no reimbursable cost other than initial and continuing contributions of labor for construction and maintenance and for transport from the source. The design minimum would depend upon the preferences and habitat of the people involved. Rudimentary improvement carries certain clear hazards: if it is regarded as offering better supplies more people will use it, and the larger the number of users of a single source the greater the epidemic when contamination occurs. Recurrent small outbreaks then may be replaced by less frequent catastrophic outbreaks. There are no fully satisfactory grounds for comparing the two, but we suspect that the latter risks may be less heavy.

2. So far as the rural population shows itself ready, over a reasonable period of repayment, to bear the whole cost of maintenance and some proportion of construction cost for simple piped schemes furnishing up to 40 liters per day with low hazard of contamination, these would be provided. The question arises whether there are distinct limits to the economy of making such improvements in relation to terrain gradient, volume of readily available supply, settlement pattern, and capacity to pay.

3. Individual homeowners would be systematically encouraged to make independent improvements. These include individual cisterns, shallow wells, spring protection, water treatment devices, and methods of handling water. Social guides would include research on new methods, information on proved techniques, and technical assistance in design and construction.

Such a policy would depart from the current tendency to focus national efforts on rural projects directly administered by national agencies. More emphasis would be placed on stimulating individuals and community groups to make their own improvements. The expensive and technically difficult projects would be undertaken only if they promised very large returns in crop and livestock production, and thus would not cause drastic increases in total expenditure levels. The shift would be from centrally planned and costly works with high standards of purity to decentralized, inexpensive works with somewhat lower standards.

In nations where only 3 to 10 percent of the total population lives in large urban areas, but where such areas are growing rapidly and disproportionately by comparison with the nation as a whole, stress in planning and investment would be laid on providing improved supplies to the rural population and safe water for the expanding group of low income workers in the cities. The choice may be between treating these people differently from higher income workers and neglecting them entirely. Assuming that the total funds available for savings, public construction, and water supply construction were to remain the same, the sums could be reallocated to achieve a major shift in aggregate national costs. This allocation would require a basic adjustment in government policy in order to reduce standards of safety for government construction and to redeploy technical services to and among rural areas. Corresponding changes would be necessary in the operating procedures of the agencies responsible for research, design, construction, and operation.

Recent rates and methods of water-supply improvement in the three East African countries, as well as in most developing countries for which data are at hand, have been insufficient or barely sufficient to keep up with the growth in population. In 1968, the annual rural population growth in major sectors of East Africa was at least four times the numbers being provided each year with new improved supplies of classes 1, 2, and 3. To maintain the proportion currently served by such supplies would require expenditures above the 1968 rate. To actually gain on the situation and bring an expansion of 25 percent in five or six years would require still larger changes in expenditure, and steps have now been taken in that direction by Kenya and Tanzania. This would involve a reorientation of aims and methods on the part of the responsible government officers and the professional consultants to whom they turn for advice. To greatly increase the proportion of the rural population having improved supplies would require still further change in budget allocations among different classes of improvements.

A few of the alternative programs from which a government can choose are shown in a hypothetical case. Assume that in a country with a total population of 9,000,000 there are 700,000 urban dwellers and 8,300,000 in rural areas, mostly in humid or semiarid dispersed settlement. A very conservative population projection for a ten-year period would see urban population raised to 1,140,000 and rural to 10,119,000. It would not be unusual for as much as 63 percent of the rural population to draw water from unimproved supplies, and for about one-third of the urban population to enjoy multiple-tap service. This distribution of water services among the total population is illustrated in the second column of Table 1. Let us now ask the minimum likely investment cost of maintaining or changing the proportion of people using the several types of services.

The estimates of public investment cost are rough but will help to suggest orders of magnitude. We have shown the great range in such costs in relation to habitat. Plumbing and sewer costs are excluded. Operation costs are not calculated: these are assumed to be covered by user contributions of services or cash. [. . .]

One aim of a government might be to preserve over the decade the same proportion of its population served by different types of water improvements. A minimum program for this purpose is suggested in alternative 1 (Table 1). This would call for expenditures of at least $10,000,000 in urban areas, the overwhelming part going to new multiple-tap services costing about $50 per capita. The rural improvements would seek to maintain the same percentage of farmers having type 1, 2, and 3 services

TABLE 1 Alternative National Water Programs

		Population Served and Mean Annual Investment at End of Ten Years					
		Alternative 1		Alternative 2		Alternative 3	
Types of Water Improvement (type number in parentheses)	Base Year Population Served (thousands)	Mean Annual Investment (thousand dollars)	Population Served (thousands)	Mean Annual Investment (thousand dollars)	Population Served (thousands)	Mean Annual Investment (thousand dollars)	Population Served (thousands)
Rural							
No improvement (0)	5,240	0	6,392	345	5,240	647	900
Individual and group (1,2)	1,800	198	2,196	198	3,348	198	4,500
Pipeline (3)	1,260	139	1,531	139	1,531	139	4,719
Total rural	8,300	337	10,119	682	10,119	984	10,119
Urban							
No improvement (0)	160	0	260	70	160	0	0
Standpipe (4)	180	79	293	79	393	262	450
Single-tap (5)	90	68	147	68	147	300	340
Multiple-tap (6)	270	850	440	850	440	150	300
Total urban	700	997	1,140	1,067	1,140	712	1,140
Total national	9,000	1,334	11,259	1,749	11,259	1,696	11,259

and would cost $3 to $7 per capita for a total of at least $3,400,000. No effort would be made to help the people now lacking improved supplies. More costly types of rural improvement would be avoided. At the end of the period, the absolute number of people lacking improved supplies would be 20 percent larger than at the outset.

If the government were to seek to prevent any larger part of the population from using unimproved sources but not reduce the proportion in each of types 3, 4, 5, and 6, it could invest capital funds as shown in alternative 2. About $3,450,000 would go to improving type 1 or 2 facilities for rural households lacking improved water supply. That expenditure is shown as rural type 0. At least $700,000 would be used to improve unimproved urban sources. Large amounts would be required to give type 1 and 2 improvements to rural dwellers and to give standpipe services to new migrants to the city. The expenditures estimated for types 1 and 2 are the amounts required to offset population growth. That, with other services, would cost a minimum of $17,000,000. The effect would be to reduce the proportion without improved water supplies to less than one-half.

The country still would be far from a goal of relatively pure water in modest amounts for all. [. . .] Since budget constraints may be severe, it may be more helpful to suggest how expenditures at a level of those in alternative 2 might be used to effect a drastic change in health costs. This is outlined in alternative 3, which would eliminate unimproved sources in urban areas and cut the rural users of unimproved sources to less than 10 percent. It would call for heavy investment in type 1, 2, and 3 improvements for people without improvements (these are shown as expenditures for type 0 in the table, and the resulting change in population served is shown for types 1, 2, and 3).

Standpipe service would be extended to 40 percent of the urban residents, and single-tap service at a cost of about $12 per capita would be provided to about 30 percent. These major expenditures would be possible because investment in multiple-tap services would be limited to 30,000 rather than 170,000 new users as contemplated in alternatives 1 and 2.

We put forward these choices not as recommendations for a particular government, but to illustrate the opportunities to change the strategy of domestic water supply without demanding wholly impractical increases in the level of public expenditure.

The practicability of reaching these service goals by the expenditures noted is still speculative. The unit costs are rough at best, as was already noted. Yet they indicate the different outcomes which might be expected if new standards of design and operation were adopted.

The evidence marshalled about the health effects of improved water supply could lead to a contrary argument on narrowly economic grounds. Since impure water supply is a principal cause of high infant mortality, the failure to prevent it relieves the society of pressures exerted by a rapid increase in population: delay in improving supplies is an aid to curbing population growth. This is clearly a huge topic that cannot be adequately considered here. Quite aside from the humanitarian considerations which would encourage any effort to prolong and enrich life, the economic effects of water supply improvement may be somewhat different from those of certain other public health measures. To the extent that time and energy spent in drawing water is liberated for other useful purposes, productivity may be enhanced beyond the prevention of disease. And to the degree that community cooperation and joint enterprises are engendered by new rural schemes, the pace of economic development may be quickened. These latter gains will hinge on the effort's being essentially self-help.

Were policy aims stated in terms of reducing net health and energy costs, the demands made upon technicians and planners as well as research units would change radically. The effects upon the quality of water supply would be wide ranging. Part of the engineering activity devoted to the design of complex new community projects would be channeled to advice on possible independent action and to the preparation of simple designs which individual water users or community groups could carry out on their own. This would focus fresh attention on devising construction methods suitable for unskilled application. For example, if the key obstacle to cistern improvement were the expense of trucking cumbersome storage tanks into the countryside, means would be found to assemble them in place at low cost, or to build them from available materials, or to substitute new materials.* If there were lively local interest in using an available shallow aquifer, methods would be developed to permit borehole drilling by relatively unskilled but specially trained workers and to finance the joint purchase of the needed rig. Another technique would be to facilitate low-cost transport of water from safe sources to delivery points. Possible new adjustments would be explored not only in design, construction methods, and transport, but in credit and in technical advice on operations and repairs. Few women are familiar with the ways water and utensils can be handled in the household to reduce disease, and there is almost no research on equipment or techniques to help.

It usually is easier to recommend expenditures from the central treasury for well-defined projects than to devise ways for local groups to willingly carry the burden of action, and the precedent for such efforts is recent. Under a policy of promoting local action, no borehole would be drilled unless the potential users clearly wanted it and were prepared to

---

*This approach to developing effective techniques with local materials has been followed by Intermediate Technology Group, Ltd., a private nonprofit organization concerned with the identification and application of small-scale, low-cost technologies in the rural areas of developing countries.

contribute to its construction. No materials would be provided for pipe or pumps unless the community were ready to take the lead in preliminary design and construction. This would be the acid test of the community's perception of the utility of the improvement and of its capacity to provide leadership in instigating and carrying out the work. But even then the sparse funds for construction materials and equipment might be better allocated to spring improvements serving a much larger population with less pure supplies. Emphasis would be placed upon sounding the views of water users about their needs and available sources and on giving them assistance in whatever steps offered reduction in health and energy costs. Insofar as manufactured equipment was to be purchased and stockpiled it would be selected to have widest use by operators having only elementary training. Special provision would be made for repair and supply service through regional networks, including private insurance schemes, without involving central agencies. The central and district technical agencies would be obliged to distribute their service differently and to schedule it so as to stimulate and coordinate local initiative without undue interruptions in the work. The Kenya experience suggests that this may be attainable.

Urban Aims and Methods

In urban areas where piped supplies are practicable, the low income consumers are bearing a disproportionately large share of the social cost, whereas the upper income consumers, who might be expected to pay heavily for the amenities they enjoy, carry a disproportionately low share. It is not uncommon for more than 40 percent of the population of an African city to be served by standpipes or unimproved sources and for this group to use about 15–20 percent of the total domestic withdrawal, and less than 10 percent of the total withdrawal.*

As an alternative to current policies, the public agencies might well consider one aimed at achieving the lowest aggregate social cost from providing water. It is important to recall that no solid evidence has been advanced showing that urban economic growth is dependent upon improvement of domestic water supply beyond the minimum standards suggested above. To be sure, amenities are involved, but basic changes in employment pattern and productivity apparently are not at stake.

---

*In Accra in 1963, 48.5 percent of the population lived in substandard housing. The standpipe service was believed to reach all of these and accounted for an estimated 17 percent of total domestic use. In Dodoma in 1967 the 36 percent of the population served by standpipes was believed to use 9 percent of the pumpage. In Kampala in 1968, standpipe customers used 7 percent of the total withdrawal.

It seems likely that the greatest human migration in history will be the movement, in the decades immediately ahead, of farm people to cities in developing countries. Raw, new housing on the outskirts of Dar es Salaam, Kampala, and Nairobi may be only the precursor of larger movements to come. Given the probable size and speed of the movement in a period when capital will continue to be short, the responsible governments will be hard put to provide the minimum of a roof and a distant water source.

The density of population in relation to the number of independent sources in urban areas is very high, and therefore human pollution is a much more serious problem than in the countryside. Whereas in rural areas quantity of moderately clean water is the chief aim, in urban areas it is at least as important to reduce the use of dangerous supplies as to provide adequate volume for use. In the absence of sewer systems in many poor areas this is more urgent, and also more difficult, since much polluted surface water results. Settled areas are much smaller than in the countryside, and a reasonable solution to the situation may be to provide at least one tap per household. There seems to be no viable substitute for the traditional chlorinated supply for two reasons: the likely defective state of sewers and pollution of carrying pipes for some years to come in the poorer urban areas, and the very serious consequences of accidental pollution of a large common source. The suggested aims for urban supply are therefore as follows.

1. A minimal pipe installation of one controlled tap per household yielding up to 40–80 liters per capita per day would be provided at a charge to cover the direct cost for supply and maintenance. This would imply allocation of joint cost in urban water accounting so that users of small amounts of water would pay according to volume withdrawn rather than according to number of connections, assessed value, or population of a household. At best, joint cost allocation is an arbitrary process reflecting public preferences. Where single-tap installation is impractical, standpipe service would be provided.
2. The remainder of the urban consumers would have more than one tap and would be expected to pay the full cost of their required system capacity, including sewer installation charges, on the basis of allocating joint costs as described above, and on a pricing schedule which would charge proportionately more for uses larger than those required for health.
3. Special efforts would be made to devise simple ways of using small quantities of water to improve household sanitation, and to bring water into the household at low cost without promoting large garden use or peak demands, as by using flow regulators rather than flow meters.

Unfortunately, such a program cannot be considered on its own, for it is limited by its institutional setting as well as by broader aspects of fiscal and welfare policy. In colonial days the heavy water users were expatriates provided with subsidized housing. This has been continued and even expanded for government office holders since independence. Commercial employers also provide housing for their more senior employees. This has several consequences. A large expenditure on multiple-tap water system installation is concealed as "housing," "company expenses," even "university budget." Salaried members of the community often pay nominal water charges and are insensitive to water rate changes intended to reduce lawn watering or make people pay heavily for it. Allocated housing tends to set the style of life of these people and minimize choice on their part. If water pricing is to be used to influence use, the system needs drastic change. Otherwise even more of the costs of multiple-tap service will fall on the government and be a charge on the public revenue, defeating its aims. The vested interests of the governing groups have so far prevented any change in this system, and to that extent seem unlikely to favor a revision.

A common method of planning for urban water supply improvement is to project future demand, canvass the available means of supplying the demand, and then choose the design assuring the desired volume at safe quality and lowest cost. Although there obviously is some limit to the amount of water a city can consume, use is seen as mounting continuously into an unspecified heaven where every day in every way people will use more and more. The decisive criterion is minimum investment, given the projected demand. This may be reasonable in areas where income is relatively high, where the tradition has been to encourage per capita use as a means of improving the financing of multiple-tap installations, and where there is no prospect of exhausting supplies or degrading downstream supplies. However, if the deciding question is posed as "What is the cheapest way of meeting minimum health standards?" in place of "What is the cheapest way of meeting projected demand?", another design emerges. In a city with 30–50 percent of its total population in low income housing or squatter quarters, the crucial aspect of design from a public health standpoint is seeing to it that the 30–50 percent are provided with pure supplies in quantities of 20–80 liters per capita daily. That minimum can generally be reached at a cost of $10–$30 per capita. An integrated system caring for the full demand may run $50–$200 per capita as a minimum.

The implications in terms of design for a hypothetical urban area would be as shown in Table 2. Here, the emphasis in alternative A, a city with a population of 200,000, such as an East African capital city, is on supplying the upper and middle income consumers with whatever water they will buy at prices sufficient to recover annual expenditures. The annual pumpage is about 2 billion gallons. In order to simplify the choice in

TABLE 2 Alternative Water Supply Investment Programs for a Growing City

	Alternative A		Alternative B	
Type of Domestic Service* (improvement type)	Percent Population Served	Percent Contribution to Annual Receipts	Percent Population Served	Percent Contribution to Annual Receipts
Unimproved sources (0)	30	0	0	0
Improved sources (1, 2)	35	0	10	0
Standpipe (4)	5	7	45	9
Single taps (5)	5	0	25	32
Multiple taps (6)	25	93	20	59
	100	100	100	100
Level of Annual Receipts and Expenditures	$560,000		$840,000	
Allocation of Annual Domestic System Expenditures	Percent		Percent	
Supply: storage, pumping and treatment	40		42	
Distribution	25		28	
Administration	20		17	
Capital fund	15		13	
	100		100	

*Large industrial users are assumed to be either self-supplied or served by a separable sector of the municipal system, and are not included in estimates of income and expenditure.

dealing with domestic use it is assumed that industrial users either are self-supplied or would be served by a separate distribution system of which almost half is industrial or waste. The standpipe services are money losers under prevailing price schedules in this city and usually are not promoted. As a result, a substantial part of the population draws from unimproved services. The small number of single-tap customers are in government estates and do not pay for water.

Under an alternative policy suggested in column B, the emphasis is on eliminating use of unimproved sources. This would be achieved by improving or closing off those unimproved sources remaining, by extending standpipe services ninefold, and by encouraging single-tap connections for a quarter of the customers. It would provide for four-fifths the number of users having multiple connections under alternative B. Charges for standpipe supplies would be no more than one-quarter of those in alternative A, or about $0.75 per capita per year. The single-tap users would pay about $5.50 per capita per year or about $0.015 per day. Charges for multiple-tap users would be 25 percent more than in the first alternative. The multiple-tap and industrial users would suffer only slightly in proportion to income, and would be stimulated in some measure to conserve their purchased supplies and to develop independent supplies, such as cisterns for lawn watering, at their own expense. The total usage would be about 13 percent larger and the revenues 50 percent larger. The capital expenditures and debt service would remain the same, but multiple-tap installations would be less, a small part would go to sealing or improvement of peripheral sources, supply would need to be expanded modestly, and much heavier expenditures would go into standpipe and single-tap service.

The greater standpipe services under alternative B would not be expected to yield equal cash income, whereas single taps might possibly pay for themselves. The multiple-tap users would pay larger rates, and the low income users who formerly carried water from unimproved or partly improved sources would be saved a major part of their transport cost but would pay at the tap. If the government wishes, it could eliminate any charges to standpipe users and offset this by increasing the charges to multiple-tap users by $0.005 per day.

Any attempt to provide piped water at low price to low income users by means of single taps raises two other problems: excessive wasteful use and the collection of water rates.

Waste can be curbed by two measures. Taps may be equipped with a control device, such as the Fordilla valve, which will prevent the tap from being left running. A periodic inspection service, using meters on line segments, will guard against leaks and illegally attached pipes.

Collection of water rates from poor areas raises problems. Metering houses under such circumstances has repeatedly been shown to be costly and inefficient, and some type of flat rate is necessary. If this rate is to be low and yet cover costs, each family should have its own tap. It follows that the area should be saturated by this type of supply and that every family must use it if the system is to be viable. Disconnection is therefore not a sound way to enforce payment of water rates, and it may be found better to collect water charges at the same time as general tax revenues or by some other means not directly linked to continuation of service. These can be effective only if ease of collection is coupled with technical means of preventing waste. It seems clear that a complicated or selective system rarely works. The simpler universal system has worked in some countries and deserves wider experimentation with a view to devising improved social and engineering techniques which will stand the test of rugged operating conditions.

At present, as shown above, the rich man pays a smaller proportion of his income for ample pure water for health and amenities than the poor man pays for his meager supplies. Two arbitrary decisions need to be made; our first is that the needs of all should precede anyone's wants, and that the rich man should be prepared to pay a larger proportion of his income for the amenities of a large water supply. Second, water should be considered as a self-contained enterprise. The rich man can be assessed a larger share of the water bill either by increasing direct taxation on property or income and leaving the pricing schedule unchanged or by altering the pricing schedule. We have chosen the latter system.

Stressing the delivery of minimum quantities of potable water to every household would alter the design of major distribution lines, for it would impose low requirements for normal as well as peak flows. It also would call for ingenuity in perfecting control valves, shower devices, billing systems, and waste disposal to meet health standards at minimum costs. Research in these fields would be needed, and the results would have to be translated into plumbing codes, import tax schedules, and assistance to local manufacturers.

The choice for a municipal government is between modest expansion of the high-cost connections to houses with multiple taps and dramatic increase in rudimentary services for low income people.

POLICY CHOICES

The World Health Organization commendably sets high standards of service as a goal for all urban populations. Less weight is placed upon the arrangements made for the great bulk of the urban population in tropical cities who cannot expect to obtain multiple-tap service for many years to come. Perhaps the greatest demands on engineering and administrative imagination in the water field are for providing acceptable and socially efficient service to those people.

It is significant that in a report to the Twenty-third World Health Assembly the director-general of the World Health Organization set very modest goals for improvement during 1971–80 of water supplies in developing member countries. Targets were proposed for raising the proportion of rural inhabitants served by safe water from less than 10 percent to 20 percent. Rural dwellers make up more than seven-tenths of the total population of those countries. For the urban dwellers, the decade targets were to raise the 25 percent supplied in house or courtyard to 40 percent, and to increase the 26 percent supplied from public standpipes to 60 percent, thus reaching all the city population. Per capita construction costs were figured at \$35–\$20 for house connections, and \$20–\$12 for standpipes, and \$14–\$8 for rural supplies, with the higher numbers applying to Latin America. The proposed program of construction would amount to \$4,340 million for urban piped connections, \$3,160 for urban standpipes, and \$1,600 for rural areas, for a total of \$9,100 million.

The proposed targets reaffirm the use of the WHO standards for drinking water but then go on to recognize that "it is obviously impracticable to attempt to maintain the same high standard in a remote village in a poor country as in the capital city of a wealthy industrial state;" but they do not say how these conflicting approaches should be resolved in practice, and they would devote seven-tenths of the capital funds to the city dwellers and leave four-fifths of those in rural areas with unimproved supplies. The emphasis is on piped supplies for cities, and in the same way most investment for waste disposal and purchase of plumbing would also benefit the middle and upper income consumers.

In terms of benefits to health for large parts of the population, a different distribution of investment would deserve serious consideration. The WHO has launched a network of collaborating research institutions based on an International Reference Centre for Community Water Supply in The Hague. This network can move either to diffuse and enforce the old standard approaches and techniques of wealthy nations or to devise genuinely imaginative solutions to fit the needs of developing countries and test them in the field.

The policy suggested here differs from the alternative proposed by [Ian] Burton and [T. R.] Lee in its lesser emphasis upon standpipe services. It contemplates an earlier and wider adoption of single-tap service in individual households for two major reasons. First, the capital cost of single-tap service does not greatly exceed the cost of a dense network of standpipes for the same area. Second, the direct cost to individual consumers may be little more than for standpipe service, when account is taken of both the cost in carrying time and purchase and the frequent use of paid carriers at high rates.

Public choice of the policy to be followed in providing new water service finally must rest on assessment of the total social impacts of the possible range of improvements. Capital and operating costs are well known. Cash and energy costs for people carrying water from the source are less well known but can be estimated. Complete health costs can be judged only on a scale which bears no direct relation to monetary measures of the effects of disease. Amenity costs can be inferred from the willingness of consumers to pay for water beyond essential health requirements. Public agencies can deal with the choice among possible combinations of improvements simply by adopting a policy followed elsewhere. Generally, such policies were set for other environments with other expectations of economic growth. Or they can try to select the combination offering the smallest deleterious effects for the particular environments concerned. Then the choice will be strongly influenced by the values society places on reduction of health costs and on provision of amenities.

As we assess the use and improvement programs in the varied environments of East Africa, we find opportunities for fruitful action especially promising in three directions. First, individuals or groups of rural water users stand to gain greatly in health from very modest improvements. Second, where settlement density and pattern permit, the development of rural distribution lines can help materially in reducing both health and energy costs. Third, in urban areas there is particular promise in simple installation of single-tap service. The first two will depend upon self-help initiative with guidance. The third will demand innovation in methods of organizing urban deliveries of water. All three will need imaginative research to perfect new equipment, techniques, and methods of management.

Some administrators look longingly to an earlier period when it was assumed that the march of change in developing countries would be slow but sure in the direction of replicating Western European material culture. Under this view it was proper to lay out a city water system with the idea that ultimately all consumers would live in multiple-tap dwellings and that makeshift service would suffice until people could pay for the best. When the realities of present urban population and economic growth rates are considered, it is more reasonable to assume that within the physical life of new water systems only a small proportion of the inhabitants will be able to enjoy such facilities. The key problem then becomes one of finding the least costly means of meeting whatever are regarded as minimum health standards.

The reader may reach this point with the feeling that we have raised more questions than we have answered, and that in some cases we have provided vague answers hedged about with reservations and exceptions in place of the clear balances of costs and benefits to be found in much of the literature justifying new municipal supplies. Yet there are more alternative forms of improvement than farmers or governments are inclined to perceive, and unequivocal statements of health benefits may provide a good brief but a poor water supply and worse science. Simple rules of thumb may be needed in daily practice, but they should avoid distorting understanding of the factors at work in shaping individual use and its social consequences.

Among nations with high losses from disease and with low resources of capital and foreign credit, it is desirable to examine the full range of alternatives for meeting health needs with a keen eye to the social returns and with openness to new approaches. If social costs are to be minimized, investment adding little to national improvement must be avoided. Innovative ways of promoting health through social as well as technical devices must be cultivated. Both investment and innovation must be sensitive to the complex ways in which domestic households respond to changes in water source, cost, and techniques for distribution. This will call for more refinement in tracing out health costs and in examining the way water users make their choices.

41

Assurance of Municipal Water Supplies

Brian J.L. Berry
and Frank E. Horton

Alongside the problem of water-*quality* maintenance and improvement, there is the associated problem of the adequacy of municipal water *supplies.* The two may be linked through recycling and renovation of wastewaters for municipal purposes. Let us turn to an examination of this case, because it raises a variety of underlying perceptual and behavioral issues and will permit a whole range of alternatives in water management to be examined.

As [James F.] Johnson notes, the problem of supplying water for municipal use is becoming increasingly difficult in the United States, and this trend is expected to continue into the foreseeable future. According to recent estimates of the Water Resources Council, several regions in the United States may experience critical problems of water shortage compounded by water-quality deterioration unless suitable measures are taken. Under certain conditions, the optimal solution to increasing municipal demands and reducing water-quality deterioration may rest with wastewater renovation. Advanced waste treatment could lower the amounts of pollutants discharged to prescribed levels, and the resultant high-quality effluent could be made available on-site for municipal use. The prospective use of renovated wastewater for municipal supply must therefore be evaluated against the range of technical, economic, and social factors which may affect its usage.

The problems associated with prospective municipal water "shortages" are not unique to any area in the country. The differential distribu-

Reprint of "Assurance of Municipal Water Supplies," Chapter 8 in *Urban Environmental Management: Planning for Pollution Control,* by Brian J. L. Berry and Frank E. Horton. Prentice-Hall, Inc., Englewood Cliffs, N.J., 1974. Chapter 8 is based on a paper by James F. Johnson, *Renovated Waste Water,* Dept. of Geography Research Paper No. 135, University of Chicago, 1971, pp. 3–23 and 160–66. Reprinted with permission of the author.

tion of water supply and demands in space and time has resulted in both seasonal and annual shortages for municipal uses in many parts of the United States. Rapidly increasing urbanization in the Southwest has severely taxed that area's permanent water supplies, and the more humid Midwest and Northeast have been subject to periodic water shortages in spite of apparently adequate resources. Several large-scale projects have been proposed for the Southwest, where emphasis has been on quenching that area's growing thirst with interbasin transfers, in spite of their questionable economic efficiency. The problem is of an equally serious nature in eastern cities such as New York, where the water "shortages" caused by the declining reservoir levels in the drought of 1965–66 could have been averted through the use of water from the Hudson River.

In these and other situations, there has been a manifest tendency to meet increasing municipal demands through conventional alternatives such as the transport of water from distant sources. At the same time, inefficiency of municipal usage and deterioration in the quality of supplies has added to the seriousness of local situations. Much of what has been wrong with past approaches to more efficient water management lies in the failure of water planners to recognize the integrated nature of water systems and the impact which each alteration of the water in these systems has upon subsequent uses and users. Greater emphasis has been placed upon the procurement of water than upon the most efficient use of supplies.

Completely renovated municipal sewage effluent in some instances could supply cities at a lower cost than conventional sources, and the impact of using such an alternative could be profound. For instance, a community that would return 80 percent of its initial water withdrawal to its system for reuse could cumulatively increase the utility of this water supply fivefold. This being so, it may be fruitful to examine the position of renovation within the framework of municipal water-supply and water-quality management systems. The range of alternatives for coping with problems of municipal water supply and water-quality deterioration is discussed in order to assess the relative status of wastewater renovation. Because of the variation in environmental conditions throughout the country, the practicality of these alternatives may vary considerably in different situations. This discussion does not attempt to specify the practicality of these alternatives; rather, it seeks to lay out the options available to communities for solving their water-supply and wastewater problems.

WATER SUPPLY

Several possible approaches are available to cope with growing municipal demands for water. Options available to any community would vary considerably throughout the country and may involve various combinations of these alternatives. These include (1) bearing shortage or pollution, (2) transporting distant sources and storing untimely sources, (3) increasing the overall water supply, (4) changing water quality, and (5) changing water use (Table 1). The alternatives may be outlined with a view to showing the distinctive role of water reuse; each has its distinctive effects upon the water system.

Bear Shortage or Pollution

Theoretically, the community has available to it the "no action" alternative of bearing shortage or pollution of its present water supply without seeking other alternatives—but whether such an option is viable is questionable. A decision to bear shortage would invoke consumer self-restraint; there is no guarantee of the effectiveness of this alternative and no measure with which to support most efficient use. Over the long run, the most productive uses would be competing for water with marginal uses without benefit of any effective market mechanism to foster efficiency. One of the more obvious drawbacks to such an alternative would

TABLE 1 Alternative for Meeting Increasing Demands

Goals	Approaches	Techniques
Bear shortage or pollution		
Use available supply	Storage	Reservoirs
		Storm catchment
	Transport	Aqueducts
		Ground pumpage
		Motive transport
Increase overall supply	Precipitation inducement	Cloud seeding
	Increase and capture snow- and ice-melt	
Change water quality	Treat influent	Freshwater purification
		Desalination
	Treat effluent	Advanced waste treatment
Change water use	Reduce use	Price curbs—metering
		Restricted use
		Recycling
	Curb waste	Evapotranspiration reduction
		Seepage reduction
	Alter distribution	Dual supply lines
		Directed pipelines
		Bottled water

be in the probability of diminished residual supply for fire protection, which would most likely be reflected in the higher cost of insurance.

Likewise, the probable community response to the bearing of increased pollution may render it infeasible.

Available Supply

Man conventionally has turned to the storage and transport of high-quality waters in order to satisfy municipal demands. This practice continues today, even where lower-quality sources are available at a more favorable cost. Whether the solution to increasing municipal demands lies in the construction of larger *reservoirs* and more distant *aqueducts* is the subject of considerable debate. As construction costs and interest rates increase, such alternatives become impractical in comparison with nonstructural alternatives. Nevertheless, these schemes continue to dominate the imagination of many planners. Projects such as the Cannonsville reservoir to supply New York City, the Feather River project to supply southern California, and the Central Arizona project have been subject to severe criticism; yet, other and more elaborate schemes appear to be in the offing. Perhaps the use of *underwater flexible piping* may be an alternative in coastal areas. One study has indicated that substantial cost savings would be realized in using this method rather than the inland route to transfer water from northern to southern California.

Groundwater pumpage has been a popular mode of municipal water supply wherever possible, owing to its generally high quality and low production costs. Because ground aquifers are spread thinly and are slow to recharge, increasing urban demands have resulted in diminishing groundwater levels in many areas. Where wells must extend to continually deeper aquifers, the production costs are likely to increase rapidly. This increase would result from lower yields, increased power and equipment requirements, and higher chloride content. Unless technological advances can improve the efficiency of deep-well drilling, it is likely that heavier urban demands upon localized groundwater sources will have to be met by supplementing with other sources or by aquifer recharge.

Motive transport has been considered for solving municipal water problems, although generally in remote locations. Tank trucks, railroad cars, and tanker vessels all have been used for this purpose, but they usually have not been designed for the job and their costs are high. Motively transported water generally has been used only where other alternatives are not available, whether due to emergencies such as drought or contamination or because of remote location. It is unlikely that this alternative will be considered by communities where other alternatives are available, especially considering the risk posed by possible failure of delivery.

Increase Overall Supply

Increasing municipal demands also may be met through increasing the overall supply of available water. This can be accomplished through precipitation inducement or through snow- or ice-melt. Precipitation inducement is a highly complex alternative, and little is known of the potential consequences. One study has indicated that while it would be more economical than conventional alternatives in some locations, it may not be as suitable elsewhere. The present limitation appears to be primarily a physical one. Its prospective use is complicated by potential litigation involving both on-site and off-site damages. Such damages could grow out of (1) conflicting weather requirements of property owners, (2) unanticipated destructive effects such as floods, and (3) deprivation of benefits of natural weather such as off-site reduction in precipitation.

Snow-melt is an important source of water supply, particularly in the West. Because storage is dependent upon regional climate, it is thought by some to be beyond the control of man. Snow accumulation can have a significant effect upon the general availability of water, seasonal low stream flows, and direct evaporation. At present, the practicality or physical capability of supplying additional demands through this alternative has not been determined; perhaps future technology will lead to its more efficient utilization. The harnessing of water contained in *ice masses* also warrants further consideration. However, it appears that the distance between massive glacial deposits and municipal demands would inhibit any such project. One interesting scheme proposed by John Isaac would offer a partial solution to the growing water demands of Los Angeles by towing icebergs from the Antarctic. However, there is some doubt whether such an alternative is physically viable.

Change Water Quality

The alternative that appears to offer the greatest potential for meeting future water needs is improving the quality of polluted waters. Major cities generally are located near or help generate vast quantities of low-quality water. Considering the trend to increasing costs for fixed capital projects such as reservoirs and aqueducts, alternatives geared to the continual refinement of purification technology and concomitant cost efficiencies would appear to be attractive.

More attention should be given to forms of catchment that are less spectacular. Paved surfaces and even roofs provide potential for meeting future demands. Low-quality waters are available as saline or brackish supplies from which inorganic material need be removed, surface supplies in which organics pose the main problem; or as sewage effluent from which organics and possible inorganics need be removed.

The purified product of *low-quality surface water* is used throughout the country, although to a lesser extent where higher-quality supplies are even remotely available. The use of these polluted waters is mostly the result of deterioration of a once-clean supply. It is likely that many water managers would opt for transporting clean waters to cities if the choice were open to them, in view of such recent expansion as that of Detroit to Lake Huron. Although the monetary costs of increasing supplies through treatment of polluted sources are less than for most transport-oriented alternatives, it is likely that costs in terms of aesthetics and hygienic risk may offset this in many situations.

The use of *desalinized seawater* has received considerable attention and should add measurably to available supplies in coastal areas once treatment costs are reduced. Apparently desalinized water bears no stigma to prospective domestic users, owing to the inorganic rather than organic pollutants. It is likely that this source will be viewed as a practical alternative for meeting future demands, especially in coastal areas with limited freshwater supplies. Its value to inland areas is quite limited by high transport costs. For instance, a study of the feasibility of transporting desalinized seawater to augment the flow of the Colorado River indicated that the transport cost would be several times that of desalination.

The use of *renovated municipal sewage effluent* would be competitive with both transport- and treatment-oriented alternatives, although the problems of aesthetics and hygienic risk associated with organically polluted sources may be an inhibiting factor. Because of its lower pollutant load, secondary sewage effluent would be less expensive to "desalinize" than brackish or saline water. With the rising costs of construction-oriented purification alternatives, it is likely that the use of renovated wastewater would be practical in a number of situations. This is especially true where high waste-treatment requirements reduce the marginal cost of providing a potable product.

Change Water Use

Municipal demands also could be met more effectively by changing the way in which water is used. This can be accomplished by reducing the amount used, by curbing waste, or by altering the distribution system in order to gear water quality to usage.

Reduction in use could be accomplished by metering or pricing curbs, use restrictions, or recycling. Both *metering* and *pricing curbs* have been found to be effective means of lowering municipal water demands, although not generally employed by water managers for this purpose. Several major cities, including New York and Chicago, do not meter their water supplies, instead charging a flat rate. The practicality of metering must be weighed according to installation and computation costs versus the increased utility of available supplies. One study indicated a 40 percent drop in per capita water consumption in Boulder, Colorado, from 1960 when only 5 percent of the city was metered to 1965, when it was fully metered. Another study indicated that the quantity of water demand for residential uses, particularly sprinkling, is affected by the price charged. [Charles W.] Howe suggests that even the magnitude of maximum-day demands responds to price charges, and this could be used by management for either increasing or decreasing average- and maximum-day demands.

Restrictions on use have been employed for temporary water shortages, but not as permanent measures. Temporary restrictions on lawn watering, car washing, and other peak uses could substantially reduce peak loading but tend to be unpopular. Such restrictions in some instances might not act in the interest of economic efficiency, in that they might penalize those users or uses that are willing and able to pay the marginal cost.

In response to the growing scarcity of available water and the increase in associated production costs in certain situations, some industrial users have begun to *recycle* water. The recycling of water for cooling and certain types of processing that have low-quality requirements is especially valuable in arid regions where the cost and quality of fresh water is too high for the needs of these uses. Perhaps more industries would gear operations to recycling if the cost of purchasing water reflected marginal production costs as it should, rather than the distribution costs that encourage large-volume usage. Nonetheless, recycling warrants serious consideration for satisfying some of the future municipal demands.

Increased municipal demands also could be satisfied in part by reducing the amount of water wastage through evaporation, transpiration, and seepage. Evaporation can be lessened by covering water surfaces, whether by chemical or structural measures. Hexadecanol has been applied to water surfaces in reservoirs as a monomolecular film and found significant in *reducing evaporation.* However, its use is not physically practical at present because it can be broken down by wind and wave action. Evaporation losses in open conduits account for some 20 percent of water flow in some parts of the Southwest. In spite of high costs, complete closure may be practical in areas of high potential evaporation that face future water scarcity. Other methods such as design of reservoirs to obtain low area-to-volume ratio, alteration of the thermal stratification of water in reservoirs, and selective withdrawal of warmer water from stratified reservoirs may be practical alternatives in certain situations.

Increased water yields also may be realized by *reducing transpiration* from vegetation, although municipalities may have little control over the most substantial sources of transpiration losses. In the arid

Southwest, for instance, the maintenance of irrigation agriculture with nearly 100 percent evapotranspiration losses ignores the economic value of water for alternative municipal and industrial uses. Unfortunately, the political factors in water development may far outweigh economic factors in such situations. Still, certain communities can increase water yields substantially through more effective watershed management. As one example, elimination of ground and forest vegetation through chemical application added 190,000 gallons of water per acre in a Newark, N.J., watershed.

Seepage is a problem in both the import and distribution of municipal water supplies. The *lining of conduits* with concrete or other impervious materials would remove the seepage losses in the import of water, but the costs may be considerable. Seepage within the distribution system also is a serious problem owing to the cracking of pipes, and losses may run from 10 to 20 percent. Where water production costs are high and seepage losses considerable, the isolation and repair of breaks may prove to be a practical alternative for meeting a portion of increasing demands. In fact, the hygienic risk posed by seepage inflow may be sufficient reason itself for greater concern with *pipeline repair.*

Another means of meeting increased municipal demands would be to alter the distribution system in order to make more efficient use of the range in quality of alternative water sources. The increased production costs for obtaining a high-quality water may not be compatible with the needs for certain uses which can utilize a low-quality product at reduced costs. The supplying of valuable high-quality water for certain industrial and domestic uses and for fire protection may not be the wisest allocation of the resource under conditions of increased scarcity. Distribution systems that allow for some greater degree of choice may improve this efficiency. Alternative means of distribution include dual supply lines, directed pipelines, and bottling.

Dual supply lines would direct two water supplies of different quality to the consumer. In such a system, lower-quality water could be used for lawn watering or flushing of wastes—uses that account for nearly one-half of residential demands. Although the costs may be excessive in presently developed areas, dual systems warrant serious consideration in newly developing areas. However, the risk associated with potential error in cross-linkage of supply lines may act as a constraint upon serious consideration of this alternative.

Directed piping of nonpotable water merits serious consideration in terms of both economic efficiency and public acceptance. It is likely that water could be directed to high-demand industrial conglomerations at low cost, especially where distances between supply and demand are minimal. Also, public reaction would not be a factor, because potential linkage with domestic systems would be nil. It has been over two decades since U.S. Steel at Sparrows Point began using Baltimore's sewage effluent; perhaps the time has arrived for broadening the scope of directed piping to provide a partial solution to increasing industrial demands.

Uses requiring potable-quality water account for a small share of residential demands. Therefore, it may be worthwhile considering a distribution scheme incorporating *bottled water.* In recent years, sales of bottled water have increased tremendously, and a range of products and distribution modes has developed. This results from apparent dissatisfaction with municipal supplies. Mass distribution of bottled water could be an effective means of freeing municipal piped supplies from the inhibiting requirements of potability.

WATER QUALITY

Several alternatives are available to communities to stem the increasing deterioration of water by municipal sewage effluent and to increase the wastable municipal supply. Essentially these involve two steps, collection and disposal (Table 2). Approaches to increase the efficiency of collection are (1) extension of sewerage pipelines and (2) preventing storm runoff from causing combined-system overload. Approaches to minimize the effect of sewage disposal include (1) concentrating disposal in specific watercourses, (2) utilizing stream purification, (3) utilizing soil purification, and (4) increased sewage treatment.

Collection

Collection involves the transfer of wastes from one location to another and is not necessarily remedial to the system as a whole. Nevertheless, much of the water-quality deterioration in developing urban areas today grows out of the inability to collect and treat municipal wastes adequately. Urban fringe areas often lack the refined treatment facilities necessary to cope with rapidly increasing waste loads. Pollution of water resources may result from the discharge of raw waste into surface streams as well as oversaturation of septic systems. Much of this pollution could be stemmed by *extending municipal sewerage facilities* to outlying areas. However, dispersion of urban settlement can make such sewage collection an expensive matter, and the problems of intercommunity politics and "equitable" service charges may severely inhibit such schemes.

Another factor that has a substantial impact on water quality is the design of collection systems with respect to storm runoff and municipal waste. At present, most systems combine both storm and sanitation sewers, and serious pollution is caused by overloading of the system during heavy storm runoff. This pollution results from the diversion of untreated sewage along with storm waters into receiving watercourses.

TABLE 2 Alternatives for Reducing Water-Quality Deterioration

Goals	Approaches	Techniques
Increase collection efficiency	Centralize waste water operations	Extend sewerage facilities
	Prevent overburden from storm runoff	Separate storm and sanitation sewers
		Temporary diversion and storage
Minimize effect of disposal	Selective pollution	Assigned waste channels
	Utilize stream purification	Flow augmentation
		Temporary waste withholding
		Effluent dispersal by pipeline
	Utilize soil purification	Land disposal—spreading
	Withholding waste	Increased waste treatment

Alternative solutions would be either separate storm and sanitation sewers, or diversion and temporary storage of storm water.

Separate storm and sanitation sewers are quite expensive because of the construction and renewal costs involved. Present research indicates that dual sewer systems are practical in some circumstances, such as newly developing urban areas. The prospects for using storm runoff as an alternative source of water supply also should be considered. In areas already developed, *temporary storage of storm water* may be a more practical solution than dual sewer systems. Two schemes presently under study appear to be of practical value for particular situations. These are the use of deep caverns for storm waste storage at Chicago and the use of inflatable bags at Washington, D.C., Sandusky, Ohio, and Cambridge, Maryland.

Waste Disposal

Communities generally have used nearby watercourses as convenient means of waste disposal. The capability of flowing waters to assimilate low-volume waste loads probably reinforced the perceived practicality of this choice. Where flows are less adequate, wastes generally are disposed of on land, utilizing the capability of soils to purify percolating waters. However, water and soil purification capabilities are limited, and communities have supplemented these with treatment systems based on similar principles. In most of these schemes, man adjusts the variables of flow and waste discharge in an attempt to optimize purification capabilities. Alternatives are (1) diversion to assigned waste channels, (2) stream flow augmentation, (3) temporary withholding of wastes, (4) dispersal of effluent by pipeline, (5) land disposal, and (6) increased waste treatment.

One approach to the problem would be to *designate particular channels for waste transport* and allow deterioration therein. Two factors support such a system. First, it may not be in the interest of economic efficiency to attempt to bring all watercourses up to habitable quality, especially those which are well entrenched in industry. It may be that the cost of waste treatment would be far greater than the benefits of water-quality improvement. In addition, such a channel may provide for regional waste disposal and may be economically practical on these additional grounds. However, it is worth noting that the inequitable distribution of benefits and costs to uses along the channel such as recreation may render such an alternative politically infeasible.

The conventional regional approach to reduction of water-quality deterioration has been *flow augmentation* of the stream. Flow augmentation distributes the flow of the watercourse evenly through a series of catchment dams, thereby maintaining levels suitable for maximum dilution of wastes throughout the year. This is generally practical where seasonal irregularities in low flow can be adjusted, but it should not be considered as a solution independent of other schemes. For instance, [R. K.] Davis has demonstrated that flow augmentation as a singular means of pollution abatement is much more costly than a combined approach with increased waste treatment.

The *temporary withholding of wastes* during periods of low stream flow also is geared to the variable assimilation capacity of the watercourse. This is generally practical where critical low flow is of short duration, but it would not be economically practical over longer periods.

Still another means toward optimizing the assimilation process is the *dispersion of effluent* by pipeline along a watercourse. One study found this to be a practical alternative to other forms of water-quality management. In each instance, however, the use of the watercourse as a cleansing agent passes the cost of purification on to other users. These costs are most evident in the reduction of recreational and aesthetic pleasures derived from the watercourse.

The *disposal of treated sewage effluent on land* is a relatively common practice in arid environments such as the Southwest that do not afford sufficient volumes of water flow for assimilation. Although this may remove the direct threat to intermittent flowing streams, care must be exercised to insure against pollution of the groundwater resources. Increased urbanization and waste loading would necessitate either increased discharge acreage or increased pretreatment if the quality of groundwater resources is to be safeguarded.

The most effective long-range alternative for restoring water quality, and that which minimizes disbenefits to downstream users, appears to be *increased waste treatment.* This includes the primary stage of solids removal, the secondary stage of biological purification, and advanced chemical techniques where warranted. Increased treatment would free greater stretches of the watercourse for various types of recreation, fish and wildlife uses, and aesthetic pleasure than would other alternatives. On the other hand, the problem of ultimate waste disposal is yet unresolved, and a continuing effort must be made to determine the best disposal sites and mode of transport.

WASTEWATER RENOVATION

The optimal solution to the problems of municipal water demands and water-quality deterioration may rest with wastewater renovation. Sewage effluent would be purified through advanced waste treatment, and this high-quality water would be made available on-site for municipal use. The idea of reusing water is neither new nor unique; the seemingly radical element is the degree and proximity of reuse. It is estimated that over 40 percent of the U.S. population reuses water that has been used for some domestic or industrial purposes including power cooling, and 60 percent of the population reuses water that has been used upstream. In some instances where the water-supply intake of one city lies immediately downstream of the sewage outfall of another, or where tidal influence returns the flow of a city's effluent to its water supply, water systems currently do use waste water.

As waste-treatment requirements increase in order to stem the growing deterioration of our waters, the quality of treated effluent will increase accordingly. On the basis of standards currently being used, as we noted earlier, municipalities discharging into streams will be required to provide a minimum of secondary treatment, and in some cases tertiary treatment. Also, there is growing awareness on the part of state governments of the need to provide for more stringent regulation of intrastate streams. As a result, treated effluent in many cities will be suitable for nonpotable municipal uses and with additional treatment would be suitable for the home.

Practicality of Use

The practicality of using renovated wastewater for municipal water supply varies with environmental conditions. In particular, it is tied closely to the quality of effluent discharged by the community and the availability of suitable alternative sources of supply.

Increasing waste-treatment requirements that limit the discharge of organic wastes and nutrients will result in the availability of a high-quality product effluent for many communities throughout the United States. In many instances, both in humid and arid environments, this effluent may be less expensive for satisfying particular urban demands than alternative sources of supply. This should become more obvious in the near future in view of the growing scarcity of good reservoir sites, the increasing costs of construction-oriented alternatives, and the growing competition for state and federal funds necessary for the construction of many of the larger projects.

The use of renovated wastewater, on the other hand, should become relatively less expensive in time, owing to the refinement in purification technology and the increasing sewage-treatment requirements. The nature of this use could vary considerably, depending upon the different water-supply conditions throughout the United States. In water-scarce areas, such as the Southwest and the Great Plains, it may be more practical for communities to consider direct aquifer recharge with renovated wastewater for municipal supply. On the other hand, advanced waste-treatment requirements in the Midwest and Northeast may make it more practical for many communities in these regions to consider at least directed piping of renovated wastewater to satisfy concentrated high-volume demands, such as for industrial usage.

Greater emphasis is needed at the national level to assure a coordinated management of water-quality control and water supply. At present, various agencies are charged with specific tasks within each of these two problem areas. In particular, more effort is needed to classify, describe, and analyze the resource situations most amenable to advanced waste treatment. Present efforts are piecemeal, apparently being limited to the funding of separate operations in particular communities, apart from any ordering by regions or conditions of environmental stress. The water-resource agencies concerned with this problem need first to improve the methods of classifying environmental situations in the United States according to the nature of resource deterioration, the alternatives available to improve the quality of these resources, and the immediacy with which these programs should be put into action. From this, it would be possible to describe more accurately the regions where high-quality effluent may be available for meeting future municipal and other water demands.

Technical and Institutional Factors Affecting Reuse

The use of renovated wastewater appears to be considered by many water managers as a desperation alternative, one more appropriate for consideration in arid environments. A reversal of thinking is required if renovated wastewater is to be considered when it is the most economical alternative rather than when it is the "only" economical alternative. Planners and managers should recognize that several alternative methods are available by which to use renovated waste water—namely: direct reuse; aquifer recharge; directed piping to high-volume users such as industry; and, possibly, systems in which bottled water is distributed for potable usage. Study has indicated that while the use of renovated wastewater at Tucson may be of more apparent practicality, it also is likely to be of practical value to communities in more humid regions of the country, such as Indianapolis and Philadelphia.

Consideration of renovated wastewater as a practical alternative may be constrained by the organization of water agencies in a community or region. In order to incorporate the use of renovated wastewater into municipal water planning in an efficient manner, administration of supply and disposal should be effectively coordinated. In communities where separate agencies are responsible for water supply and waste disposal, an effort should be made to establish liaison between them in order to make efficient use of renovated wastewater. The situation is most critical where agencies are wholly segregated—for example, where a community has a private water utility and a public sewage-disposal agency.

This may be asking too much of most communities. Nevertheless, renovated wastewater is going to be an integral part of municipal water management in the relatively near future, and we should be concerned that communities use this source wisely at the most opportune time. Because of the constraints created by the lack of administrative linkages and inadequate information flows, water-management officials may not consider the use of renovated wastewater in spite of its possible value. Federal agencies involved, therefore, should consider creation of information services which could take an active role in both disseminating information and providing technical expertise.

Consumer Attitudes Toward Renovated Wastewater

The issues of whether or not the municipal use of renovated waste water is technically feasible or economically practical lose relevance if officials responsible for water management preclude the consideration of such alternatives. Both water analysts and community water-management officials have expressed concern that consumers would not accept the use of renovated wastewater because of certain aesthetic and hygienic constraints. In fact, however, consumer attitudes are found to vary considerably according to differential perceptions of their resource situations, and certain personal factors. Perhaps the most significant finding is that some of the factors which may affect the economic practicality of using renovated wastewater, namely, the adequacy and quality of water-supply sources, also are associated with individual attitudes toward renovated wastewater.

The perceived adequacy of water-supply sources to meet anticipated future demands showed a significant association with consumer acceptance of possible community consideration of renovated wastewater. Because the scarcity of alternative sources, or the cost of developing them, may signal the need for communities to consider renovated wastewater, it is important for managers to be aware that the perceptions of these conditions also may be reflected in more favorable public support. There also is a significant association between consumer perception of the quality of the present water-supply source and attitutde toward use of renovated wastewater as reflected in willingness to pay. Where communities consider it economically practical to supplement a source of low organic quality with renovated wastewater, it is important again for managers to be aware that perception of these conditions by the public may be reflected in more favorable support.

Certain personal factors also show significant associations with attitudes toward renovated wastewater. In particular, the associations of education and knowledge of renovated wastewater with consumer attitudes may signal the possible importance of both general education and specific information programs in the prospective adoption of such innovations. Educational level shows a rather strong association with both acceptance of community consideration of renovated wastewater and the willingness to drink the product. As educational levels increase in the future, consumer attitudes may be even more favorable toward renovated wastewater, especially in view of the continually increasing public familiarity with technological achievements. There also is a significant association between knowledge of renovated wastewater and willingness to drink the product. In view of the apparent importance of both education and knowledge of the product, consideration should be given to the possible value of information programs as social guides concerning the acceptance of renovated wastewater.

Future Directions for Research

It seems clear that officials responsible for the management of municipal water supply should give greater attention to understanding consumer attitudes relevant to these and other water decisions. In fact, a greater understanding is needed of both consumer and manager attitudes, especially as they relate to one another. In such work, it may be profitable to proceed to obtain a better understanding of community acceptance, rather than that of consumers alone. This would provide officials with an appraisal of the validity of their perceptions concerning consumer attitudes and goals relevant to both the specific issue of renovation and the broader area of water management. Presumably such in-depth analysis could be extended to cover a cross section of environmental conditions in order to observe whether public-official relationships would vary with these conditions.

Community acceptance, however, falls short of community adoption. The controversy over fluoridation has left its mark in cautioning against the assumption that the one assures the other. In spite of generally favorable reactions accorded to fluoridation, it met rather resounding defeats when put to public referendums. A range of factors appeared to contribute to the defeat of fluoridation referendums. Research on issues like fluoridation may provide the basis for comparison of an innovation which, as yet, is relatively unpublicized. Much needs to be done toward evaluating the weight of factors in the fluoridation issue as they relate to the prospective adoption of renovated wastewater for municipal water supply.

Among the most significant points in favor of subsequent research on the renovation issue is the opportunity it provides for the meshing of disciplines. Technically, it serves to combine the often separate subsystems of water supply and water-quality control. To the social and behavioral sciences it offers the opportunity to observe the range of psychological, social, economic, and political impacts associated with the radical concept of ingestion of a product of human waste. Hopefully, subsequent research will lead not only to a better understanding of factors surrounding the prospective community acceptance and adoption of using this valuable resource, but also to a refinement in the techniques of water-resource management.

42

United Nations Conference on Desertification: Round-up of the Conference

United Nations

The winter rains had not ended in Kenya by the end of August when the United Nations Conference on Desertification met in Nairobi. Over the high tower of the Kenyatta Conference Centre the skies were grey and occasional showers sent people scurrying for cover along the puddled streets. Uhuru Park glistened in the rain and the jacaranda trees dripped in the gentle sun afterwards. Altogether, Nairobi seemed far removed from the problems before the desertification conference.

In fact the world as a whole seemed rather removed from the mood and dangers of the early 1970s. In 1973 the Sahelian region of Africa, the southern margin of the Sahara, had seen five years of uninterrupted drought. Lake Chad had shrunk to a third of its normal size, the Niger and Senegal rivers had not flooded, leaving barren much of the best agricultural land of the area. Shallow and seasonal wells dried up. Vegetation disappeared as hungry animals stripped the land. Patches of newly created desert seemed to grow and link with the great desert to the north. As people fled the stricken area in large numbers the world was faced with a series of unanswered questions.

Was the Sahelian drought evidence of larger changes in the global climate? Was the Sahara expanding south? What implications did this have for the countries directly involved? For their neighbors? For the international community? Most important, what could be done to cushion the impact of, or prevent, disastrous changes? It was in the absence of answers to such questions that the UN General Assembly called for a world conference on desertification. But in the year the assembly acted, the rains returned to the Sahel. The years since then have seen the slow

Reprint of "Round-up of the Conference," United Nations Conference on Desertification, 29 August–9 September 1977 (United Nations, 1978). Pp. 1–5.

but steady regeneration of the area, and no disasters of similar magnitude have occurred elsewhere.

However, even without the spur of present disaster, some 500 delegates from 94 countries gathered in Nairobi from 29 August to 9 September to discuss the problems of desertification. The reasons are evident in the documents prepared for the conference, for they show that the problems of desertification are larger, more widely shared, and require greater and longer term action than expected. The simplistic fears of a few years ago are now replaced by a well-founded sense of danger. And it is amply clear that preventing the degradation of land and reclaiming desertified land are not only highly profitable propositions, but essential for economic and social developments as well.

Before looking at some of the findings in the conference documentation, however, it would be useful to consider briefly the process by which the documents were prepared. The General Assembly resolution that called for the conference [Res. 3337 (XXIX)] delegated the responsibility of preparing for the meeting to the executive director of the United Nations Environment Program, with UNEP's 58-member Governing Council serving as the intergovernmental authority in charge. To ensure, as the assembly resolution directed, that "all available knowledge in this area is fully utilized," UNEP executive director, Mostafa Kamal Tolba, drew extensively on the resources of the world scientific community. Four scholarly reviews were commissioned that looked at the relationship of desertification to climate, ecological change, technology, and society. Underpinning these reviews were a further set of studies, funded by the UN Development Program, that looked not at the global scene but at the actual processes of desertification in a number of countries. They analyzed the processes in different ecological and socioeconomic circumstances, and looked at the efficacy of remedial action. Yet another group of scientists looked at the feasibility of transnational attempts to fight desertification. Other scientists within and outside the UN system prepared world and regional desertification maps. Based on all this an overview was prepared, which served as the main document for conference delegates.

What has emerged from all this expert work is a fascinating picture of the fluid relationships that exist between humanity and the biosphere. What has also become clear is that desertification is not a problem that concerns just a few countries. Based on climatic data, more than a third of the earth's surface is desert or semidesert and more than 15 percent of the world's population live in these areas. If we go by data on the nature of soil and vegetation, the total area is some 43 percent of the earth's land surface. The difference is accounted for by the estimated extent of man-made deserts (9,115,000 square kilometers), an area larger than Brazil. Further, some 30 million square kilometers (19 percent of the earth's land surface) are threatened with desertification, and this threatened area is distributed among more than two-thirds of the world's 150 countries.

TABLE 1 Estimates of Populations—According to Livelihood—In Areas Recently Undergoing Severe Desertification (in thousands)

Region	Total Population	Urban Based	Cropping Based	Animal Based	Area (km^2)
Mediterranean Basin	9,820	2,995 31%	5,900 60%	925 9%	1,320,000
Sub-Saharan Africa	16,165	3,072 19%	6,014 37%	7,079 44%	6,850,000
Asia and the Pacific	28,482	7,740 27%	14,311 54%	6,431 19%	4,361,000
Americas	24,079	7,683 32%	13,417 56%	2,979 12%	17,545,000
Total	78,546	21,490 27%	39,642 51%	17,414 22%	30,076,000

Of the 78 million people threatened, about a third may be in a position, because of high income or other advantages, to avoid the worst consequences of desertification. This still leaves about 50 million people who are immediately menaced through the destruction of their livelihoods and who are faced by the grim prospect of uprooting themselves from everything familiar and of migrating to other areas frequently ill-equipped to receive them.

Estimates of present losses of productive land suggest that the world will lose close to one-third of its arable land by the end of the century. Such a loss during a period of unprecedented population growth and increased demands for food could be disastrous. To assess the cost of preventing this degradation of land a group of experts were convened by the conference secretariat. They estimated that the costs of corrective measures would be far outweighed by the benefit in strictly financial terms. The many social benefits that would result from a program to save and reclaim land cannot, of course, be assessed in terms of money.

THE PROCESS OF DESERTIFICATION

To see precisely what happens when desertification occurs, attention should be focused on that shallow meeting place between soil and atmosphere, where plants thrive and where a balance is maintained between incoming and outgoing energy and between water received and lost.

When rain falls, some of the water is taken up directly by plants, some filters into the soil, where it may remain in storage, and the rest evaporates or runs off. Some soil moisture, that intercepted by plants, is put back into the atmosphere by the plants in transpiration. Some of the moisture may seep into deeper layers to collect in underground reservoirs or aquifers, where it may remain for thousands of years, or may migrate slowly from plateau to depression or back to the ocean itself.

Where Soil and Air Meet

Each region has its climate, an element in the global pattern of atmospheric circulation. There is also another climate, partly determined by the first, at the shallow meeting place of earth and air. Like the larger climate, this smaller one is ever changing, always balancing its water and energy budgets. Reaching the soil as rain or dew, water evaporates, runs off, or sinks in to be stored, with some released by plants and animals in respiration and transpiration. Energy comes from the sun. Some is reflected back into the air; some warms the soil as stored heat. Some is taken up by plants and used in the process of photosynthesis. Herbivores eat

TABLE 2 Revision of Table Prepared for the Conference, Basing Land Values on Capitalized Values and Adjusting Unit Salvage Costs to More Realistic Levels

	Initial Estimates of Orders of Magnitude of Costs and Benefits of Corrective Measures								
(1)	(2)	(3)	(4)	(5)	(6)	(7)	(8)	(9)	(10)
Type of Land[1]	Annual Rate of Land Degradation (000 hectares)[2]	Estimated Value ($ per hectare)[3]		Gain		Estimated Cost of Salvage[4] per Hectare $	Total (2 × 7) Million $	Net Gain per Hectare (5) − (7) $	Total Net Benefits (2) × (9) Million $
		If Not Salvaged	If Salvaged	(4) − (3) per Hectare $	(2) × (5) Total Million $				
Irrigated	125[5]	200	2,000	1,800	225	850 (250–2,000)	106	950	119
Range	3,200	2	20	18	58	10 (1–50)	32	8	26
Rain-fed crop	2,500	50	450	400	1,000	100 (50–150)	250	300	750
Total	5,825				1,283		388		895

[1] Arid and semiarid lands only.

[2] Annual rate of land degradation is based on annual rate of change of classes of land to more degraded conditions. The degree of degradation from higher to lower classes of land has been converted to more limited areas assumed to be deteriorating from land yielding highest net return (if salvaged) to land at the point of going out of production (if not salvaged).

[3] In view of difficulties in quantifying social values, these estimates are rough conservative approximations of orders of magnitude of capitalized values. Values are calculated using an assumed net income at half of gross income divided by an assumed opportunity cost of 10 percent, with a slight adjustment for rangelands to reflect lower opportunity costs. If social factors are included the values would be substantially higher.

[4] Figures within parentheses give ranges of salvage costs. It follows from footnote 2 that cost of salvage is the maximum, equivalent to the cost of reclamation or restoration of practically completely desertified land. Because desertification is a continuous process, the more prudent course of action would be to begin corrective investment as soon as practicable and initially to lands which offer the highest returns to ensure continued maximum production.

[5] Due to waterlogging, salinization, and, to a lesser extent, alkalinization.

the plants, and carnivores eat herbivores. Plants hold the soil in place. Their waste products, as those of animals, supply the soil with nutrients, richest in the topmost layers. There is some question as to how much the activities of man affect the large climate which determines the weather. There is no question that man has a profound impact on the small climate at the soil's surface whenever he makes use of the land.

The soil-air meeting place participates in an energy balance activated by the rays of the sun or through atmospheric heating. Some energy is reflected by the surface layer back into the atmosphere and into space. Some is held by the soil in storage, thereby warming the earth, and it is this energy and that from the sun directly that is used by plants to carry out the processes of photosynthesis and growth. Some of the plants are eaten by grazers or browsers, and these animals in turn may be eaten by carnivores, with all animals returning energy and moisture to the atmosphere in respiration and to the soil in the form of humus. The excreta of animals, their decomposing carcasses, and the decomposition of plants supply the soil with nutrients, most densely in the topmost layers and thinning out below.

In arid situations the cycling of water and energy takes on special characteristics because of deficient and variable rainfall and abundant solar energy from cloudless skies. Vegetation is generally sparser than in humid areas, provides less cover to the ground surface, and returns less organic matter to the topsoil. During occasional intense rainfall, runoff may occur in spate, but water at the surface tends rapidly to be lost through evaporation, and in the long intervening dry spells the soil is parched and heated by the powerful sun.

However scanty it may be, the dryland vegetation constitutes a fundamental resource which transforms solar energy into food and which protects and stabilizes the surface of the ground. This vegetation survives by adapting to water deficit in ways which are important because they determine seasonal differences in the usefulness of dryland pastures.

MAN UPSETS THE NATURAL BALANCE

Under natural conditions and through appropriate strategies, the dryland ecosystems maintain a balanced exchange of water and energy, but a favorable equilibrium is readily disturbed when man makes use of the land. For example, where meager vegetation is further reduced to expose the ground surface, humus will be mineralized and soil structure lost. Rain will fall directly on the soil, and break it down, and the sun will bake a thin crust which prevents additional water from sinking in. As the water budget deteriorates in the soil beneath, the level of groundwater in nearby wells may fall. The water lost to the soil store now contributes to overrapid runoff. Where the surface has been loosened or disturbed as by the trampling of animals, the topmost soil layer, that with the best structure and containing the bulk of plant food, may be washed away or blown away in dust storms. The denuded soil is essentially infertile, with poor structure and water relations. All these changes constitute a shift towards a more hostile environment for plants, with the result that the vegetation responds less well to rain and produces less biomass, and many plants tend to die off at an increasingly early stage of drought. Such changes are typical of desertification.

RAIN-FED FARMING

In areas of rain-fed farming, desertification often originates on land cleared for cultivation or left fallow. Removal of the original vegetative cover exposes the soil to accelerated wind and water erosion. The beating action of rain on naked soil puddles the surface which crusts when the sun comes out, reducing infiltration and further increasing runoff. This, in turn, leads to increased soil erosion which ultimately, unless halted by protective measures, strips away the fertile surface soil and exposes infertile subsoils. Gullies may form on the lower parts of slopes and impeded farming operations, or prevent them entirely. Sediment deposited at the foot of slopes covers plains, fills waterways, and aggravates flooding in low-lying areas which follows increased runoff from the slopes above.

WATER AND WIND EROSION

Water and wind erosion work together, as redeposited silts from surfaces stripped by water erosion are particularly vulnerable to wind transport. Wind erosion starts with the movement of coarse soil particles in one part of a field, then progresses downwind with increasing severity as bouncing soil particles knock other particles into the air in a kind of snowballing effect. Finer materials are lifted into the air and carried away over long distances as dust; coarser sandy materials drift over the surface until they are trapped by plants in accumulations as hummocks and small dunes. Removal of fine topsoil materials means the loss of the most productive and nutritious portions of the soil complex, while sterile sand accumulations cover plants and good soil. A further harmful effect of high-velocity sand drift is the destruction of young crops by the blasting impact of moving sand. Fine airborne particles may carry soil-borne diseases, irritate respiratory tracts of humans and animals, cause wear on machinery parts, and reduce visibility.

IRRIGATED LAND

The principal manifestations of desertification on irrigated lands are the salinization and alkalinization of soils, due to inadequate leaching of salts contained in the soil or added in irrigation water. Salinization and waterlogging commonly occur together. Where the soil is waterlogged, the upward movement of saline groundwater leaves salts on the surface where water evaporates. On soils that are not waterlogged, salinization can still occur when water containing soluble salts moves from irrigation furrows into the ridges where crops are planted or to high spots in poorly levelled land. Underirrigation of weakly permeable soils can also lead to salinization if the irrigation water is salty.

When left alone, dryland ecosystems disturbed by land uses or stressed by drought, will usually return to what they were. Recovery tends to advance at a slow pace because of the low productivity of drylands and is usually episodic, with more rapid recovery in years of above-average rainfall. Eventually, former water and energy balances will be restored, with the recovery of the original vegetation. This is a measure of the natural resilience of the drylands.

FACTORS INITIATING DESERTIFICATION

Where pressure of land use persists through drought, these same ecosystems are shown to be fragile, and processes can be set in motion whereby desertification becomes self-accelerating. This can occur where sand dunes are stripped of vegetation, as near watering points or other places where stock tend to congregate, and drifitng sand destroys more vegetation and mobilizes extending surfaces, and dunes slowly advance and engulf less damaged sites. It can occur where destruction of vegetation initiates accelerating erosion, removing sediment which, in turn, buries fields or pastures downstream, or in denuded areas, where hot, drying winds become increasingly prevalent. In irrigated systems, lack of drainage allows water tables to rise and waterlog and salinize fields to the point where they must be abandoned. Because self-acceleration can occur through a variety of circumstances, desertification will often advance inexorably unless preventive measures are undertaken. As it advances, it becomes ever more difficult and more expensive to treat, with the costs of reclamation continually rising until the stark equilibrium of extreme desert is reached and the land has for all practical purposes passed beyond hope of rehabilitation.

Deserts themselves are not the sources from which desertification springs. Except for hot winds, the deserts themselves supply none of the essential impetus for the processes described. Desertification breaks out, usually at times of drought stress, in areas of naturally vulnerable land subject to pressures of land use. These degraded patches, like a skin disease, link up to carry the process over extended areas. It is generally incorrect to envision the process as an advance of the desert frontier engulfing usable land on its perimeter: the advancing sand dune is in fact a very special and localized case. Desertification, as a patchy destruction that may be far removed from any nebulous front line, is a more subtle and insidious process.

MEASURES TO COMBAT DESERTIFICATION

During its two week session the Desertification Conference spent most of its time considering a plan of action. A draft plan had been prepared by the secretariat, in consultation with an international group of experts and with the help of governments at four regional meetings as well as at meetings of the UNEP Governing Council. The conference considered the draft paragraph by paragraph, strengthening, reshaping, and molding it according to the needs of governments. What resulted is a document of 104 paragraphs, containing 28 recommendations for action.

If there is one central theme to the plan, it is that action must not await complete knowledge about complex situations. The need is recognized for immediate action in applying existing knowledge, not only to stop the physical processes of desertification, but to educate people in minimizing the harm done to the fragile ecosystems of drylands by existing economic and social activities. The plan acknowledges the need to base improved systems of land use on the inevitability of periodic drought. And it acknowledges also that drylands have a low level of natural biological productivity.

Another central theme of the plan is that all measures are to be directed primarily toward the well-being and development of the peoples affected by or vulnerable to desertification. Efforts to fight desertification must thus be consistent with and part of wider development programs. In implementing programs the plan stresses the cultural and ecological variety in vulnerable areas and the overriding need for an approach that is both sensitive and flexible.

While underlining the need for urgent short-term relief measures, the plan recognizes that long-term programs to prevent desertification should not be delayed because the cost of prevention is far less than that of the cure.

V
Marine Resources

Many people around the world who have thought and written about population-resources-environment relationships during the past generation have looked to the sea as a possible solution to all of our problems. This trend is likely to continue. Indeed, in the twenty-first century we are likely to be more sea-minded than land- or space-minded. The sea certainly has great potential for more intensive human use, and we may well, as a species, begin a gradual return to the sea whence we came (as other mammals have already done). But the sea will not solve all of our problems—or even significantly mitigate them—as some of the following readings point out.

In the first article, which appeared in a journal published by the Royal Swedish Academy of Sciences, Hans A. Ackefors elaborates the common opinion that the sea can produce several times its present yield of food for human consumption—if all goes well. C. P. Idyll, who is with the National Oceanic and Atmospheric Administration in Washington, D.C., however, considering the same facts, arrives at a much less sanguine conclusion about the sea's potential food yield. The American Petroleum Institute, in an article prepared for this book, lays out the industry case for exploitation of petroleum and natural gas in the outer continental shelf of the United States. Fillmore C. F. Earney, a geographer unaffiliated with the oil industry, however, details the hazards of offshore hydrocarbon production while not denying its importance. Production of certain minerals from land mines may in the future be supplemented by production from the seabed—or it may not. John L. Mero, the American geologist who first called attention to the potentials of polymetallic (or manganese) nodules in the mid-1960s, is still upbeat about them, but the UN Secretariat is far more reserved about the future of seabed mining in view of technological and economic problems—which it presents most diplomatically.

M.C.W. Pinto, Sri Lanka's special representative to and a prominent participant in the Third UN Conference on the Law of the Sea, which ended with the adoption of the UN Convention on the Law of the Sea in 1982, puts the whole question of seabed minerals into the context of the drive of the Group of 77 for a New International Economic Order. This point was made by Tanzanian President Julius Nyerere in Section 3 of this book. Finally, we offer a warning from the Soviet Union (which has only recently joined the ranks of those concerned about environmental problems) that we should not destroy the marine environment as we seem to be destroying the terrestrial environment. If the future of Homo sapiens *really does depend on the sea, we may conclude, then it behooves us to assure that marine resources of all kinds are utilized efficiently, with the benefits distributed equitably among all the peoples of the earth and without damaging the marine environment. Otherwise, we should simply leave them alone.*

43

Production of Fish and Other Animals in the Sea

Hans Ackefors

Catches from oceans and lakes have increased greatly since the 1940s. During the 1950s and 1960s the increase was, on an average, 4.5–7.1 percent a year based on the means of five years. After 1968 the trend was interrupted, and the increase during the last period was only 1.6 percent. If we view development historically, we find that catches doubled from about 2 million tons in 1850 to about 4 million tons at the end of the century. Between 1900 and 1962 the catches increased eight-fold to about 40 million tons. During the peak years of 1970–71, the total annual catch was approximately 70 million tons, almost 18 times as great as at the turn of the century. After a decrease in the 1972–73 catches, the preliminary figures for 1976 indicate that the catch has exceeded the 1970–71 peak and amounts to 72 million tons.

The population of the world has increased at an accelerating rate. In 1650 there were 500 million people in the world, in 1830 one thousand million, in 1930 two thousand million, in 1960 three thousand million and in 1974 four thousand million. This implies that, just now, the population growth is 2.1 percent per year, i.e., there are 60 million more mouths to feed every year. During the 1960s, when fishing expanded 6–7 percent a year, the increased flow of food from the sea to a hungry world was viewed with optimism. The contribution of fishing to the economy of the world increased much more than that of agriculture. The total global increase in food was only 0.5 percent. Is the sea the source of nourishment that is to save the world?

Reprint of "Production of Fish and Other Animals in the Sea," by Hans Ackefors in *AMBIO* (Vol. 6, No. 4, 1977). Reprinted with the kind permission of *AMBIO*, the international journal of the human environment (published in Stockholm, Sweden). Pp. 192–99.

It is sometimes stated that the sea gives only 1 to 2 percent of the calories mankind consumes. This is correct, but it is wrong to discuss only calories, when it is lack of protein that mankind is suffering most. In 1960 3.2 million tons of protein were taken from the sea, 13.1 percent of all the animal protein consumed in the world.

In 1964–66, the total supply of protein was about 100 million tons, or 66 grams per day per capita, of which 21 grams was animal protein. Cereals contributed most to the total protein supply, with 48 percent. Fish accounted for about 5 percent of the total protein supply. Animal protein came mainly from meat (44 percent), milk (32 percent), and fish (14 percent). Unfortunately the whole amount of fish protein is not used directly by man. According to Food and Agriculture Organization (FAO) statistics, 67 percent, or 38 million tons, of marine catches were directly used as food for man in 1973. This corresponds to at least 4 million tons of protein after cleaning operations. The rest, 19 million tons, or 33 percent of the catch, were used for feeding such animals as broilers, pigs, etc., either directly or as fish meal. A conservative estimate indicates, that in spite of this roundabout in the food chain, man got about 5 million tons of protein from the sea. This means that 4–5 percent of the total protein resources came from the sea during that period.

Protein consists of about 20 amino acids, and some of them, the so-called essential amino acids, cannot be synthesized by the human body. Vegetable albumin (wheat, rice, etc.) lacks sufficient lysine, methionin, and tryptophane to be nutritionally satisfactory according to the FAO standard for human food. Fish, on the other hand, has a good combination of essential amino acids. No animal protein has such a high concentration of lysine as fish. The amount of lysine per 100 g fish meat is 10.6 g and the corresponding values for milk, meat, and eggs are 7.5, 8.5, and 7.2 g. Both wheat and rice have just a little more than 2 g lysine per 100 g protein, which is about half of the FAO recommended standard value for lysine in human food. The relatively small quantity of high quality fish protein consumed by the world population is therefore of utmost importance.

The aim of this paper is to describe the present catch from marine and freshwater areas in relation to the potential resources (including cultivation). The intention is also to describe in a simple way the energy flow in the marine ecosystems from solar energy to the resources available for man.

SOLAR ENERGY AND PRODUCTION IN THE SEA

Solar energy is of fundamental importance for life on earth. Radiation from the sun to the earth amounts to thousands of kilogram calories per square meter per day. On an average, the flow of energy to the earth is 5,110 kcal per square meter per day and of this, 3,400 kcal, or more than two-thirds, is retained by the surface of the earth. Half of this is visible light, which is utilized for photosynthesis in green plants on land. In the sea, on the other hand, a very small proportion of this, or only about 6 kcal m^2, is used by marine algae. Most of the energy is converted into thermal energy. Such energy steers the system of winds on earth and drives the ocean currents. Knowledge of the biological effects of these ocean currents is of fundamental importance to an understanding of production. The upwelling phenomena in the oceans are caused by a combination of the wind and current systems and the rotation of the earth. The great upwelling regions off the west coasts of South America and Africa are well known. The currents transport great amounts of nutritive salts from the deeper parts of the oceans, which give rise to a great production of plankton. The phytoplankton algae in their turn serve as food for large stocks of pelagic, or open-sea fishes. The transport of nutritive salts also occurs in regions where warm and cold currents meet. There is one such highly productive region in the North Atlantic between Iceland, Norway, and Spitsbergen.

The *FAO Atlas of the Living Resources of the Seas* shows clearly the uneven distribution of phytoplankton in the oceans. The production is often measured in milligrams of carbon (mg C), which is the main constituent of tissue in all living organisms. In the literature, references to the "barren areas of the oceans" are common—and far from false. In large parts of the Pacific Ocean, for example, the production is less than 100 mg C per square meter per day, while production in upwelling areas exceeds 500 mg C, and in most productive regions the corresponding value is 2,000 mg C. Zooplankton, which live on phytoplankton, are therefore also unevenly distributed, as well as benthos (evertebrates at the bottom), which, of course determines the production of fish, as will be discussed later.

FOOD CHAINS-FOOD WEBS

Food chains and food webs are usually depicted popularly as a pyramid with phytoplankton as the base and man as the apex. Only a very small proportion of the phytoplankton biomass remains in the catch taken by human beings, owing to the so-called "loss of energy" in each link of the food chain.

It is usual, in a food chain, to distinguish between *producers* and *consumers.* Consumers in their turn are divided into *herbivores, omnivores,* and *carnivores.* One also speaks of consumers of the *first, second, third,* and so on, *order,* to describe their place in the food chain. The term *trophic level* is used to define the distance of a consumer from the primary nourishment. The following schematic table may be used to illustrate a food chain for open water:

Producers
Trophic level No. 0. Phytoplankton

Consumers

Trophic level No. 1.	Herbivores→zooplankton, fishes Omnivores→zooplankton, fishes
Trophic level No. 2.	Carnivores→zooplankton, fishes, mammals
Trophic level No. 3.	Carnivores→fishes, mammals
Trophic level No. 4.	Carnivores→fishes, mammals

The process is far more complicated than the schematic diagram suggests. It would be more correct to use the term *food web,* which is very often used in the literature, and which indicates how complicated ecosystems are.

To describe the flow of energy from prey to predator, the term *efficiency* is used, together with several qualifying words which define different types of energy flow, *viz.: ecological efficiency, gross efficiency,* and *net efficiency.* By *ecological efficiency* is meant the flow of energy from one trophic level to another, where the energy is used for biological growth and where the time is long enough to include all developmental stages in the life cycle of both the prey and the predator. *Gross efficiency* refers to the relation of growth to food ingested, and *net efficiency* to growth in relation to food assimilated.

The degree of efficiency is very low in the link between solar energy and plant community: sugarcane cultivation 1.8 percent, tropical rainforest 3.5 percent, deserts 0.05 percent, algae cultures 3 percent, subtropical seas 0.09 percent, and so on. The corresponding value for phytoplankton in the southern Baltic proper is, on an average, 0.26 percent.

The ecological efficiency is much greater in the next link of the energy flow (plant community—herbivores). Earlier it was considered to be 10 percent. Recent studies indicate that the correct figures for terrestrial mammals are 2–5 percent, while marine organisms such as zooplankton are far more efficient and figures up to 20–25 percent are given.

In spite of the greater efficiency in water, food chains are usually longer in the sea than on cultivated land, and production on land is therefore greater. Borgström states that about six times as much vegetable albumin is involved in the marine production of food for human consumption as in the production of meat on land. The amount of protein in the form of plankton algae and macroalgae exploited in the whole annual catch of fish is equivalent to 40 world harvests of wheat or 75 world harvests of rice.

THE PRESENT CATCH FROM MARINE AND FRESH WATER

In 1975 the total catch amounted to 69.7 million tons excluding mammals, and preliminary figures for 1976 from FAO indicate a catch of 72 million tons. [The catches of mammals (whales and seals) are reported in numbers. A conservative weight estimate is 1–2 million tons.] The marine fish catches accounted for 72–78 percent, other marine catches for 12–16 percent and the freshwater catches for 11–14 percent. The proportion of evertebrates (shellfish and squids) has been 5–7 percent, salmon and related species 3–5 percent, crustaceans 3 percent, and marine algae 1.5 percent.

The main part of the marine catches has consisted of marine fish species which accounted for 49 million tons in 1975 of a total catch of 60 million tons in the sea. The clupeoids (herring, sardine, anchovy, etc.) and gadoids (cod, haddock, etc.) have dominated. Up to 1975 they accounted for 50 percent or more of the catches. The clupeoids contributed 25–39 percent and the gadoids 15–25 percent.

CATCH POTENTIALS IN THE OCEANS

Indirect Methods of Assessment

The primary production of phytoplankton algae and benthic macroalgae is of fundamental importance for the further production of zooplankton, bottom animals, fish, and so on. Quantitatively, phytoplankton are of greater importance than benthic macroalgae. Assessments of primary production have as a rule been made by the so-called ^{14}C technique. The ^{14}C method is used for measurement of primary production in aquatic ecosystems. The principle of the ^{14}C technique is: additions of $^{14}CO_2$ in the form of $NaH^{14}CO_3$ to the water sample, where during photosynthesis the algae incorporate the tracer into organic matter. After incubation, the water samples are filtered and the radioactivity of the algae is measured. If the total content of $^{12}CO_2$ in the experimental water is known, and if a known amount of $^{14}CO_2$ is added, the rate of primary production can be calculated. Since this method has been adversely criticized and is now being modified, reservations must be included in the discussion of published values of primary production.

Schaefer assessed the production of fish in the oceans on the basis of a total primary production of 1.9×10^{10} tons of carbon a year (Table 1).

TABLE 1 Production of Organic Substance Measured in Tons of Carbon at Different Trophic Levels in the Food Chain, if the Synthesized Amount of Phytoplankton is 1.9×10^{10} Tons of C Annually in the Oceans. The Calculations Were Made for Ecological Efficiencies of 10, 15, and 20 Percent.

	Tons of C Synthesized		
	10%	15%	20%
(0) Phytoplankton	1.9×10^{10}	1.9×10^{10}	1.9×10^{10}
(1) Herbivores	1.9×10^{9}	2.8×10^{9}	3.8×10^{9}
(2) 1st Carnivores	1.9×10^{8}	4.2×10^{8}	7.6×10^{8}
(3) 2nd Carnivores	1.9×10^{7}	6.4×10^{7}	15.2×10^{7}
(4) 3rd Carnivores	1.9×10^{6}	9.6×10^{6}	30.4×10^{6}

Such clupeoid species as anchovy, sardine, etc., live partly or to a great extent on phytoplankton. It is considered, therefore, that these species may be taken one and a half steps above the phytoplankton level. Of course, most of the catches are taken at higher trophic levels. If, on an average, the catch is taken at trophic level No. 3, the production potential is estimated at 190 million tons of fish at an efficiency of 10 percent and 640 million tons of fish at 15 percent efficiency [10 percent of the wet weight if fish are considered to consist of carbon molecules (C)]. Schaefer assumes that half of the potential is taken at trophic level No. 2 (first order carnivores) and half at trophic level No. 3, on an average. On the basis of efficiencies of 10 and 15 percent, the available potential should be 1,045 million tons and 2,420 million tons (wet weight) respectively. Schaefer stresses, however, several reasons why it is impossible to harvest these great volumes. It is uneconomical to fish where populations are sparse, and predators other than man take their share. He concludes that at least 200 million tons should be available for commercial fishing.

Ryther, using a somewhat different approach, reaches estimates (see Table 2) of 20×10^{9} for total production of fish in the seas, and a potential harvest of 120 million tons.

Much of the primary phytoplankton production is not utilized by the pelagic fishes. Living or dead phytoplankton (more or less decomposed detritus) fall down to the seabed and are food for bottom evertebrates (benthos). Moiseev estimated a world benthos production of $1\text{–}2 \times 10^{9}$ tons. Considering an annual consumption of 5×10^{8} tons of benthos by fish and crustacea and a conversion rate of 10 percent, the annual production of demersal, or bottom-dwelling, fish and crustacea may be estimated at 5×10^{7} tons. The present catch of these groups is about half that.

TABLE 2 Production in the Oceans According to Ryther.

Region	% of Ocean	Primary Production		P_{tot} 10^9 Tons C Year[1]†
		Area (km²)	P gC m^{-2} $year^{-1}$*	
Open ocean	90	326×10^6	50	16.3
Coastal zones	9.9	36×10^6	100	3.6
Upwelling areas	0.1	3.6×10^6	300	0.1

Total 740,000 million tons of plankton algae a year = 20.0×10^9 tons C $year^{-1}$.

*Production in grams of carbon per m² and year.

†Total annual production in tons of carbon per year.

Region	Primary Production, Tons C $Year^{-1}$	Trophic Levels	Ecological Efficiency	Fish Production, Tons Wet Weight
	Primary Production—Fish Production			
Oceans	16.3×10^9	5	10	16×10^5
Coastal zones	3.6×10^9	3	15	12×10^7
Upwelling areas	0.1×10^9	1½	20	12×10^7
			Total	24×10^7

Total: 240 million tons of fish a year.

Direct Methods of Assessment

There are several direct ways to assess fish stocks. Saetersdal gives a survey of these methods. Egg and larval surveys provide important information about spawning and distribution. The number of spawning fish may be estimated by this method. Late larval surveys, or 0-group surveys (fish younger than 12 months), are used for assessing the strength of the new year-class as well as 1-group surveys (12–24-month-old fish). Acoustic surveys (echosounder and sonar) have been used over the last 20 years for assessment of pelagic fish stocks. Visual observations of such surface-schooling fish as tunas and bonitos are also routine. Under certain circumstances aerial surveys may be used in combination with other surveys. Remote sensing by satellites may also be a tool for surveys in the future.

It seems probable that the catch potential can be assessed most reliably by exploratory fishing surveys, where each population of fish, crustaceans, mollusks, and mammals, is studied. The growth curve can be plotted and mean recruitment, natural mortality, etc., determined.

Table 3 shows in detail the relation between the actual and the potential catch in each part of the three oceans. [. . .] The Pacific has the greatest catch potential of traditional species (47.2 million tons), the Atlantic a little less, of 43.8 million tons, and the Indian Ocean 14.9 million tons.

World Potential in the Oceans

Gulland gives a survey of what species other than the traditional ones may, in the future, be exploited (Table 4). Traditional species can yield a catch of about 100 million tons a year, and there are great unexploited reserves of other species. For comparison, it may be mentioned that in 1975 the seas gave about 60 million tons excluding mammals. If whales can be saved for posterity, they can give mankind an additional supply of at least 2.5 million tons a year.

TABLE 3 Actual and Potential Catches in the Oceans. Potential Catches after Gulland.

Region		Actual Catch 1975 (millions of tons)	Percent of Potential	Potential Catch (millions of tons)
Atlantic				
Northwest		3.8	55.9	6.8
Northeast		12.1	86.4	14.0
Western central		1.6	27.6	5.8
Eastern central		3.5	97.2	3.6
Southwest		0.9	11.7	7.7
Southeast		2.6	56.5	4.6
Mediterranean + Black Sea		1.3	100.0	1.3
Total		25.8	58.9	43.8
Indian Ocean				
West		2.0	21.5	9.3
East		1.1	19.6	5.6
Total		3.1	20.8	14.9
Pacific				
Northwest	17.0			
Northeast	2.2	24.2	89.2	27.1
Western central	5.0			
Eastern central		1.3	20.3	6.4
Southwest		0.3	50.0	0.6
Southeast		4.6	35.1	13.1
Total		30.4	64.4	47.2
Grand Total		59.3	56.0	105.9

TABLE 4 The Potential of the Oceans According to Gulland. Annual Yields in Millions of Tons.

1. Traditional marine species	100
2. Whales (Antarctic)	2.5
3. Squids	10–100
4. Euphausiids (Krill)	50–100*
5. Myctophids	> 100
Total	260–400

*FAO, COFI/77/7 (1977) states that the potential catch is 50–150 million tons.

The great reserves in the sea today probably consist of squid. There is information suggesting possible catches of up to 100 million tons a year. A very cautious assessment by Voss suggests that an annual catch of at least 7.5 million tons is by no means unrealistic.

Krill is the popular name of a large group of crustaceans (euphausiids) which are represented by at least 85 species in the marine plankton all over the world. Most species are 2–5 cm long, and are known for their light-producing organs. The best-known species is probably *Euphausia superba,* common in the Antarctic, where it is an important basic diet of whales. The catch potential has been estimated at 50–100 million tons a year. Catches of up to 12 tons per trawling hour have been reported by Russian and Japanese vessels.

To exploit the myctophids living in the deep sea will be difficult. The potential has been estimated to be more than 100 million tons, which is, of course, a very uncertain and rough figure. However, it is doubtful if such fishes can be effectively exploited, due to high energy costs. In such a fishery as well as in a traditional high-seas fishery the catch, calculated in energy units, ought to be related to the amount of energy required for the catching operation. With present deep-sea fishing techniques it is possible that such a comparison will show a negative energy balance.

The total potential in the oceans, therefore, amounts to 260–400 million tons. But it will be a long time, and many technical and economic obstacles will have to be overcome, before we can exploit this potential. Realistic quarry today are, in spite of everything, the traditional species, whales, and squids. If 75 percent of the potential calculated for these could be exploited, the annual catch would increase to 85–150 million tons, i.e., at best almost 150 percent of the 1975 catch.

Unexploited Populations of Fish

A survey of the situation of known populations in different marine areas, made by the fishery committee of FAO, gives information on, among other things, unexploited or little-exploited populations. For example, in the northeast Atlantic there are still reserves of blue whiting, *Micromesistius poutassou.* Norwegian studies show that at least a million tons a year could be caught to the north and west of the British Isles. In the western part of the North Atlantic are hitherto unexploited populations of capelin, *Mallotus villosus,* and sand eels, *Ammodytes* spp. The greatest hope for the future, however, is probably the fish population off the Argentine coast. It is remarkable that there is a practically untouched population of herring left in the world. There are also great stocks of blue whiting, anchovy, and demersal fishes off Argentina.

In the Pacific Ocean there are great reserves, mainly of pelagic fishes. There, too, capelin is an unexploited species. Our knowledge of the pelagic fishes in both the Pacific and the Atlantic, however, is incomplete. Off the coasts of Brazil alone there are estimated to be about 50 species of anchovy or sardine.

Great efforts are now being made to inventory the resources of the Indian Ocean. Increased knowledge will, in the long run, make it possible to exploit these resources better. Preliminary information suggests that only about 20 percent of the potential is now being utilized.

Large Reserves of Squids

Squids occur in all large seas, from arctic to tropical marine regions. They are found near coasts and in the central parts of the great oceans, from the surface down to at least 5,400 m deep. Three different groups of squids are represented by about 650 species in different parts of the world. There is a great variety of forms. Some species are only a centimeter or so long, others more than 20 meters. Most species are predators at the top of the food chain. Benthic squids live on shrimps, lobsters, crabs, and other shellfish. Other, more pelagic, squids live on both pelagic and benthic crustaceans, fishes, and other squids.

[Evidence suggests] great potential reserves of squids in the different parts of the oceans. The assessment is a very cautious one and, as mentioned, the total might well be ten times as great. Taking the catches in the various marine regions as percentages of the potential given by Voss, we find that only the resources in the northwestern Pacific, the Mediterranean, and those off the west coast of Africa are exploited to any appreciable extent. Traditionally, squids are eaten very little in other parts of the world. Marine regions bordering these areas are therefore great reserves of valuable protein which should be utilized.

CATCH FROM ONE POPULATION

A population of fish or other animals may be exploited to an extent determined by the natural recruitment, rate of growth in various age groups, and natural mortality. [. . .] The stock of mature and young fish is being altered continuously. These alterations may be expressed mathematically. [A fundamental book for mathematical-scientific treatment of fishery-biological data was published by Beverton & Holt in 1957.] Due to the new ideas introduced in this book, the population dynamic alterations and long-term predictions to steady state situations now became possible to calculate in a more proper way. The potential catch was likely to be no more than half of the total fish production. The problem of stock and recruitment relationship was introduced by Ricker. The stock is in a steady state with its annual increment of recruits equivalent to the annual loss by fishing mortality and natural mortality and it may be considered to replace itself at any stable level of population.

A necessary condition for such predictions is the ability to mathematically determine growth curves for different species in different marine regions. [A model has been developed that] gives a simple description of how a year-class of a certain species alters in number and weight during its life. With the help of von Bertalanffy's equations for growth, alterations in an individual's weight can be determined, and thereby also the alterations in weight of the whole year-class during its life, as long as it is not influenced by fishing. A year-class reaches a maximum weight, which naturally differs between species, at a definite point of time. The maximum weight of a year-class also differs in different populations of the same species. If catches are made when the weight of a year-class reaches its maximum, the greatest possible returns will be obtained.

REGULATION AND PROTECTION OF THE LIVING RESOURCES OF THE SEA

Rational exploitation of the world's resources of fish presupposes international agreements, for most fish are caught in international water. An extension of fishing boundaries to a 200 nautical miles economic zone, as discussed at the UN Conferences on the Law of the Sea at Caracas (Venezuela) in 1974, at Geneva (Switzerland) in 1975, and in New York (United States) in 1976, will not provide adequate protection for fish populations, nor will it create conditions for their rational exploitation. Most fish populations are mobile and move from one country's territorial waters to another's during their annual migrations. If 200-mile boundaries were imposed in the entire North Sea, for example, most of the important species—herring, cod, haddock, whiting, etc.—would be within the 200-mile boundaries of two to six countries during different parts of the year. So far the 200-mile boundaries have been imposed in the North Sea area, excluding the Kattegat and the Skagerrak. International agreements are therefore absolutely necessary in regions like the North Sea if the fish population is to be utilized rationally.

The North Atlantic Fishing Convention was drawn up in 1959 on an initiative from the USSR, and the Northeast Atlantic Fishery Commission (NEAFC) was established. The region covered by the convention comprises the northeast Atlantic bounded by Greenland to the west and the sea off the coast of Spain to the south. Neither the Mediterranean, nor the Baltic with its belts are affected by this convention. A special convention was drawn up in 1973 to protect the fish populations of the Baltic.

Experts attached to the International Council for the Exploration of the Sea (ICES) report annually, by way of their liaison committee, on the status of various fish populations. These reports form the basis of action by various member states inside the NEAFC. The NEAFC has intervened in many ways—regulating minimum size of fish that may be caught, mesh size in fishing gear, etc. When the overfishing problem became acute in the northeast Atlantic towards the end of the 1960s, it became clear that radical steps would have to be taken to prevent overfishing of such pelagic species as the herring.

The year 1974 was a historic one for the NEAFC, for then Article 7 of the convention was applied for the first time. Quotas were introduced for fishing in the northeast Atlantic. A total allowable catch was fixed for herring, cod, haddock, whiting, plaice, and sole in the North Sea and later in 1975 for arctic cod.

All countries must reduce their fishing fleets, for today there is a very great excess capacity. It is a painful economic decision that must be made. It must be realized by all—fishery biologists and others—that this will take time. Unfortunately, during this time the situation of the fish populations is deteriorating, and their recovery will take longer when really effective measures can be applied. Disagreement on who is to pay for these measures nationally (compensation to fishermen) and internationally (the country most responsible for the overfishing) is great. In some cases reality is so hopeless that there is no solution. When the catastrophe for the Atlanto-Scandian herring became clear in 1971, the Soviet Union, Norway, and Iceland came to an agreement forbidding all fishing for mature herring outside the framework of the NEAFC. Later the NEAFC extended the decision to young herring.

Marine fisheries are now supervised by many international bodies. The most important problem areas in the international law governing marine fisheries can be summarized in six items:

1. The full utilization of the living resources of the high seas
2. The conservation of these resources
3. The economic efficiency of marine fisheries
4. The allocation of the catch
5. Scientific research
6. Interuse and intrause conflicts

A few of the most well-known international bodies are mentioned below:

FAO	Food and Agriculture Organization of the United Nations
ICNAF	International Commission for the Northwest Atlantic Fisheries
INPFC	International North Pacific Fisheries Commission
IOFC	Indian Ocean Fishery Commission
IPHC	International Pacific Halibut Commission
IWC	International Whaling Commission
NEAFC	North-East Atlantic Fisheries Commission
ICBF	International Commission for Baltic Fisheries

NONRATIONALLY EXPLOITED POPULATIONS

The FAO fishery committee has given, for each marine region, the status of known populations of fish and other animals. Very many populations are reported to be fully exploited, e.g., the cod population in the northeast Atlantic. [. . .]

In the northeast Atlantic the Atlanto-Scandian herring was fished so intensively during the 1960s that we do not know today whether the population can survive. For several years the remaining few seem to have failed in their reproduction, and the population seems now to be too small for reproduction. Neither larvae nor young herring were observed during the five or six years after the population crashed. [. . .] After the poor catches of mature herring in 1969–1971, herring fishing was totally prohibited in 1972, except for a certain amount of young herring. From January 1976, there is a total ban on all commercial fishing of this stock.

The future is very dark for the North Sea herring, unless very strict regulations are introduced. Since 1971 we have had closed seasons for herring fishing in the North Sea and the Skagerrak. In 1974 NEAFC introduced quotas for the North Sea herring. The total allowable catch for the first year (1974/75) was fixed at 488,000 tons. The annual total quota has been dropped to only 170,000 tons for 1976. The group of scientists working inside ICES has proposed a total ban on herring fishery in the North Sea.

The great decline of the sardine population off the coast of California at the end of the 1940s and the similar disastrous decline of the anchovy off the Peruvian coast at the beginning of the 1970s are well known, but in both cases unfavorably hydrographic conditions were a contributing factor. These are therefore not typical illustrations of the results of overfishing.

THE THREAT OF POLLUTION

Another threat to the rational utilization of the living resources in seas and lakes is pollution. Most aquatic ecosystems are very sensitive to the thousands of substances discharged into seas and lakes: organic substances, chlorinated hydrocarbons, heavy metals, acids, resins, chlorine and fluorine compounds, oils and oil derivatives, radioactive substances, etc.

Certain pollutants affect the habitat in such a way that plants and animals cannot breed or live in the area. A common example is sewage containing phosphorus and nitrogen compounds, which contribute to the eutrophication of the water. Oxygen resources are depleted when the excess of produced organic material is decomposed by bacterial activities. Due to lack of oxygen the animals emigrate from the area. Another effect of eutrophication may be an outburst of planktonic organisms such as dinoflagellates, which produce toxic substances. The acidification of lakes due to airborne sulfur produced by industrial activities is another example of an effect that will adversely influence the breeding of many fish populations. A water with low pH prevents a normal development of eggs and larvae of certain species.

Many pollutants cause an accumulation of harmful substances in the tissues of animals. The high content of mercury, chlorinated hydrocarbons, and other substances that have a long biological half-life in animals and man now prevents utilization of fish or other animals in some areas. The accumulation of mercury in the body was disastrous for the people in the Minimata Bay of Japan who ate fish with a very high concentration of mercury. Many people died or were disabled. In Sweden certain areas with high content of mercury in fish were banned for commercial fishing. Fish, birds, and mammals in the Baltic are reported to accumulate high amounts of chlorinated hydrocarbons. Cod liver from the southern Baltic is not allowed to be utilized due to high content of PCB and DDT. High concentrations of such substances prevent the use of valuable animals and plants. But the substances may also adversely affect the organisms themselves, influencing important physiological processes in the animals as well as in man.

The monitoring of such substances in different habitats is therefore extremely important. A worldwide monitoring system is necessary. Many international conferences have therefore dealt with such problems for many years to coordinate the national activities in this particular field. The increasing amounts of chemical compounds, especially in industrialized countries, force national and international bodies to introduce measures to stop the discharge of all harmful pollutants. Research work in different fields is more necessary than ever, not only technical and chemical studies but also biological studies. Biological investigations to ascertain the effect of pollutants on the organisms are as important as field studies to follow changes in species composition and abundance in different habitats. The basis for all measures to be taken must be scientific knowledge.

PROGNOSES AND PROSPECTS

The argument that the sea is not important as a source of food for the world is quite wrong. It is true that the sea can by no means solve the whole hunger problem of mankind, but neither can agriculture. There are, however, good prospects of doubling or tripling the harvest from the sea. To this must be added the cultivation of fish, which FAO considers can be increased from the present 6 million tons to 50 million tons by the year 2000. This means that a total of at least 200 million tons of fish and other animals can be taken from saltwater and freshwater by the year 2000. With an average of 20 percent protein in fish, this would imply an additional 40 million tons of animal albumin. As only half or one-third of some consumption fish can be utilized after cleaning, it seems reasonable to make a conservative estimate on the order of 20 million tons of animal protein.

It is probable that most of the people in the industrialized world will have to change their nutrition pattern in the future. "Luxury" feeding has to cease when the supply of traditional fish species becomes scarce. Plankton, krill, and small fishes will have to be accepted in the form of sausage, paste, or as an ingredient in meal intended for baking.

The heavy fishing in the North Sea has changed the composition of catches from adult and big fishes to younger and smaller fishes. In 1960, before the heavy overfishing started in the North Sea, 1.5 million tons of fish were caught, mainly adult and big fishes suitable for human consumption. The overfishing in connection with fishing for industrial purposes in the 1960s changed the whole pattern. The average length of some species decreased and the stock density of such valuable species as herring, mackerel, cod, haddock, etc., decreased. However, the total catch increased to more than 3 million tons due to the big catches of industrial fishes as sand eel (*Ammodytes* spp), Norway pout (*Boreogadus esmarcki*), blue whiting (*Micromesistius poutassou*), and sprat (*Sprattus sprattus*). A fish such as sprat, which has a short lifespan, and starts spawning at the age of one or two years, seems to be favored by the present situation, with no or very little competition from herring. During the last four eyars, the catches of sprat have increased from about 100,000 tons to more than 600,000 tons. Although we are speaking of a crisis in the North Sea fishery, we catch more than ever, but the catches consist of less valuable species, mainly used for production of fish meal and fish oil. If traditional food habits could be changed to include fish sausages, fish sticks, pastes, etc., other species, which today are considered unsuitable for human consumption, could be used as food. These species are now converted to fish meal in order to raise pigs, broilers, and even fishes in fish farms. This indirect use is a waste of biological energy.

The cultivation of plankton, mussels, crustaceans, fishes, and algae in lakes, coastal areas of the sea, ponds, tanks, silos, etc., probably belongs to the future. Today a little less than half of the catches from freshwaters are cultivated, mainly in developing countries. World production through aquaculture from marine and freshwater is about 6 million tons. An increase of up to eight times in production through aquaculture by the year 2000 has been predicted, although many technical and biological problems remain to be overcome. The main obstacle today seems to be that many aquaculture operations are uneconomical. The fish farmer in industrial countries cannot compete with the "hunted" fish. The cost of feed, seed, and labor is too high in most types of intensive aquaculture. Therefore the production of cheap feed, which is the main expense in many aquaculture operations today, could be a real breakthrough for aquaculture.

44

The Realities

C. P. Idyll

It is widely believed by the world's leaders and wise men as well as by the general public that the ocean alone can overcome present and future malnutrition and famine. One of the world's most highly respected scholars, the late Professor Arnold Toynbee, author of the monumental *Study of History*, expressed the view that the sea will eventually contribute more food than the land. Following the orbiting of the moon by astronauts in late 1968, Professor Toynbee urged that the United States (and the rest of the world) turn the enormous efforts being expended on "the dead end" of space exploration toward the solution of problems of extracting food from the sea. "Here," he said, "is a vast accessible field for mankind's enterprise, and also a sure guarantee for our race's survival even if our descendants are going to be ten times as numerous as we are today. Even in these numbers our descendants will not starve, since the quantities of edible fish will have multiplied in domestication, far more sensationally."

Fictional and pseudoscientific accounts of ocean exploitation support the same view. In his skillful novel, *The Deep Range*, Arthur Clarke describes his hero, a latter-day marine scientist, as "holding at bay the specter of famine which had confronted all earlier ages, but which would never threaten the world again while the great plankton farms harvested their millions of tons of protein, and the whale herds obeyed their masters . . . until the oceans froze [man] would never be hungry again."

Unfortunately, such hopes are unlikely to be fulfilled. Professor Toynbee made the assumption that man will abandon the process of "skimming food from the sea by the paleolithic method of hunting" in

---

Reprint of "The Realities," Chapter 13 in *The Sea Against Hunger*, by C. P. Idyll. (Thomas Y. Crowell Co.) Pp. 197–204.

favor of "farming the sea by cultivating edible seaweed and by breeding and shepherding fish, as we breed and shepherd sheep." This is undoubtedly the most widely held (or at least, hoped-for) idea about man's future in the sea, but [. . .] it is false.

In Mr. Clarke's case the false assumptions are that plankton offers an economic or nutritionally acceptable source of protein for man, and that the principal food fishes of the ocean can be successfully herded or increased by land-adapted farming techniques.[. . .]

If we cannot hope for substantial increases in food from the harvest of plankton, and we can expect only partial solutions from sea farming or the transplantation of useful animals to new parts of the ocean, we are left for a long time with the hunting of wild fish, as has been the case since the dawn of mankind.

But the situation is not as bad as unadorned statements about "primitive fishing methods" would imply. Indeed, fishing techniques are significantly improved over those of even a generation or so back, and they promise to become far better still.

The exercise of attempting to estimate the potential production of food from the ocean is frustrating because of the lack of knowledge about the basic productivity of most areas and the biology of fish stocks, especially in respect to fluctuations in abundance—information we must have to make rational calculations of these potential yields. But it is nonetheless clear that the total quantity of food material in the sea is far above that needed to meet the needs of the present world population, and even above amounts needed far into the future. So we can start from the important baseline that food material is being manufactured in the sea in very great quantities.

Yet, whatever the magnitude of this potential, it can never be fully realized because of the numerous biological, social, economic, political, and technical barriers.

One of the basic biological barriers is the fact that by removing certain species through fishing, man is often competing with ocean creatures that require these same species for food. Thus, by heavy exploitation of one fish, the harvest of another species on a higher trophic level is reduced. For example, if fishing for the sand lance, *Ammodytes*, increases substantially, enough food may be snatched from the mouths of codfish (which depend heavily on sand lance in their diet) to reduce the catch of cod. There are millions of intricate relationships that may be upset as fishing becomes heavier and more diversified.

Some of the theoretical increase in yield can come about only if much better management is applied and the waste of overfishing is eliminated. The tools to do this exist for many stocks, and failures are only the consequence of defects in administrative machinery—social and political difficulties. But for other stocks technical problems hamper the framing of effective management. When many different kinds of fishes are exploited in the same area by the same gear, fishing may be too heavy on some species—resulting in lower sustained catches—and too light on others—also resulting in yields below the potential for those stocks. An example exists in the trawl fishery off the west coast of Africa, where a considerable number of fishes of different sizes are caught together. For the overexploited species less fishing with bigger meshes would correct the problem; for the underexploited species exactly the opposite techniques are required. In the growing fishery for sand eels and sand lances in the North Sea, the small meshed trawls used to catch these species are also making sizable incidental catches of juvenile cod and haddock—to the detriment of these stocks.

Among the other technical difficulties delaying full harvest from the sea is the present lack of gear and fishing methods capable of catching certain of the unfished stocks. We cannot, for example, economically harvest the enormously abundant zooplankton (including the millions of tons of antarctic krill) nor the swarming deep-sea fishes.

In the end, when all the complex calculations have been made of the total annual production of organic material in the sea, when all the guesses have been collected about how much of this or that kind of fish might be harvested from every segment of the ocean, we are forced to adjust all of them in terms of one overriding determinant: How much of the potential food can be landed at a profit? Regardless of how many people need food, fish will not be caught unless the fisherman can sell them for more than it costs him to catch them, including a reasonable return for his labor and his investment in boat and apparatus. Ultimately, the whole equation can be in terms of efficiency of capture, since if this is high enough, so that fish can be caught at a cost low enough, sales can be made at a profit even with weak demand.

A significant amount of the projected increases from the sea would come from the remoter regions of the ocean, or from areas where fishing conditions are so unfavorable due to weather, ocean currents, depths, or types of bottom that exploitation may never be possible. These parts of the estimated potential should therefore be subtracted from the total.

The prospect of doubling or quadrupling the catch of seafood may create the misconception that these extra catches will be constituted by popular species like salmon, sole, shrimp, and lobsters. But most of the stocks of the high-value species are near full exploitation now, or are already overfished, and a high proportion of future increases in catch will consist of species of low value and demand—sand lances, squids, and sharks, for example. Many of these will be suitable for direct human consumption only if they are made into fish protein concentrate or some other, now unfamiliar product. Thus it is important to encourage public acceptance of fish in new forms.

The same species that could be transformed into FPC will more likely be manufactured into fish meal, at least for many years. This means that the fish will have to be fed first to chickens or livestock before it can benefit humans. Not only does this reduce the real food potential of an enormous quantity of the possible catch from the ocean, but it makes mankind dependent again on the land farms to serve as channels for food from the sea.

The rapid increase in human population is forcing man to make many changes in both the land and sea environments that are reducing his chances of feeding himself. Trends of land use are affecting sea harvests adversely, and threaten worse effects. Land and sea, far from being independent parts of our globe, are intimately interrelated. By far the greatest production of sea animals is supported by the shallow seas over the continental shelves. It has been estimated that as much as 90 percent of the seafood produced by U.S. fishermen is of species that must spend part of their lives in the estuaries or nearby shallow waters. But through the destructive process of harbor and land building, and the dumping of enormous quantities of killing pollutants into the estuaries and bays, we are reducing the ability of the sea to produce marine animals. This has already had undoubted effects on the salmon catch, for example, and it may be partly or mostly responsible for the disastrous drop in the landings of menhaden off the Atlantic Coast of the United States. Hence careless handling of our land resources is also destroying our sea resources, and the bright hopes for vast new harvests from the ocean may be vain unless we learn better control of activities along the shore.

It is apparent therefore, that some of the more optimistic estimates of the sea's potential assume not only a perfect world in terms of man's behavior, but the simultaneous occurrence of incompatible events. If we concede imperfection of man and the reality of nature, it is probably realistic to hope that the sea will some day produce 100 to 125 million tons of usable food—about twice the present yield. To the extent that man becomes more rational in his behavior and that he sharpens his understanding of the complexities of the ocean and his skills in fishing techniques and management, larger harvests will be possible: perhaps 400 million tons without stretching credibility.

If supplies of food from the land remain at their present level, world fish catches of 125 million tons would constitute about 4 percent of the supply of calories. But the amount of food from the land will and must increase, so that the proportion originating from the sea may rise only a little from its present 1 or 2 percent. Furthermore, there will be a great many more people to feed by the time the fishing industry has reached this level of production, since it may take many decades if it is ever achieved. Thus, the average amount of fish available per person may not rise significantly either.

It seems certain, therefore, that food from the sea scarcely constitutes "a sure guarantee for our race's survival," as Arnold Toynbee predicted.

Despite the high hopes of so much of mankind, it appears that the sea alone cannot solve the world's hunger problem. It will take every ounce of straining effort in every way that man can devise to produce the food that is needed—by land farming, by the manufacture of protein from petroleum, by algal culture, by increasing the harvest from the sea.

But this should not be a message of despair, since far greater quantities of food, especially valuable animal protein, can be harvested than is the case now, so that even if hunger cannot be banished by the fruits of the sea alone, one of its most damaging manifestations, protein deficiency, can be blunted.

These prospects make it more than worthwhile—they make it urgently necessary—that mankind put forward the necessary effort to realize the potential of the sea.

45

Oil and Gas From Under the Sea

The American Petroleum Institute

The United States is by far the largest energy user of any nation on earth. In 1981, we consumed more energy than the Soviet Union, France, Great Britain, and West Germany combined, and five times as much per man, woman, and child as the world average. In fact, each American, on the average, uses 1.1 gallons of oil and 233 cubic feet of natural gas every day of the year.

Today, petroleum—crude oil and natural gas—provides more than two-thirds of all our mechanical energy—energy to heat and cool our homes and offices, run our trains, trucks, and cars, turn the wheels of industry, and generate one-tenth of the electricity we use. Indeed, our industrialized civilization has been built, to a large extent, on a past abundance of secure, low-cost energy, much of it supplied by domestic crude oil and natural gas.

Until recently, however, we used up our reserves of petroleum faster than we found new ones. Consequently, the United States faced a period of petroleum shortfall. Demand was outstripping supply. In 1981, the level of domestic discovery just about equaled domestic production. Nevertheless, the nation's energy requirements, which have doubled over the past 20 years, are expected to increase to meet the needs of a growing population. And oil and gas are expected to continue to provide the largest portion of that energy for many years to come.

A large portion of the oil needed to provide our energy has come from foreign sources. In recent years, we have reduced that dependency from nearly one-half of our oil supply in 1977 to about one-third in 1981. Even at that lower rate, a cutoff of foreign supplies could pose a serious threat to our economic security.

Reprint of "Oil and Gas from Under the Sea," American Petroleum Institute, June 1982. Pp. 1–13.

This article tells the story of our dwindling oil and gas supplies, the potential for increasing those reserves, and the alternatives to finding new domestic sources of petroleum. It is the story of why and how we must explore for and produce from beneath our seas the oil and gas necessary to preserve the national, economic, and consumer security of the United States.

THE NEED FOR UNDERSEA DRILLING

Virtually since its founding, the United States benefited from a seemingly inexhaustible supply of cheap energy—energy from wood, coal, waterpower, and petroleum. Unfortunately, we are now faced with the reality of how finite these energy sources are. We have found that, for environmental reasons, the nation has restricted the use of coal—once the chief supplier of energy in the United States—and has slowed the construction of both hydroelectric and nuclear generating plants. As a result, the petroleum industry has been called upon to provide a greater share of America's fuels.

In 1981, for example, the United States consumed nearly 6 billion barrels of refined products (there are 42 gallons to the barrel) and more than 19 trillion cubic feet of natural gas. The major products made were gasoline, over 2.4 billion barrels, and fuel oils, over 1.75 billion barrels. Jet fuel accounted for 320 million barrels, and kerosene for 46 million barrels. The remaining 1.3 billion barrels were consumed as liquefied petroleum gas, asphalt, lubricating oils and greases, and other products.

That's a lot of petroleum. And it will require substantial exploration and production activities onshore and offshore in the United States to keep pace with our energy requirements.

Most of the readily located onshore oil and gas fields have already been found and are in production. Oil companies have had to search increasingly in more inaccessible locations—in Alaska, in deeper formations of the earth, and beneath the ocean floor. It is this third area—under the nation's outer continental shelf and continental slope to the 8,200-foot water depth—that offers one of the best opportunities for meeting our near-term petroleum needs.

The U.S. Geological Survey estimates that recoverable quantities of petroleum under these offshore areas may range from 21 to 48 billion barrels of crude oil and from 197 to 310 trillion cubic feet of natural gas. Future improvements in technology and economics could, of course, increase the recoverable amounts of petroleum.

If the full potential of the offshore shelf and slope were realized in the near future, petroleum from that source could go a long way toward meeting the nation's energy needs. Moreover, this petroleum could lessen our long-term dependence on oil imports, and the risks involved in relying too heavily on energy supplies controlled by other nations. But it takes three to ten years to bring an oil or gas field into full production, once it has been located.

EXPLORING UNDERSEA AREAS

Petroleum exploration in the marine environment is neither a new nor untried venture. The first oil wells drilled under water date back to the mid-1890s. And over 26,000 such wells have been drilled in coastal waters in depths of up to 2,600 feet. Today, oil and gas wells located offshore account for about 10 percent of the crude oil and over 27 percent of the natural gas produced in America. Worldwide undersea operations account for about 23 percent of the crude oil produced today.

Sophisticated tools and technology now enable geologists to gain a more accurate "picture" of the underwater earth formations than was possible in the past. These pictures—called "geophysical profiles"—are obtained by directing energy waves into the formations under the ocean floor, by means of devices which do not disturb the marine environment. Sensing devices pick up the returning energy waves, and the data obtained are stored on computer tapes for later analysis.

After the data are processed, maybe—just maybe—a picture will emerge that points to earth formations which may contain reservoirs of petroleum. But there is no assurance that oil and gas will be found in these structures. Scientific examination of the data obtained merely narrows the odds. The only sure way to find oil or gas is by drilling a well.

DRILLING OPERATIONS

In the simplest terms, an oil or gas well is a steel-encased hole which serves as a pipeline from the underground petroleum source to the surface. The same basic drilling principles apply whether the well is drilled onshore or under waters. A well is drilled using a series of bits that cut a hole into the rock strata. At a relatively shallow predetermined depth, the bit and drilling tools are withdrawn, and conductor or surface casing—the outer pipe of the well—is lowered into the hole and cemented into place. This casing protects against possible pollution of underground water and supports well-control equipment.

The drilling process is repeated, with the hole being drilled deeper and with other smaller casing strings placed inside the earlier ones, until the desired depth is reached.

During the entire drilling procedure, precautions are taken to prevent the uncontrolled release of fluids or gases from the well. In addition to the strings of casing, special valve systems—called "blowout preventers"—are attached to the top of the well during drilling. They remain in place to provide a means of cutting off well flow in an emergency.

A specially prepared fluid known as "mud" is forced through the drill stem—the hollow pipe that turns the bit—and up the well between the drill stem and the hole created by the bit. The mud controls pressures within the well, lubricates and cools the bit, seals the strata until the casing is in place, supports the sides of the hole, and carries the rock chips cut by the bit back to the surface. The density and other properties of the mud can be varied to meet conditions within the well.

Operations are constantly monitored during drilling. Crews are trained to operate well-control equipment and to shut down the well, if there are indications of any emergency. In a severe storm, such as a hurricane, all operations come to a halt, and the well is shut down.

UNDERSEA DRILLING

The major differences between onshore and undersea drilling are the facilities used to support the well-drilling equipment. These facilities may be of four different types:

- A floating vessel moored above the well site
- A semisubmersible vessel floating above the sea bottom
- A "jackup," where steel legs are placed on the bottom and the drilling platform is jacked up on them to a safe height above the waves
- A steel concrete platform extending from the seabed to well above storm waves

Platforms of this latter type are designed to withstand storms of the greatest intensity recorded over the previous 100 years in the area of the rig. Such platforms are constructed to withstand hurricane force winds, hurricane-driven waves, strong currents, and floating ice, where weather patterns warrant these extreme precautions.

A number of separate wells may be drilled from a single large platform. Some of these wells are drilled into different earth formations. Others are drilled into the same structure, but at different angles, so that they may "bottom" at selected locations, often more than a mile laterally from the site of the platform itself.

Drilling platforms at sea generally have fully equipped living quarters for the crews. They are also equipped with heliports and complete sewage and waste treatment systems. When such systems do not exist, onshore support facilities are used to dispose of wastes. In recent years, the industry's capability for drilling in waters of the outer continental slope (beyond the 600-foot water depth of the shelf) has substantially increased. Worldwide, more than 200 wells have been drilled in water depths exceeding 1,000 feet.

PRODUCING FROM UNDERSEA WELLS

If oil and gas, or both, are found in commercially significant quantities, preparations are made to change from drilling to production operations. Platforms may be adapted for production operations or, as in some deep-sea areas, special mooring buoys connected to subsea production systems may serve as loading points for tankers.

Once drilling is completed, production casing is placed in the hole and cemented into place. An additional, smaller pipe, called "tubing"—through which the petroleum is to flow—is usually suspended within the innermost string of casing from an assemblage of valves and other equipment at the wellhead. The wellhead assembly, called a "Christmas tree," is a series of valves, controls, and connections designed to regulate the flow of fluids from the well.

Downhole safety valves are installed in the tubing string, below the ocean floor. These devices are designed to automatically shut off the well when flow pressures vary from predicted norms. Some of the valves are designed to be operated electrically or hydraulically from the surface.

Other safety devices include automatic and manually operated valves, alarms, and monitoring and recording equipment. Navigational warning and fire detection devices also are installed. Master switches, located at various places on the rig, are designed to shut down the entire operation if an emergency should occur that might endanger life or property or cause an oil spill.

The care taken to prevent blowouts and oil spills from undersea drilling and production operations has produced an exceptional safety record. During the drilling of the more than 26,000 such wells in U.S. waters, several have experienced blowouts. However, only one platform spill—in 1969 in the Santa Barbara Channel—resulted in significant oil reaching the shore, and the damage was only temporary. In a gas well blowout, usually there is not even temporary damage to the environment.

DRILLING IS A HIGH RISK INVESTMENT

Out of every 50 wells drilled in the search for new oil and natural gas reserves, only about four, on the average, find petroleum in commercially significant quantities, and the odds are four to one against finding any oil or gas at all.

There is no sure way to predetermine whether any petroleum will be found, or whether—if found—it will be in the form of oil, natural gas, or both. And until the drilling is completed, there is no way to determine if the quantity of petroleum is sufficient to make it economically justifiable to continue the operations.

If the well is a dry hole, it is permanently plugged. This is done by pumping a cementing material into the well, to seal the layers that have been penetrated and to prevent leakage between the earth formations or into the surface waters. All casing is cut off 15 feet below the ocean floor, and the sea bottom is dragged for any remaining objects.

MOVING THE OIL OR GAS TO SHORE

Where oil or gas is produced from an undersea well, a pipeline is generally used to transport it to onshore facilities for processing or transshipment to refineries. These pipelines are weighted and, by government regulations, buried in the seabed, where the water depth is 200 feet or less. Pipelines are designed to exacting specifications to minimize risk of rupture.

Sometimes crude oil is stored and transferred to barges at the field site. Such barge operations normally are limited to shallow water areas with mild sea conditions. Where economics justify the recovery of natural gas, it is transported to shore through pipelines. Otherwise the gas that is produced with the crude oil is reinjected into the producing strata.

WHERE ARE OUR UNDERSEA RESERVES?

Thus far, offshore production in the United States has been limited to the water areas off Alaska and the West Coast states and in the northern and western sections of the Gulf of Mexico. Only about 4 percent of the continental shelf area has been opened up by the government to leasing. Yet wells drilled on this relatively small acreage produced, in 1981, almost 382 million barrels of oil and 5.5 trillion cubic feet of natural gas.

The search for new reserves has turned to four frontier areas:

- Beneath the Atlantic Ocean—near the Georges Bank (off New England), Baltimore Canyon (off the Middle Atlantic States), and Blake Plateau (off northern Florida and Georgia)
- In the northeastern Gulf of Mexico
- Along the Pacific Coast
- In the waters off the southern, western, and northern coasts of Alaska

The areas of the Atlantic outer continental shelf believed to be the most promising lie offshore, out of sight and sound of land.

Before any lease sale of potential petroleum tracts can be made in these areas, a number of actions must be taken. The petroleum industry and the public are asked to identify tracts which should, or should not, be offered for leasing. Environmental impact statements must be filed by the responsible federal agency. And public hearings must be held, at which environmental considerations are balanced with the nation's need for the fuel necessary to meet consumer, industrial, and security needs. Only after these steps are taken can designated tracts be put up by the government for competitive bidding for leases.

CAN IMPORTS FILL THE GAP?

We are now importing about one-third of our oil. Our dependence on foreign oil, over the short term, must necessarily continue to fill the gap between domestic production and demand. However, we cannot afford the luxury of permitting this dependence to become overdependence. The six-month Arab oil embargo in 1973–74 and the reduction in supplies resulting from the Iranian revolution in 1979 dramatically brought home the danger to our nation's economic and military security of prolonged cutoffs of petroleum supplies from overseas sources.

Since World War II, there have been more than a dozen disruptions in the flow of crude oil from the Middle East and North Africa. Mexico and Venezuela, our principal western hemisphere suppliers, currently do not have the capacity to fill the gap which might be created in the event of future shut-offs of eastern hemisphere supplies, even if they were willing to do so. Imports, therefore, must not be considered a substitute for the exploration and development of our domestic petroleum resources underlying the offshore waters of the United States.

CAN'T WE USE ENERGY MORE EFFICIENTLY?

We have been using energy more efficiently in recent years. Overall energy use in the United States has dropped substantially—down 6 percent in 1981 below 1979 levels. Economies in energy consumption have been achieved in homes, in transportation, in agriculture, in business and industry, and in government.

More efficient automobiles, better construction techniques, and new concepts in mass transit have played a part and can continue to do so. Each of us, too, can make a contribution toward more efficient use of energy—in our homes (through proper insulation, storm doors and windows, wise use of appliances), and in driving our cars (good driving practices, regular auto tune-ups, avoiding unnecessary trips).

All of these, together, can help slow the demand for energy. But this, alone, will not solve the problem. Even with continued conservation efforts, more energy will be needed in the future.

We must encourage the search for oil and gas, particularly at the time when this nation needs to expand its energy production to meet future environmental, social, and economic needs. These goals can be met only if there is sufficient energy available to generate the needed jobs, materials, and facilities. To fulfill these needs will require expanded, not retrenched, domestic activities of the energy-producing industries, including the exploration and development of the oil and gas deposits of our offshore waters.

PETROLEUM AND NEAR-TERM ENERGY SUPPLIES

To our society, energy—which means mainly oil and natural gas—is lifeblood. The availability and cost of energy will affect every aspect of our economy and of our daily living.

In the medium to long term, the United States has a strong energy resource base on which to call, not only oil and natural gas still awaiting discovery but very large deposits of coal and oil shale. And there are still other nonconventional energy sources—solar and geothermal power and synthetic fuels—in the more distant future.

In the near term, however—say, the next 10 to 15 years, we will have to rely on oil and natural gas as our prime sources of energy. This means finding and developing new reserves of oil and gas under our outer continental shelf and slope, from deeper horizons onshore and from remote onshore areas, such as Alaska and the Rocky Mountains.

46

Petroleum and the Environment

Fillmore C. F. Earney

Offshore development of hydrocarbons is fraught with numerous problems, including natural and man-made hazards to oil field workers and platforms, open-water and coastal ecological damage from oil spillage and waste disposal, and conflicts with other users of ocean space and resources, like the fishing and shipping industries. The international dimension of potential environmental damage from the offshore petroleum industry was early recognized under the 1958 Geneva Convention on the High Seas. The Convention stipulates that "Every state shall draw up regulations to prevent pollution of the seas by the discharge of oil from ships or pipelines or resulting from the exploitation and exploration of the seabed and its subsoil. . . ." Many world states are attempting to abide by this stricture, especially so after several subsequent oil field and tanker accidents focused world attention on the problem.

MAN-MADE HAZARDS

The offshore petroleum industry's pollution record has often been cast in a bad light, but when compared with other sources, its performance is favorable, both in maintaining control over human and industrial wastes and in preventing oil spillage. The control of these problems presents a formidable technological challenge and a major expense to producers.

Reprint of "Petroleum and the Environment," Chapter 8 in Fillmore C. F. Earney, *Petroleum and Hard Minerals From the Sea* (New York, John Wiley and Sons, 1980). Pp. 143–62.

HUMAN AND INDUSTRIAL WASTES

Numerous federal and state regulations control waste disposal in the United States' offshore petroleum fields. Drilling muds containing toxic materials or additives must be neutralized before being discharged into the ocean or they have to be backhauled to shore. Several studies have shown, however, that dumping drilling muds into the sea has no negative effect on the marine environment. Human wastes must be handled similarly to drilling muds. But on platforms having a limited amount of human waste, electrocatalytic converters, or "electric chairs" as they are known to platform workers, incinerate the waste into a vapor and then pass it through a catalyst. In areas where the weather is hot and humid, it is difficult to store a large volume of galley garbage; consequently, it too must be frequently backhauled.

OIL SPILLS

A 1975 U.S. National Academy of Sciences study has provided comparative best-estimate data showing that world offshore oil well production in the mid-1970s was annually introducing 0.08 million tons (600,000 [barrels] bbl.) or 1.3 percent of the total 6.113 million tons (45.3 million bbl.) of petroleum hydrocarbons entering the oceans. In comparison, transportation sources accounted for 34.9 percent, river runoff for 26.2 percent, atmospheric rainout for 9.8 percent, urban runoff for 4.9 percent, and natural marine seeps for 9.8 percent. Translated into percentages and assuming these values remain unchanged, the volume of offshore oil well pollution is 27 times less than that of transportation sources, nearly 4 times less than urban runoff, and 7.5 times less than pollution occurring from natural oil seeps.

Offshore oil fields spillage occurs in various ways, including blowouts, pipeline breakage, and loss during transfer, primarily from supertankers to smaller craft. Spills usually form slicks that can rapidly spread from the point of origin. Oil spill drift is normally a function of wind, current, and wave conditions. Wind accounts for most of a slick's movement, and the rate of movement is usually estimated to be approximately 3 percent of the wind speed. Subsurface currents and wind-induced surface currents also enter into the problem of predicting speed and direction of slick movement. Wave and slick movement relationships are less well understood; small waves seem to increase slick movement, whereas large waves reduce it. The oil's viscosity, density, and volatility, also, contribute to varying rates of spread.

Several major oil spill disasters have occurred in recent years, and it is these events that account for most of the total volume of spillage. Most spills, however, are small. A 1977 study shows that two-thirds of all reported oil discharges from production facilities in the United States' OCS [outer continental shelf] were caused by equipment malfunctions; 7 percent stemmed from errors made by personnel. During the years 1971–76, oil spills of 50 bbl. or more occurring on the OCS averaged five events annually. The total spillage for the five-year period was 51,311 bbl. A few large spills—50 bbl. or more—accounted for most of the spillage (Table 1).

Oil spillages may have significant impacts on marine and coastal ecosystems. Fishermen, marine biologists, and officials at all governmental levels are concerned for coastal biota viability and onshore social and financial costs. In open seas, the major problem is damage to surface organisms such as plankton and pelagic fish. In coastal waters, there may be severe but relatively localized difficulties, especially if the oil is churned into beaches or enters tidal estuaries where it often smothers crustaceans and shellfish or immobilizes and kills birds. Estuaries and beaches may take two to three years, or more, to recover. On the other hand, studies of Venezuela's Lake Maracaibo and of California's Santa Barbara Channel have demonstrated that many marine organisms' growth rates have not been diminished even when exposed to constant seepage from local oil wells or natural seeps. Under new amendments to the OCS Lands Act of 1953, passed in September 1978, a fund of $100–$200 million was established for oil spillage liability; fishermen and others suffering losses from oil spills are eligible for assistance. The fund is maintained by a 3¢/bbl. tax on all oil produced on the OCS. Platform operators are liable for damages and cleanup costs up to $35 million.

TABLE 1 Hydrocarbon Spills on the United States' OCS, 1971–76

Year	Spills of 50 bbl.[a] or More			Spills of Less than 50 bbl.[a]		
	Number	Bbl. Spilled	Tons Spilled	Number	Bbl. Spilled	Tons Spilled
1971	11	1,285	174	1,245	1,492	202
1972	2	150	20	1,159	1,032	139
1973	4	22,175[b]	2,997	1,171	921	124
1974	8	22,721[c]	3,070	1,129	667	90
1975	2	266	36	1,126	711	96
1976	3	4,714[d]	637	949	523	71

Source: Department of Interior, *U.S. Geological Survey Yearbook*, Fiscal Year 1977; *Yearbook*, Fiscal Year 1978, p. 203.

Notes: [a] 50 bbl. = 6.8 metric tons; [b] 9,935 bbl. spilled from a ruptured storage tank (Jan. 9) and 7,000 bbl. from a leaking barge (Jan. 26); [c] 19,850 bbl. spilled from a pipeline broken when a ship's anchor dragged on the seabed (Apr. 17); [d] 4,000 bbl. spilled from a pipeline tie-in broken by a shrimp trawl drag (Dec. 18).

Small-scale oil spills may go unnoticed or unreported, but major spills have had a significant impact on forming world opinion and prompting tighter offshore oil production regulations and enforcement; the Santa Barbara Channel oil spill of 1969 is a case in point. That spill is attributed to geological conditions, deficiencies in the drilling program, and human error. Without attempting to pinpoint the reason for the spill, one can safely say that it electrified public concern for coastal environments in petroleum-producing regions. Consequently, the U.S. Congress, state legislatures, and local governments and regulatory agencies at all administrative levels moved toward a more vigorous control of the offshore oil industry. The federal Water Quality Improvement Act of 1970, containing numerous cleanup and prevention regulations dealing with offshore oil discharges, exemplifies this surge of interest.

THE OCS ENVIRONMENT AND THE DOI

Since 1969, the DOI [Department of the Interior] has instituted much more stringent regulations on petroleum exploration and production safety, including changes in bore hole casing depth specifications and cementing techniques, blowout prevention equipment, well completion methods, and waste disposal practices. All significant pollution accidents must be investigated and the findings made available to the public. And accident contingency plans for oil spill containment and cleanup must be on file with the DOI. Federal regulations passed in 1978 require that before exploratory drilling can begin, oil companies must file environmental reports along with each exploration proposal and obtain an exploration permit from the USGS [U.S. Geological Survey]; and in state waters, a permit from the U.S. Corps of Engineers must also be acquired. The Corps' main concern is unobstructed navigation.

The Conservation Division of DOI's USGS is responsible for administering OCS development plans and environmental affairs. During the fiscal year of 1977, the division's officials supervised oil and gas production activities of 1,970 leases in OCS waters off the Atlantic, Gulf of Mexico, Pacific, and Alaska coasts, covering some 9,312,000 acres. A total of 540 exploration and development plans were examined and approved. Inspections of drilling rigs (2,655) and production platforms (2,250) resulted in 683 warnings for improper operations. Although the OTA [Office of Territorial Affairs] contends there are no systematically planned government inspections of the construction, installation, and operation of offshore platforms, the work of the DOI seems to have been effective in reducing the number of oil spills. Despite recent increases in OCS petroleum activities, the overall trend for oil spills is downward, as is the total tonnage lost in spills of less than 50 bbl. (Table 1).

Environmental impact studies prior to leasing. The DOI is responsible for developing very detailed environmental impact statements for all areas it proposes to lease. A good and highly important example of the studies is the BLM's [Bureau of Land Management] Environmental Impact Statement prepared for a proposed 1979 sale of tracts in the mid-Atlantic OCS, the Baltimore Canyon area. The study presents individual probability estimates for the frequencies of oil spills and their potential magnitude from platforms and pipelines.[. . .] The BLM calculated that, collectively, the expected number of spills greater than 1,000 bbl. (using pipeline transport) from areas already leased or those proposed for leasing is approximately 0.62 spills during the lease areas' production life. For the proposed lease areas, the probability that no spills will occur during the lifetime of production is 54 percent.

Hypothetical trajectories or pathways for oil spills were plotted on a digital map of the area between latitude 35° and 42°N. and between longitude 69° and 76.5°W. Trajectories from 500 hypothetical oil spills were simulated by the Monte Carlo method for each of the four seasons and for each of the 13 points in the mid-Atlantic area, "resulting in a total of 26,000 trajectories that reflect wind and current patterns." [. . .] The pathways meander, but the net movement is eastward. By combining spill frequency estimates and the probability of a spill following a particular path, the overall oil spill risk posed by oil and gas production in the sale area can be assessed. A similar study done earlier for the same general area for a mid-Atlantic lease sale held in 1976 showed a somewhat different trajectory pattern. [. . .] The summer trajectories experienced six landfalls; the winter season had one landfall. The time elapsing from spillage to landfall varied from 33 to 60 days for summer events to 18 days for the winter's one event. The total time lapse from spill to landfall is important, because the spill's impact on the coast will usually decrease as the length of time the spill is at sea increases. The authors of the 1976 study, stressing the essence of assessing potential environmental damage to coastal zones near offshore oil fields, stated: "An important fact that stands out when one attempts to evaluate the significance of accidental oil spillage for [the OCS], or any proposed lease area, is that the problem is fundamentally probabilistic." As in the study conducted for the 1979 sale, the authors calculated frequency probabilities for landings of oil spills larger than 1,000 bbl. during the proposed lease area's 25-year production life. There is a 61 percent probability that no landings of 1,000-bbl. oil spills will occur, and less than a 1 percent probability that four landings will occur. This study also generated probabilities of an oil spill episode's affecting specific biological resources and recreation areas. The probabilities were relatively low—endangered species (1.5 percent), migratory birds (4 percent), shell fisheries (1 percent), coastal finfish (7 percent), estuarine and anadromous fish (1 percent), wildlife refuges and management areas (3 percent), resort beaches (2 percent), and park and recreation areas (5 percent).

The OTA disagrees. The findings of the two studies outlined above seem to indicate that the hazard of oil spills along the mid-Atlantic coast is not excessive. But according to an independent study performed by the U.S. Coast Guard for the OTA, an oil spill occurring in the summer months, when the area is under the influence of a stagnant high-pressure system, has a very good chance of reaching shore, which could virtually wipe out the affected area's seasonal tourist income. In 1976, the OTA pointed out that it is debatable whether oil spills occurring along the Atlantic coast would be handled adequately, and it contended that the USGS did not ". . . appear to employ the best available system for establishing standards and enforcing regulations dealing with oil spill prevention and cleanup." Although oil spill control is vested in the USGS, the technical knowledge for oil spill detection and containment has been developed primarily in the Coast Guard which, until the 1978 OCS Lands Act Amendments were instituted, had no statutory authority over oil and gas development activities on the OCS. As of mid-1979, the USGS had an agreement with the Coast Guard to review its oil spillage prevention and cleanup programs.

BLOWOUTS

Most oil spillages are potentially hazardous to marine biota and coastal zones, but those associated with blowouts (an uncontrolled well) pose a special threat—explosions and fires that may destroy the rig and endanger personnel. Fortunately, blowout is less than two wells for each 1,000 drilled. Blowouts occurring during production operations are nearly always caused by fires on the platform, platform failure, or the collision of a vessel with the platform. From 1970 through 1976, the United States OCS petroleum industry experienced 173 explosions and fires, an average of 24.7 events annually, with a total of 105 injuries and 32 fatalities. Some of these fires and explosions were associated with blowouts (Table 2).

Blowout control. Trapped petroleum deposits are under pressure. Drillers control this pressure by pumping heavy drilling mud into the well to keep the oil and gas from pushing upward through the drill hole. Failure of the mud to restrain the pressurized gas or oil can result in a blowout. All oil drilling and pumping operations have safety backup systems. During drilling from floating platforms, operators attach a blowout preventer (a set of large valves) to the top of the casing on the ocean floor. During production, an elaborate system of valves and fusible plugs, a "Christmas tree," located on the deck or seabed, controls the flow of gas

TABLE 2 Fires and Explosions on the United States OCS, 1970–76

Year	Number of Events	Injuries	Fatalities
1970	12	31	17
1971	19	16	1
1972	31	9	0
1973	30	9	2
1974	22	15	0
1975	27	11	10[a]
1976	32	14	0

[a] A tanker collided with a platform. Oil escaping from the tanker ignited and set the ship on fire. Six men died in the blaze (Aug. 15).

or oil to the surface; operators also install a safety valve below the seabed. The valve sits within a series of casings set several hundred to thousands of feet into the seabed. The subsurface safety valve is kept open by hydraulic pressure maintained from the platform. If this pressure is lost, the valve closes. Needless to say, these systems sometimes fail, or human error occurs in their operation or installation. Fortunately, within 5 to 15 days, approximately 60 percent of all blowouts plug, bridging themselves by the collapse of the oil-bearing strata into the drill hole.

Ekofisk. In the North Sea, a major blowout resulted from both mechanical failure and human error on April 22, 1977. The accident occurred on the Bravo Platform of the Ekofisk complex located in the Norwegian sector. Workers, attempting to pull tubing, were replacing a down-hole safety valve when it gave way, allowing an oil and gas discharge to reach the platform deck. The discharge became so severe that, after shutting the platform's other 14 wells, all 112 men aboard evacuated the rig, using survival capsules dropped from the deck to the sea surface. To reduce the fire hazard, a fire-fighting vessel sprayed the rig with water.[1] All work in the Ekofisk area stopped for 50 hours, until it was determined that the escaping gas and oil posed no threat to the use of the field. A team from an oil well troubleshooting firm based in Texas was called in to control the blowout. Capping efforts were finally successful on April 30, although the Bravo Platform remained idle until July 19.[2]

During the blowout, 15–21,000 tons (110,000–155,000 bbl.) of oil discharged into the North Sea. It is estimated that 50 percent evaporated; only 800–1,000 tons (5,900 –7,400 bbl.) were mechanically recovered during cleanup, primarily because rough seas did not allow recovery equipment to function properly. To reduce the fire hazard, 55 tons of chemical dispersants were distributed, an amount capable of handling about 1,000 tons of oil. Fortunately, because of favorable winds and currents, the slick never reached closer than 70 nautical mi. to any shore, and by June only small (diameter 0.1 in.) scattered tar balls remained. Results of an investigation of the blowout's effects on marine life showed no significant impact, although somc bird, fish, and plankton were affected. This fortunate outcome may have resulted because of a relatively inactive level of biological processes in that portion of the North Sea at that time of year. Total oil spill cleanup costs were calculated in 1977 as probably between $5 and $10 million. Costs of lost production during the field's eight-day closure totaled at least $57 million, and control effort costs were considerable. Investigators found that human error caused the blowout. The down-hole safety valve was blown from the bore hole because it had not been locked correctly and a blowout preventer had been installed in an inverted position.

MONITORING NORTH SEA OIL PRODUCTION AND ENVIRONMENT

The Ekofisk accident caused considerable debate within government circles in Norway. Even prior to the blowout, many officials were not happy about Norway's entry into the oil producing business or about the rapid pace of the development effort.[3] The blowout cost the Norwegian government 40 million kroner ($7.48 million) in royalty fees and a tax loss of approximately 250 million kroner ($46.75 million).

Although Ekofisk's financial costs were high, some observers view the accident as having had a positive effect because executives in industry and government took a more careful look at safety procedures followed on the North Sea's platforms. Norwegian regulatory agencies have, in fact, been accused of being so obsessed with safety that North Sea oil investment and development are unnecessarily retarded. For example, Norway will not allow oil production on a platform that is also drilling at the same time: Great Britain allows this practice, which some claim increases the accident hazard. Given Norway's strict rules and considering the number of workers injured or killed annually in its oil industry, the government had reason for concern. Injuries during the period 1971–76 averaged 122 per year, rising from 21 in 1971 to 328 in 1976; fatalities averaged 2.7 each year. The average number of injuries per 100 workers during 1973–76 was 10.9 per year.[4] The United Kingdom, partly as a consequence of the accident, established a team of high-ranking government officials to coordinate control procedures, should a similar event occur in the British sector. In 1969, all states bordering on the North Sea made a pact—the Bonn Agreement—to mutually cooperate on North Sea oil pollution problems. The signatories pledged to exchange information on all oil-related accidents. Thus, within only a few hours after the Bravo blowout, all parties had been informed; they were kept posted on progress in controlling the blowout and in dispersing the oil. In a follow-up, Norway extended an invitation to the governments of Sweden, Ireland, Iceland,

France, West Germany, the Netherlands, the United Kingdom, and the United States, as well as representatives of the OECD [Organization for Cooperation and Economic Development], EEC [European Economic Community], and the Economic Commission of Europe, to meet and discuss the lessons learned from the accident. Out of this meeting came a commitment to convene yet another conference, in early 1978, to consider improved safety and pollution prevention in the North Sea oil fields. By late 1978, Norway and the United Kingdom had worked out a joint program for mutual assistance in emergencies, and they will share in the cost of construction and operation of a special emergency supoperation of a special emergency support boat.

The various states bordering the North Sea have different but for the most part, effective systems of regulating exploratory and development activities of the region's oil producers. Norway and the Netherlands have regulations placing the burden upon the producer to prove they are not damaging the environment; their regulations use words such as "all proper measures," "safe," and "best oil field practice." Norway maintains rigorous governmental inspection programs for platform safety and oil spillage.[5] Although the United Kingdom has specific stipulations for onshore zoning and land use, it holds basically to a "reasonable man" and a less direct governmental monitoring regulatory policy for safety and oil production. This method thus far has been successful in avoiding most conflicts of interest and litigation over conservation problems and among various marine resource users, although not for blowouts and oil spills. The British government has a much less restrictive regulatory scheme than the United States under its 1969 Environmental Protection Act which requires detailed examination of any likely impacts a given construction program might cause. The United Kingdom does have a Prevention of Oil Pollution Act (1971) providing for a fine up to £50,000 for an oil spill. Fines have frequently been levied at a rate less than this amount when the operator has been able to show that "neither the escape nor any delay in discovering it was due to any want of reasonable care, and that as soon as practicable after it was discovered, all reasonable steps were taken to stopping or reducing it." The United Kingdom exerts considerable local control over offshore oil producers by placing supervisory authority in the hands of port city police. Each port's police force is responsible for monitoring all oil rigs and platforms under its jurisdiction. Aberdeen's police, for example, are responsible for the surveillance of operations as far away as the East Shetland Basin.

NATURAL HAZARDS AND THE WORKING ENVIRONMENT

Offshore oil producers and workers must cope not only with manmade hazards associated with platforms—blowouts, fires, explosions, and sanitation—but also face hazards of the marine environment itself, including storms with their winds and waves, currents, scour, and ice. However, elaborate use of technical expertise and sophisticated engineering techniques and safety precautions is allowing producers to venture into areas that only a few years ago would have been economically unproductive and/or technically impossible.

Survival Systems

When hazardous conditions develop on a platform, as occurred in Ekofisk's Bravo Platform blowout, or when in danger of capsizing, drilling and production platform crews need some kind of survival system to reach the water lying more than 100 ft. below. There are several types of survival systems capable of sheltering up to 50 people. These systems are specially built to meet the needs of today's offshore oil industry; constructed of fiberglass, self-righting, self-propelled, and highly fire resistant survival vessels have already proven themselves. One unit, the Harding Safety Lifeboat, was put to a severe test on March 1, 1976, when the semisubmersible rig Deep Sea Driller went aground northwest of Bergen, Norway. Winds of 70 knots had whipped the sea into mountainous waves, pushing the drilling rig into shallow waters where it partially capsized. The crewmen managed to launch one of the rig's survival lifeboats. After launching, a huge wave overturned the lifeboat, but it righted itself and the men inside were rescued after the craft stranded on the shore. Unfortunately, six of the seven men who had chosen to cling to the outside of the lifeboat were drowned when it flipped over.

Storms

Exposed to storms moving eastward out of the North Atlantic, the North Sea frequently experiences winds of 50 knots and waves of 60 ft. In severe storms winds may reach hurricane force and waves may attain heights of 80 ft. Consequently, design engineers must plan for the "storm of the century," which might generate winds of 100 knots and waves of 100 ft. The overturning force of such waves is tremendous, ten times that of maximum waves in the Gulf of Mexico. Waves of much smaller magnitude can cause considerable downtime during drilling and supply operations. Five times more downtime occurs in the North Sea than in the Gulf of Mexico. [. . .] Because of these severe conditions, structural steel members used in North Sea platforms need to be five to ten times stronger than those required in the Gulf of Mexico.

In the early period of North Sea development, engineers and government officials did not fully recognize the severity of the area's climatic conditions and the platform design problems they faced. In 1965, because of bad weather, British Petroleum lost a rig, the Sea Gem. Forty-five men onboard were killed when the rig went down. Heavy weather off the

Shetland Islands has caused the loss of a seismic survey ship, a new semi-submersible rig, a rig-standby ship, and a barge. In the same area during rough weather, an articulated tower (owned by Mobil Oil) in the Beryl field broke loose from its concrete base and floated away. The tower was recaptured, secured, and then it broke loose again during a storm on the following day. The tower had to be towed to Stavanger, Norway, for inspection and repairs. This accident caused a six-month delay in bringing the Beryl field into production.

Engineering problems of oil rigs are highly varied in relation to weather conditions and currents. Relatively shallow waters in the southern North Sea tend to accentuate wave heights during storms; in the north, not only local storm waves but swells from distant Atlantic storms are an additional problem. Regional coastal configurations and local, fast moving depressions generate wave trains, resulting in highly complicated patterns that create severe and complex stresses on platforms and other offshore oil industry structures. Efforts are being made to computerize the stress capabilities of platforms. Instruments mounted on the platform measure stress and movements during storms. Analysis of the data can help identify the approach of the danger threshold.

A basic difficulty facing design engineers working with offshore equipment and structures is that long-term historical climatic data are unavailable. To help solve this problem, the United Kingdom's Department of Energy has been working on an oil company-sponsored meteorological and hydrological study, costing approximately £600,000. Ideally, the wave height maximum in a 100-year period should be known for relatively local areas so that the probabilities of the anticipated 20- to 30-year exposure (or lifetime) of the active platform can be calculated. Climatic and wave-height records usually cover a time span too short for statisticians to make reliable predictions. Presently, extrapolation methods (based on a measured 20-year data period) are used for projection and hindcast techniques; in hindcasting, storm conditions are constructed backwards from a known point in time. Monte Carlo simulation methods are applied by using computer calculation based on ". . . randomly drawn storm variables. . . ," winds, currents, waves, and tides.

Although the emphasis here has been on the North Sea, other offshore areas also face difficult climatic problems. During the winter, wildcatters working in the Baltimore Canyon area experience significant downtime, and hurricanes also present a major threat here and in the Gulf of Mexico. In the past, when a hurricane entered the Gulf Coast area, personnel had to be taken off the rigs and operations shut down. This procedure meant at least a five-day down period even if the hurricane veered away from the oil field. Now computerized systems have been installed by some producers so that the wells can be left operating when personnel are not on the platform. If it becomes necessary to shut the rig down, this can be done from onshore. Studies made by the European Space Research Organization have recently determined the feasibility of using aerial satellite systems to relay weather and other data instantly to onshore monitoring stations.

Frictional Drag, Currents, and Scour

A problem closely associated with wave impact (slam) as well as with currents is the frictional drag created from movement of the water across marine growth of mussels, sea anemones, and weeds on the platform's legs and cross-members. Engineers designing rigs for the North Sea at first planned for a 4-in. radial growth extending 20 ft. below the water surface. Actual growth patterns more often have an 8-in. thickness, reaching to the seabed. As of the mid-1970s, investigators were uncertain about the precise effects of this additional drag on platforms. The marine growth, however, is removed periodically, and platforms that seem to need it are reinforced.

When oceanic currents or tides flow and ebb, sand grains and other particles may be eroded from the seabed, especially where obstructions create eddies. Depending on local conditions, this erosion process may excavate large holes surrounding the legs of platforms, resulting in a lateral weakness or imbalance in the support base; it can also uncover marine pipelines. Scour is expensive to control, and in conjunction with storms may create extreme danger to platforms. As a result of Hurricane Camille in August 1969, Shell Oil and Gulf Oil each lost a platform off the Louisiana coast near the Mississippi River mouth. Researchers attribute the collapse of the Shell Oil platform to soil failure around its legs, resulting from severe seabed scour.

Scour holes can deepen only so far before reaching an equilibrium point. To allow for this point of equilibrium, engineers must carefully determine the direction and speed of currents before deciding on the depth to set the legs below the seabed. Unfortunately, current direction and speed change make the problem more complicated. Even drilling rigs, remaining stationary only for a short time, may experience scour problems if their legs do not penetrate well below the seabed floor. Sandbags and various leg nets are useful for small scour holes, but they can be expensive in the long run. Adequate protection for an eight-leg platform may require 22,000 sandbags and several divers to arrange the bags after they are dropped overboard. Gravity structures (submersibles) are sometimes ballasted down on a prelaid gravel bed or hinged mats. Both techniques help reduce scour.

Ice Floes and Icebergs

Besides bone-chilling cold and the threat of metal fatigue in platforms and machinery, oil company personnel working in the Arctic and sub-Arctic offshore face the problem of ice. When pack ice and icebergs are moved about by winds and currents, they may be pushed against a rig, either damaging or destroying it.

Conditions off Labrador and Greenland well illustrate the problem of coping with ice, especially icebergs. Icebergs create a hazard when they calve off the Greenland ice cap and move southward in the Labrador Current. In some years, as many as 3,000 icebergs cross the 48th parallel on their journey southward, whereas in other years the number may be fewer than 100. The problems of exploring for oil in this major iceberg region are making costs ten times higher than in the North Sea and 20 times higher than in Saudi Arabia. Extensive petroleum exploration began during 1976 in the Davis Strait area off Greenland. Icebergs pose such a major threat to the six oil companies with concessions in the area that they use only dynamically positioned drill ships.[6] If danger seems imminent, the ship retrieves its drill string and moves out of the area. Several techniques are currently used or are under study to reduce the iceberg hazard. Experimental work is being done to develop a 100-ft. thick rubber bumper that encircles stationary structures. Presently, drilling and production rigs maintain two radars (one as a backup) that track iceberg movements. Technicians plot an iceberg's hourly position on a master map. If operators decide an iceberg poses a threat, sonar units are used to determine its size, giving them a better indication of how much power will be required to change its course. The iceberg is then lassoed with a floating cable and attached to one or more towing vessels, a hazardous task if it is windy. Icebergs of 3 to 4 million tons have been diverted slightly from their natural trajectory, and success with those of 1 million tons or less has been good. Producers had hoped the iceberg problem would become less hazardous after the United States launched the satellite *Seasat* in June 1978. The satellite would have provided the oil companies with data needed to make more accurate predictions of iceberg movements, but, unfortunately, it developed an unexplained short circuit and quit functioning after only 106 days.

Icebergs and ice ridges can threaten not only platforms, but also damage or destroy seabed pipelines and seabed completion units. After a well has been brought in, it may be tied by pipeline to a central platform, with only a "Christmas tree" completion unit left on the well site. If the deep keels of icebergs or ice ridges scour the bottom, they may sheer off or damage completion units. To reduce the problem, oil field workers in the Beaufort Sea area encase completion systems with steel cylinders. Pipelines laid in the Newfoundland area may have to be buried as much as 50 ft. below the seabed.

Artificial sea-ice islands. The Beaufort Sea is the site of several valuable experiments that might be better termed "working with ice." During the winter of 1976–77, Union Oil Co. drillers at Harrison Bay, 18 mi. west of the Prudhoe Bay field, used a man-made ice island as a temporary drilling base. Construction took place in water 8 to 10 ft. deep. Engineers made a containment ring of snow on the sea ice, and then pumped sea water into the enclosure, allowing it to freeze. As the weight increased, the island sank deeper until it fused with the bottom. The island was designed to have a diameter of 900 ft. and to sit 5 to 6 ft. above the ocean surface; all facilities, including a mess hall, living quarters, and sewage, were contained on the island.

Natural sea ice has also been used successfully as a drilling base. In one experiment, an insulating "sandwich" pad was laid down on the sea ice. The sandwich consisted of two layers of polyethylene film, two 2-in. layers of foam polyurethane, and then two additional layers of plastic film. Finally, a 4-in. timber layer was placed on top. The plastic film was used to provide protection against polluting the ice with drilling mud and other materials.

Landfill islands. The Arctic Ocean's first artificial landfill island was built by Imperial Oil, Ltd., of Canada. The island, dubbed Immerk, took two summers (1972–73) to build; it was sited north of the Mackenzie River Delta approximately 10 mi. offshore in about 15 ft. of water. Immerk provided the base for drilling the world's first offshore exploration well in the Arctic. In contrast to Union Oil's ice island, Imperial's island was constructed from sediments dredged from the seabed. The sediments were mounded to a depth 15 ft. above sea level, becoming frozen to the seabed during the first winter. The finished work area had a radius of approximately 150 ft. To protect the island from floe ice and wave erosion, engineers built a large erosion beach seaward of the island's work area. The total cost of the Immerk project was $5 million, evidently a worthwhile exploration investment because by 1976 six additional islands had been constructed in the region's offshore. In 1979, the number of islands constructed reached a total of 15.[7]

Offshore tunneling. The petroleum potential of the Beaufort Sea area has led some engineers to suggest the use of an offshore tunneling and chamber system. Two parallel tunnels onshore would be driven seaward—one for air inflow and the other for worker access and rail lines leading to drilling chambers adjacent to the tunnels. A 10-mi.-long tunnel and its network of drilling chambers (containing up to 12 directionally drilled wells) could give access to an area of 30 mi.^{2} Advantages of this system would be (1) dry-land drilling technology could be used; (2) hydrostatic head and drilling mud relationships would be easier to manage; (3) surface weather would be avoided; (4) oil spills would present no problem; (5) ocean floor pipelines would be unnecessary; and (6) less financial risk would be involved, because of more stable working conditions. The system would present several special problems in safety, including considerations for the hazards of fire, seismic shock, gas leakage, excessive water inflow, and blowouts.

SUMMARY AND CONCLUSIONS

Oil production on the continental margins will become increasingly important in coming decades, requiring significant inputs of capital and human skills to develop environmental impact studies, pollution control devices, and cleanup, when accidents occur, as in oil spills. Considerable differences of opinion, however, prompt disagreements concerning the long-term effects of oil and other types of pollution on marine and coastal biota; clearly, more research must be done as, for example, the type pursued by the Gulf Universities Research Consortium (GURC). Participating scientists have established a comparative set of more than 1 million data points, distributed over an area of 400 $mi.^2$, in the Gulf of Mexico for which geological, biological, and chemical variables and conditions (turbidity, dissolved oxygen, trace elements, species abundance, and hydrocarbon sources) have been measured to determine man's impact on the marine environment.

Greater care must be given to avoiding offshore man-made hazards, including platform accidents, oil spillage, explosions, fires, and blowouts. Natural hazards such as storms, ice, and scour should be further studied to ensure safe platform operation and to avoid unwise siting of rigs which may put them in jeopardy or cause environmental damage. Robert M. Owen has stressed that mining companies should attempt to obtain all previously collected field data (governmental, university, and private) dealing with a proposed mine site, including hydrological, meteorological, biological, and sedimentation information. They should, also, attempt to set up mining schedules that consider such variables as spawning periods of marine biota, establish monitoring and control systems, and develop numerically computerized models of the local ecosystems' interactions and operation.

Although the task of assuring a viable environment and safe working conditions in the offshore petroleum industry is formidable, a cooperative effort of both government and industry should be able to do the job. It is imperative that this commitment continue for, as one prominent author has said, "Ocean space—and its ecology—is one and indivisible."

NOTES

1. After a blowout, an oil well often catches fire. During a fire, spray barges are used to keep the structure cool so it will not collapse.

2. Efforts to control and kill a blowout are often focused upon drilling relief wells that attempt to intersect the well out of control. Drilling mud and steel balls forced into the runaway well may control the blowout.

3. On June 3, 1979, 50 mi. offshore in Mexico's Bay of Campeche, a major oil well blowout began which eclipsed all previous oil spills. The well, Ixoc I,

spilled 20,000 to 30,000 bbl/d into the sea; currents carried the oil along the Gulf of Mexico's western shore until beaches in Texas were fouled. As of late January 1980, the blowout had yet to be fully contained. Statoil attempted (unsuccessfully) to assist Petroleos Mexicanos in cleaning up the spill. The ripples of this failure were felt in Norway by creating additional opposition to exploration north of the 62nd parallel.

4. The number of workers in the country's petroleum industry rose from 344 in 1973 to 2,635 in 1976.

5. The Norwegian government actually stopped work in the Statfjord field when it determined that living conditions were unsafe; it also requires each well to have four blowout preventers.

6. The companies include Amoco, Chevron, Arco, Mobil, TGA-Grepco, and Ultamar. One well was spudded 60 mi. north of the Arctic Circle.

7. In one instance, off Long Beach, Calif., oil companies use man-made islands as a base in directional drilling to tap reservoirs under the adjacent mainland.

47

Will Ocean Mining Revolutionize World Industry?

John L. Mero

It is now apparent that, within the next five to ten years, the mining industry will be in full-scale production of such metals as nickel, cobalt, copper, and manganese from the deep-sea metalliferous nodules. In addition to those metals, substantial amounts of such metals as molybdenum, zirconium, cerium, etc., can be produced as by-products from the nodules. Table 1 shows the possible products which can be produced by mining the nodules at an annual rate of 100×10^6 tons per year—a capacity certainly within reach of industry sometime within the next 10 to 20 years considering the very substantial interest being shown in these deposits by a wide range of natural resource companies and governments around the world. At the present time, about $\$250 \times 10^6$ has been spent or committed to the development of the nodules as a source of various metals, mainly by American corporations but substantial amounts are also being invested in the nodules by companies and governments from France, Germany, the United Kingdom, and Japan. Full-scale mining systems are presently under construction and development to mine the nodules and pilot plants are in operation to develop the process technology to industrial capacities. The stated goal of several of the companies making large investments in this field [was] to be in full-scale production by 1980. The impetus for these investments in the nodules is not due to any imminent shortage of metals per se from land sources, but due to the fact that political decisions in various metal-producing nations are making those sources of the metals in the nodules rather unstable as concerns the indus-

TABLE 1 Metal Production Statistics Involved in Mining and Processing Oceanic Metalliferous Nodules

Product Produced from the Nodules	Dry Weight Product Percentage in Typical Minable Nodule Deposit[a]	Annual Product Production Rate in Mining (100×10^6 tons/year of nodules) (10^6 tons/year)	Present Free World Product Consumption Rates (100×10^6 tons/year) (10^6 tons/year)	Products Produced from the Nodules as a Percent of Free World Consumption	Estimated Long-Term Cost of Production of Products from the Nodules ($/lb)	Present Quoted Market Price of Product ($/lb)	Product Production as a Percentage of Free World Consumption at a Mining Rate of 400×10^6 Tons/Year
$(Mn + Fe)O_x$	63	63	11.0	572	0.01	0.02	2,328
Cu metal	1.4	1.4	5.0	28	0.20	0.90	112
Ni metal	1.6	1.6	0.5	320	0.20	1.90	1,280
Co metal	0.24	0.24	0.02	1,200	0.20	3.60	4,800
Zn metal	0.14	0.14	4.0	3	0.20	0.40	12
Pb metal	0.07	0.07	3.4	2	0.20	0.25	8
MoO_3	0.10	0.10	0.10	100	0.30	2.10	400
Zr metal	0.06	0.06	0.002	3,000	?	5.00	12,000
Cerium	0.05	0.05	0.002	2,500	?	20.00	10,000

[a] Reserves of this type and grade of nodule can be measured in terms of tens $\times 10^9$ tons or in hundreds of years at present free world consumption rates at a mining rate of 100×10^6 tons per year. Reserves of all grades of minable nodules can be measured in terms of hundreds $\times 10^9$ tons.

trialized, consuming nations, and because the nodules promise to be a less expensive source of these metals, on the average, than are the bulk of the land sources. Also, there will be a much greater efficiency in the use of investment capital in developing the oceanic deposits. While it requires about $4 of investment capital to provide a facility to produce about $1 per year of products from a large land mine, about $1 of investment capital can produce at least $3 per year of products from the ocean deposits. As the nodules are found in the deep sea, they are ready for mining. There will be no development costs to speak of in opening up a deep-sea mine. There is no overburden to remove or land to despoil in developing a deep-sea nodule deposit. Within about a year of the ordering of a mechanical cable bucket (CLB) system [Continuous Line Bucket], the nodules can be being mined. The same basic mining equipment design can be used in all deposits of the nodules. No great amount of capital must be used for mine development or mining system design years before the facility can be put into production. And there is, of course, no investment required for town site preparation, road building, port facilities, or other ancillary facilities for working in the ocean. Returns from an investment in ocean mining can be generated within three years of initial planning. Essentially, the only form of transportation involved will be sea transport, the least expensive form of transport presently known. The financing requirements of new mining ventures can thus be drastically revised.

NO POLLUTION INVOLVED IN OCEAN MINING

There will be a great opportunity to substantially reduce land and atmospheric pollution in the development of the oceanic nodules as it will be possible to close down many of the pollution prone sulfide mines and smelters on land with the advent of deep-sea mining. Environmental monitoring of two deep-sea mining system tests, one of the CLB system in 4,500 meter (m) of water in the Pacific and another in a hydraulic system in 800 m of water in the Atlantic, has indicated that there will be no pollution of the ocean or environmental destruction of any kind associated with deep-sea mining. So there will be a great net gain in restoration of the quality of the atmosphere and land once we can shift copper, nickel, cobalt, and manganese mines out to sea.

The deep-sea nodules have been shown to be extremely efficient absorbers of sulfur dioxide from stack gases. Thus, there is even further promise in reducing atmospheric pollution around the world in mining the deep-sea deposits as it will be possible to use the nodules, or the manganese oxide material left over after the more valuable metals are removed, in power plant and other industrial stacks to remove the sulfur dioxide from these stack gases. Thus it will be possible to burn the much cheaper high-sulfur coals and oils in these plants without polluting the atmosphere with sulfur dioxide. The deep-sea nodules, having a specific surface area ranging from 100 to 300 m^2 per gram of nodule material, have also been shown to be highly effective converters of unburned hydrocarbons to carbon dioxide. Thus the nodules may become important in helping to reduce atmospheric pollution from automobile exhausts. The nodules may also be important in many other catalytic process applications such as the removal of objectionable metals from crude oils before refining.

POTENTIAL FUTURE EFFECTS OF NODULE MINING ON THE MINING INDUSTRY

With the CLB system now under full-scale development by a consortium of 20 world natural resource firms, it should be possible to mine the nodules at rates of 1 to 3×10^6 tons per year per mining unit at an indicated mining cost of less than $5 per ton. Because copper, nickel, and other metals can be differentially leached from the nodules with sulfuric acid without putting any appreciable amounts of the dominant metals of manganese or iron in the nodules into solution, processing capital and operating costs promise to be very low. Essentially, it now appears possible to produce such metals as nickel, cobalt, copper, etc. from the nodules at a total overall production cost of about $0.20 per lb of these metals. At present market prices, between $50 and $150 worth of metals can be won from a ton of the nodules.

The indicated total plant capital costs of mining, processing, and transport of the nodules promises to be as low as $50 per annual ton of raw nodule capacity in large-scale operations. The profit on a nodule mining venture initially, while the large, low grade land mines control the market price of the metals, should be in excess of 100 percent per year on total capital investment. Because a relatively low capital investment is required to mine the nodules and because the deposits are freely available to all companies, once nodule mining is initiated there should be a great rush to the ocean on the part of many major natural resource firms. A highly competitive situation should rapidly develop in ocean mining with great quantities of low cost metals becoming available in a relatively short time span. Thus, it would appear that the deep-sea nodule deposits can be considered as a revolutionary source of metals for the entire world population.

It is interesting to speculate on what some of the long-term effects will be on the metals industry of having an extremely stable supply and price for the metals which can be won from the nodules. With nickel and cobalt available in any quantity and under a highly competitive situation, which will take place in ocean mining sometime within the next 20 years, and priced to the consumer at about $0.40 per lb, it will be possible to use stainless steels for the construction of vehicles, ships, buildings, bridges, industrial plants and equipment, etc. Thereby society will make a great gain in overall metal utilization efficiency, for the corrosion of steel will be greatly reduced and the tonnage of steel necessary for a given vehicle, ship, or building can be substantially reduced because of the great strength of the stainless steels. The nodules would then allow a great reduction in the overall consumption of other natural resources such as iron, yet, at the same time, provide better and less expensive products for the world population. This is resource conservation in its best sense.

Nickel companies will probably not be able to continue as "nickel producers" only, but will have to become end product or stainless steel producers as the steel companies will easily be able to secure their own independent sources of this metal. Available in unlimited quantities, at a low price, from an extremely stable, yet highly flexible source relative to turning production off and on as the market demands, nickel will be able to cut into the markets for other metals such as aluminum. While per capita consumption of metals in the highly developed nations will probably go down somewhat, because of the use of longer lasting stainless steels, consumption in the developing nations can be expected to rise dramatically as these nations will be able to produce the metals with their own labor for consumption in their own markets. The hegemony which certain nations have over the rest of the world because of the accidental location of economic deposits of metals in those nations will cease to exist. All people of the world will have equal rights of access to these deep-sea deposits. This situation should cause some great changes in the flow of raw materials and products around the world and will cause some upset in the economies of certain nations. No longer will capital have to be invested in nations where the threat of confiscation of those investments is ever present. It will be a tragedy if certain nations which may feel threatened by production of metals from the deep-sea nodules succeed in their efforts in preventing the exploitation of the deep-sea deposits. Not only will their own populations be cut off from a source of less expensive metals, but they will succeed in preventing the flow of these metals to the vastly greater number of people in other developing nations which do not now have access to a low cost source of such raw materials.

Because all the companies will be competing on essentially the same footing, technology and efficiency will become the important factors in producing the profit for a company rather than the grade of the ore-body and the mining company's exclusive hold over it. In a highly competitive situation, the sales and customer service functions of the mining company will become highly important in the deep-sea mining organization with substantial benefits accruing, thereby, to the consumer.

If the nodules become the primary source of copper, as they probably eventually will be, and assuming that this metal can be produced at a total production cost of \$.20 per lb, the overall consumption of other metals such as nickel, cobalt, molybdenum, etc., which would be coproduced with the copper, will have to be drastically revised unless these metals are to be placed in a tailings dump. As indicated in Table 1, if the nodules were mined at a rate of 400×10^6 tons per year to produce 100 percent of the present free world consumption of copper, it would also be possible to produce 2,330 percent of the present free world consumption of manganese, 1,280 percent of that of nickel, 4,800 percent of that of cobalt, 400 percent of that of molybdenum, 4,000 percent of that of zirconium, etc. New uses would have to be found for these metals and there should be a great burst of physical metallurgical research to find economic and new applications for these surplus metals. If the chemical surface properties of the manganese oxide minerals in the nodules are not changed in the leaching process to recover nickel, copper, etc., it probably will be possible to use the manganese oxide tails in sulfur dioxide gas absorption applications or in other catalytic reactions, as the world steel industry would not be able to absorb all the manganese produced.

But it may be possible to solve some of the oversupply problems in another way, especially in the short run. If a production cost is assigned to the manganese in the nodules consonant with its weight percentage, this metal, unless it can be used in quantities greatly in excess of present demand, will simply not be worth the cost of bringing to market. Thus, it may be more economic and profitable to process the nodules at the mine site to recover the more valuable metals and return the manganese and iron oxide particles to the seafloor to serve as the nuclei for the formation of additional nodules for future generations, since the metal precipitation process is going on at present in the ocean. Thereby, the metals industry would experience a great gain in overall operational efficiency by not having to transport any but the valuable products any distance. Also, by removing process operations from land, there would be a great gain in reducing land pollution and in increasing land utilization efficiency, which is quite important in such nations as Japan and the Netherlands. There is no shortage of space at sea for such facilities.

EFFECTS ON MINING INDUSTRY SERVICE COMPANIES

Mining equipment companies will be very seriously affected by deep-sea mining. As the nodules are found in the sea they are ready for mining. Exploration is simple and inexpensive and does not involve any of the equipment presently used in the exploration for land mines. No rock has to be drilled or blasted or overburden removed. Thus there is no need for explosives, drills, draglines, shovels, bulldozers, graders, trucks, or other transport equipment other than the surface vessel and its simple and inexpensive CLB mining system. The nodules are soft, friable, and highly porous. For the differential leaching of metals from the nodules it has been found that crushing beyond about – 20 mesh does not increase reaction rates or overall recovery efficiencies substantially. Thus there will be no need for great amounts of crushing, grinding, classifying, and flotation equipment, smelting furnaces, etc., in ocean mining. The crushing of the nodules to – 20 mesh can be accomplished with a simple roll crusher in one pass. The mining equipment industry should start looking for other markets for their expertise and products.

With production of deep-sea nodules, there should, however, occur a substantial increase in exploration activity for certain of the metals which are now produced as by-products from nickel or copper sulfide mines, but which cannot be produced in large quantities from the nodules. An example is silver, much of which is now produced from copper or nickel ores as a by-product. So while some types of mines would be shut down, other mines will have to be found and developed on land.

The legal cornerstone of the mining industry, that of being able to gain exclusive hold on a mineral property and doing with it as the owners will, will be undermined in ocean mining. The mining companies will have to learn to live with one another and cooperate to a very high degree at sea to prevent high grading or other inefficient practices in mining in the deep ocean. Exploration will probably be done in common for it will be incredibly inefficient for each potential ocean mining company to reexplore the same ground to find essentially the same deposit. Ideally, the first of the deep-sea mining companies will band together to form a code of ethics concerning operations in the deep sea, recognizing that any group in the world will have equal access rights to the deposits. If they are to continue to operate freely in the deep sea, miners will have to regulate and police their own activities to prevent inefficient practices—practices not consonant with good conservation philosophy and any disturbance of the environment. Common standards concerning the measurement and descriptions of the deposits should be established as soon as possible. Eventually a world legal system will be developed to regulate deep-sea mining, but such a regime would probably be quite detrimental in the initial stages of the development of this industry. If such a regime is formulated before the industry is in full-scale production it will probably burden the industry with unrealistic regulations designed largely to protect vested interests in land mines and not to aid in the development of the deep-sea deposits.

SOCIAL EFFECTS OF MINING THE NODULES

With the advent of cheaper industrial metals, freely available to all the people of the world, produced by themselves for their own consumption, there will be great economic advantages gained by the poorer, developing nations. No longer will nickel, copper, or cobalt be priced for consumption in the rich nations. Everyone will have equal access to cheap metals which could greatly encourage industrialization in the developing nations. Unfortunately the approach to the mining and processing of the deep-sea nodules by some groups appears to be one of bringing the nodules into production at capital investments and operating costs which will make the metals produced from the nodules only competitive with present land sources. Such approaches, I think, are a great mistake and every effort should be made to mine and process the nodules at the least cost possible. It is such an approach with which I am concerned in this paper and only such an approach will produce a revolution in the world metals industry.

Great efforts have been made in some quarters to bring the production of minerals from the deep sea under the control of an international legal agency. Ostensibly the reason for such an agency is to collect royalties and lease fees on production of the nodules to generate funds for use in helping the poorer nations and, possibly, to secure an independent source of income for a new world legal regime. While the world could certainly use an effective and just world government, it is not likely that sufficient funds could be generated from the mining of the nodules to do much good for the poor nations. If the international bureaucrats succeed in their efforts to place a high royalty or other costs on production of metals from the oceanic nodules, they will only succeed in making nickel, copper, and other metals produced from the ocean available only to the rich nations which can afford the high prices. They will succeed in factoring the poorer nations out of the use of these metals for industrial development, and, in the long run, accomplish exactly the opposite of their stated goals. If the prices of the metals from the nodules are kept high so that only rich nations can consume them, the market for the metals produced from the nodules will continue to be relatively small, and, thus, the potential revenues to be gained from the royalties, etc., on nodule production will be minuscule, possibly amounting to only a few cents per capita per year for the people in the developing nations. Of course, some vast bureaucracy, which would be required to administer the control of production of metals from the nodules, would be greatly enriched, and, I suspect that it is the potential leaders of this bureaucracy who are promoting control of production of metals from the nodules so avidly.

When ocean mining comes into full-scale production it will upset the present structure of much of the present world mining industry. Large, old-fashioned companies with huge investments in land mines and the expertise of land mining and encrusted with the traditions which accrue over many years of operations will be somewhat at a disadvantage compared to young, more flexible companies. There should be a great rebirth of efficiency and initiative in the mining industry. It will attract brilliant engineers, for ocean mining will combine the romance of both oceanography and mining and will provide the engineer with the opportunity of working in a new, exciting and socially very worthwhile endeavor. Luck will be largely factored out as a means of getting rich in ocean mining. Initiative, good management, and hard work will be relatively much more important. Companies which are making or planning to make substantial investments in land sources of the metals which can be won from the nodules should very carefully investigate ocean mining, for their land mine investments could well be in serious jeopardy in the near future if the deep-sea nodules are successfully developed as they promise to be.

In the process of converting from land mining to ocean mining, of course, certain vested interests will be disadvantaged. But a much higher good for an infinitely greater number of people will be gained. It generally is so when great advances are made in the technology of producing material products or in the providing of mass services. The development of ocean mining will be one of the great industrial revolutions of modern world society, at least on a par with the development of the air transportation system of the world and its long-term effects on society should be equally great.

48

Seabed Mineral Resource Development: Recent Activities of the International Consortia

United Nations

INTRODUCTORY OVERVIEW OF DEEP-SEA MINING

The potato-shaped manganese nodules, rich in manganese, nickel, copper, cobalt, and other minerals, are known to be scattered over the ocean floor at depths of 3,000 to 6,000 meters. It is estimated that only about 15 percent of the seafloor (about 54 million km^2) is covered by nodules. The total volume of nodule resources meeting grade and abundance criteria for first generation mining may be on the order of 175 billion dry tons of nodules.

It should be noted, however, that the 175 billion dry tons of nodules represent only the theoretical maximum. A considerable portion of nodule resources may not be minable for reasons of topography or inadequate abundance in the minable area. Based on the definition of first-generation mine sites,[1] potential reserves are estimated to amount to 23 billion dry tons. This total amount can be translated into 290 million tons of nickel, 240 million tons of copper, 60 million tons of cobalt, and 6 billion tons of manganese.[2]

Table 1 compares the estimated potential reserves of manganese nodules with the land-based mineral reserve figures. It should be remembered that these categories are not strictly comparable, since land-based reserves exist in known or worked deposits, while no one has yet mined an ocean deposit. As an order of magnitude, however, nickel and cobalt contents in nodule "reserves" appear to be substantially larger than in land-based reserves.

Excerpt from "Seabed Mineral Resource Development: Recent Activities of the International Consortia" (United Nations, 1980). Pp. 1–8, 16.

TABLE 1 Comparison of Reserves from Land and Nodules: Nickel, Copper, Cobalt, and Manganese
(million tons metal content)

	Land-Based Reserves	Potential Nodule Reserves
Nickel	54	290
Copper	498	240
Cobalt	1.5	60
Manganese	5,440*	6,000

*Gross weight.

Source: For land-based reserve figures, U.S. Bureau of Mines, U.S. Department of the Interior, *Mineral Commodity Summaries, 1979* (Washington, D.C., U.S. Government Printing Office, 1978). Nodule reserve figures are based on Table 5 in Archer, *loc. cit.*

The complete system to transform the nodules into a commercially valuable form may be divided into three major components: mining, transportation, and processing. The mining system is composed of three components: collector, lift system, and surface system. Various collectors have been tested, both on land and at sea, on a reduced scale. Presently, it appears that the basic capability of collectors has been proven, although their operational feasibility has to be established, particularly at larger capacities.

With respect to the methods to raise the nodules collected at the bottom, two lift systems—airlift and hydrolift—are under consideration by all consortia, except for the Continuous Line Bucket (CLB) Group. A series of tests to date seem to indicate that the hydrolift system has an efficiency advantage. The hydrolift system, however, has an engineering disadvantage that arises from the use of moving, mechanical parts at great depths, whereas, in the airlift system, the air compressor is mounted on the mining ship.

Processing technology is also a key element for the economic viability of an operation. In commercial operations, the final selection of processing methods will depend on the results obtained from full-scale pilot-plant operations, as well as on decisions regarding which metals are to be recovered in what form.

One of the major concerns in international discussions is the possible economic impact of deep-sea mining on the land-based production. It is feared that an additional supply of metals recovered from the nodules may substantially reduce metal prices and revenues for land-based producers.

It is extremely difficult to estimate the magnitude of the likely impact of deep-sea mining on the markets of metals, because of the uncertainty associated with factors, including the size of each operation, the number of operations, the starting year of operations, and the growth rates of the total demand for the metals, among others. Nevertheless, according to various estimates and sensitivity studies, it appears that the possible impacts of deep-sea mining on the markets for cobalt, nickel, and manganese could be significant, while the impact on the copper market should be minimal.

Given this observation, the next question relates to examining countries which would be adversely affected by deep-sea mining. Countries which are presently major producers of nickel, copper, cobalt, or manganese for export would be adversely affected to the extent that their export earnings dropped as a result of price declines. Countries which were in the process of mine development at the time when additional metal supplies from nodules entered the market might experience financial problems from any price declines. Countries which contemplated exploiting smaller deposits before seabed mining became a reality might be described as being adversely affected. The brief survey below describes only major producing countries, since world mine production of nickel, cobalt, and manganese is concentrated in a few countries. Copper is not included in the following discussion because (1) world mine production of copper is relatively dispersed among countries, making a short treatment impossible; (2) even under very optimistic assumptions about future volumes of nodule production, the expected impact in the world copper market is relatively small.

The largest producer of nickel is Canada, accounting for about 30 percent, followed by the Union of Soviet Socialist Republics (17 percent), New Caledonia (15 percent), and Australia (11 percent). These four producers supplied almost three-quarters of the world mine production of nickel in 1977.

In the case of cobalt, Zaire is the world's leading producing country, accounting for more than one-third of the total production. Combined with the following three producers, namely, New Caledonia (14 percent), Australia (11 percent), and Zambia (7 percent), 67 percent of the world mine production of cobalt in 1978 originated from the top four producing countries.

The geographical concentration for manganese production is even more pronounced than that for nickel and cobalt. The top four producers accounted for 77 percent of the world's manganese production in 1978: the largest producer is the USSR (38 percent), followed by South Africa (23 percent), Gabon (8.4 percent) and India (8 percent).

If the distribution of mine production by the three economic groupings (developing, developed market economy, and centrally planned economy) is summarized, one finds that cobalt production is heavily concentrated in the developing countries (67 percent). On the other hand, 42 percent of nickel mine production originates from the developed market economies and 43 percent of manganese mine production originates from the centrally planned economies (see Table 2).

Examination of the geographical distribution of ore reserves reveals other features. Although the developed market economies currently produce 42 percent of the nickel ore, as compared with 34 percent from developing countries, 61 percent of nickel reserves are estimated to be in the developing countries.

The reserves of cobalt are even more heavily concentrated in the developing countries than is the distribution of current cobalt production. The developing countries account for 72 percent of the reserves, with the remainder divided between developed market economies (7 percent) and centrally planned economies (21 percent).

Half of the manganese reserves is estimated to be located in the centrally planned economies, primarily in the USSR, while the remaining half is concentrated in the developed market economies (43 percent, most of which is in South Africa), leaving only 7 percent in the developing countries (see Table 2).

It is well understood that actual developments of the potential nodule resources largely depend on the activities and decisions of the existing consortia. In this connection, the following two sections, which constitute the main body of the present report, focus on the identifica-

TABLE 2 Geographical Distribution of Mine Production and Ore Reserves—Nickel, Cobalt, and Manganese
(percentage)

	Nickel		Cobalt		Manganese	
	Mine Production	Ore Reserves	Mine Production	Ore Reserves	Mine Production	Ore Reserves
Developing countries	34*	61*	67	72	27	7
Developed market economies	42	23	21	7	30	43
Centrally planned economies	23†	16†	12	21	43	50

*Including Cuba.
†Excluding Cuba.

Source: For nickel see "Prospects for the Development of the Raw Materials Base for the Nickel Industry and the Demand for Nickel over the Next 10–15 Years" (E/C.7/102), 1978 estimates. For cobalt and manganese, see U.S. Bureau of Mines *op. cit.*, 1978 estimates.

tion of the major deep-sea mining consortia and on their recent research and development activities in various phases of deep-sea mining.

DEEP-SEA MINING INDUSTRY IN PERSPECTIVE

There are four commercially oriented consortia: the Kennecott Group, Ocean Mining Associates, Ocean Management, Inc., and the Ocean Minerals Company. In addition, France and Japan launched national programs: L'Association française pour l'étude et la recherche des nodules (AFERNOD) and the Deep Ocean Minerals Association (DOMA). Another international syndicate, the Continuous Line Bucket Group, was formed to develop the Continuous Line Bucket system.

The Kennecott Group

After 13 years of continued research and development on its own, Kennecott formed a partnership to conduct research and development on a large scale. The consortium, commonly called the Kennecott Group, was formed in January 1974, as an unincorporated joint venture. The original partners in the group were the Kennecott Copper Corporation (United States of America), Rio Tinto-Zinc Corporation, Ltd. (United Kingdom of Great Britain and Northern Ireland), Consolidated Gold Fields, Ltd. (United Kingdom), Noranda Mines, Ltd. (Canada), and the Mitsubishi Corporation (Japan). Later, it was joined by the British Petroleum Company, Ltd. (United Kingdom), making it a group consisting of six companies from four countries. Half of the budget has been borne by Kennecott, while the remainder is equally shared (10 percent each) by the other five companies.

The initial program called for a $50 million budget to be committed over a five-year period between 1974 and 1979. The period was divided into two phases: phase I (1974–75) was devoted to further exploration and research on mining and metallurgical processing techniques and phase IIA (1976–79) to engineering development of mining system components and the metallurgical processing system. The third phase, phase IIB, was to undertake large-scale prototype mining tests and to construct and operate a demonstration processing plant, both of which are essential steps before starting commercial operations.

A committee of representatives regularly meets and makes major decisions. Kennecott is the operator for the group. At the end of each phase, participants have the option to either remain or withdraw from the group.

The Kennecott Copper Corporation is engaged in development, production, and marketing of mineral resources, largely copper. It ranked fifth in copper mining capacities and third in refining capacities in the market economies in 1978. Noranda Mines, Ltd., of Canada is also principally engaged in mining and metallurgical activities. It accounted for 1 percent of world copper production and its refining capacity ranked sixth in the market economies in 1978.

Rio Tinto-Zinc and Consolidated Gold Fields are two large London-based international groups of mining and industrial companies. The activities of Rio Tinto-Zinc include significant production of aluminum, copper, gold, lead, and zinc. Consolidated Gold Fields is an international holding company with major interests in gold. The British Petroleum Company is one of the largest vertically integrated oil groups. The Mitsubishi Corporation is one of the leading general trading companies in Japan. Mitsubishi Heavy Industries, Ltd., and Mitsubishi Metal Corporation participate in the consortium through the Mitsubishi Corporation.

Ocean Mining Associates

This consortium evolved out of Deepsea Ventures, Inc., which started as a wholly owned subsidiary of Tenneco, Inc. (United States), in 1968. Deepsea Ventures, Inc., carried on the early efforts of its predecessor, Newport News Shipbuilding and Drydock Company. Tenneco decided to expand its pioneering work in manganese nodules by organizing a partnership. In May 1974, the group was first formed by Tenneco and Japanese Manganese Nodule Development Company (JAMCO), the latter consisting of five companies: Nichimen Company, Ltd., C. Itoh and Company, Ltd., Kanematsu-Gosho, Ltd. (all three are Japanese trading companies), Japan Metals and Chemicals, and Hitachi. In November of the same year, the group was joined by the United States Steel Corporation (United States) and Union Minière (Belgium).

Ocean Mining Associates (OMA) thus started with four companies with equal participation, to carry out research, development, and evaluation programs using Deepsea Ventures as a service contractor. This consortium, however, went through several changes in its composition. Tenneco and JAMCO withdrew from the group. United States Steel and Union Minière remained in the partnership, sharing the expenses equally until a third partner, Sun Company, Inc. (United States), was added in 1977. Under the present arrangement, three equal partners (33⅓ percent each) participate through their respective subsidiaries.

United States Steel is one of the largest steel manufacturing companies in the world. In addition to iron and coal mines, United States Steel owns 44 percent of interests of Compagnie Minière de l'Ogooue in Gabon for manganese ores. It also maintains minority ownerships in Ferroalloys, Ltd. (45 percent), for ferromanganese and Associated Manganese Mines of South Africa, Ltd. (20 percent), for manganese ores.

Union Minière, based in Brussels, undertakes international operations in the field of mining and metallurgy through numerous subsidiaries. Union Minière holds 45 percent shares of Métallurgie Hoboken-Overpelt S.A., whose copper refining capacity accounted for 3.9 percent of the total in the market economies in 1978.

Sun Company, Inc., is a nonoperating parent company with significant interests in oil and gas. Its subsidiaries operate in oil refining and marketing, concentrated in the United States and Canada.

Ocean Management, Inc.

Another multinational consortium, Ocean Management, Inc., was formed in February 1975, with Inco, Ltd., of Canada, the Deep Ocean Mining Company, Ltd. (DOMCO), of Japan, and Arbeitsgemeinschaft Meerestechnischgewinnbare Rohstoffe (AMR), of the Federal Republic of Germany. The group soon brought in a fourth partner, SEDCO, Inc., of the United States. Each partner equally contributed to a budget of approximately $40 million to be spent between 1975 and 1979.

All four partners had accumulated technical expertise in various phases of nodule mining prior to the formation of the consortium. Inco was one of the first companies to become interested in nodules, as early as 1959. The German consortium, AMR, has carried out extensive prospecting in the Pacific and Indian Oceans, using the sophisticated vessel *Valdivia.* The Sumitomo Group in DOMCO actively participated in the continuous line bucket [CLB] system tests. SEDCO also provided a crew to the mining test on the Blake Plateau conducted by Deepsea Ventures, Inc. in 1970.

Turning to the profiles of the participating groups, Inco, Ltd., is engaged in three principal lines of business: primary metals, batteries and dry cells, and formed metals. Inco Metals Company is a major operating unit of Inco, Ltd., and the leading producer of primary nickel in the world. Although its market share has eroded gradually over the past 20 years, Inco still provides 25 to 40 percent of nickel production in the market economies.

DOMCO was formed under the leadership of the Sumitomo Group for the purpose of participating in the consortium. It consists of 23 Japanese companies in a wide variety of fields. The shareholders include nine companies from the Sumitomo group, three other trading companies, two mining companies, two banks, and some manufacturing companies. The Sumitomo Group includes companies involved in the processing of nickel and copper and in shipbuilding.

AMR started with four German companies: Metallgesellschaft AG, Preussag AG, Salzgitter AG, and Rheinische Braunkohlenwerke AG, the latter withdrawing in 1976. Metallgesellschaft is engaged in the mining, refining, fabricating, and trading of metals. Preussag's business extends from production of nonferrous metals, coal, and petroleum to construction works. It is also engaged in the development of a mining and process system to exploit the Red Sea muds. Salzgitter AG, whose shares are wholly owned by the government of the Federal Republic of Germany, operates as a holding company in steelmaking, shipbuilding, and transportation.

SEDCO, Inc., primarily provides specialized services to the international petroleum industries, namely, contract drilling and support operation and pipeline construction. The drilling and support operations are principally performed offshore, using specially designed semisubmersible vessels and dynamically stationed drillships, one of which, SEDCO 445, was converted to a mining vessel for use by the consortium.

The Ocean Minerals Company

Under the leadership of the Lockheed Missiles and Space Company (United States), the Ocean Minerals Company (OMCO) was established in November 1977 in Mountain View, California. Technically, OMCO is a partnership between Amoco Ocean Minerals Company (a subsidiary of Standard Oil of Indiana) and Ocean Minerals, Inc., which is composed of the Lockheed Missiles and Space Company, Inc., Billiton B.V., and RBKW Ocean Minerals B.V. and the third partner, Lockheed Systems Company, Inc. (Lockheed's financial subsidiary), which joined OMCO in 1979. Lockheed Missiles and Space Company serves as a prime contractor, being responsible for technical aspects of the project. Other partners also send their experts to Lockheed. The exact percentage shares of the partners are not available, but it is believed that the combined United States interests (Lockheed and Standard Oil of Indiana) are in the range of 50 to 60 percent.

Lockheed Missiles and Space Company, Inc., is a wholly owned subsidiary of Lockheed Aircraft Corporation, whose interests are in aerospace equipment, ocean vessels, and petroleum-extracting equipment. Its diversification efforts to apply aerospace technology to the ocean has been going on for quite some time. Recently, it also became active in ocean thermal energy conversion (OTEC) technology.

Billiton B. V. is one of the numerous operating companies under the Royal Dutch/Shell Group, one of the largest international oil majors. Located in the Hague, Netherlands, it has an equity interest in the worldwide production of bauxite, lead, zinc, and tin.

Royal Bos Kalis Westminster Group N.V., which is a parent company of RBKW Ocean Minerals, grew out of a dredging company to become a public works contractor with worldwide activities. It is engaged mainly in dredging, pipelaying, and civil engineering, particularly dock and harbor facilities.

The Standard Oil Company of Indiana is a large integrated petroleum and chemical company that conducts operations on a worldwide basis. Amoco Minerals Company, one of its wholly owned subsidiaries, is engaged in exploration of mineral deposits.

L'Association française pour l'étude et la recherche des nodules

L'Association française pour l'étude et la recherche des nodules (AFERNOD) is an association between French government agencies and private industry. It started first in 1974 with Le Centre national pour l'exploitation des océans (CNEXO), La Société métallurgique le nickel (SLN), and Le Commissariat à l'énergie atomique (CEA). The first two were involved in the test of the continuous line bucket system in French Polynesia in 1972, and this experience eventually led to the formation of the association to develop the mining and processing methods for nodules.

At the end of 1975, AFERNOD was joined by Chantiers de France-Dunkerque and then in January 1977 by Bureau de recherches géologiques et minières (BRGM). Thus, AFERNOD is currently composed of three government agencies and two private companies.

The Deep Ocean Minerals Association

Established in March 1974, in Tokyo, Japan, Deep Ocean Minerals Association (DOMA) promotes the development of deep-sea manganese nodules for the national interest. Although it is not a government organization, it maintains close contacts with the Japanese government, and its activities are financed substantially by the government. DOMA consists of 35 leading Japanese companies as members, including mining, general trading, shipbuilding, and steelmaking companies. About one-third of its 35 members also have interests in DOMCO, which is a participant in another consortium with Inco, AMR, and SEDCO. Three companies from the Mitsubishi group which belong to this consortium also participate in the Kennecott group.

The Continuous Line Bucket Syndicate

In 1966, Commander Y. Masuda of Japan invented a cable-bucket system to mine the nodules. A series of tests resulted in the formation of an international syndicate in 1972 by some 20 companies from six countries, namely, Australia, Canada, France, Germany (Federal Republic of), Japan, and the United States. The group includes a number of companies which participate in the other consortia, such as United States Steel

(United States), the AMR group (Federal Republic of Germany), CNEXO (France), Inco and Noranda Mines (Canada), and DOMCO (Japan).

THE OUTLOOK FOR DEEP-SEA MINING INDUSTRY

Based on information presented in the previous section, the general picture of the deep-sea mining industry may be summarized as follows: It is felt that the extensive exploration activities of the consortia have resulted in the identification of potential nodule deposits which could be exploited as first-generation mine sites in the North Pacific Ocean. Regarding the processing techniques, metallurgical problems of recovering metals from nodules have been essentially solved. Concern is now focused on economic and operational feasibility rather than on the technical capability. A series of tests of small-scale plants have narrowed the number of possible processing routes, most of which are based on the hydrometallurgical technique.

Some of the consortia have already tested their mining systems (the collector, lifting system, and the mining vessel) at sea and have succeeded in raising nodules from a depth of around 5,000 meters. The capability of each component of the mining system has been more or less proven, although the capacity of the collector has to be scaled up five times or more in commercial operation. The reliability and maintainability of the coordinated mining system appear to be the important unknowns to be resolved in the future.

After the scaled-down mining systems were proven to be workable, the next step is the construction and testing of prototype mining equipment and processing plants. The tests of the prototype mining system over extended time periods should assure its reliability and maintainability. The larger demonstration plants should be run to process nodules on a continual basis. More detailed exploration work, including mapping, will be required on the potential mine sites. All these activities will demand substantially larger capital expenditure than what the preliminary research and development work up to now has required. As a result, a substantial slowdown of the research and development work was recently announced by the major consortia, which have been considered as industry forerunners.

None of consortia have discontinued their joint activities completely. Since their decisions to slow down current work, no participant has withdrawn from any of the major consortia. It is, therefore, clear that reactivation or disintegration of joint activities by the deepsea mining consortia will largely depend on the future development of international and/or national legal regimes and on the future outlook in the world metal markets.

NOTES

1. A first-generation mine site is described as an area where the average combined nickel and copper content is about 2.3 percent and the average abundance of nodules is about 10 (wet) kg/m^2, and from which about 60 million tons of such nodules can be recovered.

2. Alan A. Archer, "Resources and potential reserves of nickel and copper in manganese nodules," *Manganese Nodules: Dimensions and Perspectives* . . . , p. 77. The figures represent metal contents, assuming 1.26 percent of the average nickel grade, 1.03 percent of copper, 0.25 percent of cobalt and 27.5 percent of manganese.

49

The Developing Countries and the Exploitation of the Deep Seabed

M.C.W. Pinto

> The meek shall inherit the earth,
> but not its mineral rights
>
> —Attributed to J. Paul Getty

> The Area and its resources are the
> common heritage of mankind
>
> —Draft Convention on the Law
> of the Sea, article 136

An eminent international lawyer once observed that the more practical among us

> know from life that men live by their visions and that, while an imperfect vision may lead astray, where there is no vision the people perish.

So wrote the late C. Wilfred Jenks in a brief essay on "Idealism in International Law," which appeared shortly before his death. This essay is about two of the great visions or idealistic movements of the last decade, perhaps of all time: first, the "common heritage of mankind," and second, the "new international economic order." It will first deal with the "common heritage" concept in relation to the resources of the seabed beyond national jurisdiction, and then try to show how principles of the

---

Reprint of "The Developing Countries and the Exploitation of the Deep Seabed," by M.C.W. Pinto, in the *Columbia Journal of World Business* (Vol. 15, No. 4, Winter 1980). Pp. 30–38, 40–41.

new international economic order have influenced the "common heritage" concept as it has evolved at the Conference on the Law of the Sea. In doing so it attempts to present a generalized perspective of the developing countries in the current negotiations concerning the treaty regime to govern the exploration and exploitation of the deep seabed.

THE THIRD UNITED NATIONS CONFERENCE ON THE LAW OF THE SEA

From the earliest times, the sea has offered man vast resources of food, wealth, and power. Man's response to the challenge to take advantage of these resources was, until recently, limited only by his extractive capacity, by the level of technical skill he could command at any particular time for the purpose of locating and utilizing them. The rapid development of marine skills, particularly navigation and fishing, within a few countries in Western Europe led them not only to dreams of limitless riches and the belief that marine resources everywhere were theirs for the taking, but also to the belief that those resources were themselves inexhaustible. The stage was set for emergence of the concept that became known as the "freedom of the seas," a concept which implied that the seas and their resources were open to use and exploitation by all countries without distinction. What was ignored, by focusing on a notional equality, or lack of legal distinction among the nations was, of course, the existence of the factual distinction that only a handful of states had the technical skill and financial capacity to take advantage of this grant concept. This freedom made the high seas an exclusive arena for the competitive aspirations of nations with large merchant and military fleets. It was complemented by their insistence that the breadth of the sea areas adjacent to coastlines, conceded to be within the jurisdiction of the coastal state, should remain narrow, say three miles in extent, thus maximizing the area available for their purposes.

To the vast majority of nations, then in a dormant or quiescent period of a cyclic history, this "freedom of the seas" had little positive significance. The concept could last only so long as populations were relatively small or inadequately organized, and their demands for food and other resources from the sea correspondingly weak. To communities subjected to hegemonic influences and occupied with the business of survival, the sea's challenge remained at a primitive level, and widening awareness of the sea's wealth and potentialities remained within the capacity of only a few countries. With the phenomenal increase in populations, and the reemergence into the mainstream of international life of numbers of so-called "new" states, came the spread, however slow, of awareness of that wealth, and correspondingly the demand for an equitable opportunity to participate in the process of winning and sharing it.

We pass over, with great respect, the community's efforts to codify the law of the sea at the Hague Conferences in 1930, and at the first and second United Nations Conferences on the Law of the Sea in 1958 and 1960. Theirs was a contribution of inestimable value in the evolution of the law, and the social and political thought that shaped it. But Malta's initiative at the United Nations in 1967, and the drive towards a comprehensive conference on the oceans which it triggered, was nothing less than epoch-making. It brought about a historic and perhaps even apocalyptic division of time. With the focus on the oceans and their resources generated by and through the Third United Nations Conference on the Law of the Sea, man's view of the planet and his relationship to it will never be quite the same. The mass of information on the oceans and their resources, released and disseminated on an unprecedented scale by the conference, increased and sharpened as never before the level of awareness and interest of decision makers and public alike. To the newly independent countries, the conference not only conveyed anew, and amplified, the timeless challenge of the oceans; it also provided them, for the first time in history, with a forum in which their demand for the opportunity to participate in the acceptance of that challenge, and their claim to share equitably in the oceans' wealth, could be demonstrated, urged in a coordinated and efficient manner, and ultimately secured—not as a matter of chance or charity, but as a matter of legal right.

The manifestation of this demand shows two basic aspects. First, developing countries with coastlines of any magnitude sought to increase their national jurisdiction, at least for resource exploitation and regulatory purposes, beyond the confines of a "territorial sea" which they had been encouraged to think was necessarily narrow according to some preordained natural scheme of things. Second, all developing countries sought to participate in the control of activities in areas beyond their national jurisdiction in order to ensure that resources in which they perceived a particular or communal interest would not be exploited ruthlessly for selfish ends but rather on a rational and equitable basis without waste, with the needs of the whole community in mind. In addition, their right to exploit those resources on an equal footing would not be annulled or subverted by excessive and destructive exploitation by transnational companies or state enterprises which might enjoy a temporary technological advantage at any given period, and that the technology which had been developed within a few societies would be spread to all countries on fair terms so as to enable them to make a reality of the right of participation which they claimed. From the first of these aspects derives the concept of the exclusive economic zone; from the second, the idea of joint management of resources outside national jurisdiction: the idea that the decisions concerning the best interests of the community should not be taken by a select few, but by the community as a whole. In the case of living resources this meant a system, largely fragmented, of collective fishery management. In the case of nonliving resources (mainly the mineral wealth of the deep seabed), it meant recognition of the basic principles of a "common heritage of mankind" to be managed on a cooperative basis through a new International Seabed Authority with comprehensive powers.

THE SEABED BEYOND NATIONAL JURISDICTION AND ITS RESOURCES AS THE COMMON HERITAGE OF MANKIND

Resolution 2749 (XXV) of the General Assembly of the United Nations, adopted without dissent in 1970, declared the area of the seabed and the ocean floor beyond the limits of national jurisdiction, as well as the resources of that area, to be the "common heritage of mankind." The content of the Declaration of Principles, as it came to be known, is too familiar to be recounted here. But it is useful to recall the understanding of the overwhelming number of states of the world community as to the interpretation of the "common heritage" concept, and further, the fact that to them the principles contained in the declaration, were binding on all states as principles of customary international law.

For the overwhelming majority of states, the Declaration of Principles proclaims the community's recognition that the deep seabed and its resources had a reasonably clear though evolving legal status. The area and its resources were the "common heritage of mankind." This meant, inter alia, that the minerals of the area could not be freely mined. They were not there, so to speak, for the taking. The common heritage of mankind was the common property of mankind. The commonness of the "common heritage" is a commonness of ownership and benefit. In their original location, the resources of the area belong in undivided and indivisible share, to all countries—to all mankind, in fact, whether organized as states or not. "Touch the nodules at the bottom of the sea," they seemed to say, "and you touch my property. Take them away, and you take away my property."

It followed, therefore, that before anyone could mine the nodules from the bottom of the sea, mankind must have consented to the system chosen for doing so. It was so because the community as a whole had agreed in 1970 that this was the absolute, fundamental rule of the game. This was in fact the law, and states have been engaged for some ten years under aegis of the United Nations in trying to decide what method or system of resource taking should have mankind's approval. If this were not generally agreed to be the case, then states had rather pointlessly paid out a lot of money and spent a lot of time and energy over these years in an effort to establish an international regime which gave effect to the fundamental rule of the common heritage of mankind.

But all states did agree in 1970 that "All activities regarding the exploration and exploitation of the resources of the area . . . shall be governed by the international regime to be established." And they agreed that "the international regime . . . shall be established by an international treaty." They agreed that this treaty shall be "of a universal character" and that it should be agreed upon by the community in general, not by a handful of states, or even by a substantial number of them. The words of the Declaration of Principles of 1970 were there to prove it.

And so this appeared to foreclose for a large number of countries one of the major alternatives considered by some states from time to time: national regimes or systems of seabed mining. To such regimes the generality of states had not consented; for the generality of states was still in search of an "international regime" to include in its "international treaty" having already invested ten years in the process. They felt that national regimes were excluded by the declaration's very definite insistence on an "international regime." They were reluctant to go out there and mine on any basis, national or international, which had not the authority of a treaty "generally agreed upon." If they were to take the nodules, they would be taking another's property. They did not want to preempt the community through establishing a regime of their own, when the community had shown how particular, how selective, it could be by withholding its approval for a regime for the past ten years. They did not want to take the law into their own hands.

Thus, for many countries, the legal status of the resources of the deep seabed itself forbids mining under unilaterally developed individual or group regimes however well-intentioned, efficient, or designed to fit in and coalesce with some future internationally agreed regime. For those countries the "common heritage" of these resources is not *res nullius,* to be had for the taking; is not *res communis* simply for enjoyment or use in common; it is more akin to property held in trust—held in trust for "mankind as a whole," for the public. In this it resembles most closely the *res publicae,* that concept of Roman public law that held certain things to be *in patrimonio populi* and subject to administration by the state on behalf of the people. In the Roman concept *res publicae* belonged to the people while in their original location. They could become the subject of private ownership, but only after an act of conversion had taken place. Over such actions the state, as administrator, maintained control, taxing the taker for what he was appropriating for his own patrimony out of patrimony of the people. The parallel is even clearer when one recalls that the declaration, reflecting the views of all, calls for the establishment of "international machinery," a new intergovernmental organization, as an integral element of the "common heritage" concept. Such an organization must administer the exploration and exploitation of the resources of the seabed on behalf of mankind as a whole. Without such an authority, such activities would be inconsistent with the "common heritage" concept, and therefore in contravention of the rules of customary international law reflected in the declaration.

THE NEW INTERNATIONAL ECONOMIC ORDER

The "common heritage" concept was already more than three years old, and its elaboration far advanced, when the second of the two great visions was brought into focus by the world community. On May 1, 1974, the General Assembly at its Sixth Special Session adopted Resolution 3201, the Declaration on the Establishment of the New International Economic Order. That declaration has since been the inspiration and universal guide for all of the developing countries in multilateral negotiations on global economic issues. Although it contains no specific mention of the "common heritage," many of the declaration's provisions reflect ideas which had already been canvassed in negotiations on the international treaty regime to govern exploration and exploitation of the deep seabed. The focus given by the Declaration on the New International Economic Order now clarified and gave fresh impetus to the positions adopted by the developing countries at the Conference on the Law of the Sea.

Many provisions of the Declaration on the New International Economic Order correspond directly with positions held to be fundamental by the developing countries in negotiating a treaty regime for the deep seabed. They are referred to individually or in groups in the following pages to demonstrate the extent to which these positions have been accommodated in the draft treaty text nearing completion within the Conference on the Law of the Sea. These provisions fall broadly into two categories: those which are essentially operational, i.e., relate to the mechanics of a seabed mining regime; and those which are essentially organizational, i.e., relate more to political and institutional goals. Such a division is, of course, more for convenience of presentation, since no clear distinction is possible.

OPERATIONAL ELEMENTS

> *NIEO Principles:* (1) interdependence of members of the world community; (2) the duty of international cooperation for economic development; (3) active assistance to the developing countries by the whole community (para. 4[k]); and (4) preferential treatment for developing countries.

This group of fundamental principles, the aim of which is to provide assistance to the poor countries to secure their rapid economic development, is reflected in several ways in part XI of the Draft Convention. Here we shall deal with only two, viz., the Enterprise, and payments to and sharing of benefits by the Authority.

Unique among the organs of the new International Seabed Authority, and indeed, among those of the existing intergovernmental organizations, is the Enterprise, the operational arm of the Authority. Provided with the requisite finance and technology by the industrialized countries in its initial years, the organ of the Authority will carry out seabed mining processing to the metal stage, and marketing, with a view to making profits for the community as a whole. Conceived by the developing countries as early as 1971, the Enterprise represents in the highest degree, the principles of cooperation and interdependence upon which the new international economic order is based. The concept of seabed mining on a cooperative basis was at first rejected by the industrialized countries. They claimed, with some justification, that there would be little likelihood of such a venture functioning efficiently, if judgment were to be based on the performance of most existing intergovernmental organizations. Creating such an organ would mean creating a competitor for their own mining companies, and to give it the special privileged treatment that was being sought, would give rise to unfair competition contrary to their free market system.

Legally speaking, the Enterprise is something of a paradox. Structurally, it is declared to be an integral part of the Authority—an "organ of the Authority." And yet it is granted substantial autonomy in the performance of its functions, which are to carry out exploration and mining operations, and also prospecting, transportation, processing to the metal stage and marketing. It is one of the Authority's organs which clearly has functions and responsibilities that transcend the geographical limits of "The Area." As an organ of the Authority, on the other hand, it is made subject to the directives of the Council, and the members of its Governing Board and its chief executive officer, the director general, are elected by the Assembly on the recommendation of the Council.

The Enterprise is not, however, a mere commercial venture from which great financial benefits are to be expected. The return from investment in the Enterprise is not to be assessed or measured in purely financial terms. Its unique value lies elsewhere: as a funnel for the transfer of technology to the developing countries to enable and hasten their participation in seabed mining. Perhaps later it will act as a leader in the entire field of seabed technological development and marketing. But most importantly it is the first universally negotiated, agreed and implemented cooperative operational endeavor to which each country will contribute according to its capacity, and each will receive according to its needs. It is in these respects that the Enterprise represents the most significant step yet taken toward the establishment of a new international economic order.

Precisely for the reason that the Enterprise is an unique human endeavor, and perhaps the forerunner of others of the same character, the developing countries have sought to place it in a special position in relation to other seabed miners. The provisions of the convention are designed to ensure that it will receive technology and finance. The antimonopoly clause will not apply to its operations, nor to its selection of partners. The developing countries urged that the Enterprise pay no tax to any country on its income, property, assets, or transactions. This idea was resisted by the industrialized countries which argued that, while the Enterprise may in fact be unique, it would be contrary to principle to grant it such an advantage over its competitors in the seabed mining business. Further, they argued that the normal fiscal requirement of a tax on income would impose a discipline that could only enhance the efficiency, and ultimately the profitability of the Enterprise. And finally that it would be extremely difficult to secure the agreement of the fiscal authorities in most countries to a tax exemption of this kind. The current text therefore does not provide for immunity from taxation, but requires the Enterprise to negotiate for tax exemption in countries in which its offices and facilities are located, and allows states to discriminate in favor of the Enterprise in the matter of immunities of all kinds. The Enterprise will not, however, be immune from legal process.

All seabed miners are required to make payments to the Authority. The most recent revision of the Draft Convention applies this principle to the Enterprise as well, but grants it a "tax holiday" of ten years. The payments to be made by miners reflect the community's current assessment of what must be paid for conversion of what is owned and held in common, to the miner's individual use and benefit. It is related to the proportion that the value of unconverted resource bears to the value of the processed metal. The calculation of payments now set forth in Article 12 of Annex III appears to provide sufficient options to satisfy miners from different social and economic systems, and sufficient flexibility to take into account the vicissitudes that might attend early operations in a new industry conducted in a hostile and changeable environment. While the levels of payment are still the subject of negotiation, the system appears to be on the way to acceptance by all the negotiators.

The developing countries took the position that the Enterprise should be exempt from making payments to the Authority for two basic reasons: first, the unique character and social goals of the Enterprise as representing all mankind, and not merely one or a handful of states; and second, that the Authority has in any case the power to determine what portion of the net income of the Enterprise should be transferred to it, so that payment of a "tax" like other miners was superfluous. Negotiations will continue on this point, but it seems unlikely that this latter view will prevail.

While there are estimates of possible levels of revenues accruing to the Authority in the first 20 years of seabed mining operations, they show considerable divergence. Little thought has been given to the method by which financial benefits could be shared "equitably." In a recent unpublished study of the possible level of income, Dr. Alfredo Boucher of Argentina makes the following assumptions: (1) level and characteristics of production according to the original MIT model; (2) development and operational costs according to the Aachen model; (3) prices of metals (nickel, copper, cobalt) at December 1979 levels; (4) use of the so-called "mixed system" and commencement of the second period under that system in the sixth year; (5) no further difficulties in negotiating the treaty or delays in its entry into force; (6) no major changes in technology or market conditions; (7) commercial production commencing in 1990; (8) the operation of five mine sites, together with one operated by the Enterprise at the same level of profitability, and making the same payments to the Authority as the others, totaling six mining operations in 1995; and finally, that three or more sites will come into production between 1995 and 2000 so that the Authority would be receiving income from a total of nine operations by that time. On these assumptions he arrives at the following figures:

1st to 5th year — U.S. $37,080,000/year
6th to 20th year — U.S. $53,090,000/year
totaling U.S. $981,750,000 per site over the 20-year period.

Taking into account six sites on this basis, and three others commencing between 1995 and 2000, he estimates an average annual income for the Authority during the first 20 years of commercial production at U.S. $333,720,000.

Systems of "equitable" distribution which the Assembly might apply are generally likely to employ a combination of the accepted indicators such as per capita gross national product, level of protein consumption or caloric consumption, life expectancy, number of doctors per unit of the population, level of literacy, per capita energy consumption, and others. It may be possible to arrive at an index of need on this basis. On the other hand, the income estimates are of such a level as to suggest its distribution is unlikely to have a dramatic impact on the economy of any country. Dr. Boucher suggests that rather than actually provide for the distribution of the Authority's income, the term "sharing" should be interpreted as contemplating a scheme whereby these funds should be used to finance special coordinated programs useful to mankind as a whole, but oriented substantially toward assistance to the developing countries, and among these, particularly the least developed. On this interpretation, each state would forego its right to collect its share of the income, and in so doing permit the maximizing of the financial benefits accruing to the community as a whole. As on any projection, it is likely that the Authority will have no income in its first few years, and that the buildup thereafter will be slow. The matter of distribution may await developments which would form a realistic basis for evolving a system specific to contemporary needs.

While equitable sharing of financial benefits in the sense of allocation of a share, notionally or in fact, to each state, is a matter of interest to the developing countries, it will not be the only call on the income of the Authority. The present draft specifies that the administrative expenses of the Authority shall be the first call on the funds of the Authority. Presumably these expenses will be met from regular subscriptions by member states. Article 173 lists three other payments which are to be made out of the Authority's funds, viz.:

(a) income to be shared, as discussed above;
(b) funds for the initial financing of the Enterprise; and
(c) funds to be used for compensating developing countries whose economies are adversely affected by metals coming on the market as a result of seabed mining.

The present text of Article 173 assigns no priority to these calls on the Authority's funds. If it is intended to apply from the start, this provision should either specify a priority or require an organ of the Authority to do so. It would seem that among these three, compensation to adversely affected developing countries might claim first place, and funding of the Enterprise second, with distribution or allocation ("sharing") being last.

Financial benefits are not, of course, the only benefits "derived from the Area" which can be shared, although such benefits come most readily to mind. Other benefits which are to be shared are the technology (dealt with separately below), technological derivatives or "spin-offs" from the development of mining technology, the results of scientific research in the area, and the greater availability of minerals. As to technology derivatives and the results of scientific research, the Authority can and should play a significant role through ensuring the widest possible dissemination of such knowledge pursuant to Articles 143, 144, 256, 273, and 274. As to sharing of the benefit of an enhanced production of minerals, little or nothing has been said. Title to minerals may be expected to pass to the miner, and out of the Authority's jurisdiction, upon recovery from the seabed. These minerals will remain within the disposition of the miner, and may thus be expected to benefit mainly, and almost exclusively, the economies of the industrialized countries. The minerals recovered by the Enterprise are to be sold "on a non-discriminatory basis," and the Enterprise is directed "not to give commercial discounts." Some relaxation of this provision may enable the developing countries to share in the greater availability of metals, by receiving them on concessional terms whenever the Enterprise can make them available without impairing its own sound business position.

NIEO Principles: Just and equitable relationship between prices of exports (raw materials) from developing countries, and prices of imports by them; and facilitating the role of producers' associations.

Of critical importance to those developing countries which are dependent on exports of nickel, copper, and cobalt for the stability of their economies was the need to ensure that production of minerals in quantity from the seabed did not depress prices and thereby adversely affect their export earnings. This cause, vital only to a few, was supported by all the developing countries as a matter of political solidarity which had collective advantages which spread beyond the confines of the conference to all negotiations where the maintenance of remunerative commodity prices were an issue. As the result of initiatives taken by the so-called land-based producer countries and backed by all developing countries, the Draft Convention in its current revision contains substantially negotiated taxes on policies relating to activities in the Area and production policies.

Article 150 lists the goals toward which production policies must be directed, and in doing so attempts to balance the interests of the industrialized consumer countries and of the developing countries that are land-based metal producers. Thus, the requirement that seabed production be so ordered as to ensure that prices for the metals concerned remain "just and stable" and "remunerative to producers" is balanced by the requirement of "promoting equilibrium between supply and demand" in regard to those metals. The requirement that policies ensure protection of developing countries from adverse effects on their economies or on their export earnings resulting from a reduction in the price of an affected mineral . . . etc.," is balanced by the requirement that the availability of the minerals produced from the resources of the area be increased as needed "to ensure supplies to consumers of such minerals." Neither consumers nor producers would seem to have the edge in Article 150.

Article 151, however, is designed to protect developing country land-based producers of the metals concerned. The essential principle is that seabed mining must always be treated as supplementary to land-based mining, on which the economies of some developing countries depend. Article 151 in its present form provides for the periodic establishment of production ceilings for ocean mining in general and polymetallic nodule mining in particular. In relation to nodule mining, using the nickel content of nodules as the indicator, it specifies a calculation by which to arrive at the maximum tonnage to be produced, and correspondingly the maximum number of sites to be mined assuming an output of 40,000 tons of nickel per site per year. Again in relation to nodule mining, it establishes a minimum guaranteed tonnage for production in order to safeguard the interests of investors in the nodule mining industry. Finally Article 151 provides for a system of compensation to developing countries that are land-based producers in the event that seabed mining results in an adverse impact on their economies despite the imposition of the ceiling. These protective arrangements are to come into force on the date when the earliest commercial production of seabed minerals commences. They are to remain for a period of 25 years or until the end of the Review Conference provided for in Article 155 or until the date of entry into force of new commodity arrangements providing adequate safeguards for land-based producers, whichever date occurs earliest. Even after entry into force of protective commodity arrangements, the Authority has the power, if those arrangements were to lapse or become ineffective, to resume its own protective role under the convention.

Little consideration has, as yet, been given to the subject of compensation for adverse economic effects, and the method by which the export earnings of affected developing countries might be stabilized. The Draft Convention would require the Economic Planning Commission to propose a system of compensation to the Council for submission to the Assembly; and after adoption by the Assembly, to make recommendations to the Council regarding application of the system in specific cases. Opinions differ as to whether and to what extent land-based producers will be affected. Cobalt producers, it is claimed, are likely to be affected early. Two schemes of compensation could provide considerable guidance: one operated by the International Monetary Fund, the other under the Lomé Convention. What would appear to be needed for a start would be the establishment of a "reference level" of export earnings in relation to which any shortfall or loss in export earnings is to be determined; definition of the terms and conditions of access to a Compensation Fund; definition of the particular objectives for which the funds could be applied, i.e., the type of economic adjustment contemplated; the source of funds: developed consumer countries, operators in the area, the Authority; and finally the eligibility of states to receive assistance from the fund, including a restriction to developing countries and provision for a measure of discriminatory treatment in favor of the least developed.

The Draft Convention thus recognizes the rights of the producer countries collectively to safeguard their interests, and provides both for control of production from the new source, and a system of compensation in the event of adverse economic effects. The collective rights of these countries are also recognized in the production policies specified in Article 150; the establishment and operation of commodity arrangements provided for in Article 151 para. 1; the functions of the Economic Planning Commission; the composition (and, thus perhaps indirectly in the decision-making procedure) of the Council; and finally, in the policies governing the adoption of rules, regulations, and procedures which will spell out the financial incentives to seabed miners, ensuring that the latter will not be at an "artificially competitive advantage relative to land-based miners."

> *NIEO Principles:* Giving developing countries access to the achievements of science and technology; promoting the transfer of technology to the developing countries.

The obligation to give the developing countries access to the achievements of modern science and technology, and to facilitate, as far as possible, the rapid transfer of technology to them, is one of the pivotal aspects of the new international economic order. Through such technological advancement the developing countries seek to gain for themselves the tools needed for their rapid industrialization; to free themselves from dependence on the transnational corporations, or to be able to deal with them from a position of relative strength; to be able to add value, through processing, to their own raw materials; and eventually to radically alter the international division of labor which has cast them for decades in the role of suppliers of primary commodities. This same concern is shown by the developing countries at the Conference on the Law of the Sea. Through their initiative the Draft Convention now provides that every seabed miner must, under contract with the Authority, undertake to transfer to the Enterprise and to developing countries on demand, the technology it uses in its own operations on "fair and reasonable commercial terms and conditions." In addition where such technology is owned by others, it must obtain written assurances from them that on demand they will similarly transfer this technology under license or other arrangement on "fair and reasonable commercial terms and conditions" and, at the request of the Enterprise, to acquire, or facilitate through direct negotiation with the owner, acquisition of, this technology. It is also provided that where technology for either mining or processing cannot be obtained by the Enterprise on fair and reasonable commercial terms and conditions in a timely manner, the Council or the Assembly will convene a group of states which are obliged to "take effective measures to ensure that such technology is made available" to the Enterprise. "Technology" is defined to mean:

> the specialized equipment and technical know-how, including manuals, designs, operating instructions, training and technical advice and assistance, necessary to assemble, maintain and operate a viable system and the legal right to use these items for that purpose on a non-exclusive basis.

By implication, this definition covers processing technology as well as mining technology.

Dispute settlement procedures are prescribed, as well as extralegal coercive devices, aimed at making the transfer as mandatory as practicable. Other such procedures and devices may be discussed as the negotiations proceed. However, the relationships between the parties concerned, viz., the Authority, the contractor, the third party owner of technology, and the Enterprise, are such as to make a truly mandatory and legally enforceable system virtually impossible to devise at the present time. At least the concept, the need, and a rudimentary system will have been, perhaps for the first time, agreed and incorporated in a multilateral agreement.

In addition to the specific requirements of Article 5 of Annex III, general obligations on the transfer of seabed mining technology are contained in Articles 144, 273, and 274. These provisions require the Authority to play a central role in the acquisition, development, and transfer of technology and scientific knowledge to the Enterprise and the developing countries.

The initiative of the developing countries has also resulted in the inclusion in the Draft Convention of provisions concerning scientific research, and the dissemination of scientific information concerning the area and its resources. Article 143 declares that marine scientific research in the area shall be carried out only for peaceful purposes and so as to benefit mankind as a whole, while Article 256 confers on all states and international organizations the legal right to carry out scientific research in the area. Here, too, the Authority is given a central role. Not only will it carry out marine scientific research, but also "promote and encourage the conduct of marine scientific research in the area and . . . co-ordinate and disseminate the results of such research and analysis when available, and secure the development of programs designed to strengthen the research capabilities of the technologically less developed countries as well as the developing countries, and train their personnel."

NIEO Principle: prevention of waste of natural resources.

Little is said in the Declaration on the New International Economic Order in regard to environmental issues, and it is in this paragraph that it comes closest to a statement of principle. The Plan of Action calls upon all states to refrain from damaging or causing deterioration in natural resources, especially those derived from the sea, by preventing pollution and taking appropriate steps to protect and reconstitute those resources. The Draft Convention contains both general provisions as well as provisions specific to seabed mining concerning the protection of the environment. Article 150 on policies relating to activities in the area prohibits "unnecessary waste" as being inconsistent with the orderly development and rational management of the resources of the area.

The attitudes of the developing countries have been ambivalent in regard to protection of the environment generally. In discussions of the subject in the early 1970s, there was a tendency to treat environmental questions as a problem essentially for the industrialized countries, which had caused the problem and had become rich in the process. It was even suggested that the environmental issue had been raised by the developed countries as a means of delaying the industrialization of the developing countries by making that process more expensive, e.g., in demanding through international rules the application of new technological devices to prevent pollution. The developing countries regarded their relatively clear environmental conditions as a natural resource which they had the right to exploit. Some even encouraged the import of pollutive industries in an effort to increase productivity. These attitudes have now changed, and the consciousness of environmental concerns, although not yet given as much emphasis as among the industrialized countries, appears universal. Of particular concern are the environmental effects on fishing of mineral resource recovery systems through disturbance of the sediments of the deep seabed, and the methods of disposal of unprecedented tonnages of potentially toxic tailings associated with nodule processing. . . .

This essay has attempted to review the principal concerns of the developing countries as expressed by them at the Conference on the Law of the Sea, and to do so in such a way as to demonstrate how those concerns are consistent with their more general political and economic objectives as formulated in the Declaration on the Establishment of a New International Economic Order. It has attempted to assess in very general terms, the extent to which the developing countries have, thus far, been successful in moving toward the establishment of such a new order through negotiations in one field: a new order for the oceans. It has attempted to assess whether two of the world's great visions are any closer to realization. Progress toward economic and social goals has been appreciable in the context of the new order of the oceans. The meek may not yet be ready to inherit the earth, but at least much has been done to prepare the way, and to try to ensure that what they eventually succeed to will not be a *damnum hereditas.*

50

The Economics of the Ocean and Ecological Equilibrium

The business of protecting man against the elemental forces of nature, (tsunami, storms at sea, catastrophic flooding of rivers, drought, earthquakes, forest fires, torrential rain gales, etc.) has not yet been taken off the agenda, but a new problem has been added, that of protecting nature from the damage done to it by people.

Mankind has been increasing some natural "production capacities" for ages. Let us recall the raising of the yield of land, the opening up of virgin lands, the increase in the numbers of cattle, the growth in the productivity of stockraising, the draining of swamps, and the irrigation of deserts.

Yet, the high development rates in industry and transport, the destruction of great forests to increase the area of arable and meadow, the extremely intensive exploitation of land and the progressing erosion of the soil caused by these processes, and the urbanization of life in its modern forms often lead to serious, sometimes irreversible deterioration of the environment. Over the past 500 years man has destroyed up to two-thirds of the world's forests. Scientists estimate that the land destroyed by erosion is now equal to half of all the tilled area of the world.

Production systems, as a rule, give a comparatively low useful yield. The bulk of the primary material is discarded as waste and scrap. These phenomena used to be ignored, and the warnings of individual scientists seemed unjustified. Their correctness is now clear to everyone. In some countries there are symptoms of an ecological crisis, that show that nature cannot put up with everything.

Reprint of "The Economics of the Ocean and Ecological Equilibrium," Chapter 6 in *Ocean and Its Resources* (Moscow: Progress Publishers, 1979). Pp. 124–39.

Ecologists, however, have not yet determined the "breaking points" that nature can withstand, while economists continue to pay little attention to ecological consequences. The time has come to develop ecological economies, or eco-economics. Economists ought to pay attention to the ceiling of the natural environment's vulnerability and its capacity to withstand critical loads and incursions.

The illusion of the infinite patience of nature is reflected in the ocean's being thought of as immune to damage by any scale of exploitation of its resources; its forces, however, are not limitless. Harmful processes going on in one place can have an adverse effect on many others, through the mixing and agitation of its waters. We have in mind, above all, the pollution of the ocean on a vast scale through the development of several maritime industries and the effect on it of industrial activities on land; serious harm is being done to the marine biomass; it is becoming difficult if not impossible to use seawater for irrigation, desalinization, and complex extraction of resources; poisonous products are getting into people's food; and the recreational role of the sea is declining.

The greatest damage is being done by oil pollution. A single ton of oil can cover a surface of 1,200 hectares. Oil, like pesticides, mercury, fluorine, arsenic, and antimony, belongs to the category of substances that constitute a real danger to human health and the marine environment. While the light fractions of oil evaporate quickly from the ocean's surface, the heavier ones, with a higher content of sulfur, metals, and wax, gradually sink to the bottom, damaging its flora and fauna everywhere and reducing the productive-biological qualities of ocean waters. Developing organisms are especially vulnerable. Experimenters have found that when fertilized fish spawn is put into an aquarium containing a very low concentration of oil products, most of the embryos perish, while many of those that survive become freaks.

Oil also harms organisms in the upper layers of water, in particular plankton. Most species of microscopic algae are retarded or die when exposed to the effect of oil. Laboratory experiments have shown that zooplankton die quickly in water poisoned by oil. That affects the quantity of the primary food link and the rate of supply of oxygen to the atmosphere. At the same time peculiar microorganisms develop that actively flourish on various sources of carbon. Oil pollution of seas also leads to the death of many birds. Every year 200,000 sea birds perish because their feathers are stuck together by oil.

The coastal areas or the "contact zone" are most polluted by oil. It is there that drilling is done, oil produced, and ships berth or anchor. The surf concentrates films of oil and lubricants along the coastline. The effluents of industrial enterprises and domestic sewage are also concentrated in the coastal waters. This is pregnant with the most negative consequences because this area is the breeding and incubation ground for many valuable species of fish, or the zone where they live or migrate. The sanitary and hygienic aspect of the cleanliness of the ocean is of great significance for people living and resting in coastal areas.

Oil gets into the sea through accidents to tankers, by their discharging water used to wash down bulkheads and oil-polluted ballast, by breakages of submarine pipelines and leakage from big storage tanks sited along the coast, etc. Ships still sink while battling with the elements; the colliding and holing of tankers is increasing, with the growth of their tonnage and speed. Accidents to tankers are usually accompanied by pollution of large bodies of water (300,000 tons of oil get into the ocean each year, through this cause alone).

Examples of major accidents occurring in recent years can be cited. In 1970, the *Arrow,* a tanker, had an accident that resulted in a huge oil slick in the northern part of Chedabucto Bay (Novia Scotia). In 1974, a Dutch tanker, the *Metula,* which was carrying about 190,000 tons of oil, ran aground in Magellan Strait and sprang a leak. In 1974, too, an American tanker, the *TransHuron* went out of control and ran into a reef near the Laccadive Islands, where Indians, Japanese, and others traditionally fish tuna. In December 1974, a 43,700-ton Japanese tanker collided with another vessel in poor visibility and caught fire 500 kilometers off the coast of the Chiba Prefecture (Japan). To put out the fire, the tanker was blown up and scuttled. In 1975, the Japanese supertanker the *Sero Maru* of about 250,000 tons, carrying oil from [the] Middle East, ran aground in the Malacca Strait not far from Singapore; 1,000 tons of oil escaped from a crack in the hull threatening to kill everything living in the waters of the strait and to poison those on shore by contaminated fish. The same year, the *Olympic Alliance,* a 220,000-ton supertanker flying the Panamanian flag, and H.M.S. *Achilles,* a British frigate, collided in the English Channel. Both ships were able to continue on their way but left behind them a black 1,000-hectare oil slick. In late December 1975, the *Berge Istra,* a 227,000-ton tanker, sank with its cargo off Sumatra. Early in 1977, a Liberian tanker, the *Argo Margent,* had an accident off the northeastern coast of the United States, that caused a slick 150 miles long and 60 miles wide. The pollution than can result from an accident to a supertanker is comparable to the consequences of all the accidents suffered by the whole world fleet only 50 years ago. And in 1974 alone, 1,163 different tanker accidents were registered. The total number of accidents in 1975 was 9,038. It is hard to think even what an accident to a supertanker carrying a million tons of oil could do to the biomass of the ocean. For that reason, progress of the tanker fleet must absolutely be tied up with ecological guarantees.

In spite of the International Convention for the Prevention of Pollution from Ships concluded in 1973, some tankers continue to discharge oil-polluted water into the sea. This reduces their turn-round time at ports and returns their owners a high profit, especially in the case of big tankers. According to figures in *Tanker and Bulk Carrier,* the washing of tanks adds a million tons of oil to the ocean. Over 300,000 tons of oil are dumped into the Mediterranean alone in this way every year which has led to a decline of 80 percent in the fish population in the past 20 years. The Indonesian Petroleum and Gas Institute has published a statement calling the Java Sea the world's most polluted sea. The washing of tankers with seawater in Jakarta Bay has caused the disappearance of marine plant life and of all animal species around the port of Telukbetung (South Sumatra) and in the Ambon area in eastern Indonesia. There are huge polluted areas along the south coast of Newfoundland, the coast of Florida, and in the eastern part of the Sargasso Sea, where the quantity of oil products is frequently 100 times the permissible maximum.

Another 200,000 tons of oil is poured into the sea during loading, unloading, and refueling and as a result of leaks. The annual total of pollution is at least 5 million tons; some estimates put it at 12 to 15 million tons.

Yet another source of pollution is accidents during drilling and pumping on off-shore oil fields. Early in 1969, a leak occurred off the Californian coast near Los Angeles as a result of inaccurate drilling. An area of 2,000 square kilometers was covered with a layer of oil two to three centimeters thick. In 1970, shoals of dead fish were found along the Florida Peninsula in the Gulf of Mexico where U.S. oil companies were drilling. In November 1975, the drilling equipment was ejected from an oil well by the pressure of the oil in the Ekofisk oil field in the North Sea, and oil was spilled out. In April 1977 damage to a safety valve in a well at the same site caused spill of 4,000–6,000 tons of oil a day for several days.

Other wastes are also dumped into the ocean. In California discharge of copper and mercury above the permitted amounts led to the destruction of giant fucoid seaweeds. Dangerous wastes are frequently concentrated in the seaweeds on which fish feed, and in this way enter the food eaten by man. Mercury has been found in seaweeds, mollusks, and fish in the Indian Ocean and in waters off the coast of Africa. The concentration of mercury off the west coast of Ireland, the coast of Portugal, and in the eastern and central parts of the Gulf Stream is higher than the permitted quantity. Intense discharge of water saturated with mercury is taking place in Saint George's Channel, in the British Isles. In Japan mercury is poured into the sea with untreated effluent and is poisoning both fish and people. Towards the end of the 1950s discharge of waste containing mercury by the Chisso Concern into the Minimata Bay (Japan) caused mass poisoning in a nearby community with many fatalities. Fish caught off the coasts of Sweden, Finland, and Denmark contains so many poisonous heavy metals like mercury that it has been necessary to ban fishing over a broad area. In 1946 an excess of cobalt and phosphorus in wastes stimulated the development of microorganisms in Florida that paralyzed fish

(100–150 kilograms of fish per square kilometer floated on the surface). Similar occurrences have been periodically reported along the coast of North America where 60 percent of the U.S. population live.

The world's biggest dumping ground is in the ocean 20 kilometers from New York. It covers around 50 square kilometers of the ocean floor. Various wastes and impurities from New York City and neighboring cities have been dumped there over the past 40 years. For many miles around the seabed is covered with a substance that contains a huge quantity of deadly bacteria, and the area of this poisonous mass continues to expand. Some countries use the ocean to dispose of wastes from the nuclear industry. Containers with these wastes are sunk to great depths where they are continually subjected to enormous pressure, the chemical action of the water, and vertical and horizontal displacements, which entails a threat of rupture and the most serious consequences for everything living. There is a continuous exchange of bottom and surface waters. Radioactive burials could therefore sooner or later affect all layers of the ocean, while its currents could carry them to the most distant corners.

The water employed to cool nuclear reactors becomes radioactive. It is also warm, and as it is discharged into the sea it upsets the ecological balance and can produce "thermal death." The use of nuclear-powered ships and submarines, which are tending to grow in numbers, can entail dangerous consequences.

The sea is polluted in other ways apart from the direct discharge of waste. The water, land, and air interact with each other, and accidents to the reactors in power stations, even when they are located underground, eventually also affect the ocean. Rivers into which factory effluents have been dumped and toxic chemicals, fertilizers, and fetid fluids from rubbish dumps have seeped also carry much pollution into the sea.

Radioactive substances have contaminated seaweeds and benthonic organisms in the Irish Sea, areas off the coasts of North America, and in Japanese waters. In France radioactive strontium has been found in the shells of edible mollusks.

Observations and statistics both indicate that whenever coasts are polluted by untreated effluent, the danger of epidemics is increased. Particularly favorable conditions are created for the dissemination of intestinal and purulent skin diseases. The pollution also gives edible fish bad odor and flavor.

The use of artificial fertilizers with a high content of phosphorus, nitrates in farming, and of toxic chemicals to combat weeds and pests is also helping pollute the ocean. Some of these substances are disseminated by the wind and so get into water, while some are dissolved in the soil and pollute water through it. Their period of decomposition is very long, so that they cannot be counted on to disappear without harm. The concentration of DDT, copper, arsenic, lead, and zinc in marine organisms reaches very high levels, which increases their greater vulnerability to disease, and causes genetic changes in them as a result of which their hormonal balance is disturbed and reproduction slowed down.

Similar discharges of harmful wastes produce different damage in different areas of the ocean. Marine bacteria "work" well only when it is warm. As soon as the water temperature falls below 5° to 10°C the process of bacterial decomposition practically stops. In cold waters various oil products can last for decades, producing chronic pollution of the water basin. The permissible level of pollution in northern seas must therefore be minimal.

Bodies of water with limited water exchange, slow currents, and shallow depths and with small numbers of biological agents that break down pollution are particularly sensitive to pollution. Their degree of pollution is also affected by the scale of clean river discharge. When water is diverted from them for irrigation and industrial needs without compensation, it lowers the renewal of their waters and increases their salinity. In 1970 the International Council for the Exploration of the Sea (ICES) described the Baltic as the biggest weir. The causes of this are its limited communication with the ocean and the active discharge of waste by the 200 rivers falling into it. Not so long ago soundings made at a depth of 70 meters revealed around 250 species of living organisms; today there are only 30. The catch of Baltic herring has declined drastically.

In 1970 Jacques-Yves Cousteau returned from a round-the-world voyage he made on the oceanographic ship *Calypso.* In an interview with the French newspaper *L'Humanité* he said that the ocean was now ill and dying as a result of man's activities. In the past 20 years alone the volume of life in the water had fallen by 40 percent; a thousand species of marine flora and fauna have vanished over the past 50 years. Since the death of the ocean spells also the death of mankind, this tragedy must be stopped.

A whole system of measures is needed to save the ocean. The limiting possibilities of the water's natural capacity to diffuse waste and purify itself must be determined and current levels of pollution measured accurately. If the sea's self-purifying capacity is inadequate, mechanical means for purifying and disinfecting effluent will be necessary. Many such methods have now been developed that permit successive trapping of various metals, glass, oil lubricants, etc. The first steps have also been taken to introduce a completely wasteless technology, in particular to build closed water-supply systems based on repeated recycling of the same volume of water. In the USSR, during the Ninth Five-Year Plan, 9,000 big cleansing plants were commissioned at a cost around 3 billion rubles. The volume of effluent passed through such installations increased by 38 percent. Thanks to recycling there was only a 12 percent increase in the intake of water, with a 39 percent increase in consumption.

Biological methods of purification based on the use of marine microorganisms are being more and more widely used. British experts have produced a material that absorbs 30 times its own weight of oil. A blanket of this material 0.9 × 4.5 meters and 1.2 centimeters thick absorbs around half a ton of oil in ten seconds. Such blankets can be laid on oil-polluted water. Improvements are also being made in chemical methods neutralizing the oil slicks formed when tankers are involved in accidents or else when breaks occur in pipelines.

One way of rational discharge of effluents is to pipe them to great depths at long distances from the coast, especially when great pipelines are fitted with diffusors. Dilution begins at great depths. At first the effluent mixes with the colder, heavier layers of water near the bottom. As it moves upward to the surface, the resulting mixture is denser than each successive upper layer, and will continue to be diffused within an intermediate layer without reaching the top one. The effluent thus remains below the surface, which itself remains clean; so, consequently does the coast. This method also reduces the effect of pollution on the biological processes in the active surface layer.[1]

Dense (heavy, neutral) effluent will naturally remain in intermediate layers of the water for a long time. Light mixtures will tend to rise vertically. It is preferable, however, to dispose of effluent at great depths since this results in substantial dilution through turbulent diffusion. The process of deep mixing is intensified by currents, while deeply indented coastlines and the complex nature of the bottom relief along coasts produce patterns of closed circulation in the narrow coastal strip and stagnant zones in which there is not much movement of water.

Modern engineering is able not only to trap wastes but to process them into useful products. We are witnessing a shift of production systems to closed cycles. Generating incinerators are coming into use that transform waste into energy. Work is being done on decomposing plastics into their "component factors" and on trapping and use of by-products.

Improvement in the design of ships is an important and effective way of preventing pollution. Some Soviet tankers, for example, have oil-free ballast tanks. When the tanker is loaded they are empty, and when the tanker is empty they contain clean seawater. The 1973 International Convention for the Prevention of Pollution from Ships, incidentally, provides for application of this technical innovation to all tankers being built with a displacement of more than 70,000 tons. The tanker *Crimea* and many others have a double bottom. Going over to a tanker fleet of this design, which uses the intermediate space for carrying freshwater and other non-dangerous stores, will reduce oil discharges into the sea by 95 percent.

There are installations in the big ports of many countries for dealing with oil water from tankers, and floating pollution-control stations that wash the oil tanks of vessels (in the USSR, for example, in Leningrad,

Riga, Tallinn, Novorossiisk, Tuapse, Batumi, Ventspils, Klaipeda, Nakhodka, Aktau, Krasnovodsk, and Neftyaniye Kamni). Harbors and the open sea are patrolled and cleaned by vessels specially equipped to filter out products and refuse.

The exhaust gases of diesel-electric ships contaminate water with lead. In order to prevent lead getting into water, or to diminish the amount, scrubbing installations of a new design are being developed. The design of atomic engines is being improved so as to prevent interference with marine ecosystems.

In order to prevent accidents, big ships are fitted with automatic devices that help to avoid collisions with approaching vessels. The introduction of two-way traffic along strictly defined routes in especially dangerous areas is playing an essential role in making navigation safer.

Some countries, including the Soviet Union, prohibit the commissioning of newly built or reconstructed plants, factory shops, assemblies, municipal or other facilities not provided with installations to prevent pollution and contamination of waters. Disposal of effluent is only permitted in cases when it does not raise the content of pollutants above an established level. Oil wells also cannot be commissioned in the absence of appropriate measures preventing oil from getting into the sea. On existing oil fields, reliable measures have been taken that prevent leakage of oil and penetration of spent chemical reagents into the water. The floors of drilling rigs are so erected that literally not a drop of pollutants can seep out. Special absorption wells are also drilled, into which all waste produced during drilling is buried. Explosions are prohibited in oil prospecting at sea; instead the use of pneumatic sources of elastic waves are used that are harmless for fish.

The ocean is a system efficient exploitation and conservation of which is impossible without a coordinated policy of all countries. The pollution permitted by some countries or their ships, for example, does enormous harm to the coastal waters and marine flora and fauna of other countries. The radical solution of this problem lies in a global struggle against harmful pollution of the World Ocean.

The International Convention for the Prevention of Pollution of the Sea by Oil (1954) bans the disposal of oil and oil mixtures from ships in coastal areas from 50 to 150 miles off shore, discharging of tankers being forbidden in all water basins to ships of 20,000 gross register tons and upwards.[2]

In 1973, an International Convention for the Prevention of Pollution of the Sea from Ships was adopted which prohibits disposal of oil in special areas—the Baltic, Black Sea, Mediterranean, Red Sea, and Persian Gulf. The convention also provides for restrictions on the disposal of other noxious substances, effluent, and refuse.

Additional restrictions aimed at preventing pollution are provided for in regional agreements, namely, those on cooperation to prevent pollution of the North Sea by oil (1969) and on preventing pollution of the sea by substances discharged from ships and aircraft (in the northeastern Atlantic) (1972). There are regional agreements between the Soviet Union and neighboring countries, envisaging joint work to prevent pollution of and to clean the Baltic. Seven countries; viz., the Soviet Union, the German Democratic Republic, Poland, Sweden, Denmark, West Germany, and Finland, signed a convention on protecting the living resources of the Baltic and the belts.

Mediterranean countries held a conference in Rome in 1970 sponsored by the FAO, at which they agreed to cooperate in controlling pollution of the Mediterranean. Similar problems were considered in 1972 in Stockholm, at a UN conference on study of human environment. An Inter-parliamentary Conference of Mediterranean Countries (Rome, 1974) was held with the aim of protecting the sea. Its proceedings contained an appeal to declare the Mediterranean a "special area" because of the great danger of pollution by effluents, the disposal of industrial wastes, and leakage of oil, and recommended setting up a fund to combat pollution, the biggest contributions to be made by the countries actively polluting the sea. The fund is intended to finance research, exchange information, develop techniques, and train specialists in conservation of the environment. An intergovernment conference on combating pollution of the Mediterranean was held in 1975 in Barcelona, which was attended by observers from the Soviet Union, Britain, and the United States, as well as by representatives of Mediterranean countries.

The Soviet Union provides an example of a new, rational, comprehensive approach to marine resources.

The most important Soviet legislation in the field of conservation of the water environment and seabed are the Fundamentals of Water Legislation of the USSR and Union Republics, the water codes of the Union republics, the Decree of the Presidium of the USSR Supreme Soviet on the continental shelf of the USSR, issued on 6 February 1968, the Decree of the USSR Council of Ministers on the procedure for conducting work on the continental shelf of the USSR and protection of its natural wealth, issued on 18 July 1969, and so on. Nature conservancy and rational use of natural resources are a constitutional principle in the Soviet Union. Article 18 of the new Constitution of the USSR (1977) proclaims: "In the interests of the present and future generations, the necessary steps are taken in the USSR to protect and make scientific, rational use of the land and its mineral and water resources, and the plant and animal kingdoms, to preserve the purity of air and water, ensure reproduction of natural wealth, and improve the human environment."

Among recent decisions of the Communist party and Soviet government on water conservancy those introducing measures to prevent pollution of the Sea of Azov, the Black Sea, Baltic, and Caspian (passed in 1976) deserve mention. The measures planned in them are to be largely carried out before 1980. They require establishments to stop discharging untreated industrial and domestic effluent into the water basins of these seas, which is to be done by introducing progressive technologies, complex processing of raw materials, utilization of industrial waste, and the building of efficient purification and decontamination installations. All vessels are to be provided with the necessary equipment to purify or collect oily and other contaminated water, and refuse and garbage, and to deliver them to floating or shore installations. In the Sea of Azov and on certain parts of the Black Sea shelf, with important fisheries, drilling, blasting, geological prospecting, etc., injurious to marine life may only be carried on with the permission of the USSR Ministry for Land Improvement and Water Economy and the USSR Ministry of Fisheries. A general plan for conservation of the natural complex of these seas and rational use of their resources up to the year 2000 is being drafted.

The USSR Council of Ministers adopted a decision in 1968 that said that the northern part of the Caspian and the deltas of the Volga and Ural rivers must be made a nature preserve and used only for fisheries and transport purposes. It was also decided to make part of Peter the Great Bay, near Vladivostok, a marine reservation.

Since 1974, long-term and annual plans for rational exploitation of natural resources and nature conservation have been drawn up in the Soviet Union as a special part of economic development plans.

Under the Tenth Five-Year Plan, 11 billion rubles will be allocated for protection of the environment. Carrying out of the measures planned for this period (1976–80) to improve the forecasting of the impact of industry on the environment will be of great value for protection of the ocean. Measures for a drastic reduction of the noxious effect of wastes, protection of water and other resources, as well as development of specialized industries producing the equipment and machinery for building high-efficiency purification plants, etc., at industrial establishments will also be carried out and comprehensive exploration of the ocean undertaken.

It is necessary to combat pollution to protect the flora and fauna of the ocean, but it is not enough. Another indispensable condition providing for optimum amount of biomass is regulation of catches and finding their optimal size.

Biological resources, including marine ones, are reproducible. As a result of lengthy evolution optimum balances and technical proportions and connections have been developed between flora and fauna and regional ecosystems and within them. The ocean overcomes individual deviations from the normal by its own efforts, since it is a self-regulated system functioning with reserve "tolerances."

Man's intervention in extracting natural resources should also be within the limits not exceeding the "capacity" of natural reproduction. Man has the right to take from the sea only such an amount of biological resources as will not damage their reproduction.

When man, however, takes more than the optimum catch from the sea, he damages both the biological cycle and his own economy. The biological harm is that overfishing narrows the base for subsequent natural reproduction of marine products. The economic damage is expressed in that, as the catch diminishes, the available capacity and manpower employed in the fishing fleet and fishprocessing industry will be underused while society will not get the fish products it needs.

In order to regulate fisheries definite limits are imposed on catches and the amount of fishing gear is regulated and the season is begun and ended so as not to interfere with spawning. Hydraulic engineering works in estuaries must be so built as not to hamper the migration or spawning of fish, and during certain periods restrictions are imposed on their operation.

The overfishing of certain species has reached such critical dimensions that catching them has been temporarily banned altogether to promote reproduction of the biological resources. In 1971, the catching of Atlantic-Scandinavian herring in the northeastern part of the Atlantic was banned (until restoration of reserves). A limit was put on the catch of commercial fisheries in the northwestern part of the Atlantic, where there were already signs in 1969 of a diminishing of reserves. Fishing of haddock along [the] New England coast (USA) has been banned. Strict control has been introduced over the fisheries off the coast of Peru where anchovy populations have been catastrophically reduced by rapacious fishing.

Special measures have been taken to protect dolphins. In the Soviet Union the hunting of dolphins in the Sea of Azov-Black Sea Basin was banned in 1966. Similar steps have been taken by Bulgaria and Romania. Laws protecting dolphins have been passed by Australia, New Zealand, and other countries.

The effectiveness of the regulation of fisheries largely depends on coordination of the efforts of the countries involved. Without coordinated action and international agreements it will be difficult to develop aqua culture successfully.

There are many special conventions concerned with protecting the biological balance in the ocean. An international convention regulating whaling was concluded in 1946. In 1956, the Soviet Union and Japan undertook to conserve and increase salmon, crab, and herring populations in the Northwest of the Pacific. In 1957, the Soviet Union and Norway signed an agreement on measures to control sealing in the northeastern Atlantic. There are agreements between the Soviet Union and the United States on Soviet fishing of king and tanner crab on the American shelf in the eastern part of the Bering Sea, and between the Soviet Union and the United States, Japan, and Canada on the protection of fur seals in the North Pacific, signed in 1966. The fishery ministers of Bulgaria, Czechoslovakia, the German Democratic Republic, Hungary, Poland, and the Soviet Union met in Moscow in 1972 and adopted a declaration on the principles of rational exploitation of the living resources of the ocean in the common interests of all peoples of the world, and so on.

It is both possible and necessary to exploit the ocean's wealth rationally and on a scientific basis. This will involve much less expenditure than would be subsequently needed if this is not done. In some cases, moreover, the extreme state of resource depletion can result in irreversible exhaustion.

It is easier to prevent illness than to cure it. Similarly, it is cheaper to avoid the pollution of seas and the thoughtless destruction of the biomass than to eliminate their harmful consequences. The time has arrived to care for the ocean and to realize that it is not a bottomless reservoir or a dumping ground for waste products.

NOTES

1. On the other hand, oxidation will be slower in deeper layers of water since the volume of dissolved oxygen is much lower there than in the upper layers in contact with the atmosphere.

2. Disposal is allowed in exceptional cases, when necessary for the ship's safety or to save a human life, or when it is unavoidable because of damage, the springing of leaks, etc.

VI
Conclusion

In this essay Kempton E. Webb, chairman of the department of geography at Columbia University, summarizes many of the themes introduced in this book, projects Geoffrey Martin's historical overview into the future, and adds some provocative ideas of his own. His concluding sentence is really a challenge, a call to action. Will people living today respond to the challenge? Or will they leave it to the next generation to accomplish what by then will be a much more difficult—and perhaps impossible—task?

51

Global Interdependence

Kempton E. Webb

INTRODUCTION

In the final years of the twentieth century, all humanity, rich and poor, is confronted by the awesome specter of global resource scarcity. The rich countries are worried about losing their cherished standard of living, and the world's poor worry about whether their children will die because of disease or lack of food or shelter.

The challenge facing the world's nations and the people who guide them is unprecedented; some nations will rise to the challenge of resource scarcity and deal with it effectively; other countries will become economic wastelands and sewers of humanity. The pecking order of countries will change, and some surprises are in store. For example, the United States will probably decline relative to other developed countries in per capita income and other measures, and Brazil will probably become a major world industrial power by the year 2000.

The ever-quickening pace of change in relationships between people and resources took its first leap about 10,000 years ago due to the Agricultural Revolution in which the domestication of plants and animals greatly enlarged per capita food production. The eighteenth- and nineteenth-century Industrial Revolution, and its bequest to mankind of controlled inanimate energy, is still spreading geographically from its cultural hearth around the shores of the North Sea. It is this uneven impact of the industrialization process which accounts for the striking differences in economic development between countries such as Upper Volta and Nigeria, Haiti and Mexico, Portugal and Canada, or Ireland and Japan.

How each country fares will depend upon broader considerations than mere economic, political, or social ones. The success or failure of each country will turn largely upon how intelligently it defines and assesses its resource base, and how it transforms those resources into the useful materials of its society.

Although resources are physical things, they are ultimately defined by society, and it is society's political units that must take the credit or blame for the use or abuse of land and resources.

Three principles underlie the viability of all societies: (1) Society must form a workable connection with its land or resource base; (2) the definition and significance of the resource base is determined by the culture of the people who own or control it; (3) the diverse elements of the physical resource base and of society itself form a system of interconnected parts in which a change in one part will ultimately have an impact elsewhere in the system. This is the basic principle of ecology.

OVERRIDING THEMES

Among the very diverse foregoing articles, a number of recurring themes deserve emphasis.

1. *The uselessness of aggregate analysis.* It is totally irrelevant to state that the world's aggregate oil supply or grain supply per capita is adequate if there are serious shortages in specific places. Shortages occur in particular places at particular times for particular reasons; the remedies, likewise, are specific in time and place. The more aggregated the figures, the less the figures reveal. It is the differences from one place to another that illuminate scarcity problems and point to their solutions.

2. *The cultural relativity of logic in particular times and places.* Gunnar Myrdal, in the prologue to this volume, appropriately skewers the arrogant ethnocentric and ideological biases of some economists' solutions to developing countries' problems. One does not need to be proficient in mathematics to understand why an expensive $20-a-day bulldozer and operator would be shunned in a less developed country where ten men with shovels can do the same job at $1 per day per man. The machine is not necessarily better.

3. *The nature of the problem: control over the material bases of society.* Self-sufficiency in resources is a much debated topic. Fernando Belaunde Terry, twice president of Peru, once remarked that the only way for a country to be economically and politically independent was to be dependent upon many different countries.

With the exception of individual indigenous peoples living in the practically self-sufficient small communities in the interior vastness of Africa, South America, and Australia, few individuals or groups have control over the material base of their existence. The present struggle for control over resources is largely between individual countries, groups of countries (e.g., OPEC), and multinational corporations. Global control is still a dream, although the Law of the Sea is an attempt to move in that direction.

4. *Persistent paradoxes.* If countries are so rich (in resources, e.g., Bolivia, Zaire, Peru), why are their people so poor? If there is so much idle empty land, why is there so much population pressure? If there are food surpluses, why are people starving or malnourished?

5. *The essential interdependence and vulnerability of all nations.* The developed countries are vulnerable because they need such a variety of goods and resources, and they need them in large quantities. The less developed countries are vulnerable because they have so little to barter and so little bargaining power.

6. *The desirability of diversification of one's resource bases.* Strategic criteria dictate that a country should not be totally dependent on others for vital supplies of food, oil, etc.

7. *The immorality of squandering resources and money on socially dubious purposes.* The world's armaments race absorbs over $550 billion a year that might otherwise be diverted into socially and economically useful channels.

8. *The absence of an informed public.* Reducing waste and the squandering of resources requires a better educated public and electorate, one that is informed and articulate regarding the grand themes and lesser details of human resource relationships.

INTERRELATIONSHIPS AND LINKAGES

Let us now examine briefly some of the ways resources impinge directly and also less obviously upon other aspects of society. The very way in which a society defines resources is one window into that society.

Resources and Population

In any discussion of resources, on either a global or local scale, population stands in the forefront as the great denominator in the people/resources equation. The primary projections that emerged from the Global 2000 Report are that (1) the world's population will increase by almost 50 percent—from around 4.5 billion to over 6.3 billion—by the year 2000; (2) about 90 percent of that increase will occur in the world's poorest countries; and (3) by far the greater part of that increase is going to be located in urban areas.

It is obvious that the resources available to any society are going to be divided among the people who control or have access to those resources. The greater number of people, the more mouths will have to be fed with any given amount of food. It is a cruel irony that the fastest growth rates in population are occurring in the least developed economies, and marked decreases are to be found mainly in the more mature economies.

Both the quantity and the quality of a population must be considered. History shows that the flowerings of early civilizations were made possible by agglomerations of people in places where a diversity of social, economic, and political functions was possible. The early centers of Renaissance activity, whether Siena or Venice, were places of less than 40,000 inhabitants at their height. The present prospect is for more and more metropolitan centers of ever increasing size, with millions and tens of millions of inhabitants. Mexico City is projected to have over 30 million people by 2000. It is impossible to imagine the scale of squalor that that prospect conveys—and Mexico will be better off than most less-developed countries.

Migration of people from areas of perceived hardship to areas of greater perceived opportunities—the so-called rural-to-urban flow—has been the historical pathway of people seeking a better life and greater economic security. In view of the anticipated growth rates of population generally and of metropolitan areas particularly, it would seem that a primary objective in most countries should be to fix rural population in productive activities within the rural areas. This would appear not only to enhance food production, in itself a serious problem, but also to lessen the pressure on the beleaguered facilities and services in the cities.

It is only fair to point out that, among many of the world's poor, a "revolution of rising expectations" motivates them to want to enjoy the fruits of their labor. In places where people once went about on animal-drawn vehicles or on bicycles, they have moved into the era of the motorbike, and those who started with motorbikes now drive Volkswagens and Renaults. International television has communicated only too well what the material "good life" consists of, as transmitted from the United States and Western Europe.

In the opinion of F. E. Trainer, it is going to be impossible for the rest of the world's population to achieve or even come close to achieving the standard of living existing in the developed countries of the 1970s. For others even to approximate that standard of living, the developed countries would have to give up affluence and economic growth as a way of life. Given human nature, they are not likely to do so without a struggle.

Resources and Technology

In our wonderment at the technology of our modern industrial society, we tend to forget that technology is a function of culture and that technology has logic only in a given cultural setting at a certain place in time and space. For example, the vast coalbeds underlying the heartland of North America did not constitute a resource for the American Indians. Those coal deposits only became a resource during the nineteenth century, when the Industrial Revolution and the hunger for controlled inanimate energy created an ever expanding market for coal at home and abroad.

The low-grade taconite iron ore deposits underlying the richer ores in the Mesabi iron range were not a resource until a process was developed to crush and pelletize those low-grade ores, thereby rendering them usable and, in fact, ideal for the blast furnaces.

In the agricultural sector, the famous American author-farmer-agronomist-conservationist Louis Bromfield, of Malabar Farm fame, went to Brazil after World War II and proceeded to apply capital, conservation-mindedness and a scientific attitude to reclaim old worn-out coffee lands in the interior of São Paulo State. He demonstrated that eroded and leached soils could be resuscitated with impressive amounts of capital, know-how, and rigorous attention to detail. But at that time, his experience was not terribly relevant to the Brazilian scene. Brazilian farmers in the 1940s and 1950s used a hoe and a machete to do their primitive slash and burn farming—and in fact many still do. Bromfield's discoveries only became meaningful later as Brazil developed into an industrial power complete with a modern agricultural component.

Today all sorts of interesting experiments are in progress by which the hitherto ancient, sterile, and acid savanna soils of central Brazil are being made productive for the first time. Brazil is a leading producer of soybeans using some of the reclaimed soils, and selected areas of the Amazon region are also producing food.

The objectives of a society could not be more strongly contrasted than those of the United States and China. In the last few years China has made progress in raising agricultural production as well as productivity. The aims are not the maximization of profits but the provision of a subsistence floor comprising food supplies for all of the Chinese population. The "market" means something quite different in China than in the United States.

One may be surprised to learn that a so-called less developed country, or perhaps more appropriately a "middle power," Brazil, is the world's leading innovator in alcohol-powered vehicles. Some 450,000 cars and trucks in Brazil are powered by ethanol (ethyl alcohol) produced from sugarcane and manioc. Brazil exports not only Volkswagen automobiles to developing countries but also the fuel to power those vehicles. Brazil has an energy policy and is intent upon lessening its dependence upon imported oil.

Some of the most imaginative experiments in solar and wind power are being carried out in countries such as Israel and Colombia. Each country and society has a different incentive. Whereas a developed country may decide that solar power, for example, is not viable, a less developed or middle power may reach the opposite conclusion based on its level of technology, the unemployment picture, and its social objectives.

The extraordinary linkage between energy (oil) and food has been pointed out in Lester Brown's article. The link is, of course, more direct in large-scale intensive commercial agriculture, as practiced in the United States or Western Europe, where the application of petroleum-derived fertilizer is a necessary and costly part of crop production. (In the simpler societies, fertilizers—if they are used at all—are in the form of animal manure or even human waste.) In the developed countries, higher prices for fuel are translated directly into higher prices for agricultural products, and especially food.

The challenge is for each society and each country to define its resources and set its priorities.

Resources and Ecology

Barry Commoner emphasizes the ecological dimension of resources with his four pithy laws: (1) everything is connected to everything else, (2) everything must go somewhere, (3) nature knows best, and (4) there is no free lunch. Public awareness of the principles of ecology and the ecological implications of resource development is a recent phenomenon and still not common even among educated people in the developed or developing countries.

The earth's inhabitants and their resources, however defined for each culture, form a system of interconnected parts, as stated in Commoner's first principle. Changes in any one part ultimately have repercussions in other parts of the system. Take the case of U.S. agriculture. The prodigious output of American farmers—and, indeed, Canadians and Australians—has a long-term cost in terms of erosion, loss of soil nutrients, and flushing of fertilizers into streams and lakes whose ecological balance is upset. According to some critics, American farmers are really exporting more than crops; they export a nonrenewable resource, namely, valuable topsoil.

The planting of marginal drier zones west of the traditional American wheat zones in the Great Plains states has been made possible by wells tapping into groundwater, which is being pumped out faster than normal replenishment.

Some of the world's last frontier areas are undoubtedly going to be called into service in order to feed, shelter, and clothe the world's growing population. The Amazon Basin of South America is such an area, and Brazil is implementing long-range plans by which it intends to be not only a provider of a host of minerals (for example, the Carajás project—iron ore, aluminum, manganese, copper) but also a source of food, timber, and abundant hydroelectric energy. The Amazon is the last of the large frontier zones, and the future of its fragile, humid, tropical environment is a concern. Some people would like to preserve that seemingly pristine rainforest region forever from the hand of man as an inviolate "book of Genesis" which the Brazilian engineer-writer Euclydes da Cunha mentions in his turn-of-the-century book *The Margin of History.* Yet there is absolutely no possibility that the Brazilian people will not occupy that part of their national territory. It is hoped that the process of economic development will proceed with resource-conserving technologies and without violating basic ecological principles.

Brazil's example points to the possibility that the entire tropical world—that low latitude area occupied by most of the less developed countries—may be a new frontier for resources experimentation. The tropics comprise that part of the earth's surface where the largest amounts of insolation of solar radiant energy is concentrated and where the process of biomass conversion proceeds at a rapid rate. The forward-looking countries of the tropics may attempt to diversify their resource bases through the use of ethanol alcohol as a substitute for expensive imported oil and become food exporters.

Many of the developing countries may also be able to bypass the costly phases and avoid the mistakes of the developed countries that resulted in the pollution and blight that accompanied their labored progress through and beyond the industrial revolution. Their success or failure in avoiding the ecological pitfalls of development will soon be apparent. Much of the primary economic production—that is to say, the manufacture of steel, ships, machine tools, clothing, and automobiles—has already passed out of the hands of high wage workers in the developed countries to the next tier of countries—places like Taiwan, Brazil, India, South Korea, and Thailand.

Resources and Economics

Some economists such as John Kenneth Galbraith assert that in post-industrial societies, of which the United States is a prime example, true competition based on supply and demand does not exist. Galbraith writes in *A Life in Our Times* that only about 1,000 major corporations produce most of what the American people consume. Moreover, these giants exercise a large influence over their markets: They are able to develop products, set price schedules, and use advertising in a way to control the volume of demand.

According to Galbraith, the decisions regarding resource use are made in a relatively few centers of decision making: private industry, consortia of private industries, or federal and state governments or foreign and multinational companies.

Many of the defense industries consume immense amounts of money, talent, and resources and turn back very little to the public in terms of basic food, shelter, and clothing; they do not have a large multiplier effect upon the satisfaction of social needs. This principle of the dissipation of energy into incoherent and unusable forms is the second law of thermodynamics, so imaginatively applied in the book *Entropy* by Jeremy Rifkin.

Resources and Politics

The decisions regarding resource use are usually highly political, and the quality of decisions is frequently not of a high order or adequate to the challenges. The United States, despite the hardships inflicted by the oil embargo of 1973–74 and its consequences, still cannot be said to have an effective, consistent, and long-range energy policy. Politicians understandably tend to be more interested in politics than in the more mundane details of resource analysis. Their frame of reference is from two to six years at most, while key resource decisions have an impact for generations into the future.

PROJECTIONS: THE FUTURE OF RESOURCES

From the vantage point of the 1980s, the future of the world's peoples and the prospect of their being able to live satisfying lives engaged in productive activity, free from worries about physical survival, are, indeed, dim and at best uncertain. Never before has there been so much doubt and questioning regarding the future of humanity. It is ironic that man's increasing sophistication and achievements in the areas of science, technology, health care, communications, and the arts have not been accompanied by physical security and global peace. Even in the so-called developed economies it is not at all certain that the generations now living will fill out their remaining years in relative comfort and security. And for the world's poorest people, the prospects are terrible. The application of science and technology to traditional resource use has, in many instances, prolonged their lives but has not improved them. Clearly, a new approach to the exploitation of resources is needed.

The future will bring a continuing change in the definitions of resources, and the process of change will accelerate as the pace of world industrialization quickens. To cite but one example, in Latin America, the historical definition of wealth was land itself. In the hundreds of years of preindustrial life in Latin America, there was, in fact, a basis for that definition—namely, one's ability to survive physically depended upon the ability to grow food. So land was truly synonymous with wealth. Later, as industrialization appeared, economic value and, to a lesser extent, social prestige accrued also to those people who owned capital goods or the means of production. In other words, the owner of a shoe factory, textile mill, or brewery was also understood to have wealth, that is, the means of producing salable goods.

Almost every nation has its own particular definition of resources. Generally speaking, the poorer countries are those in which manufactured goods are relatively expensive and labor is cheap, possibly one dollar per day. In the developed countries, by contrast, the reverse is true. This is, of course, why much primary production has fled beyond the borders of the developed countries, and why most jobs have shifted to the tertiary or services sector.

Physical resources, which already play an important role in international affairs, will play an exceedingly important one in the future. Traditionally in developed societies, it was capital and technology rather than resources that enjoyed dominance and control. One has only to study the entrepreneurial development of North America, Western Europe, and Japan to understand this basic fact of economic history. Beginning in the 1970s, however, with the OPEC oil embargo, the importance of natural resources began to be better appreciated. Those countries possessing or otherwise controlling significant amounts of valuable energy, food, or mineral resources acquired economic and political clout, and they are increasingly aware of that clout.

Another new development on the international scene that could persist is the inflation that has engulfed practically every corner of the inhabited world. In the 1950s and 1960s Americans read about incredible inflation rates of 50 percent and even 100 percent per year in places like Chile, Argentina, and Brazil, but they had never themselves experienced an inflation rate of more than 1 or 2 percent a year. In the late 1970s and early 1980s, double-digit inflation afflicted even the developed countries, bringing an effective halt to economic growth and causing widespread bankruptcies. It also prompted people to give more serious attention to tangible capital goods and resources. If money held in a vault is going to lose purchasing power, then it is wiser to convert that money into a tangible good, which, at a later date, may be sold for a quantity of currency that may have some relationship to its true purchasing power. Hence, the investments in diamonds, coins, antiques, land, and buildings. This is standard practice in any inflationary economy.

Another recent development in international affairs that could affect the future is a reassessment of the theory of comparative economic advantage. Under the classical economic doctrine, other things being equal, the country that could grow wheat most efficiently, that is, at lowest cost, would concentrate at growing wheat and selling it to others. But the doctrine assumed that (a) there were abundant energy supplies available for transportation, (b) that it was cheap energy, and (c) that there were no serious barriers to the free movement of goods. The quadrupling of oil prices in the 1970s effectively negated much of that logic. In our one world divided, each country faces the challenging task of deciding what priorities and strategies to pursue regarding the question of interdependency with other countries, on the one hand, and self-sufficiency on the other. Arguments pro or con change from day to day, depending on access to resources, shifting costs of production and transportation, and unpredictable political developments. How many people foresaw the war over the Falkland Islands (1982) or the American hostage experience in Iran (1979–81)?

The increasing sophistication of less developed countries is another new element in international affairs. Many of their intellectuals, political leaders, and economists have been exposed to residence and education in the more developed countries, and they argue and act with increasing effectiveness in their dealings with the developed countries.

Possibility of Market Wars/Conflicts

As modern industrial societies become increasingly dependent on physical resources for their development, the likelihood of their protecting their sources of supply—fighting for them, if necessary—grows. In the 1970s and early 1980s the developed countries were embroiled in a number of major market conflicts. The United States and Japan were at odds over the highly successful penetration of U.S. markets by Japanese automobiles, transistors, TV components, etc. The United States maintained that it had not been allowed comparable access to Japanese markets due to high protective walls that favored domestic producers.

Another conflict among political allies erupted over the projected Siberian gas pipeline. Western Europeans favored the pipeline to lessen their dependence upon uncertain supplies of oil from the politically unstable Middle East-Persian Gulf region. The United States opposed the pipeline, in part to protest the Soviet invasion and occupation of Afghanistan, and forbade U.S. companies and their affiliates to sell technology that would facilitate the pipeline's construction. West Europeans noted wryly that U.S. displeasure with the Soviets did not extend to cutting off lucrative wheat sales.

If market wars are to be avoided there will have to be a change in the traditional relationship between industrialized and Third World nations. The Brandt Report presents very effectively the predicaments facing the less developed countries. Historically they have provided mostly raw materials at low prices to the more developed countries; the richer countries then sell them back expensive manufactured goods. The prices the poor countries receive for the raw material resources are never enough to cover the total costs of the range of finished goods needed by those same countries.

The call for a New International Economic Order, which the Group of 77 nations advanced, and which now is supported by well over 100 countries, essentially demands a fairer division of the profits from world resource exploitation and trade. There is a growing awareness among the leaders of all countries, rich and poor alike, that the world is "a fragile and interlocking system, whether for its people, its ecology, or its resources." It is not in the interest of either the rich or the poor nations to aggravate the resentments and strong negative feelings that the traditional attitudes have engendered. The Brandt Report argues that both the developing and the developed countries must move toward each other from fairly entrenched positions, and that the economic and social survival of both groups depends upon their being able to compromise and to work out constructive imaginative arrangements for their mutual development and improvement.

The stakes in the game of economic survival and growth are continuously rising. Some observers believe the time will come when developed countries will decide to dig in and fight to protect their hard-earned, comfortable living levels. At the same time the developing countries, having had a taste of a better material life, will be even more determined to achieve the same gains that the developed countries have enjoyed.

As bad as the current situation is in the poorer countries, with their extreme malnutrition, hunger, inflation, mounting debts, monetary disorder, and tensions between countries competing for essential supplies of energy and food, the future could be even bleaker if world population and unemployment continue to grow, with accompanying threats to the environment through the pollution of air and water.

The Possibility of Resource Wars

The likeliest candidate for a resource war is the Persian Gulf region. If its supplies of oil were interrupted, it is conceivable that Western Europe, Japan, and the United States would take united action—possibly even military force—to guarantee access to the oil. How the Soviet Union would react to such a military move is unpredictable, but there would be a grave risk of escalating conflict.

South Africa presents a different situation. There the most likely source of conflict is domestic, stemming from the white minority government's racial policies. If a race war broke out, it would affect to varying degrees most developed countries because of their interest in South Africa's rich endowment of critical minerals essential to modern industry and technology.

War over the most elemental resource—food—is an ever present danger. The dispute between El Salvador and Honduras is an example of a food resource conflict. El Salvador is a crowded country in which all of the arable land is occupied, and population pressure upon land and food resources is intolerable. Honduras is much more sparsely populated, and the pressure of an overflow of Salvadoran people has long been an irritant.

In the poorest region of Africa, that is, in the Sahel of West Africa, we have witnessed the most horrible examples of starvation and human wastage. While it is difficult to imagine those frail victims engaging in something called resource wars, starving people have been known to rise up under the stimulus of a charismatic leader to fight for survival.

The Antarctic poses a unique situation in that it is essentially uninhabited, yet it is claimed by many nations. Not all of these countries with claims to the land and resources of Antarctica have the economic or technical wherewithal to exploit their claims, e.g., Argentina. But, as the Falkland Islands war illustrated, this would not necessarily inhibit a country like Argentina from embarking upon a reckless and costly international adventure.

The prospects of an actual war being fought over resources are difficult to gauge. One of the primary factors that contributes to the likelihood of such a war is the increasing dependence of countries on others for basic necessities. In recent years countries too numerous to list have ceased to be food exporters and are now net food importers. Only a handful of countries export wheat today: Canada, the United States, Australia, and Argentina. Many nations that used to be self-sufficient in maize, rice, and wheat now import those same commodities. Uncle Ben's Converted rice from the United States floods the village markets all over Nigeria. To be dependent upon another people for food, the staff of life, is to feel insecurity, especially if the sources of supply are unreliable.

As the issues of global scarcity in our interdependent world become more sharply defined and debated, and the stakes for winners and losers more clearly understood, the threat or the risks of war will also be more apparent.

The Future of Industrial Society

The Industrial Revolution was built upon the premise of controlled inanimate energy and, ultimately, inexpensive and abundant controlled inanimate energy. Plentiful energy allowed the concentration of goods, people, and services within small areas and also permitted the transportation of the output of productive labor in those cities to the far corners of the world. Subsequent multiplication of diverse functions gave those human agglomerations their "urbane" qualities, which extended into the realms of the arts, the sciences, education, and political functions. In recent years these service functions have superseded those of the basic production of durable goods. Modern cities in many parts of the United States have become essentially service centers focused upon retailing, financial services, tourism, arts, and leisure.

Many developing countries, in attempting to duplicate what they perceive to be the advantages of the modern industrial society, have built capital cities that tend to imitate those of the developed countries, complete with the problems of traffic congestion, noise, air and water pollution, and crime. Some Third World leaders advocate a different approach. In the view of President Julius K. Nyerere of Tanzania, the purpose of economic growth and economic exchanges is to provide people with the basic requirements—food, shelter, health and education. While those basic functions, with the exception of food may be located in an urban setting, and in fact they generally are within the developed countries, they do not necessarily *have* to be. The provision of shelter, health, and education can just as well be promoted in the countryside.

Examples of developing countries that do not attempt to imitate the developed countries are rare. China is an example. An effective, even coercive Chinese population policy, which demands that each couple have but one child, under duress of harsh penalties, is expected to lower the birth rate dramatically by the year 2000. Counteracting these policies is the newly found prosperity of a small number of Chinese peasants. The incentive system, which allows them to keep their own harvest profit above and beyond the assigned production quota, has enabled them to buy not only bicycles, radios, sewing machines, and TVs but also occasionally a small truck. These prosperous Chinese can afford to have more than one child, and they do, because there is still a strong cultural bias in China toward having many sons. These politically and socially aberrant behavior patterns are a source of consternation to Chinese officials.

Brazil is an example of a fairly enlightened country rapidly moving from developing status to developed status. It has given careful attention to its inventory of resources and has planned how it will develop and make effective use of much of the national territory.

New Patterns of Resource Dependency and the Realignments of Economic and Political Power

We are now witnessing a change in the way in which nations relate to one another. Relations in former years tended to be based upon elements of cultural and political affinity, while today we see relations based more and more on resource dependency or interdependency. Take Spain and Libya, for example, which in the 1970s expounded diametrically opposed political philosophies and yet formed a trading relationship based upon the Spanish market for Libyan oil. The resource dependency picture creates strange bedfellows.

The new patterns of resource dependency have created new patterns of economic development that include international migration. Increasing numbers of people from poorer countries are discovering that the effective way to experience economic "development" or enhanced well-being is to move to a developed country by any means possible, frequently at great risk and incredible hardship. In the United States, for example, the greater Miami area of southern Florida has been "Latinized." Many thousands of people, not only Cuban refugees but people from all parts of Latin America, especially the Caribbean Basin, have settled there. Britain has experienced similar flows of migrants from former colonial areas in the Caribbean, Pakistan, India, and Africa. West Germany, Switzerland, and France have large numbers of migrant workers from Turkey, Algeria, Portugal, etc. Britain and the United States are increasingly concerned about their ability to absorb the flood of migrants at a time when they can hardly take care of their own citizens. Human resources, it is clear, are closely linked to natural resources in these new patterns of interdependency.

In the last analysis, the threats to resource access contribute to destabilization. And any form of destabilization detracts from the quality of life of a country's entire population.

Conclusions

We have discussed at length differing points of view concerning mankind's perceptions of resources, their abundance and scarcity, ways in which societies and governments address themselves to—or ignore—resources and their use and misuse. The ultimate limitation on resources is imposed by mankind itself. People, cultures, and whole countries define and therefore create their own resources. Only people can resolve the problem of resources. The greatest wisdom and courage is demanded from our leaders to make the very difficult decisions that will guarantee either human misery or survival in the coming decades.

The ultimate example of a human resource issue was presented in the 1982 publication of Jonathan Schell's *The Fate of the Earth*. The book had a profound impact upon the literate public in portraying what the actual effects of a nuclear holocaust would be and mean. The book shows how the resource of nuclear energy has been put to use by human beings to protect human beings, but, in a classic demonstration of the individual-brilliance/collective-insanity syndrome and the basic principles of ecology, the nuclear initiative, which purportedly protects human beings, ends up destroying its user and the rest of the world as well. The impact of a nuclear holocaust upon mankind and upon the earth's environment is unthinkable because no one has yet experienced it. It has not yet been subjected to experimentation, and yet the evidence presented by Schell is entirely credible. The issue, here again, is not nuclear power; it is mankind's use and abuse of it.

In the twenty-first century, the greatest frontiers will not be those of outer space but those dealing with the individual's relationship with the physical environment. At the height of the Scientific Revolution, the outpouring of technical breakthroughs accomplished many worthwhile objectives that improved the quality and quantity of life for many people, mostly in the developed world. It also produced many problems and threats to the developed world. It is only by continually examining and reexamining these questions of the individual's relationship to the physical earth, and the past, present, and future use of resources that it is possible to consider the future with any degree of informed hope.

E. F. Schumacher, author of *Small is Beautiful* and an economist who sees his field and its practitioners in an original light, stresses the need to redefine meaningful life in terms of quality and progress instead of quantity and growth. Let us face the twenty-first century with knowledge, will, and courage necessary to resolve the issues of global scarcity in ways that will enhance humanity and guarantee its survival with a degree of fulfillment and dignity.

Appendix

The lead article in Section 3, "Protecting World Resources: Is Time Running Out?" by the Foreign Policy Association, uses Global 2000 as a springboard for its analysis. Despite the criticism it has received, this report is without question one of the most important documents to emerge from the U.S. government in a very long time. It deserves careful reading, much thought, and vigorous, informed public discussion. Though the report itself may soon be forgotten, the questions it raises, the dangers it points to, will not go away. We have therefore included a portion of the summary volume of the report in this book for ready reference. For those interested in probing deeper into these questions, the entire three-volume report is worth reading—or at least scanning. It documents, as perhaps no other analysis does, the challenges of interdependence.

The Global 2000 Report to the President: Entering the 21st Century

Council on Environmental Quality and the Department of State

INCOME

Projected declines in fertility rates are based in part on anticipated social and economic progress, which is ultimately reflected in increased income. Income projections were not possible, and gross national product projections were used as surrogates. GNP, a rough and inadequate measure of social and economic welfare, is projected to increase worldwide by 145 percent over 25 years from 1975 to 2000. But because of population growth, per capita GNP increases much more slowly, from $1,500 in 1975 to $2,300 in 2000—an increase of 53 percent. For both the poorer and the richer countries, rates of growth in GNP are projected to decelerate after 1985.

GNP growth is expected to be faster in LDCs (an average annual growth of 4.5 percent, or an approximate tripling over 25 years) than in developed regions (an average annual growth of 3.3 percent, or somewhat more than a doubling). However, the LDC growth in gross national product develops from a very low base, and population growth in the LDCs brings per capita increases in GNP down to very modest proportions. While parts of the LDC world, especially several countries in Latin America, are projected to improve significantly in per capita GNP by 2000, other countries will make little or no gains from their present low levels. India, Bangladesh, and Pakistan, for example, increase their per capita GNP by 31 percent, 8 percent, and 3 percent, respectively, but in all three countries GNP per capita remains below $200 (in 1975 dollars). [. . .]

The present income disparities between the wealthiest and poorest nations are projected to widen. Assuming that present trends continue, the group of industrialized coun-

Excerpt from *The Global 2000 Report to the President: Entering the 21st Century,* Report prepared by Council on Environmental Quality (a White House agency) and the Department of State. Volume 1 (The Summary Report), U.S. Government Printing Office, 1980). Pp. 13–38.

tries will have a per capita GNP of nearly $8,500 (in 1975 dollars) in 2000, and North America, Western Europe, Australia, New Zealand, and Japan will average more than $11,000. By contrast, per capita GNP in the LDCs will average less than $600. For every $1 increase in GNP per capita in the LDCs, a $20 increase is projected for the industrialized countries. Tables 1 and 2 summarize the GNP projections. The disparity between the developed countries and the less developed group is so marked that dramatically different rates of change would be needed to reduce the gap significantly by the end of the century.[1] Disparities between the rich and poor of many LDCs are equally striking.

Updated GNP projections would indicate somewhat lower economic growth than shown in the Global 2000 projections. Projections for the member nations of the Organization for Economic Cooperation and Development (OECD) have been revised downward over the past two to three years because of the effects of increasing petroleum prices and because of anticipated measures to reduce inflation. In turn, depressed growth in the OECD economies is expected to lead to slowed growth in LDC economies. For example, in 1976 the World Bank projected that the industrialized nations' economies would expand at 4.9 percent annually over the 1980–85 period; by 1979 the Bank had revised these projections downward to 4.2 percent annually over the 1980–90 period. Similarly, between 1976 and 1979 Bank projections for LDC economies dropped from 6.3 percent (1980–85 period) to 5.6 percent (1980–90 period).

RESOURCES

The Global 2000 Study resource projections are based to the fullest extent possible on the population and GNP projections presented previously. The resource projections cover food, fisheries, forests, nonfuel minerals, water, and energy.

Food

The Global 2000 Study projects world food production to increase at an average annual rate of about 2.2 percent over the 1970–2000 period. This rate of increase is roughly equal to the record growth rates experienced during the 1950s, 1960s, and early 1970s, including the period of the so-called Green Revolution. Assuming no deterioration in climate or weather, food production is projected to be 90 percent higher in 2000 than in 1970.

The projections indicate that most of the increase in food production will come from more intensive use of yield-enhancing, energy-intensive inputs and technologies such as fertilizer, pesticides, herbicides, and irrigation—in many cases with diminishing returns. Land under cultivation is projected to increase only 4 percent by 2000 because most good land is already being cultivated. In the early 1970s one hectare of arable land supported an average of 2.6 persons; by 2000 one hectare will have to support 4 persons. Because of this tightening land constraint, food production is not likely to increase fast enough to meet rising demands unless world agriculture becomes significantly more dependent on petroleum and petroleum-related inputs. Increased petroleum dependence also has implications for the cost of food production. After decades of generally falling prices, the real price of food is projected to increase 95 percent over the 1970–2000 period, in significant part as a result of increased petroleum dependence. If energy prices in fact rise more rapidly than the projections anticipate, then the effect on food prices could be still more marked.

On the average, world food production is projected to increase more rapidly than world population, with average per capita consumption increasing about 15 percent between 1970 and 2000. Per capita consumption in the industrialized nations is projected to rise 21 percent from 1970 levels, with increases of from 40 to more than 50 percent in Japan, Eastern Europe, and the USSR, and 28 percent in the United States.[2] In the LDCs, however, rising food output will barely keep ahead of population growth.

An increase of 9 percent in per capita food consumption is projected for the LDCs as a whole, but with enormous variations among regions and nations. The great populous countries of South Asia—expected to contain 1.3 billion people by 2000—improve hardly at all, nor do large areas of low-income North Africa and the Middle East. Per capita consumption in the sub-Saharan African LDCs will actually decline, according to the projections. The LDCs showing the greatest per capita growth (increases of about 25 percent) are concentrated in Latin America and East Asia. Table 3 summarizes the projections for food production and consumption, and Table 4 shows per capita food consumption by regions.

The outlook for improved diets for the poorest people in the poorest LDCs is sobering. In the 1970s, consumption of calories in the LDCs averaged only 94 percent of the minimum requirements set by the UN Food and Agriculture Organization (FAO).[3] Moreover, income and food distribution within individual LDCs is so skewed that national average caloric consumption generally must be 10–20 percent above minimum levels before the poorest are likely to be able to afford a diet that meets the FAO minimum standard. Latin America is the only major LDC region where average caloric consumption is projected to be 20 percent or more above the FAO minimum standard in the year 2000. In the other LDC regions—South, East, and Southeast Asia, poor areas of North Africa and the Middle East, and especially central Africa, where a calamitous drop in food per capita is projected—the quantity of food available to the poorest groups of people will simply be insufficient to permit children to reach normal body weight and intelligence and to permit normal activity and good health in adults. Consumption in the LDCs of central Africa is projected to be more than 20 percent below the FAO minimum standard, assuming no recurrence of severe drought. In South Asia (primarily India, Pakistan, and Bangladesh), average caloric intake is projected to remain below the FAO minimum standard, although increasing slightly—from 12 percent below the FAO standard in the mid-1970s to about 3 percent below the standard in 2000. In East Asia, Southeast Asia, and affluent areas of North Africa and the Middle East, average per capita caloric intakes are projected to be 6–17 percent above FAO minimum requirement levels, but because the great majority of people in these regions are extremely poor, they will almost certainly continue to eat less than the minimum. The World Bank has estimated that the number of malnourished people in LDCs could rise from 400–600 million in the mid-1970s to 1.3 billion in 2000.

TABLE 1 GNP Estimates (1975) and Projections and Growth Rates (1985, 2000) by Major Regions and Selected Countries and Regions

(billions of constant 1975 dollars)

	1975 GNP	1975–85 Growth Rate	1985 Projections[a]	1985–2000 Growth Rate	2000 Projections[a]
		percent		*percent*	
World	6,025	4.1	8,991	3.3	14,677
More developed regions	4,892	3.9	7,150	3.1	11,224
Less developed regions	1,133	5.0	1,841	4.3	3,452
Major Regions					
Africa	162	5.2	268	4.3	505
Asia and Oceania	697	4.6	1,097	4.2	2,023
Latin America[b]	326	5.6	564	4.5	1,092
USSR and Eastern Europe	996	3.3	1,371	2.8	2,060
North America, Western Europe, Japan, Australia, and New Zealand	3,844	4.0	5,691	3.1	8,996
Selected Countries and Regions[c]					
People's Republic of China	286	3.8	413	3.8	718
India	92	3.6	131	2.8	198
Indonesia	24	6.4	45	5.4	99
Bangladesh	9	3.6	13	2.8	19

Pakistan	10	3.6	14	2.8	21
Philippines	16	5.6	27	4.4	52
Thailand	15	5.6	25	4.4	48
South Korea	19	5.6	32	4.4	61
Egypt	12	5.6	20	4.4	38
Nigeria	23	6.4	43	5.4	94
Brazil	108	5.6	185	4.4	353
Mexico	71	5.6	122	4.4	233
United States[d]	1,509	4.0	2,233	3.1	3,530
USSR	666	3.3	917	2.8	1,377
Japan	495	4.0	733	3.1	1,158
Eastern Europe (excluding USSR)	330	3.3	454	2.8	682
Western Europe	1,598	4.0	2,366	3.1	3,740

[a] Projected growth rates of gross national product were developed using complex computer simulation techniques described in Chapter 16 of the Global 2000 Technical Report. These projections represent the result of applying those projected growth rates to the 1975 GNP data presented in the 1976 World Bank Atlas. Projections shown here are for medium-growth rates.

[b] Includes Puerto Rico.

[c] In most cases, gross national income growth rates were projected for groups of countries rather than for individual countries. Thus the rates attributed to individual LDCs in this table are the growth rates applicable to the group with which that country was aggregated for making projections and do not take into account country specific characteristics.

[d] Does not include Puerto Rico.

Source: Global 2000 Technical Report, Table 3-3.

TABLE 2 Per Capita GNP Estimates (1975) and Projections and Growth Rates (1985, 2000) by Major Regions and Selected Countries and Regions

(constant 1975 U.S. dollars)

	1975	Average Annual Growth Rate, 1975–85	1985 Projections[a]	Average Annual Growth Rate, 1985–2000	2000 Projections[a]
		percent		*percent*	
World	1,473	2.3	1,841	1.5	2,311
More developed countries	4,325	3.2	5,901	2.5	8,485
Less developed countries	382	2.8	501	2.1	587
Major Regions					
Africa	405	2.2	505	1.4	620
Asia and Oceania	306	2.7	398	2.3	557
Latin America[b]	1,005	2.6	1,304	1.8	1,715
USSR and Eastern Europe	2,591	2.4	3,279	2.1	4,472
North America, Western Europe, Japan, Australia, and New Zealand	5,431	3.4	7,597	2.6	11,117
Selected Countries and Regions[c]					
People's Republic of China	306	2.3	384	2.3	540
India	148	1.5	171	0.8	194
Indonesia	179	4.1	268	3.1	422
Bangladesh	111	0.6	118	0.1	120
Pakistan	138	0.4	144	−0.1	142

Philippines	368	3.2	503	2.3	704
Thailand	343	3.0	460	2.2	633
South Korea	507	3.5	718	2.7	1,071
Egypt	313	2.9	416	2.2	578
Nigeria	367	3.3	507	2.2	698
Brazil	991	2.2	1,236	1.6	1,563
Mexico	1,188	2.0	1,454	1.3	1,775
United States[d]	7,066	3.3	9,756	2.5	14,212
USSR	2,618	2.3	3,286	2.1	4,459
Japan	4,437	3.1	6,023	2.5	8,712
Eastern Europe	2,539	2.6	3,265	2.2	4,500
Western Europe	4,653	3.7	6,666	2.7	9,889

[a] The medium-series projections of gross national product and population presented in Tables 3-3 and 3-4 of the Global 2000 Technical Report were used to calculate the 1975, 1985, and 2000 per capita gross national product figures presented in this table.

[b] Includes Puerto Rico.

[c] In most cases, gross national product growth rates were projected for groups of countries rather than for individual countries. Thus, the rates attributed to individual LDCs in this table are the growth rates applicable to the group with which that country was aggregated for making projections and do not take into account country-specific characteristics.

[d] Does not include Puerto Rico.

Source: Global 2000 Technical Report, Table 3-5.

TABLE 3 Grain Production, Consumption, and Trade, Actual and Projected, and Percent Increase in Total Food Production and Consumption

	Grain (million metric tons)			Food (Percent increase over the 1970–2000 period)
	1969–71	1973–75	2000	
Industrialized countries				
Production	401.7	434.7	679.1	43.7
Consumption	374.3	374.6	610.8	47.4
Trade	+ 32.1	+ 61.6	+ 68.3	
United States				
Production	208.7	228.7	402.0	78.5
Consumption	169.0	158.5	272.4	51.3
Trade	+ 39.9	+ 72.9	+ 129.6	
Other developed exporters				
Production	58.6	61.2	106.1	55.6
Consumption	33.2	34.3	65.2	66.8
Trade	+ 28.4	+ 27.7	+ 40.9	
Western Europe				
Production	121.7	132.9	153.0	14.6
Consumption	144.2	151.7	213.1	31.6
Trade	− 21.8	− 19.7	− 60.1	
Japan				
Production	12.7	11.9	18.0	31.5
Consumption	27.9	30.1	60.1	92.8
Trade	− 14.4	− 19.3	− 42.1	
Centrally planned countries				
Production	401.0	439.4	722.0	74.0
Consumption	406.6	472.4	758.5	79.9
Trade	− 5.2	− 24.0	− 36.5	
Eastern Europe				
Production	72.1	89.4	140.0	83.2
Consumption	78.7	97.7	151.5	81.7
Trade	− 6.1	− 7.8	− 11.5	
USSR				
Production	165.0	179.3	290.0	72.7
Consumption	161.0	200.7	305.0	85.9
Trade	+ 3.9	− 10.6	− 15.0	
People's Republic of China				
Production	163.9	176.9	292.0	69.0
Consumption	166.9	180.8	302.0	71.4
Trade	− 3.0	− 3.9	− 10.0	

Less developed countries				
Production	306.5	328.7	740.6	147.7
Consumption	326.6	355.0	772.4	142.8
Trade	– 18.5	– 29.5	– 31.8	
Exporters[a]				
Production	30.1	34.5	84.0	125.0
Consumption	18.4	21.5	36.0	58.0
Trade	+ 11.3	+ 13.1	+ 48.0	
Importers[b]				
Production	276.4	294.2	656.6	149.3
Consumption	308.2	333.5	736.4	148.9
Trade	– 29.8	– 42.6	– 79.8	
Latin America				
Production	63.8	72.0	185.9	184.4
Consumption	61.2	71.2	166.0	165.3
Trade	+ 3.2	+ 0.2	+ 19.9	
North Africa/Middle East				
Production	38.9	42.4	89.0	157.8
Consumption	49.5	54.1	123.7	167.3
Trade	– 9.1	– 13.8	– 29.7	
Other African LDCs				
Production	32.0	31.3	63.7	104.9
Consumption	33.0	33.8	63.0	96.4
Trade	– 1.0	– 2.4	+ 0.7	
South Asia				
Production	119.1	127.7	259.0	116.8
Consumption	125.3	135.1	275.7	119.4
Trade	– 6.2	– 9.3	– 16.7	
Southeast Asia				
Production	22.8	21.4	65.0	210.0
Consumption	19.3	17.9	47.0	163.6
Trade	+ 3.4	+ 3.7	+ 18.0	
East Asia				
Production	29.9	34.0	73.0	155.3
Consumption	38.3	42.9	97.0	164.9
Trade	– 8.8	– 9.7	– 24.0	
World				
Production/ Consumption	1,108.0	1,202.0	2,141.7	91.0

[a] Argentina and Thailand.

[b] All others, including several countries that export in some scenarios (e.g., Brazil, Indonesia, and Colombia).

Source: Global 2000 Technical Report, Table 6-5.

Note: In grade figures, plus sign indicates export, minus sign indicates import.

TABLE 4 Per Capita Grain Production, Consumption, and Trade, Actual and Projected, and Percent Increase in Per Capita Total Food Production and Consumption

	Grain (*kilograms per capita*)			Food (*Percent increase over the 1970–2000 period*)
	1969–71	1973–75	2000	
Industrialized countries				
Production	573.6	592.6	769.8	18.4
Consumption	534.4	510.7	692.4	21.2
Trade	+ 45.8	+ 84.0	+ 77.4	
United States				
Production	1,018.6	1,079.3	1,640.3	51.1
Consumption	824.9	748.0	1,111.5	28.3
Trade	+ 194.7	+ 344.0	+ 528.8	
Other developed exporters				
Production	1,015.6	917.0	915.6	– 11.3
Consumption	575.4	514.0	562.6	– 5.7
Trade	+ 492.2	+ 415.0	+ 353.0	
Western Europe				
Production	364.9	388.4	394.0	1.0
Consumption	432.4	443.3	548.8	15.5
Trade	– 65.4	– 57.6	– 154.8	
Japan				
Production	121.7	108.5	135.4	6.1
Consumption	267.5	274.4	452.3	54.2
Trade	– 138.1	– 175.9	– 316.7	
Centrally planned countries				
Production	356.1	368.0	451.1	29.6
Consumption	361.0	395.6	473.9	35.8
Trade	– 4.6	– 20.1	– 22.8	
Eastern Europe				
Production	574.0	693.0	921.9	53.3
Consumption	626.6	757.4	997.6	52.1
Trade	– 48.6	– 60.5	– 75.8	
USSR				
Production	697.6	711.2	903.2	28.1
Consumption	663.1	796.1	949.9	41.4
Trade	+ 16.1	– 42.0	– 46.7	
People's Republic of China				
Production	216.3	217.6	259.0	17.4
Consumption	220.2	222.4	267.8	19.1
Trade	– 4.0	– 4.8	– 8.8	

Less developed countries				
Production	176.7	168.7	197.1	10.8
Consumption	188.3	182.2	205.5	8.6
Trade	– 10.7	– 15.1	– 8.4	
Exporters[a]				
Production	491.0	521.9	671.7	10.4
Consumption	300.1	325.3	287.8	– 22.6
Trade	+ 184.3	+ 198.2	+ 383.9	
Importers[b]				
Production	159.4	173.8	180.7	10.8
Consumption	177.7	193.6	202.7	10.8
Trade	– 17.2	– 24.1	– 21.9	
Latin America				
Production	236.1	241.0	311.4	33.7
Consumption	226.5	238.3	278.1	25.1
Trade	+ 11.8	+ 2.7	+ 33.3	
North Africa/Middle East				
Production	217.1	214.6	222.5	– 1.8
Consumption	276.2	273.8	292.8	2.2
Trade	– 50.8	– 69.8	– 70.3	
Other African LDCs				
Production	134.9	118.3	113.2	– 15.5
Consumption	139.1	127.7	112.0	– 19.1
Trade	– 4.2	– 9.1	+ 1.2	
South Asia				
Production	161.6	162.4	170.0	4.6
Consumption	170.0	171.8	181.0	5.8
Trade	– 8.4	– 11.8	– 11.0	
Southeast Asia				
Production	244.7	214.5	316.5	35.9
Consumption	207.2	182.6	228.5	14.6
Trade	+ 37.5	+ 31.9	+ 87.5	
East Asia				
Production	137.3	136.0	163.5	22.8
Consumption	176.2	171.5	217.3	27.3
Trade	– 40.4	– 38.8	– 53.8	
World				
Production/ Consumption	311.5	313.6	343.2	14.5

[a] Argentina and Thailand.

[b] All others, including several countries that export in some scenarios (e.g., Brazil, Indonesia, and Colombia).

Source: Global 2000 Technical Report, Table 6-6.

Note: In trade figures, plus sign indicates export, minus sign indicates import.

The projected food situation has many implications for food assistance and trade. In the developing world, the need for imported food is expected to grow. The most prosperous LDCs will turn increasingly to the world commercial markets. In the poorest countries, which lack the wherewithal to buy food, requirements for international food assistance will expand. LDC exporters (especially Argentina and Thailand) are projected to enlarge food production for export because of their cost advantage over countries dependent on energy-intensive inputs. LDC grain-exporting countries, which accounted for only a little more than 10 percent of the world grain market in 1975, are projected to capture more than 20 percent of the market by 2000. The United States is expected to continue its role as the world's principal food exporter. Moreover, as the year 2000 approaches and more marginal, weather-sensitive lands are brought into production around the world, the United States is likely to become even more of a residual world supplier than today; that is, U.S. producers will be responding to widening, weather-related swings in world production and foreign demand.

Revised and updated food projections would reflect reduced estimates of future yields, increased pressure on the agricultural resource base, and several changes in national food policies.

Farmers' costs of raising—and even maintaining—yields have increased rapidly in recent years. The costs of energy-intensive, yield-enhancing inputs—fertilizer, pesticides, and fuels—have risen very rapidly throughout the world, and where these inputs are heavily used, increased applications are bringing diminishing returns. In the United States, the real cost of producing food increased roughly 10 percent in both 1978 and 1979. Other industrialized countries have experienced comparable production cost increases. Cost increases in the LDCs appear to be lower, but are still two to three times the annual increases of the 1960s and early 1970s. While there have been significant improvements recently in the yields of selected crops, the diminishing returns and rapidly rising costs of yield-enhancing inputs suggest that yields overall will increase more slowly than projected.

Since the food projections were made, there have been several important shifts in national food and agricultural policy concerns. In most industrialized countries, concern with protecting agricultural resources, especially soils, has increased as the resource implications of sustained production of record quantities of food here become more apparent. Debate on the 1981 U.S. farm bill, for example, will certainly include more consideration of "exporting top soil" than was foreseeable at the time the Global 2000 Study's food projections were made. The heightened concern for protection of agricultural resources is leading to a search for policies that encourage improved resource management practices. Still further pressure on the resource base can be expected, however, due to rising industrial demand for grain, especially for fermentation into alcohol-based fuels. Accelerated erosion, loss of natural soil fertility, and other deterioration of the agricultural resource base may have more effect in the coming years than is indicated in the Global 2000 food projections.

In the LDCs, many governments are attempting to accelerate investment in food production capacity. This policy emphasis offers important long-term benefits. Some LDC governments are intervening more frequently in domestic food markets to keep food prices low, but often at the cost of low rural incomes and slowed development of agricultural production capacity.

Worldwide, the use of yield-enhancing inputs is likely to be less, and soil deterioration greater, than expected, As a result, revised food projections would show a tighter food future—somewhat less production and somewhat higher prices—than indicated in the Global 2000 projections.

Fisheries

Fish is an important component of the world's diet and has sometimes been put forth as a possible partial solution to world food shortages. Unfortunately, the world harvest of fish is expected to rise little, if at all, by the year 2000.[4] The world catch of naturally produced fish leveled off in the 1970s at about 70 million metric tons a year (60 million metric tons for marine fisheries, 10 million metric tons for freshwater species). Harvests of traditional fisheries are not likely to increase on a sustained basis, and indeed to maintain them will take good management and improved protection of the marine environment. Some potential for greater harvests comes from aquaculture and from nontraditional marine species, such as Antarctic krill, that are little used at present for direct human consumption.

Traditional freshwater and marine species might be augmented in some areas by means of aquaculture. The 1976 FAO World Conference on Aquaculture concluded that a five- to tenfold increase in production from aquaculture would be possible by 2000, given adequate financial and technical support. (Aquaculture contributed an estimated 6 million metric tons to the world's total catch in 1975.) However, limited investment and technical support, as well as increasing pollution of freshwater ponds and coastal water, are likely to be a serious impediment to such growth.

While fish is not a solution to the world needs for calories, fish does provide an important source of protein. The 70 million metric tons caught and raised in 1975 is roughly equivalent to 14 million metric tons of protein, enough to supply 27 percent of the minimum protein requirements of 4 billion people. (Actually since more than one-third of the fish harvest is used for animal feed, not food for humans, the contribution of fish to human needs for protein is lower than these figures suggest. A harvest of about 115 million metric tons would be required to supply 27 percent of the protein needs of 6.35 billion people in 2000. Even assuming that the catch of marine and freshwater fish rises to the unlikely level of 100 million metric tons annually, and that yields from aquaculture double, rising to 12 million tons, the hypothetical total of 112 million metric tons would not provide as much protein per capita as the catch of the mid-1970s. Thus, on a per capita basis, fish may well contribute less to the world's nutrition in 2000 than today.

Updated fisheries projections would show little change from the Global 2000 Study projections. FAO fisheries statistics are now available for 1978 and show a world catch of 72.4 million metric tons. (The FAO statistics for the 1970–78 period have been revised downward somewhat to reflect improved data on the catch of the People's Republic of China.) While there has been some slight recovery of the anchovy and menhaden fisheries, traditional species continue to show signs of heavy pressure. As indicated in the Global 2000 projections, the catch of nontraditional species is filling in to some extent. Perhaps the biggest change in updated fisheries projections would stem from a careful analysis of the effects of the large increase in oil prices that occurred in 1979. Scattered observations suggest that fishing fleets throughout the world are being adversely affected except where governments are keeping oil prices to fishing boats artificially low.

Forests

If present trends continue, both forest cover and growing stocks of commercial-size wood in the less developed regions (Latin America, Africa, Asia, and Oceania) will decline 40 percent by 2000. In the industrialized regions (Europe, the USSR, North America, Japan, Australia, New Zealand) forests will decline only 0.5 percent and growing stock about 5 percent. Growing stock per capita is expected to decline 47 percent worldwide and 63 percent in LDCs. Table 5 shows projected forest cover and growing stocks by region for 1978 and 2000.

Deforestation is projected to continue until about 2020, when the total world forest area will stabilize at about 1.8 billion hectares. Most of the loss will occur in the tropical forests of the developing world. About 1.45 billion hectares of forest in the industrialized nations has already stabilized and about 0.37 billion hectares of forest in the LDCs is physically or economically inaccessible. By 2020, virtually all of the physically accessible forest in the LDCs is expected to have been cut.

The real prices of wood products—fuel wood, sawn lumber, wood panels, paper, wood-based chemicals, and so on—are expected to rise considerably as GNP (and thus also demand) rises and world supplies tighten. In the industrialized nations, the effects may be disruptive, but not catastrophic. In the less developed countries, however, 90 percent of wood consumption goes for cooking and heating, and wood is a necessity of life. Loss of woodlands will force people in many LDCs to pay steeply rising prices for fuel wood and charcoal or to spend much more effort collecting wood—or else to do without.

Updated forest projections would present much the same picture as the Global 2000 Study projections. The rapid increase in the price of crude oil will probably limit the penetration of kerosene sales into areas now depending on fuel wood and dung and, as a result, demand for fuel wood may be somewhat higher than expected. Some replanting of cut tropical areas is occurring, but only at low rates similar to those assumed in the Global 2000 Study projections. Perhaps the most encouraging developments are those associated with heightened international awareness of the seriousness of current trends in world forests.

Water

The Global 2000 Study population, GNP, and resource projections all imply rapidly increasing demands for freshwater. Increases of at least 200–300 percent in world water withdrawals are expected over the 1975–2000 period. By far the largest part of the increase is for irrigation. The United Nations has estimated that water needed for irrigation,

TABLE 5 Estimates of World Forest Resources, 1978 and 2000

	Closed Forest[a] (*millions of hectares*)		Growing Stock (*billions cu m overbark*)	
	1978	2000	1978	2000
USSR	785	775	79	77
Europe	140	150	15	13
North America	470	464	58	55
Japan, Australia, New Zealand	69	68	4	4
Subtotal	1,464	1,457	156	149
Latin America	550	329	94	54
Africa	188	150	39	31
Asia and Pacific LDCs	361	181	38	19
Subtotal (LDCs)	1,099	660	171	104
Total (world)	2,563	2,117	327	253
			Growing Stock per Capita (*cu m biomass*)	
Industrial countries			142	114
LDCs			57	21
Global			76	40

[a] Closed forests are relatively dense and productive forests. They are defined variously in different parts of the world. For further details, see Global 2000 Technical Report, footnote, p. 117.

Source: Global 2000 Technical Report, Table 13-29.

which accounted for 70 percent of human uses of water in 1967, would double by 2000. Moreover, irrigation is a highly consumptive use, that is, much of the water withdrawn for this purpose is not available for immediate reuse because it evaporates, is transpired by plants, or becomes salinated.

Regional water shortages and deterioration of water quality, already serious in many parts of the world, are likely to become worse by 2000. [. . .] Population growth alone, [by 2000,] will cause demands for water at least to double relative to 1971 in nearly half the countries of the world. Still greater increases would be needed to improve standards of living.

Much of the increased demand for water will be in the LDCs of Africa, South Asia, the Middle East, and Latin America, where in many areas freshwater for human consumption and irrigation is already in short supply. Although the data are sketchy, it is known that several nations in these areas will be approaching their maximum developable water supply by 2000, and that it will be quite expensive to develop the water remaining. Moreover, many LDCs will also suffer destabilization of water supplies following extensive loss of forests. In the industrialized countries competition among different uses of water—for increasing food production, new energy systems (such as production of synthetic fuels from coal and shale), increasing power generation, expanding food production, and increasing needs of other industry—will aggravate water shortages in many areas.

Updated water projections would present essentially the same picture. The only significant change that has occurred since the projections were developed is that the price of energy (especially oil) has increased markedly. Increased energy costs will adversely affect the economics of many water development projects, and may reduce the amount of water available for a variety of uses. Irrigation, which usually requires large amounts of energy for pumping, may be particularly affected.

Nonfuel Minerals

The trends for nonfuel minerals, like those for the other resources considered in the Global 2000 Study, show steady increases in demand and consumption. The global demand for and consumption of most major nonfuel mineral commodities is projected to increase 3–5 percent annually, slightly more than doubling by 2000. Consumption of all major steelmaking mineral commodities is projected to increase at least 3 percent annually. Consumption of all mineral commodities for fertilizer production is projected to grow at more than 3 percent annually, with consumption of phosphate rock growing at 5.2 percent per year—the highest growth rate projected for any of the major nonfuel mineral commodities. The nonferrous metals show widely varying projected growth rates; the growth rate for aluminum, 4.3 percent per year, is the largest.

The projections suggest that the LDC's share of nonfuel mineral use will increase only modestly. Over the 1971–75 period, Latin America, Africa, and Asia used 7 percent of the world's aluminum production, 9 percent of the copper, and 12 percent of the iron ore. The three-quarters of the world's population living in these regions in 2000 are projected to use only 8 percent of aluminum production, 13 percent of copper production, and 17 percent of iron ore production. The one-quarter of the world's population that inhabits industrial countries is projected to continue absorbing more than three-fourths of the world's nonfuel minerals production. [. . .]

The projections point to no mineral exhaustion problems but, as indicated in Table 6, further discoveries and investments will be needed to maintain reserves and production of several mineral commodities at desirable levels. In most cases, however, the resource potential is still large (see Table 7), especially for low grade ores.

Updated nonfuel minerals projections would need to give further attention to two factors affecting investment in mining. One is the shift over the past decade in investment in extraction and processing away from the developing countries toward industrialized countries (although this trend may now be reversing). The other factor is the rapid increase in energy prices. Production of many nonfuel minerals is highly energy-intensive, and the recent and projected increases in oil prices can be expected to slow the expansion of these mineral supplies.

TABLE 6 Life Expectancies of 1976 World Reserves of Selected Mineral Commodities at Two Different Rates of Demand

	1976 Reserves	1976 Primary Demand	Projected Demand Growth Rate	Life Expectancy in Years[a]	
				Static at 1976 Level	Growing at Projected Rates
			percent		
Fluorine (million short tons)	37	2.1	4.58	18	13
Silver (million troy ounces)	6,100	305	2.33	20	17
Zinc (million short tons)	166	6.4	3.05	26	19
Mercury (thousand flasks)	5,210	239	0.50	22	21
Sulfur (million long tons)	1,700	50	3.16	34	23
Lead (million short tons)	136	3.7	3.14	37	25
Tungsten (million pounds)	4,200	81	3.26	52	31
Tin (thousand metric tons)	10,000	241	2.05	41	31
Copper (million short tons)	503	8.0	2.94	63	36
Nickel (million short tons)	60	0.7	2.94	86	43
Platinum (million troy ounces)	297	2.7	3.75	110	44
Phosphate rock (million metric tons)	25,732	107	5.17	240	51
Manganese (million short tons)	1,800	11.0	3.36	164	56
Iron in ore (billion short tons)	103	0.6	2.95	172	62
Aluminum in bauxite (million short tons)	5,610	18	4.29	312	63
Chromium (million short tons)	829	2.2	3.27	377	80
Potash (million short tons)	12,230	26	3.27	470	86

[a] Assumes no increase to 1976 reserves.

Source: After Global 2000 Technical Report, Table 12-4, but with updated and corrected entries. Updated reserves and demand data from U.S. Bureau of Mines, *Mineral Trends and Forecasts*, 1979. Projected demand growth rates are from Global 2000 Technical Report, Table 12-2.

Note: Corresponding data for helium and industrial diamonds not available.

TABLE 7 World Production and Reserves in 1977 (Estimated), Other Resources in 1973–77 (as Data Available), Resource Potential, and Resource Base of 17 Elements

(millions of metric tons)

	Production	Reserves	Other Resources	Resource Potential (Recoverable)	Resource Base (Crustal Mass)
Aluminum	17[a]	5,200[a]	2,800[a]	3,519,000	1,990,000,000,000
Iron	495[b]	93,100	143,000[c]	2,035,000	1,392,000,000,000
Potassium	22	9,960	103,000	n.a.	408,000,000,000
Manganese	10[d]	2,200	1,100[e]	42,000	31,200,000,000
Phosphorus	14[f]	3,400[f]	12,000[f]	51,000	28,800,000,000
Fluorine	2[g]	72	270	20,000	10,800,000,000
Sulfur	52	1,700	3,800[h]		9,600,000,000
Chromium	3[i]	780[i]	6,000[i]	3,260	2,600,000,000
Zinc	6	159	4,000	3,400	2,250,000,000
Nickel	0.7	54	103[e]	2,590	2,130,000,000
Copper	8	456	1,770[j]	2,120	1,510,000,000
Lead	4	123	1,250	550	290,000,000
Tin	0.2	10	27	68	40,800,000

Tungsten	0.04	1.8	3.4	51	26,400,000
Mercury	0.008	0.2	0.4	3.4	2,100,000
Silver	0.010	0.2	0.5	2.8	1,800,000
Platinum group[k]	0.0002	0.02	0.05[l]	1.2[m]	1,100,000

[a] In bauxite, dry basis, assumed to average 21 percent recoverable aluminum.

[b] In ore and concentrates assumed to average 58 percent recoverable iron.

[c] In ore and concentrates assumed to average 26 percent recoverable iron.

[d] In ore and concentrates assumed to average 40 percent manganese.

[e] Excludes metal in deep-sea nodules and, in the case of nickel, unidentified resources.

[f] In phosphate rock ore and concentrates assumed to average 13 percent phosphorus.

[g] In fluorspar and phosphate rock ore and concentrates assumed to average 44 percent fluorine.

[h] Excludes unidentified sulfur resources, enormous quantities of sulfur in gypsum and anhydrite, and some 600 billion tons of sulfur in coal, oil shale, and in shale that is rich in organic matter.

[i] In ore and concentrates assumed to average 32 percent chromium.

[j] Includes 690 million tons in deep-sea nodules.

[k] Platinum, palladium, iridium, cesium, rhodium, and ruthenium.

[l] Approximate midpoint of estimated range of 0.03–0.06 million metric tons.

[m] Platinum only.

Source: Global 2000 Technical Report, Table 12-7.

Energy

The Global 2000 Study's energy projections show no early relief from the world's energy problems. The projections point out that petroleum production capacity is not increasing as rapidly as demand. Furthermore, the rate at which petroleum reserves are being added per unit of exploratory effort appears to be falling. Engineering and geological considerations suggest that world petroleum production will peak before the end of the century. Political and economic decisions in the OPEC countries could cause oil production to level off even before technological constraints come into play. A world transition away from petroleum dependence must take place, but there is still much uncertainty as to how this transition will occur. In the face of this uncertainty, it was not possible at the time the Global 2000 energy projections were made—late 1977—for the Department of Energy (DOE) to develop meaningful energy projections beyond 1990. Updated DOE analyses, discussed at the end of this section, extend the global energy projections available from the U.S. government to 1995.

DOE projections prepared for the Study show large increases in demand for all commercial sources over the 1975–90 period (see Table 8). World energy demand is projected to increase 58 percent, reaching 384 quads (quadrillion British thermal units) by 1990. Nuclear and hydro sources (primarily nuclear) increase most rapidly (226 percent by 1990), followed by oil (58 percent), natural gas (43 percent), and coal (13 percent). Oil is projected to remain the world's leading energy source, providing 46–47 percent of the world's total energy through 1990, assuming that the real price of oil on the international market increases 65 percent over the 1975–90 period. The energy projections indicate that there is considerable potential for reductions in energy consumption.

Per capita energy consumption is projected to increase everywhere. The largest increase—72 percent over the 1975–90 period—is in industrialized countries other than the United States. The smallest increase, 12 percent, is in the centrally planned economies of Eastern Europe. The percentage increases for the United States and for the LDCs are the same—27 percent—but actual per capita energy consumption is very different. By 2000, U.S. per capita energy consumption is projected to be about 422 million Btu (British thermal units) annually. In the LDCs, it will be only 14 million Btu, up from 11 million in 1975 (see Table 9).

While prices for oil and other commercial energy sources are rising, fuel wood—the poor person's oil—is expected to become far less available than it is today. The FAO has estimated that the demand for fuel wood in LDCs will increase at 2.2 percent per year, leading to local fuel wood shortages in 1994 totaling 650 million cubic meters—approximately 25 percent of the projected need. Scarcities are now local but expanding. In the arid Sahel of Africa, fuel wood gathering has become a full-time job requiring in some places 360 person-days of work per household each year. When demand is concentrated in cities, surrounding areas have already become barren for considerable distances—50 to 100 kilometers in some places. Urban families, too far from collectible wood, spend 20 to 30 percent of their income on wood in some West African cities.

The projected shortfall of fuel wood implies that fuel consumption for essential uses will be reduced, deforestation expanded, wood prices increased, and growing amounts of

TABLE 8 Global Primary[a] Energy Use, 1975 and 1990, by Energy Type

	1975		1990			
	10^{15} Btu	Percent of Total	10^{15} Btu[b]	Percent of Total	Percent Increase (1975–90)	Average Annual Percent Increase
Oil	113	46	179	47	58	3.1
Coal	68	28	77	20	13	0.8
Natural gas	46	19	66	17	43	2.4
Nuclear and hydro	19	8[c]	62	16[c]	226	7.9
Solar (other than conservation/ and hydro)[d]						
Total	246	100	384	100	56	3.0

[a] All of the nuclear and much of the coal primary (i.e., input) energy is used thermally to generate electricity. In the process, approximately two-thirds of the primary energy is lost as waste heat. The figures given here are primary energy.

[b] The conversions from the DOE projections in Table 10-8 were made as follows: *Oil* 84.8×10^6 bbl/day × 365 days × 5.8×10^6 Btu/bbl = 179×10^6 Btu. *Coal:* $5{,}424 \times 10^6$ short tons/yr × 14.1×10^6 Btu/short ton [DOE figure for world average grade coal] = 77×10^{15} Btu. *Natural gas:* 64.4×10^{12}ft^3/yr × 1,032 Btu/ft^3 = 66×10^{15} Btu. *Nuclear and Hydro:* $6{,}009 \times 10^{12}$ Wh [output]/yr × 3,412 Btu/Wh × 3 input Btu/output Btu = 62×10^{12} Btu.

[c] After deductions for lost (waste) heat (see note a), the corresponding figures for output energy are 2.7 percent in 1975 and 6.0 in 1990.

[d] The IIES projection model is able to include solar only as conservation or hydro.

Source: Global 2000 Technical Report, Table 13-32.

TABLE 9 Per Capita Global Primary Energy Use, Annually, 1975 and 1990

	1975		1990			
	10^6 Btu	Percent of World Average	10^6 Btu	Percent of World Average	Percent Increase (1975–90)	Average Annual Percent Increase
United States	332	553	422	586	27	1.6
Other industrialized countries	136	227	234	325	72	3.6
Less developed countries[a]	11	18	14	19	27	1.6
Centrally planned economies	58	97	65	90	12	0.8
World	60	100	72	100	20	1.2

[a] Since population projections were not made separately for the OPEC countries, those countries have been included here in LDC category.

Source: Global 2000 Technical Report, Table 13-34.

dung and crop residues shifted from the field to the cooking fire. No explicit projections of dung and crop residue combustion could be made for the study, but it is known that a shift toward burning these organic materials is already well advanced in the Himalayan hills, in the treeless Ganges plain of India, in other parts of Asia, and in the Andean region of South America. The FAO reports that in 1970 India burned 68 million tons of cow dung and 39 million tons of vegetable waste, accounting for roughly a third of the nation's total non-commercial energy consumption that year. Worldwide, an estimated 150–400 million tons of dung are burned annually for fuel.

Updated energy projections have been developed by the Department of Energy based on new price scenarios that include the rapid 1979 increase in the price of crude oil. The new price scenarios are not markedly different from the earlier estimates for the 1990s. The new medium-scenario price for 1995 is $40 per barrel (in 1979 dollars), which is about 10 percent higher than the $36 price (1979 dollars) implied by the earlier scenario. However, the prices for the early 1980s are almost 100 percent higher than those in the projections made by DOE in late 1977 for the Study. The sudden large increase in oil prices of 1979 is likely to have a more disruptive effect on other sectors than would the gradual increase assumed in the Global 2000 Study projections.

DOE's new projections differ in several ways from those reported in this Study. Using the higher prices, additional data, and a modified model, DOE is now able to project supply and demand for an additional five years, to 1995. Demand is projected to be lower because of the higher prices and also because of reduced estimates of economic growth. Coal is projected to provide a somewhat larger share of the total energy supply. The nuclear projections for the OECD countries are lower, reflecting revised estimates of the speed at which new nuclear plants will be built. Updated estimates of OPEC maximum production are lower than earlier estimates, reflecting trends toward resource conservation by the OPEC nations. The higher oil prices will encourage the adoption of alternative fuels and technologies, including solar technology and conservation measures.

ENVIRONMENTAL CONSEQUENCES

The population, income, and resource projections all imply significant consequences for the quality of the world environment. Virtually every aspect of the earth's ecosystems and resource base will be affected.

Impacts on Agriculture

Perhaps the most serious environmental development will be an accelerating deterioration and loss of the resources essential for agriculture. This overall development includes soil erosion; loss of nutrients and compaction of soils; increasing salinization of both irrigated land and water used for irrigation; loss of high-quality cropland to urban development; crop damage due to increasing air and water pollution; extinction of local and wild crop strains needed by plant breeders for improving cultivated varieties; and more frequent and more severe regional water shortages—especially where energy and industrial developments compete for water supplies, or where forest losses are heavy and the earth can no longer absorb, store, and regulate the discharge of water.

Deterioration of soils is occurring rapidly in LDCs, with the spread of desert-like conditions in drier regions, and heavy erosion in more humid areas. Present global losses to desertification are estimated at around 6 million hectares a year (an area about the size of Maine), including 3.2 million hectares of rangeland, 2.5 million hectares of rainfed cropland, and 125 thousand hectares of irrigated farmland. Desertification does not necessarily mean the creation of Sahara-like sand deserts, but rather it includes a variety of ecological changes that destroy the cover of vegetation and fertile soil in the earth's drier regions, rendering the land useless for range or crops. Principal direct causes are overgrazing, destructive cropping practices, and use of woody plants for fuel.

At presently estimated rates of desertification, the world's desert areas (now some 800 million hectares) would expand almost 20 percent by 2000. But there is reason to expect that losses to desertification will accelerate, as increasing numbers of people in the world's drier regions put more pressures on the land to meet their needs for livestock range, cropland, and fuel wood. The United Nations has identified about 2 billion hectares of lands where the risk of desertification is "high" or "very high." These lands at risk total about two and one-half times the area now classified as desert.

Although soil loss and deterioration are especially serious in many LDCs, they are also affecting agricultural prospects in industrialized nations. Present rates of soil loss in many industrialized nations cannot be sustained without serious implications for crop production. In the United States, for example, the Soil Conservation Service, looking at wind and water erosion of U.S. soils, has concluded that to sustain crop production indefinitely at even present levels, soil losses must be cut in half.

The outlook for making such gains in the United States and elsewhere is not good. The food and forestry projections imply increasing pressures on soils throughout the world. Losses due to improper irrigation, reduced fallow periods, cultivation of steep and marginal lands, and reduced vegetative cover can be expected to accelerate, especially in North and central Africa, the humid and high-altitude portions of Latin America, and much of South Asia. In addition, the increased burning of dung and crop wastes for domestic fuel will deprive the soil of nutrients and degrade the soil's ability to hold moisture by reducing its organic content. For the world's poor, these organic materials are often the only source of the nutrients needed to maintain the productivity of farmlands. It is the poorest people—those least able to afford chemical fertilizers—who are being forced to burn their organic fertilizers. These nutrients will be urgently needed for food production in the years ahead, since by 2000 the world's croplands will have to feed half again as many people as in 1975. In the industrialized regions, increasing use of chemical fertilizers, high-yield plant varieties, irrigation water, and herbicides and pesticides have so far compensated for basic declines in soil conditions. However, heavy dependence on chemical fertilizers also leads to losses of soil organic matter, reducing the capacity of the soil to retain moisture.

Damage and loss of irrigated lands are especially significant because these lands have yields far above average. Furthermore, as the amount of arable land per capita declines over the next two decades, irrigated lands will be counted upon increasingly to raise per capita food availability. As of 1975, 230 million hectares—15 percent of the world's arable area—were being irrigated; an additional 50 million hectares are expected to be irrigated by 1990. Unfortunately there is great difficulty in maintaining the productivity of irrigated lands. About half of the world's irrigated land has already been damaged to some degree by salinity, alkalinity, and waterlogging, and much of the additional land expected to be irrigated by 1990 is highly vulnerable to irrigation-related damage.

Environmental problems of irrigation exist in industrialized countries (for example, in the San Joaquin Valley in California) as well as in LDCs (as in Pakistan, where three-quarters of the irrigated lands are damaged). It is possible, but slow and costly, to restore damaged lands. Prevention requires careful consideration of soils and attention to drainage, maintenance, and appropriate water-saving designs.

Loss of good cropland to urban encroachment is another problem affecting all countries. Cities and industries are often located on a nation's best agricultural land—rich, well-watered alluvial soils in gently sloping river valleys. In the industrialized countries that are members of the OECD, the amount of land devoted to urban uses has been increasing twice as fast as population. The limited data available for LDCs point to similar trends. In Egypt, for example, despite efforts to open new lands to agriculture, the total area of irrigated farmland has remained almost unchanged in the past two decades. As fast as additional acres are irrigated with water from the Aswan Dam, old producing lands on the Nile are converted to urban uses.

The rising yields assumed by the Global 2000 food projections depend on wider adoption of existing high-yield agricultural technology and on accelerating use of fertilizers, irrigation, pesticides, and herbicides. These yield-enhancing inputs, projected to more than double in use worldwide and to quadruple in LDCs, are heavily dependent on fossil fuels. Even now, a rapid escalation of fossil fuel prices or a sudden interruption of supply could severely disturb world agricultural production, raise food prices, and deprive larger numbers of people of adequate food. As agriculture becomes still more dependent on energy-intensive inputs, the potential for disruption will be even greater.

Accelerating use of pesticides is expected to raise crop yields quickly and substantially, especially in LDCs. Yet, many of these chemicals produce a wide range of serious environmental consequences, some of which adversely affect agricultural production. Destruction of pest predator populations and the increasing resistance of pests to heavily used pesticides have already proved to be significant agricultural problems. On California farms, for example, 17 of 25 major agricultural pests are now resistant to one or more types of pesticides, and the populations of pest predators have been severely reduced. Many millions of dollars in crop damage are now caused annually in California by resistant pests whose natural predators have been destroyed.

Crop yields are expected to be increased significantly by much wider use of high-yield strains of grains. Unfortunately, large monocultures of genetically identical crops pose increased risks of catastrophic loss from insect attacks or crop epidemics. The corn blight that struck the U.S. corn belt in 1970 provided a clear illustration of the vulnerability of genetically identical monocultures.

Impacts on Water Resources

The quality of the world's water resources is virtually certain to suffer from the changes taking place between now and the year 2000. Water pollution from heavy application of pesticides will cause increasing difficulties. In the industrialized countries, shifts from widespread use of long-lived chemicals such as DDT are now underway, but in the LDCs—where the largest increases in agricultural chemical use is projected—it is likely that the persistent pesticides will continue to be used. Pesticide use in LDCs is expected to at least quadruple over the 1975–2000 period (a sixfold increase is possible if recent rates of increase continue). Pollution from the persistent pesticides in irrigation canals, ponds, and rice paddies is already a worrisome problem. Farmers in some parts of Asia are reluctant to stock paddies and ponds because fish are being killed by pesticides. This means a serious loss of high-quality protein for the diets of rural families.

In addition to the potential impacts on soils discussed above, irrigation adversely affects water quality by adding salt to the water returning to streams and rivers. Downstream from extensive irrigation projects the water may become too saline for further use, unless expensive desalinization measures are undertaken. As the use of water for irrigation increases, water salinity problems are certain to increase as well.

Water pollution in LDCs is likely to worsen as the urban population soars and industry expands. Already the waters below many LDC cities are heavily polluted with sewage and wastes from pulp and paper mills, tanneries, slaughterhouses, oil refineries, and chemical plants.

River basin development that combines flood control, generation of electricity, and irrigation is likely to increase in many less developed regions, where most of the world's untapped hydropower potential lies. While providing many benefits, large-scale dams and irrigation projects can also cause highly adverse changes in both freshwater and coastal ecosystems, creating health problems (including schistosomiasis, river blindness, malaria), inundating valuable lands, and displacing populations. In addition, if erosion in the watersheds of these projects is not controlled, siltation and buildup of sediments may greatly reduce the useful life of the projects.

Virtually all of the Global 2000 Study's projections point to increasing destruction or pollution of coastal ecosystems, a resource on which the commercially important fisheries of the world depend heavily. It is estimated that 60–80 percent of commercially valuable marine fishery species use estuaries, salt marshes, or mangrove swamps for habitat at some point in their life cycle. Reef habitats also provide food and shelter for large numbers of fish and invertebrate species. Rapidly expanding cities and industry are likely to claim coastal wetland areas for development; and increasing coastal pollution from agriculture, industry, logging, water resources development, energy systems, and coastal communities is anticipated in many areas.

Impacts of Forest Losses

The projected rapid, widespread loss of tropical forests will have severe adverse effects on water and other resources. Deforestation—especially in South Asia, the Amazon Basin, and central Africa—will destabilize water flows, leading to siltation of streams, reservoirs behind hydroelectric dams, and irrigation works, to depletion of groundwater, to intensified flooding, and to aggravated water shortages during dry periods. In South and Southeast Asia approximately 1 billion people live in heavily farmed alluvial basins and valleys that depend on forested mountain watersheds for their water. If present trends continue, forests in these regions will be reduced by about half in 2000, and erosion, siltation, and erratic streamflows will seriously affect food production.

In many tropical forests, the soils, land forms, temperatures, patterns of rainfall, and distribution of nutrients are in precarious balance. When these forests are disturbed by extensive cutting, neither trees nor productive grasses will grow again. Even in less fragile tropical forests, the great diversity of species is lost after extensive cutting.

Impacts on the World's Atmosphere and Climate

Among the emerging environmental stresses are some that affect the chemical and physical nature of the atmosphere. Several are recognized as problems; others are more conjectural but nevertheless of concern.

Quantitative projections of urban air quality around the world are not possible with the data and models now available, but further pollution in LDCs and some industrial nations is virtually certain to occur under present policies and practices. In LDC cities, industrial growth projected for the next 20 years is likely to worsen air quality. Even now, observations in scattered LDC cities show levels of sulfur dioxide, particulates, nitrogen dioxide, and carbon monoxide far above levels considered safe by the World Health Organization. In some cities, such as Bombay and Caracas, recent rapid increases in the numbers of cars and trucks have aggravated air pollution.

Despite recent progress in reducing various types of air pollution in many industrialized countries, air quality there is likely to worsen as increased amounts of fossil fuels, especially coal, are burned. Emissions of sulfur and nitrogen oxides are particularly troubling because they combine with water vapor in the atmosphere to form acid rain or produce other acid deposition. In large areas of Norway, Sweden, southern Canada, and the eastern United States, the pH value of rainfall has dropped from 5.7 to below 4.5, well into the acidic range. Also, rainfall has almost certainly become more acid in parts of Germany, Eastern Europe, and the USSR, although available data are incomplete.

The effects of acid rain are not yet fully understood, but damage has already been observed in lakes, forests, soils, crops, nitrogen-fixing plants, and building materials. Damage to lakes has been studied most extensively. For example, of 1,500 lakes in southern Norway with a pH below 4.3, 70 percent had no fish. Similar damage has been observed in the Adirondack Mountains of New York and in parts of Canada. River fish are also severely affected. In the last 20 years, first salmon and then trout disappeared in many Norwegian rivers as acidity increased.

Another environmental problem related to the combustion of fossil fuels (and perhaps also to the global loss of forests and soil humus) is the increasing concentration of carbon dioxide in the earth's atmosphere. Rising CO_2 concentrations are of concern because of their potential for causing a warming of the earth. Scientific opinion differs on the possible consequences, but a widely held view is that highly disruptive effects on world agriculture could occur before the middle of the twenty-first century. The CO_2 content of the world's atmosphere has increased about 15 percent in the last century and by 2000 is expected to be nearly a third higher than preindustrial levels. If the projected rates of increase in fossil fuel combustion (about 2 percent per year) were to continue, a doubling of the CO_2 content of the atmosphere could be expected after the middle of the next century; and if deforestation substantially reduces tropical forests (as projected), a doubling of atmospheric CO_2 could occur sooner. The result could be significant alterations of precipitation patterns around the world, and a 2°–3°C rise in temperatures in the middle latitudes of the earth. Agriculture and other human endeavors would have great difficulty in adapting to such large, rapid changes in climate. Even a 1°C increase in average global temperatures would make the earth's climate warmer than it has been any time in the last 1,000 years.

A carbon dioxide-induced temperature rise is expected to be three or four times greater at the poles than in the middle latitudes. An increase of 5°–10°C in polar temperatures could eventually lead to the melting of the Greenland and Antarctic ice caps and a gradual rise in sea level, forcing abandonment of many coastal cities.

Ozone is another major concern. The stratospheric ozone layer protects the earth from damaging ultraviolet light. However, the ozone layer is being threatened by chlorofluorocarbon emissions from aerosol cans and refrigeration equipment, by nitrous oxide (N_2O) emissions from the denitrification of both organic and inorganic nitrogen fertilizers, and possibly by the effects of high-altitude aircraft flights. Only the United States and a few other countries have made serious efforts to date to control the use of aerosol cans. Refrigerants and nitrogen fertilizers present even more difficult challenges. The most widely discussed effect of ozone depletion and the resulting increase in ultraviolet light is an increased incidence of skin cancer, but damage to food crops would also be significant and might actually prove to be the most serious ozone related problem.

Impacts of Nuclear Energy

The problems presented by the projected production of increasing amounts of nuclear power are different from but no less serious than those related to fossil fuel combustion. The risk of radioactive contamination of the environment due to nuclear power reactor accidents will be increased, as will the potential for proliferation of nuclear weapons. No nation has yet conducted a demonstration program for the satisfactory disposal of radioactive wastes, and the amount of wastes is increasing rapidly. Several hundred thousand tons of highly radioactive spent nuclear fuel will be generated over the lifetimes of the nuclear plants likely to be constructed through the year 2000. In addition, nuclear power production will create millions of cubic meters of low-level radioactive wastes, and uranium mining and processing will lead to the production of hundreds of millions of tons of low-level radioactive tailings. It has not yet been demonstrated that all of these high- and low-level wastes from nuclear power production can be safely stored and disposed of without incident. Some of the by-products of reactors, it should be noted, have half-lives approximately five times as long as the period of recorded history.

Species Extinctions

Finally, the world faces an urgent problem of loss of plant and animal genetic resources. An estimate prepared for the Global 2000 Study suggests that between half a million and 2 million species—15 to 20 percent of all species on earth—could be extinguished by 2000, mainly because of loss of wild habitat but also in part because of pollution. Extinction of species on this scale is without precedent in human history.

One-half to two-thirds of the extinctions projected to occur by 2000 will result from the clearing or degradation of tropical forests. Insect, other invertebrate, and plant species—many of them unclassified and unexamined by scientists—will account for most of the losses. The potential value of this genetic reservoir is immense. If preserved and carefully managed, tropical forest species could be a sustainable source of new foods (especially nuts and fruits), pharmaceutical chemicals, natural predators of pests, building materials, speciality woods, fuel, and so on. Even careful husbandry of the remaining biotic resources of the tropics cannot compensate for the swift, massive losses that are to be expected if present trends continue.

Current trends also threaten freshwater and marine species. Physical alterations—damming, channelization, siltation—and pollution by salts, acid rain, pesticides, and other toxic chemicals are profoundly affecting freshwater ecosystems throughout the world. At present 274 freshwater vertebrate taxa are threatened with extinction, and by the year 2000 many may have been lost.

Some of the most important genetic losses will involve the extinction not of species but of subspecies and varieties of cereal grains. Four-fifths of the world's food supplies are derived from less than two dozen plant and animal species. Wild and local domestic strains are needed for breeding resistance to pests and pathogens into the high-yield varieties now widely used. These varietal stocks are rapidly diminishing as marginal wild lands are brought into cultivation. Local domesticated varieties, often uniquely suited to local conditions, are also being lost as higher-yield varieties displace them. And the increasing practice of monoculture of a few strains—which makes crops more vulnerable to disease epidemics or plagues of pests—is occurring at the same time that the genetic resources to resist such disasters are being lost.

Notes

1. The gap would be significantly smaller—in some cases it would be reduced by about one-half—if the comparison were based on purchasing power considerations rather than exchange rates, but a large gap would remain.

2. "Consumption" statistics are based on the amount of food that leaves the farms and does not leave the country and therefore include transportation and processing losses. Projected increases in per capita consumption in countries like the United States, where average consumption is already at least nutritionally adequate, reflect increasing losses of food during transportation and processing and might also be accounted for by increased industrial demand for grain, especially for fermentation into fuels.

3. The FAO standard indicates the *minimum* consumption that will allow normal activity and good health in adults and will permit children to reach normal body weight and intelligence in the absence of disease.

4. The food projections assumed that the world fish catch would increase at essentially the same rate as population and are therefore likely to prove too optimistic on this point.

Index

About the Editor

MARTIN IRA GLASSNER is currently Chairman of the Department of Geography at Southern Connecticut State University. He holds a B.A. in Geography and Political Science from Syracuse University, an M.A. in Geography and Political Science from California State University at Fullerton, and a Ph.D. in International Relations from Claremont Graduate School. He also did graduate study at Columbia University, Syracuse University, the University of Wisconsin, and the University of the Americas in Mexico City.

Mr. Glassner's positions have included those of: Foreign Service Officer in Washington, Jamaica and Chile; Assistant Professor of Political Science and Geography in Washington State and Israel; Advisor to the government of Nepal under the United Nations Development Programme; consultant to UNDP in Afghanistan, Nepal, Laos, Pakistan, India and Thailand; Visiting Scholar, Yale Law School; and Representative of the International Law Association and advisor to the delegation of Nepal to the Third United Nations Conference on the Law of the Sea. He undertook a study tour of Morocco, Tunisia and Egypt under a fellowship from the U.S. Office of Education, and did field work in South America for a book on Bolivia under a National Geographic Society grant.

He has published numerous articles, papers, and book reviews in various fields. Books written by Martin Glassner include: *Access to the Sea for Developing Land-locked States* (The Hague: Martinus Nijhoff, 1970) *Systematic Political Geography*, 3rd edition (New York: John Wiley & Sons, 1980) and *Bibliography on Land-locked States* (Leyden: Sijthoff & Noordhoff, 1980). With Nikos Papadakis he edited *The International Law of the Sea and Marine Affairs: A Bibliography*, a supplement to the 1980 edition (Leyden: Sijthoff & Noordhoff, 1983).